Teaching Infants and Preschoolers with Handicaps

Donald B. Bailey, Jr.
University of North Carolina

Mark Wolery
University of Kentucky

Charles E. Merrill Publishing Company
A Bell & Howell Company
Columbus Toronto London Sydney

Published by
Charles E. Merrill Publishing Company
A Bell & Howell Company
Columbus, Ohio 43216

Production Coordinator: Sandra Gurvis

Cover Designer: Tony Faiola

ISBN: 0-675-20132-2

Library of Congress Catalog Card Number:
83-062504

1 2 3 4 5—89 88 87 86 85 84

Printed in the United States of America

To our wives,
Pam and Ruth
and our children,
Lara, Rebecca, Steve, and Tim

Foreword

Any good methods text in special education must provide information that leads directly to instructional procedures. However, no textbook can teach an individual to be a competent teacher. Rather, a book provides a framework for viewing the world of teaching and a body of information used to answer questions. Care must be taken not to develop a cookbook of recipes without substantial rationale for the proposed procedures. Ideally, a methods text should discuss theoretical assumptions, review relevant research, and provide concrete examples of instructional procedures. This mix of content and format are the crucial factors that make *Teaching Infants and Preschoolers with Handicaps* readable and useful. Don Bailey and Mark Wolery have succeeded in combining theoretical information with practical suggestions so the reader is provided with information to make instructional decisions and an adequate background to understand why these procedures are recommended.

The area of early childhood/special education presents an additional problem for the author of a method's text; that of great variance in both the children described and the potential users. This text addresses teachers and therapists who deal with a wide range of handicapping conditions, from children who ae "at risk" for educational failure to children with profound handicapping conditions. The material is organized in a manner that allows various professionals to find relevance for all types of handicapped children, a difficult task.

Early childhood special educators must be prepared to teach two distinct groups of young handicapped children: those with documented central nervous system damage (severely involved children) and those with problems in learning (often referred to as "at risk" or mildly handicapped). One might assume that early intervention for the severely handicapped group would be different from that for the mildly handicapped. Currently, however, few data-based studies have addressed the question of what type of programming is most appropriate for which type of student. In truth there will probably never be a clear answer provided by research. Thus professionals are faced with the problem of how to choose intervention strategies. Bailey and Wolery have directly addressed this issue throughout the text.

Very briefly, their point of view is that two basic instructional approaches are commonly used with young handicapped students: the *developmental approach,* in which the child's natural developmental patterns are facilitated through typical preschool activities, and the *functional approach,* which attempts to teach discrete skills. Instructional procedures, curricula, classroom activities, assessment procedures, and general overall classroom atmosphere may vary depending upon the philosophical approach used by the program staff. Although the mildly handicapped student seems to benefit from a developmental approach, while the more severely handicapped student requires the functional approach, aspects of each approach are relevant for all children. Most important, the program staff should selectively choose dimensions of each to meet children's individual needs.

In *Teaching Infants and Preschoolers with Handicaps,* both sides of the debate over developmental vs. functional approach are presented and the relevant research literature is analyzed. Although much work needs to be done in this area, I believe the authors' conclusions are sound.

This text provides a thorough overview of all the major content areas typically addressed when teaching infants and preschoolers with handicaps. To use the text effectively, the reader must bring a set of serious questions. Any teacher or therapist with a good set of questions about how to best instruct young handicapped children will find much of interest in this text, perhaps even a few answers. At the very least, anyone who seriously studies this book will improve their competence in attempting to best serve young handicapped children.

Finally, a comment on Don Bailey and Mark Wolery. These two young men bring to any task energy, intelligence, and a wealth of personal experience that allows them to demonstrate their understanding of the crucial issues in programming for young handicapped children. Most important, however, is the issue of integrity and intellectual honesty. Both authors are scrupulously honest and thorough. They thoughtfully consider all sides of an issue, carefully review relevant literature, and listen to colleagues. However, they do not shy away from assertive statements. We can trust their thoughts.

Eugene Edgar, Ph.D.
Professor, Special Education
University of Washington, Seattle

Teaching is the process of facilitating learning and can be accomplished in many ways: providing the proper environment, modeling desired behaviors, presenting direct instruction, and providing feedback for performance. The secret to good teaching is knowing *what* skills the young handicapped child needs to learn and *how* to select among a variety of procedures to teach those skills.

In this text we have tried to focus on three of the many roles required of a teacher of young handicapped children: assessment, environmental planning, and instruction. Each role is critical to successful teaching. Appropriate assessments must be conducted if teachers are to identify and teach important skills. Environments must be arranged to encourage learning, independence, and generalization. Environments should also be pleasant and appropriate for the ages and needs of children. Instruction must be provided for children who do not learn rapidly in normal preschool settings. Good teachers successfully blend each of these skills.

We have attempted to combine the developmental and behavioral approaches to early education. Many have said this could not be done, but it is our belief that it *must* be done if appropriate intervention is to occur. The optimal intervention program, in our opinion, successfully blends what special educators know about behavioral programming with what regular early childhood educators and child development specialists know about infants and preschoolers. Given the paucity of research addressing this area, both approaches should be viewed as viable and investigations regarding the effectiveness of each should be conducted in an open and empirical manner.

We would like to acknowledge the support and assistance of many individuals throughout the writing of this text: Dave Gast, Jim Paul, Rune Simeonsson, and George Sugai, who provided much support and encouragement; Ann Turnbull, who got us started on this project; Susan Dick, who helped with library research; Betty Wafford, who secured temporary typists; and Connie Fugate, Sylvia Mewborn, and Anita Buie, who typed numerous drafts of the manuscript. We would like to thank our numerous reviewers for their helpful comments, especially Gene Edgar and Rebecca Fewell who helped shape the final product.

Preface

Contents

1

Fundamentals of Early Intervention

Over the past 20 years, early intervention for handicapped children has moved from a state of virtual nonexistence to a broad and growing spectrum of services for infants and preschool children. This burgeoning interest in early intervention has evolved from a number of theoretical and empirical bases (cf. Hayden & McGinness, 1977) and currently enjoys wide support in public and professional circles. Although this support has yet to be translated by many states into a mandatory service delivery system for all handicapped children from birth, most states currently provide some home-based and/or center-based program options for more severely handicapped preschoolers. State Boards of Education sometimes fund early intervention services, but in most communities the programs are funded by federal grants, local governments, and local communities.

This book is about *how to teach* children enrolled in early intervention programs; this chapter describes the *origins, effects, rationale,* and *current status* of early intervention, and the *skills* and *knowledge* needed by teachers in early intervention programs.

FACTORS INFLUENCING EARLY INTERVENTION TRENDS

Thirty years ago, parents of young handicapped children were virtually unaware that their children would benefit from intervention, that intervention should begin in the first months of life, and that services could be provided in local communities. Unfortunately, many professionals in education, special education, medicine, developmental psychology, and other related fields were also unaware of these facts and recommended institutionalizing handicapped children soon after birth. As a result, many parents followed that recommendation. Although such recommendations are still reported by parents, they are infrequent and are met with astonishment by both parents and other professionals. What has caused such a profound and rapid change in thinking? In the first section of this chapter, we will describe four factors that have contributed to this change. These factors reflect a general shift in the interest and attention given to children in general, the value and worth of individual members of society and minority groups within society, the environmental influences on child development, and the importance of education.

Interest and Attention in Children

Most parents have always valued their children, but prior to the reformation in the 16th century, they viewed children as miniature adults. At least four thinkers have helped change this view and influenced the early childhood movement. Jan Amos Comenius (1592–1670) emphasized the importance of toys, play, and the first six years of life. John Locke (1632–1704) and Jean Jacques Rousseau (1712–1778) proposed new, although different, theories about how children become adults. Johann Pestalozzi (1764–1827) taught preschool children and, contrary to the prevailing practices of the time, emphasized kindness to children. He recommended that children have experience with objects prior to verbalizations about those objects.

Friedrich Froebel (1782–1852), the "father of kindergarten," was influenced by views of Comenius and Rousseau and by contact with Pestalozzi (Deasey, 1978; Evans, 1975). Since Froebel's time, the progressive change in society's view of children can be noted by historical events.

Interest and Attention in Individual Members of Society

Although the authors of the United States Constitution were keenly aware of individual rights, the needs of individual citizens and of minority groups were subservient to the perceived needs of the nation as a whole. For example, slavery was common practice in some regions until the Civil War; women were not allowed to vote until the early 1900s; child labor was common until the passage of the Fair Labor Standards Act (1938); and handicapped children were not assured of a public education until passage of the Education for All Handicapped Children's Act in 1975. However, as minority groups began to fight for their rights and have their needs met, the views of the nation began to change. The methods used by these groups included nonviolent demonstrations, informing and educating the public through the mass media, lobbying state and federal legislators, and initiating lawsuits. The leaders of the civil rights, individual rights, and women's rights movements were not necessarily directly involved in advocating early intervention programs, but they helped set the stage for society's receptiveness to the needs of various minority groups. The parents of handicapped children, and professionals interested in the care and education of such children, made up one such group. They were successful in initiating lawsuits and in motivating legislators to pass laws which improved services for handicapped children.

Perhaps the most important law ever passed for handicapped children and their families was Public Law 94–142 (the Education for All Handicapped Children's Act). This law contains several important provisions:

☐ *Zero reject*—Children have a right to a free appropriate public education regardless of the type and severity of their handicaps.

☐ *Individualized and appropriate education* —All children must have a written educational program designed to meet their particular needs.

☐ *Nondiscriminatory testing, classification, and placement*—The procedures used to assess, label, and place children in educational programs must be free of bias, and must be conducted with parental notification and consent.

☐ *Children must be placed in the least restrictive appropriate environment*— Handicapped children must be placed in regular educational settings with non-handicapped children to the maximum benefit of the handicapped children.

☐ *Rights to procedural due process*—Parents have the right to question and challenge actions by the school prior to any action that will affect their handicapped child's education.

☐ *Shared decision making*—Parents are to be involved in planning and developing state and local educational policy regarding their handicapped child, and in developing and implementing the child's educational program.

These provisions are to be implemented for all handicapped children ages 3–21. However, P.L. 94–142 does not include handicapped children from birth to 3 years, and many handicapped children from 3 to 5 years are also excluded (Hayden, 1979). If a state provides education services to nonhandicapped children in the 3 to 5 age range, then it must provide appropriate public education to a proportionate number of 3–5 year-old handicapped children; however, public education usually is not provided for nonhandicapped children under 5 years of age. Further, if the state is required by court order or state law to provide education to any type of handicapped children from 3–5 years of age, then it must provide education to all handicapped children. However, if provision of services is inconsistent with a court order in a given state, or if spending public funds for such services is not authorized or is prohibited by state law, then such services are not required. Therefore, handicapped preschoolers in many states are not guaranteed a free appropriate public education until they are 5 years of age. But by providing services to *some* preschool handicapped children, society is beginning to recognize the needs of this minority group.

Interest and Attention in Environmental Influences on Child Development

For 300 years a debate has raged concerning the influences of the environment and heredity on development, especially intellectual development. Presently most theorists agree that both are important, and argue that development is a result of a biologically maturing organism (the child) interacting with the animate (living/social) and inanimate (nonliving/physical) environment. Since we cannot, at the present time, change a child's genetic makeup, we are left with making changes (interventions) in the environment. The important question is: What environmental interventions should be made to optimally facilitate the development of handicapped youngsters?

For the first half of this century, this question would have appeared somewhat absurd, since people believed mental retardation was inherited. In 1912, Henry Goddard traced the descendants of a revolutionary war soldier named Martin Kallikak to prove this point. During the war, Kallikak fathered a son by a feeble-minded woman, and later he married and fathered children by a woman of normal intelligence. The descendants of both women were traced over five generations. Offspring of the feeble-minded woman had high incidences of criminality, promiscuity, alcoholism, and 143 of the 480 descendants were feeble-minded. The offspring of the woman of normal intelligence, on the other hand, were respectable, influential members of society and were often professional people (MacMillan, 1977). Such reports and the accompanying views began what was known as the eugenics or selective breeding movement. As a result of the movement, retarded persons were frequently sterilized, with the view that since mental retardation was inherited it could not be changed. The advent of the intelligence quotient (IQ) reinforced the belief that intelligence was fixed and unchangeable throughout life.

Assumptions about intelligence changed slowly. In 1939, Skeels and Dye took 13 children under 3 years of age out of an orphanage and placed them in a ward for older retarded women in an institution. They left 12 other children in the orphanage. At that time, orphanages were frequently understaffed and were poor environments. All children were pretested for IQ when the 13 were transferred to the institution. They were also tested 18 months to 3 years later when they were placed in foster homes. The 13 children who were placed on the ward with older retarded women had gained an average of 27 IQ points while those who remained in the orphanage lost an average of 26 IQ points.

In 1966, Skeels reported on a 21-year follow-up of the children. The findings from the follow-up study indicated that all the children who were placed in the institution were self-supporting and none were wards of the state. Of the 12 who stayed at the orphanage, 1 had died in an institution for retarded children as an adolescent, and 4 others were wards of the state and were in institutions for the retarded. Half were working, but all except 1 were unskilled laborers. The median school year completed by the institutionalized group was more than 12th grade, while the orphanage children received an average of less than a 3rd grade education.

Skeels and Dye's methodology has received considerable criticism, but the study demonstrated that environmental conditions influence development and that children's intelligence test scores may fluctuate.

The notion of fixed intelligence was dealt severe blows by two books in the 1960s. J. McVicker Hunt (1961) wrote *Intelligence and experience* in which he reviewed empirical work dealing with the effects of experience on intelligence. He also described intelligence from the perspective of Jean Piaget rather than from the typical perspective that intelligence is measured by IQ tests. Similarly, Bloom (1964) wrote *Stability and change in human characteristics* in which he asserted that experience has a substantial impact on development, especially during infancy and early childhood. Since that time, numerous studies have demonstrated that specific environmental manipulations can change specific behaviors of young children with handicaps (cf. *Journal of Applied Behavior Analysis*, 1968–1982) and the general influence of environmental living conditions on development (Elardo, Bradley, & Caldwell, 1977; Wachs, 1979; Yarrow, Rubenstein, & Pedersen, 1975; also see Chapters 5 and 6 of this text).

Interest and Attention in Education

Traditionally, education has been a valuable part of American life. In recent decades, society has become increasingly more complex, with a trend toward more sophisticated technology in the work-place and therefore greater value on education. During the 1960s, more money was spent on teacher training, research, educational media and materials, and curriculum revisions, with emphasis on science and mathematics. School failure was seen as more tragic than in earlier times. Two groups comprised the major portion of children who failed in school; socioeconomically disadvantaged (i.e., low income) children, and children with learning problems—many of whom were handicapped. In 1965, Head Start was initiated with the goal of reversing the poverty cycle by reducing school failure of low income children, thus making them competi-

tive with their middle-class peers in school and in the marketplace.

Similarly, more money was spent on research, teacher training, and model program development in special education. In 1966, P.L. 89–750 created the Bureau of Education for the Handicapped. This Bureau administered programs related to educating handicapped persons across the nation. In 1968, the Handicapped Children's Early Education Assistance Act (P.L. 90–538) created the Handicapped Children's Early Education Program (HCEEP) with the purpose of establishing model experimental programs to demonstrate the efficacy of early intervention. These programs have provided much of what we know about early intervention.

The current commitment to education is best described by the following statement from Bricker (1970):

I wish to affirm my belief in the importance of the nervous system and to indicate a conviction that a host of events can do damage to it and to its functioning. However, only the failure of a perfectly valid, perfectly reliable, perfectly efficient program of training will convince me that the identification of the deficit is sufficient reason to stop trying to educate the child (p. 20).

A timeline of influential people and events related to the education of typical and handicapped young children is shown in Table 1.1. Note how events relating to preschool handicapped children lag behind those related to typical children.

WHAT DO WE KNOW ABOUT EARLY INTERVENTION?

Now that we have traced the development of early intervention, we need to explore the effectiveness, the rationale behind, and the current status and curriculum of early intervention programs.

Is Early Intervention Effective?

As Baer (1981) states, "the basic research [evaluation] questions to ask about any intervention are Did it work? and, if the answer is yes, the second is Why did it work?" (p. 561) "Did it work?" could mean many things;

TABLE 1.1
Chronology of the development of early childhood education for handicapped and typical children

Early Childhood Education for Typical Children	Date	Special Education for Handicapped Children
	1799–1805	Jean-Marc-Gespard Itard taught the "wild boy," Victor, in France
	1817	Thomas Gallaudet founded school for deaf in Hartford, Connecticut
F. Froebel (1782–1852), "father of kindergarten," founded schools and kindergartens in Germany and Switzerland	Early 1800s	
	1829	Perkins School for the Blind was founded in Watertown, Massachusetts
	1837	Edouard Seguin, influenced by Itard, started first school for feeble-minded in France
	1840s	Jacob Guggenbuhl started first residential facility for mentally retarded in Switzerland
	1851	Howe advocated educating blind children in regular classes; however, this did not appear to occur
	1854	First educational residential facility founded in Syracuse[a]
First United States kindergarten was founded in Wisconsin by M. Schurz (1832–1876). Class was German speaking	1855–6	
First English-speaking kindergarten in U.S. founded by Elizabeth Palmer Peabody (1804–1894), Boston	1860	
	1869	First class for deaf children, Boston
First Public kindergarten founded by William Harris and Susan Blow, St. Louis	1873	
	1875	First class for mentally retarded children in U.S., Cleveland
Model kindergarten exhibited at Exposition in Philadelphia	1876	
First teacher-training program for teachers of kindergarten started, Oshkosh Normal School, Philadelphia	1880	
International Kindergarten Union founded	1892	
John Dewey (1859–1952) established what was probably the first laboratory school with pre-school children	1896	

TABLE 1.1 (continued)

Chronology of the development of early childhood education for handicapped and typical children

Early Childhood Education for Typical Children	Date	Special Education for Handicapped Children
	1896 or 1899	First special class for the blind, Chicago
	1896	Maria Montessori started class for subnormal children in Italy
	1899–1900	First class for orthopedically handicapped, Chicago
Maria Montessori worked with Rome "slum" children and started *Casa dei Bambini* (homes/ houses of children)	1907	
Arnold Gesell founded Clinic of Child Development at Yale University	1911	
Child Education Foundation of New York City founded a nursery school using Montessori's principles	1915	
Iowa Child Welfare Station founded and began a preschool lab in 1921	1917	
Harriet Johnson founded lab school which is now Bank Street	1919	
Merrill-Palmer School (later Institute) was founded	1922	
Child Study Institute of Columbia Teacher's College was founded	1924	
Childhood Education—perhaps the first professional journal in early childhood education—was first published by International Kindergarten Union (IKU)	1924	
IKU changed name to Association for Childhood Education (ACE)	1930	
National Association for Nursery Education (NANE) was organized	1930	
Nursery schools provided by WPA to provide jobs	1933–1942	
	1939	Skeels and Dye reported on the effects of living conditions on young children[b]
Lanham War Act Nurseries were provided for children of women in defense plants during WW II	1940	
Young Children—perhaps the second ma-	1944	

TABLE 1.1 (continued)
Chronology of the development of early childhood education for handicapped and typical children

Early Childhood Education for Typical Children	Date	Special Education for Handicapped Children
jor professional journal—was first published by NANE		
	1958	Kirk reported on studies with preschool educationally handicapped children[b]
	1961	President Kennedy established President's Committee on Mental Retardation Hunt published *Intelligence and experience*[b]
NANE became known as the National Association for the Education of Young Children (NAEYC)	1964	
Elementary-Secondary Education Act initiated Head Start	1965	
	1966	Bureau of Education for the Handicapped established[b]
Project Follow Through was initiated	1968	
	1968	Federal Government established Handicapped Children's Early Education Program to fund model preschool programs for handicapped children[b]
Children's Television Workshop broadcast "Sesame Street" publicly on a national level	1969	
Westinghouse Learning Corporation evaluation of Head Start was published	1969	
	1972	Economic Opportunity Act required at least 10% enrollment of handicapped children in Head Start[b]
Tremendous growth in the compensatory education movement and related evaluation studies	Early 1970s	
	1975	P.L. 94–142, The Education for All Handicapped Children Act, established educational services for some preschool handicapped children[b]
Lazar and Darlington published summary results of the lasting effects of early compensatory education	1979	
	1979	Publication of the *Journal of the Division for Early Childhood*, first professional journal expressly for handicapped preschool children[b]

TABLE 1.1 (continued)
Chronology of the development of early childhood education for handicapped and typical children

Early Childhood Education for Typical Children	Date	Special Education for Handicapped Children
	1981	Publication of *Topics in Early Childhood Special Education*, second professional journal expressly for handicapped preschool children[b]

Source: Blackhurst, A. E. and Berdine, W.H. *An introduction to special education.* Boston: Little, Brown & Company, 1981; Browman, B.L. *The early years in childhood education.* Boston: Houghton Mifflin, 1982; Deasey, D. *Education under six.* New York: St. Martin's Press, 1978; Evans, E.D. *Contemporary influences in early childhood education.* New York: Holt, Rinehart & Winston, 1975; Hayden, A.H. Early childhood education. In K.E. Allen, V. Holm, and R.L. Schiefelbusch (Eds.), *Early intervention: A team approach.* Baltimore: University Park Press, 1978; Hewett, F.M., and Forness, S.R. *Education of exceptional learners.* Boston: Allyn & Bacon, 1974.

[a]Indicates events that may have included young handicapped children.

[b]Indicates events that were directly related to services for young handicapped children.

for example, did it produce positive changes in parents, school systems, social service agencies, the number of handicapped children who are institutionalized, the number of children who were retained in grade, or society's perceptions of handicapped children? We usually define "did it work" in terms of the effects of intervention on children with handicaps and those at risk for developmental delays. Specifically, we are interested in whether children's rates of development were accelerated, whether they learned new behaviors, whether they functioned more independently, and whether the positive effects (if any) of intervention lasted or were maintained after the intervention stopped.

In this section we briefly describe evaluation results of intervention programs with two different types of children. The first set of results comes from evaluation studies of intervention programs for socioeconomically disadvantaged children, and the second deals with young handicapped children. The results from these two types of programs must be kept separate because these two groups of children have very different abilities and needs, and what works with one group may not work with the other. If intervention "X" works with young socioeconomically disadvantaged children, we cannot assume that intervention "X" will work with young handicapped children, especially young severely handicapped children. Thus, we discuss the evaluation results

of the two types of intervention programs separately.

Early Intervention and Socioeconomically Disadvantaged Preschool Children   Reviews of the evaluation results of early intervention with low income children have filled entire volumes. In an attempt to condense this information into a few paragraphs we have ignored many studies and details.[1]

An important report on the effects of Head Start was the Westinghouse Study (Cicirelli et al., 1969). This study has prompted considerable discussion and debate (cf. Cicirelli, Evans, & Schiller, 1970; Smith & Bissell, 1970), but four of the major findings were:

1   Summer Head Start programs do not produce cognitive or affective gains that persist into the early elementary grades.
2   Full-year Head Start programs do not appear to influence affective development, but have marginal effects on cognitive development which can still be detected in grades one, two, and three.
3   Head Start children are below national norms on the Stanford Achievement Test and the Illi-

---

[1]Selected examples of relevant literature are: Beller (1973), Bronfenbrenner (1975), Gotts (1981), Gray, Klaus, and Ramsey (1982), Hodges and Cooper (1981), Horowitz and Paden (1973), Klaus and Gray (1968), Miller and Dyer (1975), Schweinhart and Weikart (1980; 1981), and Stanley (1973).

nois Test of Psycholinguistic Ability—although their Metropolitan Readiness scores approach national norms.

4 Parents liked the program and participated in it. (Smith & Bissell, pp. 52–55).

There were four reactions to the Westinghouse Study:

1 Short-term gains in their own right make intervention worth the cost, and one year of preschool experience cannot be expected to produce long-term effects (Zigler & Hunsinger, 1979).
2 Intervention should begin earlier; therefore, "Home Start" for younger children was initiated and Head Start began to enroll younger children (Deasey, 1978).
3 Intervention should continue into the elementary school grades; therefore, Follow Through was initiated (House, Glass, McLean, & Walker, 1978; Stallings, 1975).
4 Early intervention does not work, thus should not be continued. The fact that parents liked and participated in Head Start was important because later studies suggested that parent involvement was necessary if gains were to endure (e.g., Bronfenbrenner, 1975).

After the Westinghouse Study, other studies of Head Start and similar preschool projects began to emerge. Evans (1975) has summarized the findings of those studies as follows:

1 For most children, and especially males, any type of Head Start program seems better than none.
2 Positive gains in academic-intellectual areas, when achieved within Head Start, usually dissipate when special services are terminated and children move on to "regular" programs. Even a K-1 Follow Through experience seems desirable for maintaining gains among children from conventional Head Start classes.
3 Upon formal school entry, Head Start children generally manifest a slight advantage over their non-Head Start peers in "school socialization," which includes adjusting to classroom routines, self-care skills, sharing behavior, and following teacher directives.

4 Only in unusually well-designed and executed programs for basic skill learning is the overall rate of disadvantaged children's educational development much accelerated. (Such programs have been rare within the mainstream of Head Start.)
5 Disadvantaged children who achieve and maintain cognitive advantages more generally attend schools which have a low proportion of low-income children in the overall student body. (pp 68–69).

The accelerated development during intervention, and the subsequent decrease in positive gains over control children after the end of intervention has become known as the "wash-out effect." Thus, early intervention with low-income children does appear to accelerate their rate of development, allow them to acquire new skills, and approach the elementary school somewhat more prepared, but the benefits are not as great as had been hoped.

Recently, attention has been given to the lasting effects of early intervention for low income children. Lazar and Darlington (1979) reviewed the lasting effects of eight well-run, well-controlled preschool projects that were similar to Head Start. The data they analyzed were collected years after the children had completed early intervention programs.

Several findings are noteworthy. Children who had attended early intervention programs were less likely than control group children (no early intervention) to be placed in special education classes in the elementary school years. This finding does not mean no early intervention children were in special education; rather, there was a statistically significant lower number when compared to the control group. Early intervention children were also less likely than control group children to be retained in grade ("held back") during the elementary years. These first two findings indicate a large cost savings for school systems when children are enrolled in early intervention programs.

Achievement test performance was measured at fourth grade. Children who attended early intervention programs scored higher than control children, but the difference was statistically significant only for the math scores. At age 6, early intervention children had higher intelligence test performance than controls, but by age 13 this difference no longer existed. Children from early intervention programs tended to be more achievement oriented than control group children, and their mothers had higher vocational aspirations for them. Lazar and Darlington were unable to identify components of any of the early intervention programs that made children in one program perform better than children in other early intervention programs.

Based on this study, it appears that early intervention programs can produce lasting effects for low income children. However, since the children in these programs were not handicapped, the findings may not apply to the handicapped. Also, Lazar and Darlington studied only well-planned, well-run programs that are not necessarily representative of average Head Start and other preschool programs. Thus, we would only expect children from similar preschool programs to perform in the manner documented in the Lazar and Darlington report.

Early Intervention and Handicapped Preschool Children Evaluating early intervention for young handicapped children is difficult. An effective intervention program must produce results that are better than those when no intervention is used. To make such comparisons control groups traditionally are used, but several factors make it difficult to obtain a control/comparison group similar to the group that receives intervention. First, many persons consider it unethical to withhold intervention from one group of handicapped children while giving it to another. Second, few programs provide different levels of the same intervention services to the same type of children. If two such programs exist, we are no longer trying to determine whether early intervention is effective, but which of the levels of intervention is more effective than the other. Third, when comparisons across children in different programs are made, it is difficult to have equal groups. Obviously, comparing the effects of intervention programs having 4- and 5-year-old children with the effects of another program on infants is invalid. Likewise, interventions would be difficult to compare across different types of handicapping conditions. We cannot validly compare the effects of an intervention program with blind children to the effects of an intervention program with mentally retarded children. Even within a single handicapping condition we cannot compare the effects of intervention programs on varying levels of severity; certainly a profoundly deaf child will respond differently than a mildly deaf child, or a profoundly disabled cerebral palsied child will respond differently than a mildly disabled cerebral palsied child. These problems are chronic because of the relatively small number of children in most intervention programs; thus, evaluators have a small number of diverse children from which to construct comparison groups (Dunst & Rheingrover, 1981; Simeonsson, Cooper, & Scheiner, 1982).

One solution for this problem may be to compare a child's performance before intervention to his or her performance during and after intervention (White, 1980). By comparing children's performance to themselves under different conditions (no-intervention and intervention) we eliminate the need for comparison groups because the children serve as their own controls. However, we do need to withhold intervention for a while, then implement it, then withhold it, and then implement it again. Or, withhold intervention from all the children, and then initiate it on a staggered basis to different children at different times. We must also measure children's performance more than once in each condition.

Besides problems with making comparisons between intervention and no-intervention, evaluation studies have the problem of maturation. Most children with handicaps will make some progress despite their handicapping conditions even when they do not receive intervention. When evaluating the effects of intervention, the problem then becomes: How much progress is due to the intervention program, and how much is due to maturation, and how much additional progress is needed before the intervention is considered effective?

Another evaluation problem involves determining what measures should be used. Should children's developmental levels and gains be the primary considerations of effectiveness, and if so, which of many developmental scales should we use? Or, should we use IQ change, or the number of objectives children met, or parents' satisfaction, or changes in the rate of given behaviors (e.g., the number of words the child speaks per hour)? Bricker and Sheehan (1981) suggest that several measures should be used to determine effectiveness. While this recommendation appears logical, it prompts an additional problem: How do we get the time and resources to use multiple measures with each child in an intervention program?

Despite these and many other problems, studies evaluating the effectiveness of intervention with young handicapped children have been conducted.[2] The results of these evaluation studies were recently reviewed by Dunst and Rheingrover (1981) and Simeonsson et al. (1982). Dunst and Rheingrover (1981) focused primarily on the strengths and weaknesses of the methods used in the evaluation studies as compared to the findings. They found that 35 of 49 studies (71%) used methods that essentially made the results scientifically uninterpretable. When taken together, the studies clearly showed progress; the question is whether the progress was a result of the intervention program or other factors. Dunst and Rheingrover recommend that the authors of the evaluation reports reexamine their studies to eliminate factors that made the results uninterpretable, and that future evaluation studies be carefully planned and implemented to control extraneous factors. Dunst and Rheingrover also suggest that there is not enough scientifically valid evidence to conclude that early intervention is effective.

Simeonsson et al. (1982) agree that the majority of the evaluation reports lack sufficient scientific rigor, but go on to state, "In spite of limitations from the standpoint of scientific criteria, the research does provide qualified support for the effectiveness of early intervention. Although only 48% of all studies yielded statistical evidence for effectiveness, this figure increases to 81% when the analysis is restricted to those studies that incorpo-

rate statistical procedures" (p. 638). They give several reasons why the 48% figure underestimates the effectiveness of early intervention with handicapped children: the small number of children used in each report would work against finding statistically significant results; children's progress may have occurred in developmental areas that were not assessed; children's progress may have occurred in areas of management rather than in developmental areas; changes may have occurred in only the family and living environment; and only a small percentage of studies utilized statistical procedures. One further consideration is the distinction between statistical and clinical significance (Kazdin, 1976; Wolery & Harris, 1982). Some changes may not be statistically significant, but may produce worthwhile changes in the child's functioning. For example, learning to feed oneself may be an insufficient statistical change on a developmental scale, but it is obviously a clinically significant change in the child's life.

From these reviews and reports, four conclusions are apparent about the effects of early intervention with handicapped children:

1 Children made developmental progress during enrollment in early intervention programs; however, in many cases it is unclear whether the progress was a result of the intervention, some specific aspect of the intervention, or other factors unrelated to the intervention.
2 Most persons, including professionals and parents, who are involved in early intervention programs believe that those programs are effective in facilitating children's development.
3 A definite need exists for well-controlled, well-run evaluation studies concerning the effectiveness of early intervention with young handicapped children.
4 Evaluating the effectiveness of early intervention is difficult because of numerous ethical, practical, and methodological problems; however, some scientifically valid evaluation reports have been conducted.

Recently researchers have begun to describe the behavior of graduates of early intervention programs. Hayden, Morris, and Bailey (1977) followed up moderately handicapped

---

[2]For examples of evaluation studies with preschool handicapped children see: Brassell (1977); Bricker and Sheehan (1981); Cooke, Ruskus, Apolloni, and Peck (1981); Clunies-Ross (1979); Hanson and Schwarz (1978); Galloway and Chandler (1978); Hayden and Haring (1977); and Sandow and Clarke (1978). For examples of the literature related to early intervention program evaluation see: Bagnato and Neisworth (1980); Bricker (1978); Garwood (1982); May (1980); Sheehan and Keogh (1982); Simeonsson, Huntington, and Parse (1980); Simeonsson and Wiegerink (1975); Strain (1981); Swan (1981); Wang and Ellett (1982); and Zigler and Balla (1982).

children who had been enrolled in preschool programs for handicapped children 1–6 years earlier. Of this group, 34% were in regular class placements and 66% were in special class placements and of the latter, 22% were functioning as well as children in regular class placements. There appeared to be no trend toward placing children from regular programs into special classrooms; rather, language remediation in preschool may have prevented later cognitive deficits which in turn may have prevented special class placements.

In a similar study, Karnes, Schwedel, Lewis, Ratts, and Esry (1981) described the performance of mildly to moderately handicapped children who had been enrolled in preschool programs 1–5 years earlier. Of these children, 48% had speech and language impairments when they were enrolled in preschool. The group benefited from early intervention as measured by changes in their Stanford-Binet Intelligence Test scores.

In this group, 8% were currently enrolled in regular class placements, 18% had been retained in grade, and 12% of those placed in regular programs upon graduation from preschool were later placed in special education classes. The academic performance of children in regular classes as measured by achievement tests was similar to that of nonhandicapped children and tended to cluster around the mean performance of elementary children.

Parents who tended to be involved in their children's preschool program continued to do so after graduation from preschool. However, no comparison group was used, making it impossible to determine the extent to which these findings were a result of the early intervention program.

Moore, Fredericks, and Baldwin (1981) described the enduring effects of early intervention with children placed in classrooms for Trainable Mentally Retarded (TMR) children. The children were 9, 10, and 11 years old at the time of the follow-up study. They compared the social, motor, academic, language, and self-help skills of children who had varying amounts of early intervention. Some children had not attended preschool programs, others had gone for one year, and still others, two years. No statistically significant differences were found between children who had

no early intervention and those who had one year of early intervention. However, the scores of children with two years of preschool experience were higher than those with no preschool, and with the exception of social skills, the differences were statistically significant. Further, on some measures such as self-help skills, motor skills, and academic skills these differences became more apparent as the years since entering public school increased. These differences were found despite the fact that many of the more advanced children who had preschool experiences were transferred to other types of classes, and thus their performance was not included in the data collection and analysis.

In addition to the above findings, Moore et al. (1981) found that the characteristics of the post-preschool classrooms that maximized gains from preschools and facilitated new skill acquisition were "(a) maximizing instructional time, (b) appropriate delivery of cues and consequences, and (c) collecting and updating instructional data" (p. 103). Although post-preschool teachers could not discriminate between children who had and had not attended preschool, they strongly supported the practice of providing early intervention programs. Parents whose children had preschool experiences felt such programs definitely accelerated their children's acquisition of self-help skills and that their children were less of a physical drain than previously.

From these three follow-up studies with handicapped children, two tentative and one irrefutable conclusion can be made about the long-term effectiveness of early intervention. The tentative conclusions are that if children are placed in regular classrooms upon leaving early intervention programs, they then appear to continue in those classrooms and are rarely placed in special education programs. Also, gains made in early intervention programs appear to be maintained across developmental areas, especially if in the post-preschool classroom teachers devote a high percentage of time to direct instruction, frequently update individual programs, and accurately present the planned antecedents and consequences during instructional activities. The irrefutable conclusion is that the data on the long-term effectiveness of early intervention with handicapped children is extremely limited. There is a significant need for studies with comparison groups as compared to descriptive studies without such controls.

Why Provide Early Intervention Services?

One of the major reasons for having early intervention programs is to produce behavior changes in children. These changes are evidenced by accelerated rates of development, acquisition of new behaviors, and increased independent functioning. Another reason for providing intervention programs is the prevention of secondary handicaps. Consider 6-year-old Sandra who did not receive early intervention services. She is a severely retarded child who has learned some adaptive skills, but she has also learned that she can get her way by biting and throwing temper tantrums. She does this if she wants to be alone and if adults make requests of her or try to get her to participate in activities. These problems are so severe that school officials want to place her in a program for behaviorally disordered children. Had she been in a good early intervention program perhaps these problems might have been prevented.

Early intervention programs can also help detect secondary handicaps. For example, Larry is a 5-year-old Down syndrome child who does not speak and has very limited communication skills which his parents thought were a result of mental retardation. However, besides mental retardation, Larry has a hearing loss common in Down syndrome children. Had he been enrolled in an early intervention program, his hearing loss would have likely been identified and his communication skills developed.

Early intervention appears to reduce later costs of educating handicapped children (Antley & DuBose, 1981; Hayden & McGinness, 1977; Hayden & Pious, 1979). It is less expensive to educate children in the community than to care for them in institutions. For example, Antley and DuBose (1981) found that in the state of Washington, 3 years of preschool intervention and 12 years of special education will cost about $68,400. If the child was institutionalized during those years, the cost would be about $570,000. There is a savings to the state of about half a million dollars when children are educated in the community. These figures vary, depending upon the type of services in the community and the instutition, the type and severity of the child's handicap, and the state in which services are provided. Nonetheless, there is a dramatic economic incentive for society to educate children in the community as compared to caring for them in institutions. When children stay in the community, however, the economic costs for the family will be greater.

Garland, Swanson, Stone, and Woodruff (1981) suggest a relationship exists between the cost of educating a handicapped child and how early intervention begins. The earlier intervention begins, the less it will cost per year to educate the child. They suggest that if a child begins to receive intervention services before age 2 as compared to at school age, the cost per year will be about half as much. As with the research on the effects of early intervention, methodological problems exist with the research on the cost of early intervention. But the current data suggest that while early intervention with handicapped preschool children is expensive, in the long run it would be more economical to provide programs than nothing at all. More research in this area clearly needs to be conducted, comparing the costs of various early intervention programs with the benefits children derive from those programs, and the costs of early intervention and later education of children whose handicaps differ in severity.

Finally, parents of handicapped children need the assistance provided by early intervention activities. Most people in our society are not really prepared to be parents, let alone take care of a handicapped child. Most new parents of a handicapped child know very little about special education, different impairments, or procedures for providing appropriate care. Early intervention may take the form of providing information and training on how to care for or teach their child, along with respite from the pressure of constant care and emotional support. These issues are discussed in greater detail in Chapter 8. Even if children's rate of development was not accelerated by early intervention programs, the help that can be given to parents may make them worthwhile.

What Is the Current Status of Early Intervention?

In this section, we look at the type of children who attend early intervention programs, the service delivery models developed to serve those children, the curriculum used in early intervention programs, and the activities of teachers in those programs.

Type of Children Served   Unlike most special education classes in public schools, early intervention programs for the handicapped serve a broad range of children from birth to school age. There is a vast difference between a 3-month-old, a 3-year-old, and a 6-year-old child. Gary is 3 months old; he does not talk, crawl, walk, dress or feed himself, play with other children, and is not toilet trained. Heather is 3 years old; she says quite a bit and can make her needs and wishes known. She not only walks but can run, jump, ride a tricycle; she plays with other children, but does not engage in pretend play; she feeds herself but is rather messy; she can put on some clothing and take it off, but she does not button or tie her shoes; and she is toilet trained but she still wets the bed sometimes. Jill, age 6, is very grown up. She can carry on a detailed conversation, is learning to play hopscotch, rides a bicycle without training wheels, and enjoys playing games and "make-believe" with her friends. She dresses herself and ties her shoes; eats neatly and cuts food with a knife; and recognizes her name and some letters, and counts to 10. Each of these children is very different from one another, but all could be in an early intervention program.

Early intervention programs also serve children with all handicapping conditions. These include children who are at risk for developmental delays, blind or otherwise visually impaired, deaf or hearing impaired, physically disabled, cerebral palsied, mentally retarded, health impaired, behavior disordered, autistic, speech and language impaired, or a combination of these disorders. Some programs, called *categorical programs*, serve only specific dis-

abilities such as the deaf-blind or the cerebral palsied. Most intervention programs, however, are *cross-categorical programs* and serve children with any disability.

Early intervention programs also serve children whose handicaps vary in severity. For example, one child may be at risk for developmental delays, another may be mildly retarded, another moderately retarded, and still another have profound retardation. They would likely be functioning at different developmental levels, yet are all served in early intervention programs and sometimes within the same program.

Thus, unlike many special education classes for school-aged children, the type of children served in early intervention programs varies greatly. They range from birth to school age, and include all handicaps and degrees of severity or functioning levels.

Service Delivery Models Used   *Model* as used here refers to a pattern or design which can be replicated and repeated. *Service delivery* is how assistance is given to people who need it, and *service delivery models* are replicable patterns or designs of getting assistance to those who need it, such as families of young children with handicaps.

A broad range of models have been developed. Each of these models has advantages and disadvantages, and some are more suited for given children, locations, and communities than others. In this section, we describe four general models: home-based, center-based, home- and center-based, and parent consultation. Many variations and combinations of these models exist. Jordan, Hayden, Karnes, and Wood (1977) provide extensive descriptions of various models; Tjossem (1976) discusses various effective early intervention programs, and descriptions of programs funded through the Handicapped Children's Early Education Program (HCEEP) are found in the *HCEEP Overview and Directory* (e.g., May & Meyer, 1980).

In the *home-based model*, as the name would imply, services are provided in the child's home. Usually a worker goes into the home one to three times a week. Home-based programs are generally in rural areas where transporting the children to a center would take a lot of time, and with a small population of handicapped preschoolers living a long distance away from each other. These programs typically direct their services to infants and children under 2 years, but some include older preschool children.

In home-based programs, professionals assess the child to determine what skills he or she needs to acquire, help the parent plan the training activities, train the parent to implement the activities, and monitor parent and child progress. The major portion of the professional's job is to train the parent. The most widely used, and probably the best procedure is to describe what you want the parent to do, show the parent how to do it, ask the parent to do it while you watch, and give parents feedback on how well they did. The parent must also be trained to collect data to assist the professional in evaluating the effectiveness of the training activities. Frequently, professionals will check the parent's and child's performance on the skill during home visits. Paraprofessionals are sometimes used as home workers, with professionals supervising their activities. Supervision includes joint planning with the paraprofessionals and accompanying them on frequent home visits.

Parents are the real workers in the home-based models and do the largest portion of the actual child training. They collect data and give the professionals feedback on the child's progress. Involving parents requires a lot of time and effort. Professionals must take care not to overburden parents and to develop teaching activities that can be done within daily caregiving routines. Soliciting the assistance of older siblings, grandparents, and on occasion neighbors can ease the demands on the parent.

The home-based model has a number of advantages. Young and frail children and families without transportation can stay at home and still receive services. Also, these programs are relatively inexpensive because they do not require large facilities that cost a lot to build and maintain. In addition, the child is in a natural setting, so generalization should be less of a problem than in center-based programs. Further, parents are involved in their child's program, and the home worker can give them the individualized information, training, and emotional support they may need. Frequently, strong friendships are established between home workers and parents.

Home-based programs have some disadvantages, the primary one being that parents are required to do so much work. Not all people are good teachers, and these include some parents of handicapped children. Because parent participation is so critical to the success of the program, an unmotivated parent makes it difficult to make the program work. Further, the parent gets no break from the caretaking responsibilities because the child does not go to school. Another disadvantage is that the programming may not be as broad as it is in center-based programs. And as the child gets older and needs more social interactions with peers, the home-based model becomes restrictive. Finally, the teacher is on the road a good bit of the time. As a result, valuable planning, teaching, and record-keeping time is lost.

A classic example of the home-based model is the Portage Project of Portage, Wisconsin developed in the late 1960s by David and Marsha Shearer (Shearer & Shearer, 1972; 1976). The Portage Project is a cross-categorical program serving handicapped children from birth to age 6 in a rural area. The project staff developed a developmental checklist and corresponding curriculum materials (Bluma, Shearer, Frohman, & Hilliard, 1976).

In the *center-based model*, services are provided in a center or school. Usually, the children are 2 or 3 years old to school age, although some centers include infants. Children frequently come to the center 4–5 days per week, but may come only 2 or 3 days. School days are usually 3–5 hours long. Center-based programs are usually urban, but there is also a large number of rural center-based programs. These programs vary considerably as to the quality of their facilities; some have beautiful physical plants and others are in the basements of old school buildings, churches, and so on. The quality of the building has very little to do with the quality of the services provided, but it can affect staff morale and influence outside visitors.

The services provided in center-based programs usually include training across all areas of development with assistance from support personnel. Professionals are heavily involved in assessing children's needs, providing instruction, supervising teacher aides who do a lot of teaching, monitoring child performance, and record keeping. Frequently teachers are involved with parents, but sometimes one staff member is assigned the role of parent worker and does all these activities. However, when teachers are directly involved in providing services to parents, they are more apt to have accurate views of what the child can do and what will work, and are able to provide parents with more realistic activities. Further, when a parent sees a teacher working with his or her child and enjoying the activities, then the parent usually appreciates the teacher's efforts and will be more receptive to his or her training suggestions.

Parent involvement in center-based programs includes the parent observing and participating in the class. Parent training is done through group meetings and through participation in the class. Sometimes the parents carry over the training at home to ensure maintenance and generalization of the skills learned in the center. Communication between the center and home is established when the parents come into the center, by telephone, or by a series of notes back and forth between the home and center.

The center-based model has several distinct advantages, including the efficient use of staff time and the ease of supervision. Team members can work closely with one another because they are all in one location. Two child-related advantages of the center-based model are an increased opportunity for socialization with other children, and if their parents are unable to be involved in training, the child still receives needed training. Finally, good public relations can be easily established. Service clubs, social clubs, the United Way, and other interested members of the community can come to the center, observe the program, become educated about early intervention, and then support the program through financial support, sharing of expertise, as volunteers, and as advocates for early intervention services. In center-based programs these groups may come to the center, but in home-based programs establishing good public relations is much more difficult.

Three major disadvantages exist in center-based programs. The first is transportation, and the problems can be overwhelming. School buses are very expensive to purchase and maintain, especially those equipped for handicapped children. Transportation can also

consume a lot of director or teacher time. Frequently a child will move and the route will have to be changed, or the driver will quit or get sick, or the bus gets stuck in the mud or snow, or breaks down. The second major disadvantage of the center-based model is the cost of the building and upkeep. The final disadvantage is that parent involvement is usually less than in home-based programs, making it harder to establish a good relationship between the teachers and parents.

A good example of a center-based program is the Model Preschool Program at the University of Washington. This project was developed by Norris Haring and Alice Hayden and is now being directed by Rebecca Fewell (Hayden & Haring, 1976; Hayden, Morris, & Bailey, 1977). The project has three programs: a program for Down syndrome and other developmentally delayed children, an integrated program, and a communication disorders program. Children are transported to the center and receive training across all areas of development. Support services from related disciplines are also available.

The third model is the combination *home- and center-based model* and there are two basic types. The first serves the younger children in the home and the older children in the center. The second places and serves the children dependent upon their individual needs. For example, one child may come to the center every day and receive a visit from a home worker once every two weeks, another child may come to the center two days a week and receive a weekly visit from the home worker, and a third child may receive a visit from the home worker every week but not attend the center.

The activities of professionals in the home- and center-based model depend upon their role, and will be similar to their counterparts in either the home or center-based programs, dependent upon which area they work. The services children receive and parents' roles also depend upon the child's placement in the program.

The advantages of the home- and center-based model are similar to the combined advantages of the home-only and center-only models. One additional advantage is the flexibility in meeting children and family needs. The disadvantages are also similar, but occur with less intensity. An added disadvantage of the home- and center-based model is the supervision and scheduling of staff members, particularly in large programs.

A classic example of the home- and center-based model is the Precise Early Education of Children with Handicaps (PEECH) at the University of Illinois, Urbana-Champaign. The project was developed by Merle Karnes (Karnes, 1977; Karnes & Zehrbach, 1977) and serves mildly to moderately multiple-handicapped children ages 3 to school age. The project has an extensive screening program and a team approach to early intervention. Children are served in one of several classrooms or in their homes.

The final model, the *consultation-to-parents model,* is very popular. Although several variations exist, it is really the reverse of the home-based model. Usually the programs are cross-categorical and frequently serve infants. The parents bring the infant to the center to be seen by the professionals about once a week. Thus, as in the home-based model, the parent does the major training of the child. Parents receive training from the professionals who conduct assessments and monitor performance.

One advantage of this model is that parents can meet with other parents while at the center, allowing them to develop useful support systems. Another advantage is that a team of professionals can see the child without visiting the home; thus, there is better utilization of staff time than in the home-based model. The disadvantage, of course, is the strong reliance upon the parents to do the child training and provide transportation.

Several examples and variations of this model exist. The Atypical Infant Development Program (AID) in Marin County, California includes a parent-infant group. AID is a cross-categorical program for handicapped and at risk children ages birth to 3 years. Parents are trained by professionals, and bring their children to the program once a week. The parents also spend an hour each week with a staff member in a discussion group (Nielsen, Collins, Meisel, Lowry, Engh, & Johnson, 1975). A similar program is the Infant Learning Program for High Risk and Handicapped Children at the University of Washington in Seattle (Gentry & Adams, 1977). In this project, parents and infants are seen individually as compared to in a group as in Project

AID. Both projects use a variety of disciplines in meeting the needs of the children.

What Is The Curriculum in Early Intervention?

The curriculum in early intervention programs depends upon the needs of the children, but generally includes the developmental areas of cognitive, social, language, motor, and self-help and subareas such as fine and gross motor skills in motor development, or eating, self-feeding, toileting, dressing, and undressing skills in self-help. The breadth and scope of the early intervention curriculum is immense. For example, in cognitive development, an appropriate objective for an infant might be to visually follow and track a slow-moving object, but for an older child it might be to verbally state which of several sets has the largest number of objects. The interactions between the curriculum areas is also considerable. For example, an apparently simple response such as waving bye-bye has motor, communication, and social components. Unfortunately, some interactions have not been clearly specified.

The purposes of the early intervention curriculum are to accelerate children's developmental progress and to maximize independent functioning. With some children (e.g., mildly and moderately handicapped children) the primary emphasis is on accelerating developmental progress. With more severely handicapped children, the emphasis is on maximizing independent functioning. This conflict between developmental and functional approaches to programming for children is discussed in detail in the next chapter.

Many published curricula will be listed throughout this text; for a review of infant curricula see Bailey, Jens, and Johnson (1983). Relatively few of the curricula have been empirically validated, although procedures for conducting such evaluations exist (Wolery, 1983; Wood & Hurley, 1977).

What do Early Intervention Teachers Do?

In a given program a teacher may serve children who have several different handicapping conditions, have various levels of severity within each condition, and represent a wide age range. The service delivery models are unique and varied, and the curriculum covers many areas with numerous skills. In addition, teachers interact almost daily with parents who have differing strengths and needs and with professionals who have different backgrounds, experiences, and viewpoints. In the final analysis, however, what teachers do in early intervention programs is *teach*. This book is about *teaching*. It is also about how young children *learn* new skills as well as how they refine and adapt old skills in new situations. The teacher can facilitate learning through a variety of techniques: providing the right toys or materials at the right time, arranging specific aspects of the environment, giving direct instruction, demonstrating a skill, and rewarding, ignoring, or punishing certain behaviors. The secret to good teaching is knowing *what* learning should occur, *when* it should occur, and the most appropriate *method* to insure that it does occur.

Teaching is a complex decision-making process that requires constant attention to different facets of children and their development. Teachers must have a basic knowledge of a wide range of concepts, theories, and strategies and must plan programs for children who have greatly diverse needs. Teachers need flexibility and alertness to make instantaneous and accurate decisions about children in a classroom situation. Read the following, considering all of the important decisions we teachers make every day:

Greg is a 3-month-old child with Down syndrome. His parents were devastated when they learned of his handicap, and refused to accept the fact that anything is wrong, denying the need for early intervention. Should the teacher advocate placing Greg in a highly stimulating early intervention program? To what extent should his parents be pushed into counseling or participating in intervention?

Alicia is 6 years old and is severely retarded. A team of experts agrees that a major goal for the coming year should be the beginnings of a communication system. Should verbal communication be the first instructional goal or should augmentative communication be considered?

These examples suggest that teaching young handicapped children is no easy job. Rather than follow a "cookbook" formula, we must continually revise, adapt, and modify procedures to meet the needs of the individual child.

AREAS OF IMPORTANCE TO TEACHERS

Understanding Theory and Research

Because of the great variability in problems and abilities of young handicapped children, teachers should not only apply instructional techniques but should also have a basic understanding of their theory and empirical support. They should also be able to describe why a particular strategy is being used. For every child who fits the textbook examples, many more demonstrate unique learning and developmental patterns. The only way a teacher can appropriately individualize instruction is to have a basic understanding of the theory behind it and a technology for adapting or modifying that theory to meet individual needs.

Many curriculum packages have been developed in an attempt to provide teachers with a series of goals and activities designed to meet the needs of young handicapped children. Although these curricula are generally useful, we feel that knowledge of available curricula is not enough. This text is an attempt to merge the basic concepts of normal and exceptional child development with what is currently known about strategies for early intervention with handicapped children. Developmental skill areas typically included in most intervention curricula, theoretical issues, and the empirical status of intervention strategies are discussed later in the text.

Unfortunately, the field of early intervention is, in many ways, still in an infant state. Although much research has been conducted over the past twenty years, many issues remain unresolved. Teachers must be aware of the current status of various theoretical and empirical issues so that new interventions can be critically evaluated as to their applicability, relevance, and logic.

Normal Child Development

Special educators sometimes have little awareness of what normal children are like. A basic understanding of normal child development is important because, to prepare handicapped children to function with nonhandicapped peers, we need to know the latter's characteristics and abilities. An understanding of normal child development can serve as a useful basis for devising instructional sequences; it can also make teachers aware of the extent to which handicapped children vary from those sequences. Modified developmental sequences can be planned to meet the needs of individual handicapped children.

In each chapter of this text, we will describe relevant sequences of normal development and provide references for further readings. In addition, we will discuss applications and implications of normal development for the instruction of handicapped children.

Planning and Assessment

Planning helps teachers, parents, and children know where they are headed in an instructional program. Through planning the teacher identifies specific instructional objectives for each child and has conceptualized and detailed a series of intervention strategies designed to meet those needs. In addition, the teacher:

1 Knows the child's current level of skill
2 Understands and identifies appropriate instructional targets
3 Specifies the degree of accuracy and fluency of the child's performance of desired instructional targets
4 Identifies and implements individually designed instructional strategies to meet the needs of each child
5 Compares progress in instructional programs with desired goals to determine if intervention is working and whether a change should be made in the strategies

The basic foundation for planning is *assessment*—the systematic gathering of information to determine the current level of functioning, identify instructional objectives, and evaluate instructional progress. Teachers must be familiar with developmental sequences and a variety of instructionally relevant assessment tools to translate assessment information into functionally useful instructional objectives. They must also be able to gather and interpret daily data on progress.

Chapter 2 is devoted to instructional planning, beginning with basic considerations in the educational assessment of young handicapped children and extending through task analysis and writing behavioral objectives. Other chapters in the text include strategies for assessment within specific skills areas and guidelines for identifying appropriate learning outcomes. Chapters 5–7 address the need for appropriate planning of preschool environments.

Learning Theory

A *behavioral principle* describes the relationship between behavior and the variables affecting it (Sulzer-Azaroff & Mayer, 1977). For example, it is a well-accepted principle that people tend to repeat those behaviors for which they have been rewarded or reinforced in the past. Behavioral principles are derived from the extensive body of literature and research on learning theory, with underlying assumption that people change their behavior (i.e., learn) through experience. The more we know about the relationship between experience and behavior, the more effectively we can design appropriate learning environments. A *behavioral procedure* is the systematic application of behavior principles to bring about change in behavior and therefore facilitate learning. Good teaching requires the application of behavioral procedures during the learning process.

Chapters 3 and 4 are devoted to more detailed descriptions and applications of learning theory and behavioral procedures. Chapter 3 provides an overview of behavioral procedures, with emphasis on the acquisition, fluency-building, and generalization processes as well as strategies for collecting and analyzing individual child performance data. Chapter 4 focuses on the specific topic of imitation and its importance in the development and teaching of young exceptional children.

Environmental Design

Programs for young handicapped children must be planned to include time and space for both *acquisition* (skill learning) and *generalization* (skill application) experiences. Acquisition often requires individual or small group instruction that is teacher-directed and focused on specific tasks. The ability to design effective acquisition programs requires an understanding of practical applications of learning theory. In contrast, generalization requires intrinsically motivating play and real-life activities that elicit and integrate a number of the acquired skills. The ability to design effective generalization experiences requires an understanding of environmental design and a recognition of the important role of parents.

Three chapters are devoted to environmental design. In Chapter 5 we address considerations in planning environments for young children, including organization, structure, and scheduling. In Chapter 6 we discuss the physical environment and provide suggestions for arranging and adapting it to meet the needs of individuals. In Chapter 7 we address the specific topic of engagement and provide strategies for encouraging appropriate engagement with materials, tasks, and persons.

Parent Involvement in Determining and Implementing Instructional Strategies

Each of us has his or her own *ecosystem* that includes the various surroundings where we live as well as the relations and interconnections existing between these environments (Bronfenbrenner, 1976). The concept of ecosystem is particularly important for very young children because of the unique nature of their relationship with their parents. During the infant and preschool years parent-child attachments form and then develop as children mature and begin to leave home for day-care and school activities. To ignore the critical role of parents would defeat one broad goal of early intervention: to have a meaningful impact upon a child's life that extends beyond the school setting.

Early intervention programs are needed to provide emotional support for parents who have only recently discovered that their child is handicapped. Programs can also provide information to families on handling children. Perhaps most importantly, early intervention specialists can help parents learn to love and accept their exceptional child at a time when emotional bonding is critical.

Early intervention programs also need parents. The critical role parents play has been

discussed by a number of specialists (e.g., Bromwich, 1981; Fraiberg, 1975; Horton, 1976; Shearer & Shearer, 1976). Committed and involved parents can facilitate generalization at home, provide the solid emotional base to help children confidently go to preschool, and assist in a variety of in-school and out-of-school activities.

In addition, parents of young exceptional children require individualized programming (Bricker & Casuso, 1979) to address their needs and concerns. These include more information about their child and his or her program, training, emotional support, or related family services. Even if the program cannot identify specific concerns, it can serve as a base of support and parents can be referred to other appropriate agencies.

Like early intervention, parent involvement should be viewed as a process. This process includes assessment of parental needs, shared goal setting and activity planning, implementation of activities to meet goals, and evaluation of activities (Munson, Neel, & Wolery, 1979). Assessment should be comprehensive and should identify parental needs. Shared goal setting should give parents the opportunity to discuss what changes, if any, should be made, based on the results of the needs assessment. Activities can include a variety of things, such as receiving training, discussing certain issues with specialists, advocating for services, and training someone to provide respite care for their child. During evaluation, parents determine whether the goals have been met and set new goals.

Chapter 8 of this text focuses on the early parent-child relationship and describes strategies and resources for encouraging and facilitating meaningful parent involvement.

SUMMARY

Society's commitment to early intervention is marked by progressive changes in its interests. People have become more aware of the importance of the childhood years and of children in general. Interest in typical preschool children preceded interest in preschool handicapped children, and awareness of the needs of individual members and of minority groups set the stage for recognizing the needs of handicapped persons. The belief that intellectual development was a fixed entity and that retardation was a result of heredity has gradually changed to the view that environment is a powerful force in shaping both intellectual and general development. Because of the increasing importance of education, society has recognized the value of providing special education, including early intervention services.

We briefly reviewed the literature on the effectiveness of early intervention with low income children noting that early intervention appears to accelerate their development. But while some positive benefits are maintained after preschool, the benefits of early intervention were not as great as expected. Similarly, with young handicapped children, early intervention appears to accelerate their development and result in more independent functioning. However, because of many methodological problems with the evaluation studies, more well-controlled and well-implemented research is needed. Long-term gains appeared to be maintained, but once again significantly more research is needed. Several additional reasons exist for providing early intervention programs: prevention of the development of secondary handicaps; identification and remediation of secondary handicaps; programs appear to be cost effective; and parents may benefit from early intervention.

Programs serve a wide age range of children with all types of handicaps, and different levels of severity within each condition. Four general service delivery models are used: home-based, center-based, home- and center-based, and consultation-to-parents. The curriculum in early intervention programs includes several interacting developmental areas, each having many objectives. Instructors in intervention programs engage in a variety of teaching behaviors.

We made several assumptions about early intervention and about teachers' knowledge and competencies in programs. These include the importance of understanding theory and research, normal child development, planning and assessment, learning theory, environmental design, and parent involvement.

REFERENCES

Antley, T.R., & DuBose, R.F. *A case for early intervention: Summary of program findings, longitudinal data, and cost-effectiveness.* Seattle: Experimental Education Unit, 1981.

Baer, D.M. Nature of intervention research. In R.L. Schiefelbusch & D. Bricker (Eds.), *Early language—acquisition and intervention.* Baltimore: University Park Press, 1981.

Bailey, D.B., Jens, K.G., & Johnson, N. Curricula for handicapped infants. In R. Fewell & S.G. Garwood (Eds.), *Educating handicapped infants.* Germantown, Md.: Aspen Systems Corporation, 1983.

Bagnato, S.J., & Neisworth, J.T. The intervention efficiency index (IEI): An approach to preschool program accountability. *Exceptional Children,* 1980, *48,* (4), 264–271.

Beller, E. Research on organized programs of early education. In R. Travers (Ed.), *Second handbook on research on teaching.* Skokie. Ill.: Rand McNally, 1973.

Bloom, B.S. *Stability and change in human characteristics.* New York: Wiley, 1964.

Bluma, S.M., Shearer, M.S., Frohman, A.H., & Hilliard, J.M. *Portage guide to early education: Manual.* Portage, Wis. Cooperative Education Service Agency, 1976.

Brassell, W.R. Intervention with handicapped infants: Correlates of progress. *Mental Retardation,* 1977, *15,* 18–22.

Bricker, D. Early intervention: The criteria of success. *Allied Health and Behavioral Sciences,* 1978, *1,* 567–582.

Bricker, D., & Casuso, V. Family involvement: A critical component of early intervention. *Exceptional Children,* 1979, *46,* 108–116.

Bricker, D. & Sheehan, R. Effectiveness of an early intervention program as indexed by measures of child change. *Journal of the Division for Early Childhood,* 1981, *4,* 11–27.

Bricker, W.A. Identifying and modifying behavioral deficits. *American Journal of Mental Deficiency,* 1970, *75,* 16–21.

Bromwich, R. *Working with parents and infants: An interactional approach.* Baltimore: University Park Press, 1981.

Bronfenbrenner, U. Is early intervention effective? In B. Friedlander, G. Sterritt, & G. Kirk (Eds.) *Exceptional infant: Assessment and intervention,* (Vol. 3). New York: Brunner/Mazel, 1975.

Bronfenbrenner, U. The experimental ecology of education. *Educational Researcher,* 1976, *5*(9), 5–15.

Cicirelli, V., et al. *The impact of Head Start. An evaluation of the effects of Head Start on children's cognitive and affective development.* Report to the U.S. Office of Economic Opportunity by Westinghouse Learning Corporation and Ohio University. Washington, D.C.: Government Printing Office, 1969.

Cicirelli, V., Evans, J., & Schiller, J. *The impact of Head Start: A reply to the report analysis.* Harvard Educational Review, 1970, *40,* 105–129.

Clunies-Ross, G. Accelerating the development of

Down's syndrome infants and young children. *Journal of Special Education*, 1979, *13*, 169–177.

Cooke, T.P., Ruskus, J.A., Apolloni, T., & Peck, C.A. Handicapped preschool children in the mainstream: Background, outcomes, and clinical suggestions. *Topics in Early Childhood Special Education*, 1981, *1*, 73–83.

Deasey, D. *Education under six*. New York: St. Martin's Press, 1978.

Dunst, C.J., & Rheingrover, R.M. An analysis of the efficacy of infant intervention programs with organically handicapped children. *Evaluation and Program Planning*, 1981, *4*, 287–323.

Elardo, R., Bradley, R., & Caldwell, B.M. A longitudinal study of the relation of infants' home environment to language development at age three. *Child Development*, 1977, *48*, 595–603.

Evans, E.D. *Contemporary influences in early childhood education* (2nd ed.), New York: Holt, Rinehart and Winston, 1975.

Fraiberg, S. Intervention in infancy: A program for blind infants. In B. Friedlander, G. Sterritt, & G. Kirk (Eds.), *Exceptional infant: Assessment and intervention* (Vol. 3). New York: Bruner/Mazel, 1975.

Galloway, C., & Chandler, P. The marriage of special and generic early education services. In M.J. Guralnick (Ed.), *Early intervention and the integration of handicapped and nonhandicapped children*. Baltimore: University Park Press, 1978.

Garland, C., Swanson, J., Stone, N., & Woodruff, G. (Eds.). *Early intervention for children with special needs and their families* (WESTAR Series Paper No. 11). Monmouth, Oreg.: WESTAR, 1981.

Garwood, S.G. (Mis)use of developmental scales in program evaluation. *Topics in Early Childhood Special Education*, 1982, *1*(4), 61–69.

Gentry, D., & Adams, G. Rationale and procedures for infant education programs. In N.G. Haring (Ed.), *The Experimental Education Training Program*. Seattle: University of Washington, 1977.

Gotts, E.E. The training of intelligence as a component of early interventions: Past, present, and future. *Journal of Special Education*, 1981, *15*, 257–268.

Gray, S.W., Klaus, R.A., & Ramsey, B.K. *From three to twenty: The early training project*. Baltimore: University Park Press, 1982.

Hanson, M., & Schwarz, R. Results of a longitudinal intervention program for Down syndrome infants and their families. *Education and Training of the Mentally Retarded*, 1978, *13*, 403–407.

Hayden, A.H. Handicapped children, birth to age 3. *Exceptional Children*, 1979, *45*(7), 510–516.

Hayden, A.H., & Haring, N.G. Early intervention for high risk infants and young children: Programs for Down syndrome children. In T.D. Tojessem (Ed.), *Intervention strategies for high risk infants and young children*. Baltimore: University Park Press, 1976.

Hayden, A.H., & Haring, N.G. The acceleration and maintenance of developmental gains in Down's syndrome school age children. In P. Mittler (Ed.), *Research to practice in mental retardation (Vol. 1): Care and intervention*. Baltimore: University Park Press, 1977.

Hayden, A.H., & McGinness, G.D. Bases for early intervention. In E. Sontag (Ed.), *Educational programming for the severely and profoundly handicapped*. Reston, Va.: Council for Exceptional Children, 1977.

Hayden, A.H., Morris, K., & Bailey, D.B. *Effectiveness of early education for handicapped children. Final Report*. Seattle: University of Washington, 1977.

Hayden, A.H., & Pious, C.G. The case for early intervention. In R. York and E.B. Edgar (Eds.), *Teaching the severely handicapped* (Vol. 4), Columbus, Ohio: Special Press, 1979.

Hodges, W., & Cooper, M. Head Start and Follow Through: Influences on intellectual development. *Journal of Special Education*, 1981, *15*, 221–238.

Horton, K. Early intervention for hearing impaired infants and young children. In T.D. Tjossem (Ed.), *Intervention strategies for high risk infants and children*. Baltimore: University Park Press, 1976.

Horowitz, F., & Paden, L. The effectiveness of environmental intervention programs. In B. Caldwell & H. Ricciuti (Eds.), *Review of child development research* (Vol. 3). Chicago: University of Chicago Press, 1973.

House, E., Glass, G., McLean, L., & Walker, D. No simple answer: Critique of the Follow Through evaluation. *Harvard Education Review*, 1978, *48*, 128–160.

Hunt, J. McV. *Intelligence and experience*. New York: Ronald, 1961.

Jordan, J.B., Hayden, A.H., Karnes, M.B., & Wood, M. (Eds.), *Early childhood education for exceptional children*. Reston, Va.: The Council for Exceptional Children, 1977.

Karnes, M.B. Exemplary early education programs for handicapped children: Characteristics in common. *Educational Horizons*, 1977, *56*(1), 47–54.

Karnes, M.B., Schwedel, A.M., Lewis, G.F., Ratts, D.A., & Esry, D.R. Impact of early programming for the handicapped: A follow-up study into the elementary school. *Journal of the Division for Early Childhood*, 1981, *4*, 62–79.

Karnes, M.B., & Zehrbach, R. Alternative models for delivering services to young handicapped children. In J.B. Jordan, A.H. Hayden, M.B. Karnes, & M.M. Wood (Eds.), *Early childhood education for exceptional children*. Reston, Va.: The Council for Exceptional Children, 1977.

Kazdin, A.E. Statistical analyses for single-case experimental designs. In M. Hersen & D. Barlow (Eds.), *Single case experiemental designs: Strategies for studying behavior change*. New York: Pergamon Press, 1976.

Klaus, R., & Gray, S. The early training project for disadvantaged children: A report after five years. *Monographs of the Society for Research in Child Development*, 1968, *53* (Serial No. 120).

Lazar, I., & Darlington, R. Lasting effects of early education: A report from the consortium for longitudinal studies. *Monographs of the Society for Research in Child Development*, 1982, *47*(2 & 3, Serial No. 195).

May, M.J. (Ed.), *Evaluating Handicapped children's early education programs*. Seattle: WESTAR, 1980.

May, M.J., & Meyer, R. *Handicapped children's early education program: 1979–1980 overview and directory.* Seattle: WESTAR, 1980.

MacMillan, D.L. *Mental retardation in schools and society.* Boston: Little, Brown & Company, 1977.

Miller, L.B., & Dyer, J.L. Four preschool programs: Their dimensions and effects. *Monographs of the Society for Research in Child Development,* 1975, *40* (Serial No. 161).

Moore, M.G., Fredericks, H.D., & Baldwin, V.L. The long-range effects of early childhood education on a trainable mentally retarded population. *Journal of the Division for Early Childhood,* 1981, *4,* 94–110.

Munson, R., Neel, R.S., & Wolery, M.R. *Training manual for teachers of autistic and severely behavior disordered children.* Olympia, Wa.: Office of Public Instruction, 1979.

Nielsen, G., Collins, S., Meisel, J., Lowry, M., Engh, H., & Johnson, D. An intervention program for typical infants. In B.A. Friedlander, G. Sterritt, & G. Kirk (Eds.), *Exceptional infant assessment and intervention* (Vol. 3). New York: Brunner/Mazel, 1975.

Sandow, S., & Clarke, A.D. Home intervention with parents of severely subnormal, preschool children: An interim report. *Child, Care, Health and Development,* 1978, *4,* 29–39.

Schweinhart, L.J., & Weikart, D.P. *Young children grow up: The effects of the Perry Preschool Program on youths through age 15* (Monograph No. 7) Ypsilanti, Mich.: The High Scope Press, 1980.

Schweinhart, L.J., & Weikart, D.P. Effects of the Perry Preschool Program on youths through age 15. *Journal of the Division of Early Childhood,* 1981, *4,* 29–39.

Shearer, M., & Shearer, D. The Portage Project: A model for early childhood education. *Exceptional Children,* 1972, *39,* 210–217.

Shearer, D., & Shearer, M. The Portage Project: A model for early childhood intervention. In T. Tjossem (Ed.), *Intervention strategies for high risk infants and young children.* Baltimore: University Park Press, 1976.

Sheehan, R., & Keogh, B. Design and analysis in the evaluation of early childhood special education programs. *Topics in Early Childhood Special Education,* 1982, *1*(4), 81–88.

Simeonsson, R.J., Cooper, D.H., & Scheiner, A.P. A review and analysis of the effectiveness of early intervention programs. *Pediatrics,* 1982, *69,* 635–641.

Simeonsson, R.J., Huntington, G.S., & Parse, S.W. Assessment of children with severe handicaps: Multiple problems—multivariate goals. *Journal of the Association for the Severely Handicapped,* 1980, *5,* 55–72.

Simeonsson, R.J., & Wiegerink, R. Accountability: A dilemma in infant intervention. *Exceptional Children,* 1975, *41,* 474–481.

Skeels, H. Adult status of children with contrasting early life experiences: A follow-up study. *Monographs of the Society for Research in Child Development,* 1966, *31,* (Serial No. 105).

Skeels, H., & Dye, H. A study of.the effects of differential stimulation on mentally retarded children. *Proceedings and Addresses of the American Association on Mental Deficiency,* 1939, *44,* 114–136.

Smith, M.S., & Bissell, J.S. Report analysis: The impact of Head Start. *Harvard Educational Review,* 1970, *40,* 51–104.

Stallings, J. Implementation and child effects of teaching practices in Follow Through classrooms. *Monographs of the Society for Research in Child Development,* 1975, *40* (Serial No. 163).

Stanley, J.C. *Compensatory education for children, ages 2 to 8.* Baltimore: Johns Hopkins University Press, 1973.

Strain, P.S. Conceptual and methodological issues in efficacy research with behaviorally disordered children. *Journal of the Division for Early Childhood,* 1981, *4,* 110–124.

Sulzer-Azaroff, B., & Mayer, G. *Applying behavior-analysis procedures with children and youth.* New York: Holt, Rinehart & Winston, 1977.

Swan, W.W. Efficacy studies in early childhood special education: An overview. *Journal of the Division for Early Childhood,* 1981, *4,* 1–4.

Tjossem, T.D. *Intervention strategies for high risk infants and young children.* Baltimore: University Park Press, 1976.

Wachs, T. Proximal experience and early cognitive-intellectual development: The physical environment. *Merrill-Palmer Quarterly,* 1979, *25,* 3–41.

Wang, M.C., & Ellet, C.D. Program validation: The state of the art. *Topics in Early Childhood Special Education,* 1982, *1*(4), 35–49.

White, O.R. Practical program evaluation: Many problems and a few solutions. In M.J. May (Ed.), *Evaluating handicapped children's early education programs.* Seattle: WESTAR, 1980.

Wolery, M. Evaluating curricula: Purposes and strategies. *Topics in Early Childhood Special Education,* 1983, *2*(4) 15–24.

Wolery M., & Harris, S.R. Interpreting results of single-subject research designs. *Physical Therapy,* 1982, *62,* 445–452.

Wood, M.B., & Hurley, O.L. Curriculum and instruction. In J.B. Jordan, A.H. Hayden, M.B. Karnes, & M.M. Wood (Eds.), *Early childhood education for exceptional children.* Reston, Va.: The Council for Exceptional Children, 1977.

Yarrow, L., Rubenstein, J., & Pedersen, F. *Infant and environment: Early cognitive and motivational development.* New York: Halsted Press, 1975.

Zigler, E., & Balla, D. Selecting outcome variables in evaluations of early childhood special education programs. *Topics in Early Childhood Special Education,* 1982, *1* (4), 11–22.

Zigler, E., & Hunsinger, S. Look at the state of American's children in the Year of the Child. *Young Children,* 1979, *34,* 2–3.

The teacher's first task in designing an appropriate intervention program is to determine the skills each child needs to master and the sequence in which those skills should be taught. Determining instructional targets requires a basic understanding of child development, a knowledge of child assessment techniques, and the ability to relate developmental skills to the everyday demands placed on children. In this chapter we review general assessment strategies for identifying skills children should be taught, discuss considerations in selecting and conducting assessments, and describe the process of developing individualized instructional plans on the basis of assessment information. The assumption underlying this chapter is that a meaningful assessment is a necessary prerequisite to appropriate intervention.

ASSESSMENT

Assessment refers to the process of gathering information for the purpose of making a decision. Different assessment strategies are appropriate for different decisions; a teacher of young handicapped children should be able to select or design assessment procedures that match specific needs for information.

At least three broad methods of obtaining information about children may be identified: direct testing, naturalistic observation, and interviews. Each procedure has its advantages and disadvantages, and may be implemented in a variety of ways.

Direct Testing

Testing is a form of assessment in which a set of standard tasks is presented using predetermined administration procedures, then interpreted in a standard manner. An assumption underlying the use of tests is that those standards are maintained in any test situation. Consistency in administration and in scoring procedures facilitates communication and allows for meaningful interpretation of test results.

Assume, for example, that five early childhood special educators are asked to determine whether Jody can cut with scissors. The results of the testing may vary considerably, depending upon the teachers' materials, procedures, and scoring criteria. One teacher might use blunt-end scissors while another

Determining Instructional Targets

uses pointed scissors. One might give Jody a piece of notebook paper while another gives her construction paper. One teacher may require Jody to cut out a shape while another asks her to cut along a straight line. The end result might be that some teachers would say that Jody could cut with scissors while others would say that she had not yet mastered the skill. The only way to resolve these differences is to specify the precise materials, procedures, and criteria by which Jody is to be tested and her performance evaluated.

Tests are developed for different purposes, and the decision to use a certain test should be consistent with the original purpose of the instrument. Tests are used for screening, diagnosis, and educational assessment. *Screening* typically refers to the assessment of a large number of children to determine those at risk for some problem. For example, a hearing screening might identify children with hearing losses. Because a large number of children usually participate in a screening program, the test used must be short, economical, and easy to administer. *Data obtained from screening should only be used to refer children for further evaluation.* A decision about the presence of a problem (e.g., hearing loss) should never be made on the basis of screening information alone. *Diagnosis* refers to the verification of a particular problem, and requires considerably more testing than screening. Diagnostic statements should be made only when the tester is quite sure that the diagnosis is accurate. For example, parents should not be told their child is mentally retarded unless the diagnostic team is certain of the conclusion. *Educational assessment* refers to the use of tests for instructional planning and represents the kind of assessment in which the teacher is most typically involved. Educational assessment also requires the collection of a considerable amount of information about the child.

In all assessment activities, the assessor must be sure that the process is conducted in a nondiscriminatory manner. See Bailey and Harbin (1980) for a discussion of this issue.

At least three broad types of tests may be identified to fulfill the basic purposes of assessment: norm-referenced tests, criterion-referenced tests, and curriculum-referenced tests.

Norm-referenced tests The primary purpose of some tests is to indicate a child's developmental level in relation to that of other children. These instruments are usually referred to as *norm-referenced* because an individual child's performance is compared with a normative group consisting of others of the same age. For example, a 3-year-old Down syndrome child might be described as having a developmental age of 22 months, which means that his performance on the test most closely approximates that of the average 22-month-old child. An IQ test is an example of a norm-referenced measure, since IQ is determined by comparing a child's performance to that of others of the same age. Some norm-referenced tests commonly used with infants and preschoolers include the Denver Developmental Screening Test (Frankenburg & Dodds, 1969), the Bayley Scales of Infant Development (Bayley, 1969), and the McCarthy Scale of Children's Abilities (McCarthy, 1972).

Norm-referenced measures serve a variety of purposes. For example, the Denver Developmental Screening Test (DDST) was designed as a *screening* instrument (Powell, 1981). Its primary purpose is to sort out, from a large group of children, those who may be at risk for developmental delays and who should be referred for further evaluation. The DDST performs this screening function well, since it is relatively short, economical, easy to use, and accurate. The Bayley Scales and the McCarthy, on the other hand, were designed to serve as *diagnostic* measures. Their primary purpose is to verify, through extensive formal assessment, the nature and extent of a child's developmental delay. Each is relatively lengthy and requires administration by a highly trained examiner.

Although norm-referenced measures may be used to help plan educational programs, they were not developed with this as their primary function. Determining a child's developmental level requires the selection of test items that meet rather rigid statistical standards. Instructional relevance of items on norm-referenced tests necessarily has been only a secondary consideration in item selection. The implication for teachers is that items on scales such as the Bayley or the McCarthy may not be good instructional targets. These scales are primarily useful for determining developmental status and indicating general areas in which instruction might be appropriate.

Criterion-referenced tests   The primary purpose of some tests is to indicate the child's specific skills. These tests are usually referred to as *criterion-referenced* measures because performance on an item is compared to a standard of mastery or sequence of skills rather than with other children. For example, Marje might be described as having mastered 75% of the steps necessary to eat with a spoon. Some of the more common criterion-referenced tests used with young exceptional children include the Uniform Performance Assessment System (White, Edgar, Haring, Affleck, Hayden, & Bendersky, 1981), the Vulpé Assessment Battery (Vulpé, 1977), the Learning Accomplishment Profile (LeMay, Griffin, & Sanford, 1977), Behavioral Characteristics Progression (Office of the Santa Cruz County Superintendent of Schools, 1973), and the Brigance Inventory of Early Development (Brigance, 1978).

Although each of these tests is unique, most have several common characteristics. Skills are usually grouped into several broad domains, the most common being cognitive (or preacademic), language, gross motor, fine motor, social, and self-help. Items are sequenced developmentally, and typically serve as instructional targets. Although some tests, such as the Learning Accomplishment Profile, suggest ways to convert performance into a developmental level, most criterion-referenced tests simply summarize performance as percentage of items passed.

Curriculum-referenced tests   Some criterion-referenced tests include suggested teaching activities for each item on the scale. Such tests are referred to as curriculum-referenced measures, although most are also criterion-referenced. Some of the more common curriculum-referenced measures include the Portage Project Checklist (Bluma, Shearer, Frosham, & Hilliard, 1976), the Hawaii Early Learning Program (Furuno, O'Reilly, Hosaka, Inatsuka, Allman, & Zeisloft (1979), the Carolina Curriculum for Handicapped Infants (Johnson, Jens, & Attermeier, 1979), and the Early Intervention Developmental Profile (Schafer & Moersch, 1981).

Naturalistic Observation

A second method for gathering information about children is through *naturalistic observation*. Although a variety of techniques for this have been developed, the essence of the procedure is the recording of behavior as it occurs in a variety of settings. Naturalistic observation has several advantages. It samples the child's *typical* behavior; it allows for the assessment of many important skills (peer interaction, inappropriate behavior, communication, independence) not covered in a testing situation; it can be used to look at the *sequence* of behaviors and the *context* in which they occur. Naturalistic observation can also be used in a wide variety of ways.

Several naturalistic observation strategies have been developed and the selection of one depends on the type of information needed. Three forms of observation are running records, event sampling, and category sampling.

Running records   The running record is an attempt to document everything that occurs within a given time period. An example of a running record, described in more detail in Chapter 13, is the language sample, a record of everything a child says. A more general example is a record of every motor behavior the child performs during morning free play.

The running record is particularly useful when the teacher is interested in what generally occurs and the sequence in which things happen. However, it can be very time-consuming and requires constant attention. It may also be difficult to interpret because the information is not organized in a meaningful fashion; the teacher must convert it to another form. For example, once the teacher has collected several running records of Tina's social behavior, he or she might conduct a secondary analysis to determine the percentage of time Tina responded when a peer spoke to her.

Event sampling   Event sampling involves the measurement of specific behaviors as they occur, either through frequency counts or through duration recording. A *frequency count* is used for behaviors that are relatively short in duration. For example, the teacher may keep a record of the number of times Jack hits another child, the number of toilet accidents Ben has, or how often Greg offers to share a toy with a peer. A *duration* measure is an indication of how long something occurs, and is used for behaviors that vary considerably in length. For example, the teacher may keep a record of the length of time Pam plays alone or the number of minutes Kim cries each day.

Category sampling When the teacher is interested in a broad category of skills that actually encompasses many different behaviors, category sampling is a useful technique. For example, a primary goal for Matt is to increase the number of times he initiates an interaction with a peer. Many different behaviors could be considered initiations, however, and it might not make sense to count each one of them separately. The category of "initiations" could then be defined as encompassing a variety of specific behaviors and could be used to simplify the observational process. Category sampling allows the teacher to record a wide variety of specific behaviors within a limited set of categories. Another example of such a category is "aggressive behavior," which could also include many different discrete behaviors.

Observational procedures Once a system for event sampling or category sampling has been developed, the time and technique for gathering data must be determined. Usually we do not have the luxury of observing all the possible times a behavior occurs, so we must be satisfied with a representative *sample* of behavior. Since we can only take data for relatively short periods of time, observation periods should be selected carefully. For example, it would not make sense to observe Matt's initiations to peers during a structured work session. A free play setting would provide a more representative sample of this behavior. The structured work session might be a better setting for counting the number of times Matt responds to a direct request by the teacher, however. The teacher should also observe only when he or she can see and record behavior acurately. If the teacher has other responsibilities, many behaviors may be missed.

One solution is to set aside short periods of time for continuous observation and recording of behavior. In event sampling, this allows the teacher to count each instance of a specific behavior. Another solution is to use a systematic *time-sampling* procedure which involves brief periods of observation at regularly scheduled intervals. For example, the teacher might set the timer and every five minutes check whether Pam is playing alone or with peers.

Parent Interview

A third procedure for gathering information is through use of parent interviews. An interview may be very structured and formal, or unstructured and informal. A number of structured assessment procedures based on parent interviews have been developed for the assessment of young handicapped children. Among these are the Carey Infant Temperament Questionnaire (Carey & McDevitt, 1978), the Developmental Profile (Alpern, Boll, & Shearer, 1980), the Vineland Social Maturity Scale (Doll, 1965), and the AAMD Adaptive Behavior Scale (Nahira, Foster, Shellhaas, & Leland, 1974). Tests that consist primarily of direct test procedures may allow some items to be scored through parental report. The Denver Developmental Screening Test (Frankenburg & Dodds, 1969) contains several such items.

The primary advantage of the interview technique is its efficiency. Ideally parents should be knowledgeable about their child's abilities and should be able to quickly describe the child's typical performance. Unfortunately, getting accurate information from parents sometimes takes a great deal of skill. Parents' response may be affected by the way in which a question is asked. "He drinks from a cup, doesn't he?" might elicit a different response than "Tell me how you get him to drink liquids." Also, although the child may be able to perform the skill, the parent may have never observed or noticed it. In some cases, parents may be reluctant to admit that their child cannot perform behaviors common to most children that age.

Selecting Assessment Procedures

Testing, naturalistic observation, and parent interviewing have advantages and disadvantages and are summarized in Table 2.1. A comprehensive assessment should use a combination of these procedures, drawing on the unique strengths of each. Some form of direct testing is needed because of the logistics in transferring and recording information about children. Parent interviews and naturalistic observation should verify the results of direct testing and measure skills that cannot easily be assessed in a direct testing situation.

DETERMINING SKILLS TO BE ASSESSED

A difficult problem confronting teachers of young handicapped children is determining which skills are important for assessment. The skills assessed often are selected as instructional targets. Different tests include different items for assessment, making it hard to evaluate the content of an assessment tool. In this section we describe basic methods for determining the skills to be assessed, evaluate each method in light of its instructional utility, and describe strategies to insure that assessment targets are meaningful instructional targets.

The basic methods are the developmental milestones model, the theory-based developmental model, and the functional model.

Developmental Milestones Approach

In the *developmental milestones approach*, the content of instructional programs is based on developmental skills derived from surveys of large numbers of children such as the Gesell Scales (Knobloch, Stevens, & Malone, 1980) or from standard tests such as the Bayley Scales of Infant Development (Bayley, 1969). Some examples of curricula and assessment tools generally based on a developmental milestones model include the Hawaii Early Learning Program (Furuno, et al., 1979), the Learning Accomplishment Profile (LeMay, et al., 1977), the Portage Guide to Early Education (Bluma, et al., 1976), and Project MEMPHIS (Quick, Little, & Campbell, 1974).

Curriculum and assessment materials drawn from surveys of normal child development

Table 2.1.
Advantages and disadvantages of testing, naturalistic observation, and interviews.

Procedure	Advantages	Disadvantages
Testing	Standard procedures allow meaningful comparisons of children. Necessary for diagnostic needs Facilitates transfer of information	Alternate procedures for children with sensory or motor impairments are not generally allowed. Some tests require considerable training. Lack of validated measures for educational planning Skills sampled are limited to those included as the test.
Observation	Measures what children do in real world settings Sensitive to changes over time Can be done during regular classroom activities	Time-consuming Requires a certain amount of skill to design a good observation system Lack of guidelines to interpret data gathered
Interview	Information comes from another's perspective. Efficient use of time	Not a direct measure of child behavior The interviewee may not accurately report skills.

typically include a wide range of developmental skills sequenced in the order in which normal children attain those skills. Although many useful skills may be identified through an analysis of developmental milestones, this approach has three major limitations. First, developmental milestones are not necessarily good instructional targets. Their original function was to differentiate between different ages, not to serve as indicators of the best skills to teach young children. Second, a naturally occurring developmental sequence of skills may not be the best teaching sequence. Finally, the sequence of development observed in normal children may not represent the sequences followed by the handicapped, particularly those who are severely or profoundly retarded or those with physical and sensory impairments.

Sequences of items taken from two curricula based on the developmental milestones approach are displayed in Table 2.2. The items listed represent the first 10 "cognitive" objectives beginning at the 12-month age level of each curriculum. Note that each sequence encompasses a wide variety of skills that do not necessarily conform to a meaningful cognitive theory. Skills are "typical" of a 1-year-old and do not allow for variation. There are also considerable differences in the kinds of skills included both within and between the two curricula.

Although the developmental milestones model appears to be most commonly used in determining instructional targets in early intervention programs, limitations are highlighted in Table 2.2. For example, stacking blocks is good for determining *developmental age* because it indicates a child's approximate level of development. This does not necessarily mean we should spend a great deal of time teaching a child to stack blocks, however, since that skill alone may not be very useful. Further, the list of milestones would not represent good teaching sequences since many diverse skills are described within each sequence. And assuming the lists did include important skills, what would the teacher do with a child with severe motor impairments, since nearly every item is a motor task?

Because of these limitations, teachers should be cautious when using assessment tools based on developmental milestones, particularly when those milestones were drawn from various surveys of child development conducted by other authors. Although teachers should be able to interpret a child's abilities

TABLE 2.2

A comparison of the first 10 cognitive items beginning at the 12-month level of two curricula based on the normal developmental milestones model.

Portage Guide to Early Education	Hawaii Early Learning Profile
1. Individually takes out six objects from container.	1. Hands toy back to adult.
2. Points to one body part.	2. Enjoys messy activities such as fingerpainting.
3. Stacks three blocks on request.	3. Reacts to various sensations such as extremes in temperature and taste.
4. Matches like objects.	4. Shows understanding of color and size.
5. Scribbles.	5. Places round piece in form board.
6. Points to self when asked. "Where's (name)?"	6. Nests two then three cans (puts the smaller cans inside the larger ones).
7. Places five round pegs in a pegboard on request.	7. Understands pointing.
8. Matches object with picture of same object.	8. Pulls string horizontally to obtain toy.
9. Points to named picture.	9. Makes detours to retrieve objects.
10. Turns pages of book two-three at a time to find named picture.	10. Looks at place where ball rolls out of sight.

from a developmental perspective, this model does not tie behaviors to a logical developmental sequence.

Theory-Based Developmental Approach

The theory-based developmental approach is similar to the developmental milestones model in using sequences of normal development to determine instructional targets. The primary difference between the two approaches lies in the source of items and the procedures by which they are selected. The developmental milestones model includes a variety of items *assumed to be* good instructional targets by virtue of their ability to discriminate between children of different ages and different abilities. The theory-based developmental approach first assumes a theory about how a specific skill develops and then generates (and hopefully tests) the sequence of development.

TABLE 2.3.
Example of a theory-based developmental sequence of cognitive skills.

Development of Means for Obtaining Desired Environment Events

---

1. Appearance of hand-watching behavior
2. Achievement of visually-directed grasping
3. Repetition of actions producing an interesting result
4. Letting go of an object in order to reach for another
5. Use of locomotion as a means (to obtain objects)
6. Use of the relationship of support (e.g., pulls a support such as a pillow to obtain the object on the pillow)
7. Understanding of the relationship of support
8. Use of string horizontally (e.g., uses string to obtain object by pulling)
9. Use of string vertically
10. Use of stick as means (to obtain desired object)

SOURCE: Uzgiris, E.C. and Hunt, J.M. *Assessment in infancy: Ordinal scales of psychological development.* Urbana: University of Illinois Press, 1975. Comments in parentheses added by Bailey and Wolery.

Perhaps the most clearly articulated example of a theory-based developmental approach is the cognitive-developmental model based on Piaget's (1963) theories. Between the ages of birth and 6 years, children are assumed to progress through the sensorimotor period (approximately birth to 2 years), and the preoperational period (approximately 2–6 years of age). Within each stage, sequences of skills are described in the order that they occur. Chapter 9 provides a more detailed description of the Piagetian view of cognitive development and the implications of that model for assessing and teaching cognitive skills.

An example of a developmental sequence based on Piaget's theory of cognitive development is displayed in Table 2.3. The theory predicts that using means to reach an end (goal) is acquired by children in a specific manner and sequence. The assessment items are selected to measure children's performance within the predicted sequence of steps for the acquisition of means-end skills.

A theory-based developmental scale should have more utility as a teaching guide than a scale based on simple milestones since the content is typically related to a specific theory and hopefully follows a logical sequence. Items are usually organized around a specific skill and sequenced in an appropriate fashion. Developmental sequences have been generated in most of the content areas discussed in this text (e.g., language, social, cognitive, motor).

A version of the theory-based developmental approach might be described as the *professional consensus* method of determining assessment sequences. Using this method, a team of professionals, including experts in the area to be assessed (e.g., speech therapists or physical therapists), develops an assessment sequence. Although the sequence may not easily be tied to one particular theory, it should reflect what is currently known about the development of that skill and should represent a consensus of the experts. Some examples of general assessment tools with developmental sequences generated by professional opinions include the Adaptive Performance Instrument (CAPE, 1980) and the Carolina Curriculum for Handicapped Infants

TABLE 2.4
Examples of developmental sequences generated by professional consensus.

Gestural Communication (CCHI)	Grouping Objects (API)
1. Shows anticipation of regularly occurring events in everyday care.	1. Forms groups of several unrelated objects.
2. Responds to being shifted from mom or care-taker to another person.	2. Responds differently to different groups of objects.
3. Anticipates frequently occurring events in games.	3. Puts similar objects together in a group.
4. Repeats activity which gets interesting reaction from others.	4. Groups functionally related objects.
5. Gets adult to continue activity by starting body movements.	5. Puts objects in usual or appropriate location.
6. Initiates activity by starting movement.	6. Matches objects according to size.
7. Holds up hands to be picked up.	7. Matches objects according to shape.
8. Consistently indicates desire to "get down".	8. Matches objects according to color.
9. Reaches toward something to indicate "get it" or "give it".	
10. Uses gestures for "word concepts" (all gone, more, eat, drink, etc.)	

SOURCE: Sequences are from the Carolina Curriculum for Handicapped Infants (Johnson, Jens, & Attermeier, 1979) and the Adaptive Performance Instrument (CAPE, 1980).

(Johnson, Jens, & Attemeir, 1979). Sample sequences from each of these instruments are displayed in Table 2.4.

The fundamental assumption underlying a developmental model, be it theory- or milestone-based, is that the sequences described are generally followed in the predicted order. Further, the sequences are assumed not only to be appropriate teaching sequences, but *necessary* ones: A child must learn the earlier skills in a sequence before moving on to more advanced skills. This assumption differentiates the developmental approach from the functional model.

Functional Approach

A third model for selecting the content of instructional programs is the *functional* or *remedial* approach (Guess, Horner, Utley, Holvoet, Maxon, Tucker, & Warren, 1978). The basic premise of this approach is that teachers of young handicapped children should identify specific skills to immediately improve the child's ability to interact with his environment (Holvoet, Guess, Mulligan, & Brown,

1980) and to increase the probability that the child will perform functional behaviors critical for success and survival in future environments.

The steps in a functional approach include identifying important skills and breaking them down into small, teachable steps. For example, Joshua is a severely retarded 4-year-old who cannot eat with a spoon. Since this is an important skill, it is selected as an instructional target. Rather than teaching the developmental prerequisites to using a spoon (e.g., grasping a variety of objects, cause and effect relationships, coordinated arm movements, etc.), a functional approach would advocate conducting a *task analysis* (defined later in this chapter) of eating with a spoon and an intervention designed to teach each step in the sequence.

Selecting Developmental Versus Functional Targets

Issues such as using developmental versus functional sequences of instructional targets are complex and may be difficult to resolve. Many professionals have suggested using normal developmental sequences to select goals for young handicapped children (e.g., Cohen & Gross, 1979; Haring & Bricker, 1976; Haring & Cohen, 1975). Research has consistently demonstrated that retarded children progress through similar developmental sequences as nonretarded children (Dunst, 1976; Kahn, 1976; Miller & Yoder, 1972; Weisz & Zigler, 1979). This evidence is considered sufficient to warrant the use of those sequences for identifying instructional targets for retarded children. Also, teaching basic developmental skills should best prepare children for the broad range of possible work, academic, recreational, and daily living tasks as they grow older. Developmental skills are prerequisites that form a foundation on which a variety of other skills are acquired.

Advocates of the functional approach, however, argue that the normal sequence of development is not an appropriate basis for making decisions about the educational needs of young handicapped children, particularly those with severe impairments (e.g., Guess, Sailor, & Baer, 1977). Given a limited amount of instructional time, coupled with the severe deficits of those children, instructional targets should be selected on the basis of their functional utility. (Guess, et. al., 1977, p. 361, define a functional response as one that will "maximally enhance control of the environment that the child encounters.")

The answer to the question of functional versus developmental sequences is not an either-or response. Many factors need to be considered in identifying appropriate instructional targets. First, the arguments for each position are basically theoretical in nature. Little, if any, research has tested empirically the assumption that one approach is superior to the other, so both approaches must be accepted as viable options. Second, effective planning and teaching of young children requires a basic understanding of the underlying developmental sequences of different, though intertwined, strands of behavior. Regardless of the model used for goal specification, the appropriateness (and possibility "teachability") of goals must at least in part be examined from a developmental perspective. Third, the value of functional considerations should never be overlooked. At every age and in every setting handicapped chil-

dren will be faced with demands far beyond their "developmental level." Some of those demands can be bypassed in many different ways, but some should not be ignored. We cannot always afford to wait until the child reaches a given level of development to teach a skill demanded by the child's environment.

The relative emphasis on functional versus developmental targets will vary as the function of both the child's age and the severity of the handicap. For example, Amy is a mildly delayed 18-month-old child who makes some vocalizations but does not yet talk and Mike is a 6-year-old severely delayed child who also utters some vocalizations but cannot yet talk. Should the same sequence of objectives be taught for both children? Although this question must be asked on a case-by-case basis, it is likely that Amy and Mike will require different sequences. Amy is young and her delay is slight. A developmental sequence should meet her emerging communicative needs. Mike, however, has demonstrated that he will not learn to talk on his own, or will do so at a very slow rate. Mike's communication objectives might focus on alternative modes, such as manual signing, or on functional communication skills that will best meet his adaptive needs rather than basic developmental skills.

The relationships between age, severity of handicap, and philosophical approach are graphically displayed in Figure 2.1. As depicted, both approaches should always be considered at any age and all levels of severity. The developmental approach is of primary importance for mildly/moderately handicapped children at the younger ages since basic developmental skills should provide the child the broadest base of skills. As these children grow older, however, the functional approach increases in relative importance. As the child's remaining years in the educational system become fewer, training should focus on specific skills required in environments in which individuals spend their time. The functional approach will be of primary importance for severely/profoundly handicapped children of all ages. Given the severity of disability and level of instruction required, even the earliest interventions should address skills that maximize independent functioning and self-care. However, carefully consider the developmental appropriateness of a given skill.

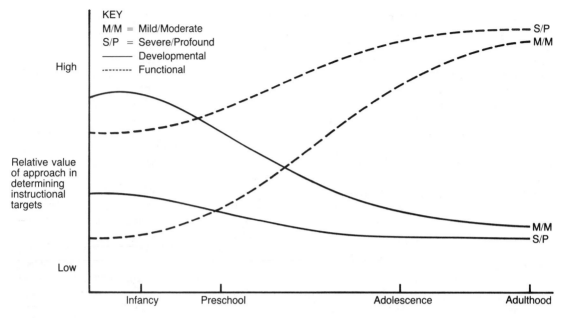

KEY
M/M = Mild/Moderate
S/P = Severe/Profound
———— Developmental
-------- Functional

High

Relative value
of approach in
determining
instructional
targets

Low

Infancy   Preschool   Adolescence   Adulthood

FIGURE 2.1.

Relative importance of functional and developmental approaches to the
assessment and identification of instructional targets, by age and severity
of handicap. Thanks to Ken Jens for helpful comments and suggestions
on this model.

Identifying Appropriate Targets

The developmental versus functional argument
will not be resolved in the near future. Teachers of young handicapped children, however,
must make immediate decisions about what
to teach. The concepts of critical function and
next-most-probable placement are useful in
making determinations. Although they are often associated with the functional approach,
their relevance to developmentally appropriate planning is significant.

Critical function Skill descriptions found in
curriculum packages of assessment tools are
usually specific in both the description of the
skill and in the procedures for determining if
the child has the skill. The concept of critical
function assumes that test items are specific
indicators of more general functions (White,
1980; White & Haring, 1980). Teachers should
understand and apply the concept of critical
function to selecting instructional targets.
Further, many items may need to be modified
for children whose ability to perform them is
precluded because of a handicapping condi-

tion. Understanding and applying the concept of critical function should facilitate generalization of acquired skills.

"Puts together a three-piece puzzle," for
example, is a common item on many preschool assessment scales. How should it be
handled in the case of a child with cerebral
palsy or one with no arms? Another example
of a smiliar problem involves the measurement of object permanence. Most children
develop this ability by 6–8 months, and usually indicate knowledge that an object removed from sight still exists. The child may
take off the cover from a toy, or look at the
correct place where an object is hidden. But
how do these visual tasks apply to an infant
who is blind? How does this child demonstrate object permanence? Should object permanence even be a goal?

Most professionals would agree that object
permanence is importance for blind children.
Knowing things exist even when you cannot
preceive their presence is essential to almost
all cognitive, language, and social skills. Blind
children simply learn and demonstrate this

skill through other senses, most notably touch and hearing. They may not learn auditory permanence at the same time nonhandicapped children learn visual permanence, or in the same sequence within the context of other skills, however. Thus, a teacher may need to adapt or modify a developmental milestone to meet the needs of the individual.

The critical skill or function of object permanence is knowing something can exist outside your perceptual field. A child finding a toy hidden under a cloth is simply indicating this cognitive skill. A blind child might indicate this skill in another way by searching for a noisy toy in the spot where he last heard it. If the critical function of "puts together a three-piece puzzle" is not a motor skill, but rather a cognitive skill involving perceptual analysis of part-whole relationships, then alternative strategies for teaching can be developed without requiring the use of hands.

Applying the concept of critical function should facilitate generalization because it encourages the teacher to consider a broader range of skills than tapped by a single item. For example, putting together a three-piece puzzle requires certain perceptual-cognitive skills. If a teacher teaches a child to build a three-piece snow figure should it be concluded that the child has these cognitive skills? If he can put together other three-piece puzzles that the teacher has not taught him to put together, then the answer may be affirmative. If not, one could only conclude that the child has learned the motor movements necessary to perform a single task, but has not generalized that skill to other puzzles. Using the concept of critical function, the teacher would realize that the child knows only the specific skill, and not the more important critical function.

Next most probable placement A second strategy for incorporating functional skills within a developmental framework is the identification of skills important for success in the child's next educational environment. Since a major goal of early intervention is to facilitate movement to less restrictive environments, the skills required for success in these programs should be identified and taught. Vincent, Salisbury, Walter, Brown, Gruenwald, and Powers (1980) refer to this process as the identification of the *criteria of the next educational environment.*

For example, Jeff is 27 months of age. He is currently being served by a local home-based intervention team. A specialist visits his home once a week, conducts several activities, and makes suggestions to his parents. In three months Jeff will be entering a preschool program serving handicapped and nonhandicapped children ages 2½ to 4½. Although the early intervention specialist should continue to focus on developmental skills, he or she should also consider demands placed on Jeff in the next program. These may include specific skills such as eating independently, or "survival" skills such as sitting in a group for short periods of time. Jeff may need to be taught and practice some of these skills at home prior to the transition.

Vincent, et al. (1980) suggest four possible strategies for determining the survival skills required in a future environment:

1 Conduct a brief "tryout" in the next placement setting. This could involve letting the child spend a short period of time over several days in his or her future kindergarten or preschool program. Such a strategy can help pinpoint specific problem areas and provide guidance for determining supplemental instructional targets.
2 Follow children who have already moved to the next placement setting. This would involve a discussion with teachers to find out the skills these students needed to insure a more successful transition.
3 Ask the teachers in the next placement setting to generate a list of survival skills. This list should include social skills (such as initiating interactions with peers or making choices during free play) that are not usually tested in the assessment process.
4 Gather objective information on survival skills actually used in the next placement setting. Observational analysis of a typical day may indicate other skills not generated by the teacher or may help to rank skills in terms of the frequency needed.

Selecting an Appropriate Test

Designing a meaningful assessment of a young handicapped child requires consideration of a variety of factors. Teachers should not waste time teaching skills that are meaningless to children. Below are a series of questions to ask when selecting assessment tools:

1 What skill areas are included? Are the broad domains (e.g., language, motor, self-help) divided into meaningful strands of behavior?
2 What age range is addressed?
3 Does the instrument generally reflect a developmental milestones model, a theory-based developmental model, or a functional model?
4 Are activities suggested for training skills included on the test?
5 Does the instrument and/or the activities provide adaptations for children with sensory or motor impairments?

In Table 2.5 several common criterion-referenced and curriculum-referenced measures are described and rated on these dimensions. Each teacher should also determine how well the items on the instrument correspond to the needs of children.

CONDUCTING ASSESSMENTS

Once a decision has been made regarding the nature and content of the assessment procedures, the teacher is ready to actually gather the information. Conducting assessments with young handicapped children requires several unique considerations, some of which are discussed in this section. Each consideration should insure that the teacher accurately determines the child's true abilities.

Assessment Situations Should be Nonthreatening

The behavior of young children can be affected by the degree of familiarity with the person conducting the assessment as well as the context in which the assessment is conducted. This concern is reduced when it is done in the classroom by the childrens' teacher. Unfamiliar teachers should plan a get acquainted period prior to conducting assessments. Also, having parents present often helps the child feel more secure and provides a better opportunity for determining optimal performance capabilities.

Conduct Multiple Assessments

Young handicapped children often exhibit variable performance patterns. Some may be on medication for seizures, hyperactivity, or illness, resulting in drowsiness or lethargy (Simeonsson & Simeonsson, 1981). Others exhibit mild seizures that may go unnoticed. Also, many children with severe impairments have less endurance than the average child. In addition, all handicapped and nonhandicapped infants exhibit rapid fluctuations in level of alertness.

Optimal assessment conditions assume that the child is in a responsive state. Teachers need to recognize those times when children are most receptive to stimulation and to capitalize on optimal states for both assessment and intervention. Brazelton (1973) describes six possible sleep and awake states observed in young children: deep sleep, light sleep, drowsy or semi-dozing, alert and focusing, alert with considerable motor activity, and crying. Simeonsson (1979) has defined nine levels of arousal in young children, as listed in Table 2.6.

The assumption underlying both the Brazelton and Simeonsson categories is that arousal levels at either end of the continuum are poor times for assessment or intervention. Responsive states are defined as those in which the child is awake, active, and aware. Assessment should only be scheduled and conducted during responsive states. Further, the state variability should be documented and will provide important information. The reduction of state variability and the increase of quiet, alert times may be essential instructional goals.

A meaningful assessment of a young handicapped child cannot and should not be conducted in one session. Multiple assessments over several days will provide a more accurate picture of a child's abilities. Although they are time-consuming, the information gained will help plan an instructional program.

Keep the Child Motivated

Young children have considerable difficulty attending to one task for an extended period of time. For this reason, assessments should not extend beyond 30–45 minutes at a time. Intersperse desk activities with activities allowing movement. Use of interesting materials and a gamelike format can increase interest levels and maintain performance over time. Many handicapped youngsters may require extra reinforcement for trying or for responding correctly. Assessments should be terminated if the teacher feels the child's performance is no longer indicative of his or her ability.

Modify Test Items

Children with sensory or motor impairments may be able to perform the critical function assessed by a test item but may not be able to perform the specific task. For example, a 4-year-old with cerebral palsy may have the cognitive skills necessary to perform tasks involving part-whole relationships but may not have the motor skills needed to assemble a three-piece puzzle. Some retarded children may not be able to perform a task independently, but could do so if given a model. Such information is important for instructional planning but may not be obtained if the teacher simply follows standard test procedure.

When the score itself is relatively unimportant and the emphasis of testing is on the instructional utility of the information gathered, McLean and Snyder-McLean (1978, pp. 132–133) suggest several modifications to increase "clinical validity." First, the teacher may want to modify the procedures for *stimulus presentation.* For example, the instructions may be simplified or repeated, or additional cues such as gestures or modeling may be used to determine the extent to which a child needs assistance in giving a correct response. Second, the teacher may modify the *topography of the required response.* For example, the child with physical disabilities may be allowed to respond by looking at the correct picture rather than pointing. Third, the *stimulus material* may need to be adapted or changed. A child with visual-perception problems may need to have pictures cut apart or spread out. Some children may require simplified pictures without the distracting background information while others may need three-dimensional objects as stimuli rather than line drawings or photographs. Finally, the teacher may need to *reinforce correct responding* in cases of apparent poor motivation or lack of comprehension of what constitutes a correct response.

McLean and Snyder-McLean argue for the appropriateness of these modifications since

the purpose of assessment should be "to obtain the most representative picture possible of the child's current level of functioning" (p. 126). Although these modifications invalidate the typical scoring procedures and standard interpretations (e.g., comparison with other children of the same age), the additional information is probably more useful than scores for determining instructional targets.

Conduct Interdisciplinary Assessments

The importance of interdisciplinary assessment and planning has become apparent in recent years (Golin & Ducanis, 1981; Orlando, 1981). The interdisciplinary process is a joint effort by several professionals to design a consistent and meaningful intervention program for a child. Because the teacher cannot be an expert in all areas, experts such as communication specialists, physical therapists, and psychologists can help facilitate understanding of the complex development of the "whole child." The interdisciplinary process should encourage generalization of skills since the application of skills in several areas would be addressed. The group interaction that is part of the interdisciplinary process serves as a forum for suggesting, evaluating, and ordering a number of alternative goals and priorities.

The interdisciplinary process is often difficult to implement because of limited resources, time, and professional "territoriality." Because of the unique needs of many handicapped youngsters, teachers should participate on an interdisciplinary team whenever possible to help themselves design meaningful objectives and intervention strategies.

Involve Parents in the Process

According to Public Law 94–142, parents have a right to participate in the assessment process. In addition, they have information about their children important to completing assessment data and selecting appropriate instructional targets.

When involving parents in planning instructional programs, inform them of their rights, both in participating in educational program planning and of due process. Because they have had limited exposure to educational programs or because they may have just learned

TABLE 2.5
Common criterion-referenced and curriculum-referenced assessment tools for young handicapped children

Instrument	Domains	Age Range	Reliability Data[a]	Validity Data[a]	Curriculum Activities Included	Assessment Adaptations Suggested for Handicapped Children	Curriculum Adaptations Suggested for Handicapped Children
Adaptive Performance Instrument (CAPE, 1980)	Reflexes & Reactions, Physical Intactness, Sensori-Motor, Social, Communication, Gross Motor, Fine Motor, Self-Care	0–2½	0	0	No	Hearing Impaired, Visually Impaired, Deaf-Blind, Motorically Impaired	NA
Behavioral Characteristics Progression (Office of the Santa Cruz County Superintendent of Schools, 1978)	Includes 2400 observable behaviors grouped into 59 behavioral strands. Skills include self-care, motor, language, social, reading, math, and prevocational	0–adult	0	0	No	None	NA
Brigance Inventory of Early Development (Brigance, 1978)	Psychomotor, self-help, speech & language, general knowledge & comprehension, & early academic	0–6	0	1	No	None	NA

						Designed for deaf-blind & severely handicapped	NA
Callier-Azusa Scale (Stillman, 1978)	Motor, Perceptual, Daily Living, Cognition/Communication/Language, & Social	0–6	A	A	No		NA
Carolina Curriculum for Handicapped Infants (Jens, Johnson & Attermeir, 1979)	Tactile Integration, Auditory Localization and Object Permanence, Visual Pursuit and Object Permanence, Object Permanence, Reaching and Grasping, Hand Watching, Space Localization, Functional Use of Objects, Control Over Physical Environment, Gestural Communication, Gestural Imitation and Imitative Play, Feeding, Vocal Imitation, Vocal Communication, Responses to Communication from Others, Social Skills, Gross Motor-Prone, Gross Motor-Supine, Gross Motor-Upright	0–2	A	A	Yes	Blind Deaf	Blind Deaf

TABLE 2.5 (continued)
Common criterion-referenced and curriculum-referenced assessment tools for young handicapped children

Instrument	Domains	Age Range	Reliability Data[a]	Validity Data[a]	Curriculum Activities Included	Assessment Adaptations Suggested for Handicapped Children	Curriculum Adaptations Suggested for Handicapped Children
Carolina Developmental Profile (Lillie, 1975)	Gross Motor, Fine Motor, Visual Perception, Reasoning Receptive & Expressive Language	2–5	A	A	Yes	None	No
Down Syndrome Performance Inventory (Dmitriev, no date)	Gross Motor, Cognitive, Fine Motor, Language, Personal/ Social	0–8	0	0	No	None	NA
Early Intervention Developmental Profile (Schafer & Moersch, 1981)	Perceptual/Fine Motor Cognition Language Social/Emotional Self-Care Gross Motor	0–36 mos.	2	1	Yes	None	Hearing Impaired Motorically Involved Visually Impaired
Early Learning Accomplishment Profile (Glover, Preminger & Sanford, 1978)	Gross Motor, Fine Motor, Cognitive, Language, Self-Help, Social, Emotional	0–3	0	0	No	None	NA
Hawaii Early Learning Profile (Furuno, et. al., 1979)	Cognitive Language Gross Motor Fine Motor Social Self-Help	0–36 mos.	0	0	Yes	None	None

Instrument	Domains	Age Range					
Learning Accomplishment Profile (LeMay, et al., 1977)	Gross Motor, Fine Motor, Cognitive, Language, Self-Help	0–6	0	0	Yes	None	None
Preschool Profile (Lynch, Rieke, Soltman, Hardman, & O'Connor, no date)	Gross Motor, Fine Motor, Pre-academic, Self-Help, Music/Art/Story, Social & Play, Understanding Language, Oral Language	0–6	0	0	No	None	NA
Programmed Environments Curriculum (Tawney, Knapp, O'Reilly, & Pratt, 1979)	Social/Language, Cognitive, Motor, Self-Help	0–36 mos.	0	0	Yes	None	None
Portage Project Checklist (Bluma, et al., 1976)	Infant Stimulation, Socialization, Language, Self-Help, Cognitive, Motor	0–6	0	0	Yes	None	No
Rockford Infant Developmental Evaluation Scale (Project RHISE, 1979)	Personal-Social Self-Help, Fine Motor/Adaptive, Receptive Language, Expressive Language, Gross Motor	0–48 mos.	0	1	None	None	NA
Uniform Performance Assessment System (White, et al., 1981)	Preacademic, Communications, Social/Self-Help, Gross Motor	0–6	2	2	None	General adaptation guidelines provided; no item-by-item suggestions	NA

TABLE 2.5 (continued)

Common criterion-referenced and curriculum-referenced assessment tools for young handicapped children

Instrument	Domains	Age Range	Reliability Data[a]	Validity Data[a]	Curriculum Activities Included	Assessment Adaptations Suggested for Handicapped Children	Curriculum Adaptations Suggested for Handicapped Children
Vulpé Assessment Battery (Vulpé, 1977)	Basic Senses & Functions Gross Motor Fine Motor Language Cognitive Organizational Behaviors Activities of Daily Living Assessment of Environment	0–5	0	0	None	None	NA

NOTE: 0—None available
1—minimal
2 = good
A = Available from author but not published in manual

TABLE 2.6
Levels of arousal observed in children

State 1—Deep sleep, eyes closed, regular respiration, no movements.

State 2—Intermediate sleep, eyes closed, few minor facial, body and/or mouth movements, respiration is "periodic," alternating periods of shallow and deep breathing.

State 3—Active sleep, eyes closed, irregular respiration, some gross motor activity (stirring, writhing, grimacing, mouthing or other facial expression).

State 4—Drowsiness, eyes open and closed intermittently, fluttering eyelids, eyes have glassy appearance, frequent relaxation followed by sudden jerks.

State 5—Quiet awake, relatively inactive, eyes open and appear bright and shiny, respiration regular.

State 6—Active awake, eyes open, diffuse motor activity of limbs or whole body, vocalizations of a content nature.

State 7—Fussy awake, eyes open, irregular respirations, diffuse motor activity, vocalizations of a fussy, cranky variety.

State 8—Mild agitation, eyes open, diffuse motor activity, moderate crying, tears may or may not be present.

State 9—Marked uncontrollable agitation, screaming, eyes open or closed, tears may or may not be present.

Source: Simeonsson (1979)

of their child's handicap, parents may be unaware of what their rights are or how to exercise them.

Treat parents as partners in determining instructional targets, and involve them in assessment activities (Powell, 1981) and in decisions based on the assessment information (Turnbull & Turnbull, 1978). Teachers should actively solicit parents' views concerning child behaviors that are necessary and functional to the home and community environment. Swick, Flake-Hobson, and Raymond (1980); Turnbull, Strickland, and Brantley (1978); and Rutherford and Edgar (1979) describe procedures and teacher behaviors to facilitate cooperative parent-teacher interactions.

USING ASSESSMENT INFORMATION

Once assessment information has been collected and parents and teachers have jointly determined the skills that the child is to learn, the teacher begins the next steps in the planning process: developing long-term objectives, breaking them down into a series of short-term objectives, and developing instructional activities based on the short-term objectives (Lynch, McGuigan, & Shoemaker, 1977). Long- and short-term objectives are statements that describe a specific behavior, the conditions or situations under which it is to be performed, and how well the child is to perform it.

Specifying Behavior

Behaviors are observable (i.e., we can see or hear them) and measurable (i.e., we can count the extent to which they occur) events. Objectives must describe behaviors so teachers can determine whether the child performs the desired skill. Descriptions of children's performance such as *discriminate, identify, recognize, know,* and *understand* are not helpful in designing instructional programs, since they are vague and do not tell precisely what we want the child to do. Although such descriptions represent desired abilities, their occurrence can be inferred from a variety of specific behaviors. For example, we infer Mike discriminates shapes because he can place similar shapes together when asked to do so. Similarly, we infer Carol recognizes pictures of her classmates when she points (behavior) to a picture of Dave, who sits across from her.

We want children to demonstrate many desirable qualities such as being cooperative, mature, friendly, or empathetic. However, what is mature for Greg, who is 2 years old, may be immature for George, who is 4. One teacher may describe a behavior as cooperative, while another teacher may feel the student shows some resistance. Before we can measure children's progress and make any necessary adjustments in instructional activities, we must define these qualities as measurable behaviors. For example, being cooperative could include giving toys to other children at their request; following one-step commands such as "come here," or "stop"; standing on the ladder of the slide waiting for a turn; and doing what the group is doing. From this array of behaviors we can begin to measure how cooperative a child is, and also determine the effects of attempts to increase the rate of cooperative behaviors.

Specifying Conditions

Conditions are the situations under which the child is to perform the desired behaviors and frequently include the materials used, the amount of verbal directions given, and the setting in which the behavior is performed. However, conditions vary depending upon the behavior and the intent of the objective. In the objective, "Susan will button her coat when getting ready to go outside within two minutes for three consecutive days," the conditions are, "her coat when getting ready to go outside." In the objective, "When given three objects (e.g., cup, shoe, and spoon) and the verbal command 'Give me_____.' Christy will give the correct object on five of five trials for each object for two consecutive days," the conditions are, "when given three objects (e.g., cup, shoe, and spoon) and the verbal command 'Give me _____.' " In the objective, "Judy will say 'thank you' when someone passes her something she has asked for during four consecutive meals," the conditions are "when someone passes her something she has asked for during meals." As illustrated in these objectives, the conditions vary, depending upon the behavior.

The intent or purpose of the objective also influences the conditions. For example, the intent of Susan's objective is speedy use of a functional behavior at a natural time (buttoning within two minutes when getting ready to go outside). If Susan could not button at all, we might teach her in a one-to-one session with a garment that was made of thinner, more easily managed material with larger buttons and loose buttonholes. The objective might be, "Susan will button a garment made of thin, easily managed material with large buttons and loose buttonholes when given the command 'Button it.' five correct of five buttons for two consecutive days." The purpose now is for Susan to learn to button, rather than to quickly button in a natural setting. As she begins to acquire the skill of buttoning, we can change the conditions of the objec-

tive to include natural times of the day and clothing she is likely to button, fading out the instructions to perform the buttoning behavior.

Specifying Criteria

The criterion of the instructional objective tells how well the child must perform the behavior before the performance is considered sufficient to proceed to the next objective. Thus, the criteria of objectives are usually numerical statements.

Frequently, criteria are difficult to state. In some cases, they should be the same level of mastery or proficiency as for nonhandicapped children. However, such levels are not well-established and show considerable variability between even these children. Thus, in the majority of cases, criteria are some indication of mastery or proficiency that allow the child to perform behaviors in his or her environment at acceptable levels, or at sufficient levels so the behavior can be used for performing or accomplishing other objectives.

Criteria vary, depending upon the behaviors specified. For example, Rick should hold his head up much longer than he should look at a spoon. Similarly, we may want Felix to count five objects in much less time than we want him to run across the gym. It is more important for Shelia to be accurate in looking both ways and crossing the street when the light is green and no cars are coming than for her to correctly label objects. If she makes a mistake when crossing the street and walks in front of a car, the results could be disastrous, but if she mislabels objects, the results are minimal.

The intent of the objective also determines the criteria. For example, increasing play skills might be appropriate for several children, but the intent and therefore the criteria of the various play objectives might be quite different. For instance, we might want Tom to play accurately with toys. Our objective for Tom might read as follows, "When presented with a model and the following toys, Tom will throw a ball, roll a toy truck with the wheels on the floor, stack blocks on top of each other, and rock a doll, *three correct movements in three opportunities with each toy for two consecutive days*" (criteria in this and other objectives are italicized). As compared to Tom, Jim plays accurately with toys but only for 2 or 3 minutes. Since we want him to play for a longer period of time, our objective might read: "When given his choice of toys, Jim will play for *7 minutes without stopping for four consecutive play sessions.*" Gene, on the other hand, plays with toys accurately and for age-appropriate lengths of time, but usually it takes about 10 minutes for him to start. Our purpose for Gene would be for him "to start playing with toys *within 4 minutes of the opportunity to play for five consecutive days.*" Although Rebecca accurately plays with toys for appropriate lengths of time, and begins when given the opportunity, she rides the tricycle so slowly that she cannot keep up with the other children and thus does not join in their activities. The purpose of our objective would be for her to ride the tricycle faster and might read: "When on the tricycle in a flat concrete play area, Rebecca will pedal with *30 rotations of the front wheel per minute.*" As illustrated, the criteria vary depending upon whether the intent of the objective is accuracy, the length of time the child performs the behavior (duration), how long it takes the child to get started performing the behavior (latency), and how quickly the child performs the behavior (rate).

When writing the criterion section of objectives, several details are important. When objectives have accuracy statements, teachers frequently write percent levels into the objectives. For example, "When asked 'What's your name?' Lisa will say 'Lisa Doe' with 100% accuracy." Although this may be a desirable objective, 100% accuracy does not indicate when the objective will be met. Does 100% mean 1 time of 1 opportunity, or 10 times of 10 opportunities? Thus, when using percent, the number of opportunities the child should perform the behavior should be specified.

With most objectives, children should perform the behaviors at criterion levels more than one time. Thus, it is wise to include statements such as "for three consecutive sessions," or "four out of five days." These statements insure that the child can consistently perform the behaviors before the objective is considered met. However, after objectives are met, we must continue to monitor them to be sure the child maintains the behavior.

Many authors have described how to write objectives; for more information the interested reader should consult the classic work by Mager (1962) as well as other sources (e.g., Popham, 1973; Ryan, Johnson, & Lynch, 1977; Vargas, 1972; Wheeler & Fox, 1972).

Task Analyzing Objectives

Task analysis involves breaking down a skill into small, teachable steps. The assumption is that the target behavior (e.g., eating with a spoon or naming the letters of the alphabet) is too large a skill to teach at one time. Dividing it into several smaller tasks should increase the probability of skill acquisition because it allows both the teacher and the child to focus on a very small component of what is, in fact, a very complex task.

The importance of task analysis was emphasized in a recent study by Fredericks, Anderson, and Baldwin (1979) which sought to determine critical competencies of teachers of severely handicapped children. Two groups of children were identified: those who made high gains and those who made low gains. Two indicators of teacher competency were identified as the major contributors to the differences between the groups: the total amount of instruction in the classroom each day and the percentage of programs task-analyzed by the teacher. Teachers of high-gain children task-analyzed significantly more programs than those of children who made low gains.

Task analysis is both a process and a product. As a *process* it is a method of breaking a long-term objective into a series of short-term objectives sequenced by difficulty, with the assumption that those short-term objectives will be more teachable. As a *product* it is a written series of learner behaviors sequenced by difficulty. Task analysis is neither a list of teacher behaviors nor of materials; rather, it is a list of short-term objectives sequenced by difficulty. The process of doing a task analysis involves five steps.

Step 1: Specify the long-term objective and look for related resources. The long-term goal should be stated in objective format, including a behavior, conditions, and criterion. The task analysis will be the steps (objectives) leading from where the child is currently functioning to the long-term objective.

Then look for resources related to teaching the objective. This includes child development literature, special education literature, and curricula for early childhood special education. If the teacher finds a task analysis of the skill he or she should consider using it. Frequently such task analyses will require adaptations for specific children, but this is usually more efficient than starting from "scratch."

Step 2: Break the long-term objective into steps. This step involves developing several small objectives from a long-term objective. At this point the teacher is only concerned with generating as many behaviors as possible. Since the behaviors of the task analysis are short-term objectives, they should be stated in instructional objective format.

Several methods may be used to break skills into small behaviors. First, watch a competent person perform the skill and write down the required behaviors. While another adult or child performs the skill, the teacher writes down the behaviors. Since we typically do many skills quickly, the person performing the skill may need to repeat it slowly several times. This way, the teacher will notice small, subtle behaviors that are needed in performing the skill. Second, the teacher should do the skill and write down the steps. As with the first method, the teacher may need to perform the skill slowly several times and record all behaviors that are needed. These first two methods are quite efficient for task-analyzing skills such as dressing, self-feeding, and grooming that involve a number of related overt behaviors.

Third, logically analyze the skill and write down the steps. A logical analysis means we identify and write down behaviors that are needed to perform the skill and/or that indicate the child can perform the steps leading to the end skill. Frequently skills in long-term objectives do *not* result in a number of overt behaviors, however. For example, when a child names a letter, the only observable behavior is stating the letter's name. We do not see the child discriminate the form of the letter or match the name to the visual stimulus of its form. Teachers must have a thorough working knowledge of the curriculum to perform logical analyses.

Fourth, copy the sequences from normal development. The sequences through which nonhandicapped children acquire given skills may be useful in determining behaviors in a given task analysis. This notion assumes children have already "described" the steps involved in acquiring a given skill. The teacher's task then becomes simply copying the developmental sequences described by researchers studying nonhandicapped children. Although developmental sequences may not always be the most efficient in teaching a behavior, they are often very helpful in designing instructional objectives. Cohen and Gross (1979) provide an exhaustive listing of developmental sequences across several domains.

Step 3: Eliminate unnecessary and redundant steps. Frequently when breaking down a skill into smaller behaviors, some unnecessary steps are listed and should be deleted from your task analysis. Likewise, a given behavior may be listed several times. Include it once, and only when it is necessary.

Step 4: Sequence steps for teaching. The most common method for sequencing behaviors is to arrange the steps by their *temporal order.* That is, behaviors are taught in the order in which they would be performed during the entire skill. Sequencing by temporal order is useful with skills comprised of several chained together behaviors such as dressing, self-feeding, and grooming.

Another method is to sequence behaviors by *response difficulty,* and is most useful in teaching "conceptual" skills that do not involve a number of related observable behaviors. For example, if we task analyze a behavior such as naming letters, we might propose the following sequence: names common objects in pictures, separates (sorts) letters, matches identical letters, points to letters when named, and names letters. In each succeeding step the response changes and becomes more difficult. This method also helps children acquire new responses.

Step 5: Specify the prerequisite behaviors. Prerequisite behaviors, sometimes called *entry behaviors,* are necessary before the child can perform the easiest step in the task analysis. Although many behaviors are desirable before training is initiated, two or three are usually critical and should be listed and the child assessed. If the child cannot perform the prerequisites, then the task analysis should be delayed until the behaviors are mastered.

According to Thiagarajan (1980), previously constructed sequences of objectives (task analyses) can be adjusted and made more suitable for individual children. One method of adjusting task analyses is to adjust the *entry point,* or the step on which instruction is initiated. If the first step is too easy, the child should begin to receive instruction on more difficult steps. If the easiest step is too difficult, that step should be further task-analyzed and instruction initiated at the child's current level of functioning.

Step size, or the amount of difficulty between steps of the task analysis, can also be adjusted. In some situations the child will need steps added to the task analysis. In other cases, the steps of the task analysis could be combined, thus consolidating more behavior and allowing for more rapid progression. For example, two sequences for tying shoes are shown in Table 2.7. The only difference between the two sequences is the size of the "chunks" to be taught. The more extensive sequence would be inappropriate for a child who can learn the larger steps. The determina-

tion of steps must be based upon each child's performance.

Thiagarajan also suggests adjusting the *prompts*—the teacher assistance provided—to the various steps. For some children, the behaviors, criteria, and size between steps may be appropriate, but they might need temporary prompts to ensure efficient acquisition. For other children, prompts might be deleted for more efficient instruction.

In addition, the *indicator behavior* can be varied. This behavior shows that the child has the conceptual knowledge addressed in the task analysis. For example, a child could use several behaviors to indicate that he or she can identify an object. Possible behaviors include pointing, touching, and looking at an object, handing it to someone, or answering "yes" and "no" if shown an object and asked, "Is this a _____?" If the purpose of the objective is identification, the manner in which it is communicated to the teacher may be a secondary consideration. Thus, the indicator behavior should be matched to the child's abilities, rather than forcing the child to con-

TABLE 2.7
Two task analyses for tying a shoe

Longer Sequence[a]	Shorter Sequence[b]
1. Pinch lace.	1. Partially tighten shoe laces.
2. Pull lace.	2. Pull shoe laces tight—vertical pull.
3. Hang lace ends from corresponding sides of shoe.	3. Cross shoe laces.
4. Pick up laces in corresponding hands.	4. Tighten laces—horizontal pull.
5. Lift laces above shoe.	5. Tie laces into a knot.
6. Cross right lace over the left to form a tepee.	6. Make a bow.
7. Bring left lace toward student.	7. Tighten bow.
8. Pull left lace through tepee.	
9. Pull laces away from each other.	
10. Bend left lace to form a loop.	
11. Pinch loop with left hand.	
12. Bring right lace over the fingers —around loop.	
13. Push right lace through hole.	
14. Pull loops away from each other.	

[a]*Source:* Smith, D. D., Smith, J. O., and Edgar, E. Research and application of instructional materials development. In N. G. Haring and L. Brown (Eds.), *Teaching the severely handicapped* (Vol. 1). New York: Grune & Stratton, 1976.

[b]*Source:* Santa Cruz County Office of Education, *Behavioral Characteristics Progression.* Palo Alto, California: VORT Corporation, 1973.

form to the indicator behavior described in the task analysis.

Thus, teachers can use a previously developed task analysis and adjust it to meet the individual needs of several children. These adjustments can be made at the entry point, or to the step size, the prompts, or the indicator behavior.

SUMMARY

In this chapter we emphasized the need for appropriate assessment prior to implementing instruction with young handicapped children. Assessment is important for individualized, efficient, and effective instruction because it helps teachers provide activities and experi-

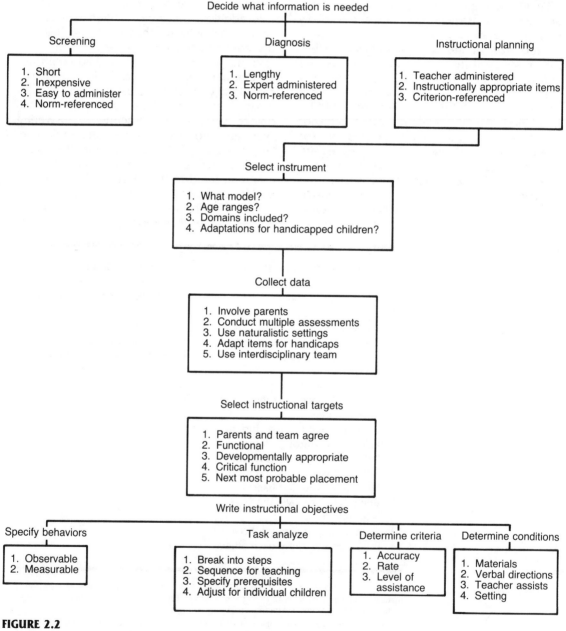

FIGURE 2.2
Steps in the Assessment Process

ences to precisely match each child's individual learning needs.

Figure 2.2 is a schematic diagram to display the steps in the assessment process. The major decision-making points are capitalized, and the basic considerations discussed in this chapter are listed inside the boxes.

REFERENCES

Alpern, G. D., Boll, T. J., & Shearer, M. S. *Developmental profile II.* Aspen: Psychological Development Publications, 1980.

Bailey, D. B., & Harbin, G. L. Nondiscriminatory evaluation. *Exceptional Children,* 1980, *46,* 590–596.

Bayley, N. *Bayley scales of infant development.* New York: Psychological Corporation, 1969.

Bluma, S. M., Shearer, M. S., Froham, A. H., & Hillard, J. M. *Portage guide to early education* (No. 12). Portage, Wis.: Cooperative Educational Agency, 1976.

Brazelton, T. B. *The neonatal behavioral assessment scale.* Philadelphia: Lippincott, 1973.

Brigance, A. H. *Inventory of early development.* Woburn, Mass.: Curriculum Associates, 1978.

CAPE Project. *Adaptive performance instrument.* Moscow: Department of Special Education, University of Idaho, 1980.

Carey, W. B., & McDevitt, S. C. Revision of the Infant Temperament Questionnaire. *Pediatrics,* 1978, *61,* 735–739.

Cohen, M. A., & Gross, P. J. *The developmental resource: Behavioral sequences for assessment and program planning.* New York: Grune & Stratton, 1979.

Dmitriev, V. *Down syndrome performance inventory.* Seattle: Experimental Education Unit, University of Washington, no date.

Doll, E. A. *Vineland social maturity scale.* Circle Pines, Minn.: American Guidance Service, 1965.

Dunst, C. J. The handicapped infant: Is there justification for cognitive intervention? *Paper presented at the 100th Annual Meeting of the American Association on Mental Deficiency.* Chicago: June 1976.

Frankenburg, W. K., & Dodds, J. B. *Denver developmental screening test.* Denver: University of Colorado Medical Center, 1969.

Fredericks, H. D., Anderson, R., & Baldwin, V. The identification of competency indicators of teachers of the severely handicapped. *AAESPH Review,* 1979, *4,* 81–95.

Furuno, S., O'Reilly, K. A., Hosaka, C. M., Inatsuka, T. T., Allman, T. L., & Zeisloft, B. *Hawaii early learning profile.* Palo Alto, Calif.: VORT, 1979.

Glover, M. E., Preminger, J. L., & Sanford, A. R. *Early learning accomplishment profile.* Winston-Salem, N.C.: Kaplan School Supply, 1978.

Golin, A. K., & Ducanis, A. J. *The interdisciplinary team: A handbook for the education of exceptional children.* Rockville, Md.: Aspen Systems, 1981.

Guess, D., Horner, R., Utley, B., Holvoet, J., Maxon, D., Tucker, D., & Warren, S. A functional curriculum sequencing model for teaching the severely handicapped. *AAESPH Review,* 1978, *3,* 202–215.

Guess, D., Sailor, W., & Baer, D. M. A behavioral remedial approach to language training for the severely handicapped. In E. Sontag (Ed.), *Educational programming for the severely and profoundly handicapped.* Reston, Va.: Council for Exceptional Children, 1977.

Haring, N. G., & Bricker, D. Overview of comprehensive services for the severely/profoundly handicapped. In N. G. Haring and L. Brown (Eds.), *Teaching the severely handicapped* (Vol. 1). New York: Grune & Stratton, 1976.

Haring, N. G., & Cohen, M. Using the developmental approach as a basis for planning and sequencing different kinds of curricula for severely/profoundly handicapped persons. In *Educating the 24-hour retarded child.* Arlington, Tex.: National Association for Retarded Citizens, 1975.

Holvoet, J., Guess, D., Mulligan, M., & Brown, F. The individualized curriculum sequencing model (II): A teaching strategy for severely handicapped students. *Journal of the Association for the Severely Handicapped,* 1980, *5,* 337–351.

Johnson, N. M., Jens, K. G., & Attermeier, S. A. Carolina curriculum for handicapped infants. Chapel Hill: Frank Porter Graham Child Development Center, University of North Carolina, 1979.

Kahn, J. V. Utility of the Uzgiris and Hunt scales of sensorimotor development with severely and profoundly retarded children. *American Journal of Mental Deficiency,* 1976, *80,* 663–665.

Knobloch, H., Stevens, F., & Malone, A. F. *Manual of developmental diagnosis.* New York: Harper & Row, 1980.

LeMay, D. W., Griffin, P. M., & Sanford, A. R. *Learning accomplishment profile: Diagnostic edition (Rev.)* Chapel Hill, N.C.: Chapel Hill Training and Outreach Project, 1977.

Lillie, D. L. *Carolina developmental profile.* Chicago: Science Research Associates, 1975.

Lynch, L., Rieke, J., Soltman, S., Hardman, D., & O'Connor, M. *Preschool profile.* Seattle: Experimental Education Unit, University of Washington, no date.

Lynch, V., McGuigan, C., & Shoemaker, S. An introduction to systematic instruction. In N. G. Haring (Ed.), *The experimental education training program* (Vol. 1). Seattle: Experimental Education Unit, 1977.

Mager, R. *Preparing instructional objectives.* Belmont, Calif.: Fearon Publishers, 1962.

McCarthy, D. *Manual for the McCarthy scales of children's abilities.* New York: Psychological Corporation, 1972.

McLean, J. E., & Snyder-McLean, L. K. *A transactional approach to early language training.* Columbus, Ohio: Charles E. Merrill, 1978.

Miller, J., & Yoder, D. On developing the content for a language teaching program. *Mental Retardation,* 1972, *10,* 9–11.

Nahira, K., Foster, R., Shellhaas, M., & Leland, H. *AAMD adaptive behavior scale.* Washington, D.C.: American Association on Mental Deficiency, 1974.

Office of the Santa Cruz County Superintendent of Schools. *Behavior characteristics progression.* Palo Alto, Calif.: VORT, 1973.

Orlando, C. Multidisciplinary team approaches in the assessment of handicapped preschool children. *Topics in Early Childhood Special Education,* 1981, *1,* 23–30.

Piaget, J. *The origins of intelligence in children.* New York: W. W. Norton, 1963.

Popham, W. J. *The uses of instructional objectives: A personal perspective.* Belmont, Calif.: Fearon, 1973.

Powell, M. L. *Assessment and management of developmental changes and problems in children* (2nd ed.), St. Louis, Mo.: C. V. Mosby, 1981.

Project RHISE. *Rockford infant developmental evaluation scales.* Bensenville, Ill.: Scholastic Testing Service, 1979.

Quick, A. D., Little, T. L., & Campbell, A. A. *Project MEMPHIS: Enhancing developmental progress in preschool exceptional children.* Belmont, Calif.: Fearon, 1974.

Rutherford, R. B., & Edgar, E. B. *Teachers and parents.* Boston: Allyn & Bacon, 1979.

Ryan, T., Johnson, J., & Lynch, V. So you want to write objectives (or have to). In N. G. Haring (Ed.), *The experimental education training program.* Seattle: Experimental Education Unit, University of Washington, 1977.

Schafer, D. S., & Moersch, M. S. (Eds.). *Developmental programming for infants and young children.* Ann Arbor: University of Michigan Press, 1981.

Simeonsson, R. J. *Carolina Record of Infant Behavior.* Chapel Hill: Frank Porter Graham Child Development Center, University of North Carolina, 1979.

Simeonsson, R. J., & Simeonsson, N. E. Medication effects in handicapped preschool children. *Topics in Early Childhood Special Education,* 1981, *1,* 61–75.

Stillman, R. (Ed.). *The Callier-Azusa scale.* Dallas: Callier Center for Communication Disorders, University of Texas at Dallas, 1978.

Swick, K. J., Flake-Hobson, C., & Raymond, G. The first step, establishing parent-teacher communica-tion in the IEP conference. *Teaching Exceptional Children,* 1980, *12,* 144–145.

Tawney, J. W., Knapp, D. S., O'Reilly, O. D., & Pratt, S. S. *Programmed environments curriculum.* Columbus, Ohio: Charles E. Merrill, 1979.

Thiagarajan, S. Individualized instructional objectives. *Teaching Exceptional Children,* 1980, *12,* 144–145.

Turnbull, A., Strickland, B., & Brantley, J. *Developing and implementing individualized education programs* (2nd ed.). Columbus, Ohio: Charles E. Merrill, 1982.

Turnbull, H. R., & Turnbull, A. *Free appropriate public education: Law and implementation.* Denver: Love, 1978.

Vargas, J. *Writing worthwhile behavioral objectives.* New York: Harper & Row, 1972.

Vincent, L. J., Salisbury, C., Walter, G., Brown, P., Gruenwald, L. J., & Powers, M. Program evaluation and curriculum development in early childhood/special education: Criteria of the next environment. In W. Sailor, B. Wilcox, & L. Brown (Eds.), *Methods of instruction for severely handicapped students.* Baltimore: Paul H. Brookes, 1980.

Vulpé, S. G. *Vulpé assessment battery.* Toronto: National Institute on Mental Retardation, 1977.

Weisz, J. R., & Zigler, E. Cognitive development in retarded and nonretarded persons: Piagetian tests of the similar sequence hypothesis. *Psychological Bulletin,* 1979, *86,* 831–851.

Wheeler, A. H., & Fox, W. L. *Managing behavior, a teachers guide to writing instructional objectives.* Lawrence, Kans.: H & H Enterprises, 1972.

White, O. R. Adaptive performance objectives: Form versus function. In W. Sailor, B. Wilcox, & L. Brown (Eds.), *Methods of instruction for severely handicapped students.* Baltimore: Paul H. Brookes, 1980.

White, O. R., Edgar, E., Haring, N. G., Affleck, J., Hayden, A., & Bendersky, M. *Uniform performance assessment system.* Columbus, Ohio: Charles E. Merrill, 1981.

White, O. R., & Haring, N. G. *Exceptional teaching* (2nd ed.), Columbus, Ohio: Charles E. Merrill, 1980.

3

Implementing Direct Instruction

Nonhandicapped preschool children are able to profit from the usual experiences of childhood and as a result learn a variety of functional and adaptive skills. Young handicapped children, however, frequently do not profit from those experiences and as a result do not learn such skills. This prompts a critical question: What can we as teachers do to facilitate the development of such skills?

Bijou and Baer (1961, 1965, 1978) proposed that an individual's behavior is changed (develops) as a result of the *functional relationships* between the behavior and environmental stimuli. Functional relationships include *reinforcing functions*, a given stimulus increases the rate of a given behavior; *discriminative functions*, a given stimulus suggests if reinforcement is available for the performance of a given behavior; *eliciting functions*, a given stimulus prompts the occurrence of a given behavior; and possibly *punishing functions*, a given stimulus decreases the rate of a given behavior. These functional relationships suggest that the stimuli come from the social, physical, or inanimate environment; the child's biological or physiological structures and processes; and the child's own behavior. By dealing only with observable behavior and the functional relationships between stimuli and behavior, Bijou and Baer explain the occurrence of many types of behavior including problem solving and other "cognitive" endeavors.

Thus, "a retarded individual, from this point of view, is one who has a limited behavioral repertoire because of deficiencies in the environment and constraints imposed on the interactions that constitute his history—the more limited and restrictive the interactions, the more underdeveloped his behavioral repertoire" (Bijou, 1981, p. 30). Bijou describes two sources that limit or restrict interactions with the environment: "abnormal anatomical structures and physiological functioning" (p. 30), and "deficiencies and marked deviations in the external conditions of development" (p. 31). Bijou suggests deficient and deviant conditions are amenable to intervention and as a result of intervention the delays can be alleviated or prevented.

ASSUMPTIONS ABOUT THE INSTRUCTIONAL PROCESS

Based on Bijou and Baer's theory and on learning theory research, six major assumptions about the instructional process can be made. First, learning is an *un*observable process and we infer it by noting relatively stable changes in performance that are due to training or environmental stimulation rather than maturation (Hilgard & Bower, 1975; Travers, 1977). Performance, of course, is children's overt behavior.

Second, performance (behavior) is influenced by many things including children's health and learning histories, the environmental setting, and the stimuli that come immediately before the behavior (frequently called *antecedents*), and after the behavior (frequently called *consequences*). As teachers we should get the desired behaviors to occur in the desired settings and in the presence of given stimuli. To accomplish this task we conduct meaningful assessments of children, arrange the environment, present activities or antecedent events, and provide consequences or reinforcing and correcting events. These manipulations are done to increase the likelihood that the desired behaviors will occur. Many of the activities or antecedents are presented by teachers, but some also occur during free play sessions and may come from materials, other children, or the environment. Likewise, some consequences come from teachers and others come from the natural interactions.

Third, instruction should be individualized and matched to children's abilities and needs. Children's abilities should be thoroughly and carefully assessed to provide precise identification of desired behaviors (those behaviors the children need to learn). Activities and environments need to be planned and implemented so that learning is facilitated.

Fourth, instruction of young handicapped children should be designed so that children can learn many behaviors in a short time. This fourth assumption requires careful and ongoing measurement of children's performance to make decisions to increase the efficiency of instruction.

Fifth, simple acquisition of desired behaviors by young handicapped children is insufficient; teachers must insure maintenance and generalization of child performance (Stokes & Baer, 1977). They also need to arrange the learning environment and design the instructional activities so children can perform desired behaviors over time (maintain or retain the behaviors) and in a variety of settings and situations (generalize the behaviors).

Sixth, the principles and procedures used in teaching skills are similar across a variety of areas. For instance, if children are reinforced for specific language behaviors, their performance of such behaviors will increase. This is also true of cognitive, social, motor, and self-help behaviors. Direct instruction procedures such as assessing children's performance, specifying behavioral objectives, conducting task analysis, and carefully planning and implementing systematic changes in antecedents and consequences are similar across developmental areas. The content may be different, but the process is basically the same.

This chapter addresses the basic skills teachers need in implementing and evaluating individualized instructional programs. Unlike one-to-one programs, individualized instruction can occur in small and large groups. Objectives and activities are specifically designed to facilitate the acquisition and use of needed, appropriate, and functional behaviors.

The focus of this chapter is on the systematic application of principles of behavior to accomplish individualized instruction. According to Sulzer-Azaroff and Mayer (1977), a *behavioral principle* is a rule describing relations (functional relationship) between behavior and the variables that control it. A *behavioral procedure* is the systematic application of behavior principles to bring about behavior change.

Good teaching may require use of behavioral procedures at many points during the learning process. Stop and think for a minute about what is involved in learning. Some of the many aspects include: attending to a set of materials or task; selecting the important aspects of those materials; profiting from various forms of assistance (e.g., teacher prompts or cues) to make a response; matching one's behavior to a model; learning from reinforcement and punishment that may follow a behavior; applying this learning when presented with the same task at a later time; and generalizing this learning to new situations or tasks. Each of these tasks may need to be analyzed and individually taught to some children.

Several theorists have suggested that learning may be conceptualized in *phases*. These phases should not be confused with the concept of stages of development that represent general characteristics of children and their behavior due to age, physical maturity, and experience. A learning phase represents a step in the process of learning one or more specific skills. The phase in which a child is functioning has implications for the types of strategies used by teachers. Haring, White, and Liberty (1978) suggest five phases of learning: acquisition, fluency-building, generalization, maintenance, and adaptation. The first three will be discussed in this chapter.

ACQUISITION

During acquisition, the child is learning the basic task requirements. This phase is most frequently thought of as *teaching*. Implementing effective instructional activities to facilitate acquisition requires several decisions such as: What will motivate the child to perform (i.e., acquire) the behavior? How should we present the activity to the child? Should teacher assistance be provided? How should the activities be scheduled within the school day? How should the learning environment be arranged? There are no clear-cut answers to these questions, and our responses must be based on the performance of individual children and on the skills we teach. However, some general information relevant to these decisions is discussed in the following sections and in Chapters 5 and 6.

Motivating Children

Ideally, we want children to be intrinsically motivated to learn new skills. However, intrinsic motivation is frequently insufficient because the children are young, handicapped, and human. Thus, we must rely on external motivation. One procedure that is often used is *positive reinforcement*, an event (praise, activity, juice, hug, candy, and others) that follows the occurrence of a behavior and increases the likelihood of its reoccurrence. Events that

serve as reinforcers for one child will not necessarily work for another, and reinforcers must be used carefully to produce the desired results (Baer, 1978).

Selecting reinforcers Many sources of reinforcers exist for most young children, including social interactions with adults and peers, food, drink, movement, toys, and activities. From these broad categories, select stimuli (reinforcers) that produce the desired result (increase the rate of the behavior); are easily given to the child; and are acceptable to the teacher, parents, and program administrators.

Stimuli that function as reinforcers can be identified through a four step process. First, attempt to use common reinforcers that appeal to most young children. These stimuli include praise; pats; tickles; "giving five"; smiles; enthusiastic facial expressions; and access to a variety of toys and objects, foods and liquids, and opportunities to move. If these events do not appear to be reinforcers, initiate the second step, asking parents about things or actions that might be reinforcing. Parents frequently know what the child likes and thus what might be reinforcing. Ask about specific categories such as, "Does she have any toys she especially likes or plays with a lot?" "What are her favorite foods and liquids?" Such questions are more apt to prompt specific answers than general queries such as, "What do you think she likes?" Third, observe the child and note any frequent behaviors. This should include two or three sessions of 10–15 minutes when the child is free to move about the room and do what she wants and some brief observations as the child moves through a typical day. The teacher should note any frequent behaviors and favorite objects; these can be used as reinforcers if access to the objects or the freedom to do the behaviors are made contingent upon the behavior you want to increase. Such arrangements are based on the Premack principle (Sulzer-Azaroff & Mayer, 1977). Fourth, if the above procedures do not result in useful reinforcers, the teacher should use a reinforcement menu, a collection of a variety of foods, drinks, toys, and so on, from which the child is allowed to choose. If the child consistently selects one or two items, then they will likely have reinforcement value.

These procedures are important because

different stimuli (reinforcers) will have different effects with different children. For example, dried pineapples are good reinforcers for Sandra, but Josh will not eat them. On the other hand, a small wind-up duck is an excellent reinforcer for Josh, but Sandra hardly even looks at the toy. These procedures are also important because some reinforcers will be very effective for a while and then begin to lose their value. When this situation occurs, the teacher should search for other reinforcers.

Once reinforcers are identified, the teacher must evaluate whether they can be easily adminsterd. For example, it is easy to give a child a small peanut or a small toy each time he responds correctly. It is very difficult to allow the child to play outside on the slide each time he responds correctly.

If an effective and easily administered reinforcer has been identified, the teacher should determine whether the reinforcer is acceptable to both the staff and parents. For example, many parents want their children to eat specific foods. In such cases, the teacher should not use edible reinforcers that are not a part of the diet. If no other reinforcers are available, the teacher should discuss the importance of the reinforcer with the parents.

Using reinforcers Reinforcers will be of little value in increasing motivation for skill acquisition unless they are used properly. The response for which the reinforcer is to be given should be clearly specified. For example, Jane's teacher wants her to learn to use two words when making requests. If at snack time Jane holds out her cup and says, "More, more," should the teacher give her more juice or should he say, "More what, Jane?" and attempt to get her to say, "More juice." The reinforcer should also be given immediately after the response. If reinforcers are not given immediately after the desired behavior, then they will not reinforce that behavior. For instance, Brian is learning to sort objects by shape. When he sorts an object correctly, the teacher records his response, gives him another object, and a few seconds later hands him a reinforcer, a small piece of fruit. In the meantime Brian begins to look out the window. If the teacher gives him the fruit at that moment, he or she is likely to reinforce looking out the window rather than correct sorting.

When reinforcers such as food, drink, and toys are used, the teacher should pair those items with social stimuli such as praise, touching, and hugs. Such pairing will result in the social stimuli becoming reinforcers. For example, if Gerard is learning to put a puzzle together, and gets a sip of milk for each correct piece, the teacher should also say, "You put it in right, Gerard!" and pat him on the back. Social reinforcers are important because they can occur in a variety of situations and are similar to the natural environment. When praise is used it should include specific statements about the child's behavior such as, "You put the puzzle together" rather than, "Good work." Further, social reinforcers should usually be given with enthusiasm; exceptions would be children with tight muscles for whom enthusiastic social stimulation increases their muscle tone.

When possible the teacher should use a variety of reinforcers, especially social ones. This will tend to increase motivation and help in keeping one or two reinforcers from losing their effectiveness. Variety in praise can be accomplished by using different words and animated facial and motor movements, and changing the volume and tone of the voice.

When possible, teachers should use natural reinforcers that occur as a result of the child's behavior or in the child's typical environment. For instance, Emily and Cathrine's teacher wants to increase the amount of time they play cooperatively together. Giving them additional toys as a reinforcer is more natural than handing each a raisin and saying, "It's good to see you play together." Likewise, if Jane says, "More juice" the natural reinforcer is to give her more rather than to say, "You're talking so nicely" while giving her "five."

Teachers should determine the best schedule of reinforcement. The schedule of reinforcement refers to how frequently the reinforcer is given in relation to how frequently the behavior occurs. Usually, during initial skill acquisition and when attempting to increase motivation, reinforcers are given each time the desired behavior occurs. Such a schedule is called a *continuous reinforcement schedule.* Once a skill has been acquired, the schedule is changed, and the reinforcement is *not* given each time the behavior occurs. This is called an *intermittent schedule*. Continuous reinforcement schedules help the child learn the skill more quickly, while intermittent schedules help the child maintain the behavior longer.

The steps for selecting and identifying reinforcers are as follows:

1   Test things and events which are reinforcers for most young children.
2   Ask the child's parents about specific types of things and activities which may be reinforcers.
3   Observe the child and identify behaviors which the child frequently does or objects the child frequently seeks.
4   Present a number of objects which may be reinforcers and allow the child to select from the objects.

Steps for using reinforcement in teaching include the following:

1   Precisely identify the behavior to be reinforced.
2   Give the reinforcer immediately after the behavior occurs.
3   Pair food, drink, and object reinforcers with social stimuli such as praise and touching the child.
4   Use a variety of reinforcers when possible.
5   Use natural reinforcers when possible.
6   Identify and use the most appropriate schedule of reinforcement.

For more detailed discussions of reinforcement, procedures for selecting reinforcers, and using reinforcement in teaching, see Baer (1978), Sulzer-Azaroff and Mayer (1977), Vargas (1977), and Wehman and McLoughlin (1981). If identified and used properly, the frequency with which the child performs the behavior should increase.

The concept of reinforcement assumes that the behavior is something the child already can do—he or she just does not do it consistently or frequently enough. However, sometimes the child is not really in the acquisition phase. Acquisition involves learning *how* to do something. The appropriate use of positive reinforcement is important in every phase of learning, but it alone will not necessarily be effective in skill acquisition. For example, if Renee does not know how to put the pieces in a puzzle, increasing reinforcement will not increase the number of pieces she puts in the puzzle. Thus, although motivation to acquire a skill is desirable and perhaps necessary, it is not sufficient. We must combine reinforcement with other techniques to ensure that acquisition occurs.

Besides the use of positive reinforcement to enhance motivation, several issues such as arranging the learning environment, presenting interesting and inviting activities, and using attractive materials are described in Chapters 5, 6, and 7. The teacher should develop skills in each of these areas.

Presenting Antecedent Events

Since reinforcement alone is insufficient in establishing acquisition of new behaviors, teachers must attend to the presentation of antecedent events. Related skills are: task analyzing skills, teaching the steps of the task analysis in the most efficient order, securing the child's attention before presenting the task, selecting the most appropriate verbal cues, and pacing the instructional activities.

As described in Chapter 2, some skills must be broken into smaller steps (task analyzed) before children can acquire them. This process is critical in facilitating acquisition. Presenting activities to teach skills that are too complex will result in ineffective and inefficient instruction, frustration for the teacher and child, and perhaps behavior problems such as inattention, noncompliance, and aggression.

If a skill has been task analyzed and involves a number of small behaviors chained together, the teacher must decide where to begin within that task sequence. The teacher usually chooses the beginning or the end of the chain. In a *forward chaining procedure*, instruction begins with the first step in the skill sequence and proceeds toward the last. For many skills the forward chaining approach is effective, particularly if the child has already mastered some of the steps.

In *backward chaining procedure*, instruction begins with the last step in the sequence and proceeds toward the first. The major advantage of backward chaining is that the child completes the task in the first lesson. The first goal is realized and the *functional relationship* begins to be established between the task completion and its natural outcomes (consequences). For example, one way to teach eating with a spoon would be to start with the first step (forward chaining) in the task sequence, such as "reaches for the spoon." Once this step has been learned, the next step is taught, and so on until the entire sequence is learned. However, it is not until the final step that the child receives the natural reward for his efforts: Independently getting food into the mouth. Furthermore, he does not practice a later skill in the sequence until it is time to teach it. If this skill were taught in a backward chain, however, the teacher might physically manipulate the child through all the steps in the sequence, and at the last step the teacher would release the spoon and the child would complete the task. The teacher says, "Alex, you ate with a spoon!" and begins the process again. Gradually the child is allowed to independently perform more steps in the sequence. A task analysis for teaching spoon feeding using backward and forward chaining is shown in Table 3.1.

Although, backward chaining seems to be quite effective with most self-help skills such as eating, dressing, and grooming, it is probably inappropriate for teaching a child to write her name, comment on her environment, match objects by color, and so on. For such skills, the behaviors from the task analysis are frequently taught in a forward chaining fashion or as individual behaviors.

Attention to the task is a critical prerequisite skill for acquisition. Although attention is difficult to measure, we can usually infer it if a child is looking at the teacher or materials and is not engaged in other behaviors, such as self-stimulation. Frequently children need help in directing their attention to the critical aspects of a task. Verbal cues such as "Connie, look" and then placing the materials in front of the child may be sufficient to secure attention. With other children however, the teacher must use more overt techniques. This can be done by moving one's hand through the child's line of vision and then to the materials, tapping or pointing to the materials, and making noises to get the child's interest. The teacher may also ask children to look at or touch each item before giving verbal directions. Besides these procedures, teachers may need to structure the instructional setting to eliminate distracting stimuli. Procedures for enhancing attention to tasks and facilitating engagement with materials are described in Chapter 7.

Verbal directions used to cue the occurrence of the behavior are a critical component of the task presentation (Etzel & LeBlanc, 1979). Verbal directions should be brief and specific, yet full of information. For example, "Put the toys on the shelves" conveys more explicit instructions than "Time to put our things away." Similarly, "Point to the big dog" is more explicit than "Where's the big one?" When the child has acquired the behavior, vary the verbal directions so that he or she

TABLE 3.1

Example of forward and backward chaining sequences for independent feeding with a spoon

Backward Chaining Sequence		Forward Chaining Sequence
1. Place spoon on table.	FIRST STEP	1. Pick up spoon from table.
2. Pull spoon out of mouth while cleaning food from spoon with lips.	TAUGHT	2. Place spoon in food.
		3. Lift spoon vertically 2–3 inches above food.
3. Put spoon in mouth.		4. Move spoon in arc toward mouth keeping the bowl of the spoon facing up.
4. Open mouth.		
5. Move spoon in arc toward mouth keeping the bowl of the spoon facing up.		5. Open mouth.
		6. Put spoon in mouth.
6. Lift spoon vertically 2–3 inches above food.		7. Pull spoon out of mouth while cleaning food from spoon with lips.
7. Place spoon in food.	LAST STEP	
8. Pick up spoon from table.	TAUGHT	8. Place spoon on table.

will perform when presented with a variety of verbal cues. Initial acquisition will be more rapid if we use one specific verbal direction, however.

Teachers sometimes want behavior to occur with only nonverbal cues. For example, we do not want children to wait for a verbal direction for each movement they make when playing with toys. However, we may initially use verbal directions when teaching a child to play with toys. Once the child acquires the play skills verbal direction could be faded out.

The pace at which direct instruction is given is another critical component of task presentation (Etzel & LeBlanc, 1979). Generally speaking, a rapid pace of instruction is preferred to a slower pace (See Chapter 6 for more detailed discussion). However, with some children such as the cerebral palsied, instruction must be slowed to allow sufficient time for them to respond. Performance is maximized by manipulating the speed of instruction. Teachers can determine the appropriate pace by systematically presenting the same task at various speeds and collecting data on the child's performance. The pace at which the child has the most correct responses should be used for instruction.

Teachers must attend to several factors when presenting antecedent events to facilitate skill acquisition. These factors include task analyzing the skill, selecting an efficient sequence, securing the child's attention, presenting verbal directions, and pacing instructional activities. A description of these factors and parts of them which can be changed if the child is not learning is presented in Table 3.2.

Using Teacher Assistance

Even if teaching conditions are optimal, many young handicapped children will continue to make errors and have slow rates of acquisition. Such situations indicate a lack of appropriate *stimulus control* which is a reliable responding in the presence of a given stimulus (Vargas, 1977). For example, if Lorraine reliably touches blue each time you ask her to "Touch the blue one" (blue stimulus) and does not touch it when you ask her to touch other colors, then stimulus control has been established. Behaviors come under the control of stimuli when they (the behaviors) are reinforced in

the presence of those stimuli. Many forms of teacher manipulations of materials and direct assistance, such as errorless learning procedures and teacher prompts, can be used to establish stimulus control.

Errorless learning procedures These procedures are based on the notion that learning will be more rapid and efficient if the teaching situation can be arranged to prevent errors. Two forms of errorless learning procedures are stimulus shaping and stimulus fading. Both involve changes in the stimuli presented to the child (frequently the materials are changed) and therefore accomplish shifts in stimulus control. In *stimulus shaping* the relevant (critical) characteristics of the stimulus (those characteristics being taught) are changed as training progresses, and in *stimulus fading* the irrelevant characteristics are gradually changed.[1] For example, if we were using stimulus shaping to train Raul to point to the set with the larger number of items, we would change the relevant characteristic, the number of items, in one of the sets. We might begin with one set of 15 items and another of 5. As training progresses, the set with 15 would be reduced to 13, 11, 9, 7, and 6 items. This shaping is used because initially it is easier for Raul to recognize that a set of 15 is greater than a set of 5, than for him to identify a set of 6 as being greater than a set of 5.

In contrast, *response shaping* involves reinforcing successive approximations of the target behavior. This means you might initially reinforce a response that is considerably inferior to the one you eventually desire. Once this relationship has been established, however, closer approximations of the target behavior are gradually required before reinforcement is presented. For example, in teaching Willie the manual sign for "toilet" you might initially reinforce any general movement of the hand and progressively require more precise hand movements before presenting reinforcement.

If we were using stimulus fading to teach Raul to identify the set with the greater number of items, we might begin with a set of six

---

[1]Although these definitions are logically correct, some authors (Dorry, 1976; Schreibman, 1975) refer to stimulus shaping as "fading in" and "fading out" given relevant characteristics.

TABLE 3.2
Steps for presenting and manipulating antecedent events to facilitate acquisition of skills

Step	Possible Modifications if the Child is Not Acquiring the Target Skill
1. Task analyze the skill.	1. Increase the number of steps in the task analysis. 2. Sequence the steps in a different order (e.g., change from temporal to response difficulty order).
2. Teach the skill in the most efficient order.	1. Change the order of teaching (e.g., use forward rather than backward chaining, and backward rather than forward). 2. Teach only a small part of the order, but retain the original sequence.
3. Secure the child's attention to the task before presenting at trial.	1. Verbally call the child's attention to task. 2. Use a gesture or other stimulus that will call child's attention to the task. 3. Eliminate distracting stimuli in the environment (e.g., move instructional situation to less distracting setting, or rearrange environment to reduce distracting stimuli). 4. Increase the attractiveness of materials (e.g., use brightly colored materials, vary materials, use novel materials, reduce the number of irrelevant characteristics in the materials). 5. Require "attention response" before presenting trial (e.g., child must point to materials and then the verbal directions are presented).
4. Use brief but specific verbal directions.	1. Increase the specificity of the verbal directions. 2. Eliminate all but the critical aspects of the verbal directions. 3. Increase the salience of verbal directions. (e.g., make them louder, vary pitch and tone of voice, eliminate distracting auditory stimuli which are not a part of the verbal directions).
5. Use an appropriate pace of presentation.	1. Present items faster. 2. Present items slower. 3. Present items at various speeds during a single session.

and another of five items. The items in the greater set might be six 4-in. by 1-in. by 4-in. blocks and the items in the smaller set might be five 1-in. cubes. As training progresses the size of the large blocks are reduced until they are 1-in. cubes. In this example we are manipulating the size of the items (irrelevant characteristic) not the number of items (relevant characteristic). Raul should shift his responding from the irrelevant characteristic of object

size to the relevant characteristic of the number of objects in each set.

Stimulus fading may take many forms and may incorporate many different dimensions of the *stimulus display* (the visual task as presented to the child). In this procedure some aspect of the stimulus display is manipulated to cue the child to the correct response. For example, if you want Fran to touch a cup, you might place the cup much closer to Fran than, for instance, a shoe. This arrangement should increase the probability of Fran touching the cup. If you want Jeremy to select his name from two cards with a name, you might have the correct choice written on a red card, his favorite color. He will probably select the red card and thus get reinforced.

Of course, we do not know if Jeremy has learned his name or is simply pointing to his favorite color. Nor do we know whether Fran really knows the concept of a cup. The way to ensure that the child is responding to the correct characteristic (dimension) is to gradually remove the incorporated cues (e.g., color and distance). For example, gradually move the shoe closer and closer (stimulus fading) until the shoe and the cup are equal dis-

tances from Fran. You could remove the color cue by gradually using lighter shades of red and pink until both names were presented on white cards. If Fran and Jeremy still respond correctly, there has been a *shift in stimulus control.* They have shifted from responding to irrelevant characteristics (distance and color) to relevant characteristics of the stimuli (cup or name).

Schreibman (1975), Etzel and LeBlanc (1979), Dorry (1976), and Schreibman and Charlop (1981) describe procedures for using stimulus shaping and fading, including examples of actual changes in the materials that facilitate learning. A variety of dimensions of stimulus fading and examples of each dimension are shown in Table 3.3.

TABLE 3.3

Dimensions and examples of stimulus fading

Dimension	Description	Examples
Position	Place the correct choice in a position that will increase the probability of the child pointing to that choice.	Target: Recognize shoe. Initially place shoe much closer to child than incorrect response. Gradually shift position so that shoe and incorrect response are equal distances from child.
Color	Highlight the correct response with a color that might increase the probability of the child pointing to that choice.	Target: Find chin on picture of person. Initially highlight the chin with a bright color. Gradually fade the color until there is no color cue.
Size	Make the correct response significantly different in size from the incorrect response.	Target: Point to triangle. Initially make triangle much larger than the incorrect shape. Gradually reduce its size until approximately equal that of other choices.
Surface	Make the texture or surface appearance of the correct response different and more appealing than that of the incorrect response.	Target: Recognize the letter A. Draw an A and another letter of equal size on two cards. Paste beans, glitter, or sandpaper on the A; do nothing to the other letter. Gradually remove these cues until the discrimination is simply between two letters.

Direct teacher assistance: Extrastimulus prompts Teachers can provide direct assistance through extrastimulus prompts. The prompt should be sufficient to produce the desired behavior, thus allowing reinforcement for performing the behavior. The prompts should also be faded as quickly as possible. Good examples of extrastimulus prompts include verbal cues, gestures, models, partial physical prompts, and full physical manipulations.

Verbal cues are extra teacher verbalizations that tell the child how to do the behavior. These prompts are minimally intrusive and can only be used with children who understand the content of the statements. For example, if Kathy is attempting to put a puzzle together, the teacher might provide verbal prompts such as, "Start with the big round piece," "Turn it more," and "Put the hat piece on the clown's head."

Gestures are nonverbal movements, usually with the hands, that are understood by most people. Pointing is a common gesture used to tell the child what to do or which of a variety of items is the correct one. Holding the palm facing the child is a common cue for him or her to stop. As with verbal prompts, gestures are minimally intrusive and require some understanding of their meaning.

Models are demonstrations of the desired behavior and are an effective means of teaching children who are imitative but who do not understand gestures or verbal cues. They are particularly efficient with complex fine motor tasks and verbal behaviors where it is difficult to provide physical prompts. Chapter 4 is devoted solely to the issue of imitation.

Partial physical prompts are brief touches by the teacher that direct the child to initiate or complete a task. Such touching may be a nudge or a small amount of pressure on the child's hand. *Full physical manipulations*, on the other hand, involve the teacher placing his hands over the child's hands and providing the complete effort required to complete the task. Usually the teacher and child should be faced in the same direction so that the prompted movements will resemble natural movements. When using full physical manipulations, the teacher should be careful not to injure the child by straining the child's muscles, holding the hands too tightly, or forcing limbs beyond their normal range of motion. Partial physical prompts and full physical manipulations are quite intrusive and require close proximity of the teacher and child, whereas verbal prompts, gestures, and models can be delivered from a distance.

Prompts must be faded. Failure to do so will keep the child from learning to perform the task independently. Extrastimulus prompts may be eliminated on some of the trials as training progresses. Eventually, the child would receive no prompts. Another method of fading is to decrease the force of the prompt. When using verbal prompts, the loudness (force) can be decreased so they are no longer audible. When using physical prompts, the pressure exerted by the teacher can be decreased until the child is no longer touched. The position of the prompt on the child's body can also be faded. For example, initially the teacher's hands are placed over the child's; then they move to the child's wrist, forearm, elbow, and finally away from the body entirely. As the position is moved back from the hand, the amount of control the teacher has over the child's arm movements is automatically decreased. Prompts can also be faded by temporal transfer of stimulus control commonly called time delay, system of least prompts, system of most to least prompts, and graduated guidance.

With *time delay*, the teacher must use a prompt that will ensure the occurrence of the behavior. This prompt is then paired with the verbal directions for the task. As training progresses, the time between the verbal directions and the prompt is progressively lengthened in small increments; that is, the prompt is delayed in time (Snell & Gast, 1981). For example, if you want Jack to give you various objects when they are named, you could use pointing as a prompt—assuming of course that Jack would respond by giving you the object to which you pointed. Initially you would say, "Give me_____." and immediately point to the object you named. In the next session, you would give the verbal direction ("Give me _____."), wait one second, and then point to the object you named. With each successive session you would add one second before pointing to the object named. As training progresses, the child should shift from responding to the pointing to the verbal cue "Give me _____."

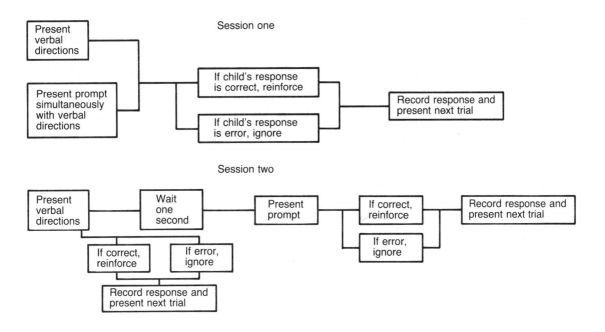

FIGURE 3.1

Flow Chart for Using the Time Delay Procedure for
Fading Extrastimulus Prompts

Verbal directions refers to the cues that the teacher wants the child to respond to when training is completed. These cues may be verbal, signed, or simply the presence of given materials or situations. One second is added for each successive session; for example, in Session 3 you would wait 2 seconds before giving the prompt and in Session 4 you would wait 3 seconds before giving the prompt.

This procedure has been used to teach many skills such as verbalizations, signing, and instruction following skills (Smeets & Striefel, 1976; Stremel-Campbell, Cantrell, & Halle, 1977; Striefel, Wetherby, & Karlan, 1976). A flow chart describing the use of time delay is shown in Figure 3.1.

In the *system of least prompts* the teacher uses a prompt hierarchy (verbal cues, gestures, models, partial physical prompts, and full physical manipulations). When the first trial is presented, the teacher provides the verbal directions, waits a few seconds and if no response occurs, repeats the directions and adds verbal cues (prompts). If the child still does not respond, then the teacher provides the verbal directions and a gesture prompt. The teacher progressively moves up the prompt hierarchy until the child performs correctly (Alberto & Schofield, 1979; Cuvo, Leaf, & Borakove, 1978). On the next trial, this progression is repeated if necessary. A flow chart describing the use of the system of least

prompts is shown in Figure 3.2. In the *most to least prompt system*, a hierarchy opposite that of the system of least prompts is used (starts with a full physical manipulation). The prompts become progressively less intrusive on each subsequent trial or each subsequent session.

Graduated guidance also involves physical prompts, but only as they are needed. Prompts can be faded at any point in the response chain (Foxx & Azrin, 1973). The procedures for using graduated guidance are as follows:

1 Begin each trial with the type and amount of assistance (prompt) required for the child to perform the task.
2 As the child begins to perform the behavior (within the trial), immediately fade the assistance.
3 If the child stops performing the behavior, immediately apply the prompts required for the child to begin performing and fade

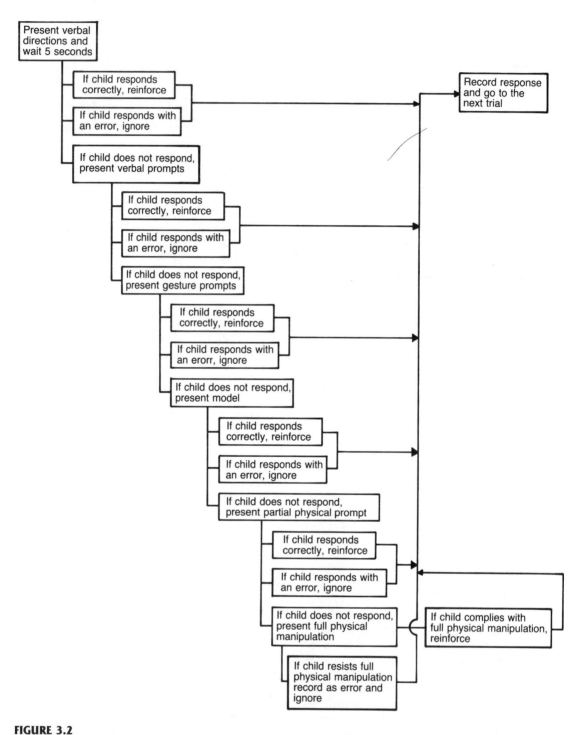

FIGURE 3.2

Flow Chart for Using the System of Least Prompts
to Fade Extrastimulus Prompts.

Verbal directions   refers to the cues that the teacher wants the child to respond to when training is completed. These cues may be verbal, signed, or simply the presence of given materials or situations.

the assistance as the child begins the task.

4 If the child starts to move in the wrong direction, the amount and type of prompt required to redirect the child should be used and faded.

5 Rewards should be given when the child independently completes the task even if a minimal amount of the final part of the task is done independently.

6 Rewards should not be given if the child is resisting assistance at the completion of the task.

All of these procedures have been effective in fading extrastimulus prompts and thus facilitating the acquisition of skills. Relatively little comparative research has been done on which procedure is most effective. In the final analysis, the selection of the "best" procedure may rest with its relative efficiency rather than its effectiveness. Each procedure may be effective, but for given tasks and given children, one may take less training time than another. Graduated guidance and the most to least system of prompts are probably the preferred procedures when children are nonimitative and when skills are comprised of behaviors chained together. For discrete behaviors, time delay and the system of least prompts are probably more effective and efficient, particularly if the child is imitative and the skills cannot be easily physically prompted (e.g., verbal skills). Nonetheless, considerable research is needed to support these statements and to identify efficient procedures.

Correcting Errors

In spite of our attempts to use errorless learning procedures and extrastimulus prompts, children will make a variety of errors. The procedures to deal with them should be as diverse as the errors themselves.

Random errors Random errors are commonly called careless errors and occur during acquisition and when practicing already acquired skills. Such errors usually occur at fairly low rates; there are relatively few when compared to the number of correct responses. In addition, no pattern of errors is apparent; the child usually performs a given response correctly.

When teachers note the occurrence of such errors, they should change the consequences for the task. For example, the teacher may change the reinforcer, the schedule of reinforcement, provide rewards for a given number of correct responses, or reinforce the child for not making errors.

Systematic errors Systematic errors usually occur during acquisition as compared to practice of an already acquired skill. Such errors are identified by their consistency. With systematic errors, children perform as though they have a rule or strategy that governs their performance. The rule is incorrect, but allows them to receive reinforcement at least some of the time. For example, if we were training Peggy to give us a spoon and a toothbrush, we might put them in front of her and say, "Give me _____." Perhaps she hands us the item to her left. If we changed the positions of the two items from trial to trial, she might be reinforced for some of her responses. She is responding to the rule, "The one on the left is correct." Peggy might also make other systematic errors that could be described by the following rules: "Only one item (e.g., toothbrush) is correct," "Select one item and then switch to the other item on the next trial, "If you are reinforced for one item (position) stay with that item or position," or "If you are reinforced for one item take the other item on the next trial." Children can also use rules that involve certain characteristics of the stimulus such as, "The big one is always correct," or, "The yellow one is always correct." Systematic errors are difficult to identify unless the teacher carefully notes the nature of the child's error, collects trial-by-trial data, and looks for patterns in the errors. Churchill (1978) identified several such errors when training language to autistic children. Guess, Sailor, Rutherford, & Baer (1968) noted that when a child was trained to add an *s* to words such as *cup* to describe plural instances of the concept (*cups*), he also generalized the form (made a systematic error) to irregular words, such as using *childs* for children.

Systematic errors can be eliminated by providing an extrastimulus prompt or using an errorless learning procedure to make the use of the incorrect rule unnecessary.

The task can also be arranged so that the incorrect rule will never result in reinforcement.

In our example of Peggy using the rule, "The one on the left is correct," we could always put the correct item on her right. In this procedure, however, be cautious that she does not learn a new incorrect rule, "The one on the right is always correct." To ensure that such a situation does not arise, wait until she makes a correct response on the right and then begin to randomly place the correct item on the left or right. Breaking children's rules can be very complex and frustrating. Children frequently move from one incorrect rule to another and may have as many as four or five. (Churchill, 1978). Use extrastimulus prompts or errorless learning procedures whenever possible.

Errors of unlearned prerequisite behaviors Errors of unlearned prerequisite behaviors are also consistent and are most obvious during the acquisition phase. Usually such errors involve one or two behaviors in a chain. For example, Ruth is learning to feed herself with a spoon. She can bring the spoon to her mouth, put it in, clean the food from the spoon with her lips, and return the spoon to her bowl, but she cannot fill her spoon unless the food sticks to it. Thus, she is unable to fill the spoon with nonsticky foods. By observing what foods she can independently feed herself and noting her behavior when she cannot, it becomes obvious why she cannot fill her spoon. The consistency of such errors and the interruptions they cause usually makes them relatively easy to identify.

Therefore, we should teach the child to perform the prerequisite behaviors. Ruth would be instructed to put her spoon into the food, make a horizontal movement, lift it straight up, and then move it to her mouth

Errors due to unlearned prerequisite behaviors are not so obvious with cognitive or language tasks. For example, in attempting to determine whether Carolyn could match objects by shape, we might give her a red square and a blue circle. We then show her a yellow circle and say, "Show me the same" (or some equivalent direction). If she performs the task incorrectly, she either cannot match by shape or she does not know what is expected of her when we say, "Show me the same." Correct performance involves pointing to one of her two shapes or placing one of her shapes on ours. We use her performance of those

behaviors to determine whether she can note similarities between the form of objects. If she cannot do such behaviors, we cannot determine what her matching skills are. To ensure that her errors are due to the inability to match by shape, use procedures that allow her to demonstrate her abilities with already acquired prerequisite behaviors or concepts (such as matching by size). Whenever errors occur on new tasks be sure the child can perform the behaviors that indicate whether he understands the concept.

Errors due to noncompliance In many instances errors due to noncompliance may be difficult to identify. Haring, White, & Liberty (1978) suggest two types of data patterns indicate that errors due to noncompliance are present: when the performance data are highly variable—on some days the child performs the task nearly perfectly, but on other days under the same circumstances he is correct on only one or two of the trials; and when there has been a stable, fairly high percent of correct responses and there is a sudden sharp drop in these responses. Existence of either of these patterns indicates possible errors due to noncompliance.

When treating noncompliance errors, Haring et al. (1978) suggest changing the consequences for the task. For example, the reinforcer, reinforcement schedule, and the behavior can change. The changes would be similar to those described for random errors. In addition, consequences can be added for error responses, such as using a full physical manipulation, reinforcing the child for not making errors, saying "No," and having the child repeat the task. Identifiable characteristics of these error types and suggested correction procedures are shown in Table 3.4.

FLUENCY BUILDING

Unfortunately many teachers stop instruction at the end of acquisition. Mastery criteria for target objectives frequently include statements such as "100% correct for three consecutive days." All too often we assume that once a child reaches a high degree of accuracy our task is done and we can move on to another skill. Obviously you cannot get more accurate,

TABLE 3.4
Correction of errors to facilitate skill acquisition

Type of Error	Identification of Errors	Correction Procedures
Random Errors	Occur during fluency-building Few errors occur No pattern of errors is apparent.	Change consequences (e.g., change reinforcer, change reinforcement schedule).
Systematic Errors	Occur during acquisition Consistent errors Appears to be an incorrect "rule" or "strategy"	Provide prompt to eliminate need for incorrect "rule" or "strategy." Arrange task so that incorrect "rule" or "strategy" is not reinforced.
Errors of Unlearned Prerequisite Skills	Occur during acquisition Consistent errors Appears as though child does not "know" how to do the task	Teach prerequisite skills.
Errors due to Noncompliance	Sharp drop in the rate of correct responses High variability, some days most responses are correct and some days most responses are errors	Change consequences (e.g., add consequences for errors, change reinforcer, change reinforcement schedule).

but you can get faster or more fluent. This is the focus of the fluency-building phase of learning.

Why should we be concerned with fluency? Should we not be satisfied that the skill has been learned? Perhaps we should teach a large number of skills and leave it up to the child and his or her environment to determine which ones will be practiced. Unfortunately for many young handicapped children, this strategy does not work. The speed with which one performs a task often bears a direct relationship to the probability that independent performance will be encouraged outside of the school. It also affects the probability that the individual will attempt to incorporate the skill into his usual repertoire.

For example, you spent three months teaching Tanya to eat with a spoon and she has reached a high degree of accuracy, so that when presented a spoon and her bowl and told to eat, she can perform the task correctly almost 100% of the time. Unfortunately it takes her 45 minutes to finish a bowl of yogurt. What are the chances that her mother, who has two other children to feed, would be willing to wait that long? Dressing is another example. If Janie can dress herself very slowly, her parents will probably not have the morning time to let her do so. In fact, they may often dress Janie themselves, simply because it is easier and faster.

Fluency may also be critical for certain skills to be safe. For example, teaching Lucy to cross the street may be a very functional objective. However, if Lucy moves very slowly, crossing the street could be dangerous.

We teach fluency through practice. The only way to become a faster guitar picker is to practice more often. It is also the only way to become faster at tying your shoes or putting on a shirt. Thus, the first rule of thumb for fluency building is to provide sufficient opportunities to perform the task each day.

Unfortunately, practice is not always exciting. In fact, repetition can rapidly lead to boredom and we can see the effects of boredom in child performance patterns: increasing errors, decreasing fluency, and increasing behavior problems. So the next rule of thumb for fluency building is to make practice rewarding. This may be accomplished by making a game out of it, or by providing some kind of reinforcement at the end of the practice period.

As mentioned earlier, reinforcement is important in every phase of the learning process; the only difference is in the way it is used. In the acquisition phase, reinforcement is important to tell the child he made a correct response and motivate the child to keep trying, but the primary teaching strategy has to do with other teacher activities such as modeling or prompting. In the fluency-building stage reinforcement is also critical, but we change the rules of the game. Reinforcement is given contingent upon *speed* rather than accuracy.

It takes a creative teacher to make daily practice of an acquired skill enjoyable. One strategy is to "beat the clock." For instance, if Maureen can tie her shoe in less than 45 seconds, she gets to play with her favorite doll. If Scott cleans up the block area before the timer goes off, he can set the table for snack time. Another strategy is to clearly point out the benefits of doing a skill rapidly. If Mark realizes he will not miss the bus if he dresses at an appropriate rate, then he may likely speed up his performance.

Fluency building not only means doing something faster but also refers to increases in duration. For example, in the acquisition phase you may teach Jerome the skills needed to play independently in the block area. In the fluency-building stage the emphasis is on playing independently for longer periods of time rather than playing rapidly. Strategies for increasing the length of time a child is engaged in an activity are described in greater detail in Chapter 7.

GENERALIZATION

Acquisition and fluency-building strategies are designed to teach children to perform skills accurately and at a reasonable rate. However, our efforts would be in vain if children only exhibited those skills with one teacher or in a particular setting or with a specific stimulus. *Generalization* occurs when a behavior learned in one situation (e.g., training situation) is performed in another situation (nontraining situation) (Sulzer-Azaroff & Mayer, 1977). The effects of teaching extend beyond the instructional setting. For example, Laura should be able to recognize the word *girls* on a bathroom door along with reading it on teaching cards.

Generalization across *settings* means that a skill taught in one setting is performed in another untrained setting. For example, Fran's teachers worked hard to teach her to pick up her toys. After training began, Fran's parents noticed she also began picking up her toys at home. Generalization across *persons* means a skill taught by one person is performed when another requests it. For example, Mark learned to slow down when his teacher asked him to stop running. The classroom aide noticed Mark also slowed down at her request. Generalization across *objects* means a skill learned with one object is applied to similar objects or tasks. For example, after Jody learned to tie her shoe, she could also tie a bow on a package. *Maintenance* is a special case of generalization over time. This means a skill learned in an instructional situation is performed even after instruction ceases.

It would be nice if all of our teaching automatically generalized to other settings. Unfortunately, consistent research has found that generalization does not just happen, particularly when teaching handicapped children. It must be as carefully planned as the initial instruction (Stokes & Baer, 1977; Wehman, Abramson, & Norman, 1977).

Stokes and Baer provide an excellent overview of alternative strategies to ensure generalization. The strategy of *training sufficient exemplars* involves sequential training of a skill in more than one setting, with more than one person, or using more than one example of the task. For example, it may be important, after Larry has learned to eat with a spoon in the classroom, that he also be *trained* to eat with a spoon in the lunchroom. After Seth has learned to add "s" to "dog" to make it plural, you should *teach* him to do the same with other nouns. If Mrs. Jones has taught Nancy to look at her upon request, then another teacher or Nancy's mother should also *teach* her to look upon request. Research has generally indicated the strategy of training sufficient exemplars results in generalization occurring after only a few exemplars have been taught (Allen, 1973; Guess, et al., 1968).

Hupp and Mervis (1981) describe a strategy that increases the probability of generalization when teaching categories of objects. According to the *best example* theory of categorization, some objects are more representative of their category than others. For example, the category *chair* is probably better exemplified by a standard wooden chair than by a bean bag chair. The implication of this theory is that objects selected for initial teaching should be those best representing the category to be taught. In selecting objects, the following factors should be considered (Rosch, 1975; Rosch & Mervis, 1975):

☐ *Family resemblance*—Objects selected should have many attributes in common with other members of the same category. For example, a football might not be the best object to use when initially teaching the concept *ball*, since most balls are round.

☐ *Contrast set*—Objects selected for initial training should have few attributes in common with members of other categories.

☐ *Saliency*—The relevant (important) dimensions of objects selected should be quite apparent.

Hupp & Mervis found that use of good exemplars resulted in greater levels of generalization than use of mixed good and poor exemplars.

Another generalization strategy is *programming common stimuli*. The generalization setting can be made similar to the training setting. Or, even better, the training setting is made as similar as possible to the setting in which the skill should be demonstrated. Some strategies suggested in the research literature include arranging for similar furniture, adding components to the training situation as skill acquisition improves (e.g., gradually change teacher/child ratio from 1:1 to 1:6 or 1:10), providing similar cues in both settings, and using similar materials.

The final strategy is wise use of schedules of reinforcement. During the acquisition phase reinforcement must be *continuous*. That is, the child should be reinforced for every correct response. If a skill is to be maintained or generalized to another setting, however, do not rely on continuous reinforcement—it is simply not practical. The alternative is to gradually switch to an *intermittent* schedule of reinforcement in which the behavior is rein-

forced only some of the time. This type of schedule happens in the real world.

The weaning process may take varying forms. One strategy is to *delay* reinforcement (Fowler & Baer, 1981). Perhaps Johnny should be required to work for 15 minutes rather than 10 before selecting a toy. Another strategy is to begin reducing the reinforcement ratio. For example, instead of reinforcing once for every correct response, you could reinforce for every two. You might also want to move to more natural reinforcement systems (e.g., verbal praise) if you have children working for edibles or tokens (Koegel & Rincover, 1977; Vargas, 1977).

Although these general procedures for facilitating generalization are applicable across a variety of skills, the manner in which they are applied may vary somewhat across developmental domains. To more thoroughly discuss generalization, examples of generalization strategies within specific skill areas are described in most of the subsequent methods chapters of this text.

EVALUATING INDIVIDUALIZED INSTRUCTION

The evaluation of children's performance ideally involves continuous, daily data collection. The primary purpose of ongoing data collection is to gather information that can be used in making decisions about changes in the instructional procedures. To implement data-based decision making, teachers must have skills in collecting, summarizing, and interpreting data. Although careful collection and use of daily data for decision making are common and expected practices in athletics and the business world, they are frequently not in education. A brief overview of collecting, summarizing, and using data in decision making will be provided. For more detailed discussions see Gentry and Haring (1976); Lynch, Flanagan, and Pennell (1977a, 1977b); Cooper (1981); White and Haring (1980); Sanders (1978); and Billingsley and Liberty (1982).

Data should be collected and used with caution, however. Teachers should use their common sense in evaluating instruction. For example, assume we are training Ron to initiate play with other children and are collecting data on the number of times he approaches another child and begins playing with the same materials. The data indicate that over a 5-day period of training Ron is initating play more frequently each day. However, we notice that he is frequently aggressive toward the child he is playing with. In spite of the fact that the data indicate he is acquiring the original objective, a sensible decision would be to change the focus of instruction to sustained *appropriate* cooperative play.

Collecting, graphing, and using data also require considerable teacher skill. After acquiring the mechanics, teachers should use those skills with one or two children on whom information for specific decisions is needed. As they become more proficient, teachers should use those skills with other children. This approach will increase the likelihood that the data-gathering activities will be implemented without detracting from other aspects of teaching, and that the data will be used for decision making.

Collecting Performance Data

Teachers must make several decisions regarding data collection. They include when, how often, and the type of data to be collected.
Frequency of data collection Frequent data collection is necessary in programs for young handicapped children. The more information you have about a child's performance, the better the position you are in to make appropriate decisions. Daily records of behavior can demonstrate *trends* in performance (is she getting better, worse, or staying the same?) as well as *variability* in performance (is she consistent in her responses or are some days much better than others?). The less frequently data are collected, the longer you have to wait before you can determine trends and variability and the longer you may continue an ineffective instructional program. One mark of excellent teachers is the frequency with which they evaluate and change children's instructional programs, continually adapting them to meet the needs of each individual.
When to collect data Data may be collected several times during the day: just before instruction, during instruction, and right after instruction. Data collection just before or after instruction is usually in the form of a probe or brief test. Probes just before instruction as-

sess the child's maintenance of the behavior since the last time instruction occurred. Probes immediately after instruction show the immediate effects of the instruction on that day. Probes should be brief, lasting 1–2 minutes. For example, Jim is learning to count objects. We might present a probe by handing him several objects and asking him to count them, giving him four or five opportunities. Data would be collected on the highest number counted before he stops or counts incorrectly, and on the average number of objects counted before he made an error. If we were concerned about whether he maintained counting behaviors from the last training session, we would present the probe just before each training session. If we were concerned about how high he could count as a result of previous training, we would present the probe just after instruction. Probes allow teachers to get some measure of a child's performance without collecting data during instructional sessions. As a result, they are particularly useful when teachers are first learning about and using data collection.

Some behaviors are likely to occur only at given times of the day such as eating during mealtimes, play during "free" sessions, and toileting behaviors during bathroom times. Data collection can occur within the entire time segment or during part of the activity such as the first 10 minutes of lunch.

When assessing children's generalization of acquired behavior, teachers should collect data on the child's performance at various times. For example, if Joan learned to sort objects using various shapes just after snack time in the morning, her sorting ability could also be assessed when she first came to school and in the afternoon. The teacher would want to assess her sorting behavior with other objects, trainers, and in various places. In addition, teachers should assess previously acquired behaviors that are no longer being instructed. Collection of such data should be done periodically; at first, once per week, then once every other week, and finally once a month. Nelson, Gast, and Trout (1979) describe a method for systematically monitoring such data.
Type of data collected The type of data will vary, depending upon the *behavior* in the instructional objective and the *intent of the*

objective. Gentry and Haring (1976) describe various critical outcomes (dimensions) of measurable behavior that require different types of data. Each dimension requires different types of data and collection procedures. Three of these—accuracy, proficiency, and duration—are frequently used in early childhood programs for handicapped children.

Accuracy refers to how well a child does a given behavior such as, "How correct are the child's responses?" Present the child with a number of opportunities to perform the behavior and then count and record how often the behavior was performed correctly. For example, Susie's teacher wants her to perform various action verbs when the teacher says them. The teacher would present action verbs to Susie and then record whether Susie actually did them. When there is a specified number of trials (opportunities) to do something, a *percentage* measure may be determined. This measure simply indicates the proportion of opportunities in which the behavior actually occurred, and is an excellent measure of accuracy. Percentage is determined by the following formula:

$$\text{Percentage} = \frac{\text{Number of occurrences}}{\text{Number of opportunities}} \times 100$$

Thus, if Susie correctly followed 15 of the 20 action verbs spoken by the teacher, her proportion correct would be 75% ($^{15}/_{20} \times 100 = 75$). One advantage of percentage measures is that they are easily understood; for example, by saying that Susie was 75% correct nearly everyone would realize that she is correct more often than not, and that she is correct about ¾ of the opportunities. Percentage measures are frequently taken during acquisition of skills, because of the need to increase the accuracy of responses.

Many teachers collect data in terms of the *level of assistance* required by a child. Level of assistance data is an approximation of an accuracy measure, and is particularly useful when working with severely handicapped children whose progress may be slow. A levels of assistance approach simply indicates the amount of help a teacher must give for the child to do a task. For example, Lisa is learning to comb her hair. During the first week of

instruction, Lisa's teacher had to fully manipulate her through the task of combing. Eventually, Lisa began to do it using a partial physical prompt, and then with just a gesture prompt, and finally she combed her hair independently. Lisa's teacher was using the most-to-least method of prompting.

When measuring speed, behavioral counts may be converted to a rate measure, which relates counts to a certain time period. Rate is a statement about the number of times a behavior happens within a given time period. The most common unit of rate is *rate per minute*, which is used as a standard for comparison against other rates. Rate per minute is determined by the following formula:

$$\text{Rate per minute} = \frac{\text{Number of occurrences}}{\text{Number of minutes}}$$

For instance, Doug's teacher wants to increase his rate of initiation behaviors during a 10-minute play period. The teacher would record the time Doug entered the play area and count the number of initiations he made in the next 10 minutes. At the end of the period the teacher would stop counting. The teacher would use a kitchen timer or a stop watch to ease the collection of rate measures. If Doug made overtures to peers 15 times during the 10-minute play period, his average rate of initiation would be 1.5 times per minute.

Proficiency can also be assessed when children make correct and error responses. For example, Betty's teacher wants her to become proficient at climbing stairs while alternating her feet on the steps. If the stairway had 10 steps, the teacher could measure the amount of time it takes Betty to climb the stairs, the number of steps where she alternated her feet, and the number of steps where she placed both feet on the same step. From this information, we could determine the rate per minute of Betty's alternating steps and how often she put both feet on the same step. If it took her 2 minutes to climb the stairs and she alternated her feet on eight of the steps, her rate of stair climbing with alternating feet would be four steps per minute

$$\left(\frac{8 \text{ alternating steps}}{2 \text{ minutes}} = 4 \text{ per minute} \right)$$

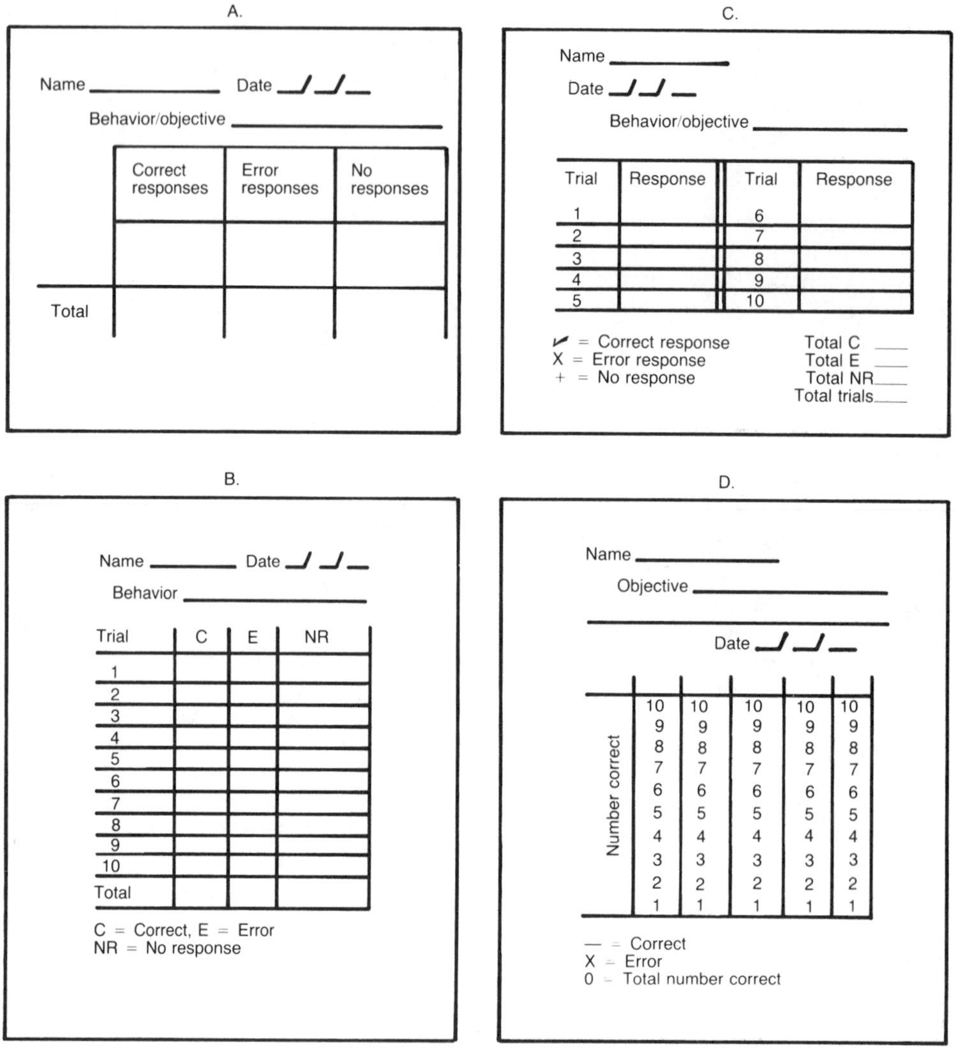

A.

Name _____ Date _/_/_

Behavior/objective _____

	Correct responses	Error responses	No responses
Total			

C.

Name _____

Date _/_/_

Behavior/objective _____

Trial	Response	Trial	Response
1		6	
2		7	
3		8	
4		9	
5		10	

✔ = Correct response   Total C ____
X = Error response   Total E ____
+ = No response   Total NR____
                     Total trials____

B.

Name _____ Date _/_/_

Behavior _____

Trial	C	E	NR
1			
2			
3			
4			
5			
6			
7			
8			
9			
10			
Total			

C = Correct, E = Error
NR = No response

D.

Name _____

Objective _____

Date _/_/_

Number correct					
	10	10	10	10	10
	9	9	9	9	9
	8	8	8	8	8
	7	7	7	7	7
	6	6	6	6	6
	5	5	5	5	5
	4	4	4	4	4
	3	3	3	3	3
	2	2	2	2	2
	1	1	1	1	1

— = Correct
X = Error
0 = Total number correct

FIGURE 3.3
Sample data collection sheets for percent data

and her rate of putting both feet on the same step would be 1 per minute

$$\left(\frac{2 \text{ steps, both feet on same step}}{2 \text{ minutes}} = 1 \text{ per minute} \right).$$

Besides accuracy and proficiency, teachers sometimes want to use a *duration* measure, an indication of how long a behavior lasts. For example, you may want to record the duration of Jody's crying episode each day during outdoor play or the length of time it takes

Jeremy to return blocks to the shelves. In such cases the teacher would start timing the behavior when it begins and stop when it ends. In cases such as Jody's crying, which may occur three or four times during one outdoor play period, the teacher may want to record the length of time Jody cried during each episode. This data could later be summarized as the average length of crying episodes per day.

Sample data sheets for percent data are shown in Figure 3.3. Sample A represents a sheet where hash marks are placed in one of three columns (correct, error, or no responses). This type of sheet is easy to use, but does not provide a record of *when* various responses occurred. It does not indicate whether the child's errors occured on the first few trials, last few trials, or throughout the instructional session. Sample B is similar to sample A but provides a record of when responses occurred in relation to other responses. Sample C provides similar information, but the child's responses are recorded with a code rather than in a specific column. Sample D is a combination data collection sheet and a graph. For example, if the child made a correct response on the first three trials, errors on Trials 4 and 6, and a correct response on Trial 5, the teacher would put an—mark through the numbers 1, 2, 3, and 5, and an *X* mark through the numbers 4 and 6. Since the child made four correct responses the teacher would circle the number 4. If 10 trials are presented, the graph can be converted to percent by simply adding a zero to each of the numbers on the graph. Rate data may be collected using these sheets if the teacher records how long it takes the child to respond.

Various specialized data sheets are shown in Figure 3.4. Sample A represents a sheet used to collect rate data. The time the observation starts is recorded in the "Start time" space, hash marks are placed in the space titled "Occurrences" each time the behavior occurs, and the end of the observation time is recorded in the space titled "Stop time." Sample B represents a data sheet used to record duration. In the column on the left the teacher records the time each behavior begins, and on the right the time the behavior ends. Each new occurrence of the behavior would result in a separate timing. The teacher can then calculate the total time the child engaged in the behavior, or the average time the behavior lasted. Sample C is a data sheet used to specify the percent of time a behavior is occurring for one or more children. The names are recorded in each of the vertical columns and at the specified times the teacher observes and records whether the behavior is occurring. For example, if the teacher wanted a group of children to engage in cooperative play during free time, he or she could record each child's activity in five-minute segments.

If the teacher is interested in a variety of behaviors for one child, he or she could write the behaviors in the vertical columns (e.g., toy play, cooperative play with peers, aggressive behaviors, self-stimulatory behaviors), and would observe and record whether the behaviors were occurring at specified times. Sample D is similar to Sample C, but instead of observing whether the behavior is occurring at a given time, the teacher records whether the behavior occurred *during* a time interval. For example, were the children playing cooperatively from 9:00–9:05? Sample D can be used with a given behavior and a number of children, or with a variety of behaviors for a given child. Sample E represents a data sheet used with levels of assistance data and with skills such as grooming, feeding, and dressing. The steps of the skill are written in the column titled *Steps*, and the teacher puts the initials of the type of assistance needed on each step of the skill for each trial.

Teachers should adapt Figures 3.3 and 3.4 to their needs. For example, spaces could be added to the data sheet, on instructional programs with more than 10 trials.

Summarizing and Graphing Performance Data

Summarizing performance facilitates decision-making and can be used to give feedback to children or parents. One way of summarizing performance is to simply compute a mean or average. For example, you might determine Jody's crying episodes dropped from an average of 3 minutes in length last week to an average of 1 minute this week. Doug may have increased his verbal initiations to peers from an average of two per day last week to an average of five per day this week. In many instances such a summarization is appropriate and useful. However, averaging performances does not say much about trend and variability. A simple mean might hide the fact that Jody's crying episodes were actually non-existent on Monday and Tuesday and quite high Wednesday through Friday.

Trend and variability in performance are best summarized through a visual display, usually some type of chart (see Parsonson and Baer, 1978, for exhaustive information on graphing

A. Rate

Name _____ Date _/_/_

Behavior _____

Start time _:_:_   Stop time _:_:_
Total time _:_:_

Occurrences

Total number of occurrences _____

B. Duration

Name _____ Date _/_/_

Behavior _____

Start time	Stop time

Total time ____

Average time per occurrence ____

C. Time sample

Date _/_/_   Behavior (or name) _____

Children's names (or behaviors)

Time						
9:00						
9:05						
9:10						
9:15						
9:20						
9:25						

✓ = Occurrence, X = Nonoccurrence

D. Interval sample

Date _/_/_   Behavior (or name) _____

Children's names (or behaviors)

Time period						
9:00–9:05						
9:10–9:15						
9:20–9:25						
9:30–9:35						
9:40–9:45						
9:50–9:55						

✓ = Occurrence, X = Nonoccurrence

E. Levels of assistance

Name _____ Date _/_/_

Objective _____

Trials

Steps	1	2	3	4	5

FM = Full physical manipulation
PP = Partial physical prompt
M = Model
G = Gesture prompt
VP = Verbal prompt
I = Independent

FIGURE 3.4
Sample data collection sheets

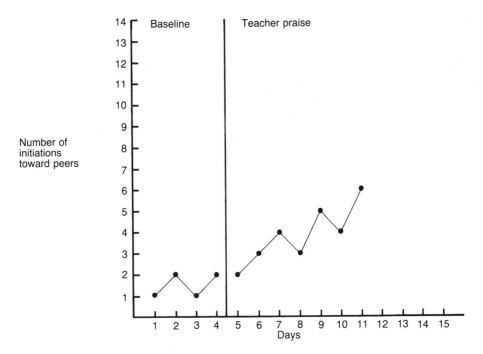

FIGURE 3.5
Number of initiations toward peers

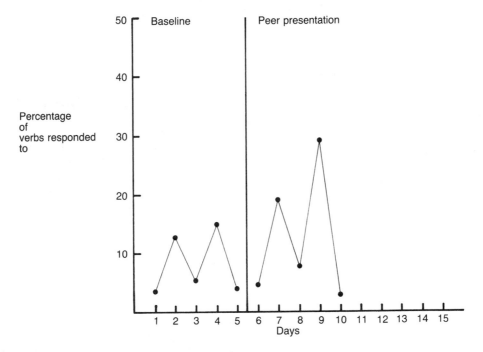

FIGURE 3.6
Percent of verbs responded to

and interpreting graphs). Sample charts for frequency and percentage are shown in Figures 3.5 and 3.6. From Figure 3.5, Doug's daily performance is relatively consistent, and after *baseline* (an initial period of data collection prior to intervention), he steadily increased his initiations toward peers, as indicated by an upward trend. It is apparent that, for Doug, teacher praise after every initiation was a useful strategy. Suzie's performance (Figure 3.6) is not as consistent. Her response to verbs is quite variable (high on some days, but low on others), and there is no clear trend in her behavior after the teacher switched from having the aide present the words (baseline) to using a nonhandicapped peer.

A chart for summarizing rate per minute measures is shown in Figure 3.7. During baseline Jeremy returned blocks to the shelves at a rate of approximately two per minute, which is very slow. When Jeremy's teacher used a "beat the clock" procedure allowing Jeremy to put snacks on the table if all the blocks were on the shelves before the bell rang, his rate increased to approximately 10 per minute.

You may have noticed that the chart in Figure 3.7 is different from other charts in that the intervals on the vertical axis are not the same distance apart. This type of chart is called a *semilogarithmic chart.* The distances are different because equal *relative* changes on the chart are represented by equal distances. For example, the distance between rates of 1 and 2 per minute is the same as the

distance between rates of 10 and 20 per minute. Both distances represent a *doubling* of the rate of performance. The distance between 1 and 3 per minute is the same as the distance between 10 and 30 per minute because both distances represent a trebling of the rate of performance. Any proportionate change (such as doubling or halving) is represented by the same distance on the chart, regardless of the absolute values of those changes. (See White and Haring, 1980, for a more detailed discussion of semilogarithmic charts).

Although these record keeping and data summary procedures may seem cumbersome and time-consuming, they are very important in teaching young handicapped children. Accurate records of child performance enhance the quality of program decisions and demonstrate their implementation and evaluation in a responsible and professional manner. Also, record keeping and data summary take less time as teachers become more proficient. Examples of charts used for recording and summarizing performance of specific types of skills (e.g., eating, toileting, communication) are described in future chapters.

Making Decisions Based on Performance Data

Collecting and summarizing data provide the information from which decisions can be made. Perhaps the most important question or decision concerns changing some aspect of the instructional process. Etzel and LeBlanc (1979) describe a method for evaluating children's performance in direct instruction. Their method is based on the principle of parsimony: when possible, use the simplest procedure to teach children. If the simplest teaching procedure is ineffective in changing performance, the next more complex procedure should be used. Etzel and LeBlanc propose three levels of simplicity. The first involves a basic trial-and-error format. The child is presented with the task and consequences are provided. If learning occurs, no adjustments are made in the instructional process. The second level is *enhanced instructional control,* which is defined as providing the instruction in a consistent manner and systematically changing any aspect of the process to improve performance. The third level is the most complex and in-

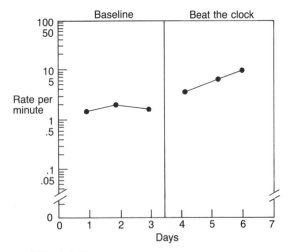

FIGURE 3.7

Rate of blocks shelved per minute

volves the use of errorless learning procedures such as stimulus shaping and fading, the extrastimulus prompt, and prompt fading procedures.

To enhance instructional control, Etzel and LeBlanc suggest that "four components of the environment should be examined: (1) the motivational system, (2) the possible presence of child responses that are incompatible with learning, (3) the presence of prerequisite skills, and (4) the effectiveness of teacher instructions, feedback, and other environmental stimuli in the learning environment" (pp. 363–364). The steps to evaluate the instructional environment when a child is not progressing as expected are described in the flow chart in Figure 3.8.

To use Figure 3.8 the teacher should begin with the first question and answer each one based on the child's performance data and the teacher's best judgment. If any part of the instructional procedures is manipulated, the teacher should collect 3–5 more days of data and evaluate the effects of the changes by starting at the first step of the flow chart. If the teacher goes through the entire flow chart and the child still is not learning, then extrastimulus prompts, stimulus fading, or stimulus shaping should be used.

Starting with the motivational system, the teacher should determine whether the stimulus being used is actually a reinforcer. The reinforcer should be assessed with a behavior easy for the child to perform. For example, if Barbara can easily put several puzzles together and do so more quickly when she receives the stimulus the teacher uses as a reinforcer, then the stimulus is a reinforcer. However, if her rate does not increase when she receives the stimulus as compared to when she does not, it is not a reinforcer. In this latter case, the teacher should search for other stimuli which have reinforcement value.

If reinforcing stimuli are identified and used and the child is not learning, the teacher should determine whether incompatible responses are interfering.

Attention (as described in Chapter 7) is critical for learning and will greatly increase correct responses. Overselective attention or stimulus overselectivity (Lovaas, Koegel, & Schreibman, 1979) occurs when children are being trained to discriminate between stimuli and frequently appear to attend and respond

to idiosyncratic aspects of the stimuli. For example, we might be training Bill to point to the word *men* in the presence of the word *women* as a prerequisite for allowing him to choose which public restroom to enter. If the card on which *men* was written had a smudge on it, Bill might be responding to the smudge rather than the word. Thus, if we presented Bill with another set of cards, he would not necessarily point to the card with *men*. Overselective attention interferes with acquisition of new discriminations and most likely with generalization of acquired discriminations (Rincover & Koegel, 1975) and has been frequently noted in autistic (Lovaas, et al.), retarded (Meisel, 1981; Wilhelm & Lovaas, 1976), and normally developing young children (Schover & Newsom, 1976). Overselectivity may be similar to the phenomenon Piaget described as *centering*. To alleviate the effects of overselectivity, use a variety of stimulus materials, conduct follow-up training, and use intermittent reinforcement during follow-up (Koegel, Schreibman, Britter, & Laitinen, 1979).

Self-stimulation such as rocking or flapping hands is another type of behavior that interferes with learning. Suppression of self-stimulatory behavior produces increases in correct discrimination responses (Koegel & Covert, 1972) and increases in spontaneous play in very structured settings (Koegel, Firestone, Kramme, & Dunlap, 1974). However, some children have acquired certain behaviors when they were allowed to engage in self-stimulation (Klier & Harris, 1977; Wolery, 1978). If the self-stimulatory behavior interferes with learning, procedures should be implemented to decrease its frequency.

Noncompliance is another type of incompatible behavior that interferes with learning (Liberty, 1977). Noncompliance may take the form of saying "No" but it is more frequently demonstrated through subtle behaviors. As described earlier, these subtle forms are identified by paying attention to the child's performance patterns.

If interfering behaviors are not present and the child is not learning, the teacher should assess whether the child has the prerequisite behaviors necessary to perform the target behavior (Etzel & LeBlanc, 1979). If the child does not display the prerequisite behaviors, the teacher would begin to teach them.

If the child still is not learning, the teacher

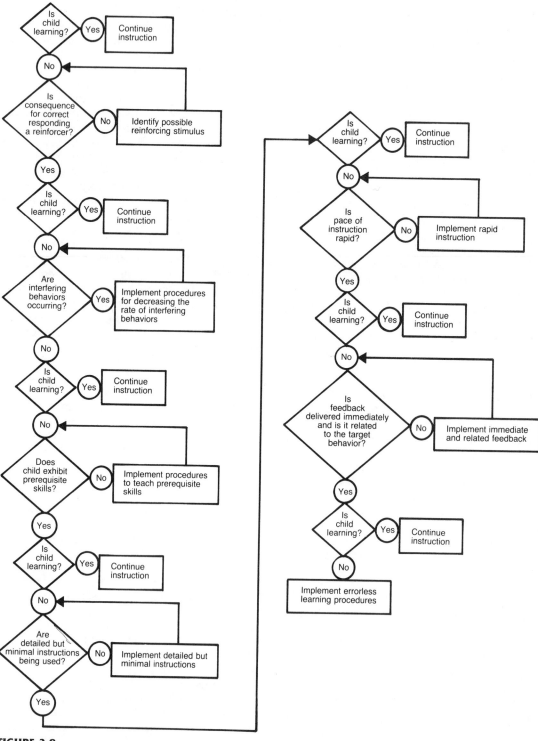

FIGURE 3.8
Flow chart describing procedures for enhancing
instructional control when using direct instruction

Source: Etzel and LeBlanc (1979)

should evaluate the instructions (directions), their timing and rate, and the method of presenting feedback for responses. Usually the instructions should be brief and explicitly communicate the expected behaviors (Becker, Engelmann, & Thomas, 1971). The pace should be brisk to increase attention and avoid interfering behaviors. (Koegel, Dunlap, & Dyer, 1980). Feedback should occur immediately after the behavior, with the behavior being reinforced and named (e.g., "Good job sorting red and green" as compared to "Good work.") (Clark, 1971). Feedback should also be varied from trial to trial.

Since errorless procedures and extrastimulus prompts should eliminate errors, the evaluation of performance data is quite straightforward. With errorless procedures, responses should be correct 100% of the opportunities. If a child moves from one shaping or fading step to another and performance drops from 100% levels, the teacher should drop back to the last shaping or fading step that was 100% correct. Two or three training sessions should be conducted at that step. If performance still drops on the next step, the teacher should create new steps between the two steps.

These issues are primarily concerned with evaluating instruction when the child is acquiring new skills. However, as described earlier, fluency-building and generalization are important phases in the instructional process. Haring et al. (1978) suggest that if the percent correct is more than 83, the teacher should probably assume the child is in the fluency-building phase of performance. Thus, if the child is not making progress, but is responding correctly more than 83% of the time, the teacher should allow the child to practice the skills and should change the consequences (reinforcers or reinforcement schedule) to ensure that the child is motivated during practice sessions.

Although no clear-cut rules exist, programming for generalization of skills should usually occur when the child has acquired the skill or is in the fluency-building phase. Generalization is assessed through periodic data collection, using different training circumstances, teachers, sections of the classroom, materials, or a combination of these. If generalization does not occur, facilitating procedures should be implemented and generalization reassessed.

SUMMARY

Teaching young handicapped children in an effective and efficient manner requires considerable teacher skill in implementing and evaluating instruction. To implement instruction, teachers must accomplish manipulations of the environment that facilitate acquisition, fluency-building, and generalization of skills. The teacher skills involved in facilitating acquisition are numerous. They include motivating children to perform new behaviors primarily through reinforcement and presenting interesting and inviting activities; and manipulating various antecedent factors such as the number of steps in the task analysis, the order of teaching, securing the child's attention, using verbal directions, and pacing the presentation of trials. Errorless learning procedures such as stimulus shaping and fading, and extrastimulus prompts and fading procedures can also be used. Errors can be identified and procedures implemented to eliminate them.

However, we simply cannot be satisfied with only skill acquisition. For skills to be functional we must also teach fluent performance and plan for generalization and maintenance. In reality these should be labeled "phases of teaching," because they clearly demonstrate a range of teaching approaches that call for different skills and strategies and depend upon the child's performance.

In evaluating the effects and efficiency of instruction, teachers must collect, summarize, and use performance data for decision making. The primary decision is whether to change some aspect of the instructional procedures to facilitate greater acquisition, proficiency, and/or generalization of skills.

REFERENCES

Alberto, P., & Schofield, P. An instructional interaction pattern for the severely handicapped. *Teaching Exceptional Children*, 1979, *12*, 16–19.

Allen, G. J. Case study: Implementation of behavior modification techniques in summer camp settings. *Behavior Therapy*, 1973, *4*, 570–575.

Baer, D. M. The behavioral analysis of trouble. In K. E. Allen, V. J. Holm, & R. L. Schieflebusch (Eds.), *Early intervention—a team approach*. Baltimore: University Park Press, 1978.

Becker, W. C., Engelmann, S., & Thomas, D. R., *Teaching: A course in applied psychology.* Chicago: Science Research Associates, 1971.

Bijou, S. W. The prevention of retarded development in disadvantaged children. In M. J. Begab, H. C. Haywood, & H. L. Garber (Eds.) *Psychosocial influences in retarded performance, Volume I: Issues and theories in development.* Baltimore: University Park Press, 1981.

Bijou, S. W., & Baer, D. M. *Child development: A systematic and empirical theory* (Vol. 1). Englewood Cliffs, N.J.: Prentice-Hall, 1961.

Bijou, S. W., & Baer, D. M. *Child development: Universal stage of infancy.* (Vol. 2). Englewood Cliffs, N.J.: Prentice-Hall, 1965.

Bijou, S. W., & Baer, D. M. *Behavior analysis of child development.* Englewood Cliffs, N.J.: Prentice-Hall, 1978.

Billingsley, F. F., & Liberty, K. A. The use of time-based data in instructional programming for the severely handicapped. *Journal of the Association for the Severely Handicapped,* 1982, 7(1), 47–55.

Churchill, D. W. *Language of autistic children.* Washington, D.C.: V. H. Winston & Sons, 1978.

Clark, D. C. Teaching concepts in the classroom: A set of teaching prescriptions derived from experimental research. *Journal of Educational Psychology Monograph,* 1971, 62, 253–278.

Cooper, J. O. *Measuring behavior* (2nd ed.). Columbus, Ohio: Charles E. Merrill, 1981.

Cuvo, A. J., Leaf, R. B., & Borakove, L. S. Teaching janitorial skills to the mentally retarded: Acquisition, generalization, and maintenance. *Journal of Applied Behavior Analysis,* 1978, 11, 345–355.

Dorry, G. W. Attention model for the effectiveness of fading in training reading-vocabulary with retarded persons. *American Journal of Mental Deficiency,* 1976, 81, 271–279.

Etzel, B. C., & LeBlanc, J. M. The simplest treatment alternative: Appropriate instructional control and errorless learning procedures for the difficult-to-teach child. *Journal of Autism and Developmental Disorders,* 1979, 9, 361–382.

Fowler, S., & Baer, D. M. "Do I have to be good all day?" The timing of delayed reinforcement as a factor of generalization. *Journal of Applied Behavior Analysis,* 1981, 14, 13–24.

Foxx, R. M., & Azrin, N. H. *Toilet training the retarded: A rapid program for day and nighttime independent toileting.* Champaign, Ill.: Research Press, 1973.

Gentry, D., & Haring, N. G. The essentials for performance measurement. In N. G. Haring & L. Brown (Eds.) *Teaching the severely handicapped* (Vol. 1). New York: Grune & Stratton, 1976.

Guess, D., Sailor, W., Rutherford, G., & Baer, D. M. An experimental analysis of linguistic development: The productive use of the plural morpheme. *Journal of Applied Behavior Analysis,* 1968, 1, 297–306.

Haring, N. G., White, O. R., & Liberty, K. A. *An investigation of phases of learning and facilitating instructional events for the severely handicapped: Annual progress report 1977–1978.* Bureau of Education for the Handicapped, Project No. 443CH70564. Seattle: University of Washington, College of Education, 1978.

Hilgard, E. R., & Bower, G. H. *Theories of learning* (4th ed.). Englewood Cliffs, N.J.: Prentice-Hall, 1975.

Hupp, S. C., & Mervis, C. B. Development of generalized concepts by severely handicapped students. *The Journal of the Association for the Severely Handicapped,* 1981, 6, 14–21.

Klier, J., & Harris, S. L. Self-stimulation and learning in autistic children: Physical or functional incompatibility? *Journal of Applied Behavior Analysis,* 1977, 10, 311. (Abstract)

Koegel, R. L., & Covert, A. The relationship of self-stimulation to learning in autistic children. *Journal of Applied Behavior Analysis,* 1972, 5, 381–387.

Koegel, R. L., Dunlap, G., & Dyer, L. Intertrial interval duration and learning in autistic children. *Journal of Applied Behavior Analysis,* 1980, 13, 91–99.

Koegel, R. L., Firestone, P. B., Kramme, K. W., & Dunlap, G. Increasing spontaneous play by suppressing self-stimulation in autistic children. *Journal of Applied Behavior Analysis,* 1974, 7, 521–528.

Koegel, R. L., & Rincover, A. Research on the difference between generalization and maintenance in extra-therapy responding. *Journal of Applied Behavior Analysis,* 1977, 10, 1–12.

Koegel, R. L., Schreibman, L., Britten, K., & Laitinen, R. The effects of schedule of reinforcement on stimulus overselectivity in autistic children. *Journal of Autism and Developmental Disorders,* 1979, 9, 383–396.

Liberty, K. A. *An investigation of two methods of achieving compliance with the severely handicapped in a classroom setting.* Unpublished doctoral dissertation, University of Washingtion, 1977.

Lovaas, O. I., Koegel, R. L., & Schreibman, L. Stimulus overselectivity in autism: A review of research. *Psychological Bulletin,* 1979, 86, 1236–1254.

Lynch, V., Flanagan, K., & Pennell, O. Implementing data collection and charting conventions: Let me count the ways, Part 1. In N. G. Haring (Ed.), *The experimental education training program.* Seattle, Wa.: Experimental Education Unit, 1977. (a)

Lynch, V., Flanagan, K., & Pennell, O. Let me count the ways (or now you've got it, use it), Part 2. In N. G. Haring (Ed.) *The experimental education training program.* Seattle, Wa.: Experimental Education Unit, 1977. (b)

Nelson, C. M., Gast, D., & Trout, D. A charting system for monitoring student performance on instructional programs. *Journal of Special Education Technology,* 1979, 3, 43–49.

Meisel, C. J. Stimulus overselectivity by mentally retarded adolescents: Effects of pretraining on cue identification. *American Journal of Mental Deficiency,* 1981, 86, 317–322.

Parsonson, B. S., & Baer, D. M. The analysis and presentation of graphic data. In T. R. Kratochwill (Ed.), *Single subject research: Strategies for evaluating change.* New York: Academic Press, 1978.

Rincover, A., & Koegel, R. L. Setting generality and stimulus control in autistic children. *Journal of Applied Behavior Analysis,* 1975, 8, 235–246.

Rosch, E. Universals and cultural specifics in human categorization. In R. Brislin, S. Bochner, & W. Lonner (Eds.), *Cross-cultural perspectives on learning.* New York: Halsted, 1975.

Rosch, E., & Mervis, C. B. Family resemblances: Studies in the internal structure of categories. *Cognitive Psychology,* 1975, *7,* 573–605.

Sanders, R. M. *How to plot data: A manual for students, researchers, and teachers of the behavioral sciences.* Lawrence, Kans.: H & H Enterprises, 1978.

Schover, L. R., & Newsom, C. D. Overselectivity, developmental level, and overtraining in autistic and normal children. *Journal of Abnormal Child Psychology,* 1976, *4,* 289–298.

Schreibman, L. Effects of within-stimulus and extra-stimulus prompting on discrimination learning in autistic children. *Journal of Applied Behavior Analysis,* 1975, *8,* 91–112.

Schreibman, L., & Charlop, M. H. S + versus S – fading in prompting procedures with autistic children. *Journal of Experimental Child Psychology,* 1981, *31,* 508–520.

Smeets, P. M., & Striefel, S. Acquisition of sign reading by transfer of stimulus control in a retarded deaf girl. *Journal of Mental Deficiency Research,* 1976, *20,* 197–205.

Snell, M. E., & Gast, D. L. Applying time delay procedure to the instruction of the severely handicapped. *The Journal of The Association for the Severely Handicapped.* 1981, *6,* 1–14.

Stokes, T. F., & Baer, D. M. An implicit technology of generalization. *Journal of Applied Behavior Analysis,* 1977, *10,* 349–367.

Stremel-Campbell, K., Cantrell, D., & Halle, J. Manual signing as a language system and as a speech initiator for the non-verbal severely handicapped student. In E. Sontag (Ed.), *Educational programming for the severely and profoundly handicapped.* Reston, Va.: Council for Exceptional Children, 1977.

Striefel, S., Wetherby, B., & Karlan, G. Establishing generalized verb-noun instruction-following skills in retarded children. *Journal of Experimental Child Psychology,* 1976, *22,* 247–260.

Sulzer-Azaroff, B., & Mayer, G. P. *Applying behavior-analysis procedures with children and youth.* New York: Holt, Rinehart & Winston, 1977.

Travers, R. M. W. *Essentials of learning* (4th ed.). New York: MacMillan, 1977.

Vargas, J. *Behavioral psychology for teachers.* New York: Harper & Row, 1977.

Wehman, P. Abramson, M., & Norman, C. Transfer of training in behavior modification programs: An evaluative review. *Journal of Special Education,* 1977, *11,* 217–231.

Wehman, P., & McLoughlin, P. J. *Program development in special education.* New York: McGraw-Hill, 1981.

White, O. R., & Haring, N. G. *Exceptional teaching.* Columbus, Ohio: Charles E. Merrill, 1980.

Wilhelm, H., & Lovaas, O. I. Stimulus overselectivity. A common feature in autism and mental retardation. *American Journal of Mental Deficiency,* 1976, *81,* 26–31.

Wolery, M. R. Self-stimulatory behavior as a basis for devising reinforcers. *AAESPH Review,* 1978, *3,* 23–29.

We all learn some skills by watching others perform. Observation is a natural means for developing new skills and for learning *when* previously acquired behaviors should be displayed.

An understanding of the imitative process is especially important for teachers of the handicapped. Many severely retarded children do not learn how to imitate, and must be taught this skill. Research has clearly demonstrated that handicapped children do not learn as efficiently through observational learning as nonhandicapped. Teachers may need to structure the environment more carefully to insure that appropriate observational learning does occur.

This chapter will discuss imitation in detail: the developmental process; techniques used for teaching; research on model characteristics; and strategies teachers can use to increase observational learning, especially in integrated handicapped/nonhandicapped settings.

THE DEVELOPMENT OF IMITATION

Imitation Defined

Parton (1976) defined imitation as "any response ... which resembles previously observed behavior and occurs as a result of that prior observation" (p. 14). Actually, determining whether or not imitation has actually occurred is sometimes difficult. The first part of the definition (resemblance to previously observed behavior) is relatively straightforward when dealing with close approximations to observed behavior. The determination of imitation is more difficult, however, when dealing with gross approximations of observed behavior. For example, a mother looks at her infant and says, "Ba, ba, ba." The infant smiles, waves her arms, kicks her feet, and then says, "Ma, ma, ma, ma, ma." Is this imitation? Although not an exact replication of behavior, it was a "molar" (general) response to observed behavior, and a response in the same general mode (speech).

The second part of Parton's definition (occurring as a result of prior observation) requires an inference: Did that behavior occur as a result of observing a model? This inference can only be made after repeated observations of behavior. For example, Mike slides down the slide and yells, "Whee!" as he goes down. Stella does the same thing. Was Stella

Teaching Imitation

imitating Mike or did the stimulus situation (slide, exhilaration, enjoyment) simply result in similar responses from both children? Answering this question requires additional information that could be obtained through further observation. For example, did Stella watch Mike go down the slide? If Mike goes down the slide again and this time yells, "Wahoo!" does Stella then do the same thing?

The identification of imitative behavior becomes even more difficult with a time period between observation of the model and actual imitation. For example, Johnny, Lou, and Tony were playing in the transportation center. Johnny took Lou's truck and Lou hit him. The next day Johnny took Tony's helicopter and Tony hit him. Was Tony imitating Lou or was he simply responding as a 3-year-old might typically respond in such a situation?

These observations demonstrate that the occurrence of similar behaviors by two persons is necessary but not sufficient in determining that imitation has occurred. A host of other variables should be considered. For example, when Lou hit Johnny did she get her truck back? If she did, and if Tony observed this, then perhaps one can infer that imitation occurred.

In any case, we must distinguish *learning to imitate* and *learning by imitation.* According to Parton (1976), learning by imitation assumes that the child knows how to imitate and uses imitative skills to learn new behaviors or how to apply and adapt previously learned behaviors. Learning to imitate, on the other hand, focuses on the infant acquiring the capacity to match his or her behavior to that of a model. Although some authors suggest the possibility of innate imitative skills (Meltzoff & Moore, 1977; Yando, Seitz, & Zigler, 1978), most agree that infants learn to imitate (e.g., Piaget, 1945, 1962).

The Developmental Course of Imitation

Knowing how to facilitate imitation requires an understanding of how it develops. Table 4.1 summarizes the major milestones between birth and 24 months of age. Newborn behavior consists primarily of reflexive behaviors, even though some appear to be imitative. For example, newborns cry when other babies

are crying or emit facial expressions resembling smiles when confronted with a smiling person. Although several studies have tried to determine the existence of true imitation during this period (Meltzoff & Moore, 1977; Jacobson, 1979), the question has yet to be resolved. Piaget (1945, 1962) suggested, however, that although these behaviors may be reflexive, they do provide the infant with an experiential base from which imitative behaviors may develop.

Between 1 and 4 months, the infant begins to demonstrate some true imitative behaviors, although sporadically. Piaget suggested that three forms of imitation occur during this stage: vocal contagion (a voice will stimulate the infant's voice, although imitation is not exact), mutual imitation (parent or teacher imitates child at the very moment he utters a sound, and the child redoubles his efforts), and sporadic imitation of a known sound (one previously practiced) even though he had not recently uttered it. An appropriate intervention strategy during this period might be to

TABLE 4.1
Developmental milestones in learning to imitate

Age	Imitation Skills
0–1 month	Primarily reflexive behavior.
1–4 months	Sporadic imitation in the form of vocal contagion, mutual imitation, and occasional imitation of a known sound even though he has not recently uttered it.
4–8 months	Systematic imitation, usually limited to sounds and movements previously performed.
8–12 months	Consistently imitates invisible movements. Begins to imitate behaviors somewhat different from those previously performed.
12–18 months	Imitates new behaviors systematically, including invisible movements.
18–24 months	Representative imitation clearly apparent. Infant is capable of delayed or deferred imitation.

frequently imitate an infant at the same time he or she is performing a behavior.

The infant's interest in the effects of his actions on objects and events shows a dramatic increase between 4 and 8 months of age (Flavell, 1977). The infant can systematically imitate by this time, although the imitation observed typically occurs only with previously performed movements and sounds (Piaget 1945, 1962).

Between 8 and 12 months of age, the infant begins to consistently imitate movements he previously demonstrated that are not visible to him (e.g., tongue protrusion) or that he cannot hear. Even more importantly, the infant begins to imitate moderately different behaviors from those he ordinarily performs. As Flavell (1977) suggests, this is "an enormously significant developmental advance" (p. 31) because the infant can now *learn* through the observation of others. The adult performs behavior that is similar, but not the same, as one previously performed by the child. According to Piaget, this immediately creates interest in the child and provides an incentive for imitation. The implication for teaching is that imitation at this stage may be encouraged by providing moderately difficult models as challenges. The teacher or parent should be aware of the infant's existing repertoire of behaviors and use this information for planning appropriate and stimulating events.

Between 12 and 18 months the infant begins to imitate new models systematically, including those involving movements invisible to the child. Finally, between 18 and 24 months the representative imitation is clearly apparent. The infant is capable of delayed or deferred imitation that may occur some length of time after the observation of the model. This critical step in cognitive development should require some form of "remembering" and is necessary for the development of meaningful language and thought.

IMITATION IN NATURAL SETTINGS

Imitation not only facilitates the development of representation and symbolic thinking but also opens up a world of potential learning opportunities.

Occurrence and Nonoccurrence of Imitation

Young children use imitation to facilitate the learning of other skills. Imitation of peers and adults is not a casual, infrequent activity in preschoolers. It is an ongoing process that occurs more often than we are aware. Abramovitch and Grusec (1978) conducted an observational study of the frequency with which children ages 4–11 imitate peers in a free play setting. Behaviors scored as imitations were limited to those occurring within 10 seconds of the modeled behavior. The observations indicated that younger children imitated much more than older children, reinforcing the importance of the imitative process at a young age. Nearly 15 imitative acts per hour were observed with the youngest children, suggesting a relatively high frequency. This figure may even be a minimal estimate since, as the authors suggest, we have no idea how much deferred imitation of peers, teachers, parents, or other models occurred.

Such imitation teaches children many important things. Bandura (1969) suggests that imitation can affect behavior through observational learning, response inhibition, and response facilitation. In *observational learning,* the child uses imitation to learn a new behavior. For example, a child might learn to set a table by observing another child. *Response inhibition* means the child uses a model to learn when certain behaviors should *not* be performed. The child also observes the consequences of that behavior. For example, a child learns that taking Danny's truck is not a good idea when she sees Danny hitting another child who took his truck. *Response facilitation* means the child uses a model to help learn when certain behaviors *should* be performed. This also assumes the observation of consequences. For example, Carrie notices that using the word "please" results in a smile from the teacher and will likely use the same word when making a similar request. Both response inhibition and response facilitation assume the child already knows *how* to perform the behavior; by observing a model the child learns the conditions under which that behavior should or should not be performed.

The potential benefits of peer imitation have been cited as one justification for the integration of handicapped and nonhandicapped children in preschool settings (Bricker, 1978; Guralnick, 1976; Snyder, Apolloni, & Cooke, 1977). The assumptions behind this rationale are that handicapped children need appropriate models for meaningful observational learning, and that children naturally tend to imitate competent persons rather than those viewed as less competent (Bricker, 1978).

Unfortunately, research to date suggests rather strongly that imitation of nonhandicapped peers by young handicapped children does not occur naturally (Cooke, Apolloni, & Cooke, 1977). Guralnick (1976), for example, investigated the effects of observing a model on the social play behavior and positive verbalization of one mildly retarded 4-year-old child, and upon the language usage of another handicapped preschooler. The first child spent virtually all of his free play time in solitary play. When asked to observe the play of nonhandicapped children for the first 5 minutes of each 15-minute play period, the child made the observations but demonstrated no change in social play behavior or in positive verbalizations to other children. Only after a more structured intervention did positive change occur. This finding was replicated with a different group of handicapped preschoolers. Likewise, simple observation of a nonhandicapped model demonstrating the appropriate use of -ing words did not change the language usage of another handicapped preschooler. More structured approaches to intervention were again necessary before a positive change was noted.

Although integrating handicapped and nonhandicapped children at the preschool level is important, simple integration may not yield all of the desired changes. A planned approach to early integration is the most effective strategy for insuring the occurrence of appropriate observational learning (Cooke, Ruskus, Apolloni, & Peck, 1981).

Factors Influencing Imitation

Imitation is an aspect of children's lives that is apparent in many of the things they do. Sometimes we notice imitation of appropriate behaviors such as speaking properly, sharing or helping, or performing a certain skill. More often we notice the unwanted instances of imitation (such as swearing, singing beer commercials, aggression) or instances that may even be hazardous to the child or other children (such as hitting or kicking, performing dangerous feats of a favorite television character). What is the basis for a young child's decision to imitate a certain behavior? What are some factors influencing imitation that might be variables to manipulate in an early intervention setting?

If the model is rewarded for behavior One factor that influences the probability of imitation is if the child observes the model being rewarded (or punished) for his behavior. This effect requires a high level of cognitive skills that allow the child to associate observed behavior with its consequences. Hartup (1978) suggests that consequences provided to the model be clearly reinforcing or punishing. He cites several studies (e.g., Geshuri, 1972) in which children are more likely to imitate a model given an obvious reward.

Similarity between model and observer Research suggests an increased probability of imitation if the observer perceives the model to be similar to himself. For example, Bandura, Ross, and Ross (1963) demonstrated that children are more likely to imitate a model of the same sex. Rosekrans (1967) described several personality characteristics and social similarities that observers notice when watching a model.

Model status A number of other model characteristics are influential to the imitative process. Abramovitch and Grusec (1978) reported that dominant children are imitated more than nondominant. Brody and Stoneman (1981) found that young children tend to imitate same age or older models rather than younger children. Bandura (1969) cites numerous studies suggesting that highly competent models, purported experts, celebrities and television heroes, as well as models with certain status symbols, are more likely to influence imitative behavior.

Research has indicated that the fear that nonhandicapped children will learn inappropriate behaviors by observing and imitating handicapped children is unwarranted. Assuming that children are more likely to imitate competent than incompetent models, nonhandicapped preschoolers generally would not imitate the inappropriate behaviors of their handicapped playmates.

Some evidence for this assumption was provided in a study of several handicapped and nonhandicapped preschoolers (Peterson, Peterson, & Scriven, 1977). The first child was taught a sequence of 10 simple behaviors by the teacher. Once the child had mastered this sequence, the second child was called in and observed the first child performing the tasks. The model then left and the second child was coached until reaching mastery. This process was repeated for all children. Both handicapped and nonhandicapped children were more likely to imitate a nonhandicapped model. The authors suggest these findings support the proposition that integration of handicapped and nonhandicapped preschoolers can have many positive outcomes and few negative side effects.

If the model imitates the observer An interesting series of publications has recently appeared suggesting that being imitated can greatly increase the probability of subsequent imitation by the observer. For example, Fouts, Waldner, and Watson (1976) investigated the effects of imitating the behavior of nonhandicapped preschool children in a simple game of dropping ball bearings into holes in a box. When the teacher consistently imitated what the child did, the child subsequently began to imitate the teacher more frequently. The authors suggest that perhaps behavioral similarity may have some reinforcing properties. Similar results were found in two studies of imitation training with retarded children (Hallahan, Kauffman, Kneedler, Snell, & Richards, 1977; Kauffman, Snell, & Hallahan, 1976). Results of these studies indicated that a teacher's imitation of a retarded child's behavior increased the probability of the child subsequently imitating the teacher. The Kauffman, et al. (1976) study further demonstrated that being imitated *and* praised was a more powerful reinforcer than being praised alone.

A study by Thelen, Miller, Fehrenback, Frautschi, and Fishbein (1980) suggests that children may even use imitation during play as a means of social influence. Children were promised a monetary incentive for each tasteless "health food" cracker that they could convince another child to eat. Prior to this time, the two children were allowed to play together. Children who knew they were soon to be placed in a position of requesting compliance from another child imitated that child more frequently than did those who did not expect to participate.

A summary of factors influencing imitation in the natural environment and related implications for teaching is found in Table 4.2. Although these factors are important variables influencing imitation, some children will require more direct instruction. Procedures for teaching children to imitate have implications for adults attempting to influence this developmental process.

TEACHING CHILDREN TO IMITATE

Although the development of imitative skills proceeds normally with most children, more severely handicapped infants may never learn to imitate or may do so at a much slower rate than nonhandicapped infants. Thus teachers of young handicapped children must plan for the facilitation of imitative skills.

A number of curricula are designed for handicapped infants and children. Comprehensive imitation training programs have been suggested by Baer and Sherman (1964), Bricker and Dennison (1978), and Tawney, Knapp, O'Reilly, and Pratt (1979).

Teaching Infants to Imitate

Imitate the child. Most curricula suggest that an important initial strategy is to imitate the child. As Piaget suggests, imitating the child may stimulate the practice of reflexive behaviors, an important experience for infants. If a child rarely vocalizes or gestures, this strategy might serve to increase these behaviors. Being imitated could also be reinforcing, even for an infant.

Provide appropriate models for the child's level of development. This requires a knowledge of both the developmental sequence of imitation and the individual child's abilities. At the 6-month developmental level the models should be sounds and motor movements the infant has repeatedly performed. The motor movements should probably be those the in-

TABLE 4.2
Findings and implications of research on imitation in natural settings

Finding	Implication for Teaching
Handicapped children may not imitate in the natural environment.	Handicapped children must be trained to imitate.
If a model is rewarded for a behavior, then observers are more apt to imitate that behavior.	Reward models for behavior that the teacher wants the handicapped child to perform. Be sure the reward for the model is clear and the behavior which is being rewarded is obvious.
If the model is similar to the observer, then the model is more apt to be imitated.	Provide models of the same sex, similar size, age, and ability levels. Provide child as compared to adult models.
If the model has high status, then the observer is more apt to imitate the model.	Bestow status on children who perform the behaviors that the teacher wants to be imitated. Use models which are more competent than the observers.
If models imitate those observing them, the observer is more apt to imitate the model.	Have competent models imitate the adaptive behavior of handicapped children.

fant can see himself perform. At the 10-month developmental level, you can begin to model movements you have seen the infant perform but which he cannot see himself do (e.g., facial expressions, mouth movements). At this age you might also provide models slightly different from those behaviors the infant typically performs.

Provide assistance when necessary to facilitate imitation. Assistance can take many forms. For example, several curricula suggest the use of a mirror in the initial stages of teaching a child to imitate gestures or facial movements he ordinarily cannot see himself perform. This approach assumes that the usual sensory cues a child receives from facial contortions are insufficient for some children; the mirror provides an additional source of feedback so the child can evaluate the accuracy of his imitations.

If a child does not accurately perform an imitative behavior, the teacher should assist him. For example, if the child does not pat the table when you pat it, you might pick up

his hand and pat the table for him. A decreasing assistance approach could be incorporated to gradually require that the child independently complete more components of the imitative act.

Make imitation a rewarding experience. Most curricula stress this point. As with any training program, the experience should be enjoyable, and some programs suggest "roughhousing" or other boisterous activities. Others stress the importance of conducting imitation training when optimal for both enjoyment and learning, such as during alert periods when the infant is not hungry or crying. In addition, contingent reinforcement can serve to increase the probability of imitative behavior and many curricula suggest contingent use of smiles or pats whenever imitation (or approximate imitation) occurs.

Evaluation   Each of these strategies appears logical when considered from the perspective of various theoretical approaches. Unfortunately we do not have sufficient data to support these practices. Minimal research has been conducted on effects of procedures such as repeating sounds the infant makes and the rate of imitation. Until such research is conducted, we must accept these as the best available knowledge and incorporate them to the extent to which they seem appropriate for any individual infant. Here is a summary of the procedures for teaching infants to imitate.

1 Imitate the child.
2 Provide models appropriate to the child's developmental level.
3 Provide assistance (prompts) when necessary (e.g., mirrors, physical prompting).
4 Make imitation activities enjoyable.
5 Reward the child's imitative responses.

Imitation for Severely Handicapped Preschoolers

Despite our best efforts, many severely handicapped children will still lack imitative skills by age 3 or 4. We do not know whether practices suggested for use with handicapped infants are appropriate for older handicapped children. Several training procedures have been designed for such children.

The developmental approach A six-stage imitation training program has been described in detail by Bricker and Dennison (1978). This program begins with an increasing vocalization phase and advances through speech sound imitation, and is primarily designed as a prerequisite training for teaching verbal skills.

1 *Increase vocalizations.* During this phase the teacher should attend to the child's vocalizations. This can be done by imitating what the child says, or by coming to him or responding in some way when he says something. Present sounds you have heard the child make at other times as a stimulus for vocalization.
2 *Gross motor imitation (familiar actions).* Training at this stage involves providing the child many opportunities to watch you copy his actions. If this does not work, step back to simultaneous imitation. The teacher should perform the child's behavior at the same time as the child. If this does not work, use the Baer, Peterson, and Sherman (1967) strategy of assisting

the child perform the movement and then gradually fading this assistance.
3 *Gross motor imitation (unfamiliar actions).* This phase of instruction teaches the child to imitate relatively easy but not previously performed motor actions. Strategies used for training are essentially those described in Phase 2.
4 *Sound imitation (self-initiated).* This is designed to teach the child the game of "vocal chaining." Intervention consists of first listening to the sounds a child makes, then imitating her. Hopefully she will repeat this sound. This should be done frequently, with particular attention to any new sounds the infant makes.
5 *Sound imitation (model-initiated).* This phase is intended to encourage the child to respond to a sound initiated by someone else. Find a time when the infant is quiet and alert, and present a sound you heard the infant make. If the infant imitates you, reinforce him with hugs, smiles, or some other appropriate reinforcer.
6 *Speech sound imitation.* The focus in this phase is upon more accurate imitation of speech sounds. Such sounds are frequently presented as stimuli. Sounds selected for initial training should be the most easily imitated English sounds (see Chapter 14). Gradually more difficult sounds can be added as the infant becomes proficient in matching.

The functional approach One of the earliest studies demonstrating the development of imitation through reinforcement was conducted by Baer, Peterson, and Sherman (1967). Although this study was conducted with severely and profoundly retarded children ages 9–12, the methods may be directly applicable to preschoolers. The three children selected for the study were observed for several days. No instances of imitation were noted for any child during the observation period. In subsequent free play and baseline sessions in which the trainer modeled certain behaviors (e.g., clapping) and told the children, "Do this," no imitative behaviors were observed.

The training program used a combination of shaping and fading procedures. Each subject was taught to respond to the instruction,

"Do this." Responding was first limited to one behavior and then gradually expanded to others. The initial training steps were as follows:

1 Teacher secures child's attention (eye contact, lack of self-stimulatory behavior).
2 Teacher says, "Do this" and then demonstrates a behavior such as raising a hand.
3 If the child makes no response, the teacher repeats the demonstration and then takes the child's hand and raises it for her.
4 Teacher immediately reinforces child.
5 After several trials the teacher gradually fades assistance by completing only part of the task for the child.
6 Teacher assistance is eventually faded until child makes the response unassisted.

Once this initial behavior had been taught, the teacher moved on to teach another response, again using "Do this" as the stimulus. As subsequent tasks were learned, new tasks were added. Throughout the training, occasional probes were conducted. A *probe* is the presentation of an untrained stimulus; it determines whether generalization has occurred. This strategy was referred to as training sufficient exemplars in Chapter 3. The trainers hoped if they taught enough responses to the same command, the children would begin to imitate other behaviors without specific training.

Other strategies were used to ensure usefulness and maintenance of skills learned. Once they mastered single step imitations, two children were taught to imitate behavioral chains (sequences of two or more behaviors) by presenting a previously learned response with a new response, and reinforcing only if the child correctly imitated both behaviors. Verbal imitations were added by chaining motor and verbal behaviors together and then fading out the motor components. Once consistent responding was obtained by one teacher, a second teacher presented the tasks and reinforced the children. This insured that correct responding would not be limited to the original teacher.

The study demonstrated each of the effects the authors predicted. Children involved in training successfully learned to imitate both single behaviors and multiple behavioral chains; this training generalized to other untrained

behaviors and across teachers. As the authors suggest, it appears that at first the children were simply learning a specific response. However, as training progressed and responding generalized to untrained behaviors, the children had obviously learned that they were supposed to imitate the teacher when he said, "Do this." In effect, the authors suggest that a stimulus class of behavioral similarity had been established. "Do this," paired with a behavior, became a discriminative stimulus for matching teacher behavior.

Using Timeout The approaches described thus far have incorporated only positive approaches to intervention. For some severely handicapped children positive approaches can be combined with other techniques to insure the development of imitative skills. One such approach has been described by Parsons and Davey (1978). The procedure used in this study was a combination of timeout and extinction in conjunction with positive reinforcement.

The child involved in the study was a 4-year-old severely retarded boy in a residential institution. The teachers trained the child to imitate four behaviors: banging the table, tapping the tummy, waving a hand in the air, and putting bricks into a container. All behaviors had six training sessions where a model was presented and then the child was physically manipulated (prompted) to perform the imitation. Following these sessions two behaviors were taught using typical training procedures. A model was presented and if the child imitated he was reinforced with popcorn and praise. Nonimitation resulted in a physical prompt that was eliminated after five consecutive correct imitations. The other two behaviors were taught in the same manner, with one exception. Nonimitation resulted in a timeout consequence, consisting of the teacher dropping her head onto her chest and not looking at the child for 30 seconds.

Results of this study indicated that reinforcement in combination with timeout was a more effective intervention for this particular child than reinforcement alone. The percentage of correct imitations for behaviors taught with the combination approach was higher than that attained with reinforcement alone.

Although this represents a more intrusive technique than is often desired, it may facilitate the discriminative process for some children because it clearly lets the child know when he has made an appropriate response to a teacher's request. Use of such aversive consequences in the early stages of the learning process may be necessary with some children to allow movement toward learning more complex and functional skills.

USING IMITATION TO TEACH SKILLS

Specific strategies can be used to facilitate appropriate imitation in early childhood settings.

Providing Appropriate Models

The provision of an appropriate model for children can be effective in some instances. At least two studies reported use of simple modeling with preschoolers in altering unusual fears and social withdrawal, problem behaviors often seen in handicapped children. **Fear reduction** Bandura and his colleagues conducted a series of studies demonstrating the effects of modeling on young children who exhibited an extreme fear of dogs (Bandura, Grusec, & Menlove, 1967; Bandura & Menlove, 1968). In the first study young children observed a peer model demonstrate progressively more involved interactions with a dog. These observations were distributed over eight brief sessions. Some children observed within a highly positive party context, while others observed in a neutral context. Over the eight session the dogs became less physically restrained, the model increased his touching of the dog, and the length of interaction with the dog was increased. In the second study, children were presented a series of brief movies rather than live demonstrations. Some children observed only one child, while others observed movies depicting several different boys and girls of varying ages playing with the dogs.

The results of the studies can be summarized as follows:

1 Both live modeling and observation of movies increased the willingness of fearful children to interact with dogs.
2 Although both were effective, observation of one live model was more effective than observing a single model in a movie.

3 Observing multiple models was more effective than observing a single model.
4 Observing within a party (as compared to a neutral) context seemed to make no difference. Apparently the children focused almost exclusively on the dog and his child companion.

These findings suggest that simple modeling can be effective in changing inappropriate behavior. The children in these studies had no other identifiable handicaps, however, and a more structured intervention may be necessary for developmentally delayed children. The procedures applied many appropriate principles in working with any child: varying the critical dimensions of the fearful object (size, proximity, restraint), gradually increasing the fear-evoking properties of these dimensions, and changing the models to increase the likelihood of generalization.

Social withdrawal A study reported by O'Connor (1969) extended the results of Bandura's studies to the problem of social withdrawal (low rates of peer interaction) in young children. Children in the experimental group were taken to a small room and told they could watch a television program. Each child saw a 23-minute sound-color film.

The film portrayed a sequence of 11 scenes in which children interacted in a nursery school setting. In each of these episodes, a child is shown first observing the interaction of others and then joining in the social activities, with reinforcing consequences ensuing. The other children, for example, offer him play material, talk to him, smile and generally respond in a positive manner to his advances into the activity. The scenes were graduated on a dimension of threat in terms of the vigor of the social activity and the size of the group. The initial scenes involve very calm activities such as sharing a book or toy while two children are seated at a table. In the terminal scenes, as many as six children are shown gleefully tossing play equipment around the room. (p. 18)

After observing the film, children were returned to class. Their social interactions were observed for an 8-minute period and showed a dramatic increase, with all children participating. The number of observed social interactions increased from an average of 1.75 to more than 11.

O'Connor suggests that behavioral inhibitions have been reduced. Initially, some children may withdraw because they fear aversive consequences from social interaction. Observing models with no aversive consequences may reduce such inhibitions. Also, according to reinforcement theory, the film provides an opportunity for observing the positive benefits of social interaction.

A logical explanation probably includes both of these notions. Regardless, the results clearly indicate the effectiveness of the procedure with young children identified as isolates by their teachers. However, these children had neither identifiable handicaps nor had been referred for special help for extreme social withdrawal. They already knew *how* to interact with peers since they did exhibit some interactions prior to the intervention; they just did not interact very often. Therefore, simple modeling alone may not be as effective for developmentally delayed or severely withdrawn children.

One question of interest is how the film was different from the day-to-day events occurring in most classrooms. These children had opportunities to observe others and enjoy the positive benefits of such interactions. Perhaps the film allowed the children to remove themselves completely from their regular environment and gave them an opportunity to view exclusively positive interactions. Although we do not have access to films to help solve every problem, perhaps important dimensions of these studies can be isolated and easily adapted to classroom situations. For example, the teacher might allow some time for children to watch each other play. The teacher could watch with the child, point out the positive aspects of child-child interactions, and then suggest some ways for the child to interact.

Observational Learning in Natural Settings

Several studies have described alternative strategies for facilitating imitation in young handicapped children.

Structure in observational settings One of the earliest studies involving the imitation of

nonhandicapped models by their handicapped peers was conducted by Guralnick (1976). As discussed earlier in this chapter, simple presentation of a model was ineffective in increasing either social play behavior or language skills of developmentally delayed 3- and 4-year-old children. In an attempt to encourage imitation and appropriate interactions, more structured approaches were attempted.

In the social play situation, role-playing and verbal descriptions were used to teach the nonhandicapped children to pay attention to the appropriate behaviors of the handicapped child and to encourage interaction. Prior to each play session the models were reminded of these strategies. In the language situation, handicapped children initially observed a nonhandicapped model using correct forms of speech (-*ing* verbs in response to action pictures). This procedure alone was ineffective in improving language usage of the handicapped youngsters. The observational situation was then altered so that the handicapped child observed the nonhandicapped model and was given specific verbal reinforcement ("Good, you are saying it the right way.") for correct responses.

In both instances, the imposition of further structure in the group was sufficient to produce the desired change in behaviors. Handicapped children demonstrated more social play, more positive verbalizations, and more appropriate language usage after the model and structure situation than in the model alone situation.

Incidental teaching and imitation An intervention to increase the imitative skills of a 4-year-old autistic child has been described by Nordquist (1978). The child's nursery school teacher and mother trained him to imitate nonverbal behaviors, using the following procedure:

If the child began to show an interest in a play material or activity, the adult would quickly place herself between the boy and the material or activity and model one of the nonverbal behaviors. If the boy did not imitate the adult, the behavior was prompted and then reinforced with verbal approval and access to the material or activity. For example, if the boy wanted to use a swing, the adult placed herself between the boy and the swing set. Then she instructed him to look at her. When he attended, she said, "———, do this. Wave good-bye." If he did not imitate, the adult quickly took his arm and moved it in the desired manner. Then she approved and placed him on the swing. Over several imitation trials adult prompts were gradually faded until the boy imitated without assistance. (p. 74)

A total of 36 nonverbal behaviors were taught in this manner. Once the child was reliably imitating these behaviors, two non-handicapped peers were trained (through role playing and modeling) to carry out the same procedures.

Results indicated that both adults and peers were able to reach a high level of imitative responding with the child. Observations of spontaneous imitation of peers (imitation occurring during free play) indicated a low level of spontaneous peer imitation during the adult training sessions. However, when peers began to conduct training, a significant increase in spontaneous imitation was noted. The author suggests that these findings support other research indicating peers may be more effective than adults in facilitating generalization of learned behaviors. It should also be noted that a more natural approach to training would be to have the child imitate behaviors that fit into the context of his own behavior. For example, if the boy wanted to use the swing, the adult could have him imitate the manual sign for swing.

Peer-imitation training. A series of investigations conducted by Apolloni, Cooke, and their colleagues have resulted in the development of a comprehensive peer imitation training program (Apolloni & Cooke, 1978; Apolloni, Cooke, & Cooke, 1977; Peck, Apolloni, Cooke, & Raver, 1978). The procedure involves verbal or physical prompts to imitate the behavior of a classmate, with adult praise provided for imitative behavior. Prompts are gradually faded as children become more responsive. For example, Peck et al. (1978) investigated the effects of peer imitation training on three young Down syndrome children, all 3 years old. The children were placed in a free play area with three nonhandicapped peers. Training consisted of a brief (4 minutes) period of time during which the teacher attempted to increase one child's level of imitative behavior. When the handicapped child was within three feet of a peer model who was engaged in appropriate play, the teacher said, "Look! See what he/she is doing?" and pointed to the peer model, "You do it." If the child imitated the behavior within 5 seconds, the teacher socially praised him and gave a pat or a hug. If the child did not imitate, the teacher physically manipulated him through the behavior and then praised him.

Observations of spontaneous imitation were conducted for 3 minutes after each training period (the teacher was out of sight at this time). As each handicapped child began to participate in training, a significant increase in imitative behavior was observed during the sessions. Further, the effects of training generalized to the free-play situation after the teacher left. Generalization was superior to that found in an earlier study where imitation was taught in a structured one-to-one setting. No instances of imitation of retarded children by peer models were observed during the training sessions, and only three instances were observed during the 246 minutes of observation during nontraining times. A second experiment reported in the Peck, et al. paper replicated this demonstration of effectiveness with a younger (25-month-old) handicapped child.

Modeling as a Teaching Strategy

Besides structuring the environment to facilitate imitation of peers in early childhood settings, modeling can be used in direct instruction to teach new behaviors. It provides teachers with a tool for *showing* children how to do tasks without using extensive physical or verbal prompts.

When children are able to imitate, the teacher can introduce new behaviors by securing the child's attention; saying either, "Do this" or "Say_____"; performing the behavior; waiting for the child to imitate the behavior; and reinforcing the child's correct responses. When used in this manner, the model serves as a prompt. These procedures have been widely used in language training programs with handicapped children (Garcia & DeHaven, 1974; Lovaas, 1977).

Several considerations are involved when modeling is used in direct instruction. Modeling is particularly useful with skills involving behaviors chained together in a sequence and provides an example of how each behavior in the chain fits with the others. This "fitting together" is frequently difficult to establish when using physical prompts, but is quite easy with modeling. However, when modeling sequences for initial acquisition, teachers should frequently model the entire sequence and then one or two behaviors in the chain. For example, if we are teaching Mike to print his name, first print the four letters in his name and then write the first letter and expect him to print another M.

When presenting a model, the teacher should show the natural cue the child should eventually use when performing a behavior. For example, if we want Mike to print his name when we say, "Print your name on your paper," we should say this sentence, and then present the model. The child should also attend to the model as it is performed. Obviously, children cannot imitate behaviors they did not see or hear. To enhance the likelihood that the child will attend to the model, present it slowly and in exaggerated form. For example, in teaching Mike to print his name, model the formation of the letters in his name with colored magic markers as compared to a pencil. Likewise, the letters might be larger than he would normally make when printing his name. We would also need to be sure that the model was presented to Mike in a manner that considers his perspective. For example, if we sit across from him and make an M, it will look like a W to him. If we sit to the side, it will look like an E. Thus, we should stand behind Mike and reach around him. The M will look like the M we expect him to make, and the motions we use in forming it will be similar to those we expect him to use in making an M.

Models can also be combined with other prompts such as verbal ones. We could tell Mike, "Start at the top, draw a line straight down, and then go back to the top and draw a slanting line," and so on. Models, of course, can also be used in combination with more intrusive prompts such as partial physical prompts and full manipulations. Thus, we would make the M and then take Mike's hand and move it in the appropriate directions to form the letter. We can also combine the verbal and physical prompts. When prompts

are used they must be faded as described in Chapter 3. The model must also be faded.

When using models, we frequently must accept approximations of eventually required behaviors. For example, Mike may make an M that has different-sized parts such as M, or the point may be below the legs such as M, or perhaps the lines will not be connected as in M. Such attempts would be initially reinforced and as training progresses only the more correct forms would be rewarded.

Generalization

Imitation in integrated settings can be viewed as an example of generalization of previously learned skills to new stimulus situations. The child already knows *how* to imitate; we would simply like to increase the frequency with which appropriate imitations occur.

As described in Chapter 3, training sufficient exemplars (Stokes & Baer, 1977) is probably the most commonly used generalization strategy, and consists of teaching sufficient examples of a class of behaviors so that responding is generalized to untrained tasks. For example, Baer, et al. (1967) demonstrated that when children were taught to respond correctly to the instruction "Do this" with several behaviors, correct imitation of untrained behaviors was also observed. The authors suggested that although the children were first simply learning specific responses, they gradually learned that "Do this" meant to do whatever the teacher does next. Thus, by directly teaching sufficient instances of imitation, generalization to untrained behaviors occurred.

Garcia, Baer, and Firestone (1971) discussed the importance of considering the *topographical similarity* between two behaviors when attempting to facilitate generalized imitative responding in severely retarded children. Topography generally refers to the configuration or form of a given response (Sulzer-Azaroff & Mayer, 1977). Garcia et al. tested the likelihood that generalization would occur if no instances of a certain topographical dimension were ever taught. Imitative responses were identified according to four topographical forms: small motor, large motor, short vocal, and long vocal responses. Four severely retarded children were taught examples of the first three forms of imitation but not the fourth. Although generalized imitation was observed (each child eventually imitated unreinforced and untrained responses), it was limited to the topographical dimensions taught.

The implication of this study is that while training sufficient exemplars is an important strategy for encouraging generalization, it may be insufficient for severely retarded children unless we consider examples of each dimension relevant to responses we eventually want children to demonstrate. In fact, we should probably go beyond an analysis of response topographies to look at characteristics of other relevant dimensions of training and generalization environments. Bandura and Menlove (1968) found that varying the model was important for ensuring the effectiveness of modeling procedures on fear reduction in children. Perhaps we also need to consider specific model characteristics (e.g., age, sex, race) and other aspects of the environment such as the teacher, dimensions of the place of training and generalization, and characteristics of materials when planning our variations.

SUMMARY

This chapter has described an evolving technology for initially teaching children how to imitate and subsequently facilitating appropriate imitation in early childhood settings. Certainly the potential for several positive outcomes of such training is great:

1 As Piaget suggests, imitation (particularly deferred imitation) surely must require some form of mental imagery (remembering the modeled behavior) and that process is a critical prerequisite to representational thinking. Deferred imitation may be higher level skill than object permanence, because the child not only remembers the existence of something but also how that something behaved.

2 Imitative skills can facilitate the learning process. If one can learn by observing, many skills become possible at a faster rate than would ordinarily be possible. Furthermore, the teacher can easily demonstrate

complex manipulative tasks (e.g., tying a shoe) as compared to physically prompting them, and can teach more than one child at a time.

3 Appropriate imitation of peers represents an independent learning process not requiring as much teacher time as direct instruction.

4 Imitation of nonhandicapped peers may have some social outcomes in integrated settings since we generally tend to like people who copy some of our own behaviors.

The issue of long-range goals and the potential for undesirable outcomes needs to be addressed. Children should not be taught to imitate the behaviors of every child or adult they meet.

Nordquist (1978) in his peer imitation training with autistic children, reports some undesirable changes in child behavior. Ritualistic and self-stimulatory behavior increased from approximately 10% during the adult imitation training periods to nearly 25% during peer imitation training. Furthermore, a substantial decrease in sustained peer interactions (interactions lasting at least 10 seconds) was observed. An analysis of other data indicated that neither of these changes could be attributed to shifts in adult or peer reinforcement contingencies. Although Nordquist offers no explanation for these findings, he suggests there may be adverse effects on handicapped children involved in peer imitation training. It is possible that the adverse effects were due to the fact that children were asked to model behaviors that were not relevant in the context of other behaviors.

Although no other authors reported negative side effects of peer imitation training, research to date has yet to clearly document long-term outcomes or outcomes other than those directly related to the variables investigated. The behavioral covariation (side effects) of an intervention procedure on positive adaptive and maladaptive behaviors needs to be studied. We know that we *can* teach young handicapped children to imitate their nonhandicapped peers in free play settings. We do not know the effect of this training in terms of long term developmental benefits.

The results of peer imitation training research have generally not been implemented in most early childhood settings for the handicapped. This may reflect the recency of the research, the fact that many handicapped preschoolers are not served in integrated settings, or simply inadequate communication of technology to direct care personnel. This research can be translated into meaningful strategies that can be incorporated in teaching and facilitating appropriate imitation.

REFERENCES

Abramovitch, R., & Grusec, J. E. Peer imitation in a natural setting. *Child Development,* 1978, *49,* 60–65.

Apolloni, T., & Cooke, S. A., & Cooke, T. P. Establishing a normal peer as a behavioral model for delayed toddlers. *Perceptual and Motor Skills,* 1977, *44,* 231–241.

Apolloni, T., & Cooke, T. P. Integrated programming at the infant, toddler, and preschool levels. In M. F. Guralnick (Ed.), *Early intervention and the integration of handicapped and nonhandicapped children.* Baltimore: University Park Press, 1978.

Baer, D. M., Peterson, R. F., & Sherman J. A. The development of imitation by reinforcing behavioral similarity to a model. *Journal of the Experimental Analysis of Behavior,* 1967, *10,* 405–416.

Baer, D. M., & Sherman, J. A. Reinforcement control of generalized imitation in young children. *Journal of Experimental Child Psychology,* 1964, *1,* 37–49.

Bandura, A. *Principles of behavior modification.* New York: Holt, Rinehart & Winston, 1969.

Bandura, A., Grusec, J. E., & Menlove, F. L. Vicarious extinction of avoidance behavior. *Journal of Personality and Social Psychology,* 1967, *5,* 16–23.

Bandura, A., & Menlove, F. L. Factors determining vicarious extinction of avoidance behavior through symbolic modeling. *Journal of Personality and Social Psychology,* 1968, *8,* 99–108.

Bandura, A., Ross, D., & Ross, S. A. Imitation of film-mediated aggressive models. *Journal of Abnormal and Social Psychology,* 1963, *66,* 3–11.

Bricker, D. A rationale for the integration of handicapped and nonhandicaped preschool children. In M. F. Guralnick (Ed.), *Early intervention and the integration of handicapped and nonhandicapped children.* Baltimore: University Park Press, 1978.

Bricker, D., & Dennison, L. Training prerequisites to verbal behavior. In M. E. Snell (Ed.), *Systematic instruction of the moderately and severely handicapped.* Columbus, Ohio: Charles E. Merrill, 1978.

Brody, G. H., & Stoneman, Z. Selective imitation of same-age, older, and younger peer models. *Child Development,* 1981, *52,* 717–720.

Cooke, T. P., Apolloni, T., & Cooke, S. A. Normal preschool children as behavioral models for retarded peers. *Exceptional Children,* 1977, *43,* 531–532.

Cooke, T. P., Ruskus, J. A., Apolloni, T., & Peck, C. A. Handicapped preschool children in the mainstream: Background, outcomes, and clinical suggestions. *Topics In Early Childhood Special Education,* 1981, *1*(1), 73–83.

Flavell, J. H. *Cognitive development.* Engelwood Cliffs, N.J.: Prentice-Hall, 1977.

Fouts, G. T., Waldner, D. N., & Watson, M. W. Effects of being imitated and counterimitated on the behavior of preschool children. *Child Development,* 1976, *47,* 172–177.

Garcia, E., Baer, D. M., & Firestone, I. The development of generalized imitation within topographically determined boundaries. *Journal of Applied Behavior Analysis,* 1971, *4,* 101–112.

Garcia, E. E., & DeHaven, E. D. Use of operant techniques in the establishment of generalization of language: A review and analysis. *American Journal of Mental Deficiency,* 1974, *79,* 169–178.

Gershuri, V. Observational learning: Effects of observed reward and response patterns. *Journal of Educational Psychology,* 1972, *63,* 374–380.

Guralnick, M. F. The value of integrating handicapped and nonhandicapped preschool children. *American Journal of Orthopsychiatry,* 1976, *46,* 236–245.

Hallahan, D. P., Kauffman, J. M., Kneedler, R. D., Snell, M. E., & Richards, H. C. Being imitated by an adult and the subsequent imitative behavior of retarded children. *American Journal of Mental Deficiency,* 1977, *81,* 556–560.

Hartup, W. W. Peer interaction and the process of socialization. In M. Guralnick (Ed.), *Early intervention and the integration of handicapped and nonhandicapped children.* Baltimore: University Park Press, 1978.

Jacobson, S. W. Matching behavior in the young infant. *Child Development,* 1979, *50,* 425–430.

Kauffman, J. M., Snell, M. E., & Hallahan, D. P. Imitating children during imitation training: Two experimental paradigms. *Education and Training of the Mentally Retarded,* 1976, *11,* 324–332.

Lovaas, O. I. The autistic child: *Language development through behavior modification.* New York: Irvington Publishers, 1977.

Meltzoff, A. N., & Moore, M. K. Imitation of facial and manual gestures by human neonates. *Science,* 1977, *198,* 75–78.

Nordquist, V. M. A behavioral approach to the analysis of peer interactions. In M. F. Guralnick (Ed.), *Early intervention and the integration of handicapped and nonhandicapped children.* Baltimore: University Park Press, 1978.

O'Connor, R. D. Modification of social withdrawal through symbolic modeling. *Journal of Applied Behavior Analysis,* 1969, *2,* 15–22.

Parsons, F., & Davey, G. C. L. Imitation training with a 4-year-old retarded person: The relative efficiency of time-out and extinction in conjunction with positive reinforcement. *Mental Retardation,* 1978, *16,* 241–245.

Parton, D. A. Learning to imitate in infancy. *Child Development,* 1976, *47,* 14–31.

Peck, C. A., Apolloni, T., Cooke, T. P., & Raver, S. A. Teaching retarded preschoolers to imitate the free-play behavior of nonretarded classmates:

Trained and generalized effects. *Journal of Special Education*, 1978, *12*, 195–207.

Peterson, C., Peterson, J., & Scriven, G.   Peer imitation by nonhandicapped and handicapped preschoolers. *Exceptional Children*, 1977, *43*, 223–225.

Piaget, J.   [*Play, dreams, and imitation in childhood.*] (C. Gattegno & F. M. Hodgson, Trans.) New York: Norton, 1962. (Originally published, 1945.)

Rosekrans, M. A.   Imitation in children as a function of perceived similarity to a social model and vicarious reinforcement. *Journal of Personality and Social Psychology*, 1967, *7*, 307–315.

Snyder, L., Apolloni, T., & Cooke, T. P.   Integrated settings at the early childhood level: The role of nonretarded peers. *Exceptional Children*, 1977, *43*, 262–266.

Stokes, T. F., & Baer, D. M.   An implicit technology of generalization. *Journal of Applied Behavior Analysis*, 1977, *10*, 349–367.

Sulzer-Azaroff, B., & Mayer, G. P.   *Applying behavior analysis procedures with children and youth*. New York: Holt, Rinehart & Winston, 1977.

Tawney, J. W., Knapp, D. S., O'Reilly, C. D., & Pratt, S. S.   *Programmed environments curriculum*. Columbus, Oh.: Charles E. Merrill, 1979.

Thelen, M. H., Miller, D. J., Fehrenbach, P. A., Frautschi, N. M., & Fishbein, M.D.   Imitation during play as a means of social influence. *Child Development*, 1980, *51*, 918–920.

Yando, R., Seitz, V., & Zigler, E.   *Imitation: A developmental perspective*. Hillsdale, N. J.: Lawrence Erlbaum, 1978.

An important tool for applying learning principles to teach young children is wise use of the preschool environment. Every aspect of the preschool experience is a dimension of the child's environment: the curriculum, the pattern and quality of interactions, the presence of other persons, the schedule, materials and space provided, and amount of structure. In this chapter we review the rationale for environmental design, identify several considerations in environmental planning, describe factors to consider in classroom organization and scheduling, and discuss the role of other persons (including nonhandicapped peers) within the environmental context. In Chapter 6 we discuss the physical setting and in Chapter 7 we focus on techniques for facilitating engagement within environments.

WHY STUDY ENVIRONMENTS?

Diverse theorists agree that the environment is a major determinant of development. Skinner (1953) emphasized the role of environment in shaping *behavior* and suggested that the consequences from interacting with one's environment affect the probability of a given behavior recurring. Piaget (1952) emphasized the role of environment in the development of *knowledge*, and suggested interactions with it confirm, deny, or challenge existing knowledge structures. Both Skinner and Piaget recognized that the critical element was not the environment alone, but rather the individual's *interactions* with that environment.

From a teaching perspective, careful planning of the environment is important in skill acquisition, skill facilitation, generalization, and nurturance. *Skill acquisition* refers to learning new skills. Learning new skills is easier when the proper materials are available. For example, although most children can learn to ride a tricycle, they must have access to one. Optimal development of expressive language skills requires an appropriate model, opportunities to talk with another person, and a variety of stimulating activities designed to elicit talking. When one or more of these factors is missing from the environment, the quality and rate of language development may be altered.

Skill facilitation refers to arrangement of the environment to increase the probability that a previously acquired skill will be demonstrated. For example, Krantz and Risley (1977)

5

Designing Preschool Environments: General Considerations

found that the percentage of time preschoolers listened to a story could be increased when the group story time was preceded by a quiet activity or rest period. When it was preceded by an active session, the percentage of time dropped considerably. Siegel (1977) sought to reduce the frequency with which retarded boys missed the toilet when urinating by simply placing an attractive floating target in the urinal. This environmental change dramatically reduced the number of misses.

Generalization means that a skill learned in one context is displayed in another. Making the training environment similar to the generalization environment should result in more generalization than when the two environments differ significantly. This observation was verified in a series of peer imitation training studies (Apolloni & Cooke, 1978; Apolloni, Cooke, & Cooke, 1977; Peck, Apolloni, Cooke, & Raver, 1978). Although training a preschool handicapped child to imitate nonhandicapped peers was effective in both free play and structured one-to-one lessons, generalization was greater in the free play setting, presumably because this environment was similar to others where generalized imitation was measured.

Careful analysis and planning of the environment is also important for *nurturance*. Risley (1981) suggests every child has a right to live in a reinforcing environment. Even if environments have little effect on behavior change, teachers should provide warm and pleasant environments to meet the children's basic nurturance needs. Special education is based on the assumption that handicapped children do not thrive in a so-called normal environment (Keith, 1979). However, Public Law 94–142 and research (Wolfensberger, 1972) give us legal and ethical mandates to provide an environment that is as close to real life as possible.

The Importance of Environmental Design

There are many ways to facilitate learning. In most teaching situations we assess the child and identify desired behaviors that need to be taught or refined and inappropriate behaviors that should be reduced. The next step is to identify a teaching strategy (e.g., prompting,

shaping, modeling, reinforcement, or punishment) to produce the desired changes. Many times teachers overlook the possibility of environmental alterations that could result in the same change with less effort. In the earlier example of attending skills during story time, the same change could have been produced through an elaborate token reinforcement system. However, a token system requires considerable planning and preparation, and may be viewed by some as an unnecessary, artificial strategy.

The environments provided for handicapped and nonhandicapped preschoolers were compared in a recent study (Bailey, Clifford & Harms, 1982). Programs for handicapped and nonhandicapped children were similar in provisions for personal care routines, language-reasoning experiences, and adult needs. However, several differences that emphasize the importance of environmental design training in special teacher education were found. The areas found to be lacking in handicapped children's programs included furnishings for relaxation and comfort, room arrangement, child-related display, art, blocks, sand/water, dramatic play, space to be alone, free play, cultural awareness, and space and scheduled time for gross motor activities.

The findings of this exploratory study raise many interesting questions regarding the nature of environments that *are* and *should be* provided for young handicapped children. Why were their programs providing significantly different environments? Are these differences appropriate for the needs of these children? Do programs for handicapped preschoolers provide other activities that actually fulfill the same functions as sand/water play, blocks, and dramatic play? As Bailey et al. (1982) suggest, such activities appear to be appropriate for *all* young children— they fulfill meaningful functions and are enjoyable. The activities can also be adapted and structured for children functioning at widely differing developmental levels. Deficiencies in environment are difficult to justify based on the argument that handicapped children require something different, particularly in the absence of supporting data.

CONSIDERATIONS IN ENVIRONMENTAL PLANNING

The next step is the identification of considerations in planning environments. At least one data-based study has addressed the question of quality in environments. Although the study dealt with the home, its implications for classrooms are readily apparent. Wachs (1979) studied 39 infants between 12 and 24 months of age in an attempt to relate dimensions of home environments to cognitive development and found a clear relationship between several dimensions. Five were positively related to cognitive growth: a physically responsive environment, presence of a stimulus shelter, lack of overcrowding, the degree to which the physical set-up permits exploration, and the degree of temporal regularity. One dimension, a high noise-confusion level, was negatively related to cognitive growth.

A Physically Responsive Environment

The dimension found to relate most consistently with cognitive growth was the presence of a physically responsive environment. According to Wachs (1979), the importance of a physically responsive environment may lie in the child's awareness that his or her behavior can affect the environment; this may encourage the child to interact even more with the environment and thus facilitate other learning.

Olds (1979) considers responsivity to be essential for children to feel competent. One way of feeling competence is to experience success—your behavior affects other people or materials around you. Having responsive materials ought to increase the probability of a child being successful and feeling competent.

A physically responsive environment is particulary important for young handicapped children. Historically society has taken a protective attitude toward handicapped individuals. Unfortunately this attitude frequently results in adults doing everything for the individual or exerting extensive control over his or her behavior. Such situations can easily lead to lack of perceived control over one's life and perhaps teach children helplessness (DeVellis, 1977; Seligman, 1975). A physically responsive environment provided during the early years may help to increase perceptions of control.

What is meant by a physically responsive environment? Wachs measured responsivity by counting the number of toys in the home that made an audiovisual response when activated. In a broader sense, a physically responsive environment allows success and independence, with materials and people who respond to the child's individual needs. A good environment should be socially as well as physically responsive. Elardo, Bradley, and Caldwell (1977) found emotional and verbal responsivity of the mother to be positively correlated with language development at age 3, and Bradley and Caldwell (1976) found the same responsivity factor to be positively correlated with mental test performance at age 4½.

The following strategies should be incorporated in designing a responsive environment: activities and materials should be appropriately challenging (frequently giving feedback) yet not so difficult that failure often occurs; the adults and children in the environment should learn to respond to verbal and nonverbal signals sent by others in that environment; and independence must be valued, encouraged, and facilitated through appropriate environmental design (such as adaptive equipment and child-sized furniture) and expected by teachers.

Overcrowding and Stimulus Shelters

Three closely related dimensions identified by Wachs were the provision of sufficient space for the people in the environment, a place where the child can be away from people and noise, and the general noise and confusion level within the environment. A number of studies investigating the effects of crowding and noise have been conducted with both animals and humans. Hutt and Viazay (1966) demonstrated that as group size within a given classroom space increased, both nonhandicapped and brain-damaged children exhibited increased aggressiveness. Kreger (1971) demonstrated that reduction of the stress from overcrowding in a residential institution resulted in decreased levels of aggression and other behavior problems. He suggested that the problems of severely retarded persons may be "the functional representation of environmental living conditions which produce degrees of stress which are beyond the retardates' ordinary capabilities to cope with effectively" (p. 29). Crowding is not merely a function of the number of people in a given space. Ittelson, Proshansky, Rivlin, and Winkel (1974) suggested that crowding results in frustration from interference of others with efforts to achieve some purpose.

Baker (1980) suggests that programs serving severely handicapped children often contribute to maladaptive social and emotional behaviors by ignoring individual needs for territoriality and privacy. The Bailey et al. (1982) comparison of preschool environments reported that more than 75% of the preschool classrooms for handicapped children in the study provided no space especially set aside for children to be alone.

In reality, we all need some space and time to be alone. Although busy, active environments can be stimulating and exciting, quiet spaces are important for relaxation and concentration. Teachers should provide a balance between stimulation and opportunities for privacy and free choice.

Harms and Cross (1977) suggest that environmental provisions for play-alone spaces be created in a number of ways:

☐ Visual barriers, high enough to give children a feeling of privacy, but low enough for adults to see over, can be created by shelves and dividers.
☐ Enclosures can be made out of cardboard boxes, wooden crates, or cable reels.
☐ Lofts or platforms can be built above part of the room. (p. 22)

Scheduling, supervision, and careful planning of space may also be useful in reducing potentially negative effects of crowding. Krantz and Risley (1977), for example, found that children were more attentive to a story when spaced equidistantly from each other (either on chairs or sitting in assigned spaces) rather than when they were allowed to randomly sit together. Harms and Cross (1977) suggest that a system for taking turns in both activities and play-alone spaces can ensure sharing and reduce competition for space and materials.

Encouraging Exploration

Another aspect of the environment that Wachs (1979) found to be important was the degree to which the physical set-up of the environment permits exploration. As Appleton, Clifton, and Goldberg (1975) suggest, freedom to explore "allows the child to process stimulation at his own pace thus producing a great probability of a match" (Wachs, 1979, p. 31).

Weisler and McCall (1976) define exploration as "perceptual-motor examination of an object, situation, or event the function of which is to reduce subjective uncertainties" (p. 493). The child uses exploration to acquire information about the properties of objects, people, or situations. A relatively consistent sequence of behaviors appears to be associated with exploration, beginning with alerting or attending to a new situation or object, and continuing with observing the new stimulus from a distance, motor-aided perceptual examination, and finally, active physical interaction.

According to Piaget (1963), active interaction with the environment is a primary learning mode for both children and adults. Active interaction requires movement and high quality (as opposed to random) exploration. In fact, Olds (1979) suggests that "to deny activity is to halt development at its source" (p. 92).

The importance of exploration and the effects of inadequate exploratory skills becomes even more apparent when considering young children with sensory or motor impairments that can reduce such opportunities. This results in the secondary handicap of deficits in experiences. How can a child in a wheelchair *really* understand the concept of "high" if he or she has never been able to explore heights through climbing?

Weisler and McCall (1976) suggest several considerations in encouraging and facilitating exploratory behaviors. First, teachers should attend to the stimulus properties of the objects or events in the environment, such as color and brightness contrasts, movement patterns, response to manipulation, and unpredictability. Second, children are more likely to explore novel stimuli. Thus some attempt should be made to vary the materials available for play. Third, children may be interested in exploring stimuli both similar and moderately discrepant with the previous stimuli. Weisler and McCall emphasize that infants may look at and explore only moderately unusual events, and cite Piaget (1963) who suggested that children will not explore anything that is very familiar (because they are satisfied with their knowledge of it) or anything that is too discrepant (because it does not fit into their knowledge structure).

Sensory or motor-impaired children may need special adaptations or encouragement to facilitate exploratory behavior. In general, an environment should minimize the dangers of exploration, maximize the reward potential of exploration, and facilitate exploration through adaptive equipment and teacher structure.

Temporal Regularity

Finally, Wachs (1979) reported the degree of temporal regularity in the home was positively related to cognitive development, although the only indicator used to measure temporal regularity was whether or not the child had a regular mealtime. Other authors, however, have also suggested the importance of temporal regularity. Harms and Cross (1977), for example, stress the importance of *predictable* environments. This does not necessarily mean the same rigid schedule should be followed every day. It suggests, however, that a relatively predictable schedule is important for children and adults to feel comfortable within a setting. Predictability would seem particularly important for children who come from unpredictable home environments.

The Wachs (1979) study should be viewed as exploratory and not definitive, particularly when inferring implications for young handicapped children. The sample size was small and all but two of the infants were Caucasian. None of the children were handicapped, and the study considered only home environments. However, the results do provide the beginnings of a data base from which meaningful suggestions regarding important dimensions of preschool environments may be generated.

CLASSROOM ORGANIZATION AND STRUCTURE

At the beginning of this chapter we broadly defined *environment* to include not only the use of space and materials but also scheduling, organization, and structural dimensions of the environment.

Scheduling of Activities

Scheduling refers to deciding who will do what and when they will do it. It is important for both adults and children, and can affect the behavior of both. A schedule provides a comfortable routine within which adults and children are able to meet a variety of needs and know that *sometime* during the day those needs will be met. A consistently followed schedule helps make a program a *predictable* setting. The best schedule specifies a sequence of activities, designates which children will be doing those activities, lists approximate time periods for activities, and specifies responsibilities for each adult in the classroom (Hart, 1982). Several factors should be considered in planning a daily schedule.

Children are probably the most alert early in the day. Structured teaching activities requiring alert concentration should be planned early in the daily schedule.

Children usually arrive at different times. Different arrival times makes conducting early structured activities difficult; the implication for scheduling is that structured play activities planned each morning and requiring minimal teacher supervision may be best. Teachers should wait to conduct structured teaching activities until most children have arrived. Such planning reduces interruptions and distractions, and frees the teacher to attend to arrival responsibilities.

Children need to be greeted appropriately when they arrive. Having "independent" activities available when children arrive does not mean the teacher is free to sit in the lounge and drink coffee. Children (and parents) need to be greeted when they arrive. Assign one or more staff members to greet children and parents each day (Harms & Clifford, 1980). Greeting time is especially important for young children. A familiar face, a smile, a directed welcome ("Hello, Mike! I am really glad to see you at school today!"), and a familiar routine at arrival time can serve to make school a pleasant experience. A procedure would include the following:

☐ Get down at the child's eye level and say, "Hello" or "Good morning," stating the child's name so that he knows you are talking to him.

☐ Assist the child as necessary in performing standard arrival behaviors such as taking off a coat or putting up a lunch box.

☐ Direct the child to a particular activity or present several optional activities from which the child may choose.

☐ Greet the parents as well, and use this time to talk and exchange information (Harms & Clifford, 1980).

☐ Children who have a long bus ride may need to go to the bathroom soon after they arrive at school.

Children need a carefully planned balance of activities. We all need and enjoy variety. Children need active as well as quiet times scheduled throughout the day. These activities should be interspersed so children will not "burn out" on tabletop activities or be too physically exhausted from motor activities.

Programs for young children must be planned to include time and space for both *acquisition* and *generalization* experiences. The environmental supports for each of these modes of instruction are somewhat different. Acquisition often requires individual or small group instruction that is teacher-directed and focuses on specific tasks. Generalization requires intrinsically motivating play and real-life activities that elicit and integrate a number of the acquired skills.

Many programs for handicapped children currently use the acquisition mode almost exclusively, whereas most programs for non-handicapped children emphasize the generalization mode. This accounts for the surprise that special education teachers feel when they see how much of the school day normal children spend in noisy, active, hands-on play. Similarly teachers of normal preschool and kindergarten-aged children are shocked to see young children with special needs sitting in chairs and being instructed for much of the school day. Yet all children need an *appropriate*

balance between instruction for acquisition and play for generalization (Olds, 1979; Piaget, 1963). The effective early childhood special educator should combine the strengths of early childhood classrooms with those of special education classrooms. A truly non-restrictive education environment for handicapped children according to Kenowitz, Zweibel, and Edgar (1979) must include activities to help prepare children to function to their capacity in the larger world.

Group Versus Individual Instruction

Grouping children for instruction can be difficult when working with those with very specific and diverse instructional needs. Given a large number of children, however, individual instruction may not always be possible. The issue of group versus individual instruction raises a variety of questions: Which procedure is the most effective method of teaching a skill? Which procedure is the most economical use of teacher time? Is it possible that some skills are best taught individually while others are just as easily taught in a group format?

Individual instruction is a primary strategy in many present-day early intervention programs. Blank (1970) made a strong case for one-to-one instruction in preschool programming, particularly language intervention. She suggested that such an approach would be preferable for children with short attention spans and should result in more effective instruction by allowing the teacher to continually diagnose difficulties and adjust the lesson to make it appropriate for each child. "There is little opportunity in the group setting for the teacher to pursue the reasons for failure and then offer him the necessary experiences to help him understand the rationale for the correct answer" (Blank, 1970, p. 30).

There may be, however, some advantages to group instruction. Brown, Holvoet, Guess, and Mulligan (1980) suggest that in an individual lesson, the teacher has little recourse with the nonresponsive or "acting out" child—the problem must be dealt with directly. In a group lesson, however, the materials, cues, or feedback given to other children can serve as potential motivators for disruptive children. For example, if Johnny knocks his chair over, the teacher could praise Susie for staying in her chair and attending to the task rather than scolding or punishing Johnny. Group instruction also provides opportunities for learning by observing peers, impossible in one-to-one instruction. Group activities predominate in nonhandicapped preschool programs, and learning to function in such a setting may facilitate movement to less restrictive environments.

In some cases group instruction can be as effective as individual instruction, even for severely handicapped children (Favell, Favell, & McGinsey, 1978; Storm & Willis, 1978). For example, Alberto, Jobes, Sizemore, and Doran (1980) found no significant differences in the effectiveness of group and individual instruction in tabletop activities involving receptive understanding of prepositions and in the discrimination of colors, even though there were more opportunities for responding in one-to-one instruction. Individual instruction resulted in more effective acquisition of dressing skills, however.

Individualized instruction should be provided within the small group setting. For example, answering questions about a story may be an appropriate goal for Roy, Larry, and Emmy. Perhaps Roy needs to answer questions about what will happen next; Larry needs to figure out what the characters did; and Emmy needs to understand who did what. While each child has a different objective, they can listen to the same story as a group and answer questions appropriate to their individual objectives.

Children need not experience a lot of "dead time" waiting for other children to complete an activity in group instruction. Activities involving children in meaningful experiences should be provided throughout the lesson. Children not directly involved with the teacher should have planned, concrete, and interesting work relating to instructional objectives. The child should be able to accomplish such activities independently.

Structure of Activities

Environmental structure provides a framework for something to happen. In a broad sense, *any* program is structured by the nature of its set-up and organization—it affects the behavior of both teacher and children. The real issue is whether the teachers are aware of the kind of structure they impose and its outcome on children. In Chapter 3, procedures used in behaviorally oriented classrooms are described; in the following section, procedures used in Piagetian classrooms are described.

The Piagetian classroom   A Piagetian model advocates self-initiated activity by children, with structure taking the form of teacher selection of appropriate materials and options for activities. The basic premise of the Piagetian model is as follows:

The concept that children—or individuals of any age—learn best from self-initiated activity is perhaps the most important single proposition that the educator can derive from Piaget's work.... Piaget places major emphasis on the role of activity—both physical and mental—in intellectual development. In Piaget's view, "to know an object, is to act on it." ... The essence of knowledge is activity (Ginsburg & Opper, 1979, p. 224).

The child must act upon the environment to construct knowledge. He or she must be able to explore, manipulate, and change objects; in short, investigate, test, retest, and question. Such activity, from Piaget's perspective, allows the child to discover knowledge and results in greater understanding and a more enduring change than knowledge we try to teach children. By providing the child with a wide range of environmental encounters, we allow the child "to come up with a variety of ideas, problems, and questions" and to "put objects and events into relationships and notice similarities and differences" (Kamii & DeVries, 1978, p. 40).

Organizing a preschool program based on these premises involves several steps. First, the *classroom environment must be arranged and equipped to invite and encourage activity.* The classroom materials should be appropriate to the children's abilities; just enough beyond their abilities to be challenging, but not frustrating. Children's products should be displayed and cultural/home environments reflected in the classroom (Elkind, 1976). It should have space for movement and should include certain "work areas," for example, block, housekeeping, construction, and sand and water areas (Hohmann, Banet, & Weikart,

1979). Hohmann et al. discuss arranging, organizing, and equipping the classroom in detail and provide suggestions for setting up the classroom for specific handicapping conditions.

Second, the *teacher must provide inviting, interesting activities.* Hohmann, Banet, and Weikart (1979) maintain that "the overriding implication of Piaget's work for educators is that the teacher is a supporter of development, and as such his or her prime goal is to promote active learning on the part of the child" (Hohmann et al., 1979, p. 3). They have designed approximately 50 *key experiences* including using language, representing experiences and ideas, developing logical reasoning (classification, seriation, number concepts), and understanding time and space. The key experiences are not behavioral objectives to be mastered, but are central themes around which an endless variety of activities can be planned regardless of the child's developmental level. The activities can be initiated by either child or teacher, but a balance between the two is desired. The key experiences allow children to constructively interact with the environment, provide the teacher with an awareness of children's cognitive processes, and serve as a means to expand activities for promoting development. The teacher is a supporter of development by doing the following:

Providing a rich array of materials and activities from which children are invited to select. Explicitly asking children to plan, in some way, what they are going to do and how they are going to do it. . . . Asking questions and making suggestions in order to set the stage for key experiences that stimulate the child's thinking processes, language development, and social development (Hohmann et al., 1979, p. 6).

Helping children plan daily activities is essential in implementing the key experiences of the book, *Cognitively Oriented Curriculum.* When children are involved in planning their activities, they begin to view themselves as capable of making and acting upon decisions. Children may also begin to construct mental pictures of the activity they are about to do (Hohmann et al., 1979).

Initially, children must learn available options in work areas, materials, and human resources. The teacher assists children in planning what they are *going to do* rather than *where* they will be working or playing. Some children indicate their plans verbally, others may point to an area, bring materials to the teacher, or report they do not know what they are going to do. The teacher should recognize how children indicate their plans and assist them in making detailed, realistic, and varied plans.

Kamii and DeVries (1978) suggest that when *beginning* an activity, the teacher should "introduce the activity in a way that maximizes children's initiative" (p. 52). This principle is implemented "by putting out materials to which children will naturally gravitate, by presenting the material and saying, 'See whatever you can think of to do with these things,' and by . . . presenting the material and saying, 'Can you find something with which you can do X?' " (p. 53). Another principle for beginning activities is "begin with parallel play" or "introduce the activity in such a way that cooperation is possible but not necessary" (pp. 53–54). Cooperation and social interaction are desirable for preschool children, but Kamii and DeVries suggest cooperation and social interactions occur as a result of children engaging in physical knowledge activities.

Kamii and DeVries (1978) also present principles for *continuing* activities. Initially, "figure out what the child is thinking and respond sparingly in his terms" (p. 54). Determining what children are thinking is not easy, and Kamii and DeVries suggest careful observation and educated guesses. Another difficult task is deciding what to do or say based on what you suppose the child is thinking. As stated, intervene sparingly. Further, the teacher must decide when to say or do something. Teachers should provide opportunities for children to note relationships between objects and events. Kamii and DeVries (1978) suggest four types of questions to help children notice relationships. Ask them the following:

1 What do you think would happen if you did (*a certain thing*) with your materials?
2 Can you do (*with a certain thing*) or can you find something to accomplish (*with a certain thing*)?
3 Can you tell how you did (*a certain thing*),

or how one way of doing it is different from another?

4 Can you explain why (*a certain thing*) happened? (This type of question should rarely be used).

Teachers also can help children with lines of experimentation impossible (or unsafe) to do alone; they can offer more materials, and model different actions or possibilities with the same material.

Another principle for continuing an activity is to "encourage children to interact with other children" (Kamii & DeVries, 1978, p. 57). Ask the type of questions just listed, but encourage children to solicit peer assistance in acting upon the question.

Still another principle is to "integrate all aspects of development in physical knowledge activities" (p. 59). Teachers should encourage growth in social, moral and language development during physical knowledge activities.

After activities are completed, the teacher should ask questions which assist children in *reflecting on* what they did and saw other children do. Emphasize honest descriptions rather than one "correct answer."

The third general characteristic of the Piagetian classroom is that *children's spontaneous play must be allowed and encouraged* (Kamii & DeVries, 1977). Piaget believed that the child uses play to gain information about objects in the environment and thus constructs knowledge. When children play, they choose activities in which they are interested. This results in motivation for continued manipulations of the environment, manipulations being the material from which intellect is constructed.

Forman and Kuschner (1977) propose guidelines for entering the child's play and assisting in constructing knowledge. Initially, the child is allowed to engage in free play. The teacher observes this and attempts to determine the specific type of knowledge the child is constructing. Based on the hypothesized explanation, the teacher makes a decision about how and when to enter the child's play. Typically, teachers enter by engaging in parallel play near enough to the child without giving the impression of forcing an interaction. Essentially the teacher is imitating the child's behavior from a "safe" distance.

The objective of imitating the child is to lead the child beyond her current knowledge. The teacher imitates what the child is doing; the child imitates the teacher's imitation of her; and then the child continues to imitate the teacher when the teacher presents novel variations on the theme of play (Forman & Kuschner, 1977, p. 132).

These novel variations allow the child to construct new notions about objects and actions possible with objects. This procedure appears very simple, but in reality involves considerable skill in rapid decision making by the teacher.

Research on structure The effects of various levels of structure in preschool programs for nonhandicapped children have been investigated in a number of ways. Johnson, Ershler, and Bell (1980) compared play behavior observed in a discovery-based preschool program with that in a formal education preschool program. The formal program emphasized Piagetian concepts but used a direct teaching approach to facilitate development. The discovery-based program focused more on the process of thinking and stressed spontaneous interactions with materials, peers, and teachers. The results suggested that the approach taken by the program could affect play behavior in a number of ways. Children in the formal program exhibited more constructive play and more transformations (changes in use of materials or the identity of people) than children in the discovery-based program. Discovery program children were observed in nonplay behavior (unoccupied or onlooking) more often than children in the formal program.

Huston-Stein, Friedrich-Cofer, and Susman (1977) compared highly structured (high percentages of adult-directed activities) Head Start classrooms with low-structure classrooms and found both positive and negative aspects. Children in high-structure classrooms were more attentive in circle time and helped to clean up more often after free play, but did not show more independent task-oriented behavior.

Doke (1975) investigated the effects of formal versus informal activity periods in a day-care treatment program for behavior-disordered preschoolers (aged 4–6 years). *Formal activities* were defined as those in which children remain in a group within a specified area and watch another person (usually the teacher) coordinate the activity. Manipulable materials are used simultaneously by all children and usually in the same way, as directed by the teacher. *Informal activities* were those in which children could obtain a variety of materials at any time and use them in a variety of ways. Formal activity periods included nursery rhymes, language lessons, and story time; informal activities included blocks, housekeeping, and manipulative play.

Doke measured the percentage of time all children were engaged in planned activities. Results indicated the amount of engagement was consistently higher during informal activities than during formal ones. This finding was consistent over several days and for most of the children. As a result of these data, Doke (1975) concluded:

Informal activities appear to hold considerable promise. Children may be worked with individually while they request materials or assistance from the caregiver. These impromptu training episodes are ideal in that the caregiver does not have to vie for the child's attention or guess about what might be reinforcing for him. The child who approaches the caregiver with a request is specifying his reinforcer and is telling the teacher that he is ready to learn. In addition, well-stocked informal activities assure that children who are not interacting with the caregiver will stay busy. Formal activities are weaker in this respect, because they often require many children to wait while the caregiver interacts with one or two children. (p. 221)

Children in this study may have been noncompliant behavior-disordered youngsters who preferred doing what they pleased rather than what someone wanted them to do. Engagement alone may be insufficient in measuring the effectiveness of informal versus formal activities.

Doke and Risley (1972) investigated required versus optional activities in organizing a day-care environment. At the beginning of the school year the children followed an "Options" activity schedule. During this period at least two optional activities were always available throughout the day, and children were free to move from one area to another after meeting simple exit requirements such as putting away materials or cleaning up. Later a "No-Options" schedule was introduced. Under this structure only one activity area was open at any given time. When that area was closed, children completed their exit requirements and then moved on to the next area which had just opened.

Doke and Risley found no significant differences in overall percentage of engagement time between the Options and No-Options arrangements. This was only true, however, when children in the No-Options schedule left the activity area as soon as they completed their individual exit requirements. When they had to wait for all children to finish, the percentage of engaged time dropped dramatically.

LeLaurin and Risley (1972) investigated "zone" versus "man-to-man" staff assignment patterns. During the zone procedure, each teacher was assigned a specific activity area. Children were required to follow a basic activity schedule at their own pace. For example, at the beginning of lunch all four teachers were in the lunch area. As soon as the first child had finished his dessert, one teacher went to the bathroom and another to the shoe area to help children moving through those sections on their way to the nap area. As more children left the lunchroom, a third teacher went to the bed area to assist children who had gone through the bathroom and shoe areas. Children were free to move through each area as they finished their responsibilities. During the man-to-man procedure, each teacher was responsible for a group of 6–12 children. The entire group had to finish a given activity before anyone in that group could proceed to the next area.

The zone procedure clearly was the superior environmental organization. The percent of engagement in appropriate activities was considerably higher when children were allowed to move at their own pace rather than wait for other children. As LeLaurin and Risley suggest, a similarly high percent of engagement probably could have been achieved using the man-to-man procedure had other procedures had been used such as providing activities for waiting children. The zone staffing pattern provides a more natural structure, however, and may be more enjoyable for children and easier for staff to implement.

Structure in programs for handicapped preschoolers Piaget's theories have caused early childhood educators to seriously examine the role of the teacher in the classroom. Many, however, would argue that a Piagetian approach to training is inappropriate in programs for handicapped youngsters. First, handicapped children may not be as likely to explore as nonhandicapped children. Second, handicapped preschoolers may not learn through simple manipulation; reinforcement and other artificial feedback may be necessary to teach desired details. Third, handicapped youngsters may not independently engage in exploratory behaviors to best facilitate long-term growth. The teacher must make sure the child is involved in activities that have a high probability of facilitating appropriate development.

In general, handicapped youngsters really do need a more structured program. The development of a sophisticated technology of teaching demonstrates the powerful effects of well-designed and systematically implemented training programs. This technology should be utilized to its maximum potential and must be applied when working with severely handicapped youngsters. The Piagetian classroom may work very well for mildly handicapped or high-risk children, but constitutes a restrictive and inappropriate setting for those who do not possess the basic skills to adapt to such an environment.

We might do well, however, when planning any intervention effort, to consider how much an environment should be structured to insure change. We often set up a contingency management program for behavior that might just as easily have been changed with a less intrusive procedure. Krantz and Risley (1977), for example, investigated the on-task behavior of preschool children during group time as a function of seating conditions. Children were more likely to attend when required to sit on pieces of masking tape spaced equidistantly apart than when allowed to sit randomly in a small area. Although similar results were obtained using a contingency management program (praise and privileges contingent upon on-task behavior), the authors suggested the environmental change was superior since it involved less planning and less teacher time for implementation, and was probably more enjoyable for the children.

HUMAN DIMENSION OF ENVIRONMENTS

In addition to physical space, scheduling, organization, and structure, a final dimension of the environment is that of other people. People are very much a part of the environment. The type, number, and relative status of other persons can affect the behavior of children and should be carefully considered. In this section we discuss the human dimension in preschool environments, including adult-child ratios, same- versus mixed-aged groupings, and integration of handicapped and nonhandicapped children.

Adult-Child Ratios

Adult-child ratios vary considerably across programs depending upon the ages of the children and the handicapping conditions. Rogers-Warren and Wedel (1980) report some generally suggested staff-child ratios—1:3 for infants, 1:5 for toddlers, 1:10 for nonhandicapped preschoolers, 1:7 for mildly handicapped preschoolers, and 1:4 for severely handicapped children. Unfortunately, little research has been done on the effects of varying ratios on child behavior. Most available research has focused on nonhandicapped preschoolers.

Ratios in infancy Fowler (1975) reviewed the influence of adult-child ratios on infant development. Although he recognized that adult-child ratios are "only one of a host of basic conditions, along with physical environment, materials, staff competencies and personalities, and programs and methods that weave together to make up the fabric of quality care" (p. 25), he concluded a high adult-child ratio was a "crucial foundation" in any infant care program. Based on his review, Fowler (1975) suggested ratios of 1:2 during the first year, 1:3 for the second, and 1:4 by the third.

As Fowler suggests, high ratios are probably necessary but not sufficient for good development. Without an adequate ratio, quality care may be difficult to provide. Being responsible for a large number of children forces the caretaker to focus on basic custodial needs and results in less time for affectionate or informational interactions. A high ratio must be combined with high quality interactions, however.

Ratios in preschool Only one study has investigated adult-child ratios during the preschool years. O'Connor (1975) compared the social and dependency behaviors of nursery school children (ages 42–60 months) placed in a classroom with a 1:3.5 adult-child ratio with those of children with 1:7 ratio. Children interacted significantly more with adults and less with peers and were more dependent upon adults in terms of more requests for assistance in the high (1:3.5) ratio settings.

Use of ratios Research on adult-child ratios is very limited, and effects of other variables have not been controlled. Fowler (1975) reviewed a wide variety of sources, but he cited no research that experimentally manipulated adult-child ratios while keeping other factors constant. For example, in the O'Connor (1975) study, the two classes differed on a second variable: one program was ungraded, with children 3–5 years of age in one classroom, while the other program grouped children according to age, with all 3-year-olds in one classroom and all 4-year-olds in the other. A mixed-age grouping can result in different interactional patterns than a same-age grouping.

A high adult-child ratio can be advantageous in any preschool program for handicapped children. Sufficient staff can conduct the necessary direct teaching sessions and work with children unable to perform self-care tasks such as toileting and feeding.

Although ratio may appear to be a dimension of the environment that the teacher has little control over, a number of strategies can be used to increase volunteers in a program. Fowler (1975) suggests both day-care cooperatives and centers as a part of high school facilities. The cooperative preschool improves adult-child ratios by systematic use of parents. Locating an early intervention program in a high school can be tied in with a parenting, teaching, or child development course for adolescents. Likewise, other volunteer programs, such as foster grandparents, should be considered as options for improving adult-child ratios.

The keys to a successful volunteer program are organization, training, and feedback. Volunteers need to know exactly what is expected of them. Teachers should set objectives and provide materials for volunteers just as they would for children. Volunteers should be trained in the basic school safety rules as well as guidelines for working with specific children (such as the physically impaired) and dealing with specific behavior problems. Finally, volunteers need supervision and feedback on their performance. A poorly run program is worse than no program at all if it results in inconsistent or inappropriate interactions with children.

Same- Versus Mixed-Age Grouping

A number of authors (Konner, 1975; Hartup, 1976) have suggested that frequent same-age interaction is a relatively recent phenomenon in evolutionary history. Hunter-gatherer societies were small and provided relatively few opportunities for same-age peer contact.

Recent research suggests the nature and effects of peer interaction may vary as a function of same- or mixed-age groupings. Lougee, Grueneich, and Hartup (1977) looked at social interaction in same- and mixed-age dyads (pairs) of preschool children. When younger (44 months) and older (58 months) children were in same-age dyads, younger children exhibited fewer positive social interactions than older children. When placed in mixed-age dyads, however, the younger children typically demonstrated more positive social interactions than their counterparts in same-age dyads; the older children demonstrated fewer positive social interactions than in the same-age dyads. Verbal communication of the younger children was more appropriate in mixed-age than same-age groupings and less appropriate for older children in mixed-age groupings. Orientation to and use of play materials did not vary as a function of dyad type.

Graziano, French, Brownell, and Hartup (1976) investigated the effects of same- and mixed-aged groupings on the peer interaction and task performance of triads of first and third grade children. Each triad was observed during a simple block-building task. No difference was found between the groups on task performance. Mixed-age groups stimulated greater task activity than same-age groups for third graders, but not for first graders. More conversation occurred with same-age triads. A single older child was more likely to take turns and be more persistent in task completion than if there was another third grader in the mixed-age triad.

Goldman (1981) observed the social behavior of 3- and 4-year-olds in same-age and mixed-age classes. Both groups spent less time in parallel play in the mixed-age classes and more time in positive interactions and solitary play. Four-year-olds spent less time under the direct guidance of an adult in the mixed-age grouping. Goldman interpreted these results to support the concept that parallel play is the least mature level of play.

Furman, Rahe, and Hartup (1979) summarized the current status of our knowledge of the effects of mixed-age groupings as follows:

(a) older children are more effective models than younger children; (b) reciprocal imitation is more characteristic of children's interactions with older children than with younger children; (c) children prefer to be taught by children older than themselves; (d) under certain conditions social reinforcement is more effective when delivered by either an older or younger child than when delivered by an age mate; (e) aggression occurs more frequently among age mates than among non-age mates; and (f) nurturance occurs more commonly in interaction with younger children. (p. 915)

Two studies examined the impact of mixed-age groupings on social withdrawal. Suomi and Harlow (1972) reared monkeys in total isolation for 6 months. Previous research suggested that such isolation results in permanent impairments in social development. Monkeys were then provided successive exposures to a normally-reared monkey (peer therapist) of only 3 months of age. The authors reported decreased self-stimulation, huddling, and other behaviors characteristic of isolate-reared animals, increased locomotion and exploration, and emergence of social contacts and play.

Furman, Rahe, and Hartup (1979) identified preschool-age children who demonstrated low rates of interaction with peers. These isolates were then paired either with a peer of the same age or with a younger child for 10 play sessions over a 4–6 week period. During this time, the mean social interaction rate among the socially withdrawn children paired with a younger child almost doubled. The interaction rates of children paired with same-age peers also increased, but not to the extent in the mixed-age. The authors concluded that the play sessions with younger children "must have provided isolates with experiences that occurred infrequently in the classroom. We believe these experiences included the opportunity to be socially assertive (i.e., to direct social activity)" (p. 921).

Peer interactions do seem to differ as a function of age. Generally these differences seem particularly favorable to the development of young and socially withdrawn children. The beneficial effects for the older children are less clear. Also, the interaction of age with developmental level has yet to be investigated. For example, would placing 3-year-old retarded children with 3-year-old nonretarded peers or older retarded children have the same effect as a mixed-age grouping? The important component of a mixed-age group may be good models who *function* higher or lower than a child, rather than chronological ages.

Integrating Handicapped and Nonhandicapped Preschoolers

The provision of nonhandicapped peers is often referred to as mainstreaming or integration. Kaufman, Gottlieb, Agard, and Kukic (1975) define *mainstreaming* as "the temporal, instructional, and social integration of eligible exceptional children with normal peers on an ongoing, individually determined educational planning and programming process" (p. 30).

Bricker (1978) identified rationales for the integration of handicapped and nonhandicapped preschoolers. They include social-ethical arguments, legal-legislative arguments, and psychological-educational arguments. From the social-ethical perspective, integration may facilitate the acceptance of handicapped children by their nonhandicapped peers. Voeltz (1980), for example, demonstrated that contact with severely handicapped students resulted in improved attitudes by their nonhandicapped peers. Nonhandicapped children also became more realistic of their perceptions regarding the abilities of handicapped children. Integration also prevents negative effects of segregation into special programs, such as labeling young handicapped children as "the slow group." Finally, the normalization principle described by Wolfensburger (1972) advocates "utilization of means which are as culturally normative as possible, in order to establish and/or maintain personal behaviors which are as culturally normative as possible" (p. 28). A complete lack of nonhandicapped or handicapped peers is a culturally abnormal situation.

The most obvious legal-legislative guidelines for mainstreaming are found in Public Law 94–142 which states that public school programs must educate handicapped children with the nonhandicapped in the least restrictive environment, according to each child's needs. This mandate implies that all children have a basic right to interact with nonhandicapped persons.

Psychological-educational arguments are based on the premise that integrating handicapped and nonhandicapped children may be of therapeutic or educational benefit for the former. Bricker (1978) suggests several reasons for this assumption. According to Piaget, children need demanding environments to grow and learn; nonhandicapped peers may create a more demanding environment. Nonhandicapped children may also serve as models for handicapped preschoolers. Imitation can be achieved with positive benefits with appropriate planning, organization, and structure. Finally, nonhandicapped peers may serve as formal and informal tutors. From an informal perspective, nonhandicapped children can appropriately adapt their behaviors to the level of the handicapped children. For example, Guralnick and Paul-Brown (1977; 1980) demonstrated that nonhandicapped preschoolers adjusted their speech to the level of handicapped children. Nonhandicapped children have been formally trained to tutor handicapped children in a structured learning environment.

Barriers to Mainstreaming

Despite the sound rationale for integrating handicapped and nonhandicapped preschoolers, relatively few mainstreamed early childhood settings exist. At least 10% of all children served by Head Start must be handicapped, but most are mildly retarded or have speech or language delays. The moderately or severely handicapped preschooler is typically served in a self-contained developmental day center designed to meet the needs of handicapped children, with little or no planned interactions with nonhandicapped children.

Why is mainstreaming the exception rather than the rule? Tawney (1981) cites several problems. Regular early childhood educators are usually not trained in techniques for developing appropriate programs for handicapped youngsters. Many regular teachers may also have negative attitudes toward handicapped children or resent their intrusion. The same may be true for parents of nonhandicapped children. In addition, mainstreaming requires a technology of teaching that has not yet been adequately developed. Often the discrepancy in skill levels of handicapped and nonhandicapped children makes planning meaningful activities for all children difficult. Sometimes mainstreaming has been accomplished by "dumping" handicapped children into regular environments without adequate planning and preparation, creating negative attitudes in everyone.

Integration of handicapped and nonhandicapped youngsters should still be attempted, despite the barriers. As Safford and Rosen (1981) suggest, "mainstreaming means providing experiences most likely to ensure that handicapped children can realize maximum potential for full participation in society and independence of functioning" (p. 3). Without classroom experiences mainstreaming outside the classroom environment may not occur.

Implementing Integration

Mainstreaming handicapped preschoolers is no easy task. Several authors such as Blacher-Dixon, Leonard, and Turnbull (1981, p. 236) have suggested general guidelines to increase the likelihood of successful integration. They conclude that several elements are critical to successful early integration: physical and cognitive adaptation of the classroom to incorporate handicapped children, provision of multisensory learning stimuli and experiences, incorporation of child strengths and weaknesses in the development of curriculum, promotion of peer tolerance and acceptance of all children, some focus on independence and exploration of the environment, and promotion of social interaction. Adequate teacher preparation is also essential and should address attitudinal as well as instructional concerns.

In other chapters we discuss, in detail, strategies for facilitating integration. Chapter 4 addressed peer imitation and described strategies for increasing the likelihood of appropriate imitation. Chapter 11 addresses strategies and issues in facilitating social interaction between handicapped and nonhandicapped preschoolers. Environmental provisions of mainstreaming can also be made. Cohen, Beer, Kidera, and Golden (1979) have developed a comprehensive set of design principles to plan mainstreamed environments. These principles suggest critical environmental factors and characteristics of settings to facilitate attainment of mainstreaming goals.

1   *Settings that are not noticeably different.* When it is necessary to make changes in school environments to accommodate handicapped children, the modified spaces and equipment should be usable by, and attractive to, all people (p. 31).
2   *Common entry and circulation.* A common entry for all students that is part of a circulation system should be usable by all children and connect the entire school building (p. 33).
3   *Linked activity areas.* Cluster regular and exceptional activity zones to link them conceptually as well as physically. Eliminate the necessity for children to move through long, undistinguished corridors (p. 34).
4   *Orderliness and consistency.* School environments should be orderly and consistent. However, environments should neither confuse exceptional children nor be too subdued for regular children (p. 35).
5   *Repetition and multiple coding.* Develop a learning environment rich with information for all the senses. Multiply code spaces and objects by color, shape, and texture; use repetition of cues and elements to help children grasp concepts and ideas; and learn to generalize (p. 37).
6   *Public display of accomplishments.* Provide places and times where good work and other accomplishments can be displayed and discussed (p. 39).
7   *Individual work areas within larger settings.* Places appropriate in scale for use by one child or a child and teacher should be created within the regular classroom (p. 40).
8   *Resource rooms for all children.* Provide instructional materials and apparatus in resource rooms useful to all children. The process of moving handicapped children to regular classrooms from resource rooms could then occasionally be reversed (p. 41).
9   *Manipulable settings.* Allow children to manipulate and make decisions about their own environment (p. 43).
10 *Predictable settings and events.* Some children must know what to expect from a situation before entering and abruptly encountering a change in activity and behavior. Maintain a degree of consistency and predictability in identification and orientation of rooms (p. 45).
11 *Retreat areas.* Small, sheltered spaces should be provided adjacent to the regular activity areas. These spaces allow children to temporarily separate themselves from the larger group to obtain relief from potential failure, anxiety, or overstimulation. The spaces should maintain some physical and conceptual connection with the activity setting (p. 46).
12 *Places for informal socialization.* Provide "informal" territories for spontaneous interactions among children (p. 48).
13 *Range of environmental stimuli.* A rich, stimulating environment can benefit the basic abilities of all children, especially if such stimuli are direct and meaningful and used to express the nature of environment. Ensure a range of stimuli from simple, bold forms with a limited message to a place filled with sounds, smells, and textures (p. 51).
14 *Settings for simultaneous activities.* Allow for different activities, including exceptional education, to occur simultaneously within regular classrooms (p. 52).
15 *Barrier-free design.* All children should be able to easily move from one area of the room to another (p. 54).
16 *Variety of teaching areas.* Within each

school, provide a range of sizes of teaching areas. In addition to large classrooms, provide smaller spaces for groups or intimate areas for individual instruction (p. 56).

17 *Personal territory and self-expression.* Provide opportunities to claim and maintain personal "territory" or objects to be recognized as belonging to particular individuals (p. 58).

These principles are not applicable to mainstreamed environments alone. They represent a conglomeration of ideas and practices appropriate for all children, and should facilitate successful integration because of the attention paid to each child.

Effects of Integration

Many other factors influence the effects of integrating handicapped and nonhandicapped children. These include the number and type of children involved, the severity of the handicaps, the ages and developmental levels of the children, the goals of the program, and the training of the teachers. Because of the diversity of influencing factors, considerable research is needed before we can predict which type of program will be best for facilitating the development of given handicapped children (Guralnick, 1981). Nonetheless, several general statements about the effects of integration can be made.

Simply mixing handicapped and nonhandicapped children will not ensure social interactions or imitation between members of the two groups. Social interactions must be planned (Guralnick, 1978). The severity of a child's handicap is also correlated with the amount of social interaction with nonhandicapped children. The more severe the handicap, the lower the percentage of social interactions with nonhandicapped children (Guralnick, 1981). In addition, the more severe the handicap the less the child will likely benefit from integration.

Another effect is that in structured skill development (i.e., intentional integration) programs, handicapped and nonhandicapped children usually make developmental gains (Cooke, Ruskus, Apolloni, & Peck, 1981; Fredericks, Baldwin, Grove, Moore, Riggs, &

Lyons, 1978; Guralnick, 1976). In some cases the developmental gains of handicapped children are equal to or greater than gains made by similarly handicapped children in segregated programs; the gains made by nonhandicapped children in integrated programs may not necessarily be greater than those made by nonhandicapped children in segregated programs, however (Cooke et al. 1981). The relative benefit of integrated over segregated settings needs more research. In addition, teachers in integrated settings require training (Fredericks, et al., 1978; Tawney, 1981). Otherwise, the handicapped child will not receive the full benefit of the integrated program. In a 3-year study of the effects of integration, Cooke et al. (1981) found that handicapped children in the third year progressed more than other handicapped children in the first year of the study. This finding suggests that their teachers became increasingly skilled at integration. Some authors (e.g., Tawney, 1981) suggest that some regular teachers may not accept handicapped children in their programs. Others are more than willing, however. For example, Harlan and Leyser (1980) found that Head Start teachers offered more support to handicapped than to nonhandicapped children; differences were noted on factors such as the "amount of encouragement and approval . . ., promotion of independence . . ., guidance toward social interaction with peers . . ., and total verbal communication" (p. 291). Yet even in this study, emotionally disturbed children received more criticism and less encouragement than any other group. In their survey of regular teachers' attitudes, Stephens and Braun (1980) found that teachers in lower grades were more receptive to handicapped children, especially if they had had a number of courses in special education. All of these findings support the notion that although some teachers are willing to integrate handicapped children, they probably need training in implemention.

Still another result of integration is the finding that nonhandicapped children do not actively reject handicapped children (Guralnick, 1981). In addition, nonhandicapped children rarely acquire the maladaptive behaviors of their handicapped peers (Bricker & Bricker, 1973). Finally, they seem to adjust their communicative attempts to the developmental levels of the handicapped children (Guralnick, 1980; 1981).

Integrated environments appear to be desirable for many young handicapped children. However, considerable research is needed to specify the limits and long-term effects of integration. The effects of integration on the nonhandicapped children and severely handicapped children should also be addressed.

SUMMARY

The environment is a powerful tool for shaping behavior and should be carefully studied and manipulated as we attempt to provide the best possible services for young handicapped children. Many strategies can be used to help children learn. At one extreme teachers can simply provide an environment and let children learn what they can; at the other, teachers emphasize direct instruction of specific skills. Teachers of young handicapped children often spend much time toward the latter end of this continuum. In most instances such an approach is appropriate as many handicapped youngsters have physical, sensory, or cognitive impairments requiring a great deal of direct teaching. To the extent possible, however, we should encourage independent learning and functioning in all children.

This chapter addressed some initial considerations in designing environments. Further considerations in physical provisions and facilitating engagement will be discussed in the next two chapters.

REFERENCES

Alberto, P., Jobes, N., Sizemore, A., & Doran, D. A comparison of individual and group instruction across response tasks. *Journal of the Association for the Severely Handicapped,* 1980, *5,* 285–293.

Appleton, T., Clifton, R., & Goldberg, S. The development of behavioral competence in infancy. In F. Horowitz (Ed.), *Review of child development research.* Chicago: University of Chicago Press, 1975.

Apolloni, T., Cooke, S. A., & Cooke, T. P. Establishing a normal peer as a behavioral model for delayed toddlers. *Perceptual and Motor Skills,* 1977, *44,* 231–241.

Apolloni, T., & Cooke, T. P. Integrated programming at the infant, toddler, and preschool levels. In M. F.

Guralnick (Ed.), *Early intervention and the integration of handicapped and nonhandicapped children.* Baltimore: University Park Press, 1978.

Bailey, D. B., Clifford, R. M., & Harms, T. Comparison of preschool environments for handicapped and nonhandicapped children. *Topics in Early Childhood Special Education,* 1982, *2,* 9–20.

Baker, D. B. Applications of environmental psychology in programming for severely handicapped persons. *Journal of the Association for the Severely Handicapped,* 1980, *5,* 234–249.

Blacher-Dixon, J., Leonard, J., & Turnbull, A. P. Mainstreaming at the early childhood level: Current and future perspectives. *Mental Retardation,* 1981, *19,* 235–241.

Blank, M. Implicit assumption underlying preschool intervention programs. *Journal of Social Issues,* 1970, *26,* 15–33.

Bradley, R. H., & Caldwell, B. M. Relation of infant's home environments to mental test performance at fifty-four months: A follow-up study. *Child Development,* 1976, *47,* 1172–1174.

Bricker, D. D. A rationale for the integration of handicapped and nonhandicapped preschool children. In M. Guralnick (Ed.), *Early intervention and the integration of handicapped and nonhandicapped children.* Baltimore: University Park Press, 1978.

Bricker, D. D., & Bricker, W. A. *Infant, toddler, and preschool research and intervention project report: Year III IMRID Behavioral Science Monograph No. 23.* Nashville, Tenn.: Institute on Mental Retardation and Intellectual Development, George Peabody College, 1973.

Brown, F., Holvoet, J., Guess, D., & Mulligan, M. The individualized curriculum sequencing model (III): Small group instruction. *Journal of the Association for the Severely Handicapped,* 1980 *5,* 352–367.

Cohen, U., Beer, J., Kidera, E., & Golden, W. *Mainstreaming the handicapped: A design guide.* Milwaukee: Center of Architecture and Urban Planning Research, University of Wisconsin—Milwaukee, 1979.

Cooke, T. P., Ruskus, J. A., Apolloni, T., & Peck, C. A. Handicapped preschool children in the mainstream: Background, outcomes, and clinical suggestions. *Topics in Early Childhood Special Education,* 1981, *1*(1), 73–83.

DeVellis, R. F. Learned helplessness in institutions. *Mental Retardation,* 1977, *15*(5), 10–13.

Doke, L. A. The organization of day-care environments: Formal versus informal activities. *Child Care Quarterly,* 1975, *4,* 216–222.

Doke, L. A., & Risley, T. R. The organization of day-care environments: Required versus optional activities. *Journal of Applied Behavior Analysis,* 1972, *5,* 405–420.

Elardo, R., Bradley, R., & Caldwell, B. M. A longitudinal study of the relation of infants' home environments to language development at age three. *Child Development,* 1977, *48,* 595–603.

Elkind, D. *Child development and education: A Piagetian perspective.* New York: Oxford University Press, 1976.

Favell, J., Favell, J., & McGinsey, J. F. Relative effectiveness and efficiency of group vs. individual training of severely retarded persons. *American Journal of Mental Deficiency*, 1978, *83*, 104–109.

Forman, G. E., & Kuschner, D. S. *The child's construction of knowledge: Piaget for teaching children.* Monterrey, Ca.: Brooks/Cole, 1977.

Fowler, W. How adult-child ratios influence infant development. *Interchange*, 1975, *6*, 17–31.

Fredericks, H. D., Baldwin, V., Grove, D., Moore, W., Riggs, C., & Lyons, B. Integrating the moderately and severely handicapped preschool child into a normal day-care setting. In M. J. Guralnick (Ed.), *Early Intervention and the integration of handicapped and nonhandicapped children.* Baltimore: University Park Press, 1978.

Furman, W., Rahe, D. F., & Hartup, W. W. Rehabilitation of socially withdrawn preschool children through mixed-age and same-age socialization. *Child Development*, 1979, *50*, 915–922.

Ginsburg, H., & Opper, S. *Piaget's theory of intellectual development: An introduction.* Engelwood Cliffs, N. J.: Prentice-Hall, 1979.

Goldman, J. A. Social participation of children in same-versus mixed-age groups. *Child Development*, 1981, *52*, 644–650.

Graziano, W., French, D., Brownell, C. A., & Hartup, W. W. Peer interaction in same- and mixed-age triads in relation to chronological age and incentive condition. *Child Development*, 1976, *47*, 707–714.

Guralnick, M. J. The value of integrating handicapped and nonhandicapped preschool children. *American Journal of Orthopsychiatry*, 1976, *46*, 236–245.

Guralnick, M. J. *Early intervention and the integration of handicapped and nonhandicapped children.* Baltimore: University Park Press, 1978.

Guralnick, M. J. Social interactions among preschool children. *Exceptional Children*, 1980, *46*, 248–253.

Guralnick, M. J. The efficacy of integrating handicapped children in early education settings: Research implications. *Topics in Early Childhood Special Education*, 1981, *1*(1), 57–71.

Guralnick, M. J., & Paul-Brown, D. The nature of verbal and nonverbal interactions among handicapped and nonhandicapped preschool children. *Child Development*, 1977, *48*, 254–260.

Guralnick, M. J., & Paul-Brown, D. Functional and discourse analyses of nonhandicapped preschool children's speech to handicapped children. *American Journal of Mental Deficiency*, 1980, *84*, 444–454.

Harlan, J. D., & Leyser, Y. Head Start teachers' use of verbal encouragement. *Exceptional Children*, 1980, *46*, 290–292.

Harms, T., & Clifford, R. M. *Early childhood environment rating scale.* New York: Teachers College Press, 1980.

Harms, T., & Cross, L. *Environmental provisions in day care.* Chapel Hill: Frank Porter Graham Child Development Center, University of North Carolina, 1977.

Hart, B. So that teachers can teach: Assigning roles and responsibilities. *Topics in Early Childhood Special Education*, 1982, *2*(1), 1–8.

Hartup, W. W. Cross-age vs. same-age peer interactions: Ethological and cross-cultural perspectives. In V.

Allen (Ed.), *Children as tutors: Theory and research on tutoring.* New York: Academic Press, 1976.

Hohmann, M., Banet, B., & Weikart, D. P. *Young children in action: A manual for preschool educators.* Ypsilanti, Mich.: High/Scope Educational Research Foundation, 1979.

Huston-Stein, A., Friedrich-Cofer, L., & Susman, E. J. The relation of classroom structure to social behavior, imaginative play, and self-regulation of economically disadvantaged children. *Child Development*, 1977, *48*, 908–916.

Hutt, C., & Vlazey, M. J. Differential effects of group density on social behavior. *Nature*, 1966, *209*, 1371–1372.

Ittelson, W., Proshansky, H., Rivlin, L., & Winkel, G. *An introduction to environmental psychology.* New York: Holt, Rinehart & Winston, 1974.

Johnson, J. E., Ershler, J., & Bell, C. Play behavior in a discovery-based and a formal-education preschool program. *Child Development*, 1980, *21*, 271–274.

Kamii, C., & DeVries, R. Piaget for early education. In M. C. Day and R. K. Parker (Eds.), *The preschool in action: Exploring early childhood programs* (2nd ed.). Boston: Allyn and Bacon, 1977.

Kamii, C., & DeVries, R. *Physical knowledge in preschool education: Implications of Piaget's theory.* Englewood Cliffs, N.J.: Prentice-Hall, 1978.

Kaufman, M. J., Gottlieb, J., Agard, J. S., & Kukic, M. B. Mainstreaming: Toward an explanation of the construct. *Exceptional Children*, 1975, *7*, 1–12.

Keith, K. D. Behavior analysis and the principle of normalization. *AAESPH Review*, 1979, *4*, 148–151.

Kenowitz, L., Zweibel, S., & Edgar, G. Determining the least restrictive educational opportunity. In N. G. Haring & D. D. Bricker (Eds.), *Teaching the severely handicapped* (Vol. III). Columbus, Ohio: Special Press, 1979.

Konner, M. Relations among infants and juveniles in comparative perspective. In M. Lewis & L. A. Rosenblum (Eds.), *Friendship and peer relations.* New York: Wiley, 1975.

Krantz, P., & Risley, T. R. Behavior ecology in the classroom. In K. D. O'Leary and S. O'Leary (Eds.), *Classroom management: The successful use of behavior modification.* New York: Permagon Press, 1977.

Kreger, K. C. Compensatory environment programming for the severely retarded behaviorally disturbed. *Mental Retardation*, 1971, *9*, 29–33.

LeLaurin, K., & Risley, T. R. The organization of day-care environments: "Zone" versus "man-to-man" staff assignments. *Journal of Applied Behavior Analysis*, 1972, *5*, 225–232.

Lougee, M. D., Grueneich, R., and Hartup, W. W. Social interaction in same- and mixed-age dyads of preschool children. *Child Development*, 1977, *48*, 1353–1361.

O'Connor, M. The nursery school environment. *Developmental Psychology*, 1975, *11*, 556–561.

Olds, A. R. Designing developmentally optimal classrooms for children with special needs. In S. J. Meisels (Ed.), *Special education and development: Perspectives on young children with special needs.* Baltimore: University Park Press, 1979.

Peck, C. A., Apolloni, T., Cooke, T. P., & Raver, S. A. Teaching retarded preschoolers to imitate the free-play behavior of nonretarded classmates: Trained and generalized effects. *Journal of Special Education*, 1978, *12*, 195–207.

Piaget, J. *The origins of intelligence in children.* New York: International Univerities Press, 1952.

Piaget, J. *Play, dreams, and imitation in childhood.* New York: Norton, 1963.

Risley, T. *Research on day-care environments.* Paper presented at Frank Porter Graham Child Development Center, University of North Carolina, July, 1981.

Rogers-Warren, A., & Wedel, J. W. The ecology of preschool classrooms for the handicapped. *New Directions for Exceptional Children*, 1980, *1*, 1–24.

Safford, P. L., & Rosen, L. A. Mainstreaming: Application of a philosophical perspective in an integrated kindergarten program. *Topics in Early Childhood Education*, 1981, *1*, 1–10.

Seligman, M. E. P. *Helplessness: On depression, development, and death.* San Francisco: W. H. Freeman, 1975.

Seigel, R. K. Stimulus selection and tracking during urination: Autoshaping directed behavior with toilet targets. *Journal of Applied Behavior Analysis*, 1977, *10*, 255–265.

Skinner, B. F. *Science and human behavior.* New York: Free Press, 1953.

Stephens, T. M., & Braun, B. L. Measures of regular classroom teachers' attitudes toward handicapped children. *Exceptional Children*, 1980, *46*, 292–294.

Storm, R. H., & Willis, J. H. Small group training as an alternative to individual programs for profoundly retarded persons. *American Journal of Mental Deficiency*, 1978, *83*, 283–288.

Suomi, S. J., and Harlow, H. F. Social rehabilitation of isolate-reared monkeys. *Developmental Psychology*, 1972, *6*, 487–496.

Tawney, J. W. A cautious view of mainstreaming in early education. *Topics in Early Childhood Special Education*, 1981, *1*(1), 25–36.

Voeltz, L. Children's attitudes toward handicapped peers. *American Journal of Mental Deficiency*, 1980, *84*, 455–465.

Wachs, T. Proximal experience and early cognitive-intellectual development: The physical environment. *Merrill-Palmer Quarterly*, 1979, *25*, 3–41.

Weisler, A., & McCall, R. B. Exploration and play: Resume and redirection. *American Psychologist*, 1976, *31*, 492–508.

Wolfensberger, W. *The principles of normalization in human services.* Toronto: National Institute on Mental Retardation, 1972.

Physical space and materials can have a significant impact on people and their behavior (Holahan, 1978; Ittelson, Proshansky, Rivlin, & Winkel, 1974; Stokols, 1976). Holahan (1978) reports that Winston Churchill once remarked, "First we shape our buildings and afterwards our buildings shape us" (p. 1). Farbstein and Kantrowitz (1978) also make the following observation:

Places are not just rooms, buildings, or outdoor spaces, but total environments made up of physical space together with people, furnishings, machines, and actions. Places form the settings for all the significant—and insignificant—events of our lives. More than just containers, they are living, changing systems which support or hinder our actions, please or disturb our emotions (p. 1).

Recent research has demonstrated numerous positive outcomes of enriching previously unstimulating environments for handicapped persons. Levy and McLeod (1977) observed the behavior of severely and profoundly retarded young adults in a dayroom before and after the room was "enriched." Enrichment consisted of room dividers, carpets, a large gross motor apparatus, and "learning booths" housing special activities such as manipulable light switches, a pulley system, a sound-activated light box, and a subject-activated music booth. Enrichment reduced neutral or stereotyped activity and increased appropriate play, resident-resident social play, and aide-resident social and training interactions. Horner (1980) conducted a similar study in the day room of a living unit for profoundly retarded children. Enrichment consisted of placing a large number of toys and objects in the dayroom. After enrichment, a higher incidence of adaptive object-directed behavior and fewer instances of self-directed maladaptive behavior (i.e., self-injurious or stereotypic) were observed.

Clearly, the physical environment can be used to change or encourage certain behaviors in handicapped children. In this chapter, we will discuss considerations in planning the physical space in preschool settings for handicapped children. Spatial arrangement, general considerations in designing activity areas, and specific considerations in setting up age-specific activity areas will be addressed. Although we attempt to provide a data base for suggestions, minimal research has been conducted on appropriate environments for young handicapped children.

6

Designing Preschool Environments: Physical Space and Materials

ARRANGING THE PHYSICAL SPACE

Space and materials within a room can be arranged in many ways. The ideal space allows the teacher to observe ongoing activities in the classroom and yet reduces distractions across activity areas. The space should be functional, comfortable, and safe for both children and adults. Finally, the space should be designed to encourage and facilitate maximum independence for children with sensory or motor impairments.

Open Space Design

Most early childhood educators who work with nonhandicapped children currently advocate an open space design for preschool classrooms. Unlike open education, which is an approach to teaching and learning focusing on self-directed learning, *open-space* refers to a large room without walls or high dividers (Rogers-Warren & Wedel, 1980). Open space architecture can be used with either an open or highly structured approach to early education. It can facilitate both staff supervision of children and children's movement to different activities and provide a context for development of care routines.

Twardosz, Cataldo, and Risley (1974) investigated the effect of an open space design on infant and toddler day-care. A large room was separated by low dividers such as shelves. The experimenters used partitions to examine the effects of open or closed classroom designs on the visibility and supervision of children and staff, infant and toddler sleep patterns, and toddler preacademic activities (puzzles, beads, coloring). The studies demonstrated that an open environment made supervision much easier because it increased the amount of time a child could be seen by an adult, and staff persons by the supervisor; moderate levels of noise, light, and visibility of center activities had no adverse effects on the sleep patterns of infants and toddlers; and engagement in preacademic tasks was similar in both an open environment and in a separate room. The authors concluded that infant and toddler day-care "definitely can and should be accomplished in an open environment" (p. 544).

Lining the walls with furniture and materials and leaving an empty area in the middle is not good use of open space, however. As Danoff, Breitbart, and Barr (1977) suggest, such a "child-sized toy cafeteria" (p. 60) may encourage children to keep moving from one activity to another without concentrating or becoming involved.

Another misuse of open space is encircling all activity areas with bookcases, storage units, or other furniture. Olds (1979) suggests that such an arrangement would make children "feel somewhat like rats in a maze, following defined pathways into enclosed, discrete boxes" (p. 109). Olds advocates increased use of *fluid* boundaries for some areas of the room. Examples of fluid boundaries include raising the floor level of an area; changing the level of the ceiling through use of canopies, streamers or mobiles; creating a "pit" with low carpeted risers to enclose a space, or painting the work surfaces, display units and dividers so that activity areas are defined by particular colors. An open space classroom should be attractively arranged into clearly differentiated, easily accessible activity areas, with sufficient dividers or boundaries to increase engagement but enough openness to allow ease of movement and adult supervision.

The appropriateness of open space design for handicapped preschoolers has yet to be empirically demonstrated. Although it has a great deal of inherent appeal, many special educators would argue that handicapped children are too distractable and that open spaces would increase hyperactivity and stereotypic behavior. A limited number of studies have addressed these issues (Gardner, Cromwell, & Foshee, 1959; Tizard, 1968; Frankel, Freeman, Ritvo, & Pardo, 1978; Adams, Tallon, & Stangl, 1980), and data suggest that, to some extent, environmental stimulation does control hyperactive and stereotypic behavior. The degree and direction of the effect depends upon the individual and the type of stimulation. Although there are no guidelines for determining appropriate levels of stimulation, Olds (1979) suggests that physical settings providing moderate levels of sensory stimulation are usually more comfortable than over- or under-arousing levels.

The safest and perhaps most ethical approach is to initially assume that the environment for a handicapped youngster should be similar to that for a nonhandicapped child. If certain aspects of the environment are subsequently suspected to be detrimental to behavior, the teacher can systematically change aspects of it to determine where the problem lies. As Keith (1979) suggests, we should seek to provide an environment that is least restrictive yet most effective for the child.

Making Space Comfortable

Olds (1979) mentions *variety* and *richness* as important in environmental planning. These can be provided by intentional variation of dimensions such as scale, floor height, ceiling height, boundary height, visual interest, auditory interest, olfactory interest, textural interest, and kinesthetic interest. Brophy, Good & Nedler (1975) suggest that the floor should be carpeted since many activities take place there. The classroom space should have good lighting, adequate ventilation and temperature control, ample storage space, and effective sound absorption.

Appropriate furnishings are also important. Child-sized furniture, including tables, chairs, and toilets should be provided. (A child-sized chair is one in which the child may sit and have his or her feet on the floor.) Each child should have a personal space, no matter how small. The locker, shelf or cubby should be easily accessible and labeled with a name card and a photograph to help the child begin to recognize his or her name. If cubbies or lockers are too expensive or unavailable, use labeled dishpans, round ice cream containers, or large shoe boxes (Harms & Cross, 1977).

Another strategy for making space comfortable is the use of child-centered displays. Bailey, Clifford, and Harms (1982) found that child-centered displays for handicapped preschoolers rarely included the children's own work. Display of children's work can be a basis for language interaction ("Tell me about this"), esteem-building ("You did that"), or comparisons ("Look, the one you made today is a different color"). Displays can also remind children of the theme or concept (e.g., animals) being emphasized during a given time period. Commercial materials and teacher-made displays facilitate some of the same functions,

so perhaps a balance between child-produced and teacher-made/commercial displays can be reached.

Keep several factors in mind when designing and planning displays. When you set them up, consider each child's eye level. This may be complex in programs for the handicapped, as eye level may vary considerably—some children are in wheelchairs, others may only crawl, still others might be unusually small. Vary the levels of display to meet the childrens' needs. Also, display each child's work, regardless of the quality. Progress will be reflected as skills are developed. Materials should be changed frequently, with the display being related to the subjects currently discussed.

Comfort considerations should not just be limited to children. The adults in the environment should also be comfortable. Regular furniture and a bathroom and lounge, an adult meeting area, and personal storage spaces should be separate from the children (Harms & Clifford, 1980).

SETTING UP ACTIVITY AREAS

One of the keys to designing a preschool environment is the effective establishment of activity areas or centers. *Activity areas* are spaces within the room designed to accommodate different types of activities for children and adults. Activities range from one-to-one tutoring or small group instruction to independent undertakings such as blocks, toy play, or art. Hildebrand (1975) suggests that organized space can serve as a stimulus for certain activities. Children can use the centers to learn how different behaviors are expected in various settings and how one changes behavior to meet changing demands.

Selecting Activity Areas

Room arrangement should provide an appropriate balance of activity areas suited to the age, skills, and interests of the children. The room should be designed to fit the routine; for example, if many structured lessons are concurrently conducted, several activity areas with tables and chairs may be needed. Such a design will limit the number of activity centers, so spread the structured lessons out over the morning, providing variety in activity centers designed for independent use and skill generalization.

Harms and Cross (1977) suggest that by age 3, most children can manage an environment with a wide variety of activity areas. However, little data exist on the ability of handicapped preschoolers to respond to a large number of choices. It may be more appropriate to provide a smaller number of activity areas and focus on advanced skill development in those areas.

In any case, several activity areas should be included in any preschool program: blocks, dramatic play, art, manipulative toys, reading/language and sensory stimulation. At least six types of activity areas should be provided in a preschool for handicapped children: a quiet, calm area, a structured materials/activities area, a crafts and discovery area, a dramatic play area, a large motor area, and a therapeutic area (Olds, 1979).

Arranging Activity Areas

Placement of activity areas within a classroom can affect the amount of use an area receives and also the level of child engagement. Brophy, Good, and Nedler (1975, pp. 140–142) suggest the following guidelines for arranging activity centers:

1 Classroom traffic should be minimized and should flow freely. Controlling traffic patterns reduces safety problems such as jostling and bumping along with wasted time. Efficient traffic management requires storing materials and equipment near the areas they will be needed, avoiding cross traffic, and suggesting routes for travel.
2 Consider the noise levels typically generated in a given activity center when determining its placement in the classroom. For example, the small group lesson area should not be located next to noisy activities such as the block/construction area or the role playing/make-believe area. Centers requiring concentration, such as the book area, should also be in quieter places in the room.
3 Consider lighting when locating classroom areas. Areas requiring close, visually demanding activities should be placed near windows or lights.

Promoting Independent Use of Activity Areas

As teachers, we want children to use centers independently. This means appropriate manipulation of materials and returning them where they belong when finished. Lack of these skills frequently keeps children from using centers and prompts many people to suggest that they are inappropriate for handicapped children. Although many handicapped preschoolers have difficulty with these skills, several environmental manipulations can be incorporated so they can be learned.

Direct teaching within a given activity area may be necessary. This may involve a combination of shaping and fading strategies designed to teach independent use of materials. Or a competent peer model may be a more appropriate strategy. Simply providing a competent peer model may be insufficient, however. The model may have to provide instructions/suggestions or reinforce the target child for appropriate imitation of modeled behavior. Detailed strategies for encouraging independent use of activity centers are described in Chapter 7.

Display and Storage of Materials

How materials are displayed and stored may affect their use and replacement. A neat, straight, and clean center is more likely to invite use and prompt replacement.

Display and visibility of materials are critical and must stimulate the child's interest. Numerous classrooms for handicapped children have closed or empty shelves or materials stored out of reach. Access is provided by the adults. The rationale for this practice is that handicapped children do not know how to make choices, select materials, or appropriately use the items. Although this may initially be true, children need to learn appropriate use by experimentation with materials and activities.

Store large items such as blocks or trucks on open shelves; place small items such as beads, cubes, or crayons in containers. Montes and Risley (1975) compared the use of shelves versus toy boxes for storing and display of materials. They found that storing manipulative toys in boxes increased the amount of time children spent selecting toys, thus reducing actual play. No difference was observed in the amount of time spent cleaning up when using either shelves or boxes. These data suggest the use of open shelves to increase the amount of time for meaningful engagement with materials.

Accessibility is a major consideration. Materials that are easy to take out and store are more likely to be used and returned than less accessible items. Materials that get dirty, such as paint brushes, are more likely to be cleaned if the sink is next to the art area than if it is on the other side of the room.

An organized center that clearly indicates to children where materials belong is important. Visible storage and display are necessary for many exceptional children who need "unambiguous physical surroundings for orientation and limit settings" (Olds, 1979, p. 116). Clearly label shelves to ensure proper placement of items. The level of representation used in labeling will depend upon the developmental level of the children. For some advanced children working on beginning reading skills, the shelves can be labeled with words or can pair words with pictures. For others, pictures or symbols alone may be more appropriate.

SETTING UP SPECIFIC ACTIVITY AREAS

Each activity area should be carefully planned and organized to meet the needs of the children using it. This requires a knowledge of the functions a given activity fulfills for children of different ages; an awareness of available materials; and the ability to plan, organize, and structure the center so it will maximally benefit all children.

Block Area

Block areas can provide opportunities to learn numerous scientific concepts (height, size, weight, etc.) and problem-solving, along with appropriate outlets for aggressive behaviors such as banging items or knocking down constructions. They can also encourage dramatic play, social interaction and cooperation, and language development. In addition, blocks facilitate muscle and eye-hand coordination, and offer a set of multisensory experiences.

The occurrence of these behaviors depends upon both the ability of the children and the teacher's planning and organization.

Block-building is an activity nearly all children enjoy. The materials are simple and can be used in many different ways from infancy to the early primary grades. Children can learn by chewing, crawling over, or dropping and banging blocks; they can also decide how many short blocks equal the same distance as three long blocks.

Block-building is a noisy activity, and thus should be located away from activities requiring concentration. It is often placed next to the housekeeping area which is also noisy. A carpet (flat nap) may be helpful in reducing the sound. Frost and Kissinger (1976) suggest that the block area be kept away from animal cages since the blocks might injure or the noise frighten the pets.

Solid wooden unit blocks and larger hollow blocks are generally found in activity centers. Each type has advantages and both should be provided. The solid unit blocks are good for small scale construction and are useful in learning "scientific" concepts, since they are carefully designed to be mathematically proportionate to one another. The large hollow blocks are better for dramatic play or role playing; children can actually create new environments to act out certain parts. Place large and small blocks in separate areas as they are used in different ways. When the two are combined, children may be less likely to appreciate the mathematical properties of the smaller units (Olds, 1979).

A sufficient number of materials in any activity area is important. Bender (1978) found that when a small number of blocks (20) were available, only one or two children used them for construction. Little cooperative conversation was observed; most comments by children were directed toward another child in an effort to maintain control of the available blocks. When the number of available blocks was increased to 70, more children were able to be actively involved in the building process and conversation primarily centered on the ongoing play rather than competition for the available blocks. Although the teachers had to settle many disputes when children were playing with 20 blocks, no disputes were observed with 70. Bender suggests that 60—80 blocks should be provided in any large area designed to accommodate more than two or three children.

A block-building area is incomplete without additional toys for children to use during constructive and dramatic play. These toys should at least include vehicles such as cars, trucks, or airplanes, as well as figures of people and animals.

Housekeeping/Dramatic Play Areas

Another activity area found in almost every preschool allows children to act out real life roles. Frequently this area takes the shape of a housekeeping center, with props such as a stove, sink, refrigerator, table, pots and pans, dishes, and so forth. Providing the opportunity for dramatic play assists children in learning and practicing appropriate societal roles, allows them to explore various roles, encourages cooperative behavior among children, and gives them a chance to apply language skills. Brophy, Good, and Nedler (1975), viewing dramatic play from more of an "inner" perspective, suggest such activity can "help a child to fulfill some of his wishes symbolically, to work through some of his fears and negative emotions, and to reduce egocentrism by allowing him to assume the perspectives of persons other than himself" (p. 137). Some of these processes are readily inferred from observing any dramatic play setting, when children become parents, teachers, or assume other community roles they have observed.

Because dramatic play is a noisy activity the area should be located in an appropriate section of the room. Many teachers place the dramatic play area next to the blocks. Dramatic play furnishings should never be lined up against a wall; a small enclosed space more closely approximates a room and facilitates fantasy (Olds, 1979). A loft area, appropriately enclosed to ensure safety, may be ideal for such activity. Unless a ramp is available or the teacher is willing to lift children, however, a loft may not be appropriate for a classroom with many physically disabled children. If it is present and used, children should never be denied access to this area because of a physical impairment. This might lead to increased feelings of rejection, isolation, and incompetence. Take appropriate safety precautions when getting children to the loft, such as lifting them in such a way to prevent back injury. Visually impaired children may also need to be closely supervised in a loft, but they too must learn to deal with different environmental structures. Climbing can provide a confidence-building experience that will hopefully facilitate general mobility around the classroom and community.

Although children do not need extensive props to participate in dramatic play activities, consider the nature and variety of materials and equipment. Factors include children's previous experience with a given setting or role, interests and needs of the children, and any themes or concepts currently being emphasized. For example, nearly all children can relate to a housekeeping area. Appropriate materials for housekeeping include dress-up clothes (men's and women's), dolls, kitchen equipment, utensils, brooms and mops, doll furniture, doll clothes, clay or other material for making "food," and recycled real-life materials such as a telephone. A full-length mirror is important so children can see how they look in different garments. Other possible props include a bed, pillows, tablecloths, and napkins.

The housekeeping materials should be supplemented by items that encourage dramatic play in other areas such as work or adventure (Harms & Clifford, 1980). One such setting is a store where children select and purchase items at a checkout counter. A variety of props should allow children to change the type of store (food for grocery store, books or magazines for bookstore, etc.). Other props and clothing for various familiar occupations are a fire hat, a police badge, or a doctor's stethoscope.

Although some stability or favorite materials are probably desirable, make provisions for varying dramatic play materials in accordance with current classroom themes or recent experiences. For example, if the group recently went on a field trip to a restaurant, make props such as a chef's hat, menus, or aprons available.

Some children will be able to take full advantage of dramatic play. Others, however, will need teacher assistance. Perspective taking is an advanced cognitive attainment that many young retarded children may not be able to understand. However, they can still enjoy dressing up or participating in dramatic play. The teacher may need to encourage the child to participate, suggest ways to become involved, or actually help the child put on clothes or begin to set up. The early childhood literature suggests teachers should observe dramatic play unobtrusively and intervene only when there is a problem or when it is important to expand upon a child-initiated theme or concept. With young handicapped children, however, the teacher may need to take a more active role. The teacher can become a participant in the center, acting as an appropriate role model and encouraging and facilitating participation as necessary. Such participation suggests teachers should dress casually and comfortably.

Sand/Water Play Areas

Sand and water play fulfills a number of important functions. It can be an excellent sensory experience, giving children the opportunity to feel and manipulate various textures of materials. Such activity facilitates what Piaget (1963) refers to as physical knowledge by providing children experience with shape, weight, and quantity. Sand or water play is also enjoyable, particularly for younger children. As with blocks and dramatic play, it can provide a setting that allows numerous opportunities for role playing, social interactions, and the development of language skills.

Sand and water areas are most appropriately placed near a sink and water faucet to encourage easy access and clean-up. A noncarpeted surface is preferable (although not essential) since some spilling is likely to occur. Children should wear plastic aprons to avoid getting wet.

The best apparatus for sand and water play is a table on locking wheels that has a drain. This type of table can be moved outdoors when the weather is suitable, and also eases the problem of dumping a heavy tub of water. If such a table is not available, any number of alternatives may be used: a plastic basin, a large tub, or a small animal feeding trough.

Although sand and water are typical substances, many other materials may also be used in setting up such an activity area. For example, a tub full of coarse salt, macaroni noodles, shells, and dried beans of different

colors is appealing to young children and provides a different set of textures. Other possibilities include leaves, sawdust, and styrofoam packing materials. Very young children should be supervised when using these materials, however, to prevent eating or choking on them. Changing tub activities prevents boredom and provides the opportunity to experience a variety of textures. A typical week in the "tub" center might include the following: Monday—water, Tuesday—sand, Wednesday—water with food coloring, Thursday—beans and noodles, and Friday—water with soap suds.

Supplementary materials are important for expanding the sensory feedback from sand and water play. Appropriate materials include cans, sponges, shovels, various floating and sinking objects, boats, mixers, beaters, funnels, squeeze bottles, straws, and buckets. Supplementary materials can also be tied to any concepts or themes being emphasized in the classroom. If a unit on the farm is being presented, small plastic farm animals can encourage generalization of concepts. If some children are working on the color red, all the materials could be red or red food coloring could be placed in the water.

A wide range of objectives may be addressed through guided sand and water play. Children beginning to develop object permanence can be taught to locate objects partially or completely hidden under sand or beans. Children with poor motor coordination can learn to dig, lift, and pour. Older children can be taught to make comparisons using volume and measurement concepts such as empty, full, more, less, and same. Means-ends behavior such as tool use can be taught by using cups and water or spoons and sand.

Sand and water play are appropriate activities for most handicapped youngsters. Physically impaired children may need special modification of the table to allow for a wheelchair or may need to have the table raised so a prone board may be propped up against it or lowered so a child on a wedge may use it. Some handicapped children may initially resist sand and water play because the sensory stimulation is aversive. Getting these children to actively participate in and enjoy sand and water play would be a major teaching accomplishment. A shaping strategy of gradually reinforcing successive approximations to sand and water play may be necessary.

Art and Crafts Areas

Art activities provide the opportunity for creative expression; practice of fine and perceptual motor skills; and the application of language concepts relating to form, shape, color, texture, and spatial relationships. The art area allows children to create products or materials to be used in other activity areas; for example, a sign for the store or a menu for the restaurant.

The art area should be located in a noncarpeted area near a sink to ease the clean-up process. Children should wear smocks to avoid getting clothes wet or stained.

The materials to be included in an art and crafts area will vary, depending upon the age and developmental levels of the children. Harms (1972) suggests the following age-appropriate activities for inclusion in the art area:

18 Months–2½ Years: The child at this age needs simple drawing materials like a soft, thick lead pencil; easel paints in 2 or 3 colors,....
2½–3½ Years: The child at this age should have available varied drawing materials including crayons and felt pens; an expanded number of colors as his experience with painting develops; varied sizes and shapes of paper and varied brush sizes; and activities involving finger-painting, clay, and salt-flour dough.
3½–4½ Years: Drawing materials should be expanded to include: paint sticks and wet chalk; very large paper and varied size brushes; art activities should include watercolor painting, collage, construction-sculpture, stringing activities, carpentry, sand-casting, salt-flour dough mixing from picture recipe, as the child seems ready for these experiences.
4½–5½ Years: Art activities that demand more technical skill should be introduced, such as stitchery, mosaics, and simple block-printing. All the basic two- and three-dimensional materials should be included (Harms, 1972, p. 97).

These suggestions may need to be modified depending upon the severity and type of handicapping conditions in a given classroom.

Store materials in an open display shelf to encourage independent use. Some materials should already be set up when children arrive. For example, paper should be on the easels, paints opened and placed on easels, and newspaper or other protective covering on the floor. To avoid competition, either have several small containers or one large container of materials available (Harms, 1972). For example, arguments will arise over only one box of crayons. Such conflicts can be avoided by making several boxes available or keeping plenty of crayons for everyone in a large box or tub. Only nontoxic paints and materials should be provided.

The degree of planning and structure in the art center will depend upon the developmental level of the children. Some handicapped children will not know how to use any of the materials (paintbrushes, crayons, scissors) and may not learn through simply observing others. The teacher may need to take an active role in instructing basic art area skills, perhaps by frequent repetition of the same type of activity (but using different materials) and initial physical manipulation of the child's hands to assist in performing a skill. An example of equipment used in teaching a child to cut is displayed in Figure 6.1. These scissors have the usual two holes for the child's fingers and an additional two holes for the teacher's fingers. Initially the teacher will do all of the cutting; the child's fingers are in the holes, however, and he or she begins to experience the movements required for cutting. Gradually the teacher performs fewer motor movements and allows the child to do more, until the child becomes independent. A similar process of fading teacher assistance can be incorporated with other materials such as crayons or paintbrushes.

Adaptations of materials, procedures, and expectations may need to be made for some physically handicapped children. Paintbrush handles can be built up with tape or other material to facilitate handling by children with motor impairments. Other children may need to paint holding the brush in the mouth, with the toes, or perhaps even using a device strapped to the head (a head-pointing device).

FIGURE 6.1
Double-holed scissors used
in teaching

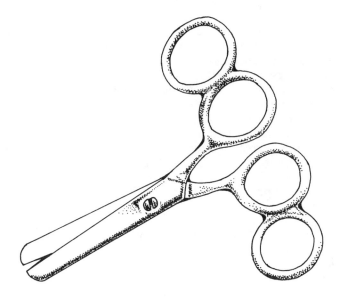

Reading/Language Areas

The reading/language arts area gives children the opportunity to relax, be quiet, and be exposed to books and other language stimulation materials. Since reading requires concentration, the reading/language area should be located in a quiet section of the room, perhaps next to the small group instructional area. A well-lighted area is essential.

The furnishings in the language center should be inviting and encourage relaxation and quiet involvement. The area should be carpeted and should contain furniture conducive to the intended activities, such as a table, bean bag and other comfortable chairs, and at least one child-sized rocking chair. Display books on an open rack with covers clearly visible at the child's height. Books that are stacked on the shelf are difficult for the child to select and may not be returned to their proper place as there is no obvious empty space.

The selection of books for this area should be a function of the age and developmental level of children as well as the relationship of materials to current topics included in the preschool program. Examples of current topics include concept units such as animals or things to ride, holidays such as Thanksgiving or Halloween, or special events such as an upcoming trip to the fire station. Small photo albums with children's pictures from past

field trips or other special days may facilitate remembering events and generate talking. Such planning can facilitate skill generalization by exposing children to concepts in a wide variety of contexts and by stimulating language experiences. Although a few favorite books should always be kept in the center, rotation of materials will maintain interest.

Brophy, Good, and Nedler (1975) suggest providing two or more copies of popular books to reduce arguments. Duplicate copies may also facilitate discussion among children as well as noting and matching pictures on similar pages.

Materials other than books should be included in the reading/language area. Some possibilities include a language master, a tape player, a flannelboard with story pictures, magazines, puppets, felt or magnetic letters, lotto games or picture word cards, and writing materials. One strategy for increasing use of the reading area (since children often prefer to play in more active areas such as housekeeping or blocks) is to conduct story time or other group activities there and leave the materials for children to use. For example, during a discussion of occupations, the teacher may tell a story about a storekeeper using flannelboard pictures, and then leave the pictures for retelling or adaptation by children.

Some adaptations to the reading/language area may need to be made depending upon the type of handicaps in the classroom. Visually impaired children may need materials with larger pictures or materials that incorporate simple, clear line drawings rather than many-hued renderings or fuzzy boundaries. Totally blind children will need materials that provide information through other senses. For example, several children's books focus on different textures. "Scratch and sniff" books incorporate smells into the reading experience. Physically handicapped children may need adaptive equipment to hold a book, to turn pages (such as a head pointer), or to activate electronic equipment such as a tape player or a language master.

Materials should be attractive to children. Books should have clear pictures, address familiar topics, and clearly portray sequences. Select books that attempt to be nonsexist and show men and women (or boys and girls) participating in a wide variety of activities, such as the switching of traditional sex-related roles (female doctors, male nurses, female truck drivers, male schoolteachers). Also books and other materials selected should portray children from a wide variety of cultural and ethnic groups, displaying both similarities and differences. Finally, select materials that picture children with handicapping conditions and/or adaptive equipment. Nonhandicapped children need to see that handicapped persons exist outside of the classrooms and handicapped children need to see that they are not the only ones who are handicapped.

Woodworking Area

Woodworking provides a setting for practicing many motor and grasping movements by giving children the opportunity to constructively use real tools and wood. Children enjoy the noise and physical movement involved. As Harms (1978) suggests, children feel competent and responsible when working with real tools, particularly when they have been told by their parents that the tools may be dangerous. Children can also learn the names and functions of tools and concepts of size and texture.

A woodworking or carpentry area will be noisy, and should be located in an isolated section of the room or outdoors. The woodworking area requires several basic components: a tool storage pegboard; a set of low shelves for tools that cannot be hung; small containers for accessories such as nails; boxes or crates for wood storage; and a table or other work space (Harms, 1981).

Miniature sets of tools purchased in department stores are inappropriate for a carpentry area. Children need real tools to perform activities such as hammering a nail or sawing wood. Harms (1981) suggests some basic tools and appropriate sizes.

- [ ] A claw hammer weighing between 10 and 13 ounces
- [ ] Some nails (Those with large heads are easier to hammer than finishing nails)
- [ ] Slotted and Phillips head screwdrivers (Short, fat-handled screwdrivers are easier for children to use. Rubber grip handles may be purchased which make screwdrivers easier to hold without slipping.)
- [ ] Screws (Raised, "round head" screws are easier to use than flat head screws.)
- [ ] Saws weighing less than 12 ounces, 12–15 inches in length, with 10 teeth per inch
- [ ] Hand drills for boring small holes
- [ ] Smoothing tools such as rasps, files, and sandpaper
- [ ] Paintbrush
- [ ] Clamps for holding woods

Only soft woods such as pine, fir, cedar, or balsam should be used.

The woodworking center is potentially dangerous and no child should use it unless an adult directly supervises the activity. Most children will not know how to use the materials properly, requiring a great deal of teacher instruction. Limit the number of children in this area to allow the adult to adequately supervise the activities.

Harms (1978) provides the following strategies for guiding activities within the woodworking/carpentry area:

1 Young children or children with poor motor skills may need to use tools with a material other than wood. Styrofoam pieces can be used for hammering, screwing, and sawing.

2 Most children will need help in getting nails or screws started.

3 Use the carpentry experience to reinforce and expand language skills.

4 Emphasize the process rather than the product.

5 Encourage girls as well as boys to use carpentry tools.

6 Provide accessories such as small pieces of rugs scraps, bottle caps, wrapped wire, or rubber bands which can serve as "add-ons" nailed to wood.

Activity Areas for Severely and Profoundly Handicapped Preschoolers

Independent or semi-independent use of the activity areas is a reasonable goal for most handicapped preschoolers. Severely handicapped, multiple handicapped, and profoundly retarded children, however, may need activity areas that address more basic skills or may need additional supports (such as an adult or adaptive equipment) to use materials.

A sensory stimulation activity area can expose severely handicapped children to a wide variety of experiences. Because these children are not as mobile, they are unable to seek out stimulation or at least have limited available experiences. A basic awareness of, sensitivity to, and responding to a variety of stimuli are prerequisites to learning more advanced skills and are enjoyable for many children.

Glover and Mesibov (1978) describe strategies for organizing a classroom into auditory, visual, tactile, kinesthetic, and gustatory-olfactory stimulation. The auditory stimulation center provides various hearing experiences and includes equipment such as a record or tape player, musical instruments, shakers/rattlers, or paper for crumpling. The visual stimulation center provides exposure to a variety of sights and should be in an easily darkened area. Materials could include a slide projector, flashlight, twinkling Christmas tree or black lights, mobiles, or bright objects such as aluminum pans or red teething rings. The tactile center provides a variety of touching and feeling experiences and includes materials such as various textures of cloth and paper products, cereals or noodles in a tub, finger paints, shaving cream, hand lotion, or foam. The kinesthetic center provides movement experiences and requires equipment such as mats, incline boards, pillows, large balls, or perhaps a waterbed. The gustatory-olfactory area provides exposure to various tastes and smells and should include a wide range of experiences within these sensory modes: sour-sweet, soft-crunchy, wet-dry, salty-not salty, warm-cool, and raw-cooked.

Obviously most activities will require a great deal of teacher involvement, particularly for children with severe motor impairments. Teachers may use a number of strategies to initially set up a center for independent or semi-independent use by severely handicapped children. For example, in the auditory or visual stimulation center, a string that activates a sound or visual display could be tied to the child's foot or hand. Or a nonhandicapped or less handicapped peer could be taught to present various stimuli in a specified manner (Glover & Mesibov, 1978).

Very little research has assessed the benefits of such activities. However, they do make good conceptual sense both from an educational and therapeutic perspective. Dunst (1981) suggests that sensory stimulation should be response-contingent as compared to response-independent. *Response-contingent stimulation* refers to intervention where the presentation of a given stimulus depends upon a particular behavior performed by the child. Response-contingent stimulation helps the child learn that his behavior can affect his environment in a predictable fashion. A variety of strategies may be used in providing response-contingent stimulation experiences. For example, Watson and Ramey (1972) designed a mobile that could be activated by changes in pressure on the infant's pillow. Any small head movements on this pressure-sensitive pillow would start the mobile moving. Watson and Ramey found that 8-week-old nonhandicapped infants quickly learned the relationship between head movement and mobile activation. Follow-up data indicated that children who had the mobile in their cribs were more active than those who did not. In addition, numerous displays of pleasure, such as smiling and cooing, were observed in these infants. In a subsequent study with retarded failure-to-thrive infants, Ramey, Starr, Phallas, Whitten, and Reed (1975) found that response-contingent stimulation resulted in significant developmental growth when comparing experimental infants with the control group.

Response-contingent stimulation facilitates the learning of contingency experiences by allowing the child to initially cause a stimulus to occur by making a random movement. Through repeated activations, the child gradually begins to associate movement with stimulus, and learns that she can control the presentation or activation of that stimulus.

Many response-contingent experiences may be devised for children at a variety of developmental levels. One simple setup is to tie a string around the child's foot and connect it to an interesting visual display such as a mobile or a picture or light. A set of bells could be tied to the child's foot, or balls or other bright objects hung so the child could hit them with random movements of his arms. Goldberg (1977) contends that such early contingency experiences are important for enhancing competence motivation in infants and may facilitate predictability and "readability" of children whose signals are unclear. These guidelines can be used in designing response-contingent stimulation experiences for handicapped children.

1 Select and arrange a display the child can perceive. A knowledge of the child's sensory abilities is crucial. A visually impaired child will need an auditory or tactile display. A hearing impaired child will need a highly visual or tactile display. The distance between the display and the child should be carefully arranged so the child can perceive the display.
2 Select and arrange a display the child will enjoy and want to perceive again, taking into consideration color, sound, contrast, and other characteristics of objects.
3 Select a behavior or movement you previously observed the child perform, which has a relatively high probability of occurring again. This will depend upon the individual's propensity and ability for movement.
4 Design an appropriate and safe connection between the movement and the stimulus display.
5 Observe the child regularly to determine any increases in the target movement (which would indicate the child may have learned the contingency).
6 Change the display if necessary to make it more appropriate or more appealing to the child.

These guidelines should aid in the identification of appropriate stimulation experiences for individuals in a program. Sayre (1981) describes a variety of automated play units for children with severe motor impairments. Involving parents in planning, designing, and constructing the apparatus for response-contingent experiences may help identify appropriate displays and child behaviors, along with giving the parents the feeling that they are contributing to their child's education and development.

Outdoor Play Areas

Every preschool should have an appropriately designed and furnished outdoor play area. Going outdoors provides a break from indoor activities for both adults and children, and has obvious health benefits (sunlight, fresh air), giving children an opportunity for exercise and movement.

Many programs for handicapped preschoolers, particularly those for the severely handicapped, have been reluctant to take children outdoors. Reasons include the need for close supervision, an unwillingness to take the time to help children get dressed and undressed, and a fear that the handicapped child may be more likely to get sick. Such attitudes are unfortunate because outdoor activities, unless specifically restricted by the child's doctor or parents, are important. Preschool-age children should go outside at least once in the morning and again in the afternoon if the program is a full day.

A good outdoor play area will provide the opportunity for several types of activities: running, climbing, swinging, games, riding, and object play. Each area should be designed to meet the developmental needs of the children and the demands of the desired activities. A variety of surface areas, such as sand, bark, sawdust or other soft materials should be available in addition to hard areas of concrete or asphalt.

Rules and areas must be clearly delineated. For example, areas appropriate for riding wheeled toys such as tricycles should be identified and limited. Identify areas that are dangerous for running and teach children to do the same.

Safety is an important consideration in outdoor play. Accidents or injuries may occur because of exposed bolts or sharp edges, improper installation or maintenance of equipment, and inappropriate use of equipment for certain developmental levels (Frost & Henniger, 1979). According to the Consumer Product Safety Commission (1975), the most frequent causes of playground injury are falling from and being struck by a piece of equipment such as a swing. Special precautions should be taken in these areas, increasing the degree of enclosure with the height of the structure. The National Recreation and Park Association (1976), as reported by Frost and Henniger, proposed that structures 4–8 feet high have railings. Those 8–12 feet should have a protective barrier, with higher structures totally enclosed. The ground surface under climbing equipment should consist of a soft material such as bark to reduce the chance of serious injury. Teach children appropriate ways to use all playground equipment, along with supervising outdoor play. For further information and examples of playgrounds for exceptional children see Gillet (1978) and Jones (1977).

Although playing outside is relaxing and enjoyable, some outdoor activities should be planned. The teacher can use this time to encourage practice of gross motor skills and social interaction or to plan a game or activity.

SUMMARY

Handicapped persons have traditionally lacked adequate physical environments. Olds (1979), for example, suggests, "schools and other institutions designed for the care of children in our society (hospitals, day care centers, special treatment facilities), can best be characterized as being environmentally barren, cold, and sterile" (p. 91). Lack of adequate financial support, the low priority given handicapped children by society, and ignorance of the importance of environmental planning have all contributed to this problem. This chapter has described the design and provision of physical space and materials that can be used by young handicapped children.

REFERENCES

Adams, G. L., Tallon, R. J., & Stangl, J. M. Environmental influences on self-stimulatory behavior. *American Journal of Mental Deficiency*, 1980, *85*, 171–175.

Bailey, D. B., Clifford, R. M., & Harms, T. Comparison of preschool environments for handicapped and nonhandicapped children. *Topics in Early Childhood Special Education*, 1982, *2*, 9–20.

Bender, J. Large hollow blocks: Relationship of quantity to block-building behaviors. *Young Children*, 1978, *34*, 17–23.

Brophy, J. E., Good, T. L., & Nedler, S. E. *Teaching in the preschool.* New York: Harper & Row, 1975.

Consumer Product Safety Commission. *Hazard analysis—playground equipment.* Washington, D.C.: Consumer Product Safety Commission, 1975.

Danoff, J., Breitbart, V., & Barr, E. *Open for children.* New York: McGraw-Hill, 1977.

Dunst, C. J. Theoretical bases and pragmatic considerations in infant curriculum construction. In J. Anderson & J. Cox (Eds.), *Curriculum materials for high risk and handicapped infants.* Chapel Hill, N.C.: Technical Assistance Development System, 1981.

Farbstein, J., & Kantrowitz, M. *People in places: Experiencing, using, and changing the built environment.* Englewood Cliffs, N.J.: Prentice-Hall, 1978.

Frankel, F., Freeman, B. S., Ritvo, E., & Pardo, R. The effect of environmental stimulation upon the stereotyped behavior of autistic children. *Journal of Autism and Childhood Schizophrenia*, 1978, *8*, 389–394.

Frost, J. L., & Henniger, M. L. Making playgrounds safe for children and children safe for playgrounds. *Young Children*, 1979, *34*(9), 23–30.

Frost, J. L., & Kissinger, J. B. *The young child and the educative process.* New York: Holt, Rinehart & Winston, 1976.

Gardner, W. I., Cromwell, R. L., & Foshee, J. G. Studies in activity level: II. Effects of distal visual stimulation in organics, familials, hyperactives, and hypoactives. *American Journal of Mental Deficiency*, 1959, *63*, 1028–1033.

Gillet, P. Classroom techniques: Retarded children need a special playground. *Education and Training of the Mentally Retarded*, 1978, *13*, 160–169.

Glover, E., & Mesibov, G. B. An interest center sensory stimulation program for severely and profoundly retarded children. *Education and Training of the Mentally Retarded*, 1978, *13*, 172–177.

Goldberg, S. Social competence in infancy: A model of parent-infant interaction. *Merrill-Palmer Quarterly*, 1977, *23*, 163–177.

Harms, T. Presenting materials effectively. In H. P. Lewis (Ed.), *Art for the pre-primary child.* Washington, D.C.: National Art Education Association, 1972.

Harms, T. Creating through carpentry. In D. Cansler (Ed.), *Programs for parents of preschoolers.* Winston-Salem, N.C.: Kaplan Press, 1978.

Harms, T. *Build and learn: Carpentry guide cards.* Chapel Hill: Frank Porter Graham Child Development Center, University of North Carolina, 1981.

Harms, T., & Clifford, R. M. *Early childhood environ-*

ment rating scale. New York: Teachers College Press, 1980.

Harms, T., & Cross, L. *Environmental provisions in day care.* Chapel Hill: Frank Porter Graham Child Development Center, University of North Carolina, 1977.

Hildebrand, V. *Guiding young children.* New York: Macmillan, 1975.

Holahan, C. J. *Environment and behavior: A dynamic perspective.* New York: Plenum Press, 1978.

Horner, R. D. The effects of an environmental "enrichment" program on the behavior of institutionalized profoundly retarded children. *Journal of Applied Behavior Analysis,* 1980, *13,* 473–491.

Ittelson, W., Proshansky, H., Rivlin, L., & Winkel, G. *An introduction to environmental psychology.* New York: Holt, Rinehart & Winston, 1974.

Jones, M. H. Physical facilities and environments. In J. Jordon, A. H. Hayden, M. B. Karnes, & M. M. Wood (Eds.), *Early education for exceptional children: A handbook of ideas and exemplary practices.* Reston, Va.: Council for Exceptional Children, 1977.

Keith, K. D. Behavior analysis and the principle of normalization. *AAESPH Review,* 1979, *4,* 148–151.

Levy, E., & McLeod, W. The effects of environmental design on adolescents in an institution. *Mental Retardation,* 1977, *15,* 28–32.

Montes, F., & Risley, T. R. Evaluating traditional day care practices: An empirical approach. *Child Care Quarterly,* 1975, *4,* 208–215.

National Recreation and Park Association. *Proposed safety standards for public playground equipment.* Arlington, Va.: National Recreation and Park Association, 1976.

Olds, A. R. Designing developmentally optimal classrooms for children with special needs. In S. J. Meisels (Ed.), *Special education and development: Perspectives on young children with special needs.* Baltimore: University Park Press, 1979.

Piaget, J. *The origins of intelligence in children.* New York: Norton, 1963.

Ramey, C. T., Starr, R. H., Pallas, J., Whitten, C. I., & Reed, V. Nutrition, response-contingent stimulation, and the maternal deprivation syndrome: Results of an early intervention program. *Merrill-Palmer Quarterly,* 1975, *21,* 45–54.

Rogers-Warren, A., & Wedel, J. W. The ecology of preschool classrooms for the handicapped. *New Directions for Exceptional children,* 1980, *1,* 1–24.

Sayre, T. *Play units for the severely handicapped.* Route 2, Box 168, Bostic, North Carolina 28018, 1981.

Stokols, D. (Ed.) *Psychological perspectives on environment and behavior: Theory, research and applications.* New York: Plenum Press, 1976.

Tizard, B. Observations of over-active imbecile children in controlled and uncontrolled environments. II. Experimental Studies. *American Journal of Mental Deficiency,* 1968, *72,* 548–553.

Twardosz, S., Cataldo, M. F., & Risley, T. R. Open environment design for infant and toddler day care. *Journal of Applied Behavior Analysis,* 1974, *7,* 529–546.

Watson, J. S., & Ramey, C. T. Reactions to response-contingent stimulation in early infancy. *Merrill-Palmer Quarterly,* 1972, *18,* 219–227.

7

Facilitating Engagement within Environments

The goal of environmental planning is to provide a setting that encourages quality interactions between children and materials, activities, and people. Risley (1981) describes such high quality interactions as *engagement*, and suggests that the amount of engagement indicates the quality of the program and predicts its effectiveness.

Engagement, or active and prolonged participation in appropriate activities, can be facilitated in many ways. Teachers would like to see high rates of *voluntary engagement*, where children independently interact with materials, activities, or people. Early childhood special educators know that high rates of voluntary engagement are not often observed in young handicapped children. The teacher must provide the necessary structure to insure that high rates of engagement occur in a variety of settings. In this chapter we review strategies for encouraging engagement in both structured teaching and free play settings. In addition we discuss hyperactivity and low engagement.

THE NATURE AND IMPORTANCE OF ENGAGEMENT

School achievement is in part a function of the time a child spends in school-related tasks. Numerous studies have demonstrated that the amount of time spent in school tasks is positively related to academic achievement (Anderson, 1976; Cobb, 1972; Lahaderne, 1968; Walker & Hops, 1976; Wyne & Stuck, 1979). Although most research has been conducted with school-aged children, the relevance to preschool-handicapped children is readily apparent. Higher amounts of engaged time should result in higher levels of developmental progress.

Carroll (1963) initially proposed the following model depicting the role of time in learning:

$$\text{Degree of learning} = f\frac{\text{Time spent}}{\text{Time needed}}.$$

The model states that the amount of learning is a function of the time spent on a task in relation to the time needed to master that task. Although subsequent publications have suggested variations in the variables affecting time spent and needed (Block, 1971; Carroll, 1971), the basic model remains applicable today.

The amount of time spent in an activity can be discussed from three perspectives: allocated time, engaged time, and academic learning time. *Allocated time* refers to the amount of time within a given schedule devoted to specific activities. For example, the preschool teacher may allocate 20 minutes for snack, 20 minutes for language instruction, 30 minutes for free play, and so forth. Research has generally indicated that although allocated time is necessary for learning to occur, it is not strongly related to academic achievement (Berliner, 1979; Borg, 1980). *Engaged time* (also referred to as time-on-task) refers to the amount of allocated time in which the student is actually engaged in the learning task. A strong relationship exists between engaged time and student achievement (Anderson, 1976; Berliner & Rosenshine, 1977; Cobb, 1972; Lahaderne, 1968; Wiley & Harnischfeger, 1974). *Academic learning time* refers to the amount of time a student is engaged with materials that are appropriate for that child's level of development. There is a strong relationship between academic learning time and achievement (Borg, 1980; Fisher, Filby, Marlowe, Cahen, Dishaw, Moore, & Berliner, 1978). Research suggests that more variability in achievement is explained by academic time than by engaged time alone.

Some evidence of the importance of engaged time for severely handicapped children was reported by Fredericks, Anderson, and Baldwin (1979). A group of teachers of severely handicapped children was divided according to whether the children in their classes made high or low developmental gains. Several teacher variables were examined to determine the reason behind the discrepancy. The factor that most clearly differentiated the two groups was the number of minutes spent on instruction each day. Children with high gains received more instructional time than those with low gains.

Teachers of young handicapped children should learn to identify and encourage high levels of academic learning time; a relatively easy task within the context of direct instruction. Early childhood, however, is typically viewed by many intervention programs as a developmental period during which children need considerable time for free play and social interaction. Such activities are felt to be important for the development of children, and the allocation of free play time is a characteristic of many early intervention programs. The complex needs of handicapped children require that teachers plan and facilitate meaningful and appropriate engagement within both free play and direct instruction contexts. A continuum of strategies can help accomplish this task.

FACILITATING ENGAGEMENT

Low levels of engagement may occur because the child has neither the skills nor the interest in performing the task. The appropriate intervention will depend on the teacher's ability to identify the reasons for low engagement.

The steps for teaching engagement include a *definition* of the skills required to participate in a given activity, an *assessment* of the child's ability to perform those skills, and an *intervention* to teach skills the child is unable to perform. A key strategy in this process is *task analysis*, which facilitates skill acquisition because it allows the child to begin instruction at the critical point and make small steps toward a final goal. The Fredericks et al. (1979) study found that the percentage of task analyzed programs was the second most important variable in differentiating high gain children from those with low gains. Children were more likely to make high gains if they had teachers who typically task analyzed instructional programs.

If the child has at least some of the prerequisite skills to participate in a given activity, the problem may be one of low motivation (activities are not reinforcing) or lack of interest. Several strategies can encourage engagement and thus increase reinforcement value and interest.

Initial Attractiveness

Children need to begin an activity before teachers encourage prolonged engagement. The natural appeal of an activity can set the stage for subsequent involvement. The following strategies may be employed to get children started:

1   *Make the materials appealing.* Colorful toys are better than drab materials. Three-

dimensional objects that can be manipulated are often more appealing than pictures or drawings. Toys or materials that provide feedback (noise, visual display, movement) are also good motivators.

2 *Make participation a privilege rather than a responsibility.* For example, everyone who helps pick up the blocks can have the privilege of coming to story time.

3 *Give the children an immediate role.* For instance, if the story is about farm animals, ask children to choose a toy animal from a box and then sit down and hold the animal in preparation for the story.

4 *Give instructions to begin or prompt initial interactions.* For example, the child who just sits in the block center may need to be told to build something, may need a model, or may need a physical prompt to begin.

5 *Identify children's preferences for materials.* Quiltich, Christopherson, and Risley (1977) described a systematic methodology for determining preferences for materials by observing the amount of time children play with available toys. Total number of minutes of child use is determined and then toys are ranked from the most to least used. Quiltich et al. found that environments with high-use toys resulted in higher levels of appropriate engagement with materials than did environments with low-use toys.

Shaping

When these strategies are unsuccessful, teachers may need to try shaping initial engagement with desired activities. *Shaping* involves the reinforcement of successive approximations to a desired response; the child is gradually required to improve the quality of a response before being reinforced.

A classic example of shaping is described in a study by Wolf, Risley, and Mees (1964). They taught a 3½-year-old boy diagnosed as childhood schizophrenic who exhibited severe tantrums and self-destructive behaviors to wear his glasses by reinforcing him for increasing amounts of contact with his glasses. Initially several empty frames were placed around the playroom and he was reinforced for picking up, holding, and carrying them.

Gradually he was reinforced for bringing the frames closer to his eyes. Through continued application of this procedure he was taught to put on and wear his glasses. Soon he had to wear the glasses during all of the activities he enjoyed, such as outdoor play, walks, and field trips.

A similar shaping procedure may be used to help children become engaged in a low preference behavior or activity. A possible sequence of steps in such a program might proceed as follows:

1 Identify a powerful reinforcer.

2 Initially deliver the reinforcer noncontingently; that is, at random intervals without requiring approximations to the target behavior. Noncontingent delivery of reinforcers establishes the teacher as a reinforcing agent and accustoms the child to receiving reinforcement.

3 Begin shaping by making reinforcement contingent on approximations to the target behavior. The degree of approximation required will depend upon the child. For example, in teaching Anna to use the housekeeping center, initially reinforce her whenever she is on the appropriate side of the room.

4 Gradually require more appropriate behavior before reinforcement is delivered. For example, a midstep in Anna's program might involve reinforcement for simply entering the center.

5 Use additional cues when needed. For example, if Anna is near the housekeeping center the teacher might say "Why don't you come in and make some cookies?" or use a light prompt to guide the child to the center.

Although such a procedure is time consuming and requires attention and skill, it is usually effective if powerful reinforcers have been identified.

Using Selective Attention

Teacher attention may be delivered contingent upon appropriate engagement. Selective attention involves ignoring the child who leaves the desired activity to pursue another activity and attending to the child when he or she is in the appropriate place. For this strategy to work, however, the following conditions must be met:

1 The child must know that he or she is expected to participate in the activity.
2 The child must like teacher attention, or more specifically, teacher attention should be a positive reinforcer.
3 Alternative activities must be less appealing.
4 When the child is appropriately engaged, the teacher must be sure to give him or her positive attention.

Selective teacher attention may be more effective in a small group format because the teacher can combine it with positive attention to other appropriately behaved children. For example, Heath frequently falls out of his chair, knocks it over, and runs away from the small group activity. Whenever Heath falls out of his chair, the teacher could turn to another child and say, "Wow, Anita, you are really working nicely!" and follow that comment with a toy or a special activity. Whenever Heath is sitting at the table, however, a special effort should be made to give him frequent attention.

Increasing Duration of Engagement

Once children are initially involved in activities, engagement can be prolonged. One strategy for increasing length of sustained activities is a changing criterion strategy. Wehman (1979) describes a sequence of such activities for increasing sustained toy play:

1 Identify an effective reinforcer for the child who demonstrates low amounts of engaged play.
2 Determine the average length of time the child currently engages in sustained play.
3 Establish a slightly longer criterion for reinforcement. For example, if the child typically engages in sustained play for an average of 15 seconds at a time, the teacher might set 20 seconds as the criterion for reinforcement. Select a criterion that is easily within the child's abilities and is demonstrated at least some of the time.
4 Begin a reinforcement schedule so the child receives reinforcement for meeting the time criterion.

5 Gradually increase the length of sustained play required before reinforcement is given.

Using the Premack Principle

The *Premack principle* involves following a low probability behavior with a high probability behavior in order to increase the rate or duration of the low probability behavior (Premack, 1959). For low rates of engagement, access to an enjoyable or familiar activity or material can be made contingent on the amount of time spent by the child in the desired activity. For example, if Matthew enjoys riding the tricycle but refuses to sit for more than one minute during art, access to the tricycle could be made contingent on longer involvement during art time.

Flexibility of the Premack principle can be extended by pairing it with tokens or other tangible symbols so the child has some concrete evidence of eventual access to the desired activity. Rowbury, Baer, and Baer (1976), for example, observed four children with behavior problems in a special preschool classroom and found that during free choice periods the children avoided preacademic materials (visual discrimination and matching items, form-insertion items, and other manipulative materials). Contact with these materials was limited to very brief encounters with few documented periods of extended engagement.

To encourage use of preacademic materials, the room was divided into two areas, a work area containing the preacademic materials and a play area consisting of several activity centers. Seven tasks were placed in the preacademic area each day. At the beginning of each "free choice" period children were told that it was actually time to work or "token time," and then led individually into the work area. Each child was invited to complete a task. While the child was doing the task, the teacher remained to demonstrate and praise. If the child completed any task, he or she was given a token to purchase five minutes of time in the play area. The token would be given to the teacher in the play area and a timer was set. At the end of five minutes, the teacher again said it was token time and returned the child to the work area. Gradually the number of task completions required for a token was increased, thus increasing the amount of task-oriented behavior required to go to the play area.

Considerable teacher guidance may be important in the initial phases of such a program. Guidance should then be faded as children gradually learn what is expected.

Switching Requirements

Jacobson, Bushell, and Risley (1969) described use of a "switching" task for children who frequently change activities. When a child wants to move from one area to another, he first has to stop at a centrally located table and complete a simple matching problem or academic task. Jacobson et al. found that when the switching task was imposed, the average number of switches to different activity areas was reduced.

Engagement in Small Groups

The small group poses unique problems in encouraging on-task behaviors, particularly when young children are expected to remain seated for extended periods of time or to wait while the teacher interacts with one member of the group. Some of these problems can be avoided by providing activities and manipulable materials for all children in the group and by reinforcing children for sitting and working. Two other strategies for increasing the likelihood of on-task behaviors in small groups are task variation and program pacing.

Task variation The typical instructional procedure in many educational settings is referred to as a *massed trial* approach to training. For example, the teacher might present 10 trials in a color recognition program, and in each trial the child is asked to point to the green object. An alternative strategy is the *distributed trials* format, in which other tasks are interspersed between two trials from the same program. For example, instead of having Anita point to the green block for 10 trials, the teacher could have her point to a green block, stack the block on top of another green block, count the blocks, and show her accomplishment to another child, then repeat the sequence. The problem with massed trials is that children stop improving their performance at a certain point in the instructional process. This does not happen so early

in a distributed trials format (Mulligan, Guess, Holvoet, & Brown, 1980).

The massed trials approach is convenient, however. The teacher does not have to constantly switch tasks and materials within a lesson. Yet tasks can also be related during a distributed trials approach. Related activities or tasks should be used with the same materials to increase skill generalization and teach children that behaviors are usually embedded within a sequence of related activities. Related goals from a variety of skill domains can then be repeated within different contexts.

For example, some of Erica's instructional targets include giving materials to peers upon request, calling peers by name, understanding basic spatial relations (on, under, behind, beside, in), and asking questions. A related sequence of tasks for Erica in a small group setting might be as follows:

1 Choose the cracker *behind* the apple.
2 Address Lisa by name and ask, "Do you want a cracker?"
3 Give the cracker to Lisa if she says, "Yes."

This sequence can interact with sequences designed for other children in the group. For example, one of Lisa's goals might be responding to simple "yes/no" questions. Dunlap and Koegel (1980) provided empirical support for task variation in a study of two methods of presenting discrimination tasks to young autistic children. In the *constant task* condition, a single task was presented in the same manner throughout an instructional session. In the *varied task* condition, the task was interspersed with a variety of other tasks. The constant task condition resulted in a gradual reduction of correct responding, whereas the varied task condition resulted in higher and more stable levels of correct responding. Further, two observers rated the children as being happier, more enthusiastic and interested, and better behaved during the varied task condition.

Program pacing A related instructional technique is the use of pacing strategies. A fast-paced approach to instruction usually results in superior performance and less off-task behavior than a more leisurely paced approach. Carnine (1976) investigated the effects of two teacher presentation rates on the off-task behaviors and rate of correct responding of two first grade children who demonstrated high levels of off-task behavior. In the slow-rate approach a 5-second delay was imposed between each child's response and the presentation of the next task; in the fast-rate approach the teacher immediately proceeded to the next task. Off-task behavior decreased and correct responding increased during the fast-paced approach. Similar results were found in a recent study by Koegel, Dunlap, and Dyer (1980).

Pacing may be particularly effective when the child does not enjoy the activity. For example, Plummer, Baer, and LeBlanc (1977) tried a time-out procedure with a 5-year-old autistic child who frequently engaged in disruptive behavior and inappropriate use of materials during instruction. The time-out procedure involved cessation of teacher interaction with the child following each occurrence of the disruptive behavior. This procedure resulted in a rapid *increase* in inappropriate behavior and was apparently serving as a negative reinforcer. Since the child disliked the activity, she increased the disruptive behavior to avoid it. When fast-paced procedures were used in combination with reinforcement of appropriate behavior, however, on-task behavior and correct responding increased and disruptive behavior disappeared.

Program pacing means that lessons should proceed at a predictable rate, keeping children active and involved. Children should not be rushed through lessons and pressured to perform rapidly. They will also become frustrated if they have to wait for the teacher to find materials or another child to respond.

The following guidelines may facilitate proper program pacing during small group instruction:

1 Be prepared for the activity. Collect and organize all necessary materials (toys, paper, crayons, data sheets, stopwatch, pencil, etc.) so you will not have to leave the activity to get a pair of scissors or rummage through the materials box for a bottle of glue.
2 Know the objectives and procedural plan for each child in the group. Follow that plan without having to refer back to the written format.
3 When possible, include some activities that all children can respond to in unison.
4 When working with one child in a group, provide interesting and relevant activities for the others to do independently.
5 Place a high priority on keeping up the flow of activities. Do not allow interruptions from other adults during structured activities.

NONCOMPLIANT, DIFFICULT-TO-TEACH CHILDREN

Every teacher of handicapped children will encounter noncompliant children who will not attend to any activities or instructions. The reasons for noncompliance and noninvolvement are many and cannot often be identified, particularly when the child is severely handicapped or autistic. The lack of involvement and responsiveness, and absence of meaningful engagement with materials, activities, and people represents a real threat to developmental progress, and with such children a more structured approach is needed to teach such skills as sitting and looking upon request.

Sitting, looking at objects, and other attending skills are not solely functional behaviors, however. Their value lies in our presumption that they will facilitate the acquisition of other useful, interesting, and functional skills. Too much emphasis on attending skills alone could actually serve to limit progress toward other targets. Whenever possible, training in these basic skills should be a part of the broader instructional context of shaping attention as a part of the more functional objective.

Sitting

Young children are naturally active and movement should be encouraged within any early intervention program. Movement can preclude the learning of some skills, however, and many noncompliant children may need to be taught to sit for a period of time. Bricker and Dennison (1978) describe an effective procedure. First, select a few toys the child enjoys. Place a toy on the table, seat the child so he or she can reach the toy, and direct the child's attention to it (shake it, point to it, etc.). This step allows the child to become accustomed to engaging in an enjoyable activity while sitting in a chair.

Second, gradually introduce another activity the child is capable of performing. After presenting this activity for a short period of time, allow the child to play with a favorite toy. This technique involves use of the Premack principle, in which a low probability behavior (sitting) is followed by a high probability behavior (playing with the favorite toy) to increase frequency of the low probability behavior. Gradually the length of time spent in working while sitting is increased to appropriate levels.

For extremely resistant children the teacher may need to use more basic reinforcers or some mild physical restraint. Kent, Klein, Falk, and Guenther (1972) suggest placing the child in the chair, saying, "Sit down," and immediately reinforcing the child's doing so with an edible or some other proven reinforcer. Sitting behavior is then shaped by gradually requiring longer intervals of sitting before reinforcement. Kent et al. suggest a target of 30 seconds of sitting, without physical restraint or prompting before reinforcement. Of course the child should be involved in an additional appropriate activity; sitting should never be taught alone for its own sake.

Bricker and Dennison (1978) suggest identifying a time when a child is relatively cooperative. Take the child to a chair and play with him or her while seated. If the child tries to get up, remove the toys from the table and use gentle restraint. When the child begins to calm down, say, "You're sitting nicely," gradually remove the restraint, and return the toys to the table.

Looking Upon Request

Another basic skill is looking at objects or the teacher when requested to do so. A typical training program is described by Kent et al. (1972):

The trainer places object on the table and points to it, saying, "Look at this." If the child looks at the object, he is reinforced. If the child does not respond or responds incorrectly, the trainer may use a physical prompt such as turning the child's head toward the object or moving the object closer to the child's face. If prompts are not effective it may be necessary for the trainer to use small boxes containing edibles rather than the standard objects. The trainer moves a small box containing a few edibles close to child's face and says, "Look." The trainer may tip the box slightly toward the child at first. If the child looks into the box, the trainer immediately reinforces him with an edible from the box. The trainer then places the box on the table and points to it, saying, "Look." If the child does not respond or responds incorrectly, the trainer may again use prompting procedures. Once the child looks at one box on the table, the trainer introduces a second and a third box spaced about the table and teaches the child to look at them.... The trainer then begins to substitute the standard objects for the boxes of edibles. The objects are introduced one at a time until all three boxes have been replaced with objects (pp. 176–177).

Kent et al. use the presentation of a "Look at that" trial as a reinforcer for correct responding to "look at me." The teacher places several objects on the table and says, "Look at me." If the child complies, the teacher immediately points to one of the objects and says, "Look at that." If the child complies again, he is immediately reinforced with a hug or edible. Once this compliance pattern has been established, the teacher begins to delay the "Look at me" request for a few seconds, in hopes that the child will look without request. Kent et al. suggest using this procedure until the child looks at the teacher without a command prior to the presentation of each of five consecutive "Look at that" trials.

Bricker and Dennison (1978) do not include the "look at objects" step in their training program. Looking at the teacher is taught immediately after sitting in a chair is learned. If a child does not respond to the request "Look at me," Bricker and Dennison suggest the following intervention:

Take the child's face between your hands and direct his face toward yours. If the child gives you even the most fleeting glance, reward him. Gradually lessen the prompts and reward the child for longer and longer gazes. Talk to the child while you are looking at each other.

If the child does not look at you following your verbal command or physical prompting, another method of attracting his attention should be used. For example, hold a toy which interests the child close to your eyes while saying, "Look at me." If he looks at the toy or your face, reinforce this by giving him the toy. Continue this procedure, varying the toys, until the child will look at your face immediately upon request. Gradually decrease the number of times the toy is used to establish eye contact (pp. 166–167).

As with sitting behavior, looking at objects and the teacher should not be taught alone. Immediately follow each trial with the opportunity to participate in a desired activity. For example, the child who is being taught to look at a toy should be allowed (and perhaps helped) to use the toy once he has looked at it.

Overcorrection Avoidance

The procedures described thus far for establishing basic attending skills have generally been positive and have relied almost exclusively on positive reinforcement and stimulating materials and activities. These programs will be effective for most handicapped children.

The range of positive approaches should be exhausted before reverting to more intrusive procedures. However, some severely retarded and autistic children are generally unresponsive to food, praise, touch, or other potential reinforcers. Because of the teacher's inability to identify effective motivators and therefore teach basic task-related skills, such children are unable to progress to more complex and functional activities.

Foxx (1977) described a procedure to teach eye contact to children who rarely respond to any identifiable social or tangible reinforcers. The strategy combines edibles and praise for eye contact with an aversive procedure for not attending. The aversive procedure, referred to as *functional movement training,* requires that the teacher manipulate the child through a series of movements that the child finds aversive.

Foxx's suggested use of functional move-

ment training for teaching eye contact is as follows. First, the teacher says "Look at me" and then waits 5 seconds. If the child does not respond, the teacher says "_____, you did not look at me" in a stern voice, and then begins functional movement training by requiring the child to move his head up, down, or straight. The teacher gives the child the instruction (e.g., "Head up") and if the child does not comply, the teacher guides the child's head manually in the desired direction, taking care not to physically hurt the child. The child is required to hold each position for 15 seconds. Shortly after functional movement training has ended, a new trial is begun. Appropriate reinforcement is given if the child complies with the "Look at me" request.

In Foxx's (1977) study all children increased their eye contact to approximately 90% or more during the avoidance training conditions. Responding to requests to look at the teacher did not generalize to other teachers, however, without further functional movement training conducted by those teachers.

This procedure provides immediate feedback to the child on his or her response to a request. If the child responds in the desired manner, he or she is immediately reinforced; if not, the child immediately receives functional movement training. The long-range goal is "to establish correct responding as an attractive alternative, so that ultimately positive consequences might gain more control over the correct response" (Foxx, 1977, p. 497).

As Foxx suggests, the functional movement training avoidance procedure should only be used after all attempts at positive approaches have been documented and have failed. Permission of parents and program supervisors must be secured since this is an aversive procedure. In addition, positive approaches should be immediately and readily available whenever correct responding occurs.

Use of aversive procedures raises moral and ethical issues about how much teachers should strive to change a child's behavior. Decisions to use aversive procedures should be made only after teachers and parents have considered these issues. If there is common agreement that a skill such as looking at the teacher upon request is critical to the attainment of future goals, then procedures such as functional movement training may be justifiable. These value judgments should be continually examined, however, because early intervention programs must be both humane and oriented towards the rights of individuals. See Chapter 12 for a more detailed discussion of this issue.

Engagement and Hyperactive Behavior

Routh (1980) has defined *hyperactivity* as "a child's frequent failure to comply in an age appropriate fashion with situational demands for restrained activity, sustained attention, resistance to distracting influences, and inhibition of impulsive response" (p. 57). Behaviors frequently associated with hyperactivity include high activity levels, low task persistence, short attention span, distractibility, and impulsive responding.

The definition and identification of hyperactivity has been a controversial topic. After extensive, though futile, attempts to define and describe a syndrome labeled as Minimal Brain Dysfunction (MBD), professionals have generally dropped this concept and focused on more specific dimensions of MBD such as hyperactivity. Although the measurement techniques typically used to identify hyperactive children are frequently lacking in terms of adequate reliability and validity data (Wallander & Conger, 1981), most professionals accept the concept of hyperactivity as educationally meaningful. Hyperactive children may exhibit higher levels of activity than normal children, particularly in situations in which the child has been asked to use restraint or slow down (Routh & Schroeder, 1976). Children who are highly distractible or have short attention spans will be less likely to make optimal use of the educational materials and activities. Further, they may detract from the learning experiences of classmates.

As a result of growing professional, parent, and public concern over hyperactive children, a number of treatment strategies have evolved. Although most research has been conducted with school-aged children, recent emphasis has focused on the preschool-aged child. Treatments emphasizing the effects of diet characteristics such as the amount of caffeine or food additives (Feingold, 1975) have yet to be adequately documented and are not discussed in this text.[1]

Drug Treatment

The most prevalent approach to the treatment of hyperactive behavior has been the administration of psychostimulant drugs, methylphenidate hydrochloride (Ritalin) and dextroamphetamine sulfate (Dexedrine). O'Leary (1980) estimates that approximately 600,000 to 700,000 children in the United States receive psychostimulant medication for hyperactivity during the school year.

Psychostimulant treatment for hyperactivity is generally very effective with a large proportion (60–90%) of children so treated (Gittelman, Abikoff, Pollack, Klein, Katz, & Mattes, 1980; Whalen & Henker, 1980). Although drug treatment does not necessarily decrease total activity levels in hyperactive children, it does have a significant impact upon on-task and goal-directed behaviors. Hyperactive children are typically rated by their teachers as more cooperative, attentive, and compliant when treated with psychostimulants (Conners & Werry, 1979). A study by Humphries, Kinsbourne, and Swanson (1978) found that when interacting with their mothers, hyperactive children on medication gave and received more praise and less criticism than when not on medication.

Although numerous positive outcomes of drug treatment of hyperactivity have been demonstrated, the widespread use of medication with young children has caused increasing concern. The issues range from concern over short-term side effects to broader social and ethical implications.

The most commonly noted short-term side effects of stimulant medication are decreased appetite and sleep disturbances. Other reported effects include headaches, stomach aches, lethargy, irritability, and sadness. Most side effects disappear rapidly with a reduc-

---

[1]However, emerging research from rigorously controlled studies *tentatively* suggests that additive-free diets may have a more positive effect on the hyperactive behavior of preschool children than on the behavior of older children (Henker & Whalen, 1980).

tion in drug dosage (Whalen & Henker, 1980). A more recent concern, however, is the finding that psychostimulants significantly increase heart rate and blood pressure in some children (Aman & Werry, 1975). Although relatively small increases may not be of short-term medical concern, long-range physical effects need to be determined.

Long-term studies have generally indicated little carry-over of positive outcomes. Psychostimulants do not increase intelligence or achievement test scores (cf. Campbell, 1976). The immediate changes in behavior observed in children do not appear to carry over into adolescence when medication is discontinued, and studies report that these children often exhibit serious social and academic difficulties (Whalen & Henker, 1980).

Long-term follow-up of negative effects suggests that children taking psychostimulant drugs over an extended period of time may suffer significant growth retardation (Safer & Allen, 1975). Although some growth may be regained during "drug holidays" such as summer vacation, it is still insufficient in bringing children to normal ranges of weight and height.

Whalen and Henker have raised a number of other issues in analyzing medication use from a social-ecological perspective, and suggest that long-term social/psychological side effects be considered in addition to the physical effects. One concern is the "message value" of medication. How does it affect peer, teacher, and parental perceptions of a child's social and academic competence? Does medication teach a child that he is not really responsible for his own behavior? Another concern is the possibility of drug abuse. Are children being taught that chemical solutions exist for problems encountered in life? Still another concern focuses on an individual's right to freedom from "chemical intrusions." Does the child have the right to refuse or accept treatment? And finally, treatment withdrawal has psychological as well as physical implications. We are telling the child it is acceptable to be one type of person in the summertime but a different type during the school year.

Hyperactivity and its treatment with psychostimulant medication imposes a number of responsibilities upon a teacher. Perhaps the most important of these is the systematic documentation of positive and negative ef-

fects of drug usage. Unfortunately teachers have traditionally not been included in this process. Bosco and Robin (1976) surveyed midwestern teachers and found that only 22% reported that physicians had requested school evaluations of children on Ritalin. Given the potential for abuse and the concern for side effects, systematic data collection is essential. Further, Whalen and Henker (1980) suggest that many children may be receiving more medication than necessary to achieve desired changes. Since greater dosages increase the probability of negative side effects, daily monitoring should be a part of any treatment program.

Although many children labeled as hyperactive will be placed on medication, teachers are still responsible for a child's behavior. Several intervention strategies can help control certain dimensions of hyperactivity. Teachers must systematically evaluate behavioral strategies prior to drug treatment to determine if psychostimulant medication is indeed necessary. A combination of medical and educational intervention may allow for smaller dosages of medication and may result in more effective intervention.

Reinforcement Training

The use of drugs implies that environmental variables have little impact on hyperactive behavior and that educational intervention may be ineffective. Such inferences are unsupported by data. For example, Ayllon, Layman, and Kandel (1975) compared a token reinforcement approach with psychostimulant medication and found that the token system was as effective as Ritalin in controlling hyperactive behavior of elementary-aged children. It also raised correct math and reading performance significantly higher than medication alone.

Shafto and Sulzbacher (1977) demonstrated how reinforcement training could be used with a hyperactive 4½-year-old preschooler. A structured intervention approach was compared with varying dosages of Ritalin and consisted of special attention from the teacher contingent on appropriate play. As soon as the child began playing appropriately, the teacher began interaction by talking about the play materials and suggesting new ways to use the material and that the child sit down.

After 15 seconds of continuous engagement, the teacher gave the child a piece of sweetened cereal and praise: "Byron, I like the way you stay and put the puzzle pieces in." Results indicated that intervention alone and in combination with medication reduced the number of activity changes to a lower level than medication alone.

Pelham, Schnedler, Bologna, and Contreros (1980) compared the effects of behavioral and stimulant treatment of hyperactive children and included parents and teachers. Parents participated in weekly training sessions and were given readings on social learning theory. Together the parents and the therapist devised programs to modify the child's specific problems. Results indicated that educational intervention alone was effective but not maximally so for most children. The authors concluded that the *combination* of psychostimulant medication and educational intervention may be more effective in treating hyperactive children than either treatment alone. Gittelman et al. (1980) found similar results in a study of a larger number of children.

The common components of each of the training programs in these studies were the same as those for any systematic intervention. Specific behaviors of concern were targeted and systematic feedback (reinforcement and punishment) was provided contingent upon appropriate and inappropriate behavior. The specific behaviors related to hyperactivity. The studies demonstrated that systematic programming can be effective, even with children whose handicaps may have a partial physiological base. For many hyperactive children, the optimal strategy will be a combination of both drug and educational treatment, reinforcing the importance of the preschool teacher's role in the treatment of hyperactive children.

Self-Control Training

Ideally children should control their own behavior without drugs or external reinforcement programs. Unfortunately, reinforcement training of hyperactive children often does not generalize to other settings or activities.

An alternative approach is to teach children to slow down and control their behavior through a self-instructional or self-control system. This approach was initially described and validated by Meichenbaum and Goodman (1971) and has since been demonstrated effective by numerous researchers (Bornstein & Quevillon, 1976; Cameron & Robinson, 1980; Camp, 1980).

Although there are minor variations, the following steps described by Bornstein and Quevillon (1976) generally constitute a self-control training program:

1 The teacher first demonstrates a task while talking aloud. The modeled verbalizations include questions about the task ("What does the teacher want me to do?"), answers to questions in the form of "cognitive rehearsal" ("Oh, that's right, I'm supposed to put together this puzzle"), self-instructions that guide through the task ("Let's see, I'll try a corner piece first"), and self-reinforcement ("Look, I got that piece in just right").
2 The child performs the task while the teacher talks aloud.
3 The child performs the task talking aloud while the teacher whispers softly.
4 The child performs the task whispering softly while the teacher makes lip movements but no sound.
5 The child performs the task making lip movements without sound while the teacher watches.
6 The child performs the task with covert self-instruction (saying the instruction to himself).

Bornstein and Quevillon (1976) applied this technique with three 4-year-old boys in a Head Start program. Each child was trained in a 2-hour self-instructional session (50 minutes of work, 20-minute break, 50 minutes of work). A number of components were added to the procedure to increase correct responding. For example, since the children did not seem motivated to work at first, the teacher paired self-praise with a small piece of candy. The teacher purposely made several mistakes and then immediately corrected ("Oh, that's not right; I'll try it this way"). Also the entire training session was conducted in a storylike manner and included a wide variety of easy and moderately difficult tasks.

For all three boys there was an immediate and significant increase in on-task behavior in the Head Start classroom, beginning from an average level of 11.6% during baseline to a post-treatment mean of 77%. Follow-up checks of on-task behavior 60 and 90 days after intervention indicated that on-task behavior was maintained at a high rate.

Self-control training is not for all children. It relies heavily on language skills and the ability to systematically use language to control behavior. Yet it can be a powerful and lasting approach to increasing on-task behavior for hyperactive children and others with the prerequisite cognitive and language skills.

SUMMARY

Engagement is a necessary prerequisite to developmental progress. Unfortunately many handicapped youngsters exhibit low rates of task persistence for a variety of reasons. This chapter described several strategies for teaching basic attending skills and encouraging prolonged and meaningful interaction with materials, activities, and people.

REFERENCES

Aman, M.G., & Werry, J. S. Methylphenidate in children: Effects upon cardiorespiratory function on exertion. *International Journal of Mental Health*, 1975, *4*, 119–131.

Anderson, L.W. An empirical investigation of individual differences in time to learn. *Journal of Educational Psychology*, 1976, *68*, 226–233.

Ayllon, T., Layman, P., & Kandel, H.J. A behavioral-educational alternative to drug control of hyperactive children. *Journal of Applied Behavior Analysis*, 1975, *8*, 137–146.

Berliner, D. C. Tempus educare. In P. L. Peterson & H. J. Walberg (Eds.), *Research on teaching: Concepts, findings, and implications.* Berkeley, Calif.: McCutchan, 1979.

Berliner, D.C., & Rosenshine, B. The acquisition of knowledge in the classroom. In R. Spiro & W. Montague (Eds.), *Schooling and the acquisition of knowledge.* Hillsdale, N. J.: Lawrence Erlbaum Associates, 1977.

Block, J. H. *Mastery learning: Theory and practice.* New York: Holt, Rinehart, & Winston, 1971.

Borg, W. R. Time and school learning. In C. Denham & A. Lieberman (Eds.),*Time to learn.* Washington, D.C.: U.S. Department of Education, 1980.

Bornstein, P. H., & Quevillon, R. P. The effects of a self-instructional package on overactive preschool boys. *Journal of Applied Behavior Analysis*, 1976, *9*, 179–188.

Bosco, J. J., & Robin, S. S. Ritalin usage: A challenge to teacher education. *Peabody Journal of Education*, 1976, *53*, 187–193.

Bricker, D., & Dennison, L. Training prerequisites to verbal behavior. In M. E. Snell (Ed.), *Systematic instruction of the moderately and severely handicapped.* Columbus, Ohio: Charles E. Merrill, 1978.

Cameron, M. I., & Robinson, V. M. J. Effects of cognitive training on academic and on-task behavior of hyperactive children. *Journal of Abnormal Child Psychology*, 1980, *8*, 405–419.

Camp, B. W. Two psychoeducational treatment programs for young aggressive boys. In C. K. Whalen & B. Hender (Eds.), *Hyperactive children: The social ecology of identification and treatment.* New York: Academic Press, 1980.

Campbell, S. B. Hyperactivity: Cause and treatment. In A. Davids (Ed.), *Child personality and psychopathology: Current topics* (Vol. 3). New York: Wiley, 1976.

Carnine, D.W. Effects of two teacher-presentation rates on off-task behavior, answering correctly, and participation. *Journal of Applied Behavior Analysis*, 1976, *9*, 199–206.

Carroll, J.B. A model of school learning. *Teacher's College Record*, 1963, *64*, 723–733.

Carroll, J.B. Problems of measurement related to the concept of learning for mastery. In J. H. Block (Ed.), *Mastery learning: Theory and Practice.* New York: Holt, Rinehart, & Winston, 1971.

Cobb, J.A. Relationship of discrete classroom behaviors to fourth-grade academic achievement. *Journal of Educational Psychology*, 1972, *63*, 74–80.

Conners, C.K., & Werry, J.S. Pharmacotherapy of psychopathology in children. In H. C. Quay & J. S. Werry (Eds.), *Psychopathological disorders of childhood* (2nd ed.). New York: Wiley, 1979.

Dunlap, G., & Koegel, R. L. Motivating autistic children through stimulus variation. *Journal of Applied Behavior Analysis*, 1980, *13*, 619–627.

Feingold, B. *Why your child is hyperactive.* New York: Random House, 1975.

Fisher, C.W., Filby, N.N., Marlowe, R. S., Cahen, L.S., Dishaw, M.M., Moore, J.E., and Berliner, D.C. *Teaching behaviors, academic learning time, and student achievement: Final report of Phase IIIB, Beginning teacher evaluation study* (Technical Report V–I). In *Beginning teacher evaluation study.* San Francisco: Far West Laboratory for Educational Research, 1978.

Foxx, R. M. Attention training: The use of overcorrection avoidance to increase the eye contact of autistic and retarded children. *Journal of Applied Behavior Analysis*, 1977, *10*, 489–499.

Fredericks, H. D. B., Anderson, R., & Baldwin, V. The identification of competency indicators of teachers of the severely handicapped. *AAESPH Review*, 1979, *4*, 81–95.

Gittelman, R., Abikoff, H., Pollack, E., Klein, D.F., Katz, S., & Mattes, J. A controlled trial of behavior modification and methylphenidate in hyperactive children. In C. K. Whalen & B. Henker (Eds.), *Hyperactive children: The social ecology of identifi-*

cation and treatment. New York: Academic Press, 1980.

Henker, B., & Whalen, C.K. The changing faces of hyperactivity: retrospect and prospect. In C.K. Whalen & B. Henker (Eds.), *Hyperactive children: The social ecology of identification and treatment.* New York: Academic Press, 1980.

Humphries, T., Kinsbourne, M., & Swanson, J. Stimulant effects on cooperation and social interaction between hyperactive children and their mothers. *Journal of Child Psychology and Psychiatry,* 1978, *19,* 13–22.

Jacobson, J.M., Bushell, D., & Risley, T. Switching requirements in a Head Start classroom. *Journal of Applied Behavior Analysis,* 1969, *2,* 43–47.

Kent, L.R., Klein, D., Falk, A., & Guenther, H. A language acquisition program for the retarded. In J. E. McLean, D.E. Yoder, & R.L. Schiefelbusch (Eds.), *Language intervention with the retarded.* Baltimore: University Park Press, 1972.

Koegel, R.L., Dunlap, G., & Dyer, K. Intertrial interval duration and learning in autistic children. *Journal of Applied Behavior Analysis,* 1980, *13,* 91–99.

Lahaderne, H. M. Attitudinal and intellectual correlates of attention: A study of four sixth-grade classrooms. *Journal of Educational Psychology,* 1968, *59,* 320–324.

Meichenbaum, D.H., & Goodman, J. Training impulsive children to talk to themselves: A means of developing self-control. *Journal of Abnormal Psychology,* 1971, *77,* 115–126.

Mulligan, M., Guess, D., Holvoet, J., & Brown, F. The individual curriculum sequencing model (I): Implications for research on massed, distributed, or spaced trial training. *Journal of the Association for the Severely Handicapped,* 1980, *5,* 325–336.

O'Leary, K.D. Pills or skills for hyperactive children? *Journal of Applied Behavior Analysis,* 1980, *13,* 191–204.

Pelham, W.E., Schnedler, R.W., Bologna, N.C., & Contreros, J.A. Behavioral and stimulant treatment of hyperactive children: A therapy study with methylphenidate probes in a within-subject design. *Journal of Applied Behavior Analysis,* 1980, *13,* 221–236.

Plummer, S., Baer, D.M., & LeBlanc, J.M. Functional considerations in the use of procedural timeout and an effective alternative. *Journal of Applied Behavior Analysis,* 1977, *10,* 689–705.

Premack, D. Toward empirical behavior laws: I. Positive reinforcement. *Psychological Review,* 1959, *66,* 219–233.

Quilitch, H.R., Christophersen, E.R., & Risley, T.R. The evaluation of children's play materials. *Journal of Applied Behavior Analysis,* 1977, *10,* 501–502.

Risley, T. *Research on day care environments.* Paper presented at Frank Porter Graham Child Development Center, University of North Carolina at Chapel Hill, July 1981.

Routh, D.K. Developmental and social aspects of hyperactivity. In C.K. Whalen & B. Henker (Eds.), *Hyperactive children: The social ecology of identification and treatment.* New York: Academic Press, 1980.

Routh, D.K., & Schroeder, C.S. Standardized playroom measures as indices of hyperactivity. *Journal of Abnormal Child Psychology,* 1976, *4,* 199–207.

Rowbury, T.G., Baer, A.M., & Baer, D.M. Interactions between teacher guidance and contingent access to play in developing preacademic skills of deviant preschool children. *Journal of Applied Behavior Analysis,* 1976, *9,* 85–104.

Safer, D. J., & Allen, R. P. Side effects from long-term use of stimulants in children. *International Journal of Mental Health,* 1975, *4,* 105–118.

Shafto, F., & Sulzbacher, S. Comparing treatment tactics with a hyperactive preschool child: Stimulant medication and programmed teacher intervention. *Journal of Applied Behavior Analysis,* 1977, *10,* 13–20.

Walker, H., & Hops, H. Increasing academic achievement by reinforcing direct academic performance and/or facilitative nonacademic responses. *Journal of Educational Psychology,* 1976, *68,* 218–225.

Wallander, J.L., & Conger, J.C. Assessment of hyperactive children: Psychometric, methodological, and practical considerations. In M. Hersen, R. Eisler, & P.M. Miller (Eds.), *Progress in Behavior Modification* (Vol. 2). New York: Academic Press, 1981.

Wehman, P. Instructional strategies for improving toy play skills of severely handicapped children. *AAESPH Review,* 1979, *4,* 125–135.

Whalen, C.K., & Henker, B. The social ecology of psychostimulant treatment: A model for conceptual and empirical analysis. In C. K. Whalen & B. Henker (Eds.), *Hyperactive children: The social ecology of identification and treatment.* New York: Academic Press, 1980.

Wiley, E.E., & Harnischfeger, A. Explosion of a myth: Quantity of schooling and exposure to instruction, major educational vehicles. *Educational Researcher,* 1974, *3,* 7–12.

Wolf, M.M., Risley, T., & Mees, H. Application of operant conditioning procedures to the behavior problems of an autistic child. *Behavior Research and Therapy,* 1964, *1,* 305–312.

Wyne, M.D., & Stuck, G.S. Time-on-task and reading performance in underachieving children. *Journal of Reading Behavior,* 1979, *11,* 119–128.

ntil recently, intervention programs for handicapped children have focused almost exclusively on the child. Within the past decade, however, family involvement has been recognized as a necessary component of early intervention. Unfortunately, this recognition has not always been translated into meaningful interactions with families. Typically, teachers are untrained in techniques for working with parents, and consequently have had to learn such skills through on-the-job experience and through trial-and-error interactions.

Several points should be made about working with families. First, dealing with parents requires sensitivity and understanding, and cannot be learned by reading a book or listening to a lecture. It takes experience, maturity, and sensitivity that can only be developed through face-to-face interaction. New teachers, particularly those who are not parents, should be aware of and open about their limitations in working with families.

Second, few parents are adequately prepared to raise a handicapped child. They may be under considerable pressure and stress. Teachers can help families by identifying strategies for reducing stress.

Third, parents have legal rights as consumers of public educational services, and the educator must serve as both an informer and an advocate of those rights. Parents can participate in planning and implementing the child's intervention program. They also have a right to due process procedures when educational practices are questioned, and can look at their child's school records at any time.

Fourth, parents of handicapped children have the same life goals as all parents. Unfortunately, the presence of a handicapped child sometimes stigmatizes all members of the family. Parents of handicapped youngsters are no different from those of typical children; they just happen to have a handicapped child. Teachers must listen, learn, and interact naturally with parents, and show a genuine interest.

Fifth, family involvement must be individualized. For several years we have realized we should individualize our instruction for handicapped children. Only recently has the professional community recognized the need for individualized family involvement. Each family has its own unique needs and a predetermined set of services cannot meet each situation.

The remainder of this chapter focuses on the specific needs of families of handicapped chil-

Working with Families

dren and strategies early childhood educators can use to address these needs. The discussion centers around parent-child social interactions, family coping skills, and parent involvement in educational programs.

PARENT-CHILD SOCIAL INTERACTIONS

The first social relationship a child establishes is with parents. A lasting bond is formed between parent and child, often referred to as *attachment* (Ainsworth, 1973; Bowlby, 1969), and serves as a basis for future social relationships with other persons. The parent-child relationship and thus the attachment process for handicapped infants is at risk from the moment of birth. An important task for the early childhood special educator may be helping families develop and maintain appropriate, mutually satisfying social relationships with the handicapped family member.

Attachment and Its Development

Ainsworth (1973) has defined attachment as "an affectional tie that one person forms to another specific person or persons, binding them together in space and enduring over time" (p. 1). Attachment is a construct; it is an intangible concept used to explain behaviors observed in parents and children. Mothers smile at babies; babies smile at mothers; babies cry when strangers pick them up or when parents leave. These and other behaviors suggest the existence of an affectional tie.

The nature and effects of attachment have been the focus of considerable interest over the last century. Freud (1905, 1915) viewed the relationship of a child with his or her parents as critical to the child's later social, emotional, and psychological development. Bowlby (1969) suggested that human attachment (as well as the attachment behavior of other animals) must be interpreted from an evolutionary perspective. He identified five infant behaviors contributing to attachment (crying, smiling, sucking, following, and clinging) and suggested that these behaviors develop naturally as a part of the evolutionary process to perform a vital function: to maintain proximity to the infant's caregiver and

thus protect the infant from dangerous predators. These instinctive behavioral patterns are still demonstrated.

Although the exact nature and consequences of attachment are still unknown, the formation of a secure bond is a process in which both partners play an active role (Bell, 1968; Stern, 1974). Mothers and fathers do things (smile, talk, coo, hold) that infants like; infants do things (smile, kick, wave, babble, cling, follow) that mothers and fathers like. Each becomes dependent upon the other and interacts with the other in a mutual communication game. This interaction begins in its earliest form with the gaze (Stern, 1974), and gradually evolves into a mature and enduring relationship.

Some major attainments in the normal development of attachments are described in Table 8.1. These attainments closely parallel the emergence of several cognitive skills. For example, early attachment behaviors require the ability to discriminate between two persons and the realization that other persons (mother, dad, or sibling) still exist even when you cannot see or hear them (Ainsworth, 1973). Later phases require the ability to view events from another's perspective and realize that the existence or quality of the relationship to the attachment figure does not change when the figure is gone for short periods of time (Marvin, 1977).

Interactional Patterns

The attachment process for handicapped infants and their families can be disrupted from birth. The interaction patterns between parents and handicapped infants are frequently different from the patterns observed in nonhandicapped infants and their families.

The effects of handicapping conditions on parent-child interactions stem from the medical needs of children or from the grief process parents experience. Many more severely handicapped infants need incubators or other self-contained life support systems. Depending upon birth weight, gestational age, physical anomalies, respiration, and weight gain, premature or handicapped infants may be kept in neonatal intensive care units for 9–12 weeks or longer. Such intervention will naturally reduce the amount of gazing, handling, and

TABLE 8.1
Some attainments in the normal development of attachments

Age	Characteristics of Attachment Relationship
0–3 months	Often referred to as the phase of "undiscriminating social responsiveness" (Ainsworth, 1973). Infant uses certain behaviors (visual fixation and tracking, listening, cooing, grasping, crying, smiling) to orient to the environment and test contingencies. Infant is more likely to respond to a human face than to a nonhuman figure but may not be able to discriminate between faces.
2–6 months	Infant responds differentially to familiar and unfamiliar faces. Begins with differentiated smiling and vocalization. Later in phase the infant cries when attachment figure leaves the room.
7–24 months	Infant actively seeks out proximity and contact with attachment figure. Behaviors include following, approaching, and clinging. Child can take action to secure proximity to attachment figure.
24–36 months	Child still seeks contact but is more likely to be satisfied with looking and verbal communication with attachment figure without requiring physical contact.
36–48 months	Child is more willing to be left for brief periods if left with friendly stranger.
48–60 months	Child finally realizes that there is "a relative invariant in their relationship between parent and child that is not dependent on physical proximity or contact" (Marvin, 1977, p. 39).

Source: Ainsworth (1973), Bowlby (1969), and Marvin (1977)

skin-to-skin contact between parents and infants, and could adversely affect future parent-child interactions.

In addition to medical needs, the birth of a handicapped child or the later diagnosis of a handicapping condition may cause parents to go through a process affecting the quality of parent-child interactions. Solnit and Stark (1961) suggested that during pregnancy parents grow to expect a normal, healthy child. When this child does not appear, parents must go through a process of mourning similar to that experienced after the death of a child. This mourning is an important experience, but may affect the bonding process.

Drotar, Baskiewicz, Irwin, Kennell, and Klaus (1975) proposed a series of five stages subsequent to the birth of a handicapped child. The first stage is overwhelming *shock*. The second stage is a period of *denial* of the reality of the handicap. The third stage is one of intense *feelings of sadness, anger, and per-* haps *anxiety* about the future well-being of the infant, which may cause parents to feel reluctant to become attached to or interact with the baby. The fourth stage is a *gradual adaptation* to the situation, and the fifth stage is that of *reorganization* and *long-term acceptance* of the child.

Not every parent goes through these stages or in this sequence. But teachers need to be aware of the range of reactions expressed by parents. Parents who appear not to accept their children need help in working through a very difficult personal situation, and the early childhood special educator must often provide counseling and support. The effects of specific handicapping conditions on the interactional skills of children have been documented by many authors. Some major findings are summarized in Table 8.2.

TABLE 8.2
Some effects of specific handicapping conditions on the interactional skills of children

Handicap	Reported Findings	Relevant Studies
Mental Retardation	Reduced responsivity to others Decreased vocalization Lack of smiling or delayed smiling More solitary play Fewer initiations to others More likely to resist or not respond to cuddling	Cicchetti & Sroufe (1976); Cunningham, Reuler, Blackwell, & Deck (1981); Kennedy (1973); Marshall, Hogrenes, & Goldstein (1973); Stone & Chesney (1978)
Hearing Impairment	Impaired communication Inconsistent responses to communicative attempts Fewer social initiations	Ferris (1980); Greenberg & Marvin (1979); Schlesinger & Meadow (1972); Wedell-Monnig & Lumley (1980)
Visual Impairment	Irregular smiling Smiling in response to auditory cues only Child must "maintain contact" by tactile and auditory (rather than visual) cues	Als, Tronick, & Brazelton (1980); Fraiberg (1974, 1975); Kastein, Spaulding, & Scharf (1980); Scott, Jan, & Freeman (1977)
Physical and Motor Impairments	Limp or physically unresponsive Difficulty in relaxing Decreased ability to laugh or smile Smile may look like a grimace Impaired communication skills Impaired locomotion skills prevent child from independently seeking out parent	Featherstone (1980); Jens & Johnson (1982); Gallagher, Jens, & O'Donnell (in press); McCubbin, Nevin, Larsen, Comeau, Patterson, Cauble, & Striker (1981); Mordock (1979); Prechtl (1963); Roskies (1972)

Improving Parent-Child Interactions

Brazelton, Koslowski, and Main (1974) observed a rhythmicity between caretaker and infant essential to the social relationship. *Rhythmicity* is the apparent mutual satisfaction with the give-and-take aspect of the interaction; parent and infant appear to read and respond to each other's cues at the appropriate times. When one member of the dyad (interactional pair) cannot or does not respond to the needs and initiations of the other, the quality of the interaction is impaired. The effects of specific handicapping conditions described in Table 8.2 make clear the impact of the handicap on the communication between parent and child. When children are or appear to be unresponsive or when the child's responses do not match the parent's expectations for a response, rhythmicity is impaired.

Bronfenbrenner (1974), in his review of the effectiveness of early intervention, reported that programs with strong parent components were more effective than those that did not emphasize parent involvement. When he conducted a more detailed examination of the important components of parent intervention, he concluded that the *interaction* between parent and child was the critical element. Early intervention should focus on assessment and, if necessary, interaction to improve the quality of parent-child interactions.

Improving the quality of interactions requires

a number of skills. Most important is the parent's ability to "read" the child. Only in this manner can the parent respond appropriately to the child's social and communicative efforts. Brazelton (1981) argues that an effective assessment procedure involving parents can be the initial basis for helping them understand their children and subsequently respond appropriately. By participating in the assessment process, parents can observe how infant behaviors vary according to "state" changes, become aware of the competence of even a newborn, and begin to recognize their infant's own unique ways of responding to the environment. The same model can be applied to older children using other assessment tools appropriate for the child's age. The purpose of the assessment is to help the parents recognize their child's abilities, to sharpen their observational skills, and to help them focus on the child's positive efforts to communicate.

The same objectives might also be accomplished by simply focusing on one aspect of the child's abilities. Fraiberg (1974), for example, taught mothers of blind infants to respond to their babies' hand signals rather than facial cues. By focusing on the mode of communication, mothers and fathers were able to more effectively interact with their children.

Often the process simply provides parents with information about their child's handicap and alerts them to differences in reaction patterns. For example, Jens and Johnson (1980) report that severely hypertonic children may actually appear to grimace when attempting to smile. Parents should be aware of unique behavioral and developmental characteristics so that they can appropriately interpret and respond to their child's handicap (see Table 8.2).

Bromwich (1976, 1981) developed an interactional model for working with parents and infants. She assumes that the quality and nature of interactions between parent and child can significantly affect the infant's development; therefore, the focus of intervention should be on this interaction. The intent of the model is to establish "mutually satisfying" interactions between parents and infants.

Bromwich's program includes the Parent Behavior Progression (PBP), an assessment tool designed to ascertain, through observations and interviews, the parents' current level of involvement with the infant and to evaluate the effectiveness of parent-infant intervention. (See Kelly, 1979, for a discussion of additional strategies for assessing parent-infant relations.) This information is then used to plan intervention programs unique to the individual needs of each parent and child. Six levels of parent behavior, briefly described in Table 8.3, are included in the PBP and are used to determine the present level of interaction. Each hierarchical level requires more competence from parents in the interactional process.

Bromwich (1981) emphasizes that only some behaviors listed in the PBP may be demonstrated by each parent. In addition, behaviors may be inappropriate when used as specific objectives. For example, for the mother of a severely handicapped infant to talk enthusiastically about how alert and responsive her child is would be a denial of reality. Bromwich further cautions that professionals should not

TABLE 8.3
Levels of the parent behavior progression

Level	Description of Parent Behavior
I	The parent enjoys the infant.
II	The parent is a sensitive observer of the infant, reads and responds accurately to behavioral cues.
III	The parent engages in quality and quantity interaction with the infant that is *mutually* satisfying and that provides opportunity for the development of attachment.
IV	The parent demonstrates an awareness of materials, activities, and experiences suitable for the infant's current stage of development.
V	The parent initiates new play activities and experiences based on internalized, personal principles or on suggested or modeled activities.
VI	The parent independently generates a wide range of developmentally appropriate and interesting activities and experiences in familiar and new situations at new levels of the infant's development.

Source: Bromwich (1981)

expect to see many behaviors in the first three levels exhibited by parents of handicapped infants, due to the stressful nature of their situation. She suggests focusing on the behaviors at Level IV in hopes that doing things with and for infants will eventually lead to mutually pleasurable interactions.

Bromwich (1981) suggests eight general *intervention modes*: listening empathetically, helping parents become sensitive observers of their children, commenting positively on parent strengths, discussing, asking questions, modeling appropriate behaviors, experimenting with different activities for the child, and encouraging the parent to follow up on previous interactions. Each mode is used selectively depending upon the parent's current level of functioning (as assessed by the PBP) and the unique needs of the infant.

Early childhood special educators can also help parents consistently respond to their children's needs. Goldberg (1977) suggests that "the central reciprocity in early social relationships is mediated by mutual enhancement of 'feelings of efficacy' " (p. 163). Both parent and child need to feel competent in the relationship, and this can be developed by having the other member of the dyad reciprocate or respond when initiations are made. Parents begin to feel competent when they are able to comfort a crying baby or make an infant laugh. Babies begin to feel competent when they learn how to call for mother or daddy or make sister smile.

Such reactions are contingency experiences. The infant usually learns that the parent's behavior is contingent upon a certain action (e.g., feeding is contingent upon loud and continuous crying). Unfortunately, handicapped children may not learn contingencies as soon or as well as other children. This is problematic for both parents and children: Recognition of the relationship between behavior and its results is essential for meaningful learning. Also, since the child has not learned to predict the parent's behavior, he or she may continue to use a variety of strategies to meet basic needs. The parents are thus unable to predict needs based on the child's behaviors and may feel incompetent because they are often unable to calm or soothe him or her. A meaningful attachment between parent and child is jeopardized because of lack of predict-

ability, routine, and give-and-take. Intervention should teach parents to be generally responsive and to design and use response-contingent stimulation experiences.

Ainsworth (1973) suggested that the best strategy for responsiveness is to try to help the parents see things from the child's point of view. Parents who know the abilities and limitations of their child can be more sensitive to needs and signals. The child also learns that he or she can be effective.

Ainsworth suggested that too many parents believe that they might spoil their infant by being overly responsive. Thus they may sometimes ignore crying. This raises a sensitive issue, requiring a variety of considerations. To ignore crying is to assume that it has no basis in need and is an attention-seeking device. This may be the case for children over 12 months, except where an obvious need exists (child is hurt, sick, afraid, or hungry). Most babies, however, do cry for a reason and Ainsworth contends that responding to a crying child does not spoil the child. Responsivity during the first months of life may lead to greater attachment between mother and child, which subsequently leads to a more independent youngster.

Unfortunately, Ainsworth's comments were based on data from nonhandicapped children. The extent to which they apply to handicapped infants has yet to be determined. Parents of handicapped infants should initially be counseled to try those strategies documented as appropriate for nonhandicapped infants. These strategies may not always be effective. Some handicapped infants are unusually irritable, others seem to cry incessantly, and still others may not enjoy being touched. For the parent's own sanity, crying must sometimes be ignored. The early intervention specialist can only help the parent accurately read the infant's signals and identify consistent ways of responding to those signals.

In addition, some authors suggest response-contingent stimulation to help the infant develop awareness of contingency experiences. Response-contingent stimulation facilitates the learning of contingency experiences by allowing the infant to initially cause a stimulus to occur through a random movement. Through repeated activations, the infant gradually begins to associate movement with stimulus, and gradually learns that he or she can control stimulus presentation or activation. Goldberg (1977) contends that such early contingency experiences enhance competence motivation in infants and may facilitate predictability and "readability" of infants with unclear signals. Guidelines for designing response-contingent stimulation experiences are described in Chapter 6. Parents should be involved in the design, construction, implementation, and evaluation of these experiences.

Quality interactions between parents and children do not end after infancy. The relationship continues to be challenged and matures as children grow older. The early childhood special educator can continue to serve as a facilitator of quality interactions between parents and children. A variety of useful strategies for improving parent-child interactions during and after infancy is described in Table 8.4.

FAMILY COPING SKILLS

The birth of any child adds stress to a family situation, including the responsibility for the welfare of an infant, the need to reallocate financial resources, changing communication systems (from dyad to triad), and changing relationships with friends and other extended family members (Wandersman, Wandersman, & Kahn, 1980). Many families have difficulty dealing with these normal stresses, as evidenced by the significant increase in divorce rates and the large number of single-parent families.

TABLE 8.4
Strategies for improving interactions between parents and their handicapped children

Strategy	Rationale
Have parents participate in the assessment process.	Parent observation and participation should help them become aware of their child's specific skills under a controlled set of stimulus conditions.
Teach parents about general response patterns unique to their child's handicap.	Knowledge of typical response patterns should help parents alter their expectations and perhaps more effectively respond to their children.
Teach parents how to design response-contingent stimulation experiences.	Through the design and implementation of these activities, parents should learn more about how their child responds to the environment and should then be able to change their own behaviors to accommodate to those response patterns. Also, children should begin to learn cause-and-effect relationships.
Conduct 1:1 modeling and interactional sessions in the home.	If teachers have learned specific ways of interacting with and responding to a certain child, those techniques should be modeled for the parents, preferably in the home.
Teach parents basic observational skills.	Parents will never learn to independently "read" their children until they become good observers of their behavior.
Emphasize the skills the infant has and can demonstrate.	Parents of handicapped children know what their children *cannot* do and may need assistance in focusing on strengths.
Teach parents how to communicate at a developmentally appropriate level.	Parents may not know how to communicate with a very young child.
Reinforce parents for appropriate interactions.	Appropriate parent behaviors will be naturally reinforced by resulting interactions. However, during the acquisition phase, parents may need feedback on how much they effectively interact with children.
Suggest activities and toys that may result in positive interactions.	Setting the stage for mutually enjoyable interactions increases the likelihood for successful intervention.

The perceived and real stress of raising a handicapped child may seem overwhelming to parents. Everything must be viewed from a different perspective, from simple tasks such as finding a good and willing babysitter to the more complicated task of planning the child's future. Although parents can and do cope with the additional stresses imposed by a handicapped child, they need support systems that help alleviate stress.

Stress in Families of Handicapped Children

The particular form and nature of stress varies as a function of the child's handicap and the family's existing support systems. Numerous authors have reviewed sources of stress in handicapped families (Beckman-Bell, 1981; Farber, 1959; Gallagher, Beckman-Bell, & Cross, in press; Gallagher, Cross, & Scharfman, 1981; Price-Bonham & Addison, 1978). In this section we focus on stress on normal family activities and routines, variations in stress on individual family members, and pressure to provide the best for the child.

Stress on normal families Handicapped children usually place stress on normal family activities and routines because of their additional needs for care, particularly basic self-help skills. Consider, for example, the difficulty of getting somewhere early if you had to awaken, dress, and feed a physically handicapped child. Stress is added when daily routines suddenly involve additional work (doing the task for the child or instructing even the most routine activities). Beckman-Bell (1980) studied the relationship between the characteristics of handicapped children and the number of family and parent problems, and found that care-giving demands accounted for 66% of the variance in stress reported by mothers.

A handicapped child, in addition to placing excess time and work demands on families, may also place limits on family opportunities and social life. For example, babysitters may not want to stay with an autistic child. Limited self-help skills may mean the family simply decides not to eat out as often. The dentist may not have the skills to effectively and humanely work with a 5-year-old retarded boy. The church nursery may be very uncomfortable about keeping a child with seizures. Just taking a walk in public can be stressful if your child does not behave like other children. Parents of handicapped children must continually struggle to achieve acceptance among their peers and gain access to the services and activities normally available to other members of society. This struggle is a source of continual stress, and is a battle which, unfortunately, must be waged over and over again.

A related form of stress comes from not knowing what to do with a child or how to handle a particular problem. For example, parents may be at a loss in conducting a toilet training program for their retarded child or may be unable to control inappropriate behavior such as tantrums or self-injury. Both the problem and the subsequent inability to deal with it impose additional stress. Further, parents may not know where to go to obtain needed information.

Stress on individual members Negative effects of a handicapped child on the family have been reported, including increased divorce and suicide rates among parents of retarded children (Price-Bonham & Addison, 1978), increased likelihood of child abuse (Embry, 1980), and a less satisfactory marriage than reported by parents of nonhandicapped children (Friedrich & Friedrich, 1981). However, each family member will be affected in a unique fashion and will require a support system to cope with stress. Daily caretaking demands of the child often become the mother's responsibility, and therefore she may be most affected (Gallagher, Cross, & Scharfman, 1981). Fathers of handicapped children have more difficulty than mothers in handling the social stigma (Tallman, 1965) and have lower self-esteem and greater depression than fathers of nonhandicapped children (Cummings, 1976). The major concerns of fathers of handicapped children include living with the uncertainty of an impairment, lack of gratification in relationships with the handicapped child (Cummings, 1976), and effects of the child on the sexual relationship with their spouse (Gallagher, Cross, & Scharfman, 1981).

Grandparents and other extended family members may also be affected, either through anger (Farber & Rykman, 1965; Pieper, 1976), mourning and grief (Solnit & Stark, 1961), or denial (Gayton & Walker, 1974). Gabel and Kotsch (1981) review the literature on extended families and conclude that the birth of a handicapped grandchild can disrupt the typical role grandchildren play in the psychological and emotional development of grandparents.

The handicapped child also has an impact on siblings. Often siblings of handicapped children must assume a greater amount of caretaking and supervision. Simeonsson and McHale (1981) suggest that a handicapped sibling can produce stress, resentment, or frustration.

Pressure to provide the best   A seldom discussed but important source of stress is the continual pressure to seek out and provide the best possible care. This is reflected in many ways. The continual search for a "cure" is one manifestation, when parents go from professional to professional in a search for the precise cause of the handicap, hoping that identification will lead to appropriate treatment. The historical lack of advocacy by schools and other educational agencies forced parents to assertively demand appropriate services for their children, placing additional stress on families.

Another form of stress is the pressure to participate in a child's educational program. Winton and Turnbull (1981) interviewed parents of handicapped preschoolers and found that 65% of the mothers felt that a major goal of an intervention program was to give them a break from the continual responsibility. Although parents wanted and appreciated the opportunity for frequent, informal contacts with the teacher, many did not want to function *as* teachers. Early childhood special educators should not force parents to participate extensively in the child's educational program if they choose not to do so.

Finally, an associated source of stress is deciding what type of educational services to advocate. For example, Turnbull and Blacher-Dixon (1980) reported that the question of mainstreaming may create a dilemma for parents who want their children to be as normal as possible but who do not want the additional stresses: the potential for teasing by peers, daily reminders of the discrepancies between their child and nonhandicapped children, and a concern that the mainstream environment may not provide the best educational setting. Parents of older handicapped children face a similar dilemma when deciding whether their child should live in a group home or move from sheltered to competitive employment.

Helping Families Cope

Early intervention programs can help parents cope with stress. Such programs should focus on identifying and predicting existing or potential sources of stress and planning strategies to deal with problems as they occur. The early childhood special educator should initially assess existing and potential stress and support systems for each family.

Assessing stress requires the consideration of a number of factors. In general, stress should be interpreted within the developmental context of each family. MacKeith (1973) suggested that four major crisis periods exist when families need strong support systems: when parents first become aware that their child is handicapped, when the child becomes eligible for educational services and the parents must begin to face the level of disability, when the child leaves school, and when parents are aging and cannot assume responsibility for their child's well-being.

Hospital support   Many parents of more severely handicapped children or those with certain genetic or physical disabilities will learn of their child's handicap at the hospital shortly after birth. Although early childhood special educators have traditionally had minimal influence over hospital practices, more hospitals are now concerned about the quality of the early parent-child relationship, particularly in the case of the high-risk child, and are beginning to change practices. The early childhood special educator can serve as an advocate for improved hospital routines for parents of handicapped infants and also as a resource for hospitals seeking advice on child and parent care practices.

One area of hospital practice where teachers can have an impact is the process of informing parents. Cunningham and Sloper (1977) interviewed parents of Down syndrome infants shortly after they were informed of the diagnosis and found that parents generally preferred to be told as early as possible. According to Cunningham and Sloper, some controversy still remains in the medical profession as to when parents should be told. The primary fear is that telling them too soon may lead to rejection of the infant. There is no research to substantiate this; in fact, post hoc interviews of parents consistently indicate that they would like to have been informed much earlier, and often suspect something is wrong before the doctor gives them the diagnosis. Nearly 63% of the parents in the Cunningham and Sloper study suspected something was wrong prior to being informed, either because of the baby's appearance or because of unusual alterations in the normal hospital routine. Unfortunately, nearly half of those parents who asked the medical staff if something was wrong were positively reassured that all was well. This false assurance proved to be devastating for some parents, and many complained bitterly.

Although most parents preferred to be told together, Cunningham and Sloper (1977) found that only 30% in their sample were together when informed of the diagnosis. Parents seem to need and want each other's support at this stressful time; the job of informing the other spouse can be particularly traumatic.

Cunningham and Sloper made several observations about how parents should be told. Privacy is important, both at the time of telling and afterwards. Many parents were told in front of a group of nurses or medical students and had no access to a private place so they could freely express their emotions without being disturbed. Parents also need the opportunity to discuss the diagnosis and ask questions. This should be followed by other opportunities for seeking information. Parents generally recalled very little information from the initial time of diagnosis, and therefore need to be told some things again. In addition, parents seem to need and want access to the baby. Many mothers felt that the baby should be present when they were told, and many wanted to hold the child immediately afterwards.

Support of parents after they have been informed of the diagnosis is important. Taylor and Hall (1980) suggest that a secure bond between parent and child cannot develop until parents have had an opportunity to work through their initial grief. "To accomplish this, we encourage parents to express and discuss their feelings of fear, anger, guilt, and sadness between themselves and with us, and let them know that their feelings are shared by most parents of premature and sick babies" (p. 321). This communication process is most important for the hospital care team. Taylor and Hall suggest principles for insuring appropriate communication with parents:

1 Determine and address the *parents'* perceptions.
2 Begin each discussion by listening to the parents' perceptions of the infant's condition and of what they have been told.
3 Check frequently during discussions to determine the parents' interpretations of what they are hearing and modify input as indicated.
4 Don't lecture.
5 Avoid information overload, statistics, vivid modifiers.
6 Regularly communicate medical information and the approach to working with particular parents to both the nursery team and referring physicians.

Parents should be allowed to participate in the initial care of their infant, regardless of the handicap. Minde (1980) reviewed the literature on bonding of parents to their premature infants and suggested that this alone may be insufficient to allay fears and anxieties. Group meetings and other counseling techniques may also be needed. Parents should be encouraged to spend time with their newborn, however, even if the child is in intensive care. Parents need to see and feel some sort of responsibility for their child.

In many cases parents are not informed of a handicap until the child is older. Although some physical or genetic anomalies are apparent at birth, evidence of delayed development cannot be assessed until later. Often the early childhood special educator will participate in a team that determines if the child is handicapped, and subsequently may participate in the informing process. Although such a situation differs considerably from informing parents at birth, many of the same principles are applicable.

Ongoing support systems The stress and needs of each family vary according to a

TABLE 8.5
Some questions to identify sources of family stress

1 Is the family a single-parent family?
2 Does the family have access to a babysitter or other respite services they can regularly use and feel comfortable with?
3 Does the family have adequate resources for food and shelter?
4 Are there any upcoming situations (meeting to plan child's Individual Educational Program (IEP), movement to public school) that may be stressful?
5 Are extended family such as grandparents, uncles, and aunts in the vicinity; if so, are they accepting and supportive?
6 Has the family been able to use normal community resources such as dentists, doctors, and churches?
7 Does the family need information related to the handicap?
8 Do family members participate in support or advocacy groups?
9 Does the family have access to transportation?

number of situational variables. A number of questions designed to identify potential sources of stress is listed in Table 8.5.

Although the teacher's ability to alter stressful situations may be limited, knowledge of community resources may allow the teacher to make helpful referrals. The bewildering number of local, state, and federal service agencies can be overwhelming for parents, and the early childhood special educator can coordinate agency services. Through referrals, early childhood special educators will be able to identify key agency personnel who support parents. Providing parents with a name and indicating this as a familiar, supportive individual will alleviate some of the stress in seeking needed services.

Other services can be provided or facilitated by the early intervention team to help parents cope. Perhaps the most important strategy is to work as an *ally* of families. All too often schools and families are viewed as having different goals. Although in some cases this may be true, families should be able to trust the educator to be their advocate.

In addition, teachers should also be good listeners. Families need time and attention so they can talk about their problems and accomplishments.

Another important strategy is participation in support groups. Often parents or siblings of handicapped children feel alone and isolated. Meeting others who have handicapped children helps family members realize they are not alone. Families under similar circumstances can be a source of support and strength and can share suggestions for coping with particular problems. Support groups often achieve objectives in the community that no individual can accomplish. Wandersman et al. (1980) suggest that support groups help create an atmosphere of trust, caring, and mutual aid; offer opportunities to share feelings and experiences; enable the family member to attain reinforcement and empathy; and provide a reference group so families can more accurately evaluate their status and performance.

The nature of the groups will vary according to the needs of families. In many communities certain types of support groups already exist, such as the National Association for Retarded Citizens, and the Parent-Teacher Association (PTA) found in public schools. However, other types of groups may need to be organized. During the preschool years families may want or need to participate in groups with other parents of young handicapped children. Individual family members may need separate groups based on their personal needs. For example, Wandersman et al. found that mothers felt that establishing a daily network available and willing to help with tasks was the most important form of support. Fathers felt that participation in a parenting group with other fathers was important to them. These preferences probably reflect the roles families allocate to the care of their children. Delaney (1978) described a model program for fathers of handicapped infants. Fathers and their infants attend a 2 hour a week class where they can discuss observations and topics of interest and have a music and exercise period, a snack, a guest speaker, and a preview and planning of the next week's activities.

In this section we briefly reviewed sources

TABLE 8.6
Some strategies for helping families cope with stress

Teacher's Strategy	Rationale
Serves as an advocate for children and families	A strong and positive parent-professional relationship built upon mutual trust and understanding can help parents feel more secure in their efforts to provide the best for their children.
Organizes support groups that meet the needs of individual family members, including fathers and siblings	Support groups allow family members to see that other families with handicapped children exist and survive, and provide reference and feedback.
Advocates appropriate hospital interventions	Since the informing process appears to be so important, hospital staff should be aware of their behavior and its impact on parents.
Helps organize respite care or train young people to work as babysitters for handicapped youngsters; maintains a file for parents	The need for respite is critical. Parents may not have access to respite services because they are unaware of available services or they cannot find a willing or competent sitter.
Prepares parents for upcoming stressful situations by suggesting strategies, describing potential problems, taking parents to observe, and talking to them and giving feedback after stressful situations have occurred	Parents need to learn to predict sources of stress and learn strategies to deal with it. Some examples of potentially stressful situations include first IEP meeting, movement from preschool to kindergarten, or taking child to church for the first time.
Maintains a file of community service agencies designed to meet specific needs not met by the school	Teachers often serve as the first contact for parents and can help refer parents to appropriate agencies or groups.

of stress and some strategies of helping families cope. These strategies are summarized in Table 8.6.

FAMILY INVOLVEMENT IN PRESCHOOL PROGRAMS

Families continue to be involved in the development of their children through educational experiences. This involvement provides a base for the child to expand his social world to others. Family involvement can also help insure more appropriate education for children by specifying goals and identifying appropriate intervention strategies, increasing the likelihood of generalization into the home, and bringing about intervention efforts. In addi-

tion to providing information to parents, intervention programs can use parents as teachers and program assistants.

Using Parents as Teachers

Many programs use parents as direct teachers of their children. Parents can teach at the center-based program or in their homes. Using parents as teachers can motivate children, can reinforce newly acquired skills at home, and can provide valuable information for others working with the child.

Rutherford and Edgar (1979) suggest that the joint determination of goals is important for rewarding and successful parent involvement in the classroom. Using parents merely as aides or for cleanup may be necessary at times but is not very rewarding. Parents can also be involved in sharing individual skills in the classroom (cooking, music, storytelling), working with their own and other children, and leading small group activities. Regardless of their role, parents should be successful. The teacher should select a skill that the child will probably learn within a relatively short period of time. Break the skill down into small steps so parents understand the strategies and techniques required to teach the skill. Model the teaching process, observe parents conducting the training session, and give feedback.

Substantial literature exists describing how parents can teach their young handicapped children (Wolery, 1979). However, as Winton and Turnbull (1981) point out, many parents prefer not to function as teachers of their own children. Further, some are unable to devote substantial time to teaching activities because of other commitments and responsibilities and yet may be actively involved with their child without engaging in formalized training activities. Even though they may not function as teachers, most parents are sincerely concerned about their child's learning, and should be involved in the assessment process and decisions.

Providing Information for Parents

Jenkins, Stephens, and Sternberg (1980) describe several strategies for meeting the information and training needs of each parent.

Individualized training may be home, media, or center based and is designed to meet the unique needs of each family. A program representative serves as the contact person with the family; conducts an individualized assessment of information and training needs; and plans activities, readings, experiences, or training sessions to meet those needs. While individualized training is flexible and relevant to the needs of the individual, it is expensive and time-consuming.

Restrictive group training involves the provision of a limited number of group training sessions. Group training is economical and provides an emotional support system with other parents of handicapped children. Jenkins et al. (1980) suggest that problems include

practical obstacles such as babysitting and transportation, difficulties in prioritizing each family's needs, and the inability to deal comfortably with individual problems in a group setting.

Continuous group training is held more frequently than restrictive group training. Weekly sessions focus on classroom activities and problems. Continuous training allows for the presentation of more information and fosters an effective communication exchange among parents and teachers. The disadvantages are similar to restrictive group training. In addition, many parents may not be able to devote so much time to the child's preschool program.

Many preschool programs use a resource room so parents can schedule their own training and obtain information to meet individual needs. A resource room should contain reading and audiovisual materials on handicapping conditions and on topics such as feeding, siblings, and behavior management. Materials should cover a range of reading skills and should be catalogued for easy reference. The room should also contain a resource directory for community services, the names and phone numbers of contact persons, and sources for obtaining additional materials and information. The room could include a library of toys, books, and other materials that can be checked out and taken home. Finally, supplies and equipment should be available so parents can make and design teaching materials either on their own or from suggestions and written instructions.

Winton and Turnbull (1981) found that parents preferred frequent, informal contacts with the teacher. Teachers should be aware of the importance of informal contacts made at arrival and departure times and should be available to talk with parents. Teacher aides or paraprofessionals should also understand the importance of these times and should be trained to interact appropriately with parents. Finally, if parents do not pick up their children at school, teachers should send information home daily on the child's present and planned activities as well as problems or achievements. Such information can be provided through a short note or by sending samples of the child's work with comments regarding goals for that activity.

The ideal parent program should encompass a variety of options, allowing parents to determine their own level of involvement. Training should be presented as a positive option. Parents' needs for information will change as the child grows and encounters new situations. A good preschool program should adapt its involvement component to meet the changing needs of families.

Parents as Program Assistants

Parents may assist preschool programs by serving on advisory boards, fund raising, participating in special projects such as field trips or playground improvement, making materials, volunteering in the classroom, cleaning up, or serving as program advocates. These activities should be carefully planned so parent involvement is successful, positive, and productive. For example, parents who work in the classroom should be familiar with classroom routines, major objectives for individual children, and standard techniques for dealing with specific behaviors. Parents who help with field trips or other outside activities should know standard safety precautions and should help plan those activities. Parents serving on advisory boards or working in fund raising or advocacy activities should be familiar with the purpose, overall philosophy, and orientation of the program, and should work with the professional staff in determining its future.

Parents should feel as if their efforts are appreciated, and that they are an important part of the program. Parents and staff can assure mutual cooperation and reinforcement by informing and involving each other.

SUMMARY

Facilitating parent-child interactions is an important but complex responsibility of the early childhood special educator. No simple solution exists, in part because the needs of each family are so unique and can be met in a variety of ways. The fundamental need is to help children and parents respond to each other in an enjoyable and meaningful fashion. Early childhood special educators must be knowledgeable of characteristic response patterns and accurately observe individual response and initiation patterns. As Robinson and Robinson (1976) suggest:

What every family of a retarded child deserves is a sort of ombudsman, an ally and advocate, to serve as a sounding board and release valve, to clarify next steps and new decisions as choice points are reached, to inform about resources and services, and to intervene when necessary (p. 414).

This role typically falls upon the preschool teacher.

This chapter has described the interaction between parents and handicapped children. It has also provided guidelines for fostering a quality relationship between parents and children, helping families deal with the stress of having a handicapped child, and involving parents in preschools.

REFERENCES

Ainsworth, M. D. S. The development of infant-mother attachment. In B. M. Caldwell and H. Ricciutti (Eds.), *Review of Child Development Research*, 1973, 1–94.

Als, H., Tronick, E., & Brazelton, T. B. Affective reciprocity and the development of autonomy: The study of a blind infant. *Journal of the American Academy of Child Psychiatry*, 1980, *19*, 22–40.

Beckman-Bell, P. *Characteristics of handicapped infants: A study of the relationship between child characteristics and stress as reported by mothers.* Unpublished doctoral dissertation, University of North Carolina, 1980.

Beckman-Bell, P. Child-related stress in families of handicapped children. *Topics in Early Childhood Special Education*, 1981, *1* (3), 45–53.

Bell, R. Q. A reinterpretation of the direction of effects in studies of socialization. *Psychological Review*, 1968, *75*, 81–95.

Bowlby, J. *Attachment.* New York: Basic Books, 1969.

Brazelton, T. B. Assessment in early infancy as an intervention. In D. Gilderman, D. Taylor-Hershel, S. Prestridge, & J. Anderson (Eds.), *The health care/education relationship.* Seattle: WESTAR, 1981.

Brazelton, T. B., Koslowski, B., & Main, M. The origins of reciprocity: The early mother-infant interaction. In M. Lewis & L. A. Rosenblum (Eds), *The effect of the infant on its caregiver.* New York: John Wiley, 1974.

Bromwich, R. M. Focus on maternal behavior in infant intervention. *American Journal of Orthopsychiatry*, 1976, *46*, 439–446.

Bromwich, R. M. *Working with parents and infants: An interactional approach.* Baltimore: University Park Press, 1981.

Bronfenbrenner, U. *Is early intervention effective? A report on longitudinal evaluations of preschool programs.* Washington, D. C.: DHEW, 1974.

Cicchetti, D., & Sroufe, L. A. The relationship between affective and cognitive development in Down's syndrome infants. *Child Development,* 1976, *46,* 920–929.

Cummings, S. The impact of the child's deficiency on the father: A study of fathers of mentally retarded and of chronically ill children. *American Journal of Orthopsychiatry,* 1976, *46,* 246–255.

Cunningham, C. C., & Sloper, T. Parents of Down's syndrome babies: Their early needs. *Child: Care, Health and Development,* 1977, *3,* 325–347.

Cunningham, E. E., Reuler, E., Blackwell, J., & Deck, J. Behavioral and linguistic developments in the interactions of normal and retarded children with their mothers. *Child Development,* 1981, *52,* 62–70.

Delaney, S. W. Fathers and infants class: A model for facilitating attachment between fathers and their infants. Unpublished manuscript, 1978. (Available from Experimental Education Unit, University of Washington, Seattle, 98195).

Drotar, D., Baskiewicz, A., Irwin, N., Kennell, J., & Klaus, M. The adaptation of parents to the birth of an infant with a congenital malformation: A hypothetical model. *Pediatrics,* 1975, *56,* 710–717.

Embry, L. Family support for handicapped preschool children at risk for abuse. In J. Gallagher (Ed.), *New directions for exceptional children* (Vol. 4). San Francisco: Jossey-Bass, 1980.

Farber, B. Effects of a severely retarded child on family integration. *Monographs of the Society for Research in Child Development,* 1959, *24* (2, Serial No. 71).

Farber, B., & Rykman, D.B. Effects of severely mentally retarded children on family relationships. *Mental Retardation Abstracts,* 1965, *11,* 1–17.

Featherstone, H. *A difference in the family.* New York: Basic Books, 1980.

Ferris, C. *A hug just isn't enough.* Washington, D.C.: Gallaudet College Press, 1980.

Fraiberg, S. Blind infants and their mothers: An examination of the sign system. In M. Lewis & L. Rosenblum (Eds.), *The effect of the infant on its caregiver.* New York: John Wiley, 1974.

Fraiberg, S. The development of human attachments in infants blind from birth. *Merrill-Palmer Quarterly,* 1975, *21,* 315–334.

Freud, S. *Three essays on the theory of sexuality.* London: Hogarth Press, 1905.

Freud, S. *Instincts and their vicissitudes.* London: Hogarth Press, 1915.

Friedrich, W. N., & Friedrich, W.L. Psychosocial assets of parents of handicapped and nonhandicapped children. *American Journal of Mental Deficiency,* 1981, *85,* 551–553.

Gabel, H., & Kotsch, L. S. Extended families and young handicapped children. *Topics in Early Childhood Special Education,* 1981, *1*(3), 29–35.

Gallagher, J. J., Beckman-Bell, P., & Cross, A. H. Families of handicapped children: Sources of stress and its amelioration. *Exceptional Children,* in press.

Gallagher, J. J., Cross, A., & Scharfman, W. Parental

adaptation to a young handicapped child: The father's role. *Journal of the Division for Early Childhood,* 1981, *3,* 3–14.

Gallagher, R. J., Jens, K. G., & O'Donnell, K. J. The effect of physical status on the affective expression of handicapped infants. *Infant Behavioral Development,* in press.

Gayton, W. R., & Walker, L. W. Family management of Down's syndrome during the early years. *Family Physician,* 1974, *9,* 160–164.

Goldberg, S. Social competence in infancy: A model of parent-infant interaction. *Merrill-Palmer Quarterly,* 1977, *23,* 163–177.

Greenberg, M. T., & Marvin, R. S. Attachment patterns in profoundly deaf preschool children. *Merrill-Palmer Quarterly,* 1979, *25,* 265–279.

Jenkins, S., Stephens, B., & Sternberg, L. The use of parents as parent trainers of handicapped children. *Education and Training of the Mentally Retarded,* 1980, *15,* 256–263.

Jens, K., & Johnson, N. Affective development: A window to cognition in young handicapped children. *Topics in Early Childhood Special Education,* 1982, *2*(2), 17–24.

Kelly, J. Focus on the parent-infant dyad. In B. L. Darby and M. J. May (Eds.), *Infant assessment: Issues and applications.* Seattle, WA: WESTAR, 1979.

Kastein, S., Spaulding, I., & Scharf, B. *Raising the young blind child: A guide for parents and educators.* New York: Human Sciences Press, 1980.

Kennedy, J. C. The high-risk maternal-infant acquaintance process. *Nursing Clinics of North America,* 1973, *8,* 549–556.

MacKeith, R. The feelings and behavior of parents of handicapped children. *Developmental Medicine and Child Neurology,* 1973, *15,* 524–527.

Marshall, N. R., Hogrenes, J. R., & Goldstein, S. Verbal interactions: Mothers and their retarded children vs. mothers and their nonretarded children. *American Journal of Mental Deficiency,* 1973, *77,* 415–417.

Marvin, R. S. An ethological-cognitive model for the attenuation of mother-child attachment behavior. In T. Alloway, P. Pliner, & L. Krames (Eds.), *Attachment behavior.* New York: Plenum, 1977.

McCubbin, H. I., Nevin, R. S., Larsen, A., Comeau, J., Patterson, J., Cauble, A. E., & Striker, K. *Families coping with cerebral palsy.* St. Paul: University of Minnesota, Family Social Science, 1981.

Minde, K. Bonding of mothers to premature infants: Theory and practice. In P. M. Taylor (Ed.), *Parent-infant relationships.* New York: Grune & Stratton, 1980.

Mordock, J. B. The separation-individuation process and developmental disabilities. *Exceptional Children,* 1979, *46,* 176–184.

Pieper, E. Grandparents can help. *The Exceptional Parent,* 1976, *6,* 7–10.

Prechtl, H. F. R. The mother-child interaction in babies with minimal brain damage. In B. M. Foss (Ed.), *Determinants of infant behavior* (Vol. 2). New York: John Wiley, 1963.

Price-Bonham, S., & Addison, S. Families and mentally retarded children: Emphasis on the father. *The Family Coordinator,* 1978, *3,* 221–230.

Robinson, H. B., & Robinson, N. M. *The mentally retarded child: A psychological approach* (2nd ed.). New York: McGraw-Hill, 1976.

Roskies, E. *Abnormality and normality: The mothering of thalidomide children.* Ithaca, N.Y.: Cornell University Press, 1972.

Rutherford, R. B., & Edgar, E. B. *Teachers and parents.* Boston: Allyn & Bacon, 1979.

Schlesinger, H. S., & Meadow, K. P. *Sound and sign: Childhood deafness and mental health.* Berkeley: University of California Press, 1972.

Scott, E. P., Jan, J. E., & Freeman, R. D. *Can't your child see?* Baltimore: University Park Press, 1977.

Simeonsson, R. J., & McHale, S. M. Review: Research on handicapped children-sibling relationships. *Child: Care, Health and Development,* 1981, *7,* 153–171.

Solnit, A. J., & Stark, M. H. Mourning and the birth of a defective child. *Psychological Studies of Children,* 1961, *16,* 523.

Stern, D. N. Mother and infant at play: The dyadic interaction involving facial, vocal, and gaze behaviors. In M. Lewis & L. Rosenblum (Eds.), *The effect of the infant on the caregiver.* New York: John Wiley, 1974.

Stone, N. W., & Chesney, B. H. Attachment behaviors in handicapped infants. *Mental Retardation,* 1978, *16,* 8–12.

Tallman, I. Spousal role differentiation and the socialization of severely retarded children. *Journal of Marriage and the Family,* 1965, *27,* 37–42.

Taylor, P. M., & Hall, B. L. Parent-infant bonding: Problems and opportunities in a perinatal center. In P. M. Taylor (Ed.), *Parent-infant relationships.* New York: Grune & Stratton, 1980.

Turnbull, A. P., & Blacher-Dixon, J. Preschool mainstreaming: Impact on parents. In J. Gallagher (Ed.), *New directions for exceptional children* (Vol. 1). San Francisco: Jossey-Bass, 1980.

Wandersman, L., Wandersman, A., & Kahn, S. Social support in the transition to parenthood. *Journal of Community Psychology,* 1980, *8,* 332–342.

Wedell-Monnig, J., & Lumley, J. M. Child deafness and mother-child interaction. *Child Development,* 1980, *51,* 766–774.

Winton, P. J., & Turnbull, A. P. Parent involvement as viewed by parents of preschool handicapped children. *Topics in Early Childhood Special Education,* 1981, *1*(3), 11–19.

Wolery, M. R. *Parents as teachers of their handicapped children: An annotated bibliography.* Seattle: WESTAR, 1979.

Interacting with the environment in adaptive and productive ways requires children to use many behaviors or skills commonly labeled *cognitive abilities*. For example, Marcy is playing peek-a-boo with her grandfather. She covers her eyes with her hands, waits an instant, throws up her hands; her grandfather stages great surprise; Marcy laughs, pauses, and repeats the sequence. After several repetitions, they stop playing peek-a-boo and begin to play with Grandfather's keys. He takes the keys, hides them in one of his hands, holds out his hands with both fists closed. Marcy opens his right hand and then his left, finds the keys, grabs them, makes eye contact, laughs, and they repeat the process. Are these activities simply games between an adoring grandfather and his granddaughter, or do they tell us something about Marcy's abilities? A few months ago when Darwin was being quiet his mother would coo and talk to him and then stop. Darwin would then coo back but he did not repeat any sounds his mother had made. Two months later if Darwin babbled and his mother repeated his sounds, he would again repeat the sounds. Now Darwin's mother can make new babbling sounds and Darwin will repeat the new sounds. Are these statements simply descriptions of a mother and infant son engaged in meaningless, albeit enjoyable, dialogue, or is Darwin learning from these experiences and do they indicate changes in his abilities?

These examples are typical activities young children and their caregivers engage in, but they are not simply games and meaningless exercises. They illustrate cognitive abilities called *sensorimotor skills*. Marcy is learning about the existence of objects not perceptually present; this skill is called *object permanence*. Darwin is learning about imitating others' behaviors and especially about imitating vocalizations.

The first section of this chapter describes various sensorimotor skills. The second section presents a rationale for teaching those skills, and the third describes procedures for assessing those skills. The fourth includes general guidelines for teaching sensorimotor skills.

Sensorimotor and other cognitive skills do not develop separately; their use depends upon interactions with the areas of social, motor, and language development. These interactions cannot be ignored when assessing and teaching young handicapped children.

9

Acquisition and Use of Sensorimotor Skills

DESCRIPTION OF SENSORIMOTOR SKILLS

Sensorimotor skills are those behaviors acquired during infancy and thought to be precursors to basic thinking and conceptual development. According to Piaget (1952), they begin as reflexes but quickly become motor schemes (patterns of behavior) which in turn become mental schemes (internal strategies for responding). By the end of the sensorimotor stage (about 2 years of age) the infant has acquired a primitive ability to symbolize or mentally represent (Coggins & Carpenter, 1979; Phillips, 1975). This accomplishment is considered the crowning achievement of the sensorimotor period.

In this chapter we describe six sensorimotor skills: object permanence, means-ends (purposeful problem solving), spatial relations, causality, schemes for relating to objects (play), and imitation (gestural and vocal). Each of these skills develops in a logical progression from motor movements to manipulations of mental representations or symbols. Some of the steps are shown in Table 9.1. These steps are ordinal. Each higher step in the skill is more complex than the previous steps, and the more complex steps incorporate or integrate the less complex steps. The less complex steps must be learned first, because they make up, in part, the more complex steps. Because of these two characteristics, the steps of the sensorimotor skills have been used as the content (sequence) of the cognitive curriculum for handicapped children (Brassell & Dunst, 1976, 1978; Kahn, 1978). The steps of the sensorimotor skills are "what" we teach young handicapped children.

Since sensorimotor skills represent a sequence from simple motor movements to mental representation, there are some similarities across skills. For example, the most complex step of each skill involves a primitive symbolic ability. Piaget (1952) grouped these similarities into six substages of the sensorimotor period (see Table 9.1, left-hand column). The relationship between the sensorimotor skills (vertical) and sensorimotor substages (horizontal) is one of ascending complexity. The first substage represents the lowest level of development; the sixth, the most complex. The simplest steps of the vertical sensorimo-

tor skills are at the base of Table 9.1 near the first substage. The most complex steps of each skill are at the top in the sixth substage.

Procedures for assessing and teaching the sensorimotor skills *rather than* the sensorimotor substages are described because children do not acquire all the skills of a given substage at the same time (Dunst, 1980; Dunst, Brassell, & Rheingrover, 1981). Thus, if we were teaching by substage, it would be difficult to determine which substage (of perhaps two or three) should be targeted for instruction. However, we can provide instruction for each skill at the appropriate step.[1]

While many of the sensorimotor skills are related to inanimate objects, such as "secures hidden object," they also have animate or social components such as "searches for mother by looking in another room." Since the steps in Table 9.1 pertain more to objects, the skills having animate components will be identified in the text.

Means-Ends Behavior

Means-ends behavior involves purposeful problem solving using both objects and people. It is the ability of the child to separate the *procedures* (means) for solving a problem from the *goal* (ends) of the solved problem. It begins with a simple reflexive response to some external stimuli and moves to repeating a behavior to make an interesting event last (hitting a mobile again to keep it moving), discovering through trial and error that a given solution will solve a particular problem (a stick can be used to obtain an object that is otherwise out of reach), and finally inventing or mentally figuring out (without using trial and error) the solution to a given problem. For example, the child would not attempt to stack a solid disk on a pole, although it might be mixed with disks with holes that the child stacks (Dunst, 1980; Uzgiris & Hunt, 1975). The animate or social aspects of means-ends behavior would involve discovering and using people to solve problems. A child may request through gestures and vocalizations some behavior (solution) from others. For example, the child might laugh and make eye contact

---

[1] See Dunst and Brassell (1975) for a detailed discussion of this issue.

TABLE 9.1

Selected steps of the sensorimotor skills throughout the sensorimotor period

Stages (age in months)	Domains of sensorimotor development						
	Purposeful problem solving	Object permanence	Spatial relationships	Causality	Vocal Imitation	Gestural Imitation	Play
VI Representation and foresight (18–24)	"Invents" means behavior, via internal thought processes, needed to obtain a desired goal	Recreates sequence of displacements to secure objects: secures hidden objects through a sequence of *invisible* displacements	Manifests the ability to "represent" the nature of spatial relationships that exist between objects, and between objects and self	Shows capacity to (a) infer a cause, given only its effect, and (b) foresee an effect, given a cause	Imitates complex verbalizations. Reproduces previously heard sounds and words from memory; deferred imitation	Imitates complex motor movements. Reproduces previously observed actions from memory; deferred imitation	Symbolic play: uses one object as a "signifier" for another (e.g., a box for a doll bed). Symbolically enacts an event without having ordinarily used objects present
V Tertiary circular reactions (12–18)	Discovers "novel" means behavior needed to obtain a desired goal	Secures objects hidden through a series of *visible* displacements	Combines and relates objects in different spatial configurations (e.g., places blocks in a cup)	Hands an object to an adult to have that person repeat or instigate a desired action	Imitates novel sound patterns and words that he/she has not previously heard	Imitates novel movements that he/she cannot see self perform (i.e., *invisible* gestures) and that he/she has not previously performed	Adaptative play: begins to use one object (e.g., doll cup) as a substitute for another (e.g., adult-size cup) during play with objects
IV Coordination of secondary circular reactions (8–12)	Serializes two heretofore separate behaviors in goal-directed sequences	Secures objects seen hidden under, behind, etc. a single barrier	Rotates and examines objects with signs of appreciation of their three-dimensional attributes, size, shape, weight, etc.	Touches adult's hands to have that person instigate or continue an interesting game or action	Imitates novel sounds but only ones that are similar to those he/she already produces	Imitates (a) self-movements that are *invisible* (e.g., sticking out the tongue), and (b) novel movements comprised of actions familiar to self	During problem solving sequences, he/she abandons the terminus in favor of playing with the means. Ritualization: applies appropriate social actions to different objects

TABLE 9.1 (continued)
Selected steps of the sensorimotor skills throughout the sensorimotor period

Stages (age in months)	Purposeful problem solving	Object permanence	Spatial relationships	Causality	Vocal Imitation	Gestural Imitation	Play
III Secondary circular reactions (4—8)	Procedures for making interesting sights last: repeats actions to maintain the reinforcing consequences produced by the action	Reinstates visual contact with objects by (a) anticipating the terminal position of a moving object, and (b) removing a cloth placed over his/her face. Retrieves a partially hidden object	Shows signs of understanding relationships between self and external events (e.g., follows trajectory of rapidly falling objects)	Uses "phenomenalistic procedures" (e.g., generalized excitement) as a causal action to have an adult repeat an interesting spectacle	Imitates sounds already in his/her repertoire	Imitates simple gestures already in his/her repertoire that are *visible* to self	Repetition of interesting actions applied to familiar objects
II Primary circular reactions (1—4)	First acquired adaptations, coordination of two behavioral schemes (e.g., hand-mouth coordination)	Attempts to maintain visual contact with objects moving outside the visual field	Reacts to external stimuli as representing independent spatial fields (e.g., visual, auditory) rather than as a spatial nexus	Shows signs of pre-causal understanding (e.g., places thumb in the mouth to suck on it)	Repeats sound just produced following adult imitation of the sound	Repeats movements just made following adult imitation of the action	Produces primary circular reactions repeatedly in an enjoyable manner
I Use of reflexes (0—1)	Shows only reflexive reactions in response to external stimuli	No active search for objects vanishing from sight	No signs of appreciation of spatial relationships between objects	No signs of understanding causal relationships	Vocal contagion: cries on hearing another infant cry	No signs of imitation of movements he/she performs	No signs of intentional play behavior

Note: From *A Clinical and Educational Manual for Use with the Uzgitis and Hunt Scales of Infant Psychological Development* by C. J. Dunst. Baltimore: University Park Press, 1980. Copyright 1980 by University Park Press. Reprinted by permission.

to get her mother to repeat some interesting game, or she might lead her father to the sink to get a drink of water.

Object Permanence

Object permanence involves the child's ability to realize that objects exist even though he cannot hear, touch, or see the object. *Object* in this case refers to both physical (things) and social objects (people). For sighted children, object permanence begins with the ability to visually fixate on something and then follow or track it as it moves, as it disappears and reappears. The next level involves searching for an object the child sees being hidden, and progresses to searching for an object the child does not see being hidden (Brainerd, 1978; Uzgiris & Hunt, 1975). For blind children, the beginning steps of object permanence may be demonstrated by the ability to locate an auditory signal and then follow it as it moves. Social object or person permanence involves "the child's recognition that his or her primary caregivers are *stable* entities who react *predictably* in response to the child's attempts to signal a desire to be attended to, cared for, picked up, etc." (Dunst, 1981a, p. 46). It would progress from recognition of the caregivers to expectations that they would behave predictably.

Spatial Relationships

Spatial relationships involve the child's recognition of an object's position in space and the recognition of one object's location in relation to another. The infant initially does not appear to be aware of spatial relationships, but later begins to track moving objects visually and through auditory signals, acts on objects as though they have a given location, rotates objects in relation to the spatial orientation (if presented a bottle with the nipple turned away the infant will turn the nipple toward him and suck it), and finally recognizes the spatial relationship between two objects without testing the relationship with his own body. For example, the child will go around a barrier to retrieve an object rather than attempting to go through it. Mental representation of space is manifested by recogni-

tion of the absence of some object usually in a given location. For example, the child notices that a certain chair is missing when it was taken to another room without his or her prior knowledge (Dunst, 1980; Uzgiris & Hunt, 1975). The social component of spatial relations deals with the infant's position in relation to objects, or the position of other persons in relation to physical objects or the infant.

Causality

Causality refers to children's recognition of causes for interesting events, particularly the infant's realization that behavior can produce changes in objects. Initially the infant shows no awareness of causal relationships, but begins to realize that a given action can cause interesting events to occur (dropping things produces interesting sounds regardless of what is dropped); that getting adults' attention can result in their making interesting things occur (patting her mother's hand to get her to reactivate a toy); that giving the adult a toy communicates the desire to have it reactivated more than simply touching the adult; and finally mentally inferring what will cause an event to occur. For example, the child may push or pull on the key of a wind-up toy to get it to work even though no one activated the toy (Dunst, 1980; Uzgiris & Hunt, 1975). The social component of causality has to do with the infant's ability to realize that other people can cause important things to occur. For example, the infant's recognition of "her mother as a primary source for satisfying bodily needs (e.g., feeding)" (Dunst, 1981a, p. 46).

Imitation

Imitation involves the ability of the child to match or copy the verbal and nonverbal behavior of a model. The course of imitation is shown in Table 9.1 and described in Chapter 4, and thus is not repeated here.

Schemes for Relating to Objects

Schemes for relating to objects involve the infant's ability to perform various behaviors on a variety of objects. These behaviors are frequently thought of as play and exploratory behaviors. Initially the child repeatedly produces enjoyable movements (sucks on fingers); then the child repeats actions with familiar objects (shakes a rattle, the bottle, Mother's keys); then begins to manipulate different objects in different ways (shakes a rattle and pushes a ball); then begins to use objects to imitate adult's use (rocks a doll, drinks from a toy cup); uses two objects together (pounds with a hammer, stirs with a spoon); and finally uses objects in a pretend fashion. For example, the child may use a chair as a car and pretend to drive it or use a stick as a vacuum cleaner (Dunst, 1980). The social component of schemes for relating to objects or social play involves the child's ability to use objects in socially meaningful ways and to engage in behaviors depicting social situations. For example, a child is engaged in social play when rolling a toy truck on the floor and making a motor-like sound, or when picking up Mother's purse and waving "bye, bye."

Sensory Organization Responses

Sensory organization responses (Robinson & Robinson, 1978) occur during the early steps of many sensorimotor skills. These are: visual fixation—the ability to visually focus on an object or person; sound localization—the ability to identify (usually by turning the head) the source and direction of auditory stimuli; visual and auditory tracking—the ability to follow (usually by moving the eyes or head) sensory stimuli as they move from one location to another; grasp maintenance—the ability to hold an object for 30 or more seconds away from support; and sensory directed reaching and grasping—the ability to note either through vision or hearing the presence and location of an object, reach for it based on sensory information, and grasp it. These behaviors may be a large part of the cognitive (sensorimotor) curriculum of neonates and profoundly handicapped children. Proficient execution of these responses will facilitate development of the sensorimotor skills of imitation, object permanence, and schemes for relating to objects as well as other areas of development such as social interactions and communication and motor development.

RATIONALE FOR TEACHING SENSORI-MOTOR SKILLS

As described in Chapter 2, three general approaches exist for deciding what to teach: the developmental milestones approach, the developmental theory-based approach, and the functional approach. The developmental theory-based and the functional approaches are preferred over the developmental milestones approach. Reasons for teaching sensorimotor skills to young handicapped children directly apply to the approach being used to determine instructional targets.

Similar Sequence Hypothesis

The *similar sequence hypothesis* is the notion that handicapped persons develop behaviors in a sequence similar to nonhandicapped persons but at a slower rate. Thus, cognitively handicapped children would develop the sensorimotor skills in a sequence similar to nonhandicapped children (i.e., similar to Piaget's descriptions of the sensorimotor period).

Weisz and Zigler (1979) reviewed a heterogeneous group of studies to determine whether the prediction of the similar sequence hypothesis would hold true for cognitively handicapped children on Piagetian tasks, including sensorimotor skills. The studies that Weisz and Zigler reviewed used a variety of mentally handicapped persons, ranging in age from children to adults, and in level of severity from mild to profound retardation. The studies used different Piagetian tasks and methods for measuring children's performance. The consistent finding was that performance of cognitively handicapped persons on Piagetian tasks followed sequences similar to typical children. Based on this finding, and given that the teacher was using the developmental theory-based approach for selecting instructional targets, sensorimotor skills should be taught to young cognitively handicapped children to accelerate their rate of development.

Functionality

Data supporting the similar sequence hypothesis would be insufficient to warrant teaching sensorimotor skills if a teacher was using the functional approach for selecting instructional targets. Some sensorimotor skills appear to have independent functional usefulness, however. For example, if Karen learned to imitate, she can use this skill to learn other behaviors such as language, social, motor, and self-help skills. Sensorimotor skills that appear to have functional importance in their own right are schemes for relating to objects (play), imitation, means-ends, and spatial relations. Thus, depending upon the child's skills and the environment, certain sensorimotor skills are useful to teach.

Sensorimotor Skills as Prerequisites

Prerequisite behaviors must be learned before other, usually more complex, behaviors. Piaget (1952) proposed that sensorimotor skills begin as reflexes, become motor schemes, and then become mental schemes so the child has a primitive ability to manipulate mental symbols. Piaget also proposed that cognitive development was invariant (Ginsburg & Opper, 1979). *Invariance* means "the sequence of development has a fixed, defined order; to reach point Z in development a child must have started at A and proceeded through B, C, D, E, and so on. Further, this order is said to be the same for all children ... although individual differences in rate are possible and likely" (Evans, 1975, p. 195). According to Piaget, the only way children can acquire mental schemes is to progress from reflexes. Invariance, or the notion of a fixed order, applies to cognitive development beyond the sensorimotor period. Thus more conceptual thinking follows the primitive ability to manipulate sensorimotor schemes acquired during the sensorimotor period. For example, at the end of the sensorimotor stage, children appear bound by perceptual rather than conceptual stimuli; things are as they appear. Suppose a teacher has three glasses; two glasses are short and wide and the other is tall and thin. The two short-wide glasses have equal amounts of fluid in them. If the teacher pours the fluid from one of the short-wide glasses into the tall-thin glass, the children at the end of the sensorimotor stage will act as though there is more fluid in the tall-thin glass than in the short-wide one. The perceptual stimulus (the height of the liquid in the tall thin glass) will override the child's ability to understand that the amount of fluid did not change when

it was poured from one glass to the other. However, to solve the problem, the child must be able to manipulate mental symbols. If early steps of the sensorimotor skills are prerequisites to later steps and the full manifestation of the sensorimotor skills is a prerequisite to later conceptual skills, then children must be taught to perform the sensorimotor skills.

Further, the sensorimotor skills of object permanence and means-ends are thought to be prerequisites or precursors for certain language skills (Bates, 1976; Morehead & Morehead, 1974). For example, Kahn (1975) noted a strong relationship between Substage VI sensorimotor skills and spontaneous language of severely and profoundly retarded children. The relationship between sensorimotor skills and later language development has not yet been clearly defined (Bowerman, 1976; Dunst, 1981a).

Mental Representation

Piaget also proposed that cognitive development was *cumulative;* that is, the quality of cognitive development at point C depends upon the earlier quality of development at point B, which in turn depends upon the quality of development at point A. The principle of cumulative development is thought to be especially true in early sensorimotor and symbolic experiences (Evans, 1975), and relates to the quality of children's thinking, reasoning, and judgments. These skills should be taught so children have the appropriate quality sensorimotor experiences. In addition, sensorimotor skill sequences are the most clearly articulated steps through which children pass in learning to think and thus should be included early in the curriculum for children with cognitive handicaps.

In general, we should use the developmental approach when selecting instructional targets for young children with mild and moderate cognitive delays. The functional approach is used for those with severe and profound cognitive delays. Instruction on sensorimotor skills should be initiated for children who are "at risk" or who have moderate or mild developmental delays. However, instruction for children with severe or profound cognitive delays should occur only if the skills result in functional, useful outcomes. For example, we might train a severely handicapped child to perform sensory organization responses to increase his or her ability to attend to environmental stimuli.

ASSESSING SENSORIMOTOR SKILLS

Measurement of intelligence has received tremendous amounts of research and rhetoric. Dunst (1978) and Lewis (1976) provide detailed discussions of the history of infant intelligence testing and related issues. Salvia and Ysseldyke (1981) describe various intelligence tests used with preschool and school-aged children; Warren (1977) and Hobbs (1975) discuss intelligence testing and special populations; Evans and McCandless (1978) and Sattler (1974, 1982) discuss related issues; and Buros (1978) provides evaluative reviews of various tests.

Teachers' involvement in assessing intelligence and cognitive functioning is usually limited to screening and determining instructional targets. When screening, teachers typically use developmental scales to provide an estimate of whether further assessment is needed. If assessment is needed, referrals are made to the appropriate services. Teachers are rarely directly involved if assessment is for placement in special intervention programs, diagnosis, or description of the child's cognitive abilities in comparison to others. Psychometric tools are used, and teachers rarely elect to receive the training required to administer such instruments.

When assessment is for instructional program planning, teachers are directly involved and should use either the developmental theory-based approach or the functional approach in determining instructional targets. The functional approach involves specifying terminal behavior to result in functional skills. The terminal behavior is then task analyzed and the child's interactions with the environment are systematically observed. For example, if the child consistently played with only one toy at a time and did not use toys in socially meaningful ways (not rolling cars on the floor or not sweeping with a broom), play with two toys at one time and in socially meaningful ways could become the instructional objective. Such toy play is functional because it allows for independent activities free of adult direction.

Teachers using the developmental theory-based approach would select an assessment tool to measure children's attainment of sensorimotor skills. Although several criterion- and curriculum-referenced tools have cognitive sections (*Hawaii Early Learning Program,* VORT, 1979; *Portage Guide to Early Education,* Bluma, Shearer, Froham, & Hilliard, 1976; *Project MEMPHIS,* Quick, Little, & Campbell, 1974; *Early Learning Accomplishment Profile,* Glover, Preminger, & Sanford, 1978), most are based on developmental milestones rather than developmental theory. Two notable exceptions are the Wabash Curriculum (Tilton, Liska, & Bourland, 1977) and the Carolina Curriculum for Handicapped Infants (Johnson, Jens, & Attermeir, 1979). Although the Early Intervention Developmental Profile (Rogers, D'Eugenio, Brown, Donovan, & Lynch, 1980) includes items from the sensorimotor skills, they are arranged by approximate developmental age. Instruction would be initiated on the skills the child is unable to perform or where performance is not at criterion levels.

Because there are so few developmental theory-based measures for the sensorimotor skills, many teachers have begun to use the Ordinal Scales of Psychological Development (Uzgiris & Hunt, 1975). These scales are based on Piaget's descriptions and on considerable empirical analysis of the sensorimotor stage. Rather than conforming to the six sensorimotor substages, however, they assess the six sensorimotor skills and consist of the following developmental phases:

1 Visual pursuit and the permanence of objects
2 Means for obtaining desired environmental events
3 Operational causality
4 Imitation: Vocal and gestural[2]
5 Object relations in space
6 Schemes for relating to objects

Uzgiris and Hunt developed 7–14 hierarchically arranged steps that detail how skills within each branch are acquired. For each step, they provide directions for administration that include:

---

[2]When using the scales, some investigators report separate data for vocal and gestural imitation as compared to combining the two (Dunst et al., 1981; Kahn, 1976).

(1) the position of the infant and the nature of the physical space around the infant, helpful in presenting the situation; (2) the object or objects suggested for use in the situation; (3) the instructions for actions to be carried out by the examiner; (4) the suggested number of times the situation is to be repeated; and (5) the various actions an infant may be expected to show in the situation (Uzgiris & Hunt, 1975, p. 145).

A sample item, the third step in the development of visual pursuit and the permanence of objects, is shown in Table 9.2.

Variations in the testing procedures are allowed to accommodate the unique needs of individual infants. For example, the examiner may vary the objects used, the order of testing, or the infant's position. Uzgiris and Hunt provide several general suggestions for administering the scales, including: testing only when the infant is fully cooperative; being sure rapport is established if the examiner is a stranger; presenting items in the infant's home or in a natural setting; varying the order of item presentation to maintain the infant's attention; using toys that are interesting to the infant; repeating presentation of the items dependent upon the infant's interest and performance; and employing scales only important to the needs of the assessment.

The Ordinal Scales are attractive to early childhood special educators because they can

TABLE 9.2
Description of an item for object permanence

═══════════════════════════════════

3. Finding an Object Which is Partially Covered

Location: The infant must be in a sitting position with both hands free to manipulate objects. A young infant may be propped up in an infant seat or on a sofa using pillows. An older infant may be seated in a high chair or on a rug on the floor. A working surface must be available in front of and to the side of the infant; it may be provided by placing a board across the infant seat, by pushing the high chair against a table, or by using the rug-covered space around the infant, if he is sitting on the floor. An infant feeding table is also suitable.

Object: Any object which the infant demonstrates interest in by reaching for it; and, for a cover or screen, a white nontransparent scarf. It is important that the object be unitary, and that no portion of the object should look equivalent to the whole. A plastic doll or animal may be used, but an object such as a necklace would be unsuitable. Use of a white nontransparent scarf for the screen helps to minimize the interest of infants in the screen.

Directions: To ascertain that an infant desires an object, place it on the surface and observe that the infant reaches for it. Take the object, while making sure the infant is focusing on it, place it on the surface within his reach and cover it with the screen in such a way that a small portion of the object remains visible (the feet of the doll, the tail of the animal, etc.). If, in his attempts to obtain the object, the infant covers it up completely, start a new presentation. If the infant's interest in the object becomes doubtful, interpose a presentation in which the object is left uncovered on the surface to determine if he will still reach for it.

Repeat: 3 times.

Infant
Actions: a. Loses interest in the object once it is partially covered.
b. Reacts to the loss of the object, but does not reach for it and does not obtain it once it is partially covered.
*c. Obtains the object by pulling it out from under the screen or by removing the screen and picking up the object.

═══════════════════════════════════

Note: Underlined infant behaviors (e.g., c) indicate the action which demonstrates the child has passed the item; items with asterisks are items used in Uzgiris and Hunt's scaling analysis to determine the ordinality of the scales.

Note: From *Assessment in Infancy* by I.C. Uzgiris and J. M. Hunt. Urbana: University of Illinois Press, 1975. Copyright 1975 by University of Illinois Press. Reprinted by permission.

be reliably administered to handicapped children (Kahn, 1976). The results obtained from the second administration of the scale will probably be similar to the first, and two people will be likely to score a child's response in a similar manner. The Ordinal Scales appear to be valid from both an empirical analysis (they are hierarchical) and a logical analysis (they generally represent Piaget's description of the sensorimotor period). The scales can also be used to plan and evaluate instructional programs (Brassell & Dunst, 1976, 1978; Kahn, 1978). Dunst (1980) developed a manual for using the Ordinal Scales in clinical and educational settings. The manual includes a performance profile that allows a visual display of a child's performance on each sensorimotor skill.

Besides the Uzgiris and Hunt (1975) Ordinal Scales, other tools can measure sensorimotor skills. The more widely known are the Albert Einstein Scales of Sensorimotor Development (Corman & Escalona, 1969; Escalona & Corman, 1966, as cited by DuBose & Kelly, 1981), and Decarie's (1965) scales (see Dunst [1981a] for other tools). The Uzgiris and Hunt Scales are the most commonly used due to their reliability, ordinality, availability, and comprehensiveness (Kahn, 1979).

TEACHING SENSORIMOTOR SKILLS

In recent years, a significant change has occurred in our view of infants and young children. Infants are seen as being much more capable and active than was previously thought (Osofsky, 1979; Stone, Smith, & Murphy, 1973), and the importance of environmental variables in promoting or retarding the attainment of cognitive competence has been recognized (cf. Wachs, 1979; Yarrow, Rubenstein, & Pederson, 1975). However, some authors (Kamii & Devries, 1977, 1978) contend that Piagetian tasks cannot be taught. This conflict leads to the issue of whether handicapped children can be taught sensorimotor skills and the need for defining general models and guidelines.

Teaching Handicapped Children

Studies with nonhandicapped children have been reviewed by Brainerd (1978) and Gelman (1978), and within general limitations it appears possible to train them to perform Piagetian sensorimotor skills. Further, living conditions affect the attainment of different cognitive skills (Dunst, 1981a; Wachs, 1979).

Data on facilitating acquisition of sensorimotor skills by handicapped children are quite limited despite relatively frequent recommendations to assess and teach such skills (D. Bricker & W. Bricker, 1973; W. Bricker & D. Bricker, 1976; Dunst, 1981a; Filler, Robinson, Smith, Vincent-Smith, D. Bricker, & W. Bricker, 1975; Kahn, 1978, 1979; Robinson, 1976; Robinson & Robinson, 1978; Stephens, 1977).[3] Robinson (1974) investigated the effects of reinforcement history on behaviors used to infer progressive acquisition of object permanence. Four young (21–32 months) developmentally delayed subjects who did not initially look and retrieve objects in the places where they observed them being hidden (substage V, object permanence) were trained to do this. The training consisted of leaving the object partially visible and over repeated trials covering up more and more of the object until it was completely hidden, with reinforcement given for correct responses. All four subjects acquired the behavior. While this finding alone was not the primary purpose of Robinson's study, it clearly indicated young handicapped children could be trained to look and retrieve objects they observed being hidden.

Brassell and Dunst (1976) compared procedures for facilitating acquisition of object permanence. They used three groups of school-aged ambulatory severely retarded institutionalized subjects. The first group, a control group, received "structured social interaction apparently unrelated to the development of the object permanence concept" (p. 524). The second group received training similar to that described by Tilton, Liska, and Bourland (1977). The third group received

---

[3]In this section, *handicapped children* refers to those on whom data have been reported. Primarily this means children with mental (cognitive) handicaps.

training in smaller steps than the second, based on the notion of shaping successive approximations of target behavior. Training occurred for eight days with each session lasting 10 minutes. Subjects in both the second and third training groups demonstrated accelerated acquisition of object permanence, with no improvement from the control group. Training was specific to object permanence; other sensorimotor skills did not differ from pretest to posttest. While the subjects were not preschool children, they functioned in the sensorimotor stage and specific, albeit minimal training accelerated their performance on object permanence tasks.

In a similar study, Kahn (1978) used two groups (four subjects each) of severely and profoundly handicapped children, 3½–7½ years of age, to assess the effects of training on the acquisition of object permanence. All subjects were given a pretest using the Uzgiris and Hunt (1975) scales and two posttests 6 and 12 months after the pretest. Kahn (1978) describes the training as follows:

The four experimental subjects received . . . individual training in an isolated room for 45 minutes a day, 3 days a week, for 6 months. . . . The training was individualized for each child and consisted of a concentrated effort to have the child improve his performance in the area of object permanence. . . . Positive reinforcement (food and praise) was used to keep the child interested in the task. The steps followed in the training procedure were those of the object permanence scale of the Uzgiris and Hunt instrument. This order was followed because the steps for this scale have been shown to be ordinal for a severely and profoundly retarded population (pp. 17–18).

All four subjects who received this training acquired all the steps on the Uzgiris and Hunt object permanence scale, a notable improvement over their pretest performance. Three of the control group subjects showed no progress from the pretest to the 6-month posttest while one showed slight improvement. Unlike the Brassell and Dunst (1976) study, the experimental subjects showed some improvement on other sensorimotor measures; all improved in means-ends and causality, and three of the four improved in spatial relations.

These studies were conducted in laboratory settings. Brassell and Dunst (1978) investigated the effects of parents teaching object permanence to young handicapped infants. Pre- and posttest measures of object permanence with the Uzgiris and Hunt scales were taken on 91 cognitively delayed infants in the Western Carolina Infants' Program.[4] After the initial assessment and instructional program planning, home trainers visited the families about once a week. Twenty-four children received training on object permanence with the remainder being taught other skills. Object permanence infants showed accelerated acquisition when their posttest scores were compared to their pretests and to posttest scores of infants not receiving object permanence training.

This experiment indicates that cognitively delayed children in a parent intervention program can show accelerated acquisition of object permanence. Sensorimotor skills can be taught by parents in natural settings, with adequate assessment and assistance from home trainers.

Specific training facilitates accelerated acquisition of sensorimotor skills for cognitively delayed children, although research is rather limited to relatively few published reports and the narrow range of skills being trained (object permanence). Nonetheless, given an appropriate assessment with a tool such as the Ordinal Scales of Psychological Development and systematic procedures, teachers can train cognitively handicapped children to perform sensorimotor skills. But is the performance maintained, and does it generalize across other skills, settings, or trainers? Data relevant to this question are severely limited. Brassell and Dunst (1976) conducted two posttests, one the day following training and the second approximately 60 days later. Unfortunately, the gains made during training did not necessarily maintain to the second posttest. Kahn (1978) also conducted two posttests, one immediately after training and one 6 months later. Object permanence performance on the second posttest was higher than performance on the pretest, but lower than on the posttest

---

[4]Brassell (1977) provides a description and evaluation data for this program.

immediately after training. Brassell and Dunst (1978) and Robinson (1974) did not report follow-up data.

In relation to generalization, Kahn (1978) found only slight transfer of object permanence training to some other sensorimotor skills. Brassell and Dunst (1976) found no transfer of training, but this may be due to the brevity of their training procedures (10 minutes per day for 8 days).

Therefore, cognitively delayed children will probably not generalize or maintain sensorimotor skills. This appears to contradict Kamii and DeVries (1977) who believe that children will not forget logico-mathematical learning. However, Kamii and DeVries (1977, 1978) strongly oppose direct instruction of Piagetian tasks, and thus might expect lack of maintenance and generalization. Also, this lack is common and not limited to training sensorimotor skills (cf. Kazdin, 1975; Stokes & Baer, 1977).

General Models and Approaches

Dunst (1981a) and Robinson and Robinson (1978) describe specific procedures for teaching each sensorimotor skill. However, two general models or approaches can be used when teaching skills.

Test/task analyze/teach The teacher can assess the child with a tool such as the Ordinal Scales. All six hierarchical scales would be used and instruction would be planned for the step (item) immediately following the child's last successfully completed step in each scale. This strategy was illustrated in the studies described earlier (Brassell & Dunst, 1976, 1978; Kahn, 1978).

Another strategy in the test/task analyze/ teach approach is recommended by Filler et al. (1975). It involves mapping or listing the sequences of the sensorimotor prerequisite behaviors and skills, and the apparent logical relationships between the steps of the sequences across different sensorimotor skills. An example of such a listing is shown in Figure 9.1. When using this strategy, assess the child to determine whether he or she could consistently perform the skills described in each of the boxes. The assessment (and, when appropriate, the instruction) would begin at the lower-center box titled *exercises reflexes.*[5]

It would progress following the arrows to the top-center box titled *differentiates actors, actions, objects of actions, as well as spatial and temporal relationships among these.* The closer a box is to the lower portion of Figure 9.1, the more basic the skill. Lower skills connected by arrows to more advanced skills are thought to be prerequisite behaviors (e.g., "visually tracks slow movements of objects and persons" and "searches for partially hidden objects"). Horizontally equal boxes represent skills that occur at roughly the same time in development (e.g., "visually tracks slow movements of objects and persons" and "visually localizes source of sounds"). Instructional activities could be initiated for both skills if the child was functioning at a given level.

Instruction based on using a tool such as the Ordinal Scales centers on developing isolated sensorimotor skills rather than the relationships between skills and prerequisite behaviors. For example, the steps for object permanence from the Uzgiris and Hunt (1975) scales and the boxes from the Filler et al. (1975) mapping that describe important behaviors to the development of object permanence are shown in Figure 9.2. The Uzgiris and Hunt sequence lists 15 steps and the skill sequence hierarchy by Filler et al. shows 16. Some of the steps are the same, whereas others represent different concepts. Therefore, teachers using either strategy are likely to omit important steps unless they combine the two sequences. A synthesis of both lists is shown in Table 9.3.

If the child is unable to acquire the steps or sequences, they can be task analyzed. Two steps (4 and 7) from Table 9.3 involve the sensorimotor prerequisite of visual tracking, and a task analysis of those two items is displayed in Table 9.4. This task analysis would be used if the child visually fixates (looks at) objects or persons, but does not visually track them when they move slowly or rapidly. Steps from this task analysis could be deleted if

---

[5]The term *exercises reflexes* is used in the Piagetian sense and means the child uses movements typical of infants such as waving arms, looking, kicking legs, moving fingers to the mouth, sucking, and turning the head from side to side. It does *not* refer to primitive postural reflexes such as the Moro or the Asymmetrical Tonic Neck Reflex. These primitive reflexes should not be stimulated or exercised; see Chapter 15 for further discussion.

performed without training. Likewise, additional "in-between" steps could be developed.

Cognitive/Linguistic Model (Dunst, 1981a)

The cognitive/linguistic model is a broader and more integrated approach than the test/task analysis/teach model. Instead of focusing on sequences within each sensorimotor skill, Dunst (1981a) identified a number of objectives/activities that facilitate development across several sensorimotor skills. For example, visually directed reaching facilitates development of means-ends, spatial relations, causality, and schemes for relating to objects. As such, the cognitive/linguistic model deals with facili-

tating a variety of sensorimotor skills. Thus, training should be more efficient than in the test/task analysis/teach model.

Dunst, working from Fischer's (1980) view of the sensorimotor period, has conceptualized the cognitive/linguistic model into three phases. In Phase I, the major goal is "to facilitate a wide variety of both social and nonsocial response contingent behaviors" (Dunst, 1981a, p. 44). The infant realizes that his or her behavior can produce changes in animate and inanimate objects. For example, a rattle will produce noise when shaken, or looking at Father, cooing, and moving arms and legs up

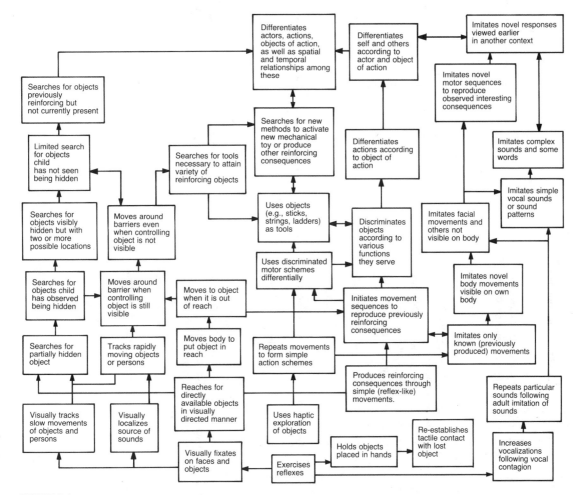

FIGURE 9.1

Schematic mapping of sensorimotor prerequisite behaviors and sensorimotor skills.

Note: From "Mental Retardation" by J. W. Filler, C. C. Robinson, R. A. Smith, L. J. Vincent-Smith, D. D. Bricker, and W. A. Bricker. In N. Hobbs (Ed.), *Issues in the Classification of Children* (Vol. 1). San Francisco: Jossey-Bass, 1975. Copyright 1975 by Jossey-Bass. Reprinted by permission.

Ordinal scales of psychological development—the development of visual pursuit and the permanence of objects[a]

15. Finding an object following a series of invisible displacements by searching in reverse of the order of hiding.
14. Finding an object following a series of invisible displacements.
13. Finding an object following one invisible displacement with three screens.
12. Finding an object following one invisible displacement with two screens alternated.
11. Finding an object following one invisible displacement with two screens.
10. Finding an object following one invisible displacement with a single screen.
9. Finding an object under three superimposed screens.
8. Finding an object after successive visible displacements.
7. Finding an object which is completely covered with a single screen in three places.
6. Finding an object which is completely covered with a single screen in two places alternately.
5. Finding an object which is completely covered with a single screen in two places.
4. Finding an object which is completely covered.
3. Finding an object which is partially covered.
2. Noticing the disappearance of a slowly moving object.
1. Following a slowly moving object through a 180° arc.

Skill sequence hierarchy for object permanence[b]

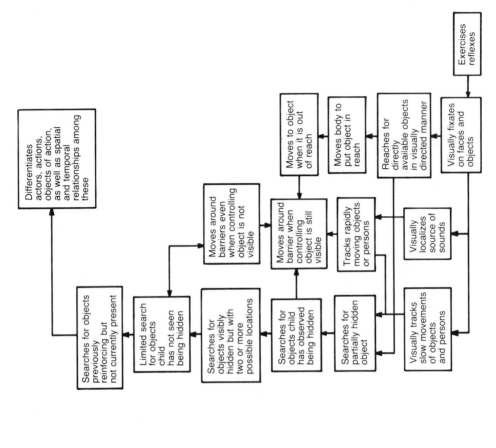

FIGURE 9.2

Comparison of Uzgiris and Hunt sequences and Filler, Robinson, Smith, Vincent-Smith, Bricker, and Bricker sequences for object permanence

[a]Adapted from Uzgiris, I.C., & Hunt, J. M., *Assessment in infancy.* Urbana: University of Illinois Press, 1975.
[b]Adapted from Filler, J.W., Robinson, C.C., Smith, R.A., Vincent-Smith, L.J., Bricker, D.D., & Bricker, W.A. Mental retardation. In N. Hobbs (Ed.), *Issues in the classification of children*

TABLE 9.3

Combination of Uzgiris and Hunt and Filler et al. sequences for object permanence

1. Exercises reflexes. F[a]
2. Visually fixates on faces and objects. F
3. Visually localizes source of sounds. F
4. Visually tracks slow movements of objects and persons. F UH[b]
5. Notices the disappearance of a slowly moving object. UH
6. Reaches for directly available objects in visually directed manner. F
7. Tracks rapidly moving objects or persons. F
8. Searches for partially hidden object. F UH
9. Moves body to put object in reach. F
10. Moves object when it is out of reach. F
11. Searches for objects child has observed being hidden. F UH
12. Moves around barrier when controlling object is still visible. F
13. Finds an object that is completely covered with a single screen in two places. UH
14. Moves around barriers even when controlling object is not visible. F
15. Finds an object that is completely covered with a single screen in two places alternately. F UH
16. Finds an object that is completely covered with a single screen in three places. UH
17. Finds an object after successive visible displacements. UH
18. Finds an object under three superimposed screens. UH
19. Limited search for objects child has not seen being hidden. F UH
20. Finds an object following one invisible displacement with two screens. UH
21. Finds an object following one invisible displacement with two screens alternated. UH
22. Finds an object following one invisible displacement with three screens. UH
23. Finds an object following a series of invisible displacements. UH
24. Finds an object following a series of invisible displacements by searching in reverse of the order of hiding. UH
25. Searches for objects previously reinforcing but not currently present. F
26. Differentiates actors, actions, objects of actions, as well as spatial and temporal relations among these. F

---

[a] F = Filler et al. item
[b] UH = Uzgiris and Hunt item
Sources: Uzgiris and Hunt (1975); Filler et al. (1975).

TABLE 9.4

Task analysis of visually tracking rapidly moving objects through an arch of 180 degrees

1. When face is turned to the left or right, will visually fixate on bright object that makes a sound.
2. When face is turned to the left or right, will visually fixate on bright object.
3. When face is at midline, will visually fixate on bright object.
4. When looking at an object with the face turned to the left, right, or at midline, will move eyes when object slowly moves in horizontal direction. (The child is not required to follow the object, only to move eyes when the object moves).
5. When looking at an object with face turned to the left or right, will follow slowly moving object toward midline about 30 degrees.
6. When looking at object at midline, will follow slowly moving object to the left or right about 45 degrees.
7. When looking at an object at midline, will follow slowly moving object 90 degrees to the left or right, but will not follow it back to midline.
8. When looking at an object with face turned to the left or right, will follow slowly moving object across midline.
9. When looking at an object with face turned to the left or right, will follow slowly moving object 180 degrees.
10. When looking at an object at midline, will follow slowly moving object to the left or right and back across midline.
11. When looking at an object at midline, will follow object moving at a moderate speed to the left or right and back across midline.
12. When looking at an object at midline, will follow a rapidly moving object to the left or right and back across midline.

and down will elicit interactions from him. In Phase II, the major goal "is to develop a wide variety of sensorimotor behaviors to be the precursors for symbolic play ... representational-problem solving ... the semantic (meaning) aspects of language, ... and the communicative aspects of language" (p. 44). The infant can profit from or change behavior as a result of feedback. Further the infant recognizes that "two or more chains or sequences of behavior [are] alternative, yet equivalent, ways of arriving at a desired terminus (end)" (p. 44). The goal of Phase III "is to develop cognitive/linguistic skills that are symbolically based, semantically organized, and used for communicative purposes" (p. 44). Children can spontaneously produce language in the absence of stimuli that elicit language responses. Thus, in the cognitive/linguistic model, teachers attempt to teach goals broader than simple attainment of specific sensorimotor skills.

The cognitive/linguistic model places more emphasis on social sensorimotor skills. Dunst (1981a) divides sensorimotor skills into psychological and psychosocial categories. *Psychological sensorimotor skills* involve children's interactions with inanimate objects and include skills such as object permanence, means-ends, spatial relationships, operational causality, and schemes for relating to objects. *Psychosocial skills* involve children's interactions with people and include skills such as person permanence, imitation, social causality, nonverbal communication, and social play.

Dunst (1981a) stresses teaching skills in their functional context. Thus, when possible, teaching should occur in the course of interactions in natural settings rather than artificial training settings and sessions. The test/task analysis/teach model can also be implemented in natural settings.

Guidelines for Teaching Sensorimotor Skills

Regardless of the approach, the teacher should follow several guidelines when attempting to facilitate sensorimotor skill development.

Teach horizontally as well as vertically. Typically teachers in early childhood special education use the developmental model as a basis for planning instruction (Bagnato, 1981;

Cohen & Gross, 1979). *Vertical instruction* occurs when emphasis is placed on accelerating children's attainment of developmental milestones, including specific sequences of sensorimotor skills. The teacher attempts to get the child to perform progressively more advanced skills. Given the similar sequence hypothesis (Weisz & Zigler, 1979) and the significant delays of many young handicapped children, vertical instruction appears to be valid and needed.

Horizontal instruction means that a child is taught to perform a given behavior in a variety of situations. For example, if Lucy was assessed on the sensorimotor skill of operational causality, she might be able to perform Item 6 from the Ordinal Scales of Psychological Development, but not Item 7. Item 6 is "behavior to a spectacle created by a mechanical object" (Uzgiris & Hunt, 1975, pp. 190–191) and involves the child's response *to the stopping* of interesting spectacles she *has seen* the examiner initiate such as when a music box or spinning toy stops. Item 7 involves the child's response *to the stopping* of a mechanical toy she has *not* seen the examiner activate. If her teacher was planning vertical instruction he would present tasks similar to Item 7 behaviors. However, the teacher would plan horizontal instruction with tasks similar to Item 6 behaviors and would emphasize Lucy performing the behaviors with a large number of objects, in a variety of settings, with more than one trainer, and in different ways. Dunst (1981b) strongly advocates teaching horizontally, and states that the failure to do so "will probably result in the facilitation of isolated, nonfunctional and nonadaptive behaviors" (p. 21). Stokes and Baer (1977), in their discussion of procedures for facilitating generalization of learned responses, recommend training sufficient exemplars, which is quite similar to teaching horizontally.

Another implication of teaching horizontally is particularly apparent when teaching sensorimotor skills and suggests we should train children to perform more than one sensorimotor skill at a time. Various sensorimotor skills appear to be independent of each other and training on one sensorimotor skill produces little if any generalization to others. Ideally, a variety of sensorimotor skills could be trained within the same activity. For example, if Kathy was playing with a small shovel and sand then she could be taught to use the shovel as a means-ends behavior. If she covers up an object with the sand, she could learn about object permanence—the object is still there when the sand is removed. She could learn about schemes for relating to objects (object play), and if a teacher or peer is actively engaged in play she would have opportunities for imitation and social play. Thus, while we want young handicapped children to advance developmentally and rapidly, we also want development to result in adaptive responses to a variety of stimulations. Therefore, activities must stimulate horizontal as well as vertical skill development.

Teach functional skills in functional settings. Determining whether a skill is functional is usually done when the teacher establishes objectives and plans activities. The teacher should consider whether the skill will be expected and reinforced in the natural environment. If not, the teacher can attempt to change the natural environment so it will reinforce the skill, or ignore and not teach the skill. If skills are not expected and reinforced, they will not be generalized and maintained in the natural environment. For example, if we teach a child to explore at school, we must also assist parents in setting limits and in allowing exploration. Teachers should also consider the effect the behavior will have on the environment. Will the sensorimotor skill give the child more opportunities to exert control over the environment? For example, teaching Leroy to point (sensorimotor skill of nonverbal communication) to objects and activities could greatly change the specificity of his requests, and is a very functional skill. In addition, teachers should consider whether the skill is a prerequisite to other functional skills. For example, teaching Sterling to imitate the vocalizations of others allows him to acquire expressive language skills.

However, as Dunst (1981a) indicates, functional skills should also be taught in functional settings. For example, Merlin should be taught the concept of *cup* while he is drinking from a cup at lunch and snack rather than in a two-choice discrimination task.

Teach animate and inanimate components. Certain sensorimotor skills (object permanence, spatial relationships, and schemes for relating to objects) have both physical (object) and social (people) components. While child-object interactions and skills are usually emphasized, the child-caregiver interactions and skills are also important because young handicapped children must function in social environments. Basic to the social and physical components of sensorimotor skills is the child's ability to identify and use *co-occurrences* (Brinker & Lewis, 1982), the association of two events. *Environmental co-occurrence* is the happening of two concurrent events external to the child: for example, the sounds of the mother's footsteps and then the appearance of the mother. *Internal co-occurrence* is when two events internal to the child occur together; for example, the infant pulls his fingers from his mouth and thus stops sucking. *Infant-environment co-occurrence* happens when events by the infant and the environment occur together; for example, when a baby moves a rattle and it makes a sound or the infant smiles at the father and is subsequently picked up. Infant-environment co-ocurrences can be subdivided into infant-object and infant-social co-occurrences, with responsive physical and social environments important to their development. Identifying and using all types of co-occurrences are critical for the development of motivational, attentional, and cognitive behaviors (Brinker & Lewis, 1982).

The handicapped infant may be less likely to notice co-occurrences because of limited response repertoires, fewer opportunities for interactions due to medical involvements, and limited ability to identify and recognize co-occurrences (Brinker & Lewis, 1982). Therefore, the social and physical environment must be structured to provide a large number of response-contingent events. In recent years there has been considerable discussion on infant stimulation with the implication that infants are delayed because they have not received enough stimulation and should be stimulated in large doses. However, recent data suggest that large amounts of stimulation are inadequate in eliminating developmental delays and "the presence of too much stimulation may be as detrimental to development as too little stimulation" (Wachs, 1976, p. 26). Likewise, response-independent or noncontingent stimulation may be detrimental (Dunst, 1981b), or at least less helpful than response-contingent stimulation (Brinker & Lewis, 1982). A social and physical environment should respond consistently and predictably to children's social and nonsocial behavior.

Besides teaching co-occurrence through response-contingent situations, children must learn that social interactions are a give-and-take or turn-taking activity. This implies that we as teachers should assist parents in reading and responding to children's cues in a consistent, appropriate, and satisfying manner. We must also teach children to play socially. This involves providing time for play and responding consistently to children's attempts at appropriate play.

Social or animate sensorimotor skills are best taught in the context of the ongoing, natural interactions (Dunst, 1981a). For example, children learn about the permanence of persons through games such as peek-a-boo and through brief separations from their parents. We should assist parents in incorporating training activities within present social interactions and provide educational environments where social interactions with teachers and peers can naturally occur. Bromwich (1981) suggests procedures for assisting parents in establishing and using interactions with infants in satisfying and beneficial ways.

Adapt activities to children with specific handicapping conditions. Handicapped children appear to develop sensorimotor skills in a sequence similar to typical children. This does not mean all handicapped children will perform or learn each step of all sensorimotor skills. For some children, physical disabilities such as blindness, deafness, and motor disabilities (e.g., cerebral palsy) will prevent them from performing some steps of the sensorimotor skills. Such disabilities will affect acquisition and demonstration of skills. We must be aware of this not only during training but also during child assessment and evaluation. For example, Ed is a cerebral palsied child who cannot roll, crawl, or walk. Thus he is deprived of experiences to assist him in using locomotion to solve problems. If, however, he can learn to operate an electric wheelchair, he will be able to participate in experiences to develop the skill of using locomotion to solve problems. During assessment, our determination is influenced by his adaptation

(wheelchair) because only through the mode of the wheelchair can he show us his cognitive ability to use locomotion to solve problems or reach goals.

Teachers should use three guidelines when deciding whether to adapt a given step or activity. First, children should not be expected to perform physically impossible skills. Second, if the skill results in functional behavior, then devise adaptations. Third, if the skill does not lead to immediate functional behavior, then consider teaching other sensorimotor skills not requiring adaptation. An example of a skill sequence for blind, deaf, and physically handicapped children is shown in Table 9.5. With some children, adaptations must be made in the method of presentation (especially with sensory-impaired children). With others, the adaptations must be made in their mode of response.

Direct instruction may be used when necessary. At times teachers may need to bring more structure to teaching sensorimotor skills. The teacher should specify the instructional objectives, select materials and activities, implement them, evaluate children's responses, and structure the environment to facilitate practice of the learned sensorimotor skills.

Specifying instructional objectives for teaching sensorimotor skills is similar to specifying objectives for other areas of development. The assessment should identify the steps of the sensorimotor skills the child performs proficiently, inefficiently, and not at all. Priorities are then established for instruction, considering such factors as the child's skill level, caregiver's concerns, the resources available to the teacher, and how functional the skill is for the child. For example, suppose we assessed Colleen using the Uzgiris and Hunt (1975) Ordinal Scales of Psychological Development. One item on the means-ends scale is the "use of locomotion as a means" (p. 168). The learned behavior shows that the infant "moves to regain the object and resumes playing with it" (p. 169). An instructional objective for this step might be: "Colleen will crawl and retrieve a toy she has been playing with when it is moved 3 feet away on 4 of 5 opportunities per day for 3 consecutive days." The above objective emphasizes that Colleen will perform the behavior and will crawl and get the toy. Depending upon the child's abilities, the teacher may want to emphasize issues other than simply performing the behavior. For example, the teacher may want Colleen to use this skill during her play time. The objective might be: "when playing by herself, if a toy moves out of her reach, Colleen will crawl and retrieve it on 4 of 5 opportunities." These objectives are based on the same sensorimotor skill, "use of locomotion as a means." However, one deals with

TABLE 9.5
Adaptation of sensorimotor skill

Objective: Child will retrieve object hidden under/behind one barrier, 5 of 5 opportunities.

Unadapted Sequence	Adaptation for Blind Child	Adaptation for Deaf Child	Adaptation for Physically Handicapped Child[a]
Visually fixates on object.	Makes body movement in response to sounds.	None necessary	None necessary
Visually tracks slow-moving object.	Makes a differential response when sound moves closer or farther away from child.	None necessary	None necessary
Turns head to maintain tracking when object goes out of visual field.	Moves or vocalizes when interesting sound stops.	None necessary	Attempts movement or vocalizes when object leaves visual field.
Looks at point of reappearance when object s/he has been tracking goes behind barrier.	Differentially responds when sound stops and starts in different location.	None necessary	None necessary
Secures object when partially hidden by barrier or screen.	Reaches for object making sound; reaches for object when sound is quieter or less frequent.	None necessary	Demonstrates increase in tone when shown partially hidden object; vocalizes when teacher reaches for object.
Secures object from behind screen.	Reaches for object when sound stops.	None necessary	Does not show surprise when hidden object is uncovered; shows anticipation when adult starts to uncover object as compared to when adult removes another screen.

[a]Assumes physically handicapped child has sensory systems intact and is unable to move arms and legs (e.g., quadriplegic).

acquisition, and the other with generalization of the response. The objectives teach Colleen an important variation of the skill; of course, others are possible.

Materials selected for instruction should assist the child in learning the response, and should be safe and easy to use and functional. For example, in instructing the visual tracking responses listed in Table 9.4, the teacher should select objects the child finds interesting. Infants initially are more apt to look at bright objects such as penlights, patterned surfaces, slowly moving objects, black and white items, curves, larger stimuli, stimuli with more parts, and external parts of patterns (Cohen & Gross, 1979). As children grow older, they readily observe different objects. The teacher should select items that solicit looking behaviors; this determination is made by measuring the accuracy, latency, and duration of the child's response. The object must be presented at such a distance from the child's face as to allow the child to focus on it.

Some objects can be moved more easily than others, such as a penlight as compared to the ceiling light. The teacher must not use stimuli that would harm the child's eyes, such as bright lights. Toys with parts that might fall on the child should also not be used.

Several factors should be considered when evaluating whether materials are functional. Are the materials similar to those in the child's natural environment? Is it more functional for a child to look at and track a three-dimensional object such as a rattle than a two-dimensional object such as a checkerboard pattern? Also, do the materials assist the child in performing a behavior to change the environment (e.g., smiling to initiate social interactions)? And do they assist the child in learning a behavior that can be used to learn other behaviors to change the environment (e.g., learning to imitate)? For example, human faces are good stimuli for tracking because infants readily look at them (Kessen, Haith, & Salapatek, 1970), they can be easily moved, they can emit sounds (the voice), and they can change their form (smiling, nonsmiling, raising and lowering the eyebrows). Faces are also functional; that is, looking and following them leads to other social interactions. Further, faces do not present safety problems.

Once instructional objectives have been specified and materials and activities selected,

the teacher *implements the instruction.* Implementing instruction for sensorimotor skills is similar to other areas of development. Stimuli should be presented to cue the occurrence of the behavior (the one stated in the objective). The behavior should result in reinforcement. For instance, in the previously mentioned means-ends objective for Colleen (Colleen will crawl and retrieve a toy she has been playing with when it is moved 3 feet away on 4 of 5 opportunities per day for 3 consecutive days), the teacher would want to position Colleen on the floor to allow her to easily and safely crawl to retrieve her toys. If she can move from sitting to the crawling position, then she could be placed in a sitting position. If she cannot easily sit or move to the crawling position, she might be placed on her stomach on the floor. Physical and occupational therapists can assist teachers in planning positions to allow maximum functional movement and safety.

In implementing instructional activities, teachers frequently need to *remove extraneous or interfering stimuli.* In the example, the teacher would remove interesting toys from the area immediately around Colleen, because she would have little reason to crawl and retrieve a toy if other interesting toys were within reach. If necessary, *prompts* should be used to insure the performance of the behavior. These prompts would of course be faded (decreased in frequency and/or intensity) as Colleen learned to move toward and retrieve the toys.

Instructional activities should include *sufficient opportunities to perform the behavior* listed in the objective. If the teacher provided Colleen one opportunity per day to crawl and retrieve toys, it would likely take her longer to learn to use locomotion than if she was given several chances. These opportunities could be provided during a relatively structured training session, but should also occur at unscheduled times. For instance, if Colleen was putting on her coat and mittens to go outside, the mittens could be placed a few feet from her and she should be cued to get them.

When the target behavior, crawling to retrieve a toy, is performed, *reinforcement should be presented.* Teacher-delivered reinforcement should be faded as children begin to consistently perform the desired responses.

Instructional activities should be conducted to *promote participation that is not necessarily a result of teacher-delivered reinforcement or prompts.* For example, if "using locomotion as a means" is to be a functional behavior for Colleen, she must do it when no one prompts her and when the teacher is not delivering the reinforcers. To increase the likelihood that the response will become a functional behavior, the teacher must select appropriate materials. In Colleen's case, materials should be ones she frequently holds, touches, or manipulates. The toys with more reinforcing value would be used, because Colleen would be more apt to crawl toward them. Toys that provide auditory and visual feedback when manipulated are usually more reinforcing; however, the reinforcement value of toys depends upon each child. Participation usually also increases with a variety of toys. Problems of boredom are alleviated and the child is further stimulated by the notion that he can crawl and retrieve a wide assortment of objects. Participation is also maximized when instructional activities are presented in a play format; the teacher and child can become actively involved in retrieving toys. If most instructional activities are enjoyable, participation will be higher.

Evaluating student responses to instruction is an important part of teaching. Cognitive skills are usually measured by motor and/or language responses, sensorimotor skills with motor responses. The teacher assumes Colleen is learning locomotion as a tool for solving problems when she crawls to obtain desired objects that are out of reach; he measures this assumption by counting the number of times she crawls and retrieves a toy. The counting or evaluating determines whether Colleen is progressively performing the behavior more accurately; if she is not, this information is used to make decisions about changing the instruction.

SUMMARY

The behaviors persons use to adapt to and master their environments have been described as cognitive behaviors. This chapter focused on describing, assessing, and teaching sensorimotor skills to handicapped children. The six sensorimotor skills are means-

ends, object permanence, spatial relationships, causality, imitation, and schemes for relating to objects (play). These skills are acquired during the sensorimotor period and evolve from simple motor movements to a primitive ability to use mental symbols. Object permanence, causality, and schemes for relating to objects have inanimate and animate (social) components. The sequences through which these sensorimotor skills are acquired can be used in the early cognitive curriculum, beginning with the sensory organization responses and moving through the steps described in Table 9.1.

There are several reasons for teaching sensorimotor skills. If we use the developmental theory-based approach for assessment, we should teach sensorimotor skills because they appear to be an accurate description of the early developmental course for cognitively handicapped and typical children. Some sensorimotor skills are also useful to the child on their own, and appear to be prerequisites for more complex skills. In addition the ability and quality of children's thinking and reasoning appear to be influenced by sensorimotor experiences. The most commonly used developmental theory-based measure is the Ordinal Scales of Psychological Development. The functional approach for determining instructional targets can also be used.

When teaching sensorimotor skills, the test/task analysis/teach model or the cognitive/linquistic model can be used. The test/task analysis/teach model tends to focus on the direct development of specific sensorimotor skills, the cognitive/linguistic model on a variety of activities to facilitate the development of several skills. Guidelines for teaching sensorimotor skills include: Teach horizontally as well as vertically, teach functional skills in functional settings, teach animate and inanimate skills, adapt the sequences and activities to children with specific handicapping conditions, and when necessary, use direct instruction.

REFERENCES

Bagnato, S.J. Developmental scales and developmental curricula: Forging a linkage for early intervention. *Topics in Early Childhood Special Education*, 1981, *1*, 1–8.

Bates, E. *Language and context: The acquisition of pragmatics.* New York: Academic Press, 1976.

Bluma, S.M., Shearer, M.S., Froham, A.H., & Hilliard, J.M. *Portage guide to early education: Manual.* Portage, Wis.: Cooperative Education Service Agency, 1976.

Bowerman, M. Words and sentences: Uniformity, individual variation, and shifts over time in patterns of acquisition. In F.D. Minifie & L.L. Lloyd (Eds.), *Communicative and cognitive abilities—Early behavioral assessment.* Baltimore: University Park Press, 1976.

Brainerd, C.J. *Piaget's theory of intelligence.* Englewood Cliffs. N.J.: Prentice-Hall, 1978.

Brassell, W.R. Intervention with handicapped infants: Correlates of progress. *Mental Retardation,* 1977, *15,* 18–22.

Brassell, W.R., & Dunst, C.J. Comparison of two procedures for fostering the development of the object construct. *American Journal of Mental Deficiency,* 1976, *80,* 523–528.

Brassell, W.R., & Dunst, C.J. Fostering the object construct: Large-scale intervention with handicapped infants. *American Journal of Mental Deficiency,* 1978, *82,* 507–510.

Bricker, D., & Bricker, W.A. *Infant, toddler, and preschool research and intervention project: Report year III.* Nashville: George Peabody College, 1973 (IMRID Behavioral Science Monograph No. 23).

Bricker, W.A., & Bricker, D.D. The infant, toddler, and preschool research and intervention program. In T.D. Tjossem (Ed.), *Intervention strategies for high risk infants and young children.* Baltimore: University Park Press, 1976.

Brinker, R.P., & Lewis, M. Discovering the competent handicapped infant: A process approach to assessment and intervention. *Topics in Early Childhood Special Education,* 1982, *2*(2), 1–16.

Bromwich, R.M. *Working with parents and infants: An interactional approach.* Baltimore: University Park Press, 1981.

Buros, O.K. (Ed). *Eighth mental measurements yearbook.* Highland Park, N.J.: Gryphon Press, 1978.

Coggins, T.E., & Carpenter, R.L. Introduction to the area of language development. In M. A. Cohen and P.J. Gross (Eds.), *The developmental resource: Behavioral sequences for assessment and program planning* (Vol. 2). New York: Grune & Stratton, 1979.

Cohen, M. A., & Gross, P.J. (Eds.). *The developmental resource: Behavioral sequences for assessment and program planning* (Vols. 1 & 2). New York: Grune & Stratton, 1979.

Corman, H.H., & Escalona, S.K. Stages of sensorimotor development: A replication study. *Merrill-Palmer Quarterly,* 1969, *15,* 351–361.

Decarie, T.G. *Intelligence and affectivity in early childhood.* New York: International Universities Press, 1965.

DuBose, R., & Kelly, J. *Curricula and instruction for young handicapped children: A guideline for selection and evaluation.* Monmouth, Oreg.: Western States Technical Assistance Resource (WESTAR), 1981 (WESTAR Series Paper No. 9.).

Dunst, C.J. The structure of infant intelligence: A historical overview. *Intelligence,* 1978, *2,* 381–391.

Dunst, C.J. *A clinical and educational manual for use with the Uzgiris and Hunt Scales of Infant Psychological Development.* Baltimore: University Park Press, 1980.

Dunst, C.J. *Infant learning: A cognitive-linguistic intervention strategy.* Hingham, Mass.: Teaching Resources Corporation, 1981. (a)

Dunst, C.J. Theoretical bases and pragmatic considerations in infant curriculum construction. In J. Anderson & J. Cox (Eds.), *Curriculum materials for high risk and handicapped infants.* Chapel Hill, N.C.: Technical Assistance Development System, 1981. (b)

Dunst, C.J., & Brassell, W.A. The utility of Piaget's concept of decalage for the construction of cognitively-based infant curricula. *North Carolina Journal of Mental Health,* 1975, *7,* 22–31.

Dunst, C.J., Brassell, W.A., & Rheingrover, R.M. Structural and organisational features of sensorimotor intelligence among retarded infants and toddlers. *British Journal of Educational Psychology,* 1981, *51,* 133–143.

Evans, E.D. *Contemporary influences in early childhood education* (2nd. ed.). New York: Holt, Rinehart, and Winston, 1975.

Evans, E.D., & McCandless, B.R. *Children and youth: Psychosocial development.* New York: Holt, Rinehart, and Winston, 1978.

Filler, J. W., Robinson, C.C., Smith, R.A., Vincent-Smith, L.J., Bricker, D.D., & Bricker, W.A. Mental retardation. In N. Hobbs (Ed.), *Issues in the classification of children.* San Francisco: Jossey-Bass, 1975.

Fischer, K. A theory of cognitive development: The control and construction of hierarchical of skills. *Psychological Review,* 1980, *87,* 477–531.

Gelman, R. Cognitive development. *Annual Review of Psychology,* 1978, *29,* 297–322.

Ginsburg, H., & Opper, S. *Piaget's theory of intellectual development* (2nd ed.). Englewood Cliffs, N.J.: Prentice-Hall, 1979.

Glover, M.E., Preminger, J.L., & Sanford, A. *Early Learning Accomplishment Profile.* Winston-Salem, N.C.: Kaplan Press, 1978.

Hawaii Early Learning Program, Palo Alto, Calif.: Vort Corporation, 1979.

Hobbs, N. *Issues in the classification of children* (Vol. 1). San Francisco: Jossey-Bass, 1975.

Johnson, N., Jens, K.G., & Attermeier, S.M. *Carolina Curriculum for handicapped infants.* Chapel Hill: University of North Carolina, 1979.

Kahn, J.V. Relationship of Piaget's sensorimotor period to language acquisition of profoundly retarded children. *American Journal of Mental Deficiency,* 1975, *79,* 640–643.

Kahn, J.V. Utility of the Uzgiris and Hunt scales of sensorimotor development with severely and profoundly retarded children. *American Journal of Mental Deficiency,* 1976, *80,* 663–665.

Kahn, J.V. Acceleration of object permanence with severely and profoundly retarded children. *AAESPH Review,* 1978, *3,* 15–22.

Kahn, J.V. Applications of the Piagetian literature to

severely and profoundly mentally retarded persons. *Mental Retardation*, 1979, *17*, 273–280.

Kamii, C., & DeVries, R. Piaget for early education. In M.C. Day & R.K. Parker (Eds.), *The preschool in action: Exploring early childhood programs* (2nd ed.). Boston: Allyn and Bacon, 1977.

Kamii, C., & DeVries, R. *Physical knowledge in preschool education: Implications of Piaget's theory.* Englewood Cliffs, N.J.: Prentice-Hall, 1978.

Kazdin, A.E. *Behavior modification in applied settings.* Homewood, Ill.: Dorsey Press, 1975.

Kessen, W., Haith, M.M., & Salapatek, P. Infancy. In P.H. Mussen (Ed.), *Carmichael's manual of child psychology* (3rd ed.). New York: Wiley, 1970.

Lewis, M. (Ed.). *Origins of intelligence: Infancy and early childhood.* New York: Plenum Press, 1976.

Morehead, D., & Morehead, A. From signal to sign: A Piagetian view of thought and language during the first two years. In R. Schiefelbusch and L.L. Lloyd (Eds.), *Language perspectives—Acquisition, retardation, and intervention.* Baltimore: University Park Press, 1974.

Osofsky, J.D. (Ed.). *Handbook on infant development.* New York: John Wiley and Sons, 1979.

Phillips, J.L. *The origins of intellect: Piaget's theory* (2nd ed.). San Francisco: W.H. Freeman, 1975.

Piaget, J. *The origins of intelligence in children.* New York: W.W. Norton, 1952.

Quick, A.D., Little, T.L., & Campbell, A. *Project MEMPHIS: Enhancing developmental progress in preschool exceptional children.* Belmont, Calif.: Fearon, 1974.

Robinson, C. Error patterns in Level 4 and Level 5 object permanence training. *American Journal of Mental Deficiency*, 1974, *78*, 389–396.

Robinson, C. Application of Piagetian sensorimotor concepts to assessment and curriculum for severely handicapped children. *AAESPH Review*, 1976, *1*, 5–10.

Robinson, C.C., & Robinson, J.H. Sensorimotor functions and cognitive development. In M.E. Snell (Ed.), *Systematic instruction of the moderately and severely handicapped.* Columbus, Ohio: Charles E. Merrill, 1978.

Rogers, S.J., D'Eugenio, D., Brown, S., Donovan, C., & Lynch, E. *Developmental programming for infants and young children: Early intervention development profile.* Ann Arbor: University of Michigan, 1980.

Salvia, J., & Ysseldyke, J.E. *Assessment in special and remedial education* (2nd ed.). Boston: Houghton Mifflin, 1981.

Sattler, J.M. *Assessment of children's intelligence.* Philadelphia: W.B. Saunders, 1974.

Sattler, J.M. *Assessment of children's intelligence and special abilities* (2nd ed.). Boston: Allyn and Bacon, 1982.

Stephens, B. A Piagetian approach to curriculum development. In E. Sontag (Ed.), *Educational programming for the severely and profoundly handicapped.* Reston, Va.: Division on Mental Retardation of the Council for Exceptional Children, 1977.

Stokes, T.F., & Baer, D.M. An implicit technology of generalization. *Journal of Applied Behavior Analysis*, 1977, *10*, 349–367.

Stone, J., Smith, H.T., & Murphy, L.B. *The competent infant: Research and commentary.* New York: Basic Books, 1973.

Tilton, J., Liska, D., & Bourland, J. (Eds.). *Guide to early developmental training.* Boston: Allyn and Bacon, 1977.

Uzgiris, I.C., & Hunt, J. McV. *Assessment in infancy: Ordinal Scales of Psychological Development.* Urbana: University of Illinois Press, 1975.

Wachs, T.D. Utilization of a Piagetian approach in the investigation of early experience effects: A research strategy and some illustrative data. *Merrill-Palmer Quarterly*, 1976, *22*, 11–30.

Wachs, T.D. Proximal experience and early cognitive-intellectual development: The physical environment. *Merrill-Palmer Quarterly*, 1979, *25*, 3–41.

Warren, S.A. Using tests to assess intellectual functioning. In P. Mittler (Ed.), *Research to practice in mental retardation: Volume II: Education and training.* Baltimore: University Park Press, 1977.

Weisz, J.R., & Zigler, E. Cognitive development in retarded and nonretarded persons: Piagetian tests of the similar sequence hypothesis. *Psychological Bulletin*, 1979, *86*, 831–851.

Yarrow, L., Rubenstein, J., & Pedersen, F. *Infant and environment: Early cognitive and motivational development.* New York: Halstead Press, 1975.

When children acquire the sensorimotor skills described in Chapter
9, their cognitive development is
not complete. Many cognitive
skills develop in the years after infancy and
before formal schooling begins at age 5 or 6.
Frequently those skills are seen as preparatory for later learning; in fact, the preparatory
nature of this entire period is evidenced by
our use of terms such as preschool, preacademic, preoperational, and readiness.
Nonetheless, many of those cognitive skills
are functional in their own right.

As with infant cognitive skills, preschool cognitive skills are not observable behaviors but
are inferred on the basis of overt behaviors.
For example, we infer Kenneth has the concept *big* because when he is asked to get a
"big glass" he gets a large one, and because
he describes a fire truck as "big" when it is
compared to his tricycle and his tricycle as
"big" when it is compared to his toy fire
truck. Frequently we say a child *has* a concept
or cognitive skill, but what we really mean is
the child performs behaviors that indicate
understanding. Many cognitive skills in the
preschool years overlap with other areas of
development, particularly language. Thus, many
of the skills described in this section appear
to be language as well as cognitive skills.

This chapter is divided into four sections.
The first section briefly describes the broad
range of skills included in common definitions of cognition. The remaining sections
describe the assumptions and strategies necessary to teach basic cognitive skills including
knowledge of concepts and classification,
preacademic skills, and reasoning and problem solving.

10

Preschool Cognitive Skills

PRESCHOOL COGNITIVE SKILLS AND PROCESSES

Early childhood education texts, child development and learning texts, and curricula for
preschool handicapped children indicate that
a variety of cognitive skills and processes are
important after infancy.

Attention, as described in Chapter 7, involves engagement or active participation. It
is also described as the "process of tuning in
to sensory information" (Jackson, Robinson,
& Dale, 1977, p. 25) and "refers to perceiv-
ing in relation to a task or goal" (Gibson &

Rader, 1979, p. 2). Attention is basic to many cognitive tasks and is an important prerequisite for instruction (Hale & Lewis, 1979).

Discrimination refers to distinguishing between two or more stimuli. Important discriminations can be made between stimuli within different sensory modalities such as vision, hearing, and touch (Meier & Malone, 1979; Stevenson, 1972; Tawney, Knapp, O'Reilly, & Pratt, 1979). Discrimination is frequently demonstrated by sorting or separating dissimilar stimuli, matching similar stimuli in the presence of dissimilar stimuli, pointing or otherwise nonverbally indicating a given stimulus from a group, and naming stimuli.

Imitation, as described in Chapter 4, refers to the child matching verbal or nonverbal behavior to that of a model (Neisworth, Willoughby-Herb, Bagnato, Cartwright, & Laub, 1980; Stevenson, 1972; Tawney et al., 1979).

Several cognitive skills have been described by Piaget and authors who have attempted to apply his theory to the education of young children. Knowledge of *spatial relationships* is evidenced by the ability to name or indicate nonverbally different body parts and realize the position of the body in relation to objects in the environment. It also is evidenced by the ability to perceive the relationships between two or more objects such as position (in, on, by), direction (up, down, toward, through), and distance (near, far, close to) (Hohmann, Banet, Weikart, 1979; Lillie, 1975). Knowledge of *temporal relationships,* as described by Lillie (1975), includes identifying the beginning and end of time intervals with statements such as "stop" or "start"; identifying the order of events with statements such as "first" or "next"; and describing different lengths of time with statements such as "a long time." Knowledge of temporal relationships also includes using instruments for describing the passage of time such as clocks and calendars and past events (Hohmann et al., 1979).

Classification of objects and events is an important preschool cognitive skill (Ginsburg & Opper, 1979; Hohmann et al., 1979; Lerner, Mardell-Czudnowski, & Goldenberg, 1981; Lillie, 1975; Neisworth et al., 1980). Lillie (1975) describes classification subgroups as follows: "(1) *relational,* that is, grouping items on the basis of common function or by

association; (2) *descriptive,* that is, grouping items on the basis of common attributes; and (3) *generic,* that is, grouping items on the basis of general classes or categories" (p. 110). Another common preschool cognitive skill is *seriation* (Ginsburg & Opper, 1979; Hohmann et al., 1979; Neisworth et al., 1980; Tawney et al., 1979), which involves ordering or ranking a group of items along a dimension such as height, length, width, or weight (Hohmann et al., 1979). *Causality* refers to learning relationships between causes and their results. In the preschool child, attempts to identify such relationships are clearly shown by the child who consistently asks, "Why?" (Brainerd, 1978). *Identity* is an extension of sensorimotor object permanence. It refers to the child understanding that some qualities of objects or people remain the same although their outward appearance or perceptual properties may change (Brainerd, 1978). For example, a *tree* remains a tree although it has no leaves in winter, buds during spring, is green during summer, and has brightly colored leaves in autumn.

Reasoning has been defined as "the process by which several pieces of prior learning are combined to produce a solution to a newly encountered problem" (Lillie, 1975, p. 109). Others describe reasoning as using previous knowledge to make decisions or generalizations (Bourne, Dominowski, & Loftus, 1979). Although the preschool child is often not credited with using reasoning in a deductive manner (going from a generalization to a specific instance) or in an inductive manner (going from a specific instance to a generalization) (Frost & Kissinger, 1976), children can *behave* in a rule-governed manner (Dale, 1976). The difference is whether the child is aware of (able to verbalize) the rule.

TEACHING CONCEPTS

Concept Development

Although *concept* is a commonly used word, it is not easily defined; Martorella (1972), for example, lists nine different definitions. However, Engelmann (1969) presents a relatively concise description: "a concept is a set of characteristics that is shared by all instances in a particular set and only by these instances" (p. 9). For any concept such as *chair* the attributes or characteristics which make it what it is can be listed. These characteristics would be present in all examples (positive instances) of chairs and would not be present in examples (negative instances) of objects other than chairs. A table is not a chair because it lacks the critical characteristics of one; it is a *negative instance* of the concept *chair*. A given kitchen chair is an example of the concept *chair* because it has the characteristics shared by all chairs; thus, it is a *positive instance* of the concept. Characteristics of concepts are described in the following paragraphs.

Concepts are classifications of ideas, symbols, objects, and events. The basic task associated with concept development is classification. The child must decide whether a given example is actually a member of a concept class. Examples of such decisions include, "Is this a *dog*?" "Is this *real*?" or "Is this something to *ride*?" Being able to answer these questions correctly requires an understanding of the *defining attributes* associated with each concept. What makes a dog a dog? What differentiates something to ride from that which a child cannot ride?

The teacher's task is to identify and teach the defining attributes of a concept. For example, a chair can be defined as a place where one person can sit that is elevated from the floor allowing the knees to bend and providing a place to rest one's back (Engelmann, 1969). All chairs have these attributes, but things that are not chairs do not have these attributes. Although a chair may possess other attributes (it rocks, or is made of wood, or squeaks, or is stained oak, or is of a certain design, etc.), all of these characteristics are *irrelevant* to its classification as chair. The identification of defining attributes is a critical step in teaching concepts and will be described later in this chapter.

Concepts themselves can be classified. Concepts can be classified as either concrete or abstract (Fallen & McGovern, 1978). *Concrete concepts* are observable and include such examples as dogs, chairs, capital letters, and numerals. *Abstract concepts* are not observable and require definitions, rules, or generalizations. Abstract concepts include examples such as big, few, ordering objects by color, or

classifying by notions such as good or appropriate. Gagne (1974) describes abstract concepts as *defined concepts.*

Concepts can also be classified as well-defined or ill-defined (Hulse, Egeth, & Deese, 1980). *Well-defined* concepts have relatively obvious features connected by clearly stated rules. Features are dimensions such as color, size, shape, and composition. The concept of "square" is well-defined because all squares have four sides of equal length and four right angles. The rule connecting the features is one of *conjunction,* that is, all three features must be added together to make a shape a square. *Ill-defined* concepts have less obvious features and rules connecting them. "Most natural language categories (e.g., game, furniture, book) are concepts of this kind" (Hulse et al., 1980, p. 213).

Regardless of the classification, certain types of concepts are more easily taught using certain procedures. For example, well-defined concepts are more easily taught by highlighting their features and presenting the connecting rules, whereas ill-defined concepts are more easily taught by showing examples (positive and negative instances of the concept) (Hulse et al, 1980).

Concepts change with experience and age. Because of different training and experiences, our concept of the atom is quite different from the nuclear physicist's. In addition, some concepts change as more knowledge is obtained. For instance, our concept of what and how much severely handicapped children can learn has changed dramatically in the last twenty years. Likewise, adults' concepts of common objects may be very different from children's perceptions. For example, an adult's concept of spoons probably includes a utensil for eating and stirring, but a child's might include eating, stirring, banging, digging, and dropping. Teachers should present concepts in the context of the learner's, not the teacher's, experience and knowledge.

Most children learn concepts through a naturally occurring process of confirmation and denial of perceptions. Rebecca, for example, has repeatedly heard her parents and sister say "doggie" whenever a dog is present. She learns to interact with the dog by pointing or patting in response to cues such as, "Where's the doggie?" or, "Pat the doggie." Finally she labels the dog as "dawdaw." Her parents get excited and make a big commotion over Rebecca's accomplishment. However, the next day Rebecca calls the kitten a "dawdaw" as well as a squirrel, a bird, and an ant. Rebecca's parents confirm or deny the accuracy of her perceptions by agreeing with her when she is right and correcting her when wrong ("That's not a dog, Rebecca, that's an ant"). Most youngsters acquire basic concepts through this natural process of experimentation and feedback.

Many handicapped youngsters do not learn concepts through such a trial-and-error process, or do so at a very slow rate. To increase the rate of acquisition of concepts, teachers of young handicapped children must plan specific instructional programs. The teacher must select the concepts and appropriate examples relating to each one. Examples should be presented to insure that the concept is learned and procedures established so the concept is generalized to other situations.

Selecting Concepts

The identification of appropriate concepts is a difficult task because of the infinite range of possibilities. Therefore, teachers should select concepts on the basis of functional utility and ease of learning.

A concept is *functional* if the child will use it in the everyday environment or if it will be required of him or her in the future environment. Parents should help identify common concepts used at home. Also, the teacher should notice what interests the child and build the training sessions around those concepts. For example, if a child seems to be especially interested in animals, the teacher might begin concept training by teaching the difference between dogs and cats. In addition, the teacher should consult checklists containing concepts important for success in kindergarten. Examples of such checklists include the Boehm Test of Basic Concepts (Boehm, 1971), the Basic Concept Inventory (Engelmann, 1967), and the Kraner Preschool Math Inventory (Kraner, 1976).

For example, the Boehm Test of Basic Concepts (BTBC) is a criterion-referenced test to assess the child's knowledge of 50 basic concepts important for later success in school. The concepts were selected by reviewing kin-

dergarten and first grade curricula and identifying the most frequently required concepts. They are grouped into broad categories of Spatial Relations, Time, Quantity, and Miscellaneous, and are listed in Table 10.1. Children display their knowledge of each concept by selecting, from three choices, the picture that most closely describes the concept. Research has demonstrated that the BTBC may be administered reliably (Levin, Henderson, Levin, & Hoffer, 1975), and that performance on the Boehm correlates with achievement in subsequent grades (Steinbauer & Heller, 1978). Ault, Cromer, and Mitchell (1977) found that the use of real objects instead of pictures did not substantially alter the scores of nonhandicapped preschoolers, implying that the procedure is valid for assessing skills of handicapped youngsters who may not respond well to several different pictures on a page or who respond better when presented with manipulable objects.

The hierarchical or taxonomical relationship of one concept to another should be considered when selecting examples for instruction. For instance, the concept of *chair* is part of the concept of *things on which to sit,* which in turn is part of the concept *furniture,* which is a part of the concept of *things in a building,* which is part of *objects made by people,* which is part of *inanimate objects.* High-order concepts such as *inanimate things* or *objects made by people* are usually more difficult to learn than lower-order concepts such as *chair* or *things to sit on* because they are less concrete and include many subconcepts (things in buildings and furniture). Usually examples should be selected and instruction initiated from a level of the child's experience in the taxonomy. Thus, for children who live in the city, the concept of *car* and *bus* may be more relevant than *tractor* and *truck,* but the reverse may be true for the child who lives on the farm. As the child acquires the concepts through experience, they can be related to higher-order concepts in the taxonomy and to concepts for which experience is limited.

Selecting Appropriate Examples

To select appropriate examples, the teacher must analyze the concept in terms of its characteristics and consider the child's level of attainment (Becker, Engelmann, & Thomas, 1975; Clark, 1971). All concepts have *defining attributes* or characteristics that distinguish examples from nonexamples (chairs from tables), and *variable attributes* that distinguish examples within a given class of the concept (wooden rocking chairs from upholstered rocking chairs). Thus, the teacher must consider the child's level of concept attainment and determine whether the child needs to learn the defining or variable attributes. If the child has no notion of the concept, instruction should begin with the defining attributes, and then move to the variable attributes. The teacher should initially select examples from a variety of classes or from the primary class. If the teacher used only rocking chairs to teach the concept *chair*, the child could incorrectly learn that a chair must rock. Some examples of a concept are better than others; for instance, a wooden, four-legged chair with a straight back is a better example of *chair*

than is a bean bag chair or a pedestal office chair. The most effective examples of a concept have a large number of characteristics shared by other examples and the defining characteristics are salient or noticeable (Rosch, 1975; Rosch & Mervis, 1975). However, all examples, even the good ones, have characteristics or irrelevant attributes that are not defining or critical (Becker et al., 1975). For instance, all chairs are made of some material and are a certain color; however, the material and the color do not define a given piece of furniture as a member or nonmember of the concept *chair*. When teaching concepts, downplay the nondefining attributes or irrelevant dimensions.

Clark (1971) suggests types of examples or instances that should be selected for instruction. The first type is a *positive-introductory instance* similar to Rosch's best example. It should have few irrelevant qualities and several defining attributes which should be more salient than irrelevant attributes. A

TABLE 10.1

Concepts included in the Boehm Test of Basic Concepts

Space	Quantity	Time	Miscellaneous
Top	Some, not many	After	Different
Through	Few	Beginning	Other
Away from	Widest	Never	Alike
Next to	Most	Always	Matches
Inside	Whole		Skip
Middle	Second		
Farthest	Several		
Around	Almost		
Over	Half		
Between	As many		
Nearest	Not first or last		
Corner	Medium-sized		
Behind	Zero		
Row	Every		
Center	Pair		
Side	Equal		
Below	Third		
Right	Least		
Forward			
Above			
Separated			
Left			
In order			

Source: Boehm (1971).

positive-introductory instance of the concept *car* might be a single-color, four-door sedan. The second type is a *positive-confirmatory instance* that also has several noncritical or irrelevant attributes. A positive-confirmatory instance of the concept *car* might be a multi-colored station wagon with a carrying rack on top. The final type of example is the *negative instance,* a nonexample of the concept. It should have some but not all of the defining attributes of the concept, and should have some of the irrelevant attributes used in the positive instances of the concept. A negative instance of the concept *car* might be a pickup truck or a multicolored van with a carrying rack. Several examples of each type should be used.

Teaching Techniques

Methods used to teach a given concept will depend upon the child's abilities and the complexity of the concept. The teacher should be sure the child has the basic sensory skills for concept discrimination and can perform certain basic operations before beginning instruction. Sensory skills include basic auditory or visual perception, and the simplest technique for assessing them is for the teacher to observe whether the child responds in different ways to various visual or auditory stimuli. The basic operations are those of matching and sorting.

Teaching basic matching and sorting   *Matching,* at its simplest level, is selecting from two or more stimuli the one more similar to a model. In this section emphasis is placed on teaching the skill of matching rather than on the concepts the child learns to match. The skill can then be used with a variety of concepts.

A sequence for teaching basic matching is displayed in Table 10.2 and includes the verbal cue used, the model or sample shown by the teacher, and the stimuli the child selects. The child should select the object like the one shown by the teacher. The same verbal cue is used throughout the teaching sequence, and is an individual decision, depending upon the motor abilities of the child. Some children may point to the correct response, others can hand it to the teacher, and still others may only be able to look at the correct response or answer a yes/no question such as, "Is this the same?"

In the first step the teacher presents an object, in this case a ball, and says, "Touch same." The child has only a ball from which to select, so he or she will either make a correct response or not comply. If the child does not comply, the teacher will need to use an appropriate form of assistance such as a model, prompt, or physical manipulation to insure correct responding. Once the child can independently complete this step, the same task should be repeated using other stimuli shown

TABLE 10.2

Steps in teaching a child to match to a sample

Step	Verbal Cue	Teacher Shows	Child Selects From
1.	"Find same."/ "Give me same."/ "Touch same."/ "Look at same."	Ball	Ball
2.	" "	Shoe	Shoe
3.	" "	Spoon	Spoon
4.	" "	Ball	Ball and car
5.	" "	Ball	Ball and shoe
6.	" "	Ball	Ball and spoon
7.	" "	Shoe	Shoe and car
8.	" "	Shoe	Shoe and ball
9.	" "	Shoe	Shoe and spoon
10.	" "	Shoe	Shoe, ball, and spoon

in Steps 2 and 3. Objects that clearly are different from each other should be used in early training.

Once the child independently performs the task across a variety of stimuli, the child should select one of two choices. For example, in Step 4 the teacher says, "Touch same" and holds up the ball. The child must select the correct answer from the possible choices of ball and car. If the child cannot perform this task, the teacher will again need to use an appropriate form of assistance to insure correct responding. For example, the stimuli from which the child can choose may be arranged so the correct answer is much closer to the child, increasing the probability of a correct choice. Gradually this *position cue* should be removed until the choices are equidistant from the child. Once the child can independently complete this step, the same task should be repeated using other stimuli, as shown in Steps 5 through 9, first varying the range of incorrect choices presented and then varying the model. The child has learned the basic operation when he or she consistently matches the sample when presented with two or three choices. At this level, the stimuli should be very different and the match should be exact. For example, the teacher should *not* present a tennis ball, say, "Touch same," and require the child to choose between a tennis ball and a baseball, since these stimuli share many similar characteristics. Likewise, it would be unwise to present a tennis shoe and have the child select from a spoon and a dress shoe. At this level we are teaching the basic operation of matching and should not confuse the child with fine discriminations or by requiring a higher level of conceptualization.

Once the child has mastered matching, he or she can move on to the basic operation of *sorting*. Sorting requires the child to initially apply matching skills to several objects and then to independently determine a dimension to sort. A sequence of steps for teaching basic sorting skills is displayed in Table 10.3. Again, the same verbal cue ("Put same with same") is used throughout the sequence, and the stimuli are quite different in nature.

In the first step the teacher gives the child several blocks, shows the child a container with one block in it, and says, "Put same with same." If the child does not place all of the blocks in the bin, use some form of assistance. Once the child has mastered this task, repeat it with another set of stimuli. Then the teacher should add a second bin, but keep the other aspects of the task the same. In Steps 5 and 6 the child is given a set of two different objects and asked to sort into bins, with a sample object in each bin. In Steps 7 and 8 the task is repeated with only one model and in Step 9 the child is asked to sort without models. If the child can perform Step 10, which requires sorting previously untrained objects with no model, the child has probably learned this basic operation.

Teaching specific concepts Once the operations of matching and sorting are mastered, they can be used to learn simple to complex concepts. A sequence of sorting, matching, identifying, and labeling can be followed. For example, assume that one of Rebecca's objectives is to identify a spoon. The concept to be taught is *spoon,* and the task is to discriminate spoon from nonspoons. The first step is to identify the defining attributes of the concept *spoon.* Webster defines *spoon* as "an eating or cooking implement consisting of a small hollow bowl with a handle," and this definition could be used to identify examples of the concept. Initially the teacher should select the best example of a spoon; generally, the spoon the child actually uses.

A sequence of steps in teaching the spoon concept is described in Table 10.4. The first is a simple sorting task. Give the child several examples of the spoon, along with some cups and say, "Put same with same." After the child can sort grossly different stimuli, then have the child sort spoons from other utensils, beginning with a knife, since it is less like a spoon than a fork (Steps 3 and 4). Once the child can sort utensils, the next task is matching. Although the first step may have to be, "Give me same," the teacher should begin as soon as possible to use the cue, "Give me the spoon." The task should first include a model (Steps 5–8) and then the model should be withdrawn (Steps 9–12). The operation in Steps 9–12 is that of identifying. *Identification* occurs when the child indicates through some

TABLE 10.3
Steps in teaching basic sorting

Step	Verbal Cue	Bins	Child Has
1.	"Put same with same."	One bin, with sample in bin	Blocks, all same
2.	" "	One bin, with sample in bin	Crayons, all same
3.	" "	Two bins, with sample in one bin	Blocks, all same
4.	" "	Two bins, with sample in one bin	Crayons, all same
5.	" "	Two bins, with sample in each bin	Blocks and crayons
6.	" "	Two bins, with sample in each bin	Blocks and cars
7.	" "	Two bins, with sample in one bin	Blocks and cars
8.	" "	Two bins, with sample in one bin	Cars and crayons
9.	" "	Two bins, with no samples	Cars and blocks
10.	" "	Two bins, with no samples	Nuts and keys

behavior, such as giving, touching, or pointing, an example of the concept named by the teacher. Usually the teacher's cue is verbal and the child's response nonverbal. However, the teacher could use a nonvocal communication system or show the child positive and negative instances of the concept and ask the child to make "yes/no" judgments. The final step in the sequence (Step 13) is having the child name the item. A similar procedure may be followed in higher-level concepts as well. Examples are provided later in this chapter.

At this point the child has simply learned the label of one object: his or her personal spoon. The child may not have learned the *concept* of spoon since they come in many different sizes, shapes, colors, and materials. The child will have learned the concept when he or she can generalize the label to new, untrained examples of spoons. As described in Chapter 3, training sufficient exemplars is an effective procedure for facilitating generalization. Anderson and Spradlin (1980), for example, trained a child to match several positive instances of six concepts (including bowls, hats, and cars) to another positive instance of each concept. The child was then trained to name one positive instance. The naming did not generalize to other positive instances of the concepts until the subject was trained to name more than one instance. Hupp and Mervis (1981) found generalization was greater when children were trained with "best example" instances of the concept than when "nonbest example" instances were used. These data suggest multiple instances that are "best examples" of the concept are likely to facilitate generalization to other instances.

Other procedures for facilitating generalization include training in the natural environment such as the home or during free play;

TABLE 10.4

A sequence of tasks for teaching the concept *spoon*

Step	General Task	Teacher Cue	Child Has
1.	Sorting	"Put same with same."	Spoons and cups
2.	Sorting	"Put same with same."	Spoons and blocks
3.	Sorting	"Put same with same."	Spoons and knives
4.	Sorting	"Put same with same."	Spoons and forks
5.	Matching	"Give me spoon" (show model).	Spoon
6.	Matching	"Give me spoon" (show model).	Spoon and cup
7.	Matching	"Give me spoon" (show model).	Spoon and knife
8.	Matching	"Give me spoon" (show model).	Spoon and fork
9.	Identify	"Give me spoon." (no model)	Spoon
10.	Identify	"Give me spoon." (no model)	Spoon and block
11.	Identify	"Give me spoon." (no model)	Spoon and knife
12.	Identify	"Give me spoon." (no model)	Spoon and fork
13.	Label	"What is this?"	Spoon

programming common stimuli, or using materials and training behaviors likely to be found and expected in the natural environment; and making contingencies indiscriminate or making it unclear which discrete behavior of several is being reinforced by using intermittent or delayed reinforcement (Stokes & Baer, 1977; Wehman, Abramson, & Norman, 1977).

Considerations in Teaching Concepts

Although the sort-match-identify-name sequence is simple, several factors influence how quickly children move through the steps. These include the number of instances used, the salience or difference between them, how closely in time various trials occur, whether one or two concepts are trained at the same time, whether instances from previous trials are visible in later trials, and what prompts (if any) are used.

At each step of the sequence, the fewer the *number of instances,* the more quickly the child learns the task. For example, the teacher's stimulus can be more easily matched if the child only has one object identical to the teacher's and another that is different than if the child had to choose from eight or nine objects. During initial instruction only one to three negative instances should be used with one positive instance, but as training progresses, use a larger number of positive and negative instances.

The *salience or difference between instances* is another factor influencing acquisition. It is easier to sort an *O* from an *X* than a *V* from an *X,* because the *V* looks more like the *X* than the *O.* Likewise, the difference in the teacher's verbal cues at the identification step is important. It is easier to hear the difference between "block" and "toothbrush" than between "block" and "clock." Initially, the differences between visual and auditory stimuli should be quite obvious, but as the child learns the discrimination, they should be made less obvious.

In initial training the defining or critical attributes of the positive instances should be accentuated. This practice will allow the child to pick up on the important aspects of the concept. This can be accomplished through methods such as extrastimulus prompting, stimulus fading, and stimulus shaping. *Extrastimulus prompts* are irrelevant to the concept being taught. They include such techniques as positioning the correct item close to the child or pointing to or verbally describing the item. Extrastimulus prompts must be faded by a decrease in provision or intensity or a delay in presentation (Snell & Gast, 1981).

Stimulus fading and *stimulus shaping* are similar processes; stimulus fading is simpler to use.

Fading ... involves the gradual shifting of control from some dominant stimulus element to a different and criterion stimulus. Fading uses an element of a stimulus that gradually changes along some physical dimension (e.g., intensity, size, color) to a point where the terminal discrimination is based on *another* dimension, usually one that is more difficult for the learner. Fading does not alter the overall configuration or topography of a stimulus (Etzel & LeBlanc, 1979, p. 369).

In both stimulus fading and shaping, characteristics of the correct choice are changed to increase the likelihood of selecting the desired example. *Relevant* characteristics of the concept are manipulated in stimulus shaping; *irrelevant* characteristics are used in stimulus fading.

For example, if a teacher is training Susie to differentiate between circles and ovals, the first step is sorting the two shapes. However, Susie cannot sort shapes when given circles and ovals of approximately the same size. One technique to help her learn naturally would be to initially make the circle bigger than the oval, accentuating the difference between the two. The teacher has changed an irrelevant dimension, because size is not relevant to the difference between a circle and an oval, and is simply used to highlight the difference between the two. Use of stimulus fading, then, would involve a gradual fading of this irrelevant dimension. The size of the circles

could gradually be made smaller until Susie is sorting circles and ovals of approximately the same size.

This strategy may be effective for many children. Some handicapped children, however (perhaps most notably autistic children), sometimes demonstrate a learning phenomenon known as stimulus overselectivity (Lovaas, Koegel, & Schreibman, 1979). In *stimulus overselectivity,* the child learns to discriminate on one dimension only, and fails to shift to another dimension. In the example of ovals and circles, use of stimulus fading (changing irrelevant dimensions) in the first step actually teaches the child to sort big and little, not oval and circle. A child who was demonstrating stimulus overselectivity might learn this discrimination, but as the teacher gradually reduces the size of the circle, the child fails to shift responding to the shape dimension as opposed to the size dimension. The child never noticed the difference between shapes, and the shift from size to shape was apparently too great.

Stimulus shaping may help avoid stimulus overselectivity because the relevant dimension is changed. For example, the teacher may initially have the child sort squares and ovals of similar size. The shape (the relevant dimension) of these two stimuli is quite different, and Susie ought to be successful in sorting them. Gradually the teacher can change the square so it more closely resembles a circle without changing the size of the shape. In this strategy the child is always sorting by shape and thus the problem of stimulus overselectivity is avoided. Examples of changing stimuli through stimulus fading and shaping procedures are displayed in Figure 10.1.

Stimulus fading and shaping, even in their simple forms as displayed in Figure 10.1, are complex procedures. The relevant dimensions of many concepts are difficult to change. Etzel and LeBlanc (1979) suggest that these procedures only be used when less complex ones are ineffective in facilitating acquisition.

The *time between presentation of instances* should be relatively short (Fallen & McGovern, 1978). If a child was given one opportunity to point to (identify) a given shape in the morning and another opportunity in the afternoon, it would take longer to learn the con-

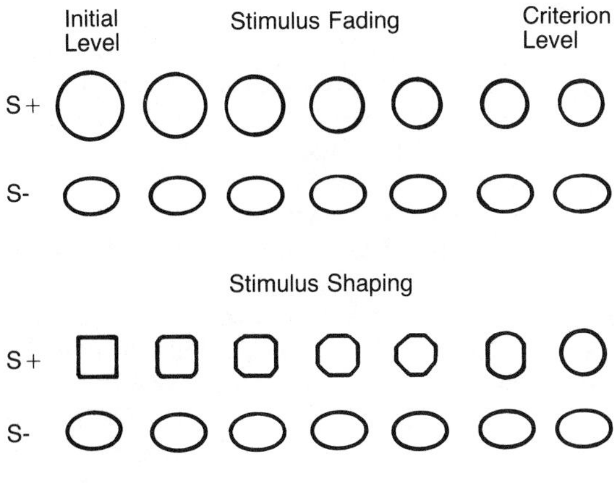

Initial Level | Stimulus Fading | Criterion Level

FIGURE 10.1

Examples of the changes in stimulus materials when using stimulus fading and stimulus shaping to teach a child to sort circles and ovals. *Note:* From "The Simplest Treatment Alternative: The Law of Parsimony Applied to Choosing Appropriate Instructional Control and Errorless Learning Procedures for the Difficult-to-Teach Child" by B.C. Etzel and J.M. LeBlanc, *Journal of Autism and Developmental Disorders,* 1979, *9,* 361–382. Copyright 1979 by Plenum Publishing Corp. Reprinted by permission.

cept than if given several opportunities in a few minutes.

The length and number of training sessions must also be considered. *Massed practice* or long concentrated training in one or two sessions and *distributed practice* or spaced training over several relatively short sessions were described in Chapter 7. Although the effects depend upon the learner and the task (Wehman & McLaughlin, 1981), distributed practice usually results in more efficient acquisition (Travers, 1977).

The *number of concepts* being trained at one time may influence the rate of acquisition. One concept will likely be acquired more quickly than several concepts that are trained at the same time. However, when two or more tasks are trained simultaneously, inattention due to boredom may be less frequent (Dunlap & Koegel, 1980). Likewise, generalization may be greater when two tasks are trained at the same time as compared to one task (Panyan & Hall, 1978; Schroder & Baer, 1972). These effects may be greater if the two tasks are different.

When *instances from previous trials are present during later trials,* acquisition of the concept will be more rapid (Clark, 1971). When exam-

ples from previous trials remain visible during later trials, the child is able to refer back to them when making judgments about later trials.

The Unit Approach

The *unit approach* is a method for teaching related concepts organized around a central theme. Themes may include specific categories such as vegetables or things to ride, special events such as holidays, or more general subject matter such as cooking. Many preschool programs organize daily activities within a unit framework, typically spending one or two weeks on a specific topic. This approach allows for correlated activities to reinforce basic concepts. For example, if the unit is jobs people do, the language lesson may involve naming common jobs, the fine motor lesson might consist of using a pencil to take the firefighter from the firehouse to the fire, story time could involve sequencing the events in the workday of a nurse, and the class could take a field trip to a factory.

The unit approach is flexible, allowing for individual instruction by providing a general framework so activities can be planned at various levels of complexity and integration. For example, while everyone is studying careers, one child may be learning to name common occupations, another may be comparing and contrasting the jobs of police and firefighters, and still another may be creating a story using miniature people and their tools. For a unit approach to be successful, use the following rules:

1 Select a concept theme or unit topic that is appropriate, of interest, and functional to the age group you are teaching.
2 Plan individual goals for children based on ability levels and instructional needs.
3 Modify instructional activities to fit within the unit concept.

Opportunistic Concept Instruction

Although every teacher should be able to implement a direct instruction strategy, the *opportunistic strategy* should also be emphasized. This strategy involves capitalizing upon any opportunity for the child to practice, learn, or generalize a previously learned skill. Capitalization can be done through incidental teaching and by taking advantage of events as they occur.

Incidental teaching, described further in Chapter 13, can occur "whenever a child initiates an interaction by specifying a reinforcer (attention, material, activity) that an adult can deliver" (Hart & Risley, 1980, p. 408). When a child initiates such an interaction, the teacher focuses attention on the child and asks a question or expands on the child's request, taking advantage of the child's immediate interest in learning a concept. Ideally, opportunistic instruction or incidental teaching should be used with most concepts. Unfortunately, many handicapped youngsters will not initiate interactions and thus teachers must turn to direct instructional strategies.

TEACHING PREACADEMIC SKILLS

Preacademic skills are skills considered necessary for success in school-related tasks. In this section we focus on the cognitive skills assumed to be important prerequisites for reading, mathematical computation, and problem solving.

Prereading

Reading involves many types of behavior; however, it is primarily a form of language use. One of the most important prerequisite skills for reading is a well-developed *language system*. The child does not necessarily have to speak, but must behave as though objects, actions, and events can be represented by symbols. According to Smith (1977), "Children need two basic insights to begin to learn to read ... they must be able to predict and make sense of language" (p. 394). Making sense of language is basically the ability to understand what is being read or said.

Some authors also consider auditory skills important. *Auditory discrimination* involves distinguishing between two or more different sounds (Cohen & Gross, 1979). *Auditory blending* refers to the child combining two or more phonemes or syllables (Williams, 1979). *Auditory segmentation* is the opposite of blending, and involves separating phrases by words, words by syllables, and syllables by phonemes (Gibson & Levin, 1975; Williams, 1979). Auditory segmentation may be a more critical skill than blending for early readers, but all three skills concern the child's perception of speech (Gibson & Levin, 1975).

Prereading also involves visual skills. *Visual discrimination* is the ability to distinguish between two or more visual stimuli. Although many visual discrimination programs and materials exist, usually visual discrimination skills required in reading are learned without formal instruction (Gibson & Levin, 1975). When children do not differentiate between given stimuli, train discriminations with materials that require little transfer to print (Williams, 1979) and emphasize the distinctive features of letters, syllables, or words being trained (Gibson & Levin, 1975). *Visual sequencing* refers to looking from left to right and is considered a prereading skill (Cohen & Gross, 1979). Besides visual sequencing, McConkie (1979) suggests the place and duration of the *visual fixation* on the page may be critical variables.

Reading also involves combining auditory and visual skills with conceptual and language skills. These include *letter-sound correspondence* or the realization that a given letter and sound stand for the same thing and that letters have names. A related skill is realizing words on a page are symbols, and those symbols (sensory stimuli) have some equivalence to the child's conceptual and language knowledge (Gibson & Levin, 1975; LaBerge, 1979; Snell, 1978).

Prereading targets A variety of skills are necessary for successful reading. A number of these skills are presented in Table 10.5 and were drawn from a variety of curricula and checklists. In Table 10.5, appropriate instructional targets are grouped into the broad areas of comprehension, visual discrimination, and sound discrimination. *Comprehension* includes such skills as describing action in pictures, sequencing events, and recalling details. *Visual discrimination* includes letter and word recognition while *sound discrimination* includes the ability to identify rhymes and matching sounds to consonants and vowels.

When identifying appropriate prereading targets, teachers should consult commercially available checklists and assessment tools. The targets described in Table 10.5 are sample

TABLE 10.5
Basic prereading skills

Comprehension	Visual Discrimination	Sound Discrimination
Finds picture to match spoken word.	Matches objects and pictures.	Adds rhyming words to familiar nursery rhyme.
Describes action in picture.	Matches shapes.	Tells whether two words sound the same or different.
Repeats simple nursery rhymes.	Selects and names shapes.	Identifies rhyming words.
Sequences pictures to tell a story.	Matches letters.	Tells which picture begins with a named consonant sound.
Recalls details of simple, unfamiliar story.	Points to named letters.	Matches consonant sound with letter.
Predicts what will happen after hearing part of a story.	Names letters.	Matches vowel sound with letter.
	Recognizes name.	Tells sound consonant makes.
	Reads common sight words.	Tells sound vowel makes.

behaviors taken from more extensive lists of skills and represent some commonly included prereading skills.

Teaching visual discrimination The procedures described for teaching basic concepts are directly applicable to many prereading skills, since reading is essentially a discrimination task.

One basic visual discrimination skill is the ability to recognize one's own name. This functional skill helps children label chairs, objects, materials, or space as their own. The child's name is a good first word to teach because it is very personal and most children are proud to recognize and show their names.

Many children can be taught to recognize their names through the match-sort-identify-label sequence described earlier. The child's name could simply be inserted in Tables 10.2, 10.3, and 10.4 instead of the objects. Objects may be used as initial distractors, but eventually the child should recognize his or her name from a group of names.

A common strategy for teaching a child is using an irrelevant but interesting cue to help the child learn to discriminate his or her name from other names. An example of the procedure is displayed in Figure 10.2. Assume that the teacher has four children in a group with name recognition an objective for each. Prerequisite skills for teaching name recognition include visual discrimination skills, knowing

you have a name, and responding consistently to your name. The first step is to select appealing and noticeable irrelevant cues. In Figure 10.2 the irrelevant cues are color and a picture of a cat. Although the cues have no relationship to his name, Tom's favorite color happens to be red and he really likes cats. The cues should therefore increase the likelihood that Tom will correctly recognize his name, particularly when the other children's names are printed on different colored cards using different symbols or pictures.

In the first step Tom is shown his name and asked to find it. This step is continued until Tom consistently picks up or points to the name card. The teacher should praise Tom for correct responding and follow it with an expanded comment such as, "Hooray, you found your name! Look, it says *Tom.*" Once consistent responding is established at this level, a distractor card (one with a different name) should be introduced. Once correct responding with a variety of distractors has been established, the teacher can then begin *fading* the irrelevant cues. First the cat is gradually removed and then the color highlighting the letters until Tom correctly discriminates his name from others written with black ink on a white card. Once this level of performance has been established, the teacher can begin generalization training, teaching Tom to recognize his name in other places and using other materials (on his cubby, on a green card, etc.).

Using and fading irrelevant cues does not work if stimulus overselectivity occurs. For example, Tom may not be paying attention to the shape of the letters at all, and when the last bit of color is removed, he may no longer be able to discriminate his name. An alternative strategy suggested by LeBlanc, Etzel, and Domash (1978) is to manipulate the actual shape of the letters to teach a word. Examples of four applications of this strategy are displayed in Figure 10.3. Initially the word is made to look very much like the object it represents. Gradually the picture is changed until the word alone remains. Obviously, this procedure is very time consuming, requires

some drawing ability, and is easier to use with nouns than other forms of words. However, when other procedures fail to work, this strategy may be successful.

Teaching sound discrimination skills To read orally, children must first be able to discriminate different sounds and then associate a specific sound with one or a combination of letters. Oral reading is more difficult to teach than visual discrimination because the teacher cannot always physically manipulate or physically prompt the correct response. The primary strategies for teaching sound discrimination are modeling and verbal cueing.

Initial skills in sound discrimination may be taught in a variety of ways. For example, in teaching rhyming words, the child can be

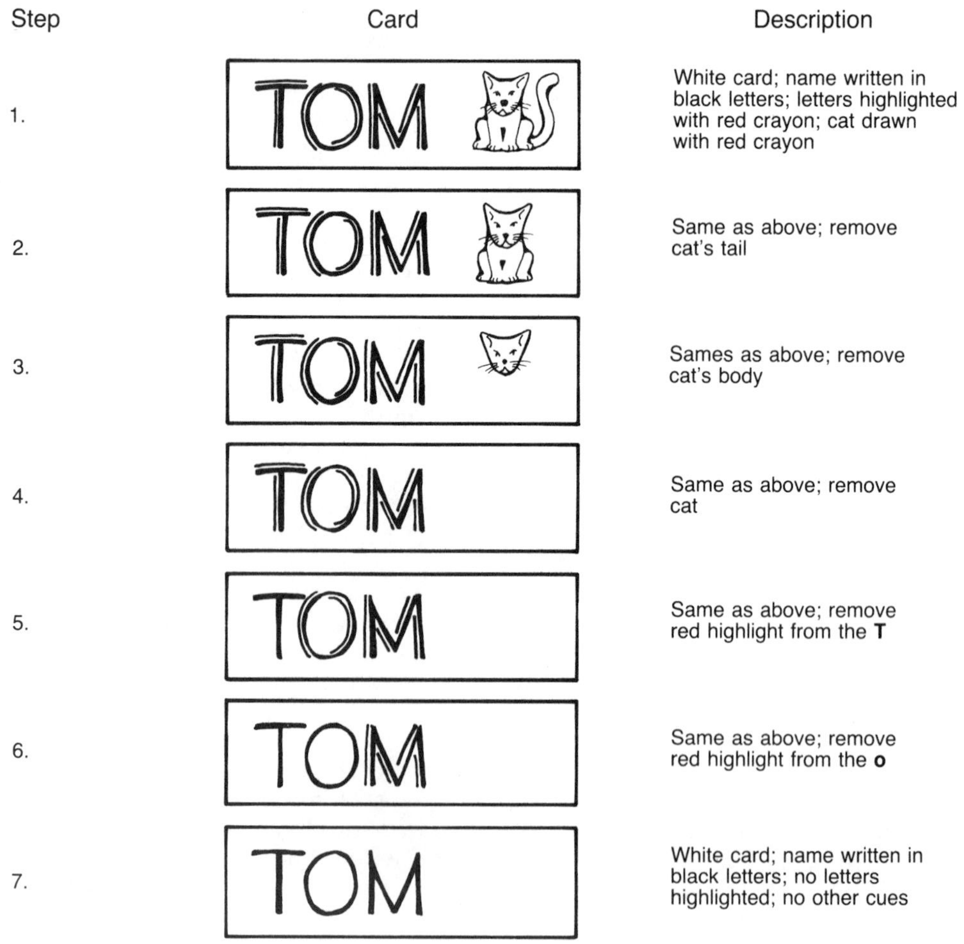

Step	Card	Description
1.		White card; name written in black letters; letters highlighted with red crayon; cat drawn with red crayon
2.		Same as above; remove cat's tail
3.		Sames as above; remove cat's body
4.		Same as above; remove cat
5.		Same as above; remove red highlight from the **T**
6.		Same as above; remove red highlight from the **o**
7.		White card; name written in black letters; no letters highlighted; no other cues

FIGURE 10.2
Use of irrelevant cues in teaching a child to recognize his name

shown two pictures, a pan and a tomato, and asked, "Which one sounds like (or rhymes with) *man*?" If the child cannot perform this task, several strategies might be used. The child can be helped in making the correct response by modelling or having the correct picture placed closer. But these cues are irrelevant to the sound discrimination task and may not help the child understand rhymes. A

more relevant strategy might be to first accentuate the stimulus word (*man*) and then say the names of the pictures, accentuating the word *pan* and saying *tomato* in a normal fashion. Such assistance helps the child focus on the importance of the sounds themselves.

Similar strategies could be used in teaching a child to recognize and associate sounds with letters. For example, if the teacher wants

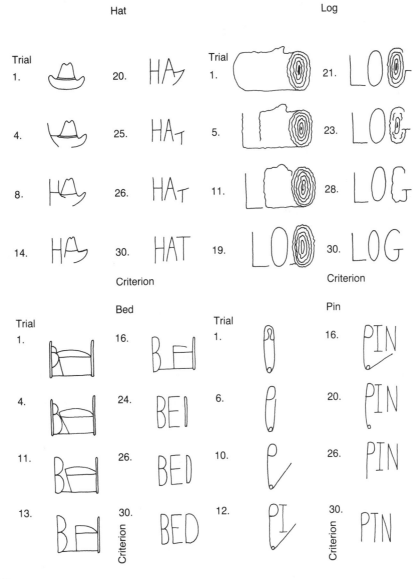

FIGURE 10.3
Manipulating letter shapes to teach words. *Note:* From "A functional curriculum for early intervention" by J.M. LeBlanc, B.C. Etzel, and M.A. Domash. In K.E. Allen, V.A. Holm, and R.L. Schiefelbusch (Eds.), *Early intervention—A team approach.* Baltimore: University Park Press, 1978. Copyright 1978 by University Park Press. Reprinted by permission.

Max to learn beginning consonant sounds, he or she might use two pictures, a moon and a car, and ask Max to "point to the one that begins with *mmm*." If Max responds incorrectly, the teacher could say the words for him, accentuating the beginning sound of *moon.*

After the child performs this skill at an acceptable level, he or she can begin to learn to associate letters with sounds. Have the child pair the letter with a picture of a word that begins with that letter. For example, a peach could be drawn on a card beside the letter *p*. LeBlanc, Etzel, and Domash (1978) suggest that if this strategy is not effective, teachers should try manipulating the shapes of the letters themselves. For example, "Mother Duh," which eventually changes into the letter *d*, is shown in Figure 10.4. The children initially respond with the sounds stimulated by the picture and gradually learn to associate the sound with the letter as the teacher gradually changes the picture to look like the letter.

Teaching children to actually say the sound a letter makes is a difficult step and often

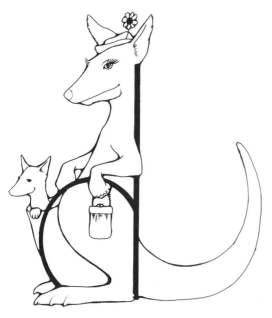

FIGURE 10.4

Manipulating letter shapes to teach letter sounds
Note: From "A functional curriculum for early intervention" by J.M. LeBlanc, B.C. Etzel, and M.A. Domash. In K.E. Allen, V.A. Holm, and R.L. Schiefelbusch (Eds.), *Early intervention—A team approach.* Baltimore: University Park Press, 1978. Copyright 1978 by University Park Press. Reprinted by permission.

requires teacher modeling and other cues. For example, Lonnie can match letters to pictures and can tell whether two sounds are the same or different. His teacher decides he is ready to learn to name consonant sounds when shown a letter. If Lonnie does not do this spontaneously, the teacher may simply have to model and say, "Lonnie, this letter says *mmm*. What does this letter say?" Once he can imitate the teacher, the model can be gradually withdrawn. For example, the teacher might not actually say the sound but could press lips together in the appropriate fashion to begin to make the sound.

Teaching comprehension skills   Reading is only functional if children understand the meaning of the words. Perhaps the most important activity facilitating comprehension is early and frequent reading of stories to children. Any child with basic auditory and visual perception skills should be read to daily even before one year of age. By sitting in an adult's lap and listening to and watching a story, young children learn the rhythm and flow of language, to associate pictures with words, and that looking at books can be fun. As children get older they learn that books tell stories, that pages can be turned, and to proceed through the book from beginning to end. Later, children use books to learn about new events, people, objects, or animals; to pretend and visualize; and to sequence events. Parents should be encouraged to read daily to their children, and preschool programs should plan daily group activities as well as quiet, individual reading times. Reading is also a lifetime recreational skill for people of all ages. Thus the basic rule for conducting any reading activity is to *make it enjoyable.*

Early signs of comprehension include behaviors such as pointing to pictures at appropriate times or filling in the word at the end of the sentence. (For example, "The duck looked in the water and saw a _____.") Later indicators of comprehension include the ability to recall facts from a story, to sequence a series of pictures to make a logical story, and to restate, evaluate, or draw inferences.

Having children fill in words of a story is an excellent beginning comprehension activity, and can be facilitated by using well-illustrated books and by pointing to the picture of the correct response. Once children can complete parts of the story with picture cues, they can be asked to predict what is going to happen in subsequent pages. This activity should be conducted using a familiar book.

Picture sequencing is a good activity to help children understand the sequence and relationship between story parts. Objectives for teaching children to sequence pictures are displayed in Table 10.6. If a child cannot sequence two simple pictures, the first step may be to have the child manipulate three-dimensional objects as the teacher reads the story. For example, if the teacher is reading *Goldilocks and the Three Bears,* the child could move a doll into a doll house and have the doll sit in the chairs, lie down in the beds, and so forth. Once the child can perform this task, the sequence of objectives with pictures may follow. Each step should begin with simple, short, familiar stories and gradually progress to longer stories involving more pictures and complex tasks.

Teachers should also write stories about activities or events that occur in the class. For example, if Tyrone has a birthday and the class celebrates it with cupcakes, candles, and

TABLE 10.6
Objectives for teaching comprehension of stories through picture sequencing

---

Prerequisite Skills: Child understands basic concepts and can follow simple directions.
Possible Sequence of Objectives:
1. Given appropriate characters and materials, child manipulates objects through the appropriate actions as the teacher reads the story.
2. Given a set of pictures, child selects picture that best represents a particular event in a story, as the teacher reads it.
3. Given two pictures (boy cooking, boy holding up a cake), child tells which comes first.
4. After hearing a complete, familiar story, child sequences pictures according to the events in the story.
5. After hearing a complete, unfamiliar story, child sequences pictures according to the events in the story.
6. Given a set of picture cards, child arranges the cards in a logical sequence to make a story (child is not told story before task).

---

punch, the teacher could write a story about what happened, using line drawings for words the children do not know. Children can be involved in writing such stories. For example, if the class went to the park for a field trip, the teacher could have each child tell what he or she did and include individual descriptions in the stories. Such involvement not only facilitates reading comprehension but assists children in realizing that symbols in print are related to their meaning. For example, the word *cake* stands for something sweet and the word *swing* stands for a piece of equipment on which one can sit and go back and forth.

Premath Skills

Premath skills focus on comparing, labeling, and measuring quantity as well as using symbols related to quantity. *Comparing quantity* includes applying basic concept judgments such as big-little, one-many, few-many, more-less, and equivalence-nonequivalence to objects and sets (Williams, Coyne, DeSpain, Johnson, Scheuerman, Stengert, Swetlik, & York, 1978); seriating or ordering objects and symbols on some dimension such as length, size, weight, number, or value (Cohen & Gross, 1979); and one-to-one correspondence (Williams et al., 1978). *Labeling quantity* includes rote counting—saying the names of the numbers in correct sequence without actually counting objects; rational counting or counting objects; and answering questions such as, "How many is this?" *Using symbols related to quantity* includes associating the written numeral such as *1, 3,* or *10,* with the correct number of objects; associating the verbal name of the number with the written numeral; and matching the verbal name of the number to the correct number of objects. *Measuring quantity* includes basic concepts used in the quantification of liquids or space (full-empty), weight (heavy-light), length (short-long), time (before-after), money (coins and their relative value), and temperature (hot-cold) (Wehman & McLaughlin, 1981).

These four basic groups of premath skills develop concurrently; each has many levels of difficulty. For example, noting that an 18-inch doll (big) is larger than a 6-inch doll (little) is much easier than recognizing that a set of two blocks, three toy animals, and four puzzle pieces has the same number of members as a set of two blocks, two toy animals, two toy cars, two puzzle pieces, and one penny. However, both involve comparing quantity.

Premath targets Mathematics includes a wide range of skills. The teacher's first task is to determine a relevant sequence of premath skills and assess the child's performance on those tasks. A possible sequence of premath instructional targets is displayed in Table 10.7.

Teaching premath targets Nonhandicapped children learn many premath concepts through discovery learning, natural experiences, and observational learning. Many theorists and practitioners suggest that teachers take advantage of children's natural interests by arranging the environment to encourage appropriate learning. For example, Forman and Kuschner (1977) believe the teacher should observe the child's play and then carefully introduce conflicting events to cause the child to notice a discrepancy. For example, Ruth thinks larger objects are heavier than smaller ones, and is putting small plastic blocks on both sides of a balance scale. The teacher should get a balance scale, sit beside Ruth, and put a few plastic blocks on one side of the balance and a smaller but heavier magnet on the other side of the scale. The teacher could repeat this process, or add enough plastic blocks for the scale to balance, and suggest that Ruth look at his scale. If Ruth notices the smaller magnet is heavier than the plastic blocks, a cognitive conflict is induced. The teacher should then provide a variety of objects for Ruth's further experimentation. Some of the objects should be large and heavy, large and light, small and heavy, and small and light. According to Forman and Kuschner (1977), if the child notices the discrepancy between what he or she thought was true and actual observation, the child will then set out to understand the discrepancy or resolve the conflict. The resolution of the conflict advances knowledge. Conflict inducement requires considerable teacher skill and rapid decision making.

Unfortunately, retarded and otherwise handicapped children often do not learn premath or other concepts through discovery learning,

TABLE 10.7
A possible sequence of premath instructional targets

Prerequisite Skills: Child demonstrates a general understanding of basic concepts such as more-less, large-small, long-short, many-few, high-low, some-none, big-little, all-none, and first-middle-last. The child responds to the perceptual attributes of objects rather than using a quantitative basis. For example, when given two sets and asked, "Which one has *more*?" child selects one that appears to have more rather than counting sets.

Possible Objectives
1. Says numerals 1–10 in order.
2. Given a set of objects, creates another set of equal number by matching objects in 1:1 correspondence.
3. Counts out number of objects specified by teacher.
4. Given a fixed, ordered set, counts objects and answers, "How many?"
5. Given a fixed, unordered set, counts objects and answers, "How many?"
6. Matches numerals.
7. Selects numeral named by teacher.
8. Reads printed numeral.
9. Places numeral in order.
10. Given two written numerals, can state which shows more or less.
11. Matches numeral to set.
12. Given two sets of objects, counts and states whether sets are same or different in quantity.
13. Given two sets of objects, counts and states which set has more or less.
14. Tells which number comes before or after number stated by teacher.
15. Identifies half.

---

conflict inducement, or by watching educational television programs. The teacher will need to use direct instruction strategies to help these children acquire basic premath skills. Natural learning experiences can then reinforce what the child has been taught.

Teaching basic premath skills involves the same basic processes used with other skills: assessment, specification of objectives, task analysis, intervention, and evaluation. For example, assume that Ted demonstrates understanding of concepts such as big-little and long-short but does not respond correctly when given two sets and asked, "Which one has more?" The teacher decides that the first objective for Ted should be to demonstrate an understanding of the general concept of *more*, although not by counting, and wants him to pick the container or set that *appears* to have more things in it. At first, the teacher should select two sets of materials where one obviously has a great deal more than the other (one bowl is full of grapes and the other has only one grape). The teacher could point to the full bowl and say "Ted, this one has *more* grapes." Then the teacher would ask Ted to point to the bowl that had more grapes. Correct answers could be reinforced with a grape; errors could be corrected through teacher assistance, including repetition of the teacher model, providing a verbal cue ("No, Ted, it is the one that has lots of grapes"), or physical manipulation (placing Ted's finger on the correct choice).

Once Ted consistently selects the correct bowl, use other sets of stimuli that are also quite different in quantity. For example, present one full and one almost empty glass of juice. Once Ted responds correctly to a wide variety of these stimuli, the task should be made more difficult by gradually decreasing the difference between the stimuli. For example, one glass could be approximately ⅓ full and the other approximately ⅔ full.

Such methods also can be used in teaching more advanced math skills. The key to successful instruction is pinpointing the child's current skills, providing a challenging yet attainable task, and giving appropriate teacher assistance. Resnick, Wang, and Kaplan (1973); Resnick and Ford (1981); Silbert, Carnine, and Stein (1981); and Williams et al. (1978) provide specific skill sequences and techniques in early mathematics instruction. Also, remember that instruction should begin with concrete objects the child can manipulate, and that functional applications of premath skills should be emphasized by providing real world opportunities to practice newly acquired skills. For example, at the grocery, Ted's mother should let Ted select the package that appears to have more strawberries in it.

PROBLEM SOLVING AND REASONING

Problems are situations where the attainment of a given goal is obstructed or where something is needed. *Problem solving* is the process used to eliminate the obstruction and secure the goal (Kodera & Garwood, 1979) or devise a method to alleviate the need. *Solutions* are devised for given problem situations, and involve combining previously learned rules or concepts "which may not have been previously applied to similar situations in the past history of the individual who is solving the problem" (Gagne & Briggs, 1979, p. 70). Gagne and Briggs (1979) maintain the solutions are devised by the "problem-solver alone, not by a teacher or other external source" (p. 70). However, Becker, Engelmann, and Thomas (1975) suggest that certain problem-analysis skills can be taught to increase the likelihood of problems being solved. Regardless of how children resolve difficulties, solutions for isolated problems frequently can be used to solve similar problems.

The phases or stages in the problem-solving process (Bourne et al., 1979; Klausmeier & Allen, 1978) have been described by Bourne and coauthors as the *preparation* phase where certain aspects of the problem are identified, the *production* phase where possible solutions are devised, and the *judgment* phase or evaluation of the generated solutions. Another way of describing problem solving is to identify the types of problems encountered. Becker et al. (1975) classify problems depending upon "whether the solution is a *fact* or a *judgment*, and in terms of what is *given* and *not given*" (p. 115). Judgment problems have more than one solution that may vary in the assumed value of each. For example, the issue of desirable free play in preschool programs for handicapped children has a variety of solutions. The value given to any one solution will vary according to the goals of the program, the philosophy of the personnel, the resources available, and the needs of children.

When teaching young handicapped children to reason and solve problems, the teacher must consider the type of problem presented and the phases or stages in the problem-solving process. In addition, the teacher should emphasize solving problems that result in func-

TABLE 10.8
Sample Unit: Musical Instruments

Level	Model Objective	Sample Objective
The *knowledge* level requires the ability to reproduce information by recognition or recall.	The child will be able to name individual items which belong in a given unit, when asked, "What is this?"	When shown object or picture, the child will be able to name the following musical instruments: Drum — Triangle Horn — Cymbal Piano — Banjo Guitar — Mandolin Harmonica — Kazoo Tambourine — Xylophone Bells — Violin
The *comprehension* level requires the ability to understand information demonstrated by reorganizing, paraphrasing, or explaining.	The child will be able to give in his own words a definition or rule for a given unit of classification.	When asked, "What is an instrument?" child should not only be able to tell that an instrument is something used to make music but also should be able to add additional ideas to this definition (i.e. used in a band, makes pretty sounds, etc.).
The *application* level requires the ability to use (learned) information (methods, rules, or abstractions) in appropriate situations where no mode of solution has been specified.	The child will be able to demonstrate understanding of a given unit by selecting, out of a group of pictures or objects, those that fit within that unit, *with no rule given.*	Given the direction, "Find all of the instruments," the child will be able to select all instruments out of a group of pictures or objects.
The *analysis* level requires the ability to identify component parts, relationships among elements, and basis for organization of whole.	Given an object or shown a picture, the child will be able to tell what it is about that object that makes it a member of a given category, and either *why* or *how.*	When asked a question such as, "Why is a guitar a musical instrument?" child will be able to tell some attribute of the guitar that lends it to being a good musical instrument (strings vibrate and make a sound, sounds pretty, easy to play, etc.).
The *synthesis* level requires the ability to uniquely organize ideas and materials or discover a unique relationship not readily apparent.	Child will be able to select objects of the same category, given no cues.	Child will find two that are alike, given a group of pictures or objects.

TABLE 10.8 (continued)
Sample Unit: Musical Instruments

Level	Model Objective	Sample Objective
The *evaluation* level requires the ability to judge value for some purpose against criteria and standards, including making comparisons and stating reasons for decisions.	Given a specific criterion, child will be able to select item best suited and give reason for selection.	In answer to questions such as the following, child will select appropriate musical instrument: a Which instrument makes the prettiest sound? b Which instrument would you be able to play if you didn't have a mouth? c Which instrument would be best to use in a marching band? After listening to excerpts of two musical selections, child will choose one best for a particular purpose.

Source: Bailey and Leonard (1977).

tional outcomes and will likely be encountered in the everyday environment.

A useful framework for teaching children various reasoning and problem-solving skills is the taxonomy of educational objectives described by Bloom (1956). Six types of cognitive reasoning skills—knowledge, comprehension, application, analysis, synthesis, and evaluation—are identified. These categories are generally hierarchical in nature, with knowledge being the most basic skill and evaluation the most advanced. For example, simple recall of facts is a knowledge level skill; evaluation requires a judgment using certain criteria for making decisions. Although the hierarchical nature of the categories has been questioned (Smith, 1968; Stedman, 1973), the categories provide a useful framework for identifying a range of appropriate cognitive objectives.

Bailey and Leonard (1977) proposed a model for adapting Bloom's taxonomy to a preschool curriculum. A set of model objectives and sample objectives for each level of Bloom's taxonomy for teaching children the concept *class of musical instruments* is shown

in Table 10.8. Basic knowledge level skills would be taught using basic concept instruction techniques. Higher-level objectives require similar techniques (modeling, cueing, providing feedback, etc.) applied to different skills.

SUMMARY

In this chapter, several cognitive abilities developing after infancy were described. Concept development, reasoning and problem solving, and preacademic skills were discussed in more detail. Sequences of instructional targets were specified and strategies for teaching those skills briefly identified.

REFERENCES

Anderson, S.R., & Spradlin, J.E. The generalized effects of productive labeling training involving common object classes. *Journal of the Association for the Severely Handicapped,* 1980, *5,* 143–157.

Ault, R. L., Cromer, C. C., & Mitchell, C. The Boehm Test of Basic Concepts: A three-dimensional version. *Journal of Educational Research,* 1977, *70,* 186–188.

Bailey, D.B., & Leonard, J. A model for adapting Bloom's taxonomy to a preschool curriculum. *Gifted Child Quarterly*, 1977, *21*, 97–103.

Becker, W.C., Engelmann, S., & Thomas, D.R. *Teaching cognitive learning and instruction.* Chicago: Science Research Associates, 1975.

Bloom, B.S. (Ed.). *Taxonomy of educational objectives, handbook 3: Cognitive domain.* New York: David McKay, 1956.

Boehm, A.E. *Test of basic concepts.* New York: Psychological Corporation, 1971.

Bourne, L.E., Dominowski, R.L., & Loftus, E.F. *Cognitive processes.* Englewood Cliffs, N.J.: Prentice-Hall, 1979.

Brainerd, C.J. *Piaget's theory of intelligence.* Englewood Cliffs, N.J.: Prentice-Hall, 1978.

Clark, D.C. Teaching concepts in the classroom: A set of teaching prescriptions derived from experimental research. *Journal of Educational Psychology*, 1971, *62*, 253–278 (Monograph).

Cohen, M.A., & Gross, P.J. *The developmental resource: Behavioral sequences for assessment and program planning* (Vols. 1 & 2). New York: Grune & Stratton, 1979.

Dale, P.S. *Language development: Structure and function* (2nd ed.). New York: Holt, Rinehart & Winston, 1976.

Dunlap, G., & Koegel, R.L. Motivating autistic children through stimulus variation. *Journal of Applied Behavior Analysis*, 1980, *13*, 619–627.

Engelmann, S. *Basic concept inventory.* Chicago: Follett Educational Corporation, 1967.

Engelmann, S. *Conceptual learning.* San Rafael, Calif.: Dimensions, 1969.

Etzel, B.C., & LeBlanc, J.M. The simplest treatment alternative: The law of parsimony applied to choosing appropriate instructional control and errorless-learning procedures for the difficult-to-teach child. *Journal of Autism and Developmental Disorders*, 1979, *9*, 361–382.

Fallen, N., & McGovern, G. *Young children with special needs.* Columbus, Ohio: Charles E. Merrill, 1978.

Forman, G.E., & Kuschner, D. *The child's construction of knowledge: Piaget for teaching children.* Monterey, Calif.: Brooks/Cole, 1977.

Frost, J.L., & Kissinger, J.B. *The young child and the educative process.* New York: Holt, Rinehart and Winston, 1976.

Gagne, R.M., & Briggs, L.J. *Principles of instructional design* (2nd ed.). New York: Holt, Rinehart and Winston, 1979.

Gibson, E.J., & Levin, H. *The psychology of reading.* Cambridge, Mass.: The MIT Press, 1975.

Gibson, E.J., & Rader, N. Attention: The perceiver as performer. In G.A. Hale & M. Lewis (Eds.), *Attention and cognitive development.* New York: Plenum, 1979.

Ginsburg, H., & Opper, S. *Piaget's theory of intellectual development* (2nd ed.). Englewood Cliffs, N.J.: Prentice-Hall, 1979.

Hale, G.A., & Lewis, M. *Attention and cognitive development.* New York: Plenum, 1979.

Hart, B., & Risley, T. In vivo language intervention: Unanticipated general effects. *Journal of Applied Behavior Analysis*, 1980, *13*, 407–32.

Hohmann, M., Banet, B., & Weikart, D.P. *Young children in action: A manual for preschool educators.* Ypsilanti, Mich.: High/Scope Educational Research Foundation, 1979.

Hulse, S.H., Egeth, H., & Deese, J. *The psychology of learning* (5th ed.). New York: McGraw-Hill, 1980.

Hupp, S.C., & Mervis, C.B. Development of generalized concepts by severely handicapped students. *The Journal of the Association for the Severely Handicapped*, 1981, *6*, 14–21.

Jackson, N.E., Robinson, H.B., & Dale, P.S. *Cognitive development in young children.* Monterey, Calif.: Brooks/Cole, 1977.

Klausmeier, H.J., & Allen, P.S. *Cognitive development of children and youth: A longitudinal study.* New York: Academic Press, 1978.

Kodera, T.L., & Garwood, S.G. Cognitive processes and intelligence. In S.G. Garwood (Ed.), *Educating young handicapped children: A developmental approach.* Germantown, Md.: Aspen Systems Corporation, 1979.

Kraner, R. *Kraner preschool math inventory.* Boylston, Mass.: Teaching Resources, 1976.

LaBerge, D. The perception of limits in beginning reading. In L.B. Resnick and P.A. Weaver (Eds.), *Theory and practice of early reading* (Vol. 3). Hillsdale, N.J.: Lawrence Erlbaum Associates, 1979.

LeBlanc, J.M., Etzel, B.C., & Domash, M.A. A functional curriculum for early intervention. In K.E. Allen, U.A. Holm, & R.L. Schiefelbusch (Eds.), *Early intervention—A team approach.* Baltimore: University Park Press, 1978.

Lerner, J., Mardell-Czudnowski, C., & Goldenberg, D. *Special education for the early childhood years.* Englewood Cliffs, N.J.: Prentice-Hall, 1981.

Levin, G.R., Henderson, B., Levin, A.M., & Hoffer, G.L. Measuring knowledge of basic concepts by disadvantaged preschoolers. *Psychology in the Schools*, 1975, *12*, 132–139.

Lillie, D.L. *Early childhood education: An individualized approach to developmental instruction.* Chicago: Science Research Associates, 1975.

Lovaas, O.I., Koegel, R.L., & Schreibman, L. Stimulus overselectivity in autism: A review of research. *Psychological Bulletin*, 1979, *86*, 1236–1254.

Martorella, P.H. *Concept learning designs for instruction.* Scranton, Pa.: Intext Educational, 1972.

McConkie, G.W. What the study of eye movements reveals about reading. In L.B. Resnick & P.A. Weaver (Eds.), *Theory and practice of early reading* (Vol. 3). Hillsdale: N.J.: Lawrence Erlbaum Associates, 1979.

Meier, J.H., & Malone, P.J. *Facilitating children's development: A systematic guide for open learning* (Vols. 1 & 2). Baltimore: University Park Press, 1979.

Neisworth, J.T., Willoughby-Herb, S.J., Bagnato, S.J., Cartwright, C.A., & Laub, K.W. *Individualized education for preschool exceptional children.* Germantown, Md.: Aspen Systems Corporation, 1980.

Panyan, M.C., & Hall, R.V. Effects of serial versus concurrent task sequencing on acquisition, maintenance, and generalization. *Journal of Applied Behavior Analysis*, 1978, *11*, 67–74.

Resnick, L., & Ford, W. The psychology of mathematics for instruction. Hillsdale, N.J.: Lawrence Erlbaum Associates, 1981.

Resnick, L., Wang, M., & Kaplan, J. Task analysis in curriculum design: A hierarchially sequenced introductory mathematics curriculum. *Journal of Applied Behavior Analysis*, 1973, *6*, 679–710.

Rosch, E. Universals and cultural specifics in human categorization. In R. Brislin, S. Bochner, & W. Lonner (Eds.), *Cross-cultural perspectives on learning*. New York: Halsted, 1975.

Rosch, E., & Mervis, C.B. Family resemblances: Studies in the internal structure of categories. *Cognitive Psychology*, 1975, *7*, 573–605.

Schroeder, G.L., & Baer, D.M. Effects of concurrent and serial training on generalized vocal imitation in retarded children. *Developmental Psychology*, 1972, *6*, 293–301.

Silbert, J., Carnine, D., & Stein, M. *Direct instruction mathematics*. Columbus, Ohio: Charles E. Merrill, 1981.

Smith, F. Making sense of reading—and of reading instruction. *Harvard Educational Review*, 1977, *47*, 386–395.

Smith, R.B. Empirical Examination of the Assumptions Underlying the Taxonomy of Educational Objectives: Cognitive Domain. *Journal of Educational Measurement*, 1968, *5*, 125–128.

Snell, M.E. *Functional reading*. In M.E. Snell (Ed.), Systematic instruction of the moderately and severely handicapped. Columbus, Ohio: Charles E. Merrill, 1978.

Snell, M.E., & Gast, D.L. Applying time delay procedure to the instruction of the severely handicapped. *Journal of the Association for the Severely Handicapped*, 1981, *6*, 1–14.

Stedman, C.H. An analysis of the assumptions underlying the Taxonomy of Educational Objectives: Cognitive Domain. *Journal of Research in Science Teaching*, 1973, *10*, 235–241.

Steinbauer, E., & Heller, M.S. The Boehm Test of Basic Concepts as a predictor of academic achievement in grades 2 and 3. *Psychology in the Schools*, 1978, *15*, 357–360.

Stevenson, H.W. *Children's learning*. New York: Appleton-Century-Crofts, 1972.

Stokes, T.F., & Baer, D.M. An implicit technology of generalization. *Journal of Applied Behavior Analysis*, 1977, *10*, 349–367.

Tawney, J.W., Knapp, D.S., O'Reilly, C.D., & Pratt, S.S. *Programmed environments curriculum*. Columbus, Ohio: Charles E. Merrill, 1979.

Travers, R.M.W. *Essentials of learning* (4th ed.). New York: MacMillan, 1977.

Wehman, P., Abramson, M., & Norman, C. Transfer of training in behavior modification programs: An evaluative review. *Journal of Special Education*, 1977, *11*, 217–231.

Wehman, P., & McLaughlin, P.J. *Program development in special education*. New York: McGraw-Hill, 1981.

Williams, J. The ABD's of reading: A program for the learning disabled. In L.B. Resnick & P.A. Weaver (Eds.), Theory and practice of early reading (Vol. 3). Hillsdale, N.J.: Lawrence Erlbaum Associates, 1979.

Williams, W., Coyne, P., DeSpain, C.J., Johnson, F., Scheuerman, N., Stengert, J., Swetlik, B., & York, R. Teaching math skills using longitudinal sequences. In M.E. Snell (Ed.), *Systematic instruction of the moderately and severely handicapped*. Columbus, Ohio: Charles E. Merrill, 1978.

Although the early parent-child relationship lays an important foundation for social development, the child's social world soon expands beyond the immediate family. This chapter focuses on related strands of social development, toy play skills and social interaction with peers, and addresses the acquisition of positive social skills. Chapter 12 deals with reducing inappropriate behaviors that interfere with positive social development.

PLAY SKILLS

What is Play?

Play has many different definitions. Piaget (1945, 1962) considered play to be *assimilation*, one of two processes that all individuals use to achieve balance or equilibrium in their lives. It is through *accommodation* the other process, that people change their behaviors and knowledge to match their perceptions of the world. Imitation is an example of accommodation. Through assimilation we change the world to match our present cognitive abilities. In playing the child takes the world and makes it into whatever he or she wants it to be. A box becomes a race car, a blanket becomes a house, or the child becomes a fantasy figure or superhero. Play for Piaget consisted of activities done "for the mere pleasure of mastering them and acquiring thereby a feeling of virtuosity or power" (Piaget, 1945, 1962, p. 89).

Weisler and McCall (1976) reviewed several definitions of play and offered the following:

Play consists of behaviors and behavioral sequences that are organism dominated rather than stimulus dominated, behaviors that appear to be intrinsically motivated and apparently performed for "their own sake" and that are conducted with relative relaxation and positive affect (p. 494).

Weisler and McCall's definition requires some subjective interpretations by the observer (Is this behavior organism dominated? Is this person exhibiting positive affect?)

In this chapter, play is limited to play with objects, although clearly social play is frequently observed in young children. Social play will be discussed later as peer interaction.

11

Play and Social Interaction with Peers

Why Do Children Play?

Theories regarding *why* children play abound and are reviewed by Weisler and McCall (1976). Early theories focused on the genetic or physiological functions of play. For example, Spencer (1855) believed that play served simply to release "surplus energy." G. Stanley Hall (1906) suggested that play is the child's way of reenacting the interests and occupations of evolutionary predecessors, and the child does so in the same evolutionary sequence (swinging from our monkey predecessors, water play from our aquatic origins, etc.).

More recent theories tend to describe the functions play fulfills for children without trying to describe a causal relationship (children play *because* ...). For example, through play children learn many things about the characteristics and properties of people, animals, and objects. Many early intervention curricula are based on the assumption that improving the play experiences for children can lead to cognitive gains and improved social/emotional development. Play also may facilitate the gradual process by which the infant becomes more independent of parents. Finally, play may allow a child to exercise control that ordinarily is impossible (Weisler & McCall, 1976).

Play is important because children spend a great deal of time occupied with it. The challenge for early childhood special educators is to take advantage of the inherent appeal of play to create meaningful learning experiences.

The Developmental Course of Play

The manner and sequence in which play skills develop has been conceptualized in many ways by different authors. Piaget (1945, 1962) described the levels of play behaviors in children as practice games, symbolic games, and games with rules. Each level represents a higher quality of play and requires a higher level of cognitive skills. Practice predominates during the sensorimotor period. As the child begins to develop a representational system, symbolic play allows the child to use an object as a symbol for something else (a stick can be a spoon or a pencil). Finally, the child begins to learn games with rules; he or she can accept constraints imposed on an activity and is gradually able to handle rules of increasing difficulty, complexity, and levels of competition (Ellis, 1975).

Smilansky (1968) expanded Piaget's descriptions of play and identified four categories. *Functional play* is observed first in children and consists of simple repetitive motor movements which involve the use of objects; *constructive play* occurs when the child uses objects to make something; during *dramatic play*, the child uses imagination to create objects or situations; and while playing *games with rules*, the child begins to accept and participate in competitive activities with other children. These types of play develop sequentially in the order described. Although lower levels of play may be observed at older ages, more advanced play should predominate. For example, the child does not leave the functional play stage completely. Even adults occasionally display simple repetitive motor movements. Hopefully though we are generally engaged in more productive or more complex activities. The sequential nature of these categories has been supported by several studies (Rubin & Maioni, 1975; Rubin, Maioni, & Hornung, 1976).

Wehman (1977) has described several play skill hierarchies for use with severely or profoundly retarded young children. Hierarchies for exploratory and toy play are discussed here. Wehman described four levels of exploratory play:

Level I—Orientational Responses: Changes in behavior as a result of a gross stimulus change in the environment. Examples of orientational responses include turning to a light or sound.
Level II—Locomotor Exploration: Movement within an environment that results in sensory feedback.
Level III—Perceptual Investigation and Manipulation: Examination of an object.
Level IV—Searching: Seeking out new stimuli for exploration.

Weisler and McCall (1976) define exploration as "relatively stereotyped perceptual-motor examination of an object, situation, or event the function of which is to reduce subjective uncertainty (i.e., acquire information)" (p. 493). Exploration is an important component of play because it is only after a child becomes aware of and familiar with an environment that he can relax and play in it. Wehman (1977) suggests that severely handicapped children do not explore in sufficient detail or duration and must be trained in this skill.

Exploration and play are not always easy to differentiate and in some instances the same behavior (e.g., mouthing) could be considered as either. Perhaps this differentiation is irrelevant, since the important issue is the identification of meaningful sequences of development in exploration and play for use as a basis for planning interventions. In bridging the transition between exploration and play, Wehman (1977) describes nine levels of toy play. We group these into six levels:

Six Levels of Toy Play

Level I—Repetitive Manual Manipulations; Oral Contacts: The child at this level interacts with toys on a sensory basis, either repeating the same motor pattern with it or mouthing it.
Level II—Pounding; Throwing; Pushing or Pulling: The child still interacts with toys on a sensory level, although more gross motor movement is involved. During this period the child begins to become aware of cause-effect relationships.
Level III—Personalized Toy Use: The child begins to perform acts upon himself with toys. For example, the child may comb his hair or put a ring on his arm.
Level IV—Manipulation of Movable Parts of Toys
Level V—Separation of Parts of Toys
Level VI—Combinational Use of Toys: The child begins to use different play materials together.

Sutton-Smith (1970) suggests that although different levels of play predominate at different ages, each type of play follows a developmental sequence in its own right, cutting across the infant and preschool years. Sutton-Smith identified four modes of children's play (excluding social play). These include *imitation* —copying the behavior of others, *exploration* —finding out what can be done with things and how they work, *prediction*—testing assumptions about the effects of behavior, and *construction*—putting things together. Sutton-Smith described how each mode changed and developed between 1–5 years of age. Changes in behaviors within each of these sequences are related to changes in cogni-

tive development. Table 11.1 represents an adaptation of information taken from Sutton-Smith and other sources describing the development of play and demonstrates how different yet parallel forms of play and preferences change and are displayed within different preschool age ranges.

Play and Cognition

Many authors emphasize the important interrelationship between cognitive and play development. The effect of cognitive development on play skills was demonstrated by Lowe (1975), who conducted an observational study of developmental trends in representational play in infants. Children between the ages of 12–36 months were observed in a free play setting with four sets of materials. Three sets included a doll and several common objects such as a spoon, cup, bed, blanket, and table. The fourth set consisted of a truck, trailer, man, and four small wooden logs. Children were allowed to spontaneously play with the materials. The most striking and consistent trend was the tendency for younger children to perform symbolic (representational) activities on themselves. For example, the child might use the spoon to pretend to feed himself or use the toy comb on his own hair. As children matured, there was a marked decrease in self-related behavior and a marked increase in doll-related behavior. Older children were more likely to feed the doll than to feed themselves. This transition was observed at approximately 21 months, when self-related and doll-related behavior were approximately equal in observed occurrence. Analogous results were observed in the truck and trailer materials. Although younger children played with and moved the truck and trailer, it was not until the 21-month age level that the child put the little man into one of them, an act requiring a higher level of representational thought.

Advanced play skills require an increased capacity for representational thought. Critical cognitive skills leading to advanced levels of play begin with the acquisition of object permanence and also include the development of language as a symbol system, the ability to imagine things or events not present and represent them in some way, and reduced egocentrism (inability to see something from another person's perspective).

Handicapping Conditions and Play

A handicap can adversely affect both a child's early social development, and the early and subsequent play behavior. Li (1981) reviewed the literature on play and the mentally retarded child and concluded that the play behaviors of retarded children differ both qualitatively and quantitatively from those of nonretarded children. For example, Weiner, Ottinger, and Tilton (1969) showed that the

TABLE 11.1
The developmental course of several types of play

Age	Exploration/Manipulation	Construction	Dramatics	Games
12–24 months	Sensorimotor/perceptual examination of objects. Modes of exploration include banging, inserting in and pulling out, tasting, creeping and crawling through, emptying and filing, tasting and scribbling.	Simple towers with blocks, primarily exploration and manipulation.	Imitates own behavior but in different situations. Themes center on simple adult routines. Late in this year child begins to perform activities with doll.	Appearance/ disappearance (peek-a-boo); strange appearance, chase and capture.
24–36 months	Exploration becomes integrated with other types of play such as construction and dramatics. Child can manipulate and observe the results of behavior at the same time.	Block building, painting, pasting, clay, puzzles. Child is pleased with whatever he or she makes.	Assumes more complete adult roles, usually pretending to be adult doing things to other children. A toy can symbolize another object.	Participation in story telling; rhyme games.
36–48 months	Becomes very interested in exploring new places, although usually prefers to have an adult companion. Field trips begin to be meaningful and exciting experiences.	Drawing, cutting, advanced puzzles, coloring, diverse structures with blocks.	Increased variety of themes; creation of imaginary characters. Wants some outstanding prop (shoes, hat) to aid in role play. Enjoys puppet play.	Imaginary monsters, friends and enemies, singing and chanting.
48–60 months	Enjoys exploring increasingly greater range of experiences and places.	Collages, painting, complex puzzles. Child begins to be critical of own workmanship.	Dramatic play becomes very social and at times cooperative. More advanced themes. Child is more likely to want more than one prop or piece of clothing to aid in role play.	Simple board games, hunts for hidden treasures, prisoners, hide-and-seek.

toy contacts of retarded children were typically brief when compared with the toy contacts of nonretarded children. Ray (1975) observed the free-play behavior of normal and Down syndrome toddlers and found that the latter exhibited total play behaviors (get object, carry object, hold object, drop object, push object, give, play) significantly less often than their nonhandicapped peers. Weiner and Weiner (1974) found that when compared with nonretarded children of the same age, 6-year-old retarded children exhibited the combinational use of toys less frequently.

The explanation for retarded play skills in these children lies primarily in the close relationship between play and cognitive development. For example, Wing, Gould, Yeates, and Brierley (1977) studied severely mentally retarded children 5–14 years old and found that symbolic play occurred only when children had mental and language comprehension development scores of 19 months or more. Hill and McCune-Nicolich (1981) investigated the relationship between pretend play and patterns of cognition in young Down syndrome children and found that the observed level of symbolic play was more highly related to the child's cognitive abilities than to chronological age.

Sensory and physically impaired children may also be deficient in play skills. Children with motor impairments cannot explore the environment as other children can. They may in some cases require special toys or other adaptive equipment to facilitate appropriate interaction. Visually and hearing impaired children may also exhibit delays or deficiencies, particularly in symbolic and social play.

Improving Skills and Encouraging Play

Many children must be taught *how* to play with toys. They must also be taught to interact with toys for an extended period of time with minimal adult assistance. Techniques for facilitating extended engagement with toys are described in Chapter 7. In this chapter the focus will be on helping children acquire specific toy play skills.

The first step in designing a training program is to assess the child's current level of play skills. This assessment should include a determination of the nature and extent of the child's exploratory behaviors, the child's ability to use a variety of age-appropriate toys, the length of time the child plays with toys, and the level of symbolism, construction, and combinations in the child's play. Generally this information is gathered by observing children during play and will depend upon the individual child. The play hierarchies proposed by Wehman (1977) are useful for determining general levels of functioning for very young and more severely handicapped youngsters. They allow for the determination of the child's general level of exploratory and toy play, and provide a basis for setting objectives to facilitate movement to the next level of skill development.

A sample observation form using Wehman's (1977) levels of exploration and play is displayed in Figure 11.1. The form uses an event sampling format (see Chapter 2) where each occurrence of a given category of behavior is recorded on the form. The teacher also records the specific object or toy used by the child and notes any interactions with peers. When using this form the numbers may not be as important as the broad picture of overall functioning. The goal of the assessment is to determine the child's range of play skills and deficits so more specific assessments can be made and appropriate instructional targets identified.

For example, the child whose behaviors are recorded in Figure 11.1 exhibits a range of exploratory skills but predominately plays with objects using repetitive manipulations and oral contacts. The goal for Eddie is to increase the variety and appropriateness of basic motor movements with objects. Subsequent assessment of specific skills may be needed to determine more adequately Eddie's level of skill. For example, Wambold and Bailey (1979) divide toy manipulations into 10 levels to determine the kinds of motor manipulations performed by the child. They assess the behaviors of touching, grasping, holding, carrying, shaking, pounding, squeezing, pushing, pulling, and turning. A sample observation form using these categories is displayed in Figure 11.2 and follows an event sampling format noting each occurrence of a specific behavior. Analysis of the data presented in Figure 11.2 indicates that Eddie usually shakes objects when he manipulates them. Appropriate instructional objectives for Eddie might include pounding

Child: Eddie
Date: 8/1/82
Time: 9:00–9:30

Description of environment: Block and toy centers in classroom

Observer: DB

	Exploratory play						Toy play				
	Orienta-tional responses	Locomotor explora-tion	Perceptual investigation and manipulation	Searching	Repetitive manipula-tions/oral contacts	Pounding through pushing/ pulling	Persona-lized toy use	Manipula-tion of movable parts of toys	Separation of parts of toys	Combina-tional use of toys	Other
	Looks at visual changes in environment ЦТ I Responds to sounds III	Moves to another area of center IIII	Rubs carpet II	Looks for rattle II	Shakes rattle ЦТ Bangs block on floor III	Pushes car I					
Total number	9	4	2	2	8	1					
Percentage of behaviors	35	15	8	8	31	4					

Notes: _____

Favorite objects: Rattle, blocks _____

Any interactions with peers? None _____

FIGURE 11.1
Sample observation form using Wehman's (1977) levels of exploratory and toy play

Child: Eddie
Date: 8/3/82
Time: 9:00 - 9:30

Description of environment: Block and toy centers
Observer: DB

	Touches	Grasps	Holds	Carries	Shakes	Pounds	Squeezes	Pushes	Pulls	Turns	Other
	II	III	I	II	~~IIII~~ IIII	I		I	I		
Total number	2	3	1	2	9	1		1	1		
Percentage of behaviors	10%	15	5	10	45	5		5	5		

Notes:

Favorite objects: Rattle, blocks
Any interactions with peers? None

FIGURE 11.2
Sample observation form using Wambold & Bailey's (1979) system for assessing toy manipulation skills

and squeezing clay or pushing and pulling toy vehicles.

Assessment of toy play skills of older or more advanced children should focus on the child's ability to use a variety of age-appropriate toys and games, participate in pretend play activities, or use construction materials such as pencils, crayons, clay, scissors, or blocks. First determine whether the child naturally participates in these activities. If not, present specific activities such as puppets or drawings to the child to determine level of use. If the child does not know how to use the material, conduct a task analysis of relevant skills and then teach the skills. Some common games, construction materials, and dramatic materials for children ages 3–6 are provided in Table 11.2.

Once a comprehensive assessment has been conducted, specify goals and objectives for each child. Give consideration to the child's ability to do something with a toy, the length of time the child can interact with it, and the age-appropriate nature of the toys. The latter point is particularly important when dealing with older preschoolers (5–6 years of age) in mainstream settings. Although the toy play skills of some handicapped children may be severely delayed, identify age-appropriate toys that fulfill the developmental functions needed by the child. Although the goal for a 5-year-old severely retarded girl might be to shake a toy, use a tambourine rather than a rattle.

Once goals and objectives are specified, begin instruction. Several strategies are described here.

Select materials appropriate to the child's level of cognitive development. Wehman (1976) suggests it is often difficult to identify appropriate play materials for handicapped children. Very little research documents the most effective toys for eliciting appropriate play behaviors in handicapped children. Commercial toy manufacturers do not make appropriate toys for severely retarded or impaired preschoolers. Often the teacher must design new materials or adapt existing toys.

However, appropriate play materials are important. Phinney (1976), for example, found that children received maximum benefit from playing with materials that matched their level of cognitive development. In addition to matching toys with developmental level, materials should be colorful, distinctive, and durable. Most toys should be reactive (do something in response to the child's action), and should be selected keeping the individual's preferences in mind.

Insure availability of toys. Toys must be accessible to children. Access to toys may be denied by sensory or motor impairments, or by environmental restrictions. Enough toys should be available to encourage a variety of play forms. Provide duplicates of some toys to encourage parallel play and reduce arguments between young children. Wehman (1978) demonstrated that mere proximity to toys increased the play of severely handicapped children. Reid, Willis, Jarman, and Brown (1978) showed that simply increasing the number of toys available will increase the extent to which severely retarded persons play with them.

TABLE 11.2
Common play materials for preschool-aged children

Gross Motor	Games	Construction	Dramatics
Tricycles	Lotto	Pencils/crayons	Puppets
Swings	Don't Spill the Beans	Felt tip pens	Dolls/dollhouses
Sliding boards	Pick-up sticks	Clay	Dress-up clothes
Monkey bars	Hide and seek	Fingerpainting	Model persons,
Climbing areas	Board games	Scissors	buildings, and
		Glue/paste	objects
		Puzzles	Cars and trucks
		Building blocks	
		Construction sets	

Teach toy skills. Many children do not know how to play with or show no interest in a given toy. Further, they do not learn well by watching others play. These children need to be taught specific toy skills. A straightforward approach to training can consist of task analysis, direct teaching, providing assistance when necessary, and positive reinforcement. Assume, for example, that you observed Rebecca and determined that you must teach her to manipulate toys. You decide to begin with shaking toys. The following represents a typical series of steps:

1 *Conduct a baseline* to be sure that Rebecca does not demonstrate this skill. Identify several toys that react in some way when shaken and make them easily accessible. If over several observations Rebecca does not manipulate them or does so at a more basic level (puts them in her mouth), then shaking is probably an appropriate goal for intervention.

2 The simplest teaching strategy is *modeling,* in which you actually perform the expected task. For example, you might pick up a rattle, shake it, get a surprised look on your face, and say, "Oh my goodness! It shakes!" This may be a sufficient stimulus for some children.

3 If modeling does not work, the next level of assistance is the *partial physical assist* or the *use of prompts.* Using the prompt strategy, you might demonstrate, give a verbal cue ("Rebecca, shake!"), and then lightly touch Rebecca's arm to begin her movement. If she does not pick up the toy, place it in her hand first and then go through the sequence.

4 If prompting or partial physical assistance does not work, the next level of assistance is *full manipulation.* Using this strategy, the teacher fully assists the child in performing the task. For example, place the rattle in Rebecca's hand, give a verbal cue, and then shake her hand yourself.

5 In each of these techniques *positive reinforcement* is essential. Natural or functional reinforcement is a consequence that occurs naturally as a result of the child's behavior. The child may hear the toy make a noise or may see it react in another fashion. This may be reinforcing if the child

likes the toy or being able to make something happen. Natural reinforcement fosters independence since children are not relying on the teacher for enjoyment. Use of natural contingencies makes the task of appropriate materials selection even more important.

For some children, however, the natural consequences of behavior are not powerful enough to affect behavior or learning. The teacher may then need to use an artificial or contrived reinforcer. Although this is not very appealing to many early childhood educators and defies the typical definitions of play (e.g., an activity performed for its own sake), teachers should use procedures that have a high probability of working for a given child. Contrived techniques for teaching play may help the child acquire basic skills and eventually enjoy various activities.

The usual rules for using reinforcement techniques should be followed. Reinforcers should be identified and selected. The reinforcer should motivate the child to obtain the toy, should be presented immediately after the desired behavior, and should be paired with verbal praise and a description of the child's action ("Good shaking, Rebecca!"). During the initial phases of skill acquisition, present the reinforcer every time the child responds appropriately. Once consistent responding is achieved, start an intermittent schedule.

6 Gradually *reduce dependency* on teacher assistance. Children should play independently. For example, Rebecca should pick up the rattle and other toys and shake them without any teacher assistance. Fading and time delay can be used in reducing teacher assistance. In *fading,* gradually decrease the amount of assistance provided. For example, if you are working at the full manipulation level, assist the child through all but the last step in the sequence and let him or her perform the last step. In *time delay,* gradually impose a time period between the cue and the assistance. For example, hand Rebecca the rattle, say, "Shake, Rebecca," and then wait two seconds before giving any further assistance in hopes that she will go ahead and begin to shake independently. Successful appli-

cations of both fading (Wehman, 1979) and time delay (Snell & Gast, 1981) have been described.

7 Encourage *generalization* of this skill to other toys. This can be accomplished by gradually introducing new toys to the training setting, by reinforcing shaking in non-training settings, and by providing more shakeable toys in the environment.

The sequence of steps for assessing and teaching toy play skills is summarized in the following:

1 Observe what the child naturally does or does not do in an environment with toys.
2 Determine what the child does when presented a specific toy.
3 Identify general levels of skills using one of the play hierarchies described.
4 Conduct a more specific assessment of a range of skills within the child's general play level.
5 Identify specific toy play skills to be taught.
6 Task analyze each skill.
7 Conduct an appropriate intervention, and evaluate its effectiveness.
8 Gradually remove teacher assistance to insure generalized and independent use.

Toy play is an extremely important area for teacher analysis and planning. Children enjoy spending time with toys, and appropriate planning for play can serve to facilitate learning. Furthermore, play with toys serves as a basis for the development of social interaction with peers.

PEER INTERACTION

As the developing child grows and matures, he or she begins to become interested in other children. This interest is evidenced during the first year of life, and subsequently peer relations begin to play a major role in shaping behavior and attitudes. This section discusses the developmental course of early peer relations and strategies teachers can use in promoting peer interaction in handicapped children.

Developmental Course of Peer Interactions

Parten (1932) suggested sequential categories describing the child's play: unoccupied behavior, solitary independent play, onlooker, parallel activity, associative play, and cooperative or organized supplementary play (Table 11.3). Parten's research generally supported the sequential nature of these categories: As children grow older they become more social toward peers. The most commonly observed category for 24–30-month-olds was solitary play; children aged 30–42 months most often exhibited parallel play; and those aged 42–54 months were most frequently involved in associative play.

Parten's scale has been a standard for describing social play, planning interventions, and evaluating the effects of various intervention strategies such as peer interaction. Wintre and Webster (1974) demonstrated that the scale could be used to describe the social play of handicapped children and that the descriptions of the categories were clear enough to reliably classify children's behaviors. Barnes (1971) observed a more recent sample of young children than Parten's original group and found that although the categories were generally hierarchical or sequential in nature, the norms for play behaviors described by Parten did not apply. Yet the conceptual and descriptive characteristics of the Parten scale provide a basis for evaluating current behaviors and planning intervention efforts. Appropriate use of Parten's scale requires the consideration of three topics: the relationship of social play categories to cognitive schemes, the value of solitary play, and the early social play of infants and toddlers.

Social play and cognitive development Social play is inherently linked to the cognitive development of children. Odom (1981), for example, found a significant relationship between the developmental level of preschool retarded children and their social play as measured by Parten's scale. Rubin et al. (1976) combined Parten's categories of social play with the cognitive play schemes described by Smilansky (1968)—functional play, constructive play, dramatic play, and games with rules—in observations of preschoolers. This study demonstrated the interaction between

TABLE 11.3
Descriptions of Parten's categories of social play

Unoccupied Behavior	The child apparently is not playing, but occupies himself with watching anything that happens to be of momentary interest. When there is nothing exciting taking place, he plays with his own body, gets on and off chairs, just stands around, follows the teacher, or sits in one spot glancing around the room.
Solitary Independent Play	The child plays alone and independently with toys that are different from those used by the children within speaking distance and makes no effort to get close to other children. He pursues his own activity without reference to what others are doing.
Onlooker	The child spends most of his time watching the other children play. He often talks to the children whom he is observing, asks questions, or gives suggestions, but does not overtly enter into the play himself. This type differs from the unoccupied in that the onlooker is definitely observing particular groups of children rather than anything that happens to be exciting. The child stands or sits within speaking distance of the group so that he can see and hear everything that takes place.
Parallel Activity	The child plays independently, but the activity he chooses naturally brings him among other children. He plays with toys that are like those which the children around him are using, but he plays with the toy as he sees fit, and does not try to influence or modify the activity of the children near him. He plays beside rather than with the other children. There is no attempt to control the coming or going of children in the group.
Associative Play	The child plays with other children. The conversation concerns the common activity; there is a borrowing and loaning of play material; following one another with trains or wagons; mild attempts to control which children may or may not play in the group. All the members engage in similar if not identical activity; there is no division of labor, and no organization of the activity of several individuals around any material goal or product. The children do not subordinate their individual interests to that of the group; instead, each child acts as he wishes. By his conversation with the other children one can tell that his interest is primarily in his associations, not in his activity. Occasionally, two or three children are engaged in no activity of any duration, but are merely doing whatever happens to draw the attention of any of them.
Cooperative or Organized Supplementary Play	The child plays in a group that is organized for the purpose of making some material product, or of striving to attain some competitive goal, or of dramatizing situations of adult and group life, or of playing formal games. There is a marked sense of belonging or of not belonging to the group. The control of the group situation is in the hands of one or two of the members who direct the activity of the others. The goal as well as the method of attaining it necessitates a division of labor, taking of different roles by the various group members, and the organization of activity so that the efforts of one child are supplemented by those of another.

Source: Parten, 1932, pp. 249–252

social play and cognitive skills. For example, solitary, parallel, and associative play can be functional, constructive, or dramatic in expression.

True social play involving interaction with other children and cooperation requires several cognitive abilities not necessarily required for the lower levels of social play. Garvey (1974) discussed the fact that children must be able to differentiate play from nonplay. In a dyad, children must recognize play and must consent to participate. Otherwise, true social play is not occurring. The child must also know the rules. Garvey further suggests that the child must be able to abstract the general rule rather than simply respond to a directly taught instance. For example, the most basic rule of social play is that of reciprocity or taking turns. Finally, Garvey believes that the child must identify a theme of the interaction and participate accordingly.

Critical cognitive skills must be developed before true cooperative social play results. However, handicapped children can be taught cooperative play behaviors even though they may not possess cognitive skills. Many specific behaviors (smiling, imitating contacts, sharing) necessary to social interaction can be directly taught.

Solitary play Solitary play is given a low score on Parten's scale and is certainly not social play. Several authors, however, have recently suggested that a greater value should be placed on solitary play. Moore, Evertson, and Brophy (1974) found that over 50% of solitary play behavior of preschoolers was of an educative or goal-directed nature. Solitary play is purposeful and can teach the child many things. Rubin et al. (1976) contend that parallel play, not solitary play, is the least mature level of play for 3- and 4-year-olds.

Because low functioning handicapped children sometimes exhibit neither solitary nor parallel play, the issue arises as to which should be taught first. Solitary play can be viewed as a level of toy play and as such is valued as an independent skill. Therefore, it should be included in a broad curriculum for handicapped youngers simultaneous with social play. The teacher should strike a balance between toy and social play.

Social skills for infants and toddlers Although Parten's scale is useful for classifying the behavior of preschoolers 2 years and older, it is more limited in describing social behaviors of infants and toddlers. Recent research has begun to document the interesting developmental course and characteristics of the social play of very young children.

Mueller and Lucas (1975), drawing from the early work of Piaget (1945, 1962), suggest that early interactions with peers are similar in structure to early interactions with objects. An infant interacts with another because that infant is an interesting stimulus to be explored. Social behaviors toward peers by 6-, 9-, and 12-month-old infants have been documented by Vandell, Wilson, and Buchanan (1980). Vocalizations, smiles, and touches were the most frequently observed social acts and occurred even in 6-month-old babies.

Toys appear to change the nature of early infant interaction. Vandell et al. found that very young infants preferred to interact with interesting toys rather than peers. More and longer interactions between infants occurred when no toys were present. By the end of the first year, however, object-centered social acts begin to increase. Eckerman and Whatley (1977) observed the social behavior of pairs of unacquainted infants either 10–12 or 22–24 months of age with and without toys. When toys were not available, infants of both ages were more likely to imitate each other's actions, smile or gesture to each other, and make contact. When toys were present, both groups showed and exchanged toys and manipulated similar play materials in parallel fashion. Jacobson (1981) observed pairs of infants at 10, 12, and 14½ months of age. At the 10-month level most social interactions occurred when children were not playing with the same toy. By 14½ months, however, the longest social exchanges occurred during play with a common toy.

Mueller and Lucas (1975) describe three stages in the development of peer interactions in 1-year-olds. These stages are summarized in Table 11.4. Stage I is Object-Centered Contacts:

A cluster at the play group's toy train engine exemplifies an object-centered contact . . . Basically one child discovers the engine, squats down, and makes the engine's whistle sound repeatedly. All other children in the room immediately toddle over to the engine and either sound the whistle or manipulate the steering handle, an action introduced by a second child. During the 68 seconds that several children are at the train, three children never look at their peers' faces and the other two children look only once or twice, and get no responses to their looks (p. 229).

Although interactions do not typically occur at this age, there is contact between children and it centers not on the object alone, but on the action toward that object performed by another child.

Stage II is described as Simple and Complex Contingency Interchanges. In this stage children begin to interact in social fashion. Early in Stage II this interaction typically involves one initiation and one response, although it may be circular in nature. For example, one child falls down and the other laughs and the first child falls down again.

Later in Stage II the interchanges between children become longer and involve different behaviors. According to Mueller and Lucas, children in this stage can take turns but cannot exchange roles.

In Stage III, Complementary Interchanges, the participants "do different but intercoordinated or reciprocal things" (p. 247). Chasing and throwing balls to each other are examples of Stage III behaviors. Further, interchanges may require a reversal of roles. For example, Jimmy chases Daniel and then Daniel chases Jimmy.

Handicaps and Social Interactions

A handicapping condition can affect a child's social skill development in a variety of ways. It may limit the specific behaviors important to social interactions. Ray (1975), for example, conducted a detailed observation of the free

TABLE 11.4
Peer interactions in one-year-olds

Stage	Description	Example
I—Object Centered Contacts	Contacts between peers typically center around an object or a child's actions with an object.	Matt sees Pam opening the jack-in-the-box and runs over to look at the box.
II—Simple Contingency Interchanges	Beginnings of peer interaction. At this level true interaction does not occur, but rather a simple initiation-response sequence.	Kimberly sees Rebecca's ball, walks over and holds out her hands, asking for it. Rebecca clutches the ball and says, "Mine".
III—Complex Contingency Interchanges	Interchanges between children become longer and more sophisticated.	Mary looks at Valerie, Valerie waves, Mary offers a toy, Valerie shakes toy and hands it back to Mary. Mary gets another toy and repeats sequence.
IV—Complementary Interchanges	True interaction and role sharing.	Jimmy chases Daniel, then Daniel chases Jimmy.

Source: Mueller and Lucas (1975)

play behaviors of Down syndrome toddlers. Delayed toddlers exhibited low rates of many specific social behaviors. Nondelayed toddlers had twice as many peer contacts and were more likely to point to other persons or objects, wave at other persons, and smile or laugh. Down syndrome children talked significantly less than their nondelayed peers and social interactions were more likely to be with adults.

Physically handicapped children may lack the motor movements such as waving or smiling related to social interaction. Their limited play repertoire will also limit social interaction. Further, their different appearance caused by severe physical impairments and adaptive equipment could serve as a barrier to social interaction. Other children may be fearful or uncertain of the child's appearance or may feel it would lower their status with their peers if they interacted with the handicapped child. Fortunately this does not often occur in very young children, but often the reverse problem exists when children tend to baby the handicapped child.

Children with sensory impairments may also be deficient in social skills. For example, blind children may not look toward others and typically will not smile. Delayed communication skills in hearing-impaired children can also serve to limit interactions. Vandall and George (1981) observed dyads of hearing and deaf preschoolers and found that the number and length of interactions observed were greater in like (deaf-deaf or hearing-hearing) dyads than in mixed dyads. In both situations deaf children were observed to make frequent and persistent social initiations. However, the initiation attempts of deaf preschoolers were more likely to be actively refused by the hearing child. The authors also observed many instances when social initiations were made toward the deaf child but the deaf child could not receive them (gestures or vocalizations behind the child's back). Thus the hearing-impaired children often were not able to respond to others' attempts at social interaction.

Assessment of Social Skills

Unfortunately a comprehensive assessment of social skills has not been created. The development of such an instrument would be difficult because social behavior must be observed in naturalistic settings and not in test situations.

Many professionals use the Parten scale as one component of a comprehensive assessment strategy. This scale can describe the child's general level of social play and since it is so commonly used, information can usually be easily shared with others who work with the child. The teacher should be aware of its limitations, however. The scale does not provide a description of a child's specific behaviors. Also, it gives the solitary play category more value when considering toy play skills. Finally, other categories may be needed to broaden the scale's usefulness and provide a more complete picture of the child's social activities. For example, Wintre and Webster (1974) suggested adding a category called Adult-Directed Behavior, since this is a form of social interaction. Copeland and Golden (1979) use the Parten categories but add Fighting as an inappropriate form of social behavior.

A sample observation form using Parten's (1932) play categories plus a category for Adult-Directed Behavior is displayed in Figure 11.3. The form uses a time-sampling format (see Chapter 2) in which the teacher looks at the target child every 30 seconds and records the level of play the child is engaged in at that moment. The 10-minute observation period is summarized by determining the percentage of time the child spent engaged in each category of play. In this example Jonathan demonstrated a range of social skills with peers although he never engaged in cooperative play. His most frequent form of social play was parallel play.

Although use of the Parten scale can give a general picture of the child's social level, teachers often need more specific information for planning and evaluating appropriate interventions. For example, based on the data presented in Figure 11.3, Jonathan's teacher determined that Jonathan needed to learn to engage in associative play behaviors. However, the information obtained thus far does not tell us very much about the specific nature of Jonathan's behaviors toward peers or their frequency. Copeland and Golden (1979) suggest a scale to supplement Parten's scale by assessing the child's actual social interactions

Child: Jonathan				Environment: House Keeping			
Date: 7/15/82				center			
Time: 10:00 - 10:10				Observer: DB			

Time	Unoccupied	Solitary play	Onlooking	Parallel play	Associative play	Cooperative play	Adult-directed behavior
:30				✓			
1:00	✓						
:30		✓					
2:00		✓					
:30				✓			
3:00				✓			
:30				✓			
4:00			✓				
:30			✓				
5:00				✓			
:30					✓		
6:00				✓			
:30			✓				
7:00				✓			
:30				✓			
8:00				✓			
:30			✓				
9:00			✓				
:30		✓					
10:00				✓			
Total no.	1	3	5	10	1		
Percentage	5	15	25	50	5		

FIGURE 11.3
Sample observation form using Parten's (1932) play categories.

with others. This observational system breaks down social interactions into categories such as: no response to initiations by others; responds to initiations by others; initiates toward others; and continues an interaction with others. Each of these categories is further coded according to whether the interaction is with an adult or with a peer. Such a system extends the Parten analysis by providing spe-

cific information on the child's behavior toward and in response to others.

A sample observation form using Copeland and Golden's (1979) categories is displayed in Figure 11.4. The form follows an event sampling format in which each occurrence or nonoccurrence of a response is recorded. Observation of Erin's social interactions indicates that she will respond verbally or nonverbally

Child: Erin
Date: 7/20/82
Time: 11:15 – 11:30
Environment: Snack Table
Observer: DB

Peer interactions				Adult interactions			
No response to peers' initiations	Responds to peer initiations	Initiates towards peers	Continues interaction with peers	No response to adults' initiations	Responds to adult initiations	Initiates toward adults	Continues interaction with adults
III	V V V N N N N			II	V V V N N	I	

V = Verbal response or initiation
N = Nonverbal response or initiation

Summary

- Total number of initiations by peers: 10
- Percentage responded to verbally: 30
- Percentage responded to nonverbally: 40
- Total number of initiations toward peers: 0
- Number of times continues an interaction with a peer: 0

- Total number of initiations by adults: 7
- Percentage responded to verbally: 43
- Percentage responded to nonverbally: 29
- Total number of initiations toward adults: 1
- Number of times continues an interaction with an adult: 0

FIGURE 11.4
Sample observation form using Copeland and Golden's (1979) categories of social interactions.

when a peer or adult initiates an interaction, but she does not initiate or continue interactions beyond an initial response. Based on this observation an appropriate goal would be to encourage Erin to actively approach other people. Perhaps she needs to be taught a specific technique for getting an interaction started such as showing another child something she has drawn or constructed.

Mueller and Brenner (1977) provide an alternative observational system that focuses on social behavior directed toward others and measures the number of interactions in a given sequence. This system incorporates the following categories:

Socially Directed Behavior (SDB)—Any behavior accompanied by or immediately preceded by looking at another person, subject to two constraints: (1) it is potentially perceivable by the other person, (2) it is a discrete, rather than as giving continuous action.

SDB Type—(1) Simple, composed of a single act such as waving, (2) coordinated, composed of two or more acts performed in unison or in immediate ... succession such as waving and saying "hi."

Social Interaction—A contingency or series of contingencies between the mutually directed SDBs of two children. SDBs are contingent when they are contiguous in time, i.e., within 10 seconds.

Interaction Length—Number of chained SDBs composing an interaction (p. 856).

This system differentiates socially-directed behavior from social interaction. Although every social interaction is made up of SDBs, not every SDB results in interaction. This distinction helps differentiate two children with low levels of social interaction, one who does not exhibit any SDBs and another who exhibits SDBs but fails to secure a response from others.

A sample observation form using Mueller and Brenner's (1977) categories for Socially Directed Behavior is displayed in Figure 11.5. The form follows a running record format (see Chapter 2) where each behavior in a social interaction chain is recorded. The teacher can then determine the length of interactions between children. For example, Alex responded to initiations from others and even initiated toward others. However, he did not usually keep the interaction going. A goal for Alex would be to increase the number of chained SDBs.

Even this system, however, may need to be expanded to meet the needs of some children. For example, SDB type may need to be assessed more specifically by actually recording instances of specific important behaviors such as looking at others, smiling, verbal and physical initiations, handing materials to others, etc. Low-frequency behaviors can then be identified and appropriate steps taken to teach them.

The assessment of peer interaction skills is time consuming but provides a basis for designing instructional strategies for increasing appropriate peer interaction. Instructional strategies include environmental considerations, modeling, and contingency management/direct instruction.

Environmental Considerations

Chapters 5–7 identified a variety of environmental dimensions that can be manipulated to increase social interaction among young children. A series of guidelines for environmental planning of social behavior follow.

Provide social toys. The research of Quiltich and Risley (1973) clearly documented the effects of toy characteristics on social behavior. Children were observed in a free play situation where "isolate" toys (usually played with by one child at a time) were used. These observations were compared with a free play setting where the available toys were "social" toys and usually required interaction between two or more children. Social play occurred only 15% of the time when the children were provided isolate toys and 78% of the time when they were given social toys.

A social toy requires or encourages interaction among children. Crayons, for instance, usually encourage solitary independent activity. A game, on the other hand, usually requires at least two participants. Dramatic play clothes typically encourage social play because children use the clothes to act out daily routines. Often this acting out is with a peer. Examples of isolate and social toys for preschool-aged children are displayed in Table 11.5.

Child: Alex
Date: 7/21/82
Time: 9:45 – 10:00

Environment Free play in all centers

Observer DB

Interactions initiated by target child

Initial SDB	Response	SDB	Response	SDB	Response	Interaction length
Handed toy to Erin	Took Toy					
Looked at Mike and said "ball"	"No, mine!"					
Handed jar to teacher to open	"You want it opened?"	Nods	"Here it is"			

Interactions initiated by peers

Initial SDB	Response	SDB	Response	SDB	Response	Interaction length
Lisa pats Alex on head	Pushes hand away	Pats shoulder	Ignores			
Mark hands ball to Alex	Looks at Mark and takes	Holds out hand to Alex and says "no"	Clutches ball and says "no"			

FIGURE 11.5
Sample observation form using Mueller and Brenner's (1977) categories for coding social behavior and interaction length.

TABLE 11.5
Examples of social and isolate toys for preschoolers

Social Toys	Isolate Toys
Don't Spill the Beans	Building blocks
Pick-up sticks	Construction sets
Lotto games	Crayons
Dramatic play clothes	Pencils
Other dramatic props	Felt-tip pens
Puppets	Sticker books
Boardgames	Books
	Clay

The determination of whether or not a toy is a social toy will vary depending upon the age of the children. For example, a good social toy for a toddler would make a noise or other action and subsequently attracts the attention of others. Also the same toy might be an isolate toy at one age level and a social toy at another age level. For example, toddlers usually play with dolls in a solitary fashion, holding and manipulating the doll, whereas older preschoolers are more likely to use the doll in social/dramatic role play.

Match toys and materials to the developmental level of children. Assessment data on social play levels of children can be used to identify appropriate toys to facilitate the kind of play the child can demonstrate. For example, to encourage parallel play in low-functioning children, provide duplicates of popular toys. If you want to encourage cooperative play, provide a variety of materials centering around a particular theme (housekeeping, construction).

Consider the effects of spatial organization on social play. For example, Kinsman and Berk (1979) investigated social behavior in the block and housekeeping areas in a preschool classroom. More solitary pursuits were observed in the housekeeping area while more social play was observed in the block corner. When the two areas were combined, solitary play and associations with children of the same sex decreased, while social play in mixed-sex groups increased.

A spatial organization facilitating positive social interactions would have the following characteristics:

1 Materials that would ordinarily stimulate solitary use are placed near more social materials or areas to encourage interactions.
2 Sufficient space is provided in high social areas to allow several children to play comfortably.
3 Access to areas is limited to a specific number of children to prevent overcrowding.

Provide at least some low-structure time each day. Most children need some time each day that is not completely adult-directed. Huston-Stein, Friedrich-Cofer, and Susman (1977) observed high-structure and low-structure preschool classrooms and found more prosocial behavior and more imaginative play in low-structure classrooms. Although we do not advocate a total day of low structure in early intervention programs for handicapped children, clearly some free play time is important and may encourage peer interaction.

Modeling

A considerable body of research focuses on the use of models in training social skills. This research addresses a diverse range of topics, including general effects of peer models and integration of handicapped and nonhandicapped preschoolers.

Effects of peer models Chapter 4 briefly discussed the use of filmed models in treating social withdrawal. O'Connor's (1969) study is an example of filmed models interacting appropriately with other children. Watching the film served to increase the number of social interactions with peers. Evers and Schwarz (1973) conducted a follow-up to this study and compared the presentation of the film with the film plus teacher praise for appropriate social interaction, and found no differences between the two. Both approaches increased social interaction with peers. Conger and Keane (1981), in a review of this and other research on social skills intervention in the treatment of isolated or withdrawn children, conclude that exposure to modeling films does have a positive effect on children who initially exhibit low levels of social interaction, although the reasons for effectiveness are unclear. Research in this area has been conducted almost exclusively with children with no other handicapping conditions, however.

Pairing withdrawn and competent children in a dyadic situation was described in Chapter 5. Furman, Rahe, and Hartup (1979), for example, paired isolate children with same-aged or younger children for 10 free-play sessions and found that both pairings increased the social behavior of withdrawn children. The effects were greatest when the withdrawn child was paired with a younger child.

When a child is handicapped simple observation of a model may not be sufficient, however. Guralnick (1976), for example, observed a handicapped child and found that the child engaged primarily in solitary play. Having the child observe two peers playing associatively or cooperatively had no effect on social play. When peer modeling was combined with reinforcement, however, significant increases in associative and cooperative play were noted.

Given the right conditions, peers can be used in a variety of ways. The target child should want to interact with the peer. In addition, the peer must be able to follow directions consistently. Finally, the peer should be carefully trained to fill the desired role prior to implementation. This training should be very specific, should include plenty of practice, and probably should demonstrate to the peer that following the procedures has a reinforcing outcome. Some examples of using peers as models and trainers for children with low social skills are displayed in Table 11.6.

Integration of handicapped/nonhandicapped preschoolers An early study designed to determine the extent to which social interactions occur in mainstreamed settings was conducted by Devoney, Guralnick, and Rubin (1974). The social behavior of a group of seven handicapped preschoolers was found to be low using Parten's play scales. In the first intervention the children were combined with a group of nonhandicapped peers. Social play improved somewhat, although the change was not substantial. In the second intervention the teacher structured the environment to encourage interactions, and significant increases in social play were found.

Peterson and Haralick (1977) demonstrated that interactions between handicapped and nonhandicapped children do occur in mainstreamed settings. More than half of all observed interactions of nonhandicapped youngsters were with handicapped children or with a small group that included at least one handicapped child. When handicapped children were the only available playmates, however, the nonhandicapped children were most likely to play alone. In those situations isolate play occurred approximately 62% of the time.

Guralnick (1980) suggested that most of the integrated interactions in the Peterson and Haralick study might have been with the mildly handicapped children to the exclusion of the more severely handicapped. To test this assumption, Guralnick (1980) observed 37 children, 4–6 years of age, in an integrated preschool. Each child was classified as nonhandicapped (n = 12), mildly handicapped (n = 9), moderately handicapped (n = 5), or severely handicapped (n = 11). Children were observed in a free play setting for positive and negative motor, gestural, and vocal or verbal communication. Numerous interactions were observed between nonhandicapped and mildly handicapped children. Even the mildly handicapped children preferred their nonhandicapped peers over the more severely involved children. Moderately and severely handicapped children interacted about equally with all developmental levels. Guralnick suggests these children may not have been able to differentiate among playmates and their skill levels.

Integration of mildly handicapped and nonhandicapped children can result in frequent social interactions between the two groups with little teacher intervention. The first choice for mildly handicapped children should be a preschool program for nonhandicapped children. However, integration of moderately and severely impaired children is not as likely to result in social interactions without additional structure and teacher training. Such an integrated setting is only possible if parents and teachers realize that it will require substantial efforts for it to work.

Integration of handicapped children whose problems extend beyond a mild developmental delay can be facilitated by teaching them specific social skills. Examples of such skills and strategies are discussed in the next section. Nonhandicapped children can be prepared for integration by being trained in sensitivity and by learning specific skills such as manual signing. Questions about handicapped children and their adaptive equipment should be answered in a positive and honest fashion. Examples of how each of us has different strengths and weaknesses should be given. Also, several books that show handicapped and nonhandicapped children playing together are available (Beuin, 1951; Fassler, 1969, 1975; Green, 1960; Grollman & Perske, 1977; Heide, 1970; Litchfield, 1976; Salazar, 1967; Stein, 1974).

Teachers should follow general guidelines throughout the preschool day for facilitating social and language behavior. Fredericks, Baldwin, Grove, Moore, Riggs, and Lyons (1978) describe a set of guidelines used to integrate moderately and severely handicapped children into a normal day-care setting.

Guidelines for Facilitating Social Behavior
Using the Parten scale as a developmental guide, general procedures were developed for the staff in order to facilitate movement through the categories of social behavior. The facilitation program was designed to change children's social behavior to the next, more advanced, Parten category. Examples of the facilitation procedures follow:

TABLE 11.6
Examples of using peers to improve social skills

Problem	Possible Intervention Using Peers
Justin will not share toys or materials with other children.	Identify a peer model who does share or stimulate the peer to demonstrate sharing. Overtly reinforce the peer for sharing. Be sure Justin observes this sequence of events and perhaps even call it to his attention ("Look, Justin, Reggie shared some blocks with Mike!")
Adrian will not respond when a peer approaches or initiates an interaction.	Teach peers to be persistent when attempting to interact with Adrian (ask a question more than once). Teach peers to give Adrian positive feedback for responding.
Bobby does not wave or smile at other children.	Train peers to initiate waving or smiling behaviors directed specifically at Bobby. Reinforce Bobby for responding in a similar fashion.
During free play Debbie will not respond to requests from peers.	Use peers in small group instruction to present initial tasks to Debbie. For example, if Debbie is working on naming pictures of animals, have peer hold up the picture and ask Debbie to name it.
Katie is extremely shy and has no friends.	Encourage one peer to regularly spend time with Katie. Organize the daily schedule so Katie and the peer have some time alone, perhaps with the teacher present to model, stimulate, and reinforce interchanges between the children.

1   To facilitate movement from unoccupied behavior into solitary independent play, or even onlooker activity, the child is placed near other children and is encouraged to participate with a toy or an object. The child is reinforced for manipulating that toy or object while remaining within that environment or observing other children.

2   To facilitate movement to parallel activity from either the onlooker or solitary play levels, the adult reinforces the child for proximity to other children and for playing with toys similar to the others. The adult encourages the normal children to share toys with the handicapped children, and reinforces the children when they do share. During this type of activity the child should be placed among the normal children, not on the fringes of the group. For instance, if there are five children sitting at a rectangular table, the child should not be placed at the end of the table but in a position where normal peers are on all sides.

3   To facilitate associative play, the adult arranges a setting where all normal peers are engaging in play with the handicapped peer, and reinforces the normal peers for conversation and sharing of objects with the handicapped child. The handicapped child is also reinforced for playing with normal peers. During associative play, if the handicapped child steps out of the setting, the adult should direct the handicapped child to engage in that activity once again and reinforce when the child enters or reenters the group.

Guidelines for Facilitating Language Behavior
The procedures to facilitate the increase in appropriate language interactions were as follows:

1   The adult reinforces all verbal and nonverbal communication emitted by the handicapped child while in the treatment setting.

2   The adult directs child-child interactions. For example, if the handicapped child is standing back as an onlooker, the adult directs the nonhandicapped peers to verbalize to the handicapped child and reinforces the peers for these interactions.

3   The adult reinforces nonhandicapped children when they initiate and/or respond to handicapped children in the treatment setting.

4   To increase the percentage of time that a handicapped child interacts with a nonhandicapped child, the adult should encourage and/or direct the handicapped child into appropriate play situations. For example, if a child is playing with a given toy, the adult could direct a peer to play with the child with that toy or vice versa.

5   If a peer does not respond to the handicapped child, the adult should model a response for the peer. If the peer adopts the response, the adult should then reinforce the peer for responding to the handicapped child.

6   The handicapped child should be encouraged to increase usage of word phrases at all times when interacting with peers. If a child does not use spontaneous intelligible language with word phrase lengths appropriate for the child's current level of language development, then the adult should model this usage and encourage the handicapped child to imitate the adult's language. The child is then reinforced for appropriate language.[1]

These procedures were successful in increasing the social play as measured by Parten's scale of moderately and severely handicapped children. Substantial increases in interactions and verbal initiations to others were observed in each of the handicapped children and also generalized from a trained setting (the motor room) to an untrained setting (the art room).

Applying the procedures suggested by Fredericks et al. (1978) requires an initial assessment of the child and individualizing intervention. Jonathan, for example (see Figure 11.4) needed to learn to engage in associative play behavior. During free play, his teacher identified an area with a number of nonhandicapped peers and directed Jonathan to go there. Any positive social behavior directed toward Jonathan by a peer is reinforced, and Jonathan is reinforced for any positive social behavior. The teacher serves as a role model, offering toys to Jonathan and other children, modeling responses, and encouraging interactions.

---

[1] From "Integrating the Moderately and Severely Handicapped Preschooler into a Normal Day-Care Setting" by H.D.B. Fredericks, V. Baldwin, D. Grove, W. Moore, C. Riggs, and B. Lyons, In M.J. Guralnick (Ed.), *Early Intervention and the Integration of Handicapped and Nonhandicapped Children,* Baltimore: University Park Press, 1978. Copyright 1978 by University Park Press. Reprinted by permission.

Contingency Management/Direct Instruction

Children may need to be taught basic skills for social interaction. Such teaching can take the basic forms of contingency management or direct instruction. *Contingency management* refers to controlling the consequences of behavior in an effort to change that behavior. For example, to increase smiling, you might somehow reinforce the child each time smiling is observed. Reinforcement is contingent upon the child smiling. *Direct instruction* involves the teacher performing activities prior to the demonstration of a desired behavior. For example, if Robin never waves goodbye when her mom leaves her at school, the teacher might say, "Robin, wave bye-bye," demonstrate a wave, and then give Robin a physical prompt or perhaps even wave Robin's hand for her. Usually direct instruction is paired with contingency management so the child is reinforced for some level of compliance with instructions.

When retarded or otherwise developmentally handicapped children do not possess specific social skills, a combination of direct instruction and reinforcement may be necessary. Techniques can be used to teach a variety of skills, including smiling and sharing.

Teaching children to smile Smiling indicates enjoyment, acceptance, and approval. The first time that a young infant appears to smile responsively is exciting for most parents because it is one of the first indications that the child is truly a social being. Unfortunately, as discussed in Chapter 8, many handicapped children (particularly retarded children) smile less frequently than their nonhandicapped counterparts (Cicchetti & Sroufe, 1976; Stone & Chesney, 1978). A low rate of smiling can affect the relationship with parents and peers.

Hopkins (1968) attempted to increase the very low rates of smiling in two retarded boys. The frequency of smiling was initially raised by giving instructions to smile and providing candy reinforcers. Social reinforcement (smiling and verbal praise by the teacher) was paired with the candy. The author demonstrated that increased smiling was maintained by social reinforcement alone after the candy was gradually withdrawn.

Cooke and Apolloni (1976) tested the effectiveness of instructions, modeling, and social praise on the smiling behaviors of learning disabled children ages 6–9 who also demonstrated low rates of appropriate social behavior. Training began with the following instructions:

Making friends is important. One way to make friends is to smile at other people. Watch me smile (trainer models smiling). Now, (turning to a subject) let me see if you can smile (p. 67).

The trainer frequently smiled throughout the lesson and often verbally prompted the children to smile. Social praise was intermittently delivered, contingent upon appropriate smiling. These techniques were successful in substantially increasing the rate of smiling for each child, and smiling behaviors generalized to an untrained free play setting. Further, increased smiling seemed to have a positive side effect because untrained children also began to smile more often when playing with this group.

A sequence of procedures to teach smiling includes several important steps. The teacher should begin by determining the natural rate of smiling exhibited by the target child as well as typical rates shown by peers, siblings, and adults in the home and school environment. Smiling behavior may be targeted for intervention if the following conditions are met:

1 A discrepancy exists between the target child's rate of smiling and rates observed in the other persons in the environment.
2 The child needs to improve social interaction skills.
3 The teachers and parents agree that smiling is an important skill to emphasize.
4 Increased rates of smiling will probably have an indirect influence on acceptance by and interaction with others.

Once smiling has been targeted as an appropriate behavioral objective, specific strategies for increasing it can be implemented. Some suggested strategies include the following:

1 Reinforce the child whenever he or she smiles appropriately.
2 Model appropriate smiling behavior.

3 Tell the child how important it is to smile at other individuals. Have the child practice smiling at the teacher and reinforce.

4 Prompt smiling in natural play situations through direct instruction, such as, "Larry, smile when you look at Teresa."

5 Prompt smiling in natural play situations through indirect comments or noticing another child smiling, such as, "Larry, look at Teresa's big smile."

When applying these strategies the teacher should attempt to maintain the naturalness of the situation. Also, teach children appropriate times for smiling, since they should not smile indiscriminately or continuously.

The strategies just described are appropriate for children who smile infrequently. In younger or more severely impaired children, smiling is a difficult behavior to manipulate. For these children, the teacher will probably need to select other behaviors such as waving or patting that fulfill a similar function.

Teaching children to share Sharing is difficult to teach because the child must give up something. However, it can build an initial bond between children. If early peer interaction does center around objects (Mueller & Lucas, 1975), then sharing becomes even more important.

Several studies documented the effectiveness of direct instruction and contingency management on sharing. The Cooke and Apolloni (1976) study also taught children to share and used the same strategies of instruction, modeling, and reinforcement. Rogers-Warren and Baer (1976) demonstrated that simple modeling and reinforcement (praise) could be effective with nonhandicapped preschoolers. Barton and Ascione (1979) compared the training strategies of teaching children to share *physically* (handing a material to another child or allowing the child to take his or her material), *verbally* (verbal attempts at initiating physical sharing or acceptance of such requests), or *both*. All treatments served to initially increase physical sharing. However, durable sharing which generalized to other settings only occurred when children were taught to share verbally. This study emphasizes the importance of the communicative component of social interaction.

The direct teaching of sharing, as any skill, should follow a carefully planned course of action. Note the initial rates of sharing by the target child and peers to determine whether a problem exists and identify typical rates of sharing in the preschool. If it is an appropriate objective, then specify the form and nature of sharing expected; for instance, whether it is to be verbal or nonverbal, or independent or a response to another's request. Interventions to teach sharing should then be implemented and evaluated according to their effectiveness. Several strategies for teaching sharing are listed.

1 Reinforce the child for any observed instances of sharing.

2 Reinforce peers for sharing. Be sure the target child observes peer reinforcement.

3 Serve as a model for sharing, verbally describing what you are doing and why.

4 Practice individually with the child through role play. Teach the child how to share; also teach appropriate responses when the child is not ready to share ("I am not quite finished, but I will let you use it in a minute").

5 Prompt appropriate responses or initiations during free play. For example, if Nancy is apparently finished with a toy, the teacher could say, "Nancy, since you are done with the tricycle why don't you ask Leonard if he wants to use it?"

SUMMARY

Social skills can be taught following many of the basic processes used in any skill. The child's behavior is assessed to determine current social skills. Specific social acts are clearly defined and identified as targets. These targets are chosen based on what is known about development and on the kinds of skills needed in the child's environment. An instructional strategy is then implemented and evaluated.

But there is another side to teaching social skills. Strain and Shores (1977) suggest the following as being of primary importance in designing a social skills training program: "Each child must be a reinforcing agent as well as being reinforced by other children" (p. 498). This statement reflects *reciprocity*, the basic component of social interaction. In communicating and interacting there must be give and take on both sides. Each person must view the other in a positive manner and want to interact.

Nonhandicapped children need to be taught how to interact with handicapped peers to encourage reciprocity. For example, Strain, Shores, and Timm (1977) selected two bright peers in a preschool program and conducted four 20-minute training sessions using role playing. The children were then encouraged to initiate social play, and were frequently reminded that although their attempts would be ignored, they should try to maintain social contact. The teacher verbally praised them for learning specific skills. This intervention increased peer initiations to withdrawn children, which in turn increased the social initiations by the withdrawn children.

Another method of initiating reciprocity is to raise the status of handicapped children among their peers. This can be done by directing positive teacher attention towards the handicapped child. As a result, nonhandicapped peers will be more likely to initiate to the target child (Strain, Shores, & Kerr, 1976). Other strategies include giving the handicapped child a valued responsibility (setting the table or leading the group) or pointing out the unique abilities of each child.

The ability to interact appropriately with another child is an important adaptive behavior. Social acceptance of handicapped persons is highly related to their ability to relate well to others. Specific social skills should be taught at all age levels but particularly during the preschool years since the child is learning lifelong response patterns. In this chapter the developmental course of toy play and peer interactions, techniques for assessing play and interaction skills, and specific strategies for teaching play and interaction behavior were described and identified.

Interactions will only occur in an environment responsive to social initiations. The current level of reciprocity and strategies for increasing reciprocity should be analyzed.

REFERENCES

Barnes, K. E. Preschool play norms: A replication. *Developmental Psychology, 1971, 5,* 99–103.

Barton, E. J., & Ascione, F. R. Sharing in preschool children: Facilitation, stimulus generalization, response generalization, and maintenance. *Journal of Applied Behavior Analysis, 1979, 12,* 417–430.

Bevin, J. *The smallest boy in the class.* New York: William Morrow, 1951.

Cicchetti, D., & Sroufe, L. A. The relationship between affective and cognitive development in Down's syndrome infants. *Child Development, 1976, 47,* 920–929.

Conger, J. C., & Keane, S. P. Social skills intervention in the treatment of isolated or withdrawn children. *Psychological Bulletin, 1981, 90,* 478–495.

Cooke, T.P., & Apolloni, T. Developing positive social-emotional behaviors: A study of training and generalization effects. *Journal of Applied Behavior Analysis, 1976, 9,* 65–78.

Copeland, A. P., & Golden, D. B. Assessing and facilitating play in handicapped children. *Child: Care, Health and Development, 1979, 5,* 335–346.

Devoney, C., Guralnick, M. J., & Rubin, H. Integrating handicapped and nonhandicapped preschool children: Effects on social play. *Childhood Education, 1974, 50,* 360–364.

Eckerman, C. O., & Whatley, J. L. Toys and social interaction between infant peers. *Child Development, 1977, 48,* 1645–1656.

Ellis, M. *Why people play.* Englewood Cliffs, N. J.: Prentice-Hall, 1975.

Evers, W. L., & Schwarz, J. S. Modifying social withdrawal in preschoolers: Filmed modeling and teacher praise. *Journal of Abnormal Child Psychology, 1973, 1,* 248–250.

Fassler, J. *One little girl.* New York: Behavioral Publications, 1969.

Fassler, J. *Howie helps himself.* Chicago: Albert Whitman, 1975.

Fredericks, H. D. B., Baldwin, V., Grove, D., Moore, W., Riggs, C., & Lyons, B. Integrating the moderately and severely handicapped preschool into a normal day care setting. In M. J. Guralnick (Ed.), *Early intervention and the integration of handicapped and nonhandicapped children.* Baltimore: University Park Press, 1978.

Furman, W., Rahe, D., & Hartup, W. Rehabilitation of socially withdrawn preschool children through mixed-age and same-age socialization. *Child Development, 1979, 50,* 915–922.

Garvey, C. Some properties of social play. *Merrill-Palmer Quarterly, 1974, 20,* 163–180.

Green, M. *Is it hard? Is it easy?* New York: William R. Scott, 1960.

Grollman, S. H., & Perske, R. *More time to grow: Explaining mental retardation to children: A story.* Boston: Beacon Press, 1977.

Guralnick, M. J. The value of integrating handicapped and nonhandicapped preschool children. *American Journal of Orthopsychiatry, 1976, 46,* 236–245.

Guralnick, M. J. Social interactions among preschool children. *Exceptional Children*, 1980, *46*, 248–253.

Hall, G. S. *Youth: Its education, regimen and hygiene.* New York: Appleton, 1906.

Heide, F. *Sound of sunshine, sound of rain.* New York: Parents' Magazine Press, 1970.

Hill, P. M., & McCune-Nicolich, L. Pretend play and patterns of cognition in Down's syndrome children. *Child Development*, 1981, *52*, 611–617.

Hopkins, B. L. Effects of candy and social reinforcement, instructions, and reinforcement schedule on the modification and maintenance of smiling. *Journal of Applied Behavior Analysis*, 1968, *1*, 121–129.

Huston-Stein, A., Friedrich-Cofer, L., & Susman, E. S. The relationship of classroom structure to social behavior, imaginative play, and self-regulation of economically disadvantaged children. *Child Development*, 1977, *48*, 908–916.

Jacobson, J. L. The role of inanimate objects in early peer interaction. *Child Development*, 1981, *52*, 618–626.

Kinsman, C. A., & Berk, L. E. Joining the block and housekeeping areas: Changes in play and social behavior. *Young Children*, 1979, *39*, 66–75.

Li, A. K. F. Play and the mentally retarded child. *Mental Retardation*, 1981, *19*, 121–126.

Litchfield, A. B. *A button in her ear.* Chicago: Albert Whitman, 1976.

Lowe, M. Trends in the development of representational play in infants from one to three years—an observational study. *Journal of Child Psychology and Psychiatry*, 1975, *16*, 33–47.

Moore, N. V., Evertson, C. M., & Brophy, J. E. Solitary play: Some functional reconsiderations. *Developmental Psychology*, 1974, *10*, 830–834.

Mueller, E., & Brenner, J. The origins of social skills and interaction among playgroup toddlers. *Child Development*, 1977, *48*, 854–861.

Mueller, E., & Lucas, T. A developmental analysis of peer interaction among toddlers. In M. Lewis & L. A. Rosenblum (Eds.), *Friendship and peer relations.* New York: Wiley, 1975.

O'Connor, R. D. Modification of social withdrawal through symbolic modeling. *Journal of Applied Behavior Analysis*, 1969, *2*, 15–22.

Odom, S. L. The relationship of play to developmental level in mentally retarded preschool children. *Education and Training of the Mentally Retarded*, 1981, *16*, 136–141.

Parten, M. B. Social participation among preschool children. *Journal of Abnormal and Social Psychology*, 1932, *27*, 243–269.

Peterson, N. L., & Haralick, J. G. Integration of handicapped and nonhandicapped preschoolers: An analysis of play behavior and social interaction. *Education and Training of the Mentally Retarded*, 1977, *12*, 235–245.

Phinney, J. S. Match between play materials and age: Its relevance to spontaneous play and to classification learning. In M. K. Poulsen, J. F. Magary, & G. I. Lubin (Eds.), *Piagetian theory and the helping professions.* Los Angeles: University of Southern California Press, 1976.

Piaget, J. [*Play, dreams and imitation in childhood*] (C. Gattegno & F. M. Hodgson trans.). New York: Norton, 1962. (Originally published, 1945.)

Quilitch, H., & Risley, T. The effects of play materials on social play. *Journal of Applied Behavior Analysis*, 1973, *6*, 573–578.

Ray, J. S. *Free-play behavior of normal and Down's syndrome toddlers.* Paper presented at the Annual Meeting of the Animal Behavior Society, Wilmington, N.C. May 24, 1975.

Reid, D., Willis, B. S., Jarman, P., & Brown, K. Increasing leisure activity of physically disabled retarded persons through modifying resource availability. *AAESPH Review*, 1978, *3*, 78–93.

Rogers-Warren, A., & Baer, D. M. Correspondence between saying and doing: Teaching children to share and praise. *Journal of Applied Behavior Analysis*, 1976, *9*, 335–354.

Rubin, K. H., & Maioni, T. L. Play preference and its relationship to egocentrism, popularity, and classification skills in preschoolers. *Merrill-Palmer Quarterly*, 1975, *21*, 171–179.

Rubin, K. H., Maioni, T. L., & Hornung, M. Free play behaviors in middle- and lower-class preschoolers: Parten and Piaget revisited. *Child Development*, 1976, *47*, 414–419.

Salazar, V. *Squares are not bad.* Racine, Wis.: Golden Press, 1967.

Smilansky, S. *The effects of sociodramatic play on disadvantaged children: Preschool children.* New York: Wiley, 1968.

Snell, M. E., & Gast, D. L. Applying time delay procedure to the instruction of the severely handicapped. *Journal of the Association for the Severely Handicapped*, 1981, *6*(3), 3–14.

Spencer, H. *The principles of psychology* (Vol. 1). London: Longman, 1855.

Stein, S. B. *About handicaps: An open family book for parents and children together.* New York: Walker, 1974.

Stone, N. W., & Chesney, B. H. Attachment behaviors in handicapped infants. *Mental Retardation*, 1978, *16*, 8–12.

Strain, P. S., & Shores, R. E. Social interaction development among behaviorally handicapped preschool children: Research and educational implications. *Psychology in the Schools*, 1977, *14*, 493–502.

Strain, P. S., Shores, R. E., & Kerr, M. M. An experimental analysis of "spillover" effects on the social interaction of behaviorally handicapped preschool children. *Journal of Applied Behavior Analysis*, 1976, *9*, 31–40.

Strain, P. S., Shores, R. E., & Timm, M. A. Effects of peer social initiations on the behavior of withdrawn preschool children. *Journal of Applied Behavior Analysis*, 1977, *10*, 289–298.

Sutton-Smith, B. *A descriptive account of four modes of children's play between one and five years.* New York: Columbia University Teachers College, 1970.

Vandell, D. L., & George, L. B. Social interaction in hearing and deaf preschoolers: Successes and failures in initiations. *Child Development*, 1981, *52*, 627–635.

Vandell, D. L., Wilson, K. S., & Buchanan, N. P. Peer

interaction in the first year of life: An examination of its structure, content, and sensitivity to toys. *Child Development,* 1980, *51,* 481–488.

Wambold, C., & Bailey, R. Improving the leisure-time behaviors of severely/profoundly mentally retarded children through toy play. *AAESPH Review,* 1979, *4,* 237– 250.

Wehman, P. Selection of play materials for the severely handicapped: A continuing dilemma. *Education and Training of the Mentally Retarded,* 1976, *11,* 46–50.

Wehman, P. *Helping the mentally retarded acquire play skills.* Springfield, Ill.: Charles C. Thomas, 1977.

Wehman, P. Effects of different environmental conditions on leisure activities of the severely and profoundly handicapped. *Journal of Special Education,* 1978, *12,* 183–193.

Wehman, P. Teaching recreational skills to severely and profoundly handicapped persons. In R. York & E. Edgar (Eds.), *Teaching the severely handicapped* (Vol. 4). Seattle: AAESPH, 1979.

Weiner, B. J., Ottinger, D. R., & Tilton, J. F. Comparison of the toy-play behavior of autistic, retarded, and normal children: A reanalysis. *Psychological Reports,* 1969, *25,* 223–227.

Weiner, E. A., & Weiner, B. J. Differentiation of retarded and normal children through toy-play analysis. *Multivariate Behavioral Research,* 1974, *9,* 245–252.

Weisler, A., & McCall, R. B. Exploration and play: Resume and redirection. *American Psychologist,* 1976, *31,* 492–508.

Wing, L., Gould, J., Yeates, S. R., & Brierley, L. M. Symbolic play in severely mentally retarded and in autistic children. *Journal of Child Psychology and Psychiatry,* 1977, *18,* 167–178.

Wintre, M. G., & Webster, C. D. A brief report on using a traditional social behavior scale with disturbed children. *Journal of Applied Behavior Analysis,* 1974, *7,* 345–348.

Despite our best efforts to teach appropriate skills, inappropriate behaviors are bound to occur in most programs for young handicapped children. The most frequently observed inappropriate behaviors, especially in severely handicapped children, are noncompliance, physical aggression, self-stimulation (frequently called stereotypic behavior), and self-injurious behaviors (Wehman & McLaughlin, 1979). Other possible inappropriate behaviors include destruction of materials, temper tantrums, and a host of annoying actions ranging from teeth grinding to throwing toys.

Many textbooks and papers have addressed strategies and considerations for reducing the occurrence of such behaviors (cf. Alberto & Troutman, 1982; Kazdin, 1975; Krumboltz & Krumboltz, 1972; Sulzer-Azaroff & Mayer, 1977). This chapter provides a description of the process of behavior management, a four level system for selecting intervention strategies, guidelines for using intervention strategies, and a description of the negative side-effects of punishment.

PROCESS FOR REDUCING INAPPROPRIATE BEHAVIORS

The process for reducing behaviors is similar to the process for teaching new behaviors; essentially it involves assessing the current rate of the behavior, developing an appropriate intervention plan, implementing the plan, and evaluating the results. However, because reducing behavior rates involves changing inappropriate behavior, some checkpoints in the process need to be included so appropriate procedures are used to produce the desired effects. The process for reducing the occurrence of inappropriate behaviors is shown in the flow chart in Figure 12.1. This flow chart is designed to be used with a four level system of intervention options described in the next section.

The behavior reduction process has 18 steps. In many cases the problem situations (Step 1 of the flow chart in Figure 12.1) will identify themselves. For example, if a child is being self-injurious or is engaging in destructive behaviors, then the teacher will easily be able to identify problem situations. However, some children are quite withdrawn or rarely initiate social interactions, and problem situa-

12

Reducing the Occurrence of Inappropriate Behaviors

tions are less obvious. Thus, teachers should use the assessment and intervention procedures described in Chapter 11.

Step 2 involves defining the problem behaviors. As described in Chapter 2, behaviors are observable, measurable events. Problem situations must be described in terms of reliably measurable behaviors to appropriately im-

plement and evaluate intervention strategies.

The teacher should evaluate whether the behavior should be changed (Step 3 of Figure 12.1). At this step, several considerations are important and are discussed in the next paragraphs.

Consider the immediate effects of the behavior. The teacher should determine whether

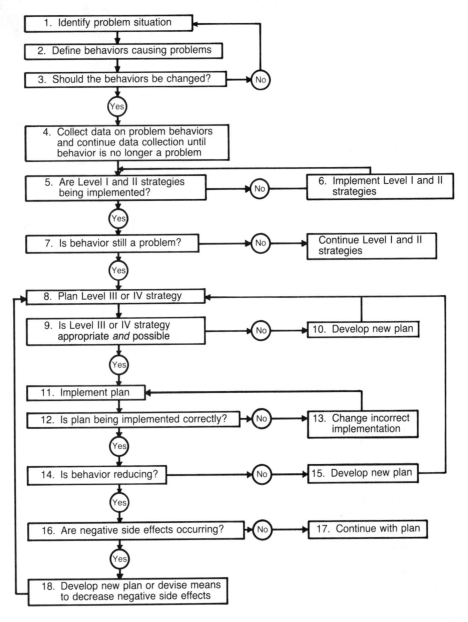

FIGURE 12.1
The process of reducing the occurrence of inappropriate behaviors

the behavior is interfering with the child's ability to learn adaptive behaviors or with other children's learning, causing injury to the child or to other children or staff members, resulting in conditions that have safety risks such as dangerous climbing, or causing others (caregivers and peers) to avoid the child. Intervention may not be necessary if these effects are not exhibited.

The behavior may occur as a result of skill deficits. Some inappropriate behaviors occur as a result of skill deficits in areas other than social skills. For example, Fred is learning to put on his clothing, and can put on his pants, shoes, socks, and shirt, but he cannot tie his shoes. He attempts to tie his shoes but fails, and after three or four unsuccessful attempts he screams, throws his shoes, and runs out of the room. Fred's inappropriate behavior appears to be a result of failure to complete the task successfully. Teachers commonly attribute such inappropriate behaviors to frustration. In such cases, the teacher should teach Fred to tie his shoes or to request assistance, instead of developing a behavior reduction program for his inappropriate behaviors.

Similarly, many children with limited communication skills engage in inappropriate behaviors as a means of communication. For example, when Bruce wants to stop activities or be "left alone," he pinches people near him. His pinching usually results in the activities being stopped or in people moving away from him. In such cases, teachers should concentrate on training him to perform some nonaggressive communication response to allow him to make his requests known without performing an inappropriate behavior (Carr, Newsom, & Binkoff, 1980). Support for this recommendation is found in data showing that, as autistic children learned communicative behaviors, there was a parallel decrease in the frequency of inappropriate behaviors (Casey, 1978).

The frequency, intensity, and durability of the behavior should be considered. Many times young children display inappropriate behaviors that rarely occur, happen for a short period of time and then stop, or are not intense. For example, Anthony sometimes pushes other children, but this behavior only occurs once or twice a month and his pushes do not appear to be malicious. Although

Anthony's teacher should monitor the pushing, he or she should not implement a behavior reduction program at this time. Similarly, Katie sometimes tells adults, "No," but she usually is compliant. She has also been observed telling dolls, "No" and saying, "No" when asked whether she wants more of her favorite juice. Her teacher should not develop a behavior reduction program for noncompliance at that time, but should realize that Katie is learning about the different uses of the word *No.*

Some behaviors occur for a period of time and then cease. For example, preschool children who are learning about differences between boys and girls may ask seemingly inappropriate questions about sexual differences such as, "Do boys have penises?" "Does John have a penis?" and so on. They may repeatedly ask such questions for a few weeks, but because the behavior is transient, the development and implementation of a behavior reduction program would be inappropriate.

Thus, behavior reduction programs should be developed when behaviors occur frequently, last a long time, are performed with concentrated force, and have the probability of continuing. However, some low frequency behaviors may require intervention, particularly if injury may result to the child or others, if the behaviors are particularly intense and harmful, and if they are likely to continue indefinitely.

The age-appropriateness of the behavior should be considered. Some behaviors are appropriate at some ages and inappropriate at others. For example, crying is appropriate for a child functioning at about a one-year level when Mother leaves for a few hours. However, if a 4-year-old child cries when Mother leaves, the behavior may be inappropriate. With handicapped children it is sometimes difficult to determine whether a given behavior is age-appropriate. If the child's chronological age is used, many of the behaviors will be considered inappropriate; but if the developmental level is used, the behaviors may appear age-appropriate. Generally speaking, the child's developmental age should be considered when attempting to determine whether a given behavior is age-appropriate.

Consider the effects of the environmental structure. The environment has a powerful influence on behavior, and many times slight changes in the setting and antecedent events will reduce inappropriate behaviors. Krantz and Risley (1977) found that a rest period before story time resulted in fewer inappropriate behaviors and more attention rather than when the story was preceded by vigorous activity. Thus, a simple manipulation of the classroom schedule resulted in a reduction of the inappropriate behaviors. Weeks and Gaylord-Ross (1981) found that inappropriate behaviors occurred more frequently in more demanding and difficult training conditions. They also documented that an errorless learning procedure could reduce errors during the difficult tasks and as a side effect lowered the rate of inappropriate behaviors. Thus, a simple manipulation of antecedent events (addition of the errorless learning procedure) resulted in the control of inappropriate behaviors. Other setting events that influence the rate of inappropriate behaviors include the amount of space; type of materials available; temperature in the room; the number, type, and proximity of other people; and biological factors such as hunger, health, fatigue, and physical stamina. For example, restricted space tends to increase the occurrence of aggression, and most parents are aware that a child who misses a nap and is hungry is apt to display inappropriate behavior if taken shopping. When inappropriate behaviors occur, teachers should consider whether those behaviors are prompted by the structure of the environment. Wahler and Fox (1981) describe procedures and issues related to evaluating the effects of setting (environmental) events on behavior. Generally, teachers should structure the environment to prevent inappropriate behavior. Although inappropriate behaviors should not dictate the environmental structure, however, teachers should structure the classroom to maximize the likelihood of the child engaging in adaptive rather than maladaptive interactions.

Thus, when determining whether a behavior should be changed, consider its immediate effects; the possibility that it occurs as a result of skill deficits; its frequency, intensity, and durability; age-appropriateness; and the effects of the environmental structure. If after careful consideration of these issues, the teacher determines the behavior should be changed, proceed to the fourth step of the flow chart in Figure 12.1.

In Step 4, the teacher begins to collect data to evaluate the effects of interventions for reducing the behavior. The teacher should also note setting events, and events that consistently occur before or after the behavior and appear to have a functional relationship with it (Gelfand & Hartmann, 1974; Wahler & Fox, 1981).

Once data have been collected, the teacher should ensure the presence of Levels I and II of the system for selecting interventions. (Steps 5 and 6). Level I involves providing a predictable, consistent environment, and activities that are functional, worthwhile, interesting, and at the child's developmental level; Level II involves having rules, reinforcing appropriate behaviors, and providing instructions not to perform the inappropriate behaviors. If Levels I and II are in effect, the teacher should determine whether the behavior remains a problem. If it does, then more intrusive strategies (Levels III and IV) should be devised (Step 8). Level III involves response shaping, contingency contracting, extinction, peers as behavior change agents, differential reinforcement of other behavior, and self-instruction/control procedures. Level IV involves verbal reprimands, timeout, overcorrection, and direct application of aversive stimuli. More intrusive procedures should be used only when warranted, and used only after less intrusive procedures have failed (Step 9). Also determine whether intrusive procedures can be used (Step 9) by getting informed permission from the parents and administrators. Also determine if you can actually do the procedures in your setting. For example, procedures such as overcorrection require one person who is responsible for implementing the procedure. If the child-to-staff ratio is so high that a person cannot be free to implement the overcorrection, then it should not be used. If the planned procedure is inappropriate or impossible, develop a new plan (Step 10).

Steps 11 and 12 involve implementing the plan and determining whether it is being implemented as planned. If it is not correctly implemented, then it should be changed (Step 13). Correctly implementing a plan involves consistently using it every time it is needed.

For example, each time Kenny throws a toy, suppose he is to sit for one minute and watch others play. Are there times when Kenny throws toys but is not required to sit and watch others play? Does he sit for exactly one minute each time?

Once procedures have been correctly implemented, determine whether the rate of the behavior is decreasing (Step 14). This determination is made, of course, by examining data. If the data do not indicate behavior reduction after 3 or 4 days of correct implementation, develop a new plan (Step 15). If the occurrence of the behavior is reducing, attempt to determine whether any negative side effects such as withdrawal, increased aggression, or new inappropriate behaviors are resulting (Step 16). Procedures should then be developed to eliminate the negative side effects or a new procedure implemented (Step 18). However, if no negative side effects exist, and the rate of the behavior is decreasing, then the procedures are successful and should be continued (Step 17).

Careful use of the process in Figure 12.1 will result in systematic attempts to reduce the occurrence of inappropriate behaviors. This process can be used with a variety of behaviors, settings, and intervention procedures.

LEVELS OF INTERVENTION OPTIONS

Ideally all children should develop *internal controls* and exhibit self-control. Very young children, however, do not have the cognitive skills necessary for complete self-control. Teachers need to help children learn self-control techniques by providing an appropriate environment that facilitates the transition from external controls to internal controls.

Four levels of intervention strategies are shown in Table 12.1 and are designed to facilitate children's development of self-control and assist teachers in selecting procedures for decreasing inappropriate behaviors. These levels are arranged from being minimally to quite intrusive. Level I should always be in place and Levels II through IV should be used as needed. Levels III and IV should not be used in the absence of Levels I and II. Use the

steps described in Figure 12.1 in implementing the strategies in Levels I–IV.

Level I

In Level I, children should be involved throughout the day in functional, worthwhile, interesting activities appropriate to their developmental levels; and the environment should be predictable. These strategies assist children in learning self-control and prevent many behavior problems.

The first strategy is based on the notion that busy children have little time for inappropriate behaviors. The teacher should attend to the procedures described throughout this text for assessing children's skills: planning, implementing, and evaluating instruction; scheduling activities; and arranging the environment. Failure to attend to these issues

TABLE 12.1
Level system of strategies for reducing the occurrence of inappropriate behaviors

Level	Strategy
Level IV	Direct application of aversive stimuli Overcorrection Timeout Verbal reprimands
Level III	Self-instruction/control procedures Peers as behavior change agents Contingency contracting Extinction Vicarious reinforcement Differential reinforcement of other behaviors
Level II	Rules Reinforcement for appropriate behaviors Instructions not to perform inappropriate behaviors
Level I	Provide a predictable, consistent environment Provide activities that are functional, worthwhile, and interesting and at the child's developmental level

may result in the following situations that produce inappropriate behaviors:

☐ When tasks are too difficult, easy, or repetitive, children quickly lose interest and frequently begin to engage in inappropriate behaviors (Weeks & Gaylord-Ross, 1981).

☐ When the classroom space is insufficient, aggression and other inappropriate behaviors are likely to increase.

☐ When there are insufficient materials, fighting, negative interaction patterns, and other maladaptive behaviors are likely to occur. For example, if most children are functioning at the parallel play level, duplicates of toys should be available. Young children often want what others have, and the easiest solution is to provide sufficient materials for everyone. Of course children need to learn to take turns and share, but enough equipment should be available so they are not engaging in maladaptive behaviors.

The importance of being aware of children's abilities in preventing behavior problems is also illustrated in the following example. At snack time cookies are distributed and some are big, others are small; some are broken, and others whole. Each child's cognitive abilities in attributes, classification, and number will affect their response to the type and number of cookies they get. Some children want a big cookie; others want lots of cookies, regardless of size. Only the most advanced children in a preschool realize that three broken cookies may really be the same as a whole one.

Another strategy used in Level I is that environments should be predictable. The worst possible situation for developing self-control is an environment with no predictability. For instance, suppose Ronnie bites other children. Sometimes the children laugh; other times the teacher runs over, comforts the hurt child, and scolds Ronnie. Or Ronnie gets punished by being removed from the play area, and every once in a while nothing happens. Ronnie's environment is unpredictable, without clearly defined and enforced rules or limits. He is neither learning the effects of his behav-

ior nor does he know what will happen when he bites another child.

To change Ronnie's biting behavior, follow the steps described in the flow chart in Figure 12.1. The problem situation is Ronnie's biting (Step 1), and it would be defined as closing his mouth with someone's body part in it (Step 2). The issues related to Step 3 should be considered. Biting harms others and may cause children to avoid him. The possibility that he bites because of skill deficits should be explored, as should the events that occur when he bites (does he bite when others are near him, when someone has taken his toy, during specific activities, at given times of the day, after specific events, etc.). Further, consider how often and how hard he bites, and how long he has been doing it. If after considering these issues, you decide that it must be eliminated, collect data on how frequently he bites (Step 4). After a few days of this, make sure that Level I procedures are being used (Steps 5 & 6). Ronnie should be engaged in appropriate, interesting activities throughout the day, in a predictable environment. Therefore, each time he bites, plan to comfort the child who was bitten and continue to collect data to evaluate the effects of Level I procedures (Step 7).

Consistency helps make an environment predictable and is particularly important with young children because they cannot reason out the chances of "being caught." They must experiment and experience the results of their behavior. Therefore, teachers and parents must respond to a given behavior in a similar fashion each time it occurs. This type of consistency is desirable and requires communication between parents and teachers. In the example of Ronnie's biting, talk with his parents about whether he bites at home, what happens when he bites, how they have attempted to control it, and what both the parents and teachers will do when he bites. Every time Ronnie bites, parents and teachers should follow the plan and ignore him and comfort the other child.

Level I is designed primarily to prevent behavior problems. Children tend to behave appropriately if they are engaged in functional, worthwhile, interesting activities at their developmental levels in predictable environments. If such circumstances do not exist, the teacher should implement them before using other procedures for controlling inappropriate behaviors.

Level II

Level II involves using reinforcement correctly, setting rules and limits, and instructing children *not* to perform inappropriate behaviors. As described in Chapter 3, reinforcement is the process of presenting an event (stimulus) to the child immediately after a behavior occurs that has the result of increasing the rate of that behavior. When appropriate behaviors increase, the child will have less time to engage in inappropriate behaviors. In preschool programs for handicapped children, common reinforcers are activities, toys, praise, peer and teacher attention, smiles, nods, winks, small pieces of food, and sips of drinks such as juice. The reinforcers for each child should be determined individually.

Several factors are important when using reinforcement. The reinforcer should be delivered immediately after the behavior occurs to produce rapid effects. It should also be delivered consistently so, as described in the section on Level I, children will learn appropriate behaviors. In addition, reinforcement should be varied, especially when using praise and other verbal reinforcers. For example, many preschool teachers say, "Very good" or, "I like the way So-And-So did X" several hundred times a day. While it is important to use praise, the same words, tone of voice, and inflection can soon become more irritating than reinforcing. Praise should also be specific to increase the likelihood that the child will understand exactly what he or she has done correctly and therefore repeat the behavior. For example, "Good job" is less specific than, "You put your arm through the sleeve!!" Specificity is also important when providing verbal instructions and corrective feedback. For example, "I want you children to be nice to each other" gives the children little direction concerning specific behaviors. General corrective feedback such as, "You have been a bad boy" does not tell the child what he did that was bad. However, comments such as, "No pinching, George; you must leave the play area" label the inappropriate behavior and connect it with the consequences.

Another strategy would be to set rules or limits in the preschool classroom. Those rules should be in the child's language to facilitate understanding; should be few in number (three or four); and should be specific but cover a "multitude of sins." For example, "Do what you are supposed to do," "Stay in the room," and "Don't bother other people" can be used to cue preschool children to perform appropriate behaviors. Rules should also be consistently enforced. When an infraction occurs, children should be able to predict that the consequences will be administered. When children have limited language abilities, stating rules will be ineffective. Nonetheless, most can learn the limits (rules) if the teacher knows and systematically enforces them. For example, although Danny is nonverbal and has minimal receptive language, he can learn not to hit others if he is rewarded when he does not hit and is punished when he does.

The final strategy in Level II is to instruct children *not* to do inappropriate behaviors. Many behaviors are only inappropriate in some situations and not in others. For example, balls can be kicked outside on the playground, but another child's toy cannot be kicked in the classroom. Thus, tell children when and where certain behaviors are appropriate. For example, if Helen climbs up on the table and jumps off, the teacher should stop her, look her in the eye, and matter-of-factly say, "We don't climb on tables in the classroom." Such instructions should not involve long explanations, but should be given as a statement of fact. Teachers should use this strategy once or twice before using more intrusive procedures.

If, in the example of Ronnie's biting, the data indicate that Level I procedures are ineffective, implement Level II procedures. A variety of reinforcers would be identified and delivered immediately and consistently after he performs adaptive behavior. Praise should be varied and specific. If Ronnie had sufficient language, the general rules would be stated at the beginning of the day. A special rule for Ronnie such as "Do not bite children" would also be included. In addition to the reinforcement and rules, he would be instructed not to bite. For example, if he bit someone, the teacher would take him aside, look him in the eye, and say, "Ronnie, do not bite." This instruction would be used once or twice. While Level II procedures were implemented, data would be collected on the number of times he bit other children, and the effectiveness of the Level II procedures would be evaluated (Step 7).

Level III

Level III is a collection of strategies teachers can and do use to reduce inappropriate behaviors. These strategies include Differential Reinforcement of Other behaviors (DRO), response shaping, extinction, vicarious reinforcement, contingency contracting, self-instruction/control procedures, and using peers as behavior change agents (for a discussion of the latter, see Chapter 11 and Nordquist, 1978; Strain & Shores, 1977; Strain, Shores, & Timm, 1977).

Even when preventive strategies fail, numerous positive procedures may reduce inappropriate behaviors. Differential Reinforcement of Other behaviors (DRO) is one such technique. In this strategy the teacher would provide a reinforcer when the child is doing anything other than the target behavior to be reduced. Differential Reinforcement of Incompatible behavior (DRI) is a similar strategy, except that the teacher reinforces the child when he or she is doing something incompatible with the target behavior. Incompatible means it is impossible to do an appropriate and inappropriate behavior at the same time. For example, sitting is incompatible with standing, playing with toys is incompatible with self-stimulatory behavior, and talking is incompatible with being quiet. The teacher ignores the inappropriate behavior when it occurs. For example, Harris, Johnston, Kelley, and Wolf (1964) used a DRI strategy for reducing the inappropriate crawling of a young girl in a preschool classroom. When the child was crawling, all of the teachers ignored her. When she was standing or walking the teachers gave her lots of attention. Attention was reinforcing for this child. This simple intervention reduced her crawling behavior and increased the desired behaviors (standing, walking, and running). The use of frequent intensive reinforcement would be

faded as the inappropriate behavior was eliminated. DRO has been successfully used with a variety of behaviors such as increasing language behaviors (Olenick & Pear, 1980), increasing adaptive object-directed behaviors while reducing maladaptive behavior (Horner, 1980), decreasing stereotypic behaviors (Singh, Dawson, & Manning, 1981), and decreasing aggressive and self-injurious behaviors (Repp & Deitz, 1974).

When using DRO or DRI, the teacher may also be using response shaping. *Response shaping* involves reinforcing successive approximations of a target behavior. The teacher not only increases the rate of "other" and "incompatible" behaviors through reinforcement but also increases the complexity of these behaviors. For example, if a child has been using aggression to request more juice, the teacher might differentially reinforce more adaptive communicative responses (verbalizations or signs), and also reinforce (shape) more complex communicative responses. Initially the teacher might reinforce the child if he approximated the sign "More," later providing reinforcement only if he performed an accurate sign of "More," and finally, only if he signed "More juice." Such a procedure might also involve prompts that are faded. The result of these procedures is reduction of the child's aggressions, and an increase in the rate of appropriate communicative responses.

Extinction is a process that technically means the reinforcement for performing a given behavior is removed. In many cases inappropriate behaviors occur because they are reinforced. For example, even though Brian can talk appropriately, when he does not get his way he begins to whine and the teacher gives him what he wants. After collecting data, the teacher decided that letting Brian get his way is actually reinforcing his inappropriate whining. Thus, the teacher decided to use extinction; when Brian whines, he will not have his way. At times extinction works slowly and may even result in a temporary increase in the inappropriate behavior, but when used correctly it can produce relatively permanent changes in behavior. However, if you cannot control the source of reinforcement, such as the children letting Brian get his way when he whines, extinction will be unsuccessful. Reinforcement for Brian's appropriate behavior, especially talking, should be given when extinction is used. Frequently extinction is equated with ignoring, and when teacher attention is a strong reinforcer, withholding such attention (ignoring) will result in extinction. However, teacher attention *must* be a reinforcer for this to work.

Extinction has been used alone and with other procedures such as reinforcement. Extinction appears to be more effective when used with reinforcement. For example, Allen, Hart, Buell, Harris, and Wolf (1964) used extinction and reinforcement for a preschool girl who interacted only with adults. They ignored her child-adult interactions and reinforced (attended to) her child-child interactions. As a result, her social interactions with peers increased. Similar procedures have been used to decrease disruptive classroom behaviors and increase attention and on task behaviors (Becker, Madsen, Arnold, & Thomas, 1967). Extinction has also been used to decrease persistent crying of young children (Hart, Allen, Buell, Harris, & Wolf, 1964) and aggression (Carr et al., 1980; Pinkston, Reese, LeBlanc, & Baer, 1973).

Vicarious reinforcement is a procedure where children who *are not doing* the inappropriate behavior are reinforced. For example, Margaret frequently bangs puzzle pieces on the table when she is supposed to be putting them together. Although the teacher has ignored her, she continues the banging behavior. When the teacher praises Kathy and Sandy for correctly working puzzles, Margaret begins to stop banging the pieces and put them in the puzzle. After Margaret puts in a few pieces, the teacher should praise her. Vicarious reinforcement cues the child to the behaviors expected in the task, and shows them that reinforcement is available. It has been used to increase attention (Kazdin, 1973), and perhaps social interactions (Strain & Timm, 1974) and maintenance of following instructions (Weisberg & Clements, 1977).

Another positive procedure for reducing inappropriate behaviors is contingency contracting (Homme, Csanyi, Gonzales, & Rechs, 1969). *Contingency contracting* is essentially a contract between the child and teacher. If the child performs a given behavior, then the teacher will deliver a given reinforcer. With older children these contracts can be in writing, but with preschool children the contracts should be verbal. For example, Joyce usually hits children during a 15 minute free play session just before snack time. The teacher has decided to use contingency contracting, and will use the fact that Joyce likes to pass out the napkins at snack time as a reinforcer. Thus, just before free play, he states the contract to Joyce: "If you play with the children, but don't hit anyone, you can pass out the napkins at snack." If Joyce successfully completes her part, the teacher allows her to pass out the napkins at snack. If children are able, they should be allowed to specify the reinforcer.

A positive Level III procedure that has recently been used with preschool children is the self-instruction/control (see the section on controlling hyperactive behavior in Chapter 7). Recent data suggest that the procedures can be used to decrease errors and increase preschoolers' accuracy on preacademic tasks (Bryant & Budd, 1982). For reviews of these procedures see O'Leary and Dubey (1979) and Rosenbaum and Drabman (1979).

Level III involves some specific positive procedures for reducing inappropriate behaviors. These procedures require careful implementation, and should be used after Levels I and II and before more intrusive procedures. The process of reducing inappropriate behaviors shown in Figure 12.1 should be followed with Level III procedures.

Level IV

Level IV strategies are the most intrusive and negative of all intervention described in this chapter. Thus, the definition of, possible negative effects of, and general guidelines for using punishment are described prior to discussing Level IV strategies.

Punishment is the presentation of a stimulus following a behavior that results in a decrease in the rate of that behavior. Punishment does not mean corporal punishment, and does not need to be perceived as negative by persons using it. Procedures that commonly function as punishments are verbal reprimands, timeout, overcorrection, and direct application of aversive stimuli.

Punishment has numerous negative side effects. First, when punishment is used the teacher models undesirable interactions. For example, if the teacher uses a verbal reprimand of, "No!" when a child does a given behavior, he or she is modeling a behavior children are apt to imitate and use in their social interactions with peers and adults. Frequent imitation of such behaviors may result in the development of a problem behavior.

The child may also avoid the person administering the punishment. This situation is undesirable because children should initiate social interactions and not withdraw from their caregivers. In addition, punishment may result in a general decrease in responding. A reduction in both appropriate and inappropriate behaviors may occur.

Punishment teaches the child what he should *not* do rather than what he should do. The task of early intervention is to accelerate the acquisition of appropriate adaptive behaviors and punishment may interfere with this process.

Punishment changes both teacher and child behaviors. When teachers are faced with numerous children who present problems, they may be tempted to use punishment procedures instead of the positive procedures described earlier. However, using punishment procedures will result in inordinate negative interactions between children and teachers. Further, the use of punishment can be very reinforcing to the teacher because it may result in rapid changes in child behavior, making it more likely that the teacher will use it again, perhaps without the necessary cautions. For a review of the issues related to punishment see Wood and Lakin (1978) and Gaylord-Ross (1980).

Regardless of the behavior, guidelines should be followed when using punishment. One rule is to *respond early in a sequence of behaviors.* Assume that Albert has decided that today he will test you. He comes into the classroom, you greet him with a hug and a smile and then tell him to hang up his coat. He takes off his coat, gets half way to the coat rack, drops it on the floor and runs to the block center. You do not want to start the day off on a bad note, particularly since Albert's mom is still there, so you pick up his coat and hang it up for him. When it is time to clean up and come to the circle, Albert continues to play and does not clean up his area. Finally, your aide

goes over and helps him put the blocks away and leads him over to the circle. By now the picture is probably clear. This pattern continues until at 10:30 you decide to set some limits. Unfortunately Albert has already had two hours of noncompliance; you and Albert would have been better off if you had set and enforced the limits early in the day.

Many reasons exist for responding early. Teachers' frustrations, the possibility for reinforcing inappropriate behaviors, and out-of-control emotional reactions of children are eliminated, and time is saved. Sometimes it is safer to stop behaviors early in a sequence. For example, Dickie likes to run out of the classroom. Unfortunately, there is a busy street nearby and Dickie goes right out in the street. Dickie also likes to be chased. Thus, there are many good reasons to stop Dickie's running early in the sequence. Usually when Dickie gets ready to run he follows a consistent pattern: he gets up from where he is, walks over to the sink which is near the classroom door, gets a drink, looks around, and then runs. To reduce his running and to catch the behavior early, visually scan the classroom. Several procedures described in Level III could be used. A contingency contract could be developed for him not running; vicarious reinforcement could be given to other children when he is moving toward the sink; differential reinforcement could be given to Dickie when he does not run. However, once he gets to the sink you must act. You might call to him as he nears the sink and tell him to get a drink and then come and play; you might prompt another child to go to the sink and talk to Dickie; and you might move toward the door and place yourself between the door and Dickie. Obviously, you must act quickly and make several decisions, but failure to stop the behavior early in the sequence may produce disastrous results.

Be consistent. If you decide that Ronnie should leave the play area each time he bites, then follow up on your decision. Sometimes this action will be inconvenient as when your aide is taking some children to the bus and you are conducting a small group session. However, Ronnie must be moved from the play area *each* time he bites. If he is to change his behavior, he must meet with consistent consequences.

Consistent use of an intermittent schedule is an inappropriate strategy for generalizing an effective behavior reduction program. This is the opposite of the suggested procedure for generalizing skill acquisition programs. In a positive skill training program, the frequency and amount of reinforcement for appropriate behavior is gradually reduced. In a behavior reduction program, however, the consequences should always be applied each time the behavior occurs.

Administer punishment in a calm and cool fashion. Thus, when Ronnie bites, walk over to him and say, "Ronnie, no biting; leave the play area." Say this firmly, without anger or other emotion. Likewise, physically prompt him if he does not move. Do not engage in a wrestling match with him, rather, use graduate guidance as described in Chapter 3. When teachers respond with anger, they weaken their position as an authority figure, and it can be quite reinforcing for some children to see adults lose control. Some teachers actually model the behaviors they want to reduce. For example, the teacher who yells, "I want it quiet in here!" is demonstrating the behavior he or she wants to reduce (loud talking). Children should quietly, gently, briefly, but firmly be told what they did and why they should not do it, with immediate implementation of the consequences.

Deliver punishment immediately after the inappropriate behavior. A delay between the behavior and the consequence (punishment) often means young children will not associate the two. By the time the punishment is administered, the child may be engaged in another behavior that would inadvertently be punished.

The number of negative stimuli (punishments) should be much lower than the number of positive stimuli. Every time punishment is used, the teacher should give the child more positive consequences. When Ronnie bites, move him out of the play area, but after he has been out of the play area and comes back and begins to play, reinforce his play behaviors several times.

Finally, *children must be reinforced for the positive (adaptive) behaviors they do.* As noted in the section on Level II, reinforcement for appropriate behaviors should always be available. It is unethical to use punishment pro-

grams in place of frequent positive reinforcement and a concerted effort to teach new adaptive behaviors.

A list of additional questions regarding any behavior reduction program are presented in Table 12.2. A decision to reduce behavior is a value judgment and often means imposing unpleasantness on the child. Although appro-

TABLE 12.2
Behavior reduction program checklist

1. Does the reduction program and its goal appear in the child's IEP, and do parents understand the program and consent to its use?
2. Is the target behavior *written* in explicit behavioral terms?
3. Were baseline data collected?
4. Is there documentation of ongoing data collection?
5. If the program is not a positive approach (DRO, DRI), does documentation show that positive behavior change projects were implemented and failed?
6. Does evidence exist to indicate that data are frequently analyzed to determine program effectiveness?
7. Does the reduction program exist in written form?
8. Does the written description of the conditions for implementation of procedures include:
   a. A description of the physical environment?
   b. A definition of the behavior to be modified?
   c. A step-by-step decription of the intervention strategy?
   d. Identification of the person to carry out the program?
   e. Identification of the person to supervise the intervention to ensure written procedures are followed?
   f. A statement of procedural safeguards?
   g. A listing of ongoing classroom programs that have positive consequences?
   h. A statement that defines the termination point of the program? If unsuccessful at termination, are alternative strategies listed?
9. Does evidence indicate that, if necessary, the program has been approved by the appropriate institutional review procedures?

SOURCE: Adapted and modified from Tawney (1980).

priate behavior reduction programs are usually justified, the team (including the parents) responsible for the child's program must agree that the goal is important and the program is necessary, sufficient documentation of the problem and its course must exist, appropriate safeguards must be followed to control negative side effects, and the behavior reduction process and intervention strategies should be used.

Two Level IV procedures are timeout and overcorrection. Other Level IV procedures not discussed in this chapter are verbal reprimands (cf. Van Houten, Nau, MacKenzie-Keating, Sameoto, & Colavecchia, 1982) and direct application of aversive stimuli such as contingent restraint (Favell, McGimsey, & Jones, 1978; Hamilton, Stephens, & Allen, 1967), contingent exercise (cf. Luce, Delquadri, & Hall, 1980), contingent ammonia (Doke, Wolery, & Sumberg, in press), contingent electric shock (Lichstein & Schreibman, 1976), and contingent lemon juice (Sajwaj, Libet, & Agras, 1974). Direct application of aversive stimuli should rarely be used. If it is considered, then careful planning, implementation, and consultation with experts and professional literature should occur.

Timeout Timeout is one of the most frequently used yet misunderstood procedures for reducing inappropriate behaviors in early intervention programs. In many cases of inappropriate behavior, the consequences controlling that behavior can be identified and removed (i.e., use extinction as described earlier). In some instances, however, you may be unable to identify the reinforcer for a given behavior or you may be able to identify the reinforcer but cannot control it. For example, Amy may hit Lara because it is exciting to hear Lara scream, or Nathan may enjoy yelling curse words because the other children laugh. It is difficult for the teacher to control those reinforcers, and when these situations occur a timeout may be necessary.

In timeout, the opportunity for almost all reinforcement is removed for a certain period of time; thus the name, *timeout* from positive reinforcement. Timeout may be exclusionary (child is removed from the environment for a given period of time) or nonexclusionary (child remains in the environment but is denied access to reinforcement for a given pe-

riod of time). An example of exclusionary timeout would be removing the child from the classroom upon the occurrence of some inappropriate behavior, and an example of nonexclusionary timeout is asking the child to sit quietly in a chair in the classroom for a given period of time.

Perhaps the most important consideration in deciding when to use timeout is being sure the child is removed from a reinforcing environment. Timeout should not be used if it gives the child an opportunity to get out of activities he or she does not find reinforcing in the first place. For example, if Jamie does not like the story period, a timeout procedure for disruptive behavior at story time would probably reinforce rather than reduce disruptive acts. Do not use timeout if the child can perform the same behaviors in the timeout area and get the same reinforcement as in the classroom. Examples of such behaviors may be self-stimulatory and self-injurious behaviors. The child must be able to clearly discriminate between the reinforcing properties of the timeout environment and the regular environment. The classroom must be full of reinforcers whereas the timeout environment must be void of reinforcers. Timeout will likely be inappropriate for severely retarded children who cannot clearly distinguish between time out of and time in reinforcement conditions (Solnick, Rincover, & Peterson, 1977). The following guidelines should be used to design and apply a timeout procedure (cf. Gast & Nelson, 1977a, b):

1 Eliminate potential reinforcing characteristics of the timeout environment. For example, it should not have toys with which the child can play. Further, it should severely limit social interactions; other children should not be able to talk with the child in timeout.

2 Make sure the child has been informed of the undesirable behavior and its consequences. The child should be told in a calm, firm manner that if the inappropriate behavior occurs, timeout will result.

3 When the behavior occurs, gently but firmly tell the child, "No (<u>hitting, etc.</u>), go to timeout." It is preferable not to use physical contact to move the child to timeout, but if it is required, use graduated guidance.

4 Timeout should be as long as necessary to be effective; with very young children 30 seconds to one minute is sufficient. Determining the length is a value judgment; however, if long periods are initially used, shorter periods are apt to be ineffective (White, Nielsen, & Johnson, 1972). But if short time periods are used and do not function as punishers, and the time is gradually lengthened, the child may learn to tolerate rather long timeout periods. Generally, timeout periods should be short because, while the child is in timeout, the opportunity to learn new adaptive behavior is lost.

5 Do not remove the child from timeout if he or she is misbehaving, as the inappropriate behavior might be reinforced. Let the child know what he or she needs to do (e.g., be quiet for 10 seconds) before timeout is over. Various criteria have been used to determine when the child can leave timeout. Usually, the child should stay the specified time plus a short period (10–15 seconds) of relative inactivity and quiet.

6 As soon as the child returns from timeout, find something appropriate he has done and reinforce him for it. Children should have more positive interactions than negative interactions, especially when timeout is being used (Solnick et al., 1977).

If after using Level I, II, and III procedures to reduce Ronnie's biting, and the data at Step 14 of the behavior reduction process indicate that he still bites, timeout can be used. Decide whether Ronnie needs exclusionary or nonexclusionary timeout. If nonexclusionary is used, begin by preparing a timeout area free of reinforcement. This area might be a chair in the corner near a metal cabinet to block his view of other children and activities, but still permit you to observe him. At the beginning of the day tell him if he bites he will go to timeout. If he does in fact bite, move immediately over to him and say, "Ronnie, no biting, go to timeout." Point to the timeout area and if necessary use graduated guidance to get him there. The duration of (1 minute) and the criteria for leaving timeout (e.g., 10 seconds of no vocalizations and continuous sitting in the chair at the end

of the 1-minute period or the first 10 seconds of quiet and sitting after the 1-minute period) were previously planned. When he gets to timeout unobtrusively observe him to be sure that he stays in the area and that others are not interacting with him. When his time has been served, and the exit criteria have been met, go over to him and say, "Ronnie, you can come play now." Once he is playing, provide reinforcement several times during the next few minutes.

Timeout has been used with a variety of behaviors. In preschool children, it resulted in decreases in aggressive and disruptive behaviors (Clark, Rowbury, Baer, & Baer, 1973), inappropriate language responses (Wulbert, Nyman, Snow, & Owen, 1973), tantrums (Solnick et al., 1977), and oppositional behavior (Wahler & Fox, 1980). However, if the classroom environment is not rich in reinforcement, it may be ineffective (Solnick et al., 1973).

An effective variation of the timeout procedure is *contingent observation.* Porterfield, Herbert-Jackson, & Risley (1976) used contingent observation to reduce disruptive behavior of 1- and 2-year-old children in a day-care setting. Caregivers responded to disruptive behaviors by describing the inappropriate behavior and telling the child the appropriate alternative (e.g., "No, don't take toys from other children, ask me for the toys you want"); moving the child to the periphery and telling him or her to watch the appropriate behaviors of others (e.g., "Sit here and watch how the other children ask for the toys they want"); allowing the child to return after a brief period of quiet watching (usually less than 1 minute); and giving positive attention when the child demonstrates the appropriate behaviors.

Another frequently used technique is *redirection,* in which the child is told the inappropriate behavior and then a different activity is suggested. Porterfield et al. found that contingent observation proved to be more effective than redirection in reducing disruptive behaviors.

Foxx and Shapiro (1978) describe a *timeout ribbon* that does not require removing the child from the environment. Each child is given a ribbon to wear on the wrist, around the neck, or on the shirt (Velcro wrist bands are the most effective). The ribbon is established as a signal for reinforcement; only when the child wears the ribbon can he or she be rewarded for good behavior. When the inappropriate behavior occurs and the timeout procedure is implemented, the child's ribbon is removed for a period and the child remains in the activity but is ineligible for reinforcement. When timeout is over, the ribbon is returned and the child can once again receive reinforcement. This procedure reduces inappropriate behaviors, can be used with several children, and does not involve physically moving the child. Although it relies on external reinforcement from the teacher, the child is allowed to participate in the ongoing activities.

Overcorrection   Another Level IV procedure is overcorrection. In Chapter 7 overcorrection was described as a technique for teaching eye contact to severely retarded children who rarely respond to any identifiable reinforcers (Foxx, 1977). Restitutional overcorrection and positive practice overcorrection were also differentiated (Axelrod, Brantner, & Maddock, 1978; Ollendick & Matson, 1978). *Restitutional overcorrection* requires the child to correct the consequences of behavior and return the situation to a condition better than before the inappropriate behavior occurred. For example, a child who spills juice might be required to wash several tables. *Positive practice* requires the child to repeatedly practice a positive behavior incompatible with the inappropriate behavior. The child who spills juice might be required to repeatedly grasp, lift, place, and release a cup of water without spilling.

Overcorrection has emerged as an increasingly popular behavior reduction technique when other strategies fail. It has been used to reduce the occurrence of self-stimulatory behavior (Epstein, Doke, Sajwaj, Sorrell, & Rimmer, 1974; Foxx & Azrin, 1973), aggressive and disruptive behaviors (Foxx & Azrin, 1972; Matson & Stephens, 1977), self-injurious behaviors (Azrin, Gottlieb, Hughart, Wesolowski, & Rahn, 1975; Conley & Wolery, 1980; Harris & Romanczyk, 1976), and many other deviant behaviors such as public disrobing (Foxx, 1976), food stealing (Azrin & Wesolowski, 1974), and repeated vomiting (Azrin & Wesolowski, 1975). Harris and Wolchik (1979), for example, compared three treatment procedures (timeout, DRO, and over-

correction) in an attempt to reduce the self-stimulatory behavior of four autistic children. During DRO each boy was reinforced frequently for periods of time when no self-stimulatory behaviors occurred. During the timeout treatment the teacher would respond to each incident of self-stimulatory behavior by sternly saying, "No hand play" and turning his or her head away from the child for 10 seconds. During overcorrection treatment the teacher would respond to each incident of self-stimulation by sternly saying, "No hand play" and then briskly guiding the child's hands through an "exaggerated hand clap" with the arms stretched over the child's head for 10 seconds. The overcorrection procedure resulted in the most consistent and obvious changes in behavior, with an immediate and substantial decrease in self-stimulatory behavior in all four children. Some reduction in responding was observed in three boys during the timeout procedure, although the effect was not as great as for the overcorrection treatment.

One child was also observed to significantly increase appropriate play behaviors during overcorrection. Recent research by Carey and Bucher (1981) further substantiates the potential of overcorrection as an educative technique that can have positive effects beyond the suppression of inappropriate behavior.

Overcorrection is a complex, potentially aversive procedure that warrants careful consideration and implementation. Popovitch (1981) suggests that parental and administrative approval should be sought beforehand. If the teacher is following the process for reducing behaviors, such approval will be obtained.

The following guidelines should be followed in designing any overcorrection program:

1   Design the overcorrection procedure so behaviors required are directly related to the child's inappropriate behavior. For example, if the inappropriate behavior is throwing toys, the behavior required may be picking up toys; if the inappropriate behavior is hitting other children, the behaviors required could be nicely patting other children, saying, "I'm sorry," and giving toys to the hit child; if the inappropriate behavior is arm flapping (a self-

stimulatory behavior), the behaviors required should be appropriately moving objects with the arms.

2 Tell the child what constituted the inappropriate behavior. The teacher should stop the child, and firmly say, "No _____" (inappropriate behavior).

3 Apply the overcorrection procedures immediately after the inappropriate behavior, telling the child what he or she did wrong. Manipulate the child through the required behaviors using graduated guidance if necessary, but do not hurt the child.

4 Do not allow any reinforcement to occur during the time the overcorrection is actually being implemented. The child's behaviors should be done without reinforcement.

5 Return the child to the ongoing activity. When the child has performed an appropriate behavior, he or she should be reinforced.

Some authors suggest that the duration of overcorrection must be lengthy in order to insure it is aversive. The procedures described by Harris and Wolchik (1979), however, lasted only 10 seconds and were quite effective. The length of time necessary should probably be determined on an individual basis, but shorter times are desired. The actual effort the child must expend may be a critical factor in determining how aversive the procedure is.

SUMMARY

This chapter includes a description of the process by which teachers can reduce the occurrence of inappropriate behaviors. This process includes identifying the problem situation, defining the problem behaviors, considering whether it is appropriate to change the behavior, collecting data on the rate of the behavior, and systematically selecting and implementing intervention strategies from a four-level hierarchy of intervention options. Level I should always be in classrooms for young children with handicaps; it includes providing a predictable environment and implementing activities that are functional, interesting, and at appropriate developmental levels. Level II involves providing reinforcement for appropriate behaviors, establishing rules, and instructing children not to engage in inappropriate behaviors. Level III includes a number of useful and positive strategies such as DRO, extinction, contingency contracting, response shaping, vicarious reinforcement, using peers as change agents, and using self-instruction/ control procedures. Level IV involves procedures such as timeout, overcorrection, verbal reprimands, and direct application of aversive stimuli. Positive procedures should be used, but if punishment is necessary, follow specific guidelines and watch for possible negative side effects.

REFERENCES

Alberto, P., & Troutman, A. *Applied behavior analysis for teachers: Influencing student performance.* Columbus, Ohio: Charles E. Merrill, 1982.

Allen, K.E., Hart, B., Buell, J.S., Harris, F.R., & Wolf, M.M. Effects of social reinforcement on isolate behavior of a nursery school child. *Child Development,* 1964, *35,* 511–518.

Axelrod, S., Brantner, J.P., & Maddock, T. Overcorrection: A review and critical analysis. *Journal of Special Education,* 1978, *12,* 367–392.

Azrin, N.H., Gottlieb, L., Hughart, L., Wesolowski, M.D., & Rahn, T. Eliminating self-injurious behavior by educative procedures. *Behavior Research and Therapy,* 1975, *13,* 101–111.

Azrin, N.H., & Wesolowski, M.D. Theft reversal: An overcorrection procedure for eliminating stealing by retarded persons. *Journal of Applied Behavior Analysis,* 1974, *7,* 577–581.

Azrin, N.H., & Wesolowski, M.D. Eliminating habitual vomiting in a retarded adult by positive practice and self-correction. *Journal of Behavior Therapy and Experimental Psychiatry,* 1975, *6,* 145–148.

Becker, W.C., Madsen, C.H., Arnold, C.R., & Thomas, D.R. The contingent use of teacher attention and praising in reducing classroom behavior problems. *Journal of Special Education,* 1967, *1,* 287–307.

Bryant, L.E., & Budd, K.S. Self-instruction training to increase independent work performance in preschoolers. *Journal of Applied Behavior Analysis,* 1982, *15,* 259–271.

Carey, R.G., & Bucher, B. Identifying the educative and suppressive effects of positive practice and restitutional overcorrection. *Journal of Applied Behavior Analysis,* 1981, *14,* 71–80.

Carr, E., Newsom, C.D., & Binkoff, J. Escape as a factor in the aggressive behavior of two retarded children. *Journal of Applied Behavior Analysis,* 1980, *13,* 101–117.

Casey, L.D. Development of communication behaviors

in autistic children: A parent program using manual signs. *Journal of Autism and Childhood Schizophrenia*, 1978, 8, 45–59.

Clark, H.B., Rowbury, T., Baer, A.M., & Baer, D.M. Timeout as a punishing stimulus in continuous and intermittent schedules. *Journal of Applied Behavior Analysis*, 1973, 6, 443–455.

Conley, O.S., & Wolery, M. Treatment by overcorrection of self-injurious eye gouging in preschool blind children. *Journal of Behavior Therapy and Experimental Psychiatry*, 1980, 11, 121–125.

Doke, L.A., Wolery, M., & Sumberg, C. Effects and side-effects of response-contingent ammonia spirits in treating chronic aggression. *Behavior Modification*, in press.

Epstein, L.H., Doke, L.A., Sajwaj, T.E., Sorrell, S., & Rimmer, B. Generality and side effects of overcorrection. *Journal of Applied Behavior Analysis*, 1974, 7, 385–390.

Favell, J.E., McGimsey, J.F., & Jones, M.L. The use of physical restraint in the treatment of self-injury and as positive reinforcement. *Journal of Applied Behavior Analysis*, 1978, 11, 225–241.

Foxx, R.M. The use of overcorrection to eliminate the public disrobing (stripping) of retarded women. *Behavior Research and Therapy*, 1976, 14, 53–61.

Foxx, R.M. Attention training: The use of overcorrection avoidance to increase the eye contact of autistic and retarded children. *Journal of Applied Behavior Analysis*, 1977, 10, 489–499.

Foxx, R.M., & Azrin, N.H. Restitution: A method of eliminating aggressive-disruptive behaviors of retarded and brain-damaged patients. *Behavior Research and Therapy*, 1972, 10, 15–27.

Foxx, R.M., & Azrin, N.H. The elimination of autistic self-stimulatory behavior by overcorrection. *Journal of Applied Behavior Analysis*, 1973, 6, 1–14.

Foxx, R.M., & Shapiro, S.T. The timeout ribbon: A nonexclusionary timeout procedure. *Journal of Applied Behavior Analysis*, 1978, 11, 125–136.

Gast, D., & Nelson, C.M. Legal and ethical considerations for the use of timeout in special education settings. *Journal of Special Education*, 1977, 11, 457–467. (a)

Gast, D., & Nelson, C.M. Time out in the classroom: Implications for special education. *Exceptional Children*, 1977, 43(7), 461–464. (b)

Gaylord-Ross, R. A decision model for the treatment of aberrant behavior in applied settings. In W. Sailor, B. Wilcox, & L. Brown (Eds.), *Methods of instruction for severely handicapped students*. Baltimore: Paul H. Brookes, 1980.

Gelfand, D.M., & Hartmann, D.P. *Child behavior: Analysis and treatment*. New York: Pergamon Press, 1974.

Hamilton, J., Stephens, L., & Allen, P. Controlling aggressive and destructive behavior in severely retarded institutionalized residents. *American Journal of Mental Deficiency*, 1967, 71, 852–856.

Harris, F.R., Johnston, M.K., Kelley, C.S., & Wolf, M.M. Effects of positive social reinforcement on regressed crawling of a nursery school child. *Journal of Educational Psychology*, 1964, 55, 35–41.

Harris, S.L., & Romanczyk, R.G. Treating self-injurious behavior of a retarded child by overcorrection. *Behavior Therapy*, 1976, 7, 235–239.

Harris, S.L., & Wolchik, S.A. Suppression of self-stimulation: Three alternative strategies. *Journal of Applied Behavior Analysis*, 1979, 12, 185–198.

Hart, B., Allen, K.E., Buell, J.S., Harris, F.R., & Wolf, M.M. Effects of social reinforcement on operant crying. *Journal of Experimental Child Psychology*, 1964, 1, 145–153.

Homme, L. Csanyi, A.P., Gonzales, M., & Rechs, J. *How to use contingency contracting in the classroom*. Champaign, Ill.: Research Press, 1969.

Kazdin, A.E. The effect of vicarious reinforcement on attentive behavior in the classroom. *Journal of Applied Behavior Analysis*, 1973, 6, 71–78.

Kazdin, A.E. *Behavior modification in applied settings*. Homewood, Ill.: The Dorsey Press, 1975.

Krantz, P., & Risley, T.R. Behavior ecology in the classroom. In K.D. O'Leary and S. O'Leary (Eds.), *Classroom management: The successful use of behavior modification*. New York: Pergamon Press, 1977.

Krumboltz, J., & Krumboltz, H. *Changing children's behavior*. Englewood Cliffs, N.J.: Prentice-Hall, 1972.

Lichstein, K.L., & Schreibman, L. Employing electric shock with autistic children: A review of the side effects. *Journal of Autism and Childhood Schizophrenia*, 1976, 6(2), 163–173.

Luce, S.C., Delquadri, J., & Hall, R.V. Contingent exercise: A mild but powerful procedure for suppressing inappropriate verbal and aggressive behavior. *Journal of Applied Behavior Analysis*, 1980, 13, 583–594.

Matson, J.L., & Stephens, R.M. Overcorrection of aggressive behavior in chronic psychiatric patient. *Behavior Modification*, 1977, 1, 559–564.

Nordquist, V.M. A behavioral approach to the analysis of peer interactions. In M.F. Guralnick (Ed.), *Early intervention and the integration of handicapped and nonhandicapped children*. Baltimore: University Park Press, 1978.

O'Leary, S., & Dubey, D.R. Applications of self-control procedures by children: A review. *Journal of Applied Behavior Analysis*, 1979, 12, 449–465.

Olenick, D.L., & Pear, J.J. Differential reinforcement of correct responses to probes and prompts in picture-naming training with retarded children. *Journal of Applied Behavior Analysis*, 1980, 13, 77–89.

Ollendick, T.H., & Matson, J.L. Overcorrection: An overview. *Behavior Therapy*, 1978, 9, 830–842.

Pinkston, E.M., Reese, N.M., LeBlanc, J.M., & Baer, D.M. Independent control of a preschool child's aggression and peer interaction by contingent teacher attention. *Journal of Applied Behavior Analysis*, 1973, 6, 115–124.

Popovitch, J.O. *Effective educational and behavioral programming for severely and profoundly handicapped students*. Baltimore: Paul H. Brookes, 1981.

Porterfield, J.K., Herbert-Jackson, E., & Risley, T.R. Contingent observation: An effective and acceptable procedure for reducing disruptive behavior of young children in a group setting. *Journal of Applied Behavior Analysis*, 1976, 9, 55–64.

Repp, A.C., & Deitz, S.M. Reducing aggressive and self-injurious behavior of institutionalized retarded children through reinforcement of other behaviors. *Journal of Applied Behavior Analysis*, 1974, *7*, 313–325.

Rosenbaum, M.S., & Drabman, R.S. Self-control training in the classroom: A review and critique. *Journal of Applied Behavior Analysis*, 1979, *12*, 467–485.

Sajwaj, T., Libet, J., & Agras, S. Lemon-juice therapy: The control of life-threatening rumination in a six-month-old infant. *Journal of Applied Behavior Analysis*, 1974, *7*, 557–563.

Singh, N.N., Dawson, M.J., & Manning, P. Effects of spaced responding DRL on the stereotyped behavior of profoundly retarded persons. *Journal of Applied Behavior Analysis*, 1981, *14*, 521–526.

Solnick, J.V., Rincover, A., & Peterson, C.R. Some determinants of the reinforcing and punishing effects of timeout. *Journal of Applied Behavior Analysis*, 1977, *10*, 415–424.

Strain, P.S., & Shores, R.E. Social reciprocity: A review of research and educational implications. *Exceptional Children*, 1977, *43*, 526–530.

Strain, P.S., Shores, R.E., & Timm, M.A. Effects of social initiations on the behavior of withdrawn preschool children. *Journal of Applied Behavior Analysis*, 1977, *10*, 289–298.

Strain, P.S., & Timm, M.A. An experimental analysis of social interactions between a behaviorally disordered preschool child and her classroom peers. *Journal of Applied Behavior Analysis*, 1974, *7*, 583–590.

Sulzer-Azaroff, B., & Mayer, G.P. *Applying behavior analysis procedures with children and youth.* New York: Holt, Rinehart, and Winston, 1977.

Tawney, J.W. *Comprehensive analysis of special education.* Final Report. Washington, D.C.: Office of Education, 1979.

Wahler, R.G., & Fox, J.J. Solitary toy play and time out: A family treatment package for children with aggressive and oppositional behavior. *Journal of Applied Behavior Analysis*, 1980, *13*, 23–39.

Wahler, R.G., & Fox, J.J. Setting events in applied behavior analysis: Toward a conceptual and methodological expansion. *Journal of Applied Behavior Analysis*, 1981, *14*, 327–338.

Weeks, M., & Gaylord-Ross, R. Task difficulty and aberrant behavior in severely handicapped students. *Journal of Applied Behavior Analysis*, 1981, *14*, 449–463.

Wehman, P., & McLaughlin, P.J. Teachers' perceptions of behavior problems with severely and profoundly handicapped students. *Mental Retardation*, 1979, *17*, 20–21.

Weisberg, P., & Clements, P. Effects of direct, intermittent, and vicarious reinforcement procedures on the development and maintenance of instruction-following behaviors in a group of young children. *Journal of Applied Behavior Analysis*, 1977, *10*, 314. (Abstract)

White, G.D., Nielsen, G., & Johnson, S.M. Timeout duration and the suppression of deviant behavior in children. *Journal of Applied Behavior Analysis*, 1972, *5*, 111–120.

Wood, F.H., & Lakin, K.C. (Eds.). *Punishment and aversive stimulation in special education: Legal, theoretical and practical issues in their use with emotionally disturbed children and youth.* Minneapolis: Advanced Training Institute, 1978.

Wulbert, M., Nyman, B.A., Snow, D., & Owen, Y. The efficacy of stimulus fading and contingency management in the treatment of elective mutism: A case study. *Journal of Applied Behavior Analysis*, 1973, *6*, 435–441.

Van Houten, R., Nau, P.A., MacKenzie-Keating, S., Sameoto, D., & Colavecchia, B. An analysis of some variables influencing the effectiveness of reprimands. *Journal of Applied Behavior Analysis*, 1982, *15*, 65–83.

ommunicating with others is an important and enjoyable activity. Consider two boys, Tyrone and Bobby, who are playing in the sand. Suddenly, Tyrone says, "Hey, see my mountain!" Bobby looks at the "mountain," notices a stick on the top, points to the stick and says, "What's that?" Tyrone answers, "That's my TV antenna." Bobby nods and says, "Let's make the mountain bigger." Tyrone responds by grabbing a big handful of sand and dropping it on the top of the mountain. With unified purpose, both boys begin putting handfuls of sand on the top of Tyrone's mountain. These boys are obviously engaged in an enjoyable activity and communicating with each other.

Consider another example. Jeanie is a child who, because of her severe motor disabilities, must be fed by her teacher. Her teacher gets the feeding area ready, positions Jeanie for feeding, she smiles at him, and he says, "You're ready to eat, aren't you, Jeanie?" Jeanie repeats her smile. The teacher presents the first spoonful of oatmeal (one of her favorite foods) and Jeanie takes it, but when he presents another she closes her mouth, her muscles tense, and she attempts to turn her head. He presents the spoon again and she repeats these behaviors. The teacher is puzzled. He puts the spoon back in the bowl and notices the rising steam. He touches the oatmeal and realizes that it is far too hot. Jeanie's use of her communicative abilities was critical in keeping her from being burned further by the oatmeal.

SKILLS INVOLVED IN COMMUNICATION

Communication is the process by which two or more individuals exchange information, needs, feelings, or desires. Communication is a social act, and is comprised of two subcomponents, mode and language. *Mode* refers to the motor acts required to express representational symbols, and speech is the usual mode through which communication occurs. In the first example, Tyrone and Bobby were speaking or using the speech mode. *Speech* is defined as the unique sounds produced by the passage of air through the throat and mouth. While speech is not the only mode of communication, as we saw in Jeanie's case, it is an efficient means or tool for communicating.

13

Acquisition and Use of Communication Skills

Other modes are described in Chapter 14. Communication between individuals requires both a mutually understood system of motor acts and language. *Language* is a conventional symbol system used for communication (Bloom & Lahey, 1978). *Symbols* are signals (words, gestures, signs, other motor responses) that stand for or represent ideas, feelings, needs, and events understood by those who use them. The symbols do not have meaning in and of themselves. For example, if Tyrone spoke only Spanish and Bobby spoke only English, they would not be able to successfully communicate by using speech sounds because they do not share a mutually understood symbol system. The word *system* refers to the rules for organizing the symbols so that they can be used for communication. Rules exist for combining pieces of meaning into words, and for putting words together into meaningful sentences. Pieces of meaning in words are known as *morphemes,* the smallest unit of meaning in a language that can be a single word or part of a word. For example, when Tyrone said, "See *my* mountain," the word *my* is a single morpheme that indicates Tyrone possesses something. When Bobby said, "Let's make the mountain bigger," he combined two units of meaning (morphemes) in the word *bigger. Big* refers to something large, and *er* refers to a comparison of two things; in this case, the relative size of the mountain before and after they added handfuls of sand. When morphemes are combined they change the meaning of words. The rules that govern combining morphemes are a part of the mutually understood language system. The development of meaning in language is known as *semantics.* Most theorists believe semantics is separate from but closely related to cognition, and that semantic abilities are a result of a child's interactions with objects and people in the environment.

The rules of the language system also determine how words are combined in sentences. If Tyrone had said, "Mountain see my," Bobby would probably not have understood what he meant. Bobby may have known the meaning of each word, but this combination of words would not follow the rules of the system, thus leading to confusion. The order of words in sentences and the related grammar is called *syntax.* As with the acquisition of meaning, the forces causing children to learn and use the rules for placing words in their most communicative sequence are not totally clear. However, children do attempt to find the most efficient means of communicating given meanings and become more efficient communicators as their language conforms with the rules governing syntax.

Pragmatics is the study of communication in its social context, and deals with the purposes, intentions, or functions of communication. For example, when Tyrone said, "Hey, see my mountain," his intention was to call Bobby's attention to the thing he made. When Bobby said, "What's that?" and pointed to the stick, he was requesting information about the stick in the sand. Tyrone gave a response, "That's my TV antenna," to provide the answer to Bobby's request for information. In the example of the teacher getting the feeding area ready, Jeanie's smile may have been to indicate approval or to signal she wanted to eat. However, after her first bite, Jeanie's closed mouth, tense muscles, and attempts to turn her head indicated that she did not want that food.

We must know what children's intentions or purposes for communicating are. Although it is impossible to *really* know what another person's communicative intentions are, we can infer their intentions from their communicative behaviors, the results of those behaviors, and their reactions to the results. Teachers should consider the parts of communication separately as well as in relation with each other when conducting assessments and planning interventions.

Considerable research describes and explains the sequences through which children develop various communication abilities (Bloom & Lahey, 1978; Dale, 1976; Schiefelbusch & Bricker, 1981). From this research we know that communication development is closely related to social and cognitive development; communication abilities are frequently first expressed in nonverbal behaviors and then in verbal (symbolic) behaviors; and the complexity and variety of communicative abilities increases as children grow older.

The social interactions occurring during infancy appear to form a basis for the social aspects of communication (pragmatics). Skills such as initiating, responding to others' initiations, and maintaining interactions are important for developing conversational skills. Likewise, sensorimotor skills children acquire during infancy form a basis for symbolic behaviors. The sensorimotor skills are the essence of what children "know" about their animate and inanimate worlds, and likely influence the meaning aspects of communication (semantics). Object permanence, means-ends, schemes for relating to objects (play), and imitation are sensorimotor skills impor-

TABLE 13.1

Taxonomy of early pragmatic functions

Category	Description
Requesting	Solicitation of a service from a listener. Three types of requests are delineated: *Requests for Objects:* Requests are gestures and/or utterances which direct the listener to provide some object for the child; the object is usually out of reach because of some physical or spatial barrier. *Requests for Action:* Requests are gestures and/or utterances which direct the listener to act upon some object in order to make the object move. The child's interest appears to be in the action of an object rather than the object *per se.* *Requests for Information:* Requests are gestures and/or utterances which direct the listener to provide information about an object, action or location.
Protesting	Gestures and/or utterances which express disapproval of an adult action or utterance.
Commenting	Direction of the listener's attention to some observable referent. Two types of comments are delineated: *Comments on Objects:* Comments are gestures and/or utterances which appear to call the listener's attention to some object identified by the child. *Comments on Action:* Comments are gestures and/or utterances which appear to call the listener's attention to the movement of some object rather than the object *per se.*
Greeting	Gestures and/or utterances, subsequent to the entrance of a person into a situation, which express recognition.
Transferring	Primarily a gesture, the intent of which is to place an object in another person's possession.
Showing Off	Gestures and/or utterances that appear to be used to attract attention.
Acknowledging	Gestures and/or utterances which provide notice that the listener's previous utterances or gestures were received.
Answering	A gesture and/or utterance from the child in response to a request for information from a listener.

Note: Supplement to presentation, "A System for Coding Pragmatic Behaviors in Preverbal Children," by T. Coggins & R. Carpenter, American Speech and Hearing Association Annual Convention, San Francisco, 1978. From "Communication Development, Assessment, and Intervention," by N. Nichols. In B.L. Darby & M. May, *Infant Assessment: Issues and Applications.* Seattle: WESTAR, 1979. Copyright 1979 by WESTAR. Reprinted by permission.

TABLE 13.2
Nonverbal behaviors and one-word statements which express semantic functions

Examples of Nonverbal Behaviors	General Relation-ship and Function	Single Word Statement	Function/Meaning of Single Word Statements
Child directs attention to object which moves or makes a sudden sound; seeks out desired objects when they are out of sight.	Existence	"there" "uh-oh"	To point out objects—particularly those which startle child
Enjoys repeating actions; indicates desire for more of an object or activity when stopped; enjoys collecting multiple examples of a type of object.	Recurrence	"more"	First to request and later to comment on the recurrence of an activity or object
	Disappearance	"away"	To comment on the disappearance of object which had existed in context
Shows surprise or disappointment if object is not found where expected; indicates that cup is empty.	Nonexistence	"a' gone" "no"[2]	(same as above) To comment on nonexistence where existence had been expected
	Cessation	"stop"	To comment on the cessation of an activity
Gesturally or physically rejects a toy, food, or activity not desired.	Rejection	"no"[1]	To protest undesired action or comment on forbidden object (e.g., stove)
When an object is handed to the child, he looks to the place where it was previously; goes to seek a desired object in the place where it is usually kept; returns object to place from which it was taken.	Location	"up"[2]	To comment on spatial location
Selects his own cup, coat, shoes, etc. when several are available. Hands an object which belongs to another to that person.	Possession		
	Action	"up"[1]	To request the action of being picked up
Attempts to perform an action performed.			

TABLE 13.2 (continued)
Nonverbal behaviors and one-word statements which express semantic functions

Examples of Nonverbal Behaviors	General Relationship and Function	Single Word Statement	Function/Meaning of Single Word Statements
Attempts to perform an action performed by another; participates in alternating, role-exchanged reciprocal play (e.g., ball rolling).	Agency		
Given an object, demonstrates an action typically carried out upon that object (e.g., kicks a ball, pushes a truck, opens a book).	Objective		

Note: From *A Transactional Approach to Early Language Training* by J. McLean and L.K. Snyder-McLean, Columbus, Ohio: Charles E. Merrill, 1978. Copyright 1978 by Charles E. Merrill. Reprinted by permission. Data from *One Word at a Time: The Use of Single Word Utterances Before Syntax* by L. Bloom, Hawthorne, N.Y.: Mouton, 1973.

[1]First use of word generally observed
[2]Second use of word generally observed

tant for communication development (Bloom & Lahey, 1978; Bricker & Carlson, 1980).

Pragmatic functions such as calling someone's attention to an object or event, protesting, and making requests illustrate the general observations based on research in communication development. Initially only a few functions are used and are expressed nonverbally. As children grow older, they use more pragmatic functions and express them verbally. A classification of various verbal and nonverbal pragmatic functions of young children is shown in Table 13.1 (page 257).[1]

Semantic functions also illustrate the general observations based on communication research. Children initially respond with consistent nonverbal behaviors that illustrate various semantic functions as shown in the left-hand portion of Table 13.2. As children begin to speak they express these same functions verbally as shown in the right-hand portion of Table 13.2. These and other semantic relationships are later expressed with two-word statements and still later the relationships are combined and expressed with two or more

words as shown in Table 13.3 on pages 260–261. (Bloom, 1973; Bloom & Lahey, 1978; McLean & Snyder-McLean, 1978).

Morphology and syntax become increasingly complex and varied. Coggins and Carpenter (1979) provide detailed descriptions of sequences of these aspects of language development.

ASSESSING CHILDREN'S COMMUNICATION SKILLS

Each aspect of children's communication abilities may require assessment. In this section, we provide information for using direct observation to assess communication and procedures for assessing children's semantic and pragmatic abilities. Assessment issues related to mode are described in Chapter 14; social skill and sensorimotor assessment were described in Chapters 9 and 11, respectively.[2]

Teachers and communication specialists should conduct assessment jointly, since they

[1]For more information related to pragmatics see Bates (1976); Schiefelbusch & Bricker (1981); Chapman (1981); Rees (1978); Dore (1975); and Dunst (1978).

[2]For information related to identification, diagnosis, and comparison of children's communication abilities see Bloom & Lahey (1978); Darley (1979); and Wiig & Semel (1980).

TABLE 13.3
Description and examples of semantic expressions in two- and three-word utterances

Type of Statement	Description	Example and Context
Introducer + Entity	Used to call attention to someone or something. The *introducer word* calls attention to the person, thing, or activity, and the *entity word* names the person, thing, or activity	"This shoe," as the child shows shoe to an adult "It doggie" as the child points to a dog in the yard
More + Entity	Used to request more of something or some activity, or to comment on something or some event that just recurred	"More milk," when child's glass is empty and she wants more milk "Another truck," as child rides in a car and sees another truck pass
Negation + Entity	Used to describe the nonexistence of, reject, or deny something	"No cookie," when child has eaten the cookie (nonexistence) "No cookie," when the child does not want an offered cookie (rejection) "No cookie," when child has cookie but does not want someone else to know it (denial)
Agent + Action	Used to describe someone doing some action or initiating some process	"Doggie eat," as child watches a dog eat "Kitty run," as child watches a kitten run
Action + Object	Used to describe something or someone who is moved or on which (whom) an action or process is initiated	"Drop cookie," as child comments on a dropped cookie "Drink water," as child watches a dog drink from a bowl
Agent + Object	Used to describe something or someone involved with another thing or person	"Doggie ball," as a child watches a dog play with a ball "Mommy car," as a child watches Mother wash the car
Action + Locative	Used to describe the site of an action or process	"Sit chair," as child climbs up on a chair to sit "Eat table," as child sees parents eating at the table
Entity + Locative	Used to describe the position of someone or something in a given location	"Coat bed," as child goes to get his coat off the bed "Ball box," as child's ball bounces into the box

TABLE 13.3 (continued)

Description and examples of semantic expressions in two- and three-word utterances

Type of Statement	Description	Example and Context
Possessor + Possession	Used to describe something owned by someone	"My coat," as child takes his coat from the coat rack "Daddy shoe," as the child picks up her father's shoe
Entity + Attribute	Used to describe a quality or quantity of someone or something	"Big shoe," as child picks up father's shoe "Pretty purse," as child looks at mother's purse

Note: These relationships are combined in three-word statements; for example, "Mommy sit chair" is a combination of Agent + Action + Locative.
Source: Semantic relations taken from Coggins and Carpenter (1979).

both have unique information about children's communication abilities. The assessment should focus on children's ability to communicate since that is the ultimate goal of communication skills training. This assessment should occur in a low structure situation where the child communicates naturally. The context of each statement should be considered when interpreting the meaning and communicative intent of children's statements. As Dale (1978) explains, "The utterance 'baby blanket' contains two nouns, but the nature of the relationship between the two is not yet specified. The utterance can be possessive ('baby's blanket'), an agent-object construction ('baby is pulling the blanket'), or a locative ('baby is under the blanket')" (p. 221). It may also serve the functions of commenting ("Look at the baby with the blanket"), requesting ("Can I have my baby blanket?"), or protesting ("No, that's my baby blanket"). Clearly, the same utterance can have many different meanings to both the speaker and listener. The assessment of context in which communication occurs allows the teacher to infer the meaning and communicative intent of the speaker. In addition, the expectations of persons that the child is to communicate with in his or her environment should be addressed. If direct testing with norm-referenced tools occurs, adaptations may be made in the stimulus presentation, stimulus materials, topography of

the required responses, and feedback given to children for their responses.

When using direct observation to assess communication skills, teachers may use language sampling and behavior codes. Language samples are a means of collecting information about the frequency and manner of the child's communication and are especially useful as a technique for assessing child-initiated production of language. Language samples are a less thorough measure of children's comprehension skills, however. Although the extent of the child's response to other's communication should be recorded, this information is limited since the observer does not attempt to present a structured set of stimuli to measure comprehension. Miller (1981) describes considerations when collecting language samples (see Table 13.4).

Miller (1981) also provides the following suggestions for encouraging children to talk while collecting a language sample:

1 Say nothing beyond friendly greetings for the first 5 minutes. This approach is particularly effective with children who are recalcitrant or self-conscious about their speech.
2 Parallel play with little talking during the first few minutes. Any talking done is directed at toys rather than the child. This approach is effective with young children functioning at 30 months or below on cognitive tasks.

3 Interactive play with little talking during the first few minutes. Toys can be shared by simply announcing "I'm going to play with my gas station. You can play with it too." There is no need to ask if the child wants to play, since he or she will likely say no. This approach is effective with children of cognitive level 3 to 5 years.

4 Interactive play without an introduction. The clinician and child can work together drawing pictures or molding playdough. Participation and discussion can be invited after the activity is completed (p. 10).

After the language sample is completed, the teacher must transcribe it into a useable

TABLE 13.4
Considerations for collecting language samples

General Considerations	Implications for Assessor
Interact with child so typical communication behaviors are observed.	Follow the child's lead in play and conversation. Refrain from questioning the child. Ask only open-ended questions ("Tell me more"). Listen closely to what the child says.
Use low structure situations.	Make situation similar to natural environment. Provide comfortable and relaxed atmosphere.
Use materials that stimulate conversation.	Use life-like toys such as dolls, cars, and puppets. Use toys that allow for themes of play and talking.
Record children's statements accurately.	Use video and audio recording equipment if possible. Make notes about the context of each statement. Record antecedents and consequent events. Record nonverbal communicative behaviors.
Observe long enough to get a representative sample of the child's communicative abilities.	Use more than one observation session. Use longer (e.g., 30 minutes) and more (3–4) sessions if the number of statements is small. Depending upon the child, plan sessions to last 15–30 minutes.
Transcribe the language sample into a usable form for decision making.	Transcribe utterances in relation to antecedent and consequent events. Complete transcription immediately after language sample is collected. Transcribe inappropriately used words, mispronounced words, etc., as they occur.

Source: Miller (1981)

form. McLean and Snyder-McLean (1978) recommend using a three-column format (see Figure 13.1).

Teachers can also use behavior codes designed to measure specific categories of behavior. With language samples, any statement the child makes is recorded verbatim; with behavior codes, frequently only the occurrence or nonoccurrence of behaviors that fit given categories are recorded. The categories are mutually exclusive (any behavior observed will fit in only one of the categories) and frequently they are also inclusive (any behavior observed will fit in a category). Behavior codes can be useful in determining the overall picture of the child's communicative efforts in a preschool or home environment.

When using behavior codes, teachers usually employ a time-sampling or interval sampling technique. In the time-sampling technique the teacher records the occurrence or nonoccurrence of given behaviors at a given time. When using the interval sampling technique, the teacher observes for a given interval—for example, for 30 seconds—and then records the responses that occurred. Interval sampling is usually preferred over time-sampling

because of the low rate of language behaviors. See Chapter 3 for sample data collection forms.

When using behavior codes, use the conditions described in Table 13.4 for collecting language samples. For example, the situation should be a low structure situation, materials should prompt communication, and the observation length should be determined by how well data represent the child's usual behavior. Behavior codes can also be used during a school day. Although they are useful for certain aspects of language, they do not provide the amount or type of information that language samples do.

Assessing Semantics

Assessment methods will vary depending upon the child's communicative abilities. For example, if a child is nonverbal, observe the child in a low structure situation in a natural environment to determine if he or she performs nonverbal behaviors that indicate understanding of the semantic functions listed in the left-hand portion of Table 13.2. If the child does not demonstrate these functions,

Child's Name: Paul Adult with child: Teacher Page 1 of 1 pages Date: 3/4/82 Setting: Block Center Analyzed by: M. Wolery			
Teacher's utterance number	Antecedent context (* = consequence of preceding utterance)	Child's utterance	Consequent event(s) (occurring within 5 sec. after child's utterance)
1	Teacher (T) says, "I'm going to build."	"Me too"	T says; "oh, good!"
2	T says: "What's that?"	"A house"	T: "It's a tall one."
3	*	"I like tall houses"	T: "You do?"
4	*	"Yeh"	T: "I like them too."
5	Child notices T's instruction	"You make a house?"	T: "No, it's a car."
6	*	"Oh"	T: "Vroom! Vroom!"

FIGURE 13.1
Suggested format for three-column transcription of language-sample data
Source: McLean & Snyder McLean (1978). Child data added by present authors.

then establish instructional objectives targeting manipulation, exploration, and functional use of real objects. In addition, target the sensorimotor skills described in Chapter 9. If the observation indicates that the child demonstrates some, but not all, of the nonverbal semantic functions, then initiate training on the unmastered functions. Those mastered functions should be targeted for being marked with words. *Marked* means that the teacher should label these functions for the child with words when the child exhibits the nonverbal behaviors demonstrating the functions.

For children using primarily single-word statements, collect a language sample and transcribe it using the form found in Figure 13.2. This form can be used for noting given words and contexts during observation, and also for analyzing the results of a language sample, such as the number of different meanings the child expresses. The number of times a child uses the word when it "makes sense" is another important consideration. For example, Ellen has consistently held up her arms to adults to be picked up for several weeks. It is important to know how frequently she also expresses her request by saying "up." Further, we would want to know whether she uses "up" to express the meaning of "up" in other situations such as when going up steps or wanting to get up on a chair to look out of the window. If a word is used only in one

context ("up" only means "Pick me up"), then the semantic function may not be present or may have a very restricted meaning and an appropriate instructional objective would be to expand the meaning.

As children begin to use two-word phrases to express semantic relations, a language sample can determine the relationships expressed and used most often. A form for analyzing such a language sample is in Figure 13.3. The semantic relations were listed in Table 13.3; Figure 13.3 includes data from three different 20-minute observations for two children, Rodney and Lisa. Rodney used most of the various relationships in each session, whereas Lisa used a much more restricted set of relationships. Lisa's language sample showed that she expressed many relationships with single-word statements. Thus, our objectives for the two children would be quite different. For example, with Rodney we may target expressing relationships such as Agent-Action-Object ("Daddy go car") and Action-Object-Locative ("Read book chair"). With Lisa we may target expressing semantic relations with two-word statements in those areas where she is only using one word.

Other semantic taxonomies are described by Bloom (1973), Dale (1976), and McLean and Snyder-McLean (1978). Teachers need to be aware of semantics in communication assessment and instructional planning. Such

---

Child's name: ___Ellen___ Date collected: ___5/6___ Analyzed by: ___D. Bailey___ Page __1__ of __2__ pages
Total number of utterances: __14__ (I); Produced in imitation (R): Produced in response to adult prompt or question

Categories:	Existence	Recurrence	Disappearance	Nonexistence	Cessation	Rejection	Action	Location
Descriptions:	Child points out or labels objects or people.	Child requests or comments on the recurrence of an activity or object.	Child comments on disappearance of object or person.	Child comments on nonexistence where existence had been expected	Child comments on cessation of activity.	Child protests undesired action or comments on something forbidden.	Child requests action.	Child comments on spatial location.
Examples:	"Ball" "There" "Dada"	"More"	"Away" "Gone bye-bye"	"No"	"Stop"	"Hot" "No" "Stove"	"Up" "Eat"	"Up"

FIGURE 13.2
Suggested format for semantic analysis of language-sample data: Primarily single-word utterances. *Source:* Adapted from McLean & Snyder-McLean (1978). Definitions of categories and examples of behaviors were added based on Bloom (1973).

Semantic relationship	Child's name _Rodney_ Date collected _10/29/82_	Child's name _Lisa_ Date collected _10/29/82_
Introducer + Entity	⫫⫭ ⎮	⎮⎮
More + Entity	⎮⎮	⎮
Negation + Entity		
Nonexistence	⎮⎮⎮	⎮
Rejection	⎮	
Denial	⎮⎮	
Agent + Action	⫫⫭ ⎮⎮⎮	⫫⫭ ⎮
Action + Object	⎮⎮⎮	
Agent + Object	⎮	
Action + Locative	⎮⎮⎮⎮	
Entity + Locative	⎮⎮⎮⎮	⎮
Possessor + Possession	⎮⎮	
Entity + Attribute	⫫⫭	

Observer _Sugai_   Observer _Gast_

FIGURE 13.3
Sample form and summary data for semantic relations

information provides a framework for interpreting skills and selecting developmentally appropriate instructional targets.

Assessing Pragmatics

Pragmatic functions can be assessed in several ways. Parents can describe how the child communicates in response to specific questions by the teacher. For example, the teacher can ask, "How does Doug let you know he wants something?" "How does he let you know he wants you to stop something?" "How does he get your attention?" or "How does he greet you when you return?" The answers usually provide a general description of the child's communicative functions.

Teachers can also design situations that encourage the child to communicate. For example, what does the child do when adults and other children enter the room and speak to him or her, when given toys or materials needing more materials (giving a puzzle with some pieces missing, or paintbrush but no paint), when asked questions by others, and when shown a novel toy or some interesting event? The child's responses would be recorded and instructional objectives determined.

In addition, the child's use of language can be assessed through observation in the natural environment and/or from the language sample. The classification of pragmatic functions described by Coggins and Carpenter (1978; Table 13.1) can be used to analyze how young children use the pragmatic functions. Summary data for three different children are shown in Figure 13.4. The summary data for Doug indicate that he used only nonverbal behaviors to communicate. Sara, on the other hand, used verbal and nonverbal behaviors, with a very restricted range of functions. Jerry also used verbal and nonverbal behaviors and a wide range of pragmatic functions. Instructional objectives for Doug may be to increase his use of verbal behaviors to

Pragmatic functions	Child Doug Date 9/2/82		Child Sara Date 9/3/82		Child Jerry Date 9/1/82	
	V	NV	V	NV	V	NV
Requesting						
Requesting objects		III	III	I	II	III
Requesting actions		I		I	III	I
Requesting information					I	
Protesting		III	II	I	I	
Commenting						
Comments on objects					I	
Comments on actions		II				II
Greeting		I			II	
Transferring		I				I
Showing Off						
Acknowledging					II	
Answering		II			III	I

Observer Nelson Settings Free play in classroom; snack; outdoor play; lunch period; sand table

FIGURE 13.4
Sample form and summary data for pragmatic functions

perform the functions, but Sara may need her range of pragmatic functions increased. Based on this assessment information, we may choose not to intervene with Jerry's use of functions and may concentrate on some other communication targets.

Assessing children's pragmatic functions requires close attention and observation of behavior. As noted in Chapter 12, some behaviors considered inappropriate and maladaptive may be used to communicate specific functions. In such cases, the teacher's task is therefore not to teach a pragmatic function, but a more acceptable behavior to express that function.

Assessing Syntax

Typically, language pathologists assist teachers in assessing syntax. Because of the complexity of syntactic analysis and the importance of semantic and pragmatic functions, proce-

dures for assessing syntax are not described here. Refer to Miller (1981); Lee (1974); Tyack and Gottsleben (1974); and Crystal, Fletcher, and Garman (1976) for more information.

FACILITATING ACQUISITION AND USE OF COMMUNICATION SKILLS

Once an assessment of communication skills has been conducted and communication objectives specified, implement an appropriate instructional program. Principles of communication training are mentioned before discussing procedures for teaching communication skills and facilitating their use at home and in school.

One general principle is that teachers should find an appropriate balance between developmental and functional communication targets. Although basic developmental sequences should be used as a foundation for communication training, teachers should focus on sequences that directly relate to semantic and pragmatic development, since they deal with meaning and intent of communicative efforts. Teachers should also always assess the basic communication requirements within a given environment, be it home, school, or community, and attempt to fit those demands into the developmental sequences.

Another general principle is that most training efforts should be conducted in natural environments. The child should spontaneously interact and communicate with people in the environment. Parents, siblings, and peers should be involved in many aspects of communication training. Although isolated sessions may be required for the initial acquisition of some communication skills, such training should be heavily supplemented with training in naturally occurring environments.

The final general principle is that generalization of training must be carefully planned. Considerable research, to be reviewed later in this chapter, suggests that most handicapped children do not apply their newly acquired communication skills in new environments or with new persons unless generalization is planned and trained. Teachers of young handicapped children need to be aware of this problem and know how to arrange environments and instruction to insure generalized use of acquired skills.

Training procedures can be applied to two distinct groups of children—those with severe and those with moderate/mild communication delays. Because of their different needs, each group should receive different types of communication training. Researchers using the developmental and functional approaches have developed training programs for each group of children.

Children with Severe Communication Deficits

The training programs and procedures described in this section are designed for children who show a restricted range of pragmatic functions; use inappropriate, maladaptive behaviors to express pragmatic functions (biting to protest); do not use a conventional symbol system (words, signs, or other augmented systems) for communicating; have limited range of nonverbal or verbal semantic functions; and demonstrate severe deficits in cognitive, social, and adaptive areas of development. These categories are not all-inclusive; children may exhibit a variety of different behaviors and have severe communication deficits. Many are potential candidates for alternative modes of communication (see Chapter 14).

Important communication skills Although specific behaviors taught will vary with children and environments, certain behaviors should have a high priority. Sensorimotor skills such as imitation, play, means-ends, and object permanence and social skills such as attending and interacting with others may be prerequisites to communication. Children who perform these sensorimotor and social skills usually perform more advanced language behaviors. Thus, if children do not perform these cognitive and social skills, and have severe communication deficits, then initiate training in sensorimotor and social skills (see Chapters 9, 10, and 11) along with training in the communication skills. If the child is to be trained to verbally perform communication skills, then vocal imitation may be necessary, since it is difficult to physically prompt vocal behaviors.

Labeling is one of the most important communication skills and is the ability to associate a given symbol (word, sign, etc.) with a given object or event. Children should be able to express the label when the object is shown to them, and to indicate which of several objects another person has labeled. Training objects should be common (food, liquids, toys, clothing, other people), preferred and frequently interacted with, and individually geared to the child. The child should also learn to label important events or activities (play time, bathroom, snack, riding in a car). Children should also learn the *functional use* of objects. For example, a cup is used for drinking, a block for stacking and building, a comb for combing hair, and different toys for various kinds of play. Functional use of objects should facilitate attachment of a label and allows children experiences to associate various action labels (drinking, stacking, etc.).

Children with severe communication deficits also need to learn to *request objects, actions* (activities), and *assistance.* Requests, of course, can be nonverbal such as pointing at or leading an adult by the hand to a desired object. They can also be done with conventional signals such as saying or signing, "more." Requests that can be used to acquire a variety of objects or actions should be trained. For example, the word *more* can be used to request more food, more toys, more rides on the merry-go-round, and so on. *Help* is a word used to request assistance for a variety of problems ranging from being unable to open a milk carton to snapping one's pants to putting a puzzle together. Requests should be trained that result in functional outcomes for the child. For example, children are more apt to request activities they enjoy, assistance if it is immediately given, and objects they prefer.

Children also need to *follow instructions* presented by others. The complexity of instructions can vary considerably and may be presented in a variety of modes including gestures, signs, and verbal. Instructions such as, "come," "stop," and "sit" are important for making caregivers' lives easier as well as for children's safety. Other instructions such as, "Do this" with imitative children can be used to get children to perform a variety of behaviors in a number of settings. Likewise, instructions such as, "Get _____" or "Give me _____" can be used in a variety of training tasks and in daily interactions. Teachers can use these instructions to allow children to indicate what they know. Children should know the meanings of words used in instructions. For example, if the teacher asks Jack to get his coat, Jack should already know that the word *coat* applies to his personal coat. Initially, instructions should be quite brief and directed towards one behavior. As children learn the labels for more objects and actions, the instructions should become more complex and require more behaviors. Examples can include, "Jack, get your coat and lunchbox" or "Larry, come here and get the ball."

In addition, children with severe communication deficits should learn to *greet* others. Such verbal or nonverbal greetings should occur soon after a person enters the room. Children should also learn to respond appropriately to others' greetings.

Protesting and answering are other impor-

tant communication skills. *Protesting* refers to indicating "no" or telling someone to "stop" something. While many children with severe communication deficits protest, we must teach them to do so appropriately. *Answering* is obviously a complex skill, because an answer requires understanding the question. However, some questions can be asked simply ("Want more milk?" "Want to play?"). When children learn to answer "yes" and "no" questions correctly, communication is greatly expanded.

All these communication skills should be selected for initial training with children with severe deficits. These skills can be made progressively more complex by adding words to the child's vocabulary. Examples include labeling an actor and an action ("John run") or an action and an object ("Hold kitty"); expanding requests from "more" and "want" to "more milk" or "want truck"; describing objects and events; and asking more complex questions and giving more complex instructions.

Published curricula Children with severe deficits need to establish a useful communication system. To accomplish this goal, several authors have developed communication training programs.

Functional Speech and Language Training. Guess, Sailor, and Baer (1976a, 1976b, 1977b, 1978b) developed a 60-step training sequence to teach basic communication skills to severely handicapped children. The steps are divided into persons and things (Steps 1–9); actions with persons and things (Steps 10–29); possession and color (Steps 30–42); and size, relation, and location (Steps 43–60).

The Functional Speech and Language Training program is based on an operant theory approach to speech and language training. Anyone using it should have a basic understanding of operant techniques. According to this program, the primary goal of intervention is to teach children to use communication to control the environment. Speech taught to a child must also be functional. Although the initial sequencing was based on normal developmental data, considerable revisions based on the performance of severely handicapped children were made (Guess, Sailor, & Baer, 1978a). The authors of the program assume that generalization will not occur without training, and thus generalization strategies are provided for many steps. Finally, children beginning the sequence are expected to imitate verbal utterances. Although some instances of successful movement through the curriculum by children originally thought to be nonimitators were reported, the authors suggest that the poor performance of these children in imitation training was due to motivational problems rather than the inability to imitate (Guess, Sailor, & Baer, 1977a).

Five basic functions of communication are incorporated across the 60 steps of the curriculum. *Reference* skills are used to describe or label objects or actions. *Control* skills are the ability to make a request. The *extended control* dimension is designed to teach children to "request more specific information based upon their own determination of what they do not know from what they already know" (Guess et al., 1977a, p. 365). For example, children are taught to ask, "What is that?" in regard to objects they do not know, or "What are you doing?" in response to unknown actions. *Integration* teaches children to discriminate when to ask questions, when to respond, and how to chain skills together for simple conversations. *Reception* skills, taught after expressive skills, help the child respond appropriately to others' utterances.

Each step in the curriculum has several parts. A *training goal* describes the skill to be taught. When appropriate, specific *training items* are listed and described. A detailed *procedures and training instructions* section describes the sequence of teaching activities within each step. Typically, the teacher presents the child with a stimulus (question, command) and uses reinforcement or correction procedures following the child's response. *Scoring forms and summary sheets* are provided for recording and analyzing performance date at each step. Finally, *generalization strategies* are suggested for many of the curriculum steps.

The Functional Speech and Language Training program offers many advantages. The procedures are clearly specified, the content focuses on functional use of communication, generalization is planned in a systematic fashion, and teachers are encouraged to collect and use child performance data to make instructional decisions. The program is probably not appropriate for mildly or moderately handicapped children because of its structure and the emphasis on initial training in a one-to-one formal instructional situation. Also, McLean and Snyder-McLean (1978) suggest that the program addresses only a limited range of communication functions and ignores the possible cognitive prerequisites to many targeted skills.

Stremel-Campbell and Waryas's Program. An intervention program that uses operant techniques to teach pragmatics and semantics within the context of specific syntactic structures has been proposed by Stremel-Campbell and Waryas (Stremel & Waryas, 1974; Waryas & Stremel-Campbell, 1978). The program is divided into three sections. The first section, *Early Language-Training Program,* teaches the child nouns, verbs, and adjectives and refines speech to increase intelligibility. These words are then used in two-word combinations (Noun-Noun, Noun-Verb, and Adjective-Noun) and the child is taught the use of first person pronouns (I, me). In the last phase of the Early Language-Training Program the child is taught to use three-word combinations (Noun-Verb-Noun, Verb-Adjective-Noun, Noun-Verb-Adverb), Wh-questions (why, who, where), and statements of negation (using *no* and *not*). These sequences of syntactic structures form a framework for superimposing content and meaning, using the child's environment as a guideline. Prerequisites for this section include basic attending skills and the ability to follow simple instructions and to label at least 10 objects or pictures.

Waryas and Stremel-Campbell (1978) describe the second and third sections of their training program as follows:

[The second phase is called] *The Early Intermediate Language-Training Program.* The length of the student's utterances is extended by expanding the classes of content words and introducing function words. At this stage the student learns to incorporate internal markers of questions and negation into his utterances. He also learns to use the optional replacive pronouns and to use a variety of different utterances for the same communicative function. [The third phase is called] *The Late Intermediate Language-Training Program.* The student's language is refined by training more complex structures. He learns to transform existing structures into others and to acquire additional syntactic rules for refining structure. An emphasis is placed on training the student to use his language to gain additional information for learning new skills (pp. 163–164).

Waryas and Stremel-Campbell emphasize a broad-based and detailed assessment of basic preverbal skills (response to gestures, imitation, and matching), basic syntactic forms, understanding of meaning, and use of language as a tool for communication. After the assessments are completed and an instructional plan developed, training is initiated. Although training is conducted in structured and unstructured environments, each approach follows a basic stimulus-response-reinforcement paradigm. Specific criterion levels are identified and prompting procedures, shaping procedures, and tangible reinforcement are the basic techniques used.

This program uses specific grammatical structures for teaching language meanings and usage. McLean and Snyder-McLean (1978) suggest that syntactic structure is not "a good representation of a child's reality in language" (p. 219). Although Waryas and Stremel-Campbell emphasize the semantic and pragmatic functions, the program and the instructional sequences are dominated by syntactic guidelines. Insufficient guidelines are provided for incorporating semantic and pragmatic considerations into the syntactic framework.

Environmental Language Intervention Program. The Environmental Language Intervention Program (Horstmeier & MacDonald, 1978; MacDonald & Horstmeier, 1978) facilitates language and communication skills in young language-delayed children. This program uses detailed assessment procedures and emphasizes semantic functions and the social-play context for language training.

The first component of the Environmental Language Intervention Program (Horstmeier & MacDonald, 1978) addresses basic prelanguage skills and includes an assessment tool (Environmental Prelanguage Battery) and a series of individual programs to be implemented by parents, teachers, or therapists (Ready, Set, Go—Talk to Me). The second component (MacDonald & Horstmeier, 1978) addresses more formal language skills and also includes an assessment tool (Environmental Language Inventory) and a set of training guides (Environmental Language Intervention Program).

The prelanguage program teaches preliminary skills (eye contact, sitting, on-task behavior, gestural communication), functional play, motor imitation, recognition of objects, understanding of action words, following directions, sound imitation, single words, and beginning social conversation. Each section includes a data sheet for recording daily performance and suggestions for applying learned skills to the environment. The language program is based on semantic-grammatical rules. These rules are taught in a structured play format, although intervention is conducted in the natural environment. For example, if a child is learning to express object-locative (location) relationships, the play activities would center around finding and labeling the location of various objects.

The Environmental Language Intervention Program has a strong assessment and theoretical (developmental) foundation. The emphasis on training within the social play context would encourage the generalization of newly acquired communication skills. Guess (1980) suggests that such an approach could help the child immediately use newly acquired skills. McLean and Snyder-McLean (1978) describe the assessment tools as "exemplary" and generally suggest that the program rests on a sound theoretical and practical foundation. They do suggest that the pragmatic functions of communication training need to be emphasized.

The Bricker, Dennison, and Bricker Program. Bricker, Dennison and Bricker (1976) developed a curriculum that blends a Piagetian approach to cognitive development, a psycholinguistic approach to grammatical development, and a behavioral approach to intervention. The cognitive base of language acquisition, including acquisition of sensorimotor skills and cognitive skills related to social interactions (Bricker & Carlson, 1980) is heavily emphasized. Prerequisites to the formal language training component have been described by Bricker and Dennison (1978) and include on-task behavior (sit in chair, look at trainer, work on task), imitation of motor movements and speech sounds, discriminative use of objects (using a block to stack, a truck to roll on the floor, and a cup to drink from), and word recognition (responding appropriately to words such as *hi, bye-bye,* or *night-night*). Training of these prerequisites follows a behavioral format, with prompting and use of natural reinforcers.

The language training program consists of a sequence of training phases emphasizing the semantics of language and application of these meanings in the natural environment. A language training lattice showing critical steps in the training program is shown in Figure 13.5. Intervention strategies again focus on a behavioral approach.

The early language training program proposed by Bricker et al. (1976) represents an important contribution to communication curricula because of its unique emphasis on Piagetian conceptions of cognitive development in tandem with a behavioral approach to intervention. The program has been through numerous revisions and adaptations, and is geared to the needs of young children with severe communication delays. Guess (1980) suggests that the program may be *too* comprehensive and thus overwhelming for some users. McLean & Snyder-McLean (1978) concur, although they suggest perhaps such comprehensiveness is necessary to appropriately serve the full range of children with communication deficits.

Each of the programs has unique strengths. The Functional Speech and Language Program develops functional speech to allow children to control their environments. It is designed for low-functioning children and requires staff members who can implement operant techniques successfully. The Waryas and Stremel-Campbell program emphasizes the syntactic aspects of communication and may be most useful with children who will be fairly competent communicators. Staff members are also required to be familiar with operant procedures. If children already have verbal semantic functions, and do not appear to have difficulties expressing pragmatic functions, more emphasis may be needed on the syntactic approach. The Environmental Language Intervention Program emphasizes the semantic aspects of communication, and may be appropriate for children who have difficulty with the semantic aspects of language. Further,

it should be used with children with good communication potential. The Environmental Language Intervention Program does not require staff to be as skilled in implementing operant procedures, but requires considerable staff skills in training activities in play situations. The Bricker et al. program emphasizes the cognitive skills thought to be prerequisites to communication development. The detailed curriculum requires staff to develop fewer programs. Because of its developmental orientation, it should probably be used with children with good communication potential. Once again, staff must have skill in implementing operant procedures.

Other training programs exist for children with severe communication deficits (Gray & Ryan, 1973; Kent, 1974; Kent, Klein, Falk, & Guenther, 1972; Lovaas, 1977; Miller & Yoder, 1974). Many curricula for young handicapped children include sections for communication development (Fredericks, Riggs, Furey, Grove, Moore, McDonnell, Jordan, Hanson, Baldwin, & Wadlow, 1976; Neisworth, Willoughby-Herb, Bagnato, Cartwright, & Laub, 1980; Tawney, Knapp, O'Reilly, & Pratt, 1979). Since research comparing the relative value of these and other communication curricula has not been done, the teacher must select the program on the basis of other considerations. Considerations should include children's immediate and potential communication abilities and the skills and philosophic orientation of the staff.

No single communication program is appropriate for the full range of children. Thus, teachers should become familiar with each program and select them for individuals rather than using one with all children. The descriptions provided present a general flavor of the various curricula. Interested readers should consult the respective authors for more information.

Procedures and examples of teaching Much of the research for teaching communication skills has used operant techniques. Because such procedures are successful, examples of the operant procedures and cases where important communication skills were trained are provided.

Although authors from behavioral and developmental perspectives disagree on an ex-

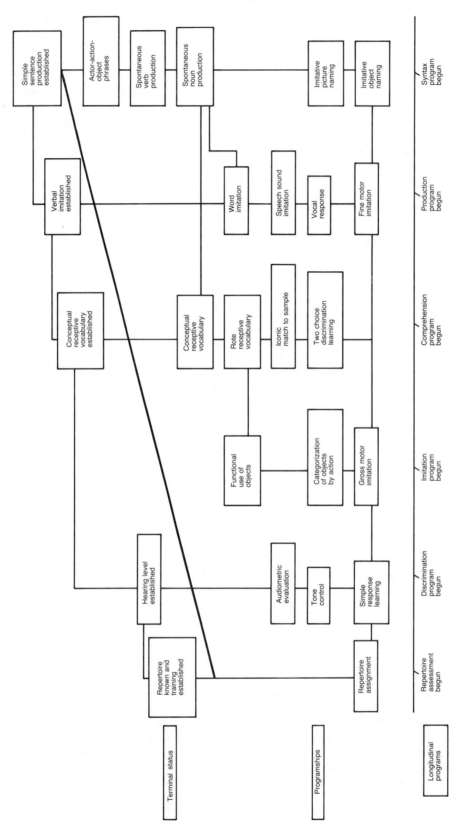

FIGURE 13.5

Language training lattice of the Bricker & Bricker Language Program. *Note:* From "An Early Language Strategy" by W. Bricker and D. Bricker. In R.L. Schiefelbusch and L. Lloyd (Eds.), *Language Perspectives—Acquisition, Retardation, and Intervention.* Baltimore: University Park Press, 1974. Copyright 1974 by University Park Press. Reprinted by permission.

planation for language acquisition, both use operant procedures. These procedures include specifying the behaviors to be trained through task analysis, presenting specific antecedent stimuli (verbal cues, objects, pictures, etc.), modeling or otherwise prompting the response to be performed by the child, reinforcing or correcting the child's response, and fading the prompts and models over successive training trials. They have been mostly used in individual sessions, but can also be successful with small groups.

Specifying behaviors to be taught through task analysis. Many of the communication behaviors such as commenting and requesting must be broken into smaller steps. A task analysis of requesting food and toys is shown.

1 Child identifies (through pointing or some other response) various foods named by another person (milk, juice, cookie, apple, orange, grapes).

2 Child identifies (through pointing or some other response) various toys named by another person (wind-up chicken, blocks, busy box, clay, toy truck).

3 Child names (verbally, signs, or other conventional system) items of food shown by another person.

4 Child names (verbally, signs, or other conventional system) various toys shown by another person.

5 Child imitates another person's model of "want" (verbally, signs, etc.).

6 Child says (verbally, signs, etc.) "want" when shown one item (food, toys, etc.).

7 Child says, "Want (food or toy)" when shown same.

8 Child says, "Want (food or toy)" when not shown same but when asked, "What do you want?"

9 Child says, "Want (food)" during snack and lunch times and when hungry.

10 Child says, "Want (toy)" during play times.

Items, of course, should be selected individually for each child. This task analysis should also be used to teach the child how and when to request objects. Training in communication skills must include not only how to do the behaviors, but when the child should perform the behavior.

Presenting specific antecedent stimuli. Antecedent stimuli must be presented so the child realizes it is his or her turn to respond, and the item to be responded to must be obvious. Verbal cues such as, "Give me," "Do this," and "What's this?" frequently cue children that it is their turn and focus their attention on the relevant stimuli. When such cues are used they must be faded, or the child will learn to respond only to them. Procedures for presenting antecedents were described in Chapter 3. Children must also learn to respond to given stimuli in the presence of other stimuli. For example, if Crystal learned to label cups when there are only cups on the table, she may also correctly identify a cup when a glass, plate, spoon, and fork are also present. If she does not, she really has not learned the concept of *cup.* Cups alone should be present at the beginning of training, later, other items should be added.

Modeling and prompting children's responses. Procedures for using and fading prompts are described in Chapter 3. Procedures for using imitation in direct instruction were presented in Chapter 4 and are reviewed in relation to speech in Chapter 14.

Reinforcing and correcting children's communicative responses. The role of reinforcement in the natural development of language is a controversial issue. However, reinforcement can be useful for teaching language and communication skills to children who have not developed those skills in a typical fashion. One issue is the nature of the reinforcement. Many of the curriculum packages suggest using primary reinforcers such as food or drinks or social praise with more responsive children. For many children these procedures may be necessary to insure initial responding, and for some children they may always be necessary. However, for children to actually use the acquired skills, they must receive reinforcement directly related to their communicative efforts. Studies have demonstrated the importance of this principle.

Janssen and Guess (1978) compared procedures for teaching profoundly retarded children to point to selected objects named by the teacher. In one procedure (Label Only) the child was shown three objects and asked to point to one labeled by the teacher. If the child did so an individually identified rein-forcer was given. In another procedure (Function Plus Label) the same pattern was followed except that after a correct response, and in addition to the usual reinforcer, the child was shown the function of the object and allowed to perform the action. Items included a stapler, record player, pencil, tape dispenser, hole punch, broom, and others. The results indicated that the children learned object labels faster when they could engage in the object's function contingent upon correct responding.

Saunders and Sailor (1979) compared procedures for teaching severely retarded children to point to toys named by the teacher. In the *specific reinforcement* condition the child was given the toy (if correctly pointed to) and allowed to play with it for 15 seconds. In the *nonspecific reinforcement* condition the child was handed a toy not in the original stimulus set and allowed to play with it for 15 seconds. In the *variable reinforcement* condition the child was given the choice of playing with the toy he or she had correctly pointed to or the toy not in the original stimulus set. Results indicated that the percentages of correct responses for each of the three children in the study were highest during the *specific* reinforcement condition.

Although these studies were conducted with small numbers of children, they demonstrate the effectiveness of using natural reinforcers (reinforcers directly related to a child's communicative response such as using an object after pointing to it). Thus, when possible, teachers should use natural reinforcers. Such reinforcers usually result in more generalization of acquired behaviors to other environments.

Besides reinforcing correct responses, teachers must respond to incorrect responses. In Chapter 3, procedures were described for eliminating errors. These procedures should be used in communication training programs. However, usually during structured communication training the teacher takes the materials away from the table and turns his or her head away from the child for 10–15 seconds. Any error correction procedure should be evaluated by how it affects the occurrence of errors.

Fading prompts and models over successive trials. Procedures for selecting, using, and fading prompts are described in Chapter 3. Readers should review the time delay, system of least prompts, system of most to least prompts, and graduated guidance procedures for fading prompts.

Implementing operant procedures in language training requires efficient practice. Teachers must develop and use such skills when training children with severe communication deficits. Several different communicative behaviors such as labeling, requesting/asking questions, answering questions, greeting others, following instructions, and describing things are important for young handicapped children including those with severe communication deficits. The operant procedures described above have been used to train children with severe communication deficits to perform these types of behaviors. Examples of these studies are in Table 13.5.

As seen in Table 13.5, children with severe deficits can learn communicative skills. When training communication behaviors in structured situations, as in the studies listed in Table 13.5, teachers must be particularly sensitive to generalization. Procedures for facilitating generalization will be described later in this chapter.

Children with Mild and Moderate Communication Delays

Although communication is important for all children, the form and nature of intervention for children with mild or moderate communication delays will differ considerably from those with severe delays. In this section, published curricula and specific training and assistance procedures are described.

Important communicative behaviors The goal of training for children with mild/moderate delays is to accelerate their communicative development. Teachers should follow developmental sequences to determine the content of instructional programs. Other goals suggested by Warren and Rogers-Warren (1980) include increasing the *rate of talking*, and *carrying on conversations*. Both of these behaviors require teachers to structure the environment to promote children to talk. Providing interesting topics of discussion and reinforcing children should increase their rate of talking. Allowing children to talk, responding

TABLE 13.5
Using operant procedures to train children with severe communication deficits to perform important communicative behaviors

Communicative Behavior	Type of Subject	Procedures Used	Reference
Labeling objects (receptive)	Four profoundly retarded children	Reinforcement Prompting Functional use of object as consequence	Janssen & Guess (1978)
Labeling objects (expressive)	Four severely retarded children	Reinforcement Modeling/fading	Welch & Pear (1980)
Requesting/asking questions for information ("What is [name of object] for?")	Four autistic children	Reinforcement Modeling/fading Verbal cues	Hung (1977)
Requesting actions ("Please tray," or "Want food")	Six severely retarded children	Reinforcement (meal) Time delay Modeling	Halle, Marshall, & Spradlin (1979)
Asking question/commenting on answer/answering another question (conversational sequence)	Two severely retarded children	Reinforcement Modeling/fading	Garcia (1974)
Greeting response (waving)	Four severely to profoundly retarded persons	Reinforcement Physical prompting/fading	Stokes, Baer, & Jackson (1974)
Following instructions with spatial location ("Put _____ on top of the _____")	One moderately and two severely retarded children	Reinforcement Physical prompting/fading	Frisch & Schumaker (1974)
Following instruction with verb-noun form ("Point to ear," "Push car")	Three retarded persons	Reinforcement Modeling/fading	Striefel, Bryan, & Aikins (1974)
Describing events (Agent-is-Active Verb-Article-Object)	Three developmentally delayed children	Reinforcement Modeling/fading	Hester & Hendrickson (1977)

to the content of their statements by making additional statements ("Tell me more"), and asking questions ("What happened next?") that allow children to respond will facilitate their ability to carry on conversations.

Published curricula Although the programs described earlier, with the possible exception of the Functional Speech and Language Program, may be used with children whose com-

munication delays are moderate and mild, the DISTAR Language Program and the Peabody Language Development Kit can also be used.

DISTAR Language Program. A series of highly structured language programs for high-risk preschoolers and kindergarten and elementary-aged children has been developed by Engelmann and Osborn (1972, 1976,

Point to each container and say:
This is a container.

c. Point to the bag.
    Is this a container? Touch. *Yes.*
    Say the whole thing. Touch.
    This is a container.

d. **What kind of container is this?** Touch.
    A bag. **Yes, this container is a bag.**
    Say the whole thing about this container.
    Touch. *This container is a bag.*

e. Repeat *c* and *d* until all children's responses are firm.

f. Point to the box.
    Is this a container? Touch. *Yes.*
    Say the whole thing. Touch.
    This is a container.

g. **What kind of container is this?** Touch.
    A box. **Yes, this container is a box.**
    Say the whole thing about this container.
    Touch. *This container is a box.*

h. Repeat *f* and *g* until all children's responses are firm.

i. Point to the cup.
    Is this a container? Touch. *Yes.*
    Say the whole thing. Touch.
    This is a container.

j. **What kind of container is this?** Touch.
    A cup. **Yes, this container is a cup.**
    Say the whole thing about this container.
    Touch. *This container is a cup.*

k. Repeat *i* and *j* until all children's responses are firm.

l. Point to the glass.
    Is this a container? Touch. *Yes.*
    Say the whole thing. Touch.
    This is a container.

m. **What kind of container is this?** Touch.
    A glass. **Yes, this container is a glass.**
    Say the whole thing about this container.
    Touch. *This container is a glass.*

n. Repeat *l* and *m* until all children's responses are firm.

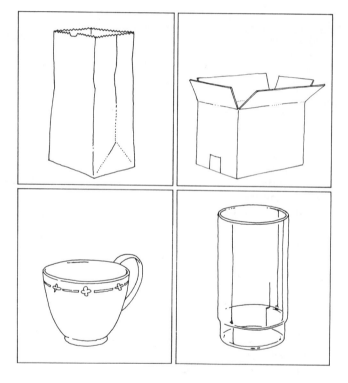

FIGURE 13.6

Sample lesson from DISTAR language program *Note:* From DISTAR® LANGUAGE 1, Teacher Presentation Book C, by Siegfried Engelmann and Jean Osborn. Copyright © 1976, 1972, 1969 by Science Research Associates, Inc. Reprinted by permission of the publisher.

1977). Osborn and Becker (1980) describe an application of the DISTAR curriculum.

Prerequisite skills for the preschool level include the ability to imitate a word or phrase, answer simple questions ("What is this?" "What are you doing?"), answer yes-no questions, and point to and label common objects and actions (Osborn & Becker, 1980). The content of Level I (preschool) includes teaching the following skills:

- ☐ Use of prepositions to describe spatial relations (under, beside)
- ☐ Understanding and use of polar opposites (long-short, big-little)
- ☐ Classification and understanding of concepts
- ☐ Proper verb tense
- ☐ Fine relations (before, after)
- ☐ Part-whole relations
- ☐ Same, different
- ☐ Basic information (days of the week, months, seasons, colors, shapes, etc.)

Level II (kindergarten) addresses problem-solving tasks, absurdities, if-then statements, synonyms, true-false propositions, and questioning skills. A sample DISTAR lesson is shown in Figure 13.6.

A DISTAR training program at the preschool level is conducted in a large group format (5–15 children) for approximately 30 minutes per day. Characteristics of training include a brisk pace and precise teacher-pupil interchanges—the teacher presents a specific concept and then asks questions of the group. All children respond in unison so each child practices saying each response. The group responses are signaled by the teacher, and occur frequently throughout the lessons. This statement-repetition format is typically followed by an application activity, usually written.

DISTAR represents a highly structured program with explicit instructions for teachers which makes it easy to implement. Many researchers and practitioners have criticized the approach because of the fast pace and high structure. The evaluation research on DISTAR, however, has generally been quite positive. Evans (1975) concluded that the program was effective in achieving its specified goals, although broader effects (improved intelligence test scores) did not necessarily occur. A re-

cent Follow Through study concluded that the Direct Instruction Model, upon which DISTAR is based, produced the best student progress in reading, arithmetic, and language by the end of the third grade (Becker, 1978). Perhaps one reason for this success is that DISTAR is a functionally-based curriculum and teaches specific, necessary language concepts for school success. Few data indicate its utility as a tool for teaching broader social communication skills such as initiating and maintaining conversations.

Peabody Language Development Kit. The Peabody Language Development Kit (PLDK) (Dunn & Smith, 1965) presents language activities in a gamelike atmosphere and uses a variety of colorful materials such as picture cards, posters, puppets, plastic fruits and vegetables, and magnetic geometric shapes. Level P of the program is addressed toward children ages 3 to 5. As with DISTAR, the research on the PLDK generally indicates that children in the program improve in their oral language skills, but this may not be reflected in intelligence test scores (Evans, 1975).

The PLDK is based in psycholinguistic theory. Children are stimulated through visual, auditory, and tactual modes, and express themselves vocally and motorically. The purpose is to stimulate divergent, convergent, and associative thinking. Sample activities include classification, conversation, critical thinking, describing, following directions, listening, naming, problem solving, and sentence building. A sample lesson is shown in Figure 13.7.

Many other programs have been developed (Blank & Soloman, 1968; Clark, 1981; Dunst, 1981; Karnes, 1968; Lavatelli, 1971). Consult the primary sources for more information.

For many teachers, published curricula have been invaluable. Obviously most teachers do not have the time or resources to develop curriculum materials. Communication and its development is so complex and varied that valid curricula should be developed by knowledgeable persons. A theoretically sound curriculum, providing sequences of meaningful communication skills with associated assessment and instructional procedures, is frequently an essential component of a well-organized early intervention program.

Although curriculum packages can be useful, most research efforts have focused on their

14

Materials

ACTIVITY I	ACTIVITY 2
None	None

1. Focus: Imitating pantomimed actions, and then identifying the actions and body parts used

Ask the children to stand before you. Say:

> **We can use our body parts to do many different things.**
> **Watch carefully, and then do what I am doing.**

Pretend to smell something. Encourage the children to join you. Then ask:

> **What were we pretending to do?** (Pause) **Yes, we were pretending to smell something. Which body part do we use to smell?** (Pause) **Yes, we use our noses to smell.**

Continue with these actions and body parts:

1. **Walking** (legs, knees, feet, toes)
2. **Bending** (elbows, knees, fingers, wrists, neck, waist)
3. **Eating** (mouth, lips, tongue, teeth, jaws)
4. **Listening** (ears)
5. **Picking up** (fingers, hands, arms, mouth, toes if we must)
6. **Blinking** (eyes, eyelids)
7. **Kicking** (feet, legs, toes)
8. **Stretching** (all body parts)

End by inviting the children to stand on tiptoe and stretch.

2. Focus: singing an action song about uses of the *mouth, feet,* and *hands*

With the children still standing, say:

> **I know a song that is fun to sing and act out. Please listen as I go through it for you the first time. Then we will do it together.**

Sing or chant the following words to the tune or rhythm of "The Farmer in the Dell":

> **We use our mouths to sing,** (point to mouth)
> **We use our mouths to sing,**
> **Hi-ho the derry-o,**
> **We use our mouths to sing.**

Continue with verses that begin as follows:

> **We use our feet to march, etc.** (March in place)
> **We use our hands to clap, etc.** (Clap hands)

Invite the children to join you in repeating the verses and movements. Ask volunteers to lead the group as everyone sings the song again.

VARIATION: To make the activity *harder,* invite the children to make up more verses.

FIGURE 13.7

Sample Lesson from Peabody Language Development Kit—Level P (Revised) *Note:* From *Peabody Language Development Kit—Level P (Rev.)* by L. Dunn, K. B., Horton, and J. O. Smith. Circle Pines, Minn.: American Guidance Service, 1981. Copyright 1981 by AGS. Reprinted by permission.

development rather than evaluation. Few comparisons have been made between programs. Therefore, curriculum selections are based on the logic of the developers and teacher knowledge of communication. Teachers must often select curriculum materials on the basis of factors other than data, including perceived usability, attractiveness of the curriculum package, whether the teacher understands the technical language, and the perceived match between the theoretical perspective of the curriculum developer and the teacher's own ideas. Extensive data are needed to document the types of children and conditions that make a curriculum effective, especially when children have severe deficits.

Also, comprehensive curriculum packages often give teachers a false sense of security. The teacher is still responsible for individual assessment of progress and adaptation of sequences and materials to meet individual needs. The Functional Speech and Language Program; Environmental Language Intervention Program; Bricker, Dennison, and Bricker's program; and Waryas and Stremel-Campbell's program encourage both initial and ongoing assessment. DISTAR and the PLDK are less suited for either initial assessment or the ongoing modifications necessary with handicapped children. Handicapped children demonstrate developmental and behavioral patterns that frequently do not fit those described in a given curriculum. Further, since their environments vary, some curriculum sequences may be more suited to their needs than others.

Teachers need to have a basic understanding of communication and its development and the ability to implement a variety of intervention strategies to adequately select appropriate programs from a myriad of curriculum materials. Furthermore, teachers must appropriately adapt instructional sequences and activities for children who do not seem to "fit in" the curriculum or who need different or additional activities.

Strategies for facilitating communication
Modeling and reinforcement are appropriate for children with mild and moderate delays, and are described in Chapters 3 and 4. The strategies of using expansions, extensions, and recast sentences and the use of incidental teaching are described.

Using Expansions, Extensions, and Recast Sentences. Expansions, extensions, and recast sentences are methods whereby adults verbally respond to children's statements and thus attempt to provide the child with additional information about communicating, particularly about the syntactic aspects. Expansions are used to make children's statements more complex, to add more descriptors, or to more fully express communicative intent. Nelson, Carskadden, and Bonvillian (1973) describe an *expansion* as using the child's words in the child's order, but also including new words to make an expanded, grammatically complete sentence. For example, when the child says, "Baby ball" the mother might say, "Baby has the ball." An expansion is different from an *extension* in that the latter follows the child's statement with different words. For example, when the child says, "Baby ball" the adult might say, "Oh, it is a big ball!"

Expansions and extensions build on the child's communicative efforts; they occur naturally; they may serve as reinforcers (for attempting to communicate) and as models for more appropriate communicative behavior; and their use may facilitate the eventual development of conversational skills. Research indicates that parents naturally expand between 25% and 30% of their young children's utterances (Schumaker, 1976; Slobin, 1968).

Some early studies, however, questioned the value of expansions in facilitating communication development. Cazden (1965), for example, compared expansions and extensions and found no differences between children exposed to expansions and extensions and a control group who received no intervention. Only one small, questionable difference was found between the extension and expansion groups on a sentence imitation measure.

More recent research, however, demonstrated the possible effectiveness of these procedures. Nelson et al. (1973) compared the extension procedure with a procedure described as recast sentences. Using *recast sentences* involves the teacher using expansions and other sentence forms to display the same general meaning, but providing new syntactic information. For example, if the child says, "The blocks fell down" the teacher might recast this sentence by saying, "The blocks did fall down, didn't they?" Results indicated that the recast sentence group was superior to a control group (no intervention) on utterance length and other measures of syntactic complexity.

Nelson (1977) examined the effect of recast sentences on complex questions and verbs. Each form was recast during different phases of intervention. For example, in the complex question intervention phase, the statement, "The donkey ran" might be recast as, "The donkey did run, didn't he?" During the complex verb phase the same statement might be recast as "The donkey ran and jumped" (p. 102). Results indicated that spontaneous use of the targeted structures increased following the periods of recasting.

Studies by Schumaker (1976) and Howell, Schumaker, and Sherman (1978) also documented the potential for expansion to facilitate the language development of children with communication delays. The data suggest that teachers and parents should consider systematic use of expansions and recast sentences with children beginning to learn the basic structure of language. McLean and Snyder-McLean (1978) offer guidelines for deciding when to use expansions. "At best it seems that this behavior (expansion) when exhibited by adults, is only useful when: (1) the child is already producing at least two-word utterances which afford grammatical expanding, (2) the expansion includes structures which the child is 'ready' to begin producing and (3) the expansion remains within the child's receptive competence" (p. 65). Although expansions, extensions, and recast sentences help increase syntactic complexity, teachers should respond to the meaning and intent of children's statements. For example, if a child says, "I want a drink," the teacher might respond by saying, "You want a drink of cool water, don't you?" but should also assist the child in getting a drink.

Schumaker and Sherman (1978) provide the following guidelines for using expansions and extensions:

☐ Expansions should be used when the child spontaneously initiates a few words.[3]
☐ To facilitate imitation, expansions should be slightly more complex than the child's statements.
☐ Expansions and extensions should relate to the child's meaning and communicative intent.
☐ Extensions can be accomplished "by substituting a pronoun or synonym for the word(s) the child used." e.g., Child: "Shoe." Adult: "Let's put it on." Child: "Look doggie." Adult: "I see him, he's a nice dog" (p. 303).

Data have not yet suggested that expansions significantly affect children's understanding of their communicative efforts, although this issue certainly deserves research.

Using Incidental Teaching. For programs serving children who can initiate very simple communication attempts, the incidental teaching model developed by Hart and Risley (1974, 1975, 1980) can effectively increase the appropriate use of language. *Incidental*

teaching* is defined as "the interaction between an adult and a single child, which arises naturally in an instructional situation such as free play and which is used by the adult to transmit information or give the child practice in developing a skill" (Hart & Risley, 1975, p. 411).

In incidental teaching the child initiates the interaction, usually by a verbal or nonverbal request for assistance, an activity, or a reinforcer. The teacher then decides whether to use the situation for incidental teaching. If so, the teacher must recall a specific language behavior the child should learn or practice. This information should have been previously determined through a communication assessment of each child. The adult initially responds to the child with focused attention and perhaps a verbal cue. For example, if the child points to something and says, "Dat," the teacher might say "What do you want?" If the child does not respond appropriately, the teacher may use a minimal prompt (request for the desired language behavior such as, "You need to tell me with words"), a medium prompt (request for partial imitation such as, "I _____"), or a full prompt (a specific request for imitation such as, "Say, 'I want ball' "). If the child responds correctly the teacher confirms the behavior ("Oh, you want the ball") and then reinforces the child by complying with the request.

Hart and Risley (1974, 1975, 1980) have demonstrated the effectiveness of incidental teaching and present a manual for using incidental teaching (1982). In their initial study (Hart & Risley, 1974) children were prompted to expand their requests for play materials. In the first phase children were required to ask for the object by name. In the second phase the object had to be requested by its name plus a word that described the material (Adjective-Noun combination such as, "Big truck"). In the third phase, children had to add color to the Adjective-Noun combination ("Big red truck"). In the final phase children were required to also state with whom they were going to use the materials. Incidental teaching proved to be effective in teaching each of these skills.

Hart and Risley (1975) expanded the initial study to further examine the potential for teaching compound sentences and to deter-

---

[3]Schumaker and Sherman (1978) recommend using expansions when the child says a few words, whereas McLean and Snyder-McLean (1978) recommend using expansions after the child has begun to use two-word statements. Where the instructional objective is to increase syntactic complexity, expansions, extensions, and recast sentences should be used. When children are using only a few single words, the instructional objective should *not* be to increase syntactic complexity; rather, the child should label more semantic functions. In such cases, teachers should mark (through modeling) additional semantic functions—whether expansions, extensions, and recast sentences serve this purpose remains an empirical question. However, given how often parents use them, they may well serve a marking function. More research is needed.

mine the generalized effects of incidental teaching. The toys for high risk 4- and 5-year-olds were placed beyond reach, but within sight of the children. After incidental teaching for use of object labels, children were also taught to use compound sentences first directed toward teachers and later toward other children. Again, incidental teaching increased compound sentences to both teachers and peers. Furthermore, all children increased their unprompted use of compound sentences.

Hart and Risley (1980) further investigated the generalized effects of incidental teaching by observing the communication behaviors of young children in an untrained, free play environment. The authors report that the average number of words per child, of different words, of sentences, and of elaborate sentences increased in a program using incidental teaching procedures, compared with stable rates in other preschool settings not using incidental teaching. These effects may be because incidental teaching incorporates many of the generalization strategies suggested by Stokes and Baer (1977) such as training conducted in natural settings and throughout the day, and using natural reinforcers (Hart & Risley, 1980).

Although early childhood special educators have often advocated naturalistic language training, such training has not been systematic. One-to-one teaching, naturalistic teaching, and incidental teaching (referred to as milieu teaching) are compared along several dimensions in Table 13.6. Incidental teaching incorporates positive aspects of both one-to-one teaching and natural settings.

Incidental teaching is a powerful strategy for encouraging and expanding the functional use of communication in preschool settings. Since the child is required to initiate the interaction, it may be inappropriate for more severely delayed children, especially those who do not initiate. Effective use of incidental teaching requires the teacher (or parent) to be available and free to respond. Further research is needed to determine whether incidental teaching can be useful in teaching other social/communication skills. Although Hart and Risley (1980) provide some indication that generalized effects may occur, specific pragmatic and semantic functions are yet to be documented.

Involving Parents in Communication Training

The final general strategy for teaching communication skills to young children with handicaps is the involvement of parents in training. General parent involvement has been discussed in Chapters 1 and 8. Parent involvement in communication training is especially important, however, because parents probably spend more time vocalizing with their children than any other adult or child during the early years of life. Children first learn the "communication game" through interactions with parents and begin to experience the enjoyment of mutual communication. Schumaker and Sherman (1978), in a review of research on parental influence on language development, conclude that parental vocabulary, praise, corrective feedback, prompts, instructions, and rationales constitute a set of experiences highly predictive of children's later performance on language measures and intelligence tests. In addition, direct involvement of parents is one of the best procedures in facilitating generalization to the home environment.

Facilitating positive affective interactions

The affective dimension addresses the parents' attitudes toward and interactions with the child. This dimension should frequently receive more attention from parents of handicapped infants. Unlike parents who must cope for the first time with handicapped babies, parents of older preschoolers have likely developed mutually satisfying interactions.

Clezy (1979), for example, suggests that the parents of any language delayed child are likely to be anxious about their child's development. High levels of anxiety can potentially have a negative impact on the social relationship between parents and child, subsequently affecting their communication system. These problems are multiplied with parents of handicapped children, since they may be angry, resentful, or sad. Further, they may be unsure about what to do with their child. These feelings can interfere with communication.

Parents and children may need to improve their social relationship. The assessment and intervention strategies suggested by Bromwich (1976, 1981) and discussed in Chapter 8 can be incorporated. Bromwich's program is designed primarily for infants and parents. An-

TABLE 13.6
Comparison of one-to-one instruction, naturalistic teaching, and milieu teaching (incidental teaching)

Aspect	One-to-one teaching	Natural settings	Milieu teaching settings
Language to the child	Highly specified and structured according to particular training program.	Varied. Content determined by the objects, events, and persons in the setting.	Controlled and balanced to coincide with both the child's skills and the objects, events, and persons present in the setting.
Models of specific language	Presented discretely. The child's attention is directed toward them. Imitations are consequated and matched systematically to the child's skill level.	Occur irregularly. The child's attention may not be directed toward them. They vary in complexity so that many of them may be beyond the child's skill level.	Specific. Delivered in a context that functionally reinforces imitation. Models are provided only when the child is attending. Complexity and frequency of presentation are determined by the child's skills.
Consequences for language usage	Frequent and immediately following child's verbal response.	Vary in frequency but are typically unsystematic. Functional reinforcers are attention from adults and peers, acquisition of needed materials and services, participation in social-verbal interaction.	Frequent and systematic. Same functional reinforcers as found in natural settings.
Demand for language usage	High. The child is required to respond many times during a relatively short period of time.	Low. The child may infrequently be required to verbalize or elaborate his verbalizations.	Selectively high, when it is functional for the child to respond.
Opportunities for language usage	Many opportunities to respond but few opportunities to initiate with descriptions or requests.	Opportunities to ask questions, request needed objects and services, and to engage in social conversation are all present in the setting although the child may not utilize the opportunities.	Same opportunities are present as in the natural setting. The child is prompted to make appropriate responses when these opportunities arise.

TABLE 13.6 (continued)
Comparison of one-to-one instruction, naturalistic teaching, and milieu teaching (incidental teaching)

Aspect	One-to-one teaching	Natural settings	Milieu teaching settings
Language teaching	Systematic but occurring during a small portion of the child's day.	No systematic teaching.	Systematic and occurring during a moderate portion of the child's day.
Emphasis of teaching	Form, correct structures, etc.	If it occurs, the focus is likely to be communicative function.	Communicative function is primary. Form is secondary.

Note: From "A Milieu Approach to Teaching Language" by B. Hart and A. Rogers-Warren. In R.L. Schiefelbusch (Ed.), *Language Intervention Strategies,* Baltimore: University Park Press, 1978. Copyright 1978 by University Park Press. Reprinted by permission.

other strategy is to analyze the nature of the feedback parents give to their children and emphasize the importance of positive rather than negative or critical comments in teaching communication (Cevette, 1979). Seitz and Hoekenga (1974) and Seitz and Marcus (1976), for example, had parents and teachers watch a child and another teacher in a play situation either from an observation room or on videotapes. The observation-teacher described the other teacher and child's interactions to the parent, and in some cases the parents described the interactions. Through these descriptions, parents were trained to interact more positively as evidenced by changes in the parent-child interactions. Parents used less directive behaviors and increased mutually satisfying interactions.

Facilitating parents' training skills As described in Chapters 1 and 8, teachers should be careful not to try to make parents into teachers. However, some parents may want and need to develop skills in facilitating their children's communicative development. McLean and Snyder-McLean (1978) reviewed Bruner's (1974, 1975) work, which identified skills or strategies parents use within the context of interactions. These referencing strategies orient or reference the child to a specific object, action, or component of communication. Several strategies are used in referencing by indicating that the parent infers and notes the child's "line of focus." *Marking* is

the behavior of manipulating an object or exaggerating an action to attract the child's attention (shaking a rattle, tapping on the window). *Naming* is the attachment of labels to objects or actions. McLean and Snyder-McLean (1978) conclude that the appropriate teaching strategies parents should use in facilitating the early communicative development of their children are

(1) linguistic and extralinguistic marking of the segments of the interactions (for example, mother raises her eyebrows, throws up her hands, and says "aboom!" after a stack of blocks has tumbled to the floor); (2) establishing joint reference or directing the child's attention to relevant elements of an event or relationship; and (3) demonstrating, encouraging, and providing opportunities for the child to explore, manipulate, and discover the relational and dynamic properties of objects in his world (p. 70).

These strategies should be conducted within the context of the social interchanges (give and take) between parents and children.

Parents can also be taught skills associated with the general strategies of modeling, reinforcement, recast sentences, and incidental teaching. For further information on involving parents, consult Chapter 8; Schumaker and Sherman (1978); Snow and Ferguson (1977); and Wolery (1979).

Generalized Use of Communication Skills

Generalization occurs when a response or behavior trained under one set of circumstances is exhibited under another. For example, Susan is taught to say, "Hi" to the teacher each morning when she arrives at preschool. If Susan also begins to say, "Hi" to her mother when she gets home, even though she was never specifically trained to do so, generalization has occurred. Generalization is an important consideration in any program, but it is especially critical in training communication skills since one main objective of communication is to interact with others in any situation. In this section suggestions for facilitating generalized use of acquired communication skills are reviewed. For more detailed discussion, see reviews of broad issues in generalization (Stokes & Baer, 1977; Wehman, Abramson, & Norman, 1977) and specific reviews of issues and strategies in language and communication training (Cooke, Cooke, & Apolloni, 1976; Garcia & DeHaven, 1974; Warren, Rogers-Warren, Baer, & Guess, 1980).

Occurrence and nonoccurrence of generalization Handicapped learners, particularly those who are more severely so, are often able to learn specified behaviors under a controlled set of circumstances, but can only perform these behaviors in other settings if they have been trained to do so (Stokes & Baer, 1977; Wehman et al., 1977). Warren et al. (1980) suggest that prevailing conceptualizations of generalized communication skills are limited in scope and often do not address the real issues of meaningful generalization. For example, many studies examined how much training of specific labels or syntactic forms has generalized to other trainers, objects, or conditions. Generalization has been established in imitative motor behavior (Baer, Peterson, & Sherman, 1967; Garcia, Baer, & Firestone, 1971), morphology (Baer & Guess, 1973; Guess, 1969), syntax (Bennett & Ling, 1971; Lutzker & Sherman, 1974), articulation training (Bennett, 1974), and language use (Clark & Sherman, 1975). It has been shown in simple tasks such as labeling by size and color (Martin, 1975) and sign labeling of different colored shapes (Smeets & Striefel, 1976), and in difficult skills such as past and

present tense verb inflections (Schumaker & Sherman, 1970). However, few studies have examined how much communicative functions have generalized, regardless of the syntactic forms used. Warren et al. report preliminary data suggesting that some handicapped children can show considerable semantic and pragmatic generalization without concurrent syntactic generalization. Since using language is a primary goal of communication training, assessment and training for generalization should focus largely on the pragmatic dimensions of development. Warren and Rogers-Warren (1980) suggest generalization must be assessed across the dimensions of other trainers (people), settings, and stimuli (materials).

Facilitating generalization in communication Although many different strategies have been suggested for facilitating generalization (see Stokes & Baer, 1977, or Warren et al., 1980), providing sufficient examplars and programming common stimuli are approaches that are often used.

Provide sufficient examplars. One broad strategy is to train enough examples of a concept so the probability of generalized performance is very high. For example, if only blocks were used in teaching *red,* the probability of generalization would be less than if a variety of red objects was used.

Many studies have demonstrated the value of training sufficient examplars. Guess, Sailor, Rutherford, and Baer (1968) trained a retarded girl to produce a plural form of a word, but her newly acquired skill did not generalize; after being trained to produce several plurals, she generalized the skill to untrained words. Stokes, Baer, and Jackson (1974) used prompting and shaping to develop hand waving as a greeting response in retarded children in an institution. When just one teacher trained the response the child systematically greeted that teacher with a wave but not any of the other institutional staff. When a second teacher trained and maintained the response, however, high levels of generalized greeting to other untrained staff members were observed.

Wetherby and Striefel (1978) have proposed a matrix-training procedure to improve the probability of generalization by varying the examplars of receptive language skills. Earlier studies (Striefel, Bryan, & Aikins, 1974; Striefel & Wetherby, 1973) indicated that although profoundly retarded children could be taught to follow verb-noun instructions ("push car") the skill did not generalize to untrained objects. "The subject always performed the behavior that had been associated with the noun during training, regardless of the action specified by the verb in the generalization item" (Striefel & Wetherby, 1973, p. 669). For example, two of the trained items were "lift block" and "push car." When told to "push block" (generalization item), however, the children lifted the block instead.

To avoid such problems, Wetherby and Striefel (1978) propose a matrix-training procedure. For example, given a set of verbs and a set of nouns, the teacher constructs a matrix with the verbs on the side and the nouns on top, so the resulting matrix is composed of all possible combinations of nouns and verbs (see Figure 13.8). Instruction should proceed through the matrix in a stepwise fashion. The teacher initially teaches the verb *touch* with the noun *ball,* followed by the verb *touch* with the noun *cup.* Then the second verb is taught with the first noun and subsequently with the third noun and so forth. A more comprehensive approach might be to teach verb A across the matrix until the response generalizes to untrained nouns and then begin verb B with the last trained noun. The procedure provides enough examples of an action so the action is not associated with a specific object. Striefel, Wetherby, and Karlan (1978) found such an approach to be successful in establishing generalized instruction following skills.

Program common stimuli. Another strategy, programming common stimuli, requires the teacher to make the training environment as similar as possible to the environments where generalized skill performance is desired. Conversely, characteristics of the training environment may be added to the generalization environment. Several strategies for programming common stimuli have already been discussed (using parents as trainers, using incidental teaching in natural environments), but a few additional studies are noted.

Halle, Marshall, and Spradlin (1979) attempted to teach severely and profoundly retarded children to ask for their tray of food at mealtime. Initially a 15-second time delay strategy was used. When the child reached the counter, the cafeteria worker held the child's tray for 15 seconds or until the child made a verbal request for the tray, whichever came first. This procedure alone was ineffective in training verbal requests. Then a delay plus a modeling procedure was used, resulting in consistent performance in all but one child. Observations at untrained meals indicated that requests for food did not generalize to those meals. However, when a part of the initial training (15-second delay only) was added to those meals, consistent generalized requests were observed.

Handleman (1979) taught four autistic boys to respond to common questions. Training occurred in a one-to-one format in a small cubicle. Although all boys learned the responses, three of them showed little or no generalization to the home environment. When training occurred in varied sites within the school (lounge, bathrooms, coat rack), however, greater generalization was observed at home.

Finally, Welch and Pear (1980) compared stimuli (picture cards, photographs, and real objects) for training object labels. Although there were no differences in the number of trials children needed to learn the specific stimuli, three of the four children in the study displayed considerably more generalization to real objects in the natural environment when they were trained with real objects.

Based on these and other findings, Spradlin and Siegel (1982) provide guidelines for maximizing the likelihood of generalization in language training. These and other guidelines

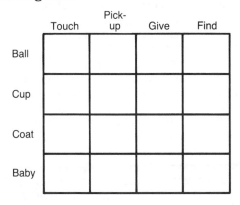

FIGURE 13.8

Sample matrix for teaching generalized verb-noun instructions

TABLE 13.7
Conditions in training and natural environment that increase the likelihood of generalization

Natural (Generalization) Environment	Training ("Artificial") Environment
Expect child to perform acquired behavior in natural environment; arrange conditions so behavior is performed.	Train useful/functional language behaviors that can be used in the natural environment.
Provide cues that "tell" the child to perform the acquired behavior in the natural environment.	Use multiple trainers, training settings, training times, training materials; vary when these various factors are used.
Reinforce communicative attempts and respond to their content.	Use and vary functional reinforcers; delay and fade reinforcement.
Assist persons in the natural environment to provide opportunities for the acquired behavior to occur and be practiced.	Tell the child to use the behavior in other settings.
	Use materials that are apt to be found in the natural environment.
Reinforce child for persistent attempts to communicate.	Be sure behavior is acquired thoroughly so the child can perform it fluently and proficiently.
Decrease reinforcement as child begins to perform desired behavior in natural environment.	Train child to keep trying rather than stopping when an error is made—train task persistence.

Sources: Marholin, D., II, & Siegel, L.J. Beyond the law of effect: Programming for the maintenance of behavior change. In D. Marholin II (Ed.), *Child Behavior Therapy,* New York: Garaner, 1978; Spradlin and Siegal (1982); Strokes and Baer (1977).

are included in Table 13.7. Generalization does not always occur, but a variety of techniques can be used to increase the probability of generalization.

SUMMARY

This chapter focused on the development of communication skills by young children with handicaps. Children must have a mode of communication and must understand and use the rules related to the symbol system of their community. Children can use language to communicate a variety of intentions, and this ability was seen as originating in cognitive (sensorimotor) and social behaviors.

Communication skills of children should be assessed through systematic observation in low structure settings if the goal of assessment is instructional program planning. The context of children's statements must be noted and considered so the observer can infer the child's meaning and communicative intent. Besides assessing children's abilities, assess the expectations of the environment. Emphasis should be on semantic and pragmatic functions; that is, how children communicate meaning and use language to meet different goals. Syntax is also important, but is viewed as less important than semantics and pragmatics.

Children with severe communication deficits should receive training on a variety of important behaviors such as labeling, requesting, and following instructions. This training can be accomplished through a variety of published curricula. The use of operant procedures such as modeling, fading, and reinforcement helps develop the critical communicative skills of children with severe deficits. Children with moderate and mild delays in communication skills should receive training to increase the rate of development, rate of talking, and ability to carry on a conversation. This can be accomplished through using published curricula, expansions, and incidental teaching.

Parents may need assistance in establishing positive affective interactions to resolve difficulties in communicating with their children. Some parents may need and want training to develop their children's specific communication skills.

Unfortunately, generalized use of communication frequently does not occur. Procedures were presented for changing both the training and natural environments to facilitate generalization.

REFERENCES

Baer, D.M., & Guess, D. Teaching productive noun suffixes to severely retarded children. *American Journal of Mental Deficiency*, 1973, *77*, 498–505.

Baer, D.M., Peterson, R., & Sherman, J.A. The development of imitation by reinforcing behavioral similarity to a model. *Journal of the Experimental Analysis of Behavior*, 1967, *10*, 405–416.

Bates, E. Pragmatics and sociolinguistics in child language. In D. Morehead and A. Morehead (Eds.), *Normal and deficient child language*. Baltimore: University Park Press, 1976.

Becker, W.C. The national evaluation of Follow Through—behavior theory based programs come out on top. *Education and Urban Society*, 1978, *10*(4), 431–458.

Bennett, C.W. Articulation training of two hearing-impaired girls. *Journal of Applied Behavior Analysis*, 1974, *7*, 439–449.

Bennett, C.W., & Ling, D. Teaching a complex verbal response to a hearing impaired girl. *Journal of Applied Behavior Analysis*, 1971, *4*, 321–328.

Blank, M., & Soloman, F. A tutorial language program to develop abstract thinking in socially disadvantaged preschool children. *Child Development*, 1968, *39*, 379–390.

Bloom, L. *One word at a time: The use of single word utterances before syntax*. The Hague: Mouton, 1973.

Bloom, L., & Lahey, M. *Language development and language disorders*. New York: Wiley, 1978.

Bricker, D.D., & Carlson, L. An intervention approach for communicatively handicapped infants and young children. In D. Bricker (Ed.), *New directions for exceptional children: Language intervention with children* (No. 2). San Francisco: Jossey-Bass, 1980.

Bricker, D.D., & Dennison, L. Training prerequisites to verbal behavior. In M.E. Snell (Ed.), *Systematic instruction of the moderately and severely handicapped*. Columbus, Ohio: Charles E. Merrill, 1978.

Bricker, D.D., Dennison, L., & Bricker, W.A. *A language intervention program for developmentally young children*. Miami Mailman Center for Child Development, University of Miami, 1976. (MCCD Monograph Series No. 1)

Bromwich, R. Focus on maternal behavior in infant intervention. *American Journal of Orthopsychiatry*, 1976, *46*, 439–446.

Bromwich, R. *Working with parents and infants: An interactional approach*. Baltimore; University Park Press, 1981.

Bruner, J.S. From communication to language—A psychological perspective. *Cognition*, 1974/75, *3*, 255–287.

Cazden, C. Environmental assistance to the child's acquisition of grammar. Unpublished doctoral dissertation, Graduate School of Education, Harvard University, 1965.

Cevette, M.J. Analysis of mother-child interchange. In G. Clezy (Ed.), *Modification of the mother-child interchange in language, speech, and hearing*. Baltimore: University Park Press, 1979.

Chapman, R.S. Exploring children's communicative intents. In J. Miller (Ed.), *Assessing language production in children*. Baltimore: University Park Press, 1981.

Clark, C. *Clark Early Language Program*. Hingham, Mass.: Teaching Resources Corporation, 1981.

Clark, H.R., & Sherman, J.A. Teaching generative use of sentence answers to three forms of questions. *Journal of Applied Behavior Analysis*, 1975, *8*, 321–330.

Clezy, G. *Modification of the mother-child interchange in language, speech, and hearing*. Baltimore: University Park Press, 1979.

Coggins, T., & Carpenter, R. A system for coding pragmatic behaviors in preverbal children. American Speech and Hearing Association Annual Convention, San Francisco, 1978.

Coggins, T., & Carpenter, R. Introduction to the area of language development. In M. Cohen & P. Gross (Eds.), *The developmental resource: Behavioral sequences for assessment and program planning*. New York: Grune & Stratton, 1979.

Cooke, S., Cooke, T., & Apolloni, T. Generalization of language training with the mentally retarded. *Journal of Special Education*, 1976, *8*, 299–304.

Crystal, D., Fletcher, P., & Garman, M. *The grammatical analysis of language disability: A procedure for assessment and remediation*. New York: Elsevier-North Holland, 1976.

Dale, P.S. *Language development: Structure and function* (2nd ed.). New York: Holt, Rinehart and Winston, 1976.

Dale, P.S. What does observing language mean? In G.P. Sackett (Ed.), *Observing behavior: Theory and applications in mental retardation*. Baltimore: University Park Press, 1978.

Darley, F.L. *Evaluation of appraisal techniques in speech and language pathology*. Reading, Mass.: Addison-Wesley, 1979.

Dore, J. Holophrases, speech acts and language universals. *Journal of Child Language*, 1975, *2*, 21–40.

Dunn, L., & Smith, J. *Peabody language development kits.* Circle Pines, Minn.: American Guidance Service, 1965.

Dunst, C.J. A cognitive-social approach for assessment of early nonverbal communication behavior. *Journal of Childhood Communication Disorders*, 1978, *2*, 110–123.

Dunst, C.J. *Infant learning: A cognitive-linguistic intervention strategy.* Hingham, Mass.: Teaching Resources Corporation, 1981.

Engelmann, S., & Osborn, J. *DISTAR Language Level III.* Chicago: Science Research Associates, 1972.

Engelmann, S., & Osborn, J. *DISTAR Language Level I* (2nd ed.). Chicago: Science Research Associates, 1976.

Engelmann, S., & Osborn, J. *DISTAR Language Level II.* (2nd ed.). Chicago: Science Research Associates, 1977.

Evans, E.D. *Contemporary influences in early childhood education* (2nd ed.). New York: Holt, Rinehart and Winston, 1975.

Fredericks, H.D., Riggs, C., Furey, T., Grove, D., Moore, W., McDonnell, J., Jordan, E., Hanson, W., Baldwin, V., & Wadlow, M. *The teaching research curriculum for moderately and severely handicapped.* Springfield, Ill.: Charles C. Thomas, 1976.

Frisch, S.A., & Schumaker, J.B. Training generalized receptive prepositions in retarded children. *Journal of Applied Behavior Analysis*, 1974, *7*, 611–621.

Garcia, E.E. The training and generalization of a conversational speech form in nonverbal retardates. *Journal of Applied Behavior Analysis*, 1974, *7*, 137–149.

Garcia, E.E., Baer, D.M., & Firestone, I. The development of generalized imitation within topographically determined boundaries. *Journal of Applied Behavior Analysis*, 1971, *4*, 101–112.

Garcia, E.E., & DeHaven, E.D. Use of operant techniques in the establishment of generalization of language: A review and analysis. *American Journal of Mental Deficiency*, 1974, *79*, 169–178.

Gray, B., & Ryan, B. *A language program for the nonlanguage child.* Champaign, Ill.: Research Press, 1973.

Guess, D. A functional analysis of receptive language and productive speech: Acquisition of the plural morpheme. *Journal of Applied Behavior Analysis*, 1969, *2*, 55–64.

Guess, D. Methods in communication instruction for severely handicapped persons. In W. Sailor, B. Wilcox, & L. Brown (Eds.), *Methods of instruction for severely handicapped students.* Baltimore: Paul H. Brookes, 1980.

Guess, D., Sailor, W., & Baer, D.M. *Functional speech and language training for the severely handicapped. Part 1: Persons and things.* Lawrence, Kans.: H & H Enterprises, 1976. (a)

Guess, D., Sailor, W., & Baer, D.M. *Functional speech and language training for the severely handicapped. Part 2: Actions with persons and things.* Lawrence, Kans.: H & H Enterprises, 1976. (b)

Guess, D., Sailor, W., & Baer, D.M. A behavioral remedial approach to language training for the severely handicapped. In E. Sontag (Ed.), *Educational programming for the severely handicapped.* Reston, Va.: Division of Mental Retardation, Council for Exceptional Children, 1977. (a)

Guess, D., Sailor, W., & Baer, D.M. *Functional speech and language training for the severely handicapped. Part 3: Possession and color.* Lawrence, Kans.: H & H Enterprises, 1977. (b)

Guess, D., Sailor, W., & Baer, D.M. Children with limited language. In R.L. Schiefelbusch (Ed.), *Language intervention strategies.* Baltimore: University Park Press, 1978. (a)

Guess, D., Sailor, W., & Baer, D.M. *Functional speech and language training for the severely handicapped. Part 4: Size, relation, and location.* Lawrence, Kans.: H & H Enterprises, 1978. (b)

Guess, D., Sailor, W., Rutherford, G., & Baer, D.M. An experimental analysis of linguistic development: The productive use of the plural morpheme. *Journal of Applied Behavior Analysis*, 1968, *1*, 297–306.

Halle, J.W., Marshall, A.M., & Spradlin, J.E. Time delay: A technique to increase language use and facilitate generalization in retarded children. *Journal of Applied Behavior Analysis*, 1979, *12*, 431–439.

Handleman, J.S. Generalization by autistic type children of verbal responses across settings. *Journal of Applied Behavior Analysis*, 1979, *12*, 273–282.

Hart, B., & Risley, T. Using preschool materials to modify the language of disadvantaged children. *Journal of Applied Behavior Analysis*, 1974, *7*, 243–256.

Hart, B., & Risley, T. Incidental teaching of language in the preschool. *Journal of Applied Behavior Analysis*, 1975, *8*, 411–420.

Hart, B., & Risley, T. In vivo language intervention: Unanticipated general effects. *Journal of Applied Behavior Analysis*, 1980, *13*, 407–432.

Hart, B., & Risley, T. *How to use incidental teaching for elaborating language.* Lawrence, Kans.: H & H Enterprises, 1982.

Hester, M., & Hendrickson, J. Training functional language: The acquisition and generalization of five-element syntactic response. *Journal of Applied Behavior Analysis*, 1977, *10*, 316.

Horstmeier, D., & MacDonald, J.D. *Ready, set, go—Talk to me.* Columbus, Ohio: Charles E. Merrill, 1978.

Howell, M.V., Schumaker, J.B., & Sherman, J.A. A comparison of parent models and expansions in two-year-old children's acquisition of color and size adjectives. *Journal of Experimental Child Psychology*, 1978, *25*, 41–57.

Hung, D. Generalization of "curiosity" questioning behavior in autistic children. *Journal of Behavior Therapy and Experimental Psychiatry*, 1977, *8*, 237–245.

Janssen, C., & Guess, D. Use of function as a consequence in training receptive labeling to severely and profoundly retarded individuals. *AAESPH Review*, 1978, *3*, 246–258.

Karnes, M.B. *Helping young children develop language skills.* Reston, Va.: Council for Exceptional Children, 1968.

Kent, L.R. *Language acquisition program for the severely retarded.* Champaign, Ill.: Research Press, 1974.

Kent, L.R., Klein, D., Falk, A., & Guenther, H. A language acquisition program for the retarded. In J.E. McLean, D.E. Yoder, & R.L. Schiefelbusch (Eds.), *Language intervention with the retarded*. Baltimore: University Park Press, 1972.

Lavatelli, C. A systematized approach to the Tucson method of language teaching. In C. Lavatelli (Ed.), *Language training in early childhood education*. Urbana: University of Illinois Press, 1971.

Lee, L.L. *Developmental Sentence Analysis*. Evanston, Ill.: Northwestern University Press, 1974.

Lovaas, O.I. *The autistic child: Language development through behavior modification*. New York: Irvington, 1977.

Lutzker, J.R., & Sherman, J.A. Producing generative sentence usage by imitation and reinforcement procedures. *Journal of Applied Behavior Analysis*, 1974, 7, 447–460.

MacDonald, J.D., & Horstmeier, D.S. *Environmental language intervention program*. Columbus, Ohio: Charles E. Merrill, 1978.

Martin, J.A. Generalizing the use of descriptive adjectives through modeling. *Journal of Applied Behavior Analysis*, 1975, 8, 203–210.

McLean, J.E., & Snyder-McLean, L.K. *A transactional approach to early language training*. Columbus, Ohio: Charles E. Merrill, 1978.

Miller, J.F. *Assessing language production in children*. Baltimore: University Park Press, 1981.

Miller, J.F., & Yoder, D.E. An ontogenetic language teaching strategy for retarded children. In R.L. Schiefelbusch & L.L. Lloyd (Eds.), *Language perspectives—Acquisition, retardation, and intervention*. Baltimore: University Park Press, 1974.

Neisworth, J.T., Willoughby-Herb, S.J., Bagnato, S.J., Cartwright, C.A., & Laub, K.W. *Individualized education for preschool exceptional children*. Germantown, Md.: Aspen Systems Corporation, 1980.

Nelson, K.E. Facilitating children's syntax acquisition. *Developmental Psychology*, 1977, 13, 101–107.

Nelson, K.E., Carskadden, G., & Bonvillian, S. Syntax acquisition: Impact of experimental variation in adult verbal interaction with the child. *Child Development*, 1973, 44, 497–504.

Nichols, N. Communication development, assessment, and intervention. In B.L. Darby & M. May (Eds.), *Infant assessment: Issues and applications*. Seattle: WESTAR, 1979.

Osborn, J., & Becker, W.C. Direct instruction language. In D. Bricker (Ed.), *New Directions for Exceptional Children: Language Intervention with Children* (No. 2). San Francisco: Jossey-Bass, 1980.

Rees, N.S. Pragmatics of language: Applications to normal and disordered language development. In R.L. Schiefelbusch (Ed.), *Bases of language intervention*. Baltimore: University Park Press, 1978.

Saunders, R.R., & Sailor, W. A comparison of three strategies of reinforcement on two-choice learning problems with severely retarded children. *AAESPH Review*, 1979, 4, 323–333.

Schiefelbusch, R.L., & Bricker, D. *Early language: Acquisition and intervention*. Baltimore: University Park Press, 1981.

Schumaker, J. *Mother's expansions: Their characteristics and effects on child language*. Unpub-

lished doctoral dissertation, University of Kansas, 1976.

Schumaker, J.B., & Sherman, J.A. Training generative verb usage by imitation and reinforcement procedures. *Journal of Applied Behavior Analysis*, 1970, 3, 273–287.

Schumaker, J.B., & Sherman, J.A. Parents as intervention agents from birth onward. In R.L. Schiefelbusch (Ed.), *Language intervention strategies*. Baltimore: University Park Press, 1978.

Seitz, S., & Hoekenga, R. Modeling as a training tool for retarded children and their parents. *Mental Retardation*, 1974, 12, 28–31.

Seitz, S., & Marcus, S. Mother-child interactions: A foundation for language development. *Exceptional Children*, 1976, 42, 445–449.

Slobin, D.T. Imitation and grammatical development in children. In N.S. Endler, L.R. Boulton, & H. Osser (Eds.), *Contemporary issues in developmental psychology*. New York: Holt, Rinehart and Winston, 1968.

Smeets, P., & Striefel, S. Acquisition of sign reading by transfer of stimulus control in a retarded deaf girl. *Journal of Mental Deficiency Research*, 1976, 20, 197–204.

Snow, C.E., & Ferguson, C.A. *Talking to children: Language input and acquisition*. New York: Cambridge University Press, 1977.

Spradlin, J.E., & Siegel, G.M. Language training in natural and clinical environments. *Journal of Speech and Hearing Disorders*, 1982, 47, 2–6.

Stokes, T.F., & Baer, D.M. An implicit technology of generalization. *Journal of Applied Behavior Analysis*, 1977, 10, 349–367.

Stokes, T.F., Baer, D.M., & Jackson, R.L. Programming the generalization of a greeting response in four retarded children. *Journal of Applied Behavior Analysis*, 1974, 7, 599–610.

Stremel, K., & Waryas, C. A behavioral-psycholinguistic approach to language training. In L. McReynolds (Ed.), *Developing systematic procedures for training children's language*. American Speech and Hearing Association Monographs, 1974 (No. 18).

Striefel, S., Bryan, K.S., & Aikins, D.A. Transfer of stimulus control from motor to verbal stimuli. *Journal of Applied Behavior Analysis*, 1974, 7, 123–135.

Striefel, S., & Wetherby, B. Instruction-following behavior of a retarded child and its controlling stimuli. *Journal of Applied Behavior Analysis*, 1973, 6, 663–670.

Striefel, S., Wetherby, B., & Karlan, G.R. Developing generalized instruction-following behavior in the severely retarded. In C.E. Meyers (Ed.), *Quality of life in severely and profoundly mentally retarded people: Research foundation for improvement*. Washington, D.C.: Monographs of the American Association on Mental Deficiency, 1978 (No. 3).

Tawney, J.W., Knapp, D.S., O'Reilly, C.D., & Pratt, S.S. *Programmed environments curriculum*. Columbus, Ohio: Charles E. Merrill, 1979.

Tynack, D., & Gottsleben, R. *Language sampling, analysis, and training*. Palo Alto, Calif.: Consulting Psychologists Press, 1974.

Warren, S.F., & Rogers-Warren, A. Current perspectives in language remediation. *Education and Treatment of Children*, 1980, *3*(2), 133–152.

Warren, S.F., Rogers-Warren, A., Baer, D.M., & Guess, D. Assessment and facilitation of language generalization. In W. Sailor, B. Wilcox, & L. Brown (Eds.), *Methods of instruction of severely handicapped students*. Baltimore: Paul H. Brookes, 1980.

Waryas, C.L., & Stremel-Campbell, K. Grammatical training for the language delayed child: A new perspective. In R.L. Schiefelbusch (Ed.), *Language intervention strategies*. Baltimore: University Park Press, 1978.

Wehman, P., Abramson, M., & Norman, C. Transfer of training in behavior modification programs: An evaluative review. *Journal of Special Education*, 1977, *11*, 217–231.

Welch, S.T., & Pear, T.T. Generalization of naming responses to objects in the natural environment as a function of training stimulus modality with retarded children. *Journal of Applied Behavior Analysis*, 1980, *13*, 629–643.

Wetherby, B., & Striefel, S. Application of miniature linguistic system of matrix-training procedures. In R.L. Schiefelbusch (Ed.), *Language intervention strategies*. Baltimore: University Park Press, 1978.

Wiig, E.H., & Semel, E.M. *Language disabilities in children and adolescents*. Columbus, Ohio: Charles E. Merrill, 1980.

Wolery, M.R. *Parents as teachers of their handicapped children: An annotated bibliography*. Seattle: WESTAR, 1979.

ommunication *mode* refers to "the form in which the content of a message is expressed" (Sailor, Guess, Goetz, Schuler, Utley, & Baldwin, 1980, p. 72). Most of us use speech to express messages (output mode) and hearing to receive messages (input mode). Although we certainly use other modes such as body language, facial expressions, and physical touching, the speech mode is the primary target of most language intervention programs.

For many handicapped children, speech is difficult, if not impossible, to develop because of sensory and motor impairments and severe retardation. As technologies supporting alternative modes of communication develop, professionals increasingly realize the importance of applying the technologies with young children.

This chapter will examine the role of the preschool special educator in developing a communication mode. The first section addresses considerations in facilitating speech in nonspeaking children, those with low rates of speech, and those with articulation problems. The second section addresses considerations in selecting and teaching alternative communication modes to children for whom speech is a low probability behavior.

Selection of a communication mode and strategies for teaching its use should be an interdisciplinary endeavor. Yoder (1980) suggests that while the augmentative communication team should be led by a speech and language specialist, other important team members include the child's parents, the teacher, and if there are motor or physical problems, the physical therapist. If a complicated electronic communication system is needed, an augmentative communication specialist should also consult with the team.

Each team member is vitally important. Communication is a daily activity that touches the lives of each person and critically affects relationships with others. The importance of the team rests not only on its technical expertise but also on the ability of important persons in the child's life to identify functional modes for daily expression of needs, communicate ideas, and understand the communicative intent of others.

14

Developing the Mode of Communication

TEACHING ORAL COMMUNICATION

Oral communication is the most frequently used form of exchanging information. It is understood by nearly everyone and is an efficient mode of communication. Most children learn to talk through natural processes of maturation and experience. Many retarded children, however, may not learn to speak or may do so at a delayed rate. Delayed onset of speech is one of the most frequently observed indicators of developmental problems, particularly mental retardation.

Since speech is such an important and universally accepted mode of communication, teachers of young handicapped children should make every effort to teach it. The normal course of speech development, strategies for encouraging speech in handicapped youngsters, and the teacher's role in working with speech disorders will be discussed.

Normal Development of Speech

Phonology refers to the speech sounds a child makes. Speech consists of sequences of *phonemes* (sound units) joined together in various ways. Although more than 80 phonemes have been described and used in various languages, most languages only use a few dozen. American speakers typically use between 40 and 45 speech sounds (Brown, 1965). Although teachers are rarely involved in articulation therapy, a basic knowledge of phonological development is necessary so the teacher can understand reports from clinicians dealing with articulation assessment and training. Knowledge of developmental sequences of phonology should assist the teacher in selecting the initial training vocabulary to maximize ease of pronunication and in identifying children who need to be screened for articulation disorders.

Learning to speak involves receptive as well as expressive communication skills. For example, learning to speak and use speech appropriately requires at least the ability to differentiate speech from nonspeech sounds, to identify differing tones of voice, and to differentiate one speech sound from another. These abilities are evidenced soon after birth by typical infants.

In nonhandicapped children the development of speech sounds follows a relatively predictable pattern. Ferguson (1978) describes stages in the early development of speech sounds. By the second month of life infants usually exhibit some form of cooing. The second stage consists of babbling with an observed diversity in cooing and other sounds. The child repeats sounds, apparently for his or her own enjoyment, in a form of vocal play. Between 10 and 14 months the child displays use of what Ferguson (1978) refers to as "early vocables"—sounds that function communicatively like first words but which have no apparent similarity to adult words. Finally, during the latter part of this 10–14-month period the child typically utters the first adult-modeled word. Typically this word is of a consonant-vowel form or perhaps a repeated consonant-vowel form such as "ma-ma" or "daw-daw."

After this point children typically demonstrate a rapid rate of acquisition of a variety of speech sounds. All basic vowel sounds are exhibited between 12 and 24 months of age. Consonant sounds typically begin with easier sounds and progress to more difficult ones including blends. Although the precise sequence of sounds displayed varies with children, sound acquisition follows a general order. For example, Bricker (1967) grouped consonant sounds according to difficulty of expression. In Level I, the sounds first observed in children include *b, w, m, t,* and *d.* Level 2, slightly more difficult than Level 1, includes *h, n, k,* and *p.* Level 3 includes *g, s, f,* and *d.* Level 4 includes *sh, r, l, ch,* and *z.* The most difficult level includes two variations of *th* (e.g., *th*at and *th*in), *v, y,* and *ng.*

Teaching Speech to Nonspeaking Children

Speech is difficult to teach to nonspeaking children because, unlike most self-help or motor skills, the child cannot be physically assisted in making sounds and must generate the initial sound. Although the lips can be manipulated to form some sound patterns, the teacher must rely on other techniques. Teaching basic imitation and pairing speech with another mode are two approaches.

Teaching basic imitation The role of imitation and models in the normal development of language is controversial. Dale (1978) suggests that research and observation data clearly indicate that most children do not initially acquire language by imitation. Other theorists (Whitehurst, 1977) believe imitation is more important. However, most theorists agree that models and imitation are important teaching strategies for children who do not develop language in the normal fashion. Curricula described in Chapter 13 require imitation as a prerequisite or include it as one of the first steps in precommunication training. Imitation is also discussed in Chapter 4.

If the child vocalizes but is not imitative, two procedures can be followed to establish verbal imitation. First, *imitate the child's vocalizations.* Initially, the teacher selects a time when the child vocalizes, then imitates the child's sounds. The purpose of this step is to get the child to make a vocalization in response to the adult's vocalization. After the child consistently repeats a sound the teacher imitated, the teacher should imitate sounds the child previously produced when the child is quiet. When the child consistently imitates these sounds, the teacher models sounds slightly different from those the child previously produced. Finally, the teacher introduces new sounds.

If these steps are not successful, the teacher should use another procedure, *response shaping.* Initially a baseline is collected on the child's rate of vocalizations. Then the teacher reinforces each vocalization until vocalizations occur about six times per minute. Reinforcement can be contrived (candy, nuts, or toys) but, as discussed in Chapter 4, Bricker and Dennison (1978) recommend that the teacher imitate the child whenever spontaneous vocalizations occur. The teacher vocalizes and then reinforces the child's first imitative vocalization. Gradually the teacher reinforces vocalizations that become more immediate to and sound more like the model (Lovaas, 1977). Finally, only child verbalizations that occur immediately after and are identical to the teacher's would be reinforced.

If these procedures do not result in verbal imitation, the teacher should use procedures for teaching imitation to children who are not

vocal. With nonverbal children *verbal imitation is established by initially establishing motor imitation* (Baer, Peterson, & Sherman, 1967; Bricker & Bricker, 1970; Lovaas, 1977; Sloane, Johnston, & Harris, 1968). As discussed in Chapter 4, Baer et al. (1967) suggest that this procedure establishes a stimulus class of behavioral similarity. "Do this" paired with a behavior becomes a discriminative stimulus for matching the teacher's behavior. If sufficient motor examples are taught, the child should develop a generalized response class in which he or she imitates verbal and other behaviors when the teacher says, "Do this" and then performs a behavior. The first step in teaching gross motor imitation is to establish attending skills such as looking at the teacher and sitting (see Chapter 7). The teacher should teach gross motor, then fine motor imitation, imitation of mouth movements and finally of speech sounds. Initially, familiar gross motor behaviors that the child can see himself perform should be selected for training. Familiar, visible actions that involve objects may be the easiest to imitate (cf. Abravanel, Levan-Goldschmidt, & Stevenson, 1976). As the child begins to imitate such behaviors, the focus of training should shift to unfamiliar, less visible, and more complicated gross motor behaviors. Fine motor skills such as manipulation of objects and pointing to various places on the face should then be trained. Imitation of movements such as opening the mouth, moving the lips, and placing the tongue on the alveolar ridge should be trained after fine motor imitation. Physical prompts can easily be used and faded with gross and fine motor behaviors (see Chapter 3). Likewise, some of the mouth movements can be prompted. If these procedures are not effective in establishing motor imitation, then procedures described by Baer (1978) should be used. Baer (1978) suggests starting by handing an edible reinforcer to the child, and then shaping the child's reaching response by gradually increasing the complexity required before reinforcement is given.

These procedures are used with the assumption that imitation of gross and fine motor movements will generalize to speech sounds; however, such generalization does not always occur. Garcia, Baer, and Firestone

(1971) found that with severely retarded children motor imitation generalized to other untrained motor responses of similar topography, but not to untrained vocal responses. Generalization to untrained vocal responses did not occur until establishment of some vocal imitation. If generalization does not occur, the teacher could pair a vocalization with a gross motor behavior the child already imitates. For example, the teacher could raise his or her hand (assuming that the child has already demonstrated successful imitation of hand-raising) and at the same time say, "Ahhh." The child would be reinforced only if hand-raising is paired with some attempt at vocalization. In addition, the shaping strategy described earlier for increasing the rate of children's vocalizations could be used in conjunction with this procedure. Obviously many young children who need imitation training are not going to make perfect responses,

particularly in the early phases. Shape the quality of responding by initially reinforcing any attempt at imitation and then gradually require more precise replications of modeled behavior. McLean and Snyder-McLean (1978) suggest several strategies for enhancing the appropriateness of the models. Exaggeration of normal stress and intonation in speech helps children identify the important components of an utterance. Also, speech directed toward language-learning children should be reduced in length and complexity. Although utterances should not be simplistic, they should be understandable.

A summary of guidelines for facilitating vocal imitation in nonspeaking children is provided in Table 14.1. Remember that each child is different and will probably require a uniquely designed intervention program.

Pairing speech with another mode   A second strategy for encouraging speech in non-

TABLE 14.1
Guidelines for teaching nonspeaking children to imitate speech sounds

Guidelines for children who vocalize	Guidelines for children who do not vocalize
1. Imitate the child's vocalizations.	1. Teach imitation of familiar, visible gross motor movements with objects.[a]
2. Use response shaping to increase the rate of child vocalizations.	2. Teach imitation of familiar, visible gross motor movements without objects.
3. Use response shaping to increase the rate of child vocalizations immediately following adult vocalizations.	3. Teach unfamiliar and invisible gross motor movements with objects.
4. Use response shaping to gradually require closer approximations of the requested sound.	4. Teach unfamiliar and invisible gross motor movements without objects.
5. If the above procedures are unsuccessful, then use guidelines for children who do not vocalize.	5. Teach fine motor movements with objects.
	6. Teach fine motor movements without objects.
	7. Teach fine motor movements in the mouth area.
	8. Pair speech sounds with gross and fine motor movements.
	9. Initially reinforce any attempts at vocal imitation.
	10. Use response shaping to gradually require closer approximations of requested sound.
	11. Initially reinforce with primary reinforcers if necessary. However, a vocal response should be made to any attempts by the child to vocalize. The response should initially be an imitation of the child's vocalization.

[a]Physical prompts as described in Chapter 3 should be used and faded to teach gross and fine motor imitation.

speaking children is to pair it with another mode of communication. A child should acquire a symbol system early because of the importance of symbols to cognitive, social, and communicative development. Since speech is so difficult to manipulate physically, teach the high-risk child another mode that is more easily learned (manual signing), simultaneously pairing speech with the other system. By pairing speech with the child's preferred mode of input, the probability that speech itself becomes understood and perhaps used is increased (Bricker, 1972; Grinnel, Detamore, & Lippke, 1976; Kahn, 1977; Kohl, Karlan, & Heal, 1979; Stremel-Campbell, Cantrell, & Halle, 1977). Techniques for teaching alternative communication modes are described later in this chapter.

Speech Disorders

Some children speak but demonstrate speech disorders. Van Riper (1972) suggests that "speech is defective when it deviates so far from the speech of other children that it calls attention to itself, interferes with communication, or causes its possessor to be maladjusted" (p. 29). Incorrect expressions of speech are common in young children and are a natural part of the process of learning to talk. Normal disfluency or mispronunciations should be ignored; the teacher can simply repeat the child's statement or question, modeling the appropriate expression.

More serious speech disorders, however, are more commonly observed in handicapped children. These include articulation and voice disorders, and disorders of rate, rhythm, and timing. *Articulation disorders* are associated with speech sound production and include sound distortion, omission, and substitution and the addition of extra sounds to words. A *voice disorder* is a chronic condition that involves the quality, pitch, or loudness of the child's voice. For example, the child's voice may be too loud or soft, may be hoarse, too deep or high, or may be nasal. Some common causes of voice disorders include hearing impairments and cleft palate. Disorders of *rate, rhythm, and timing* include stuttering, stammering, blocking, or talking unusually fast or slow. The causes of these disorders are unknown. Cerebral palsy can affect all areas of speech disorders.

The early childhood special educator can deal with children who have speech disorders by screening and referral, cooperative intervention, and working with peers.

Screening and referral Often a thorough medical, audiological, or speech and hearing examination identifies the cause and aids in developing an intervention for speech disorders. For example, hearing impairment is a common secondary handicapping condition in mentally retarded children, particularly children with Down syndrome. The teacher should observe the child, noting behavioral characteristics associated with a speech disorder. Parents should be consulted, and if a potential problem exists, the child should be referred for further examination by a specialist.

Cooperative intervention Speech disorders can be complex and may require cooperative planning and intervention efforts of a variety of professionals. For example, the child with a hearing impairment will need an audiologist to design an appropriate hearing aid, a communication disorder specialist to assist in planning and implementing specific treatment, and a preschool teacher to insure generalization of hearing aid use and therapy to the preschool. The teacher can facilitate cooperation among professionals by participating fully on the intervention team. The teacher can also serve as an advocate, ally, and interpreter for parents.

Working with peers Speech disorders are relatively obvious and children can easily become the targets of peer attention, criticism, ridicule, or teasing. The teacher must help the child achieve understanding and acceptance by peers by pointing out positive aspects of the handicapped child, reinforcing the child for attempts at communication, and reinforcing peers for positive social interactions.

ALTERNATIVE COMMUNICATION MODES

Unfortunately, some children will never learn to speak, or will do so at such a slow rate that speech is not functional. Therefore, some form of augmentative communication system or device is necessary. Characteristics of children, options, strategies, and guidelines for teaching augmentative communication are reviewed in this section.

Who Needs Augmentative Communication?

Shane (1981) reports that augmentative communication techniques have been particularly useful with children with cerebral palsy, children with mental retardation (particularly severe cases), and autistic children. However, because many of these children can learn to speak, Shane (1981) suggests considering specific factors before determining whether the child needs an augmentative communication system. Initially, children should be carefully evaluated. The persistence of obligatory oral reflexes (rooting, biting, or an overactive gag reflex) beyond 9–12 months of age is strongly related to later speech failure as this indicates a lack of normal control over the oral musculature system. Also, children who exhibit frequent cessation or blocking of the voice when attempting to vocalize are at risk for speech failure. This laryngeal blocking is particularly common in children with cerebral palsy. In addition, children with significant delays in or problems associated with basic eating skills (sucking, swallowing, chewing) have a high likelihood of speech failure. Shane suggests that such eating problems indicate a significant neuromotor problem. The child's age and corresponding physical development is another factor. Many youngsters will not have the motor skills required to use a particular kind of augmentative system such as manual signing or a communication board. The child's level of cognitive development should be considered. For example, a child who has not demonstrated acquisition or use of abstract representational symbols would be an inappropriate candidate for Non-SLIP or Bliss symbols. In addition, verbal/vocal imitation appears to be a strong predictor of successful speech use. If, after trying strategies similar to those described earlier, the child still cannot imitate any vocalizations, consider an augmentative communication system. Response to previous intervention should also be evaluated to determine the potential for success in learning oral communication skills. Finally, the environment should be evaluated when considering an augmentative communication system. Consult parents and other significant persons to determine their willingness to use a particular system. These considerations should be useful in identifying children who need an augmentative communication system.

Once it has been decided that a given child needs an alternate mode of communication, a specific strategy must be selected. A helpful decision-making model has been proposed by Sailor, Guess, Goetz, Schuler, Utley, and Baldwin (1980) (see Figure 14.1). In using this chart the teacher and the communication team should begin at the top and answer the first four questions. If the answer to each of these questions is "yes," then speech should be considered. If "no," then the various options described on the chart should be evaluated and a decision made as to the best strategy for meeting the individual child's needs. For young children, the two primary options are manual communication or a direct selection communication board. Considerations associated with the selection of each of these techniques are discussed in the following sections of this chapter.

Manual Signing

Manual signing, although initially designed for deaf persons, has recently also been used as a communication aid for severely retarded and autistic children. This section will briefly review research on the rationale and effects of manual signing and techniques for teaching.

Definition of manual signing   *Manual signing* is the representation of communicative content through movement and positioning of hands. General use of the term *sign language* is confusing because several different systems are used in this country. American Sign Language is the system typically used by deaf adults, and is a language in its own right, differing in vocabulary, syntax, and morphology from spoken English (Hollis & Carrier, 1978). Hollis and Carrier suggest that the unique characteristics of American Sign Language make it difficult to teach the handicapped child because it does not have a one-to-one relationship to English. Consequently many educators have turned to the second major sign system, Signing Exact English (Gustasum, Pfetzig, & Zawolkow, 1972), which does have a direct correspondence between the signs and the spoken words. Another alternative is to use signs from American Indian Sign Language. These signs appear to be

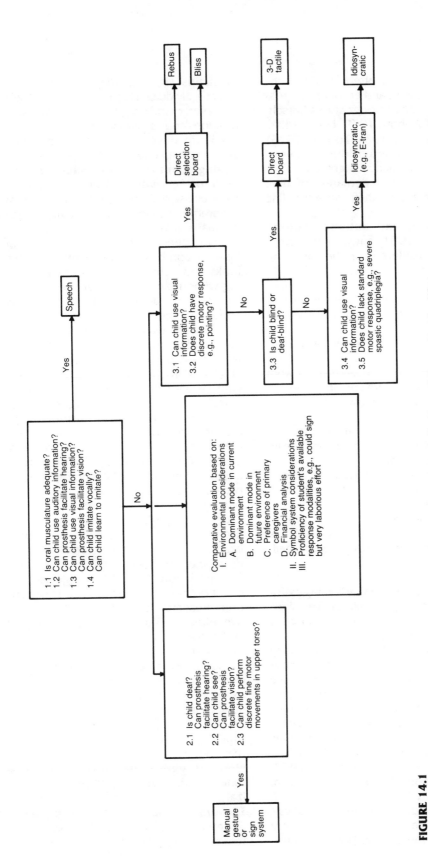

FIGURE 14.1

Steps in determining the best output mode. *Note:* From "Language and Severely Handicapped Persons: Deciding What to Teach to Whom" by W. Sailor, D. Guess, L. Goetz, A. Schuler, B. Utley, and M. Baldwin. In W. Sailor, B. Wilcox, and L. Brown (Eds.), *Methods of Instruction for Severely Handicapped Students.* Baltimore: Paul H. Brookes, 1980. Reprinted by permission from W. Sailor, D. Guess, L. Goetz, A. Schuler, B. Utley, and M. Baldwin.

easier to learn and use, often look like the concept they represent, and emphasize gross motor rather than fine motor gestures (Kirschner, Algozzine, & Abbott, 1979; Lombardino, Willems, & MacDonald, 1981; Topper, 1975). Many severely handicapped children may need individually designed manual signs that obviously relate to functional demands of their environments and match their individual fine motor skills.

Use with retarded and autistic children Lombardino et al. (1981) suggest that signing should be considered for the following groups of children:

(a) individuals who have remained at the single or two-word expressive level for an extended period of time;

(b) individuals using vocal language with long-established unintelligible speech;

(c) individuals having difficulty understanding word reference association through oral language training (e.g., learning that the word "car" stands for the object "car");

(d) individuals who have long communicated effectively through gestures and demonstrate no inclination to learn speech;

(e) individuals who are slowly acquiring a vocal language system but are in need of an immediate interim system of communication; and

(f) individuals restricted from adequate speech because of brain dysfunction, oral musculature problems, laryngeal limitations, or sensory deficits (p. 456).

Manual signing has several advantages for the teacher of handicapped children. The signs are visible and the child can see how they are formed and how well he himself forms the sign. Also, many signs are iconic; that is, they look like the concepts they represent. Unlike oral language training, the teacher can use physical prompts or full manipulation to actually form the sign for a child. Numerous studies demonstrate that nonverbal handicapped children can learn and use manual signing as a basic communication system (Benaroya, Wesley, Ogilvie, Klein, & Meaney, 1977; Bonvillian & Nelson, 1976; Salvin, Routh, Foster, & Lovejoy, 1977).

Disadvantages include the need for physical dexterity and the fact that only a very limited portion of the general population understands signs, limiting communication to select individuals. Despite these disadvantages, however, manual signs can provide a communication and a symbol system for children unable to develop oral communication skills at a reasonable rate.

Pairing manual signing with speech The term *total communication* refers to the simultaneous use of manual signs and spoken words in communication training. Pairing speech with manual signing should increase the probability that speech will be understood and used. Speech combined with manual signing also looks and sounds more "normal" than signing without speech. Use of speech lets other children and adults in the room know the content of the message.

Research relating to the notion that total communication should increase the probability of speech use is not yet definitive. Kohl et al. (1979) found that although pairing signs with verbal signals was more effective than verbal signals alone in teaching severely handicapped children to follow instructions, generalization to expressive speech occurred with only two of the four children in the study. Stremel-Campbell et al. (1977) reported that, after training in a total communication approach, several nonverbal children began pairing word approximations with signs. Creekmore (1982), however, reviewed the use of signs alone and signs plus speech in language training of nonverbal autistic children and concluded that no clear pattern emerged. Jones (1980) suggests that the question is a "non-issue" with retarded children. Research has not suggested any negative effects of pairing speech with signing, and total communication has several potential benefits.

The decision to use total communication depends upon certain characteristics. For example, stimulus overselectivity, often observed in autistic children, means that the child can only "tune in" to one sensory modality. Presenting a multisensory message may be more confusing than helpful. Carr (1979) suggests that many autistic children tune in to the sign only; subsequently generalization to speech is rarely observed.

Techniques used in teaching manual signs Stremel-Campbell et al. (1977) describe a systematic strategy for training signs using a time-delay procedure. The program follows the following sequence:

1 The desired sign is modeled and then the teacher immediately shapes the child's hand to form the correct response. The child is then reinforced for a correct response (not resisting the hand shaping).
2 Once the child reaches a level of 90% correct, the teacher moves to a 1-second time delay procedure. The model is presented and the teacher waits 1 second before hand shaping the sign.
3 Time delays are increased by 1-second intervals each time the child reaches 90% correct over two 10-trial training blocks.
4 Once a 5-second interval is reached, the child is no longer reinforced for prompted responses.

Stremel-Campbell et al. report that the majority of students began imitating at least one sign in the 2-second interval and imitated all signs at a 90% level at or before the 4-second delay.

Carr, Binkoff, Kologinsky, and Eddy (1978) describe a slightly different procedure for teaching autistic children. In Step 1 the teacher presented the object and stated the label for the object. If the child failed to produce the sign, the teacher repeated the stimulus and then immediately hand-shaped the response for the child. In Step 2 the prompt was gradually faded until the child was able to independently make the sign. A new sign was taught using the same procedures in Step 3. Also, trials involving previously mastered signs were interchanged for practice and discrimination. The steps were effective in teaching signs to all children in the study.

Communication Aids

Manual signing is an appropriate augmentative communication strategy for children with adequate fine motor skills to form the various signs and the visual skills to understand others' signs. Children with cerebral palsy or other motor impairments may not be able to form enough signs to make manual signing a functional communication mode. Also, Shane (1981) reports that parents and professionals increasingly request other systems even for children who are effective manual communicators because of the limited number of nonhandicapped persons who know sign language. A number of communication aids and prostheses are used instead.

What is a communication aid? A *communication aid* is an object used to display pictures, symbols, or words. It is made up of symbols used to represent communicative intent and a technique for selecting the desired symbol. Often such devices are referred to as *communication boards.* The board has a set of symbols; the child selects those symbols that represent the content of a communicative attempt.

Symbol systems used in communication boards In its simplest form a communication board will consist of several pictures denoting common activities, routines, or objects at home or at school. For example, it may have a picture of a toilet, a glass of juice, some toys, the television, and other frequently used items. Other boards may have written words or letters so the child can actually spell out a message.

Carrier and Peak (1975) have designed the Non-Speech Language Initiation Program (Non-SLIP) as an alternative symbol system for severely retarded children not likely to learn speech. Non-SLIP utilizes word symbols printed on plastic chips, and is based on Premack's (1970) efforts to teach communication skills to chimpanzees.

The authors suggest that this system permits the child to express a concept without having to produce (speak, write, or sign) the symbol. Further, manipulation or placement of the symbols requires only gross motor movments of the hands and fingers. Non-SLIP has been criticized because only persons with special training can interpret its messages. Guess (1980) suggests that the program requires too many prerequisite skills (discriminating symbols on the basis of shape, color, and stripes and learning which symbols stand for what concepts) and that the teacher may spend more time teaching the prerequisites than on actual communication skills. McLean and Snyder-McLean (1978) suggest that the structural grammar approach taken by Non-SLIP is inappropriate given what is now known about language development, and conclude that Non-SLIP is "a syntax-teaching program of considerable elegance but limited scope currently directed toward a population for whom its value is greatly in doubt" (p. 226).

Bliss symbols were originally devised by Charles Bliss (1965) in an effort to develop an international symbol system. McNaughton and Kates (1974) first suggested the use of Bliss symbols with handicapped persons. Bliss symbols represent concepts of ideas; some look like the object they are designed to represent.

McNaughton (1975) suggests that Bliss symbols can be easily learned. Although Harris-Vanderheiden (1975) reports the successful application of Bliss symbols in training handicapped children, little research has been conducted on the use of the system with young children. Chapman and Miller (1980) suggest that Bliss symbols require cognitive skills at the late preoperational or early concrete operations stage, thus implying that most preschool handicapped children would not be good candidates.

How children select symbols   Vanderheiden and Grilley (1975) state children select symbols by scanning and direct selection. The mode used will depend primarily on the child's motor skills. *Scanning* requires the child to respond to sequential selections presented by an electronic display. For example, some boards have a light under each letter of the alphabet or under each word or picture on the board. The child activates the scanner and the lights turn on and then off under each symbol. When the light reaches the desired symbol, the child activates a stop signal. At this point the adult can read the symbol and the child can move on to the next symbol or, if a sophisticated electronic system is available, a printer can automatically print the symbol, providing a permanent copy of the communication. The scanning technique helps children with severe motor impairments because an activation switch can be designed for almost any part of the body with motor control (e.g., toe, tongue). However, this procedure is expensive and requires considerable cognitive skills. Kucherawy and Kucherawy (1978) describe a relatively inexpensive and simple electrical system and demonstrate its application with a nonverbal, profoundly retarded spastic quadriplegic child. For detailed

reviews of electronic communication systems, see Schiefelbusch (1980), Musselwhite and St. Louis (1982), Vanderheiden and Grilley (1975), and Vanderheiden (1978).

The more common selection procedure for very young children is *direct selection*, in which the child directly indicates the desired symbol. The child usually just points with the hand or finger. Some children may not have the motor coordination to accomplish this, and may have to resort to using a head pointer, pointing with toes, or staring at the desired quadrant of the communication board. Zucker, D'Alonzo, McMullen, and Williams (1980), for example, demonstrated that eye-pointing behavior could be taught to a nonambulatory profoundly mentally retarded child using contingent vibratory stimulation as a reinforcer. Although direct selection is probably easier to teach than scanning and is more appropriate for young children, it does not provide permanent results. The adult must be present to immediately interpret and recall selected symbols.

Selecting and using communication aids   Teaching a child to use a communication aid such as a communication board follows the basic pattern of any good instructional program. The target behaviors should be clearly specified. For example, identify the specific symbols, pictures, or other referents the child is to use and specify the behavior (pointing, slapping, looking) by which the child is to select the symbol. Then the behavior should be broken down (task analyzed) into a meaningful teaching sequence. The first skill in the sequence should be taught and its functional utility immediately made clear. For example, the child could be taught through modeling to point to a picture of food or juice and immediately be presented with food or juice. Likewise the child could be taught to point to a picture of a favorite toy and immediately be allowed to play with that toy. The functional consequences of the communication aid are critical to its subsequent use. Finally, progress throughout the sequence of instructional steps should be monitored frequently to determine whether or not intervention is effective.

In designing and teaching use of communication aids the teacher should remember the following:

1 The child must have ready access to the system for it to become a meaningful communication tool. If the communication board is only used during language training, the probability of generalization becomes very small. If the board itself is not readily available, the child should always have a signal (light or buzzer) to indicate a desire to use the board.
2 The symbol system used on the board should be appropriate to the child's level of cognitive development. Pictures will be appropriate for most preschoolers.
3 The symbols on the board should represent ideas or wishes the child frequently wants or needs to express.
4 The child should be positioned to facilitate optimal use of the board.
5 The family and other significant persons in the child's environment should find the aid or system acceptable.

SUMMARY

This chapter has provided a brief overview of strategies for identifying and training a specific mode for communication. Although the decision as to type of mode should be made by the intervention team, the teacher is responsible for daily implementation. Teachers of young exceptional children should be aware of the various options for communication modes, the advantages and disadvantages of each, and techniques for ensuring their functional use.

REFERENCES

Abravanel, E., Levan-Goldschmidt, E., & Stevenson, M.B. Action imitation: The early phase of infancy. *Child Development*, 1976, *47*, 1032–1044.

Baer, D.M. The behavioral analysis of trouble. In K.E. Allen, V.A. Holm, & R.L. Schiefelbusch (Eds.), *Early intervention—A team approach*. Baltimore: University Park Press, 1978.

Baer, D.M., Peterson, R.F., & Sherman, J.A. The development of imitation by reinforcing behavioral similarity to a model. *Journal of the Experimental Analysis of Behavior*, 1967, *10*, 405–416.

Benaroya, S., Wesley, S., Ogilvie, H., Klein, L.S., & Meaney, M. Sign language and multisensory input training of children with communication and related developmental disorders. *Journal of Autism and Childhood Schizophrenia*, 1977, *7*, 23–31.

Bliss, C.K. *Semantography-Bliss symbols*. Sydney, Australia: Semantography Publications, 1965.

Bonvillian, J.D., & Nelson, K.E. Sign language acquisition in a mute autistic boy. *Journal of Speech and Hearing Disorders*, 1976, *41*, 339–347.

Bricker, D.D. Imitative sign training as a facilitator of word-object association with low functioning children. *American Journal of Mental Deficiency*, 1972, *76*, 509–516.

Bricker, D.D., & Dennison, L. Training prerequisites to verbal behavior. In M. E. Snell (Ed.), *Systematic instruction of the moderately and severely handicapped*. Columbus, Ohio: Charles E. Merrill, 1978.

Bricker, W.A. Errors in the echoic behavior of preschool children. *Journal of Speech and Hearing Research*, 1967, *10*, 67–76.

Bricker, W.A., & Bricker, D.D. A program of language training for the severely language handicapped child. *Exceptional Children*, 1970, *37*, 101–111.

Brown, R.W. *Social psychology*. New York: Free Press, 1965.

Carr, E.G. Teaching autistic children to use sign language: The research issue. *Journal of Autism and Developmental Disorders*, 1979, *9*, 345–359.

Carr, E.G., Binkoff, J.A., Kologinsky, E., & Eddy, M. Acquisition of sign language by autistic children. I: Expressive labelling. *Journal of Applied Behavior Analysis*, 1978, *11*, 489–501.

Carrier, J.K., & Peak, T. *Nonspeech Language Initiation Program*. Lawrence, Kans.: H & H Enterprises, 1975.

Chapman, R.S., & Miller, J. F. Analyzing language and communication in the child. In R. L. Schiefelbusch (Ed.), *Nonspeech language and communication: Analysis and intervention*. Baltimore: University Park Press, 1980.

Creekmore, N.N. Use of sign alone and sign plus speech in language training of nonverbal autistic children. *Journal of the Association for the Severely Handicapped*, 1982, *6*(4), 45–55.

Dale, P.S. What does observing language mean? In G.P. Sackett (Ed.), *Observing behavior: Theory and applications in mental retardation*. Baltimore: University Park Press, 1978.

Ferguson, C.A. Learning to pronounce: The earliest stages of phonological development in the child. In F.D. Minifie & L.L. Lloyd (Eds.), *Communicative and cognitive abilities—early behavioral assessment*. Baltimore: University Park Press, 1978.

Garcia, E., Baer, D.M., & Firestone, I. The development of generalized imitation within topographically determined boundaries. *Journal of Applied Behavior Analysis*, 1971, *4*, 101–112.

Grinnell, M.F., Detamore, K.L., & Lippke, B.A. Sign it successful—Manual English encourages expressive communication. *Teaching Exceptional Children*, 1976, *8*, 123–124.

Guess, D. Methods in communication instruction for severely handicapped persons. In W. Sailor, B. Wilcox, & L. Brown (Eds.), *Methods of instruction for severely handicapped students*. Baltimore: Paul H. Brookes, 1980.

Gustasum, G., Pfetzig, D., & Zawolkow, E. *Signing Exact English.* Rorsmoor, Calif.: Modern Signs Press, 1972.

Harris-Vanderheiden, D. Bliss symbols and the mentally retarded. In G. C. Vanderheiden & K. Grilley (Eds.), *Nonvocal communication techniques and aids for the severely physically handicapped.* Baltimore: University Park Press, 1975.

Hollis, J.H., & Carrier, J.K. Intervention strategies for nonspeech children. In R. L. Schiefelbusch (Ed.), *Language intervention strategies.* Baltimore: University Park Press, 1978.

Jones, T.W. It is necessary to decide whether to use a nonoral communication system with retarded children? *Education and Training of Mentally Retarded,* 1980, *15,* 157–160.

Kahn, J.V. A comparison of manual and oral training with mute retarded children. *Mental Retardation,* 1977, *15*(3), 21–23.

Kirschner, A., Algozzine, B., & Abbott, T. Manual communication systems: A comparison and its implications. *Education and Training of the Mentally Retarded,* 1979, *14,* 5–9.

Kohl, F.L., Karlan, G.R., & Heal, L.W. Effects of pairing manual signs with verbal cues upon the acquisition of instruction following behaviors and the generalization to expressive language with severely handicapped students. *AAESPH Review,* 1979, *4,* 291–300.

Kucherawy, D.A., & Kucherawy, J.M. An electrical communication system for a nonverbal, profoundly retarded spastic quadriplegic. *Education and Training of the Mentally Retarded,* 1978, *13,* 342–344.

Lombardino, L.J., Willems, S., & MacDonald, J.P. Critical considerations in total communication and an environmental intervention model for the developmentally delayed. *Exceptional Children,* 1981, *47,* 455–461.

Lovaas, O.I.-*The autistic child: Language development through behavior modification.* New York: Irvington, 1977.

McLean, J.E., & Snyder-McLean, L.K. *A transactional approach to early language training.* Columbus, Ohio: Charles E. Merrill, 1978.

McNaughton, S. Bliss symbols—An alternative symbol system for the nonvocal pre-reading child. In G. C. Vanderheiden & K. Grilley (Eds.), *Nonvocal communication techniques and aids for the severely physically handicapped.* Baltimore: University Park Press, 1975.

McNaughton, S., & Kates, B. *Visual symbols: Communication system for the prereading physically handicapped child.* Paper presented at the AAMD Annual Conference, Toronto, June 5, 1974.

Musselwhite, C. R., & St. Louis, K. W. *Communication programming for the severely handicapped: Vocal and non-vocal strategies.* Houston: College-Hill Press, 1982.

Premack, D. A functional analysis of language. *Journal of the Experimental Analysis of Behavior,* 1970, *14,* 107–125.

Sailor, W., Guess, D., Goetz, L., Schuler, A., Utley, B., & Baldwin, M. Language and severely handicapped persons: Deciding what to teach to whom. In W. Sailor, B. Wilcox, & L. Brown (Eds.), *Methods of instruction for severely handicapped students.* Baltimore: Paul H. Brookes, 1980.

Salvin, A., Routh, O. K., Foster, R. E., & Lovejoy, K. M. Acquisition of modified American Sign Language by a mute autistic child. *Journal of Autism and Childhood Schizophrenia,* 1977, *7,* 359–371.

Schiefelbusch, R. L. (Ed.) *Nonspeech language and communication: Analysis and intervention.* Baltimore: University Park Press, 1980.

Shane, H. C. Decision making in early augmentative communication system use. In R. L. Schiefelbusch & D. Bricker (Eds.), *Early language: Acquisition and intervention.* Baltimore: University Park Press, 1981.

Sloane, H., Johnson, M., & Harris, F. Remedial procedures for teaching verbal behavior to speech deficient or defective young children. In H. Sloane & B. MacAuley (Eds.), *Operant procedures in remedial speech and language training.* Boston: Houghton Mifflin, 1968.

Stremel-Campbell, K., Cantrell, D., & Halle, J. Manual signing as a language system and as a speech initiator for the non-verbal severely handicapped student. In E. Sontag (Ed.), *Educational programming for the severely and profoundly handicapped.* Reston, Va.: Council for Exceptional Children, 1977.

Topper, S. T. Gesture language for a nonverbal severely retarded male. *Mental Retardation,* 1975, *13*(1), 30–31.

Vanderheiden, G. C. (Ed.). *Non-vocal communication resource book.* Baltimore: University Park Press, 1978.

Vanderheiden, G. C., & Grilley, K. (Eds.). *Nonvocal communication techniques and aids for the severely physically handicapped.* Baltimore: University Park Press, 1975.

Van Riper, C. *Speech correction: Principles and methods* (5th Ed.). Englewood Cliffs, N.J.: Prentice-Hall, 1972.

Whitehurst, G. Comprehension, selective imitation, and the CIP hypothesis. *Journal of Experimental Child Psychology,* 1977, *23,* 23–28.

Yoder, D. Communication systems for non-speech children. In D. Bricker (Ed.), *New directions for exceptional children: Language intervention with children* (No. 2). San Francisco: Jossey-Bass, 1980.

Zucker, S. H., D'Alonzo, B. J., McMullen, M. R., & Williams, R. L. Training eye-pointing behavior in a nonambulatory profoundly mentally retarded child using contingent vibratory stimulation. *Education and Training of the Mentally Retarded,* 1980, *15,* 4–7.

Motor skills, those skills involved in the movement of the body and body parts, are important for young children. Behaviors such as locomotion (moving independently from one place to another), reaching, grasping, and maintaining one's body position and orientation in relation to objects in the environment allow children to master, control, and interact with the environment. Motor skills are also important in performing behaviors of other developmental areas. For example, speaking involves precise movements of the lip and tongue muscles; social skills such as play frequently involve movement of objects; self-help skills such as dressing involve reaching, grasping, and removing clothing; cognitive skills such as object permanence are usually demonstrated by performing certain motor behaviors. In addition, motor movements are thought by some theorists to be the basis for later perceptual and conceptual development (Ayres, 1972a; Piaget, 1952).

Many young handicapped children demonstrate motor delays and deficits (Bigge & O'Donnell, 1976; Garwood, 1979; Goldenson, 1978; Langley, 1979). With many physically and severely handicapped children, the treatment of motor deficits will be a major portion of early intervention, requiring a team effort by teachers and physical therapists, occupational therapists, or physical educators. Team members should understand each others' language; thus, the techniques and terms used by occupational and physical therapists and physical educators are discussed in this chapter.

This chapter also contains general statements concerning motor development and intervention and sections addressing major areas of motor development, including reflexes, reactions, and tone; locomotion and other gross motor skills; and fine motor skills. Each section includes a description and examples of deviations from normal development, assessment guidelines, and suggestions for intervention and adaptive equipment.

GENERAL STATEMENTS CONCERNING MOTOR DEVELOPMENT

Certain facts need to be recognized and understood when assessing and intervening in motor development. Three general statements

15

Acquisition and Use of Motor Skills

are provided to establish a foundation for the remainder of the chapter.

Motor Development in Nondelayed Children Follows Orderly Progressions

The sequences in which most children accomplish various developmental milestones are relatively consistent. Although the rate or age at which children perform those milestones varies widely (Evans & McCandless, 1978), and some exceptions may exist (McCandless, 1961), at least five general progressions of motor development may be described.

Development proceeds in a cephalo-to-caudal direction. This principle of motor development means that the head (cephalo) portion of the body develops first and then development proceeds toward the tail (caudal) portion of the body (Ford, 1975). This principle is seen in the relative size of the infant's head and body as compared to those of grown adults (Vander Zanden, 1981). Proportionally the infant's head is large compared to body size; however, as the child grows older, the proportional size of the head to the rest of the body changes as the body grows faster than the head. The cephalo-to-caudal direction of growth is also seen in the infant's mastery of motor milestones. Initially, the infant can lift his chin, then his chest, and then can sit up, using his entire trunk. The baby then creeps, finally walking in an upright manner.

Development proceeds in a proximal-to-distal direction. This principle describes the direction of development from the midline of the body (*proximal*, or close to the trunk) outward toward the end of the fingers (*distal*, or away from the trunk) (Ford, 1975), and is especially important in the development of reaching. Initially, an infant's shoulder is the most active arm joint; later, the elbow becomes more active, and finally, wrist bending and rotation (the ability to twist the forearm without moving the elbow) develops.

Development proceeds from flexion to extension. Flexion is bending at the joints, and *extension* is straightening at the joints. Newborns frequently assume the fetal position, characterized by flexion of the neck, with the chin tucked toward the chest, flexion of the elbow, with the arms drawn in toward the chest, and flexion of the hips and knees, with the legs drawn up toward the body trunk. Throughout the first 12 to 15 months the child begins to assume positions gradually involving more extension. This trend is seen when the infant is laid prone (face and stomach down) and supine (on the back), or is in a sitting position (Cohen & Gross, 1979).

Motor development proceeds from reflexive to volitional movements. At birth or soon thereafter the infant displays a number of primitive reflexes. Reflexes "are involuntary, stereotyped responses of a limb or the whole body to a specific environmental stimulus" (Swanson, 1979, p. 84). During the first year many of those reflexes are integrated and children gradually acquire greater voluntary control of their movements.

Development proceeds from undifferentiated responses to differentiated responses to complex behavior. This statement is based on Heinz Werner's *orthogenetic principle*:

Differentiation is the process by which basic behaviors and abilities are broken down into smaller and more refined components *which can be used* separately. Integration is the process by which these differentiated components are recombined into more complex behaviors and abilities (Cooper, 1977, p. 2).

An example of the differentiation process is illustrated in the development of grasp patterns. From an initial reflexive palmar grasp children acquire a variety of separate individual grasps to be used at will. The integration process is illustrated when a young child visually notices a small toy, elects to use a radial palmar grasp, picks it up, moves the toy to his mouth, sucks it, removes it from his mouth, looks at the toy, and then with a pincer grasp attempts to pull at some part of the toy. Both processes are important in assessment and intervention with children's motor development; however, the activities used to facilitate the two processes might be quite different.

Motor Delays and Atypical Motor Development Frequently Accompany Certain Handicapping Conditions

In this section, we review the motor functioning of children with mental retardation, visual impairments, hearing impairments, cerebral palsy, and other physical and health disorders.

In *mental retardation* the severity of the cognitive deficits is usually correlated with the severity of the motor delays and deviations (Robinson & Robinson, 1976); if the cognitive deficit is severe, so are the motor delays. The motor deficiencies in children with retardation may be due to general neurological damage (Robinson & Robinson, 1976), restricted interactions with the environment (Bijou, 1981), and/or other factors such as smaller body size. Children with conditions such as Down syndrome usually exhibit delayed motor development and muscle tone (tension) that is hypotonic (low tone or "floppy") (Eipper & Azen, 1978; Harris, 1981; LaVeck & LaVeck, 1977).

Blind children frequently show "selective lags in developing certain motor and locomotor behaviors" (DuBose, 1979a, p. 337). DuBose (1979a) reviews data presented by Fraiberg (1977) and concludes that for blind children the motor behaviors

falling within the normal range were rolling, independent sitting, and independent standing behaviors, as well as taking stepping movements when hands were held. These motor performances required a low and relatively stable center of gravity and could be performed by blind children with little risk or danger, since they did not require leaving the immediate base of support.

Lags were reported in behaviors requiring the infant to project his body into space (elevating upper torso by arm support, raising self to sitting, pulling to stand, crawling, or walking) (DuBose, 1979a, p. 337).

DuBose (1979a) also describes several delays and deviations in reaching and grasping. The blind infant frequently maintains the hands in the fetal position (near the shoulders) much longer than nonhandicapped children. Intentional reaching and moving the hands to midline are also delayed. Although blind children's grasps develop within normal limits, they are

characterized as "clumsy and unpracticed" (p. 338).

Although *deafness* alone probably does not result in motor delays or deviation, children with inner ear damage may have difficulties with tasks requiring balance (DuBose, 1979b). Lindsey and O'Neal (1976) assessed 8-year-old deaf and hearing children on measures of *static balance* (balance needed when the body is in one position such as sitting or standing) and *dynamic balance* (balance needed when the body is moving such as in walking or jumping). The deaf children had hearing losses at the 65 decibel level or greater, and the hearing children heard at the 25 decibel level or better. Sixteen skills were assessed, such as "standing on one foot with the eyes open or closed" (static balance) and "jumping into a square from one, two, or three feet" (dynamic balance). Deaf children performed more poorly on all tasks than their hearing counterparts. When blindfolded, both groups performed more poorly, but the decrement in deaf children's performance was larger. These findings were consistent for both static and dynamic tasks and across race and sex.

A variety of physical handicaps have accompanying motor delays and deviations. Perhaps the most common is *cerebral palsy.* Cerebral (brain) palsy (paralysis) "is a nonprogressive disorder of movement or posture beginning in childhood due to a malfunction or damage of the brain" (Bleck, 1975, p. 37).

This damage can occur before birth (prenatally), during birth (perinatally), or soon after birth (postnatally). Common causes are anoxia (lack of oxygen), prematurity, Rh incompatibility, and trauma (Langley, 1979). Cerebral palsy can be classified by the type of motor involvement and by the area of the body that is paralyzed. Six types of cerebral palsy representing different types of motor involvement and various areas of the body affected with paralysis are shown in Table 15.1. The type and severity of the cerebral palsy will determine how the child's balance, gross motor, and fine motor performance are affected.

Many other physical disorders and conditions influence children's motor performance such as muscular dystrophy, myelomeningocele (spina bifida), scoliosis (curvature of the spine), kyphosis, clubfoot, poliomyelitis, juvenile rheumatoid arthritis, hip dislocations, and Legg-Perthes disease. Several health conditions also affect motor performance or restrict the type and intensity of movement and activity. These include cystic fibrosis, hemo-philia, diabetes, and heart disease and defects. It is impossible to describe these disorders and their effect on motor performance here, but discussions may be found in Bigge and O'Donnell (1976), Bleck and Nagel (1975),

TABLE 15.1

Cerebral palsy classified by types of motor involvement and the area of the body affected

Type	Motor Involvement
Spastic	Characterized by loss of voluntary motor control; frequent co-contractions: muscles used in flexion and extension contract at the same time resulting in tense, jerky movements which are poorly controlled. If startled the child's posture may be fixed and rigid. Limb deformities are possible as children grow older.
Athetosis	Characterized by involuntary, purposeless limb movements; fluctuating muscle tone affects deliberate muscle extensions resulting in writhing irregular movements; throat and diaphragm muscles frequently involved producing drooling and labored speech.
Ataxia	Characterized by balance problems, staggering gait, slurred speech, poor depth perception, and poor gross and fine motor movements.
Rigidity	Characterized by extreme stiffness and appears to be severe spasticity; difficult for child to bend limbs, and when bent they tend to stay in that position.
Tremor	Characterized by shakiness of limbs; shakiness frequently only present during intentional movements; limb movements are small and rhythmic.
Mixed	Characterized by more than one of the above types.
Area of Body Affected with Motor Involvement	
Monoplegia	Only one limb of the body has paralysis.
Hemiplegia	Limbs on one side are affected; trunk muscles are also frequently affected.
Paraplegia	Lower limbs (legs) are affected, but arms are not.
Diplegia	All limbs are affected with paralysis, but the legs are more seriously affected than the arms.
Quadriplegia	All four limbs are affected with paralysis.

Source: Cross, D. P. Physical disabilities. In A. E. Blackhurst & W. H. Berdine (Eds.), *An introduction to special education.* Boston: Little, Brown, 1981.

and Goldenson (1978). Although teachers cannot be thoroughly knowledgeable concerning the description, etiology, diagnosis, treatment, and effects of these conditions, they should seek more information when they have a child with a given condition. Sources include references just cited, the child's parents, and physicians.

REFLEXES, REACTIONS, AND TONE

Motor development normally progresses from primitive reflexive behaviors to automatic reactions and volitional movements. A *reflex* is a response that is a result of a specific stimulus and is believed to be inborn. It is also a response over which the infant has no control. For example, if you place your fingers in the palm of an infant's hand and press, the infant will reflexively close all of his fingers around yours (palmar grasp reflex).

As the infant matures, reflexes become integrated and automatic reactions and volitional movements begin to occur. *Automatic reactions* are "involuntary, unconscious responses of the body and limbs to changes in the position of the body in relation to gravity and to changes in alignment of the body parts" (Swanson, 1979, p. 85). Automatic reactions make the postural adjustments to help maintain balance during movement. These reactions also align the body with itself and provide support when someone is knocked off balance or falls. Examples of automatic reactions include reaching to the floor to break a fall or turning the head upright when the body is turned sideways. These reactions are thought to be absent at birth and are gradually acquired as children move about (Swanson, 1979).

Volitional movements are intentional movements children can perform at any time. Most of the movements performed by adults (sitting down, reaching, walking, grasping, and manipulating objects) are volitional movements. Like automatic reactions, volitional movements gradually become more frequent during the first few months of life. The relative frequency and intensity of the reflexes, automatic reactions, and volitional movements are described in Figure 15.1. Infants are not totally reflexive; however, in proportion to automatic reactions and volitional movements, reflexes are initially more frequent. The proportional frequency changes during the first few months.

Muscle tone refers to "the degree of tension in the muscles when an individual is at rest" (Swanson, 1979, p. 82). Muscle tone can either be *hypertonic* (high muscle tension and tightness), normal, or *hypotonic* (low muscle tension, flaccid). Extreme hypertonicity or extreme hypotonicity can prevent the acquisition of many functional motor skills.

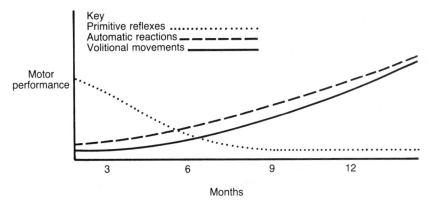

FIGURE 15.1
Relative frequency of primitive reflexes, automatic reactions, and volitional movements during the first year of life. *Source:* Adapted from O'Doherty, R. J., Neurological foundations of motor behavior in infancy. *Physiotherapy,* 1971, *57,* 144–148.

Assessing Common Reflexes

Physical and occupational therapists traditionally assess primitive reflexes. Unfortunately, many preschool teachers will have limited or no access to a therapist. Teachers of handicapped children should identify the more common reflexes and know general strategies for working with children who demonstrate those reflexes beyond the age the reflexes are normally integrated. The presence of reflexes can serve to inhibit or prevent the learning of volitional behaviors.

Many reflex patterns can be observed in newborns. Brazelton (1973); Capute, Accardo, Vining, Rubenstein, Walcher, Harryman, and Ross (1978); and Utley, Holvoet, and Barnes (1978) provide detailed descriptions. The reflexes most commonly observed in physically handicapped children are the startle reaction, the Moro reflex, the asymmetrical tonic neck reflex, the symmetrical tonic neck reflex, and the tonic labyrinthine reflex (Bigge & O'Donnell, 1976; Capute et al., 1978; and Utley et al., 1977).

Startle reaction The startle reaction consists of clenched fists and a rapid movement of the arms and legs to a flexion (close to the body) pattern. It is usually stimulated by rapid movement toward the face, loud noises, or bright lights and can interfere with the child's body position, particularly if the child is prone as in creeping or crawling. Bigge and O'Donnell (1976) suggest that the teacher should try to avoid loud noises such as slamming doors and should move slowly toward the child who frequently exhibits the startle reaction.

Moro reflex The Moro reflex consists of throwing the arms out and up and the head back. It can be stimulated by pushing a sitting child backwards, or by simply allowing the sitting child's head to drop backwards. The Moro reflex can interfere with body position as well as eye-hand coordination. Bigge and O'Donnell (1976) describe the importance of providing adequate head and trunk support for a child with the Moro reflex. Finnie (1975) emphasizes that particular care should be taken when lifting a child with the Moro reflex since tilting the head back could stimulate the reflex and the subsequent extension could cause the teacher or parent to drop the child.

Asymmetrical tonic neck reflex (ATNR) The ATNR is typically observed when a child is lying on his or her back and occurs when the head is turned to either side. The child will extend an arm and leg on the side he or she is facing and will flex the arm and leg on the opposite side. The ATNR is normally observed between birth and 4 months of age, gradually diminishing after that. This reflex is frequently observed in children with cerebral palsy and interferes considerably with the development of many functional motor skills. For example, rolling over is virtually impossible. Self-feeding is also difficult because when the child turns to a spoon, that arm extends. Utley et al. (1977) also report that the ATNR causes the child to collapse if the head is turned while the child is on all fours and may make using hands at the midline (middle of the body) difficult or impossible.

Bigge and O'Donnell (1976) suggest that if the ATNR is typically observed on only one side of the body, the teacher should present objects or feed the child from the side opposite to which the child usually looks. Adaptive equipment such as a wedge or prone board (described later in this chapter) may also be useful.

Symmetrical tonic neck reflex (STNR) While the ATNR is a function of turning the head to the left or right, the STNR is observed when the child moves his or her head up or down. The result of raising the head is extension of the upper extremities and flexion of the lower extremities. Lowering the head (bending toward the chest) results in the opposite reaction: flexion in the upper extremities and extension in the lower extremities. The STNR is normally observed between 2 and 4 months of age, after which it gradually diminishes.

The STNR interferes with functional movement. For example, the child on all fours who lifts the head to see where he or she is going may spread the arms out. The STNR can also interfere with normal sitting posture and task orientation. As Utley et al. (1977) describe, "bending the head forward to look at an object increases extension of the hips causing the student to sit with rounded back, the hips sliding forward in the chair" (p. 281). The primary intervention for adapting to the STNR is to present objects and other stimuli at a level that does not require the head to be raised or lowered.

Tonic labyrinthine reflex (TLR) The TLR refers to changes in flexion or extension as a function of whether the child is prone (on the stomach) or supine (on the back). When placed in the supine position a child with TLR will generally demonstrate an extension pattern in which arms and legs straighten, the back arches, and the head pushes back. When placed in the prone position the child with TLR will generally demonstrate a flexion pattern, with arms and legs bent and the head on the chest. The TLR is seen in normal infants up to 4 months of age and prevents the child from turning over, makes it difficult to raise the head or to come to an all fours position, and interferes with bringing hands to the midline. Interventions for the TLR include not letting the child stay in prone or supine positions for long periods of time, providing some support for sitting, and using a prone board or wedge to facilitate hand activities (Bigge & O'Donnell, 1976).

General considerations in assessing reflexes
The process of assessing these and other reflexes involves positioning the child, presenting the environmental stimulus, and observing and recording the child's response to the stimulus. The child's position and the specific environmental stimulus presented vary from reflex to reflex. Recording of the child's response varies across examiners. For example, some therapists choose to note only the presence or absence of the reflex, and others also attempt to quantify the intensity of the reflex. A rating of intensity indicates whether the reflex is an obligatory reflex—"one that controls the patient"—or one that is present but not obligatory (Capute et al., 1978, p. 1064). Nonobligatory reflexes also require treatment. The following description of a nonobligatory symmetrical tonic neck reflex illustrates this point. The symmetrical tonic neck reflex occurs

when the head tilts backward, the arms extend (stretch out) and the legs flex (bend), while the reverse occurs when the head tilts forward. If even partial components of this primitive organization are present, the ordinary business of looking up at chalkboard and then down to the desk will play havoc with the muscle tone and movement of the arms and fingers. The child will display awkward movements, impaired attention, frustration, or

withdrawal (Freides, Barbati, van Kampen-Horowitz, Sprehn, Iversen, Silver, & Woodward, 1980, p. 161).

Assessing Automatic Reactions

Assessment of automatic reactions typically is the responsibility of physical or occupational therapists. However, facilitating the development of these reactions is frequently shared by the therapist and the early childhood special educator. Automatic reactions make the postural adjustments that assist in maintaining balance during movement, maintain the body in alignment with itself, and provide support when you are knocked off balance and/or falling. Swanson (1979) states that automatic reactions are absent at birth, but Utley et al. (1977) suggest that some are present at birth. Nonetheless, they become more frequent and efficient as the child grows older.

Righting, equilibrium, and supportive reaction are automatic reactions. *Righting reactions* assist in maintaining body alignments. For example, when you are upright, righting reactions keep the head faced toward the front of the trunk with the eyes and mouth horizontal to the floor. *Equilibrium reactions* are compensatory movements of the trunk and limbs in response to changes of the "center of gravity caused by displacement of the body or movement of the supporting surface" (Swanson, 1979, p. 86). These reactions assist us in maintaining balance. For example, if you are standing in a boat and someone else in the boat begins to move, you automatically throw out your arms and spread your feet to retain your balance. *Supportive reactions* are movements of the legs and arms that assist in preventing and breaking falls. They include abduction (movement of limbs away from the midline of the body) and extension (straightening) of the arms and legs when falling.

Automatic reactions are usually tested with checklists and observation of the child's responses to specific stimuli (Harris & Tada, 1983). This assessment should occur in a variety of positions (Swanson, 1979). Righting reactions are assessed by placing the body out of alignment and observing the child's attempts to realign the body. Equilibrium reactions are measured by disrupting equilibrium and observing the child's adjustment to this disruption. Supportive reactions are frequently

TABLE 15.2
Righting and equilibrium reactions

Reflexes and reactions	Age of appearance and inhibition in normal development	Stimulus that elicits reflex	Description
Neck righting reflex	Present from birth to 4 months, then gradually diminishes.	Place the student on his or her back and turn the head to one side.	The body rotates as a whole toward the side to which the head is turned.
Body righting reflex acting on the body	Emerges between 6 to 8 months and is present until 3 years of age.	Place the student on his or her back and turn the head to one side.	This reflex modifies neck righting by the addition of rotation of the trunk between the shoulders and pelvis. (Rather than the body turning as a whole unit, the head turns to one side, then the shoulder girdle and finally the pelvis.)
Body righting reflex acting on the head	Emerges between 4 to 6 months and inhibited between 1 to 5 years.	Place the student's feet on the ground or lay the student on either side on a hard surface.	This reflex "rights" the head in space by bringing it into alignment with the trunk of the body.
Equilibrium reaction in lying on abdomen and back	On abdomen, this response emerges between 4 to 6 months; on the back, between 7 to 10 months. Normal throughout life.	Place the student on a tilt board on the abdomen or back and tilt to one side.	The head bends and the body arches toward the raised side. The arms and legs straighten and come out from the midline of the body.
Quadrupedal equilibrium reaction	Appears between 10 to 12 months. Normal throughout life.	Place the student on hands and knees and tip gently to one side.	The arm and leg on the raised side straighten out from the midline; the opposite arm also extends out from the midline as a protective reaction.
Sitting equilibrium reaction	Appears between 12 to 14 months. Normal throughout life.	1) Place the student in a sitting position and push gently to one side.	The head moves to the raised side; the arm and leg of the raised side straighten out from the midline of the body as do the opposite arm and leg.
		2) Push the student backward from a sitting position.	The head, shoulders, and arms move forward and the legs straighten.

TABLE 15.2 (continued)
Righting and equilibrium reactions

Reflexes and reactions	Age of appearance and inhibition in normal development	Stimulus that elicits reflex	Description
		3) Push the student forward.	The legs flex, the spine and neck extend, and the arms move backward.
Standing equilibrium reaction	Appears between 12 to 18 months. Normal throughout life.	1) Place the student in a standing position, straighten and pull outward on either arm.	The opposite arm and leg straighten outward and the head "rights" itself to maintain the normal position in space.
		2) Hold the student under the armpits and tip him backward.	The head, shoulders, and arms move forward, and the feet point upward bending at the ankles.

assessed by placing the child on the stomach on a large ball and observing whether extension (protective extension) of the arm occurs as the child is rolled toward the floor, or by placing the child in a sitting position and observing extension of the arms when the child is pushed gently off balance from the front, left, right, and back. The abduction (movement of the limbs away from the midline) and extension of the legs called *parachuting* is tested by lowering the child feet first toward a surface and noting the movement of the legs. Various righting and equilibrium reactions are shown for different positions in Table 15.2. The course of development for the reactions, the stimuli that elicit the reactions, and a description of the reaction are also shown.

Assessing Volitional Movements

Volitional movements, as described in Figure 15.1, are relatively infrequent at birth but become quite common as the child grows older. When assessing volitional movements, developmental scales are frequently used and teach-

ers frequently are directly involved. In addition to the child's responses on the developmental scales, give attention to the quality of the child's movements, such as extension, symmetry, independent movements, and rotation of the body and body parts (Swanson, 1979). *Extension* is assessed by noting the attainment of various developmental milestones as illustrated in Figure 15.2. *Symmetry* refers to the equal function and use of the two sides of the body. "Normal development is symmetrical with no significant discrepancy between rate or quality of development on the two sides of the body" (Swanson, 1979, p. 89). *Independent movements* refer to the ability of the child to move one part of the body without moving another part. For example, being able to reach for a cup with the right arm and hand without the left arm or hand also moving means the child has independent movement of the right arm and hand. When one part of the body moves and there is a related movement in another part, this related movement is an *associated reaction*. Finally, observation of the child's ability to rotate his or her trunk should be assessed. *Rotation* is the separation or independent movement of the shoulder girdle from the hips, allowing the trunk to twist. If rotation is not observed, passive manipulation should be used to determine whether the movement is possible (Swanson, 1979).

A recently developed assessment instrument is the Movement Assessment of Infants (MAI) (Chandler, Andrews, & Swanson, 1980). The purpose of the MAI is to objectively assess infants up to 1 year of age in "four areas of movement—muscle tone, primitive reflexes,

automatic reactions, and volitional movements" (Harris & Tada, 1983, p. 6). The purpose of the MAI is to identify problems preventing infants from acquiring developmental milestones at the appropriate or expected rate. The MAI is not yet standardized, but Harris and Tada (1983) report that validity and reliability studies are being conducted.

Assessing Muscle Tone

The objective measurement of muscle tone is difficult in clinical settings (Harris, 1981) since

A. Intermittent neck extension, allowing nose to clear the surface.

D. Creeping, a child frees one or two extremities from the supporting surface to move forward, balancing on the remaining limbs.

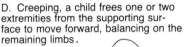
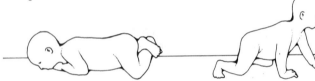

B. Head is effectively held up against gravity; arms beginning to push body away from the surface.

E. Plantigrade walking demonstrates a variation of creeping (stomach off surface).

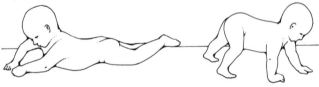

F. Using an object, a child can now pull himself on to his feet, showing controlled extension down through the legs.

C. Hips are now sufficiently under control to support lower body against gravity but not coordinated enough to move alternately.

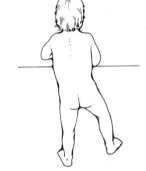

FIGURE 15.2

Progression from flexion to extension when child is prone. *Note:* From *The Developmental Resource: Behavioral Sequences for Assessment and Program Planning* (Vol. 1) by M. Cohen and P. Gross. New York: Grune & Stratton, 1979. Copyright 1979 by Grune & Stratton. Reprinted by permission.

it requires the therapist to "feel" the child and interpret the degree of tension. Accurate interpretation requires considerable experience with a variety of handicapped children. Many handicapped children may also have fluctuating tone.

Swanson (1979) describes four methods of assessing children's tone. The first method is to *feel the consistency of the child's muscles.* Normal muscles should feel firm and have "some definite bulk" (p. 83). Hypertonic muscles feel hard and "stony"; hypotonic muscles feel "flabby and soft." The second method is to *observe the range of motion or extensibility of the joints.* Range of motion is the number of degrees in the arc of motion allowed by the joint. Hypertonic children will have a restricted range of motion, whereas hypotonic children will have an exaggerated or larger than normal range. The third method is to *determine the passivity of the muscles.* This measurement is done by shaking the wrists and ankles, or by moving the child through their full range of motion. Hypertonic children will appear to resist movement of their limbs and their muscles will tighten; hypotonic children will be passive with little resistance, will allow easy movement through the range of motion, and the hands and feet will be quite floppy. The fourth method is to *observe the child's posture.* This will assist in determining whether the child is hypo- or hypertonic. Hypertonic children will appear rigid, flexed, and tight. Hypotonic children will "appear to 'melt' into the supporting surface" (Swanson, 1979, p. 83). Assessment of tone helps determine how to handle children, whether and what type of adaptive equipment should be used, and the type of treatment to be given.

Interventions and Adaptive Equipment

Reflex and tone assessment are important because abnormal patterns prevent the acquisition of functional skills. Because reflexes cannot be "unlearned," the primary intervention strategy is positioning and use of adaptive equipment. *Positioning* refers to the use of appropriate body positions in teaching children and helps insure that the child is in the optimal position for learning. An *optimal position* reduces the likelihood of interfering re-

flexes and adjusts for extreme deviations from normal muscle tone. Positioning may also help minimize deformities. For example, children who have been allowed to practice abnormal movement patterns or remain in abnormal positions may have severely contracted (permanently shortened) muscles.

Although the procedures for positioning come from many sources, much of the theory behind them comes from the Neurodevelopmental Treatment Approach (NDT). This approach was developed by Karel and Berta Bobath (B. Bobath, 1963, 1969, 1971; K. Bobath & B. Bobath, 1964) for the treatment of children with cerebral palsy, although it may be used with other children (Harris & Tada, 1983). Utley et al. (1977) describe the NDT approach as having the following goals:

(a) Normalize muscle tone: proper positioning and handling can minimize abnormality of tone; (b) inhibit abnormal reflexes: positioning and handling can help minimize the occurrence of abnormal reflex patterns; and (c) facilitate active movement along the normal developmental sequence: after normal muscle tone is established, the student can more freely engage in voluntary movements (pp. 280–281).

Included in the notion of facilitating active movement is the facilitation of automatic reactions (K. Bobath & B. Bobath, 1964). The NDT approach should be more than "therapy" administered in a separate room and can be used by teachers in the classroom and parents at home.

Common forms of adaptive equipment In recent years many types of adaptive equipment have been developed for physically handicapped children. Basic types include the wedge, the bolster, the prone board, and modified chairs.

The *wedge*, pictured in Figure 15.3, is a sloped piece of equipment usually made of foam rubber or wood covered with padding. The wedge is used to normalize tone, increase neck strength, and facilitate working at midline rather than to the side. A wedge should be constructed so the high end is equal to the length of the child's arms when extended (Campbell, Green, & Carlson, 1977) and long enough so the child's feet will hang over the other end. A foam rubber wedge is used for hypertonic children, while the more solid wooden wedge is used for hypotonic children (Campbell et al., 1977). The child should be properly positioned on the wedge so arms and shoulders are over the edge. A roll or small pillow is often placed on the front edge for additional comfort and support. The surface on which the child manipulates objects should be placed high enough so the child does not have to fully extend his arms to use it.

with asymmetrical sitting postures. Precautions in using the prone board include stabilizing it so it will not tip over, gradually introducing it to the child who may be fearful, placing the footplate so the child can learn to use his or her feet for support rather than hanging from the top, and placing the board so the child can use his or her arms to manipulate objects on the table (Campbell et al., 1977).

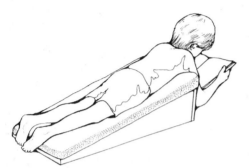

FIGURE 15.3
Example of a wedge.

The *bolster*, pictured in Figure 15.4, is actually a generic term for a roll or pillow used to fulfill a similar function as the wedge or to provide support for other positions. The bolster is often easier to use than the wedge, and can also be used as a support. For example, the child who is lying on his side may need some back support to keep from rolling over onto his back.

FIGURE 15.5
Example of a prone board.

Modified chairs are for children who have difficulty sitting well or who have abnormal hip and leg patterns. Examples of modified chairs are displayed in Figure 15.6 and provide shoulder and hip support. Posts can be used to move the legs toward or away from the midline as necessary.

Several issues to be considered when deciding to use adaptive equipment include the child's range of motion, strength, volitional movements, primitive reflexes, muscle tone, and any special precautions; the financial, social, and psychological effects of the equipment on the family members; and the durability and service requirements of the equipment (Andrews & Down, 1977).

Teachers should consult with therapists when using adaptive equipment. Therapists will help correctly fit the child to the equipment so it will benefit motor performance. Venn, Morganstern, and Dykes (1978) provide checklists for evaluating certain orthoses,

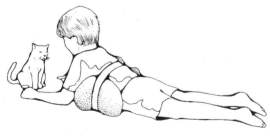

FIGURE 15.4
Example of a bolster.

The *prone board*, pictured in Figure 15.5, is used for children whose typical pattern is one of flexion (Finnie, 1975). The prone board helps the child reach forward and use the hands, and helps prevent hip and knee contractures (permanent shortenings) for children

prostheses, and other adaptive equipment pieces. Therapists can also assist teachers in identifying the purpose of a given piece of adaptive equipment and the type of equipment to use for each child depending upon the motor difficulties. In addition, therapists can provide direction as to how long the child should be placed in or on the equipment, the child's position on the equipment, the type of activities to be presented, and any special precautions while the child is on the adaptive equipment.

Adaptive devices present some major problems. They are expensive, large, and heavy, and children frequently outgrow them. Kasari and Filler (1981) describe the use of inflatable swim rings for positioning infants and smaller preschool children in lieu of larger, more expensive pieces of adaptive equipment. DuBose and Deni (1980) describe several pieces of adaptive equipment and include a listing of the purposes of the equipment and the specifications for making them. Teachers and therapists can use persons who are skilled with tools to make adaptive equipment and save a considerable amount of money.

Teachers with physically or severely handicapped children need to learn about and use adaptive equipment. This equipment can be used to normalize muscle tone, inhibit primitive reflexes, allow the child to use volitional movements with a greater range of motion, increase strength of muscles such as in holding up one's head, and provide the child with different positions to receive stimulation from the environment and perform adaptive responses. However, when using any piece of adaptive equipment, examine the child for "red spots" that indicate the early development of pressure sores.

Positioning Techniques and Principles

Although positioning techniques used must be individualized, several general principles are identifiable. One principle is to provide support at key points to help the child relax and thus normalize tone. According to Bobath & Bobath (1964), the neck, shoulders, hips, and knees are "key points" that control the amount of muscle tone. Rather than trying to manipulate the child's extremities, provide support at these key points and then allow the child to attempt voluntary movements (Utley et al., 1977).

Another principle is to use positioning to inhibit primitive reflexes. If, for example, when a child looks to the side he or she is habitually influenced by the asymmetrical tonic neck reflex, the teacher should introduce activities in the child's midline rather than at the side. Thus the child would be better able to engage in activities without the interfering influence of the ATNR. Another positioning strategy to reduce the effects of the ATNR is to have the child lie comfortably on his side.

Campbell et al. (1977) suggest that for most handicapped children, particularly those with spastic tendencies, lying on the back is a poor position, since it tends to increase stiffness and thus interferes with reaching. Whenever possible these children should be on their stomachs (on a wedge, bolster, or prone board) or on their sides.

When handling children, do not use force

FIGURE 15.6
Two examples of modified chairs.

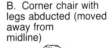

A. Corner chair with legs adducted (moved toward midline)

B. Corner chair with legs abducted (moved away from midline)

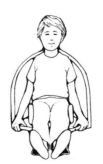

to manipulate limbs. Rather the teacher should provide support at the key points of control and move the limbs once the muscles have relaxed (Johnson, 1978). In addition, when handling spastic or hypertonic children, the teacher should not make quick movements that tend to stimulate abnormal muscle tone (Utley et al., 1977). When carrying children, provide support at the key points of control. Finnie (1975) describes appropriate proce-

TABLE 15.3

Normal sequences of gross motor skills

Age	Sample Locomotion Skills	Examples of Other Gross Motor Skills
0–6 months	Chin up Chest up Rolls over Sits with support	
6–12 months	Sits alone Moves to all fours position Crawls Creeps Walks when led Pulls to stand	Bangs large objects Attempts to "throw"
12–18 months	Stands independently Walks independently Walks up steps with help Sits self in chair Begins stiff running	Rolls ball
18–24 months	Runs well Climbs steps independently, but one foot at a time Jumps from bottom step	Throws ball overhand
2–3 years	Jumps Walks backwards Walks on tiptoes	Catches large ball with arms straight out Kicks ball forward Begins to pedal tricycle
3–4 years	More fluent running Walks straight line Stands on one foot (1–2 seconds) Hops "Skips" on one foot	Rides tricycle well Throws, maintaining balance Catches bounced ball
4–5 years	Skips, alternating feet Running or standing broad jumps Marches Walks backward heel-to-toe Jumps over 10″ high object	Throws overhand well Turns somersault

dures for holding, moving, and carrying children. Teachers should also consult with therapists about lifting and carrying children for both the child's and the teacher's safety.

TEACHING GROSS MOTOR SKILLS

Gross motor skills require large muscle movements. For example, *locomotion* is the ability to move from one place to another. Other gross motor skills include jumping, throwing, catching, and riding. Nonhandicapped children progress through relatively predictable sequences of these skills. Descriptions of some of the major milestones and the approximate ages of their appearance are displayed in Table 15.3. Many handicapped children, however, do follow these sequences or do so slowly. Teachers may need to encourage the development of basic gross motor skills, facilitate the acquisition of more advanced motor attainments, or improve the accuracy or speed of already acquired movements.

Assessing Gross Motor Skills

In the assessment of gross motor skills, the teacher should initially determine the child's abilities within the normal developmental sequence. Then the teacher should determine the presence and quality of functional movements. Finally, the teacher should determine the environmental opportunities and expectations for gross motor skills.

Assessing developmental skills Assessment of developmental levels of motor performance specifies the existence and extent of motor delays and helps interpret the child's abilities and plan an instructional program for children. The child should be compared with children who do not have motor delays by means of broad checklists, criterion-referenced tests, and norm-referenced tests. For example, the Bayley Scales of Infant Development (Bayley, 1969), the Gesell Developmental Test (Gesell & Amatruda, 1942), and the McCarthy Scales of Children's Abilities (McCarthy, 1972) have sections for assessing fine and gross motor skills.

The Peabody Developmental Motor Scale (PDMS) (Folio & DuBose, 1974) has a separate scale that assesses fine and gross motor skills from birth to 7 years. The gross motor scale has 170 items and the fine motor scale has 112. Each item is rated on a 1–5 scale where "1" is scored when total manipulation by the examiner is needed and "5" when the child performs the behavior without assistance. The scale was standardized nationally on a population of 617 children. The PDMS yields age scores, differential motor quotients, T scores, and Z scores. Programmed activities translate assessment data into instructional activities.

Broad developmental items may need to be broken down into smaller steps for instructional purposes. For example, Table 15.4 displays a list of 12 skills demonstrated by infants from 0–12 months when placed in a prone (on stomach) position.

Assessing functional movements When assessing functional movements, the *result* rather than the *form* of the movement is important. For example, locomotion, or the ability to get from place *A* to place *B*, is a functional skill, with the result of arriving at point *B*. To get from *A* to *B*, one might use a variety of forms, such as rolling, creeping, walking unassisted or with crutches, using a wheelchair, or perhaps asking someone to help them get to *B*.

TABLE 15.4
Sequence of gross motor-prone (on stomach) skills

a.	Lifts head, freeing nose
b.	Lifts head to 45° angle; support on elbows
c.	Alternates between "arms back" and elbows support
d.	Rolling from stomach to back
e.	Reaching, support on elbow
f.	Support on hands, arms extended, head at 90°
g.	Child locomotes using arm and then arms and legs
h.	Child pulls self to hands and knees
i.	Forward-backward rocking in all-fours position
j.	Child plays with toys in an asymmetrical half-sitting, half side-lying position
k.	Moves forward on hands and knees
l.	On all fours, supports weight on one hand and reaches for an object with the other hand

Source: Johnson, N.M., Jens, K.G., and Attermeir, S.M. *Carolina curriculum for handicapped infants.* Chapel Hill: University of North Carolina, 1979.

When determining whether a child's form is functional, observe several dimensions of behavior, including accuracy, duration, endurance, fluency, and flexibility. *Accuracy* refers to the child's ability to use any behavior to consistently achieve the desired goal (move 15 feet). *Duration* is the length of time a behavior lasts. For example, one might be interested in how long a child could maintain a given position. *Endurance* is the ability to repeat a behavior a number of times without stopping. For example, in order for a child to locomote, he or she must likely repeat a small behavior a number of times; either have the strength to take several steps, make several crawling movements, or roll over and over. *Fluency* or speed measures whether the child can perform the behavior fast enough to be useful. In the example of locomotion, the teacher would be interested in whether the child can use a given form (creeping) fast enough to get him to where he wants to go within a reasonable period. *Flexibility* involves the number of different forms or categories of movement a person performs per unit of time (Dodds, 1978). Obviously the child who can accomplish a given result with a variety of accurate and fluent forms will have more adaptive and functional responses than the child with only one form. For example, John can maintain balance when moving if the movement is reaching, walking, and crawling, but Jane can only maintain balance while reaching. John obviously has more functional balance abilities than Jane.

In motor performance, a variety of skills are considered functional. These skills include locomotion, reaching/grasping (procurement of objects), moving grasped objects, maintenance of position, shifts in position without loss of balance, and maintenance of balance during locomotion. Although these skills have direct counterparts in developmental progressions, a variety of forms should be used.

Assessing environmental demands and opportunities Whether the environment provides opportunities for functional movement is important in assessment. That is, does the child have opportunities to use existing functional motor skills and learn new ones? Thus, determine whether opportunities for movement are built into the schedule, if children are given time during transitions between activities for movement, and whether activities used to teach skills from other developmental areas include movement.

Another aspect of measuring the environment involves determining whether movements are expected and demanded. *Demanded*, as used here, means the environment is structured to set the occasion for movement, reinforces movement when it occurs, and prompts its occurrence when it does not. More than simply providing the opportunity for movement, the teacher expects, accepts, encourages, and reacts to movement as though it is the intended, usual, and desired response. For example, Joe has the ability to locomote, but does not do so quickly. When Joe is done with his snack, he has the opportunity to go to the free play area. If after snack, Joe sits in his chair and asks the teacher to carry him to the free play area, and the teacher complies, movement is not expected or demanded in this situation. However, if the teacher verbally cues Joe to find something fun to play with and physically assists him in getting out of his chair and into his locomotion position, then the teacher expects and demands movement from Joe.

Facilitating Gross Motor Skills

When designing environments to encourage and facilitate gross motor skills, teachers should consider children and movement when equipping and arranging the classroom and provide abundant opportunities for those skills.

Consider children and movement when equipping and arranging the classroom. Issues related to equipping and arranging the preschool environment to facilitate skill development were discussed in Chapters 5 and 6. Child-sized equipment should be used and the environment structured to stimulate and allow movement.

When selecting child-sized equipment, the teacher should remember that not all children are the same size. Chairs should allow children to comfortably place their feet on the floor. If the chairs are too tall, blocks or small wooden platforms can be placed on the floor in front of the chairs. Tables should be about as high as the children's elbows when children are seated. Adjust tables that are too high or too low to prevent abnormal movement patterns.

As described in Chapters 5 and 6, activity areas in the classroom should be arranged to allow for easy movement. Some areas should invite fine motor movements and others should invite gross motor movements. Materials within the activity areas should be at eye level and easily accessible to children. Consider safety when structuring the home and school environment for movement. Wolinsky and Walker (1973) provide a checklist for parents of preschool handicapped children to evaluate the safety of their homes. Many items can also be adapted for the classroom.

Provide abundant opportunities for movement. For most children, acquisition and refinement of movement skills occur throughout preschool years. Thus, opportunities for activities involving movement are appropriate and important for most handicapped preschool children. In implementing this guideline, the teacher should consider that *movement is a high probability behavior* for preschool children. Their play frequently involves movement of objects. Teachers should use this propensity for movement as a reinforcer; the opportunity for movement can be given contingent upon children's successful completion of other, less likely behaviors that involve less movement. Further, opportunity for movement can be given contingent upon the occurrence of adaptive behaviors (Homme, deBaca, Devine, Steinhorst, & Rickert, 1963). These arrangements are applications of the Premack principle (see Chapter 7).

The teachers should also be aware that *movement and the training of specific movements should be embedded into training activities to teach other skills.* Training children to perform specific movements can easily be accomplished by making the movements a part of another activity. This practice not only facilitates acquisition of specific movements but can facilitate acquisition of behaviors from other developmental areas. For example, in training children to receptively label objects, Janssen and Guess (1978) found that allowing the children to functionally move the objects as a consequence for correct labeling resulted in faster acquisition of labels. Similarly, training children in social skills such as turn taking, sharing, and participating in a group can naturally be accomplished through movement activities. For example, rolling or throwing a ball between two or three children and sliding on a playground slide can provide opportunities to teach turn taking and sharing. Preschool teachers frequently attempt to teach social skills such as participating in a group and cognitive skills such as spatial relationships through songs involving actions.

In addition, the teachers should provide *a variety of structured (teacher-directed) and unstructured (child-directed) opportunities for movement.* Schedule time each day for outdoor, gross motor, and play activities. Some activities will need to be structured to facilitate acquisition of specific skills. However, time should also be allowed for children to engage in self-directed activities to practice previously learned behaviors that are apt to have more reinforcement value than structured activities. When using either structured or unstructured activities, the teacher may be an observer or participant, and can extend the child's play or attempt to induce cognitive conflict as described in Chapter 5. When activities involve gross motor behaviors, children's participation can be increased by adult participation. The teacher can also model a variety of new behaviors and thus increase the types of children's movements. However, teachers should avoid wearing easily damaged and unsafe shoes, clothing, and jewelry when participating in active behaviors.

At other times the teacher may choose to systematically observe the children play. Such observation allows excellent opportunities for assessing and monitoring child-child interactions, communicative behaviors, and motor performance.

Teaching Functional Movement Skills

Skills such as walking, running, hopping, jumping, catching and throwing balls, and riding tricycles are common preschool gross motor behaviors. As a result, teachers of preschool handicapped children frequently attempt to teach these skills. Several issues should be considered when attempting to teach such behaviors.

As suggested before, *consult with a physical or occupational therapist.* Therapists may provide essential information for teachers teaching major steps in a new skill. For example, a child who does not sit up probably

TABLE 15.5
Sequence of steps in teaching a child to crawl on stomach

Stimulus	Behavior	Criteria
1. Provide stimuli so that S continues to support his weight on his forearms to maintain his position.	1. S *supports his weight on his forearms* (chest on floor) for 1 minute.	At least 5 times
2. Provide stimuli so that S raises his chest and straightens his arms (e.g., hold a toy at eye level and move it above S's head so that he raises his head to see it, thus raising his chest and arms).	2. S *straightens his arms* and *raises his chest* to support his weight on his hands for 1 minute.	At least 5 times
3. Provide stimuli so that S reaches forward (e.g., place a toy just out of reach in front of S's arm). Repeat for the other arm. Give trials for each arm alternately.	3. S *scoots slightly forward by reaching.*	At least 5 times for each arm
4. Provide stimuli so that S moves forward. S will scoot forward by alternating his arms.	4. S *pulls himself forward about 2 feet, using his arms* (pull first with one arm, then the other; OR pull with both arms at once).	At least 5 times
5. Provide stimuli so that S moves forward at least 2 feet. S will push himself forward with his feet. (Tap his feet as a cue to get him started.) Assist S to move his arms only if necessary.	5. S *pushes himself forward about 2 feet, using his legs.*	At least 5 times

TABLE 15.5 (continued) Sequence of steps in teaching a child to crawl on stomach	Stimulus	Behavior	Criteria
	6. Provide stimuli for S to move forward at least 5 feet, using his arms and legs.	6. Target—S crawls forward 5 feet on his stomach unassisted.	4 correct out of the last 5 trials

Note: From *Programmed Environments Curriculum* by J. W. Tawney, D. S. Knapp, C. D. O'Reilly, and S. S. Pratt, Columbus, Ohio: Charles E. Merrill, 1979. Copyright 1979 by Charles E. Merrill. Reprinted by permission.

should not be taught to do so by being placed in a sitting position and then reinforced. This may cause long-term problems. Instead, many therapists would suggest providing exercises and experiences to strengthen muscles necessary for sitting. When these muscles are strong enough, sitting will be more likely to occur naturally.

Also, *systematic application of procedures that include precise specification and reinforcement of target behaviors, task analysis, and prompting may be used to teach gross motor skills.* Eyman, Silverstein, and McLain (1975) state that "changes in ambulation (walking) over a 3-year period ... suggest that little progress can be expected for some retarded children unless special programming" is presented (p. 580). A variety of studies have been conducted to teach preschool handicapped children gross motor behaviors. Hardiman, Goetz, Reuter, and LeBlanc (1975) used verbal cues, physical prompts, and contingent reinforcement to teach a 4-year-old cerebral palsied child to step through the rungs of a ladder, alternate feet while walking up steps, slide down the slide, and roll on the ground. O'Brien, Azrin, and Bugle (1972) trained four preschool children with mental retardation to stop crawling and use walking as a major means of locomotion. Likewise, Haavik and Altman (1977) used operant procedures to train severely retarded children to walk. Westervelt and Luiselli (1975) trained a physically handicapped child to stand and walk. Bragg, Houser, and Schumaker (1975) trained cerebral palsied children to sit in positions other than a reverse tailor sitting (*W* position). Bunker (1978) describes issues and procedures related to teaching gross motor skills,

and several curricula for young handicapped children also describe various procedures. Examples are the *Programmed Environments Curriculum* (Tawney, Knapp, O'Reilly, & Pratt, 1979), the *Hicomp Curriculum* (Neisworth, Willoughby-Herb, Bagnato, Cartwright, & Laub, 1980), the *Teaching Research Curriculum* (Fredericks, Riggs, Furey, Grove, Moore, McDonnell, Jordan, Hanson, Baldwin, & Wadlow, 1976), and the *Wabash Curriculum* (Tilton, Liska, & Bourland, 1977). A sample sequence of steps for teaching a child to crawl forward on his or her stomach (as suggested in the Programmed Environments Curriculum) is displayed in Table 15.5.

Still another issue to be considered is that *skills selected for training should be functional;* that is, serve a useful purpose in the child's life and enlarge control of the environment. Behaviors such as proficient locomotion and head control are more functional than standing on one foot or jumping from an 8-inch platform. Teachers should be sure to select functional target behaviors when evaluating curricula that accompany developmental checklists.

Also, *maintenance and generalization of gross motor behaviors do not necessarily occur.* For example, two of the subjects in the O'Brien et al. (1972) study did not maintain walking as a means of locomotion after the training was complete. Reintroduction of the contingencies for walking resulted in maintenance. Generalization of sitting in positions other than the reverse tailor position occurred for some subjects but not for all in the Bragg et al. (1975) study. Thus, teachers should be sure they train behaviors that will be expected and reinforced in other situations and after training is completed. To accomplish maintenance and generalization of gross motor behaviors, teachers should work with parents in selecting skills to be trained and then expecting and reinforcing those skills in other situations.

Finally, *when possible, motor skills should be trained in a game format* (e.g., Russo, 1979). The game format increases the likelihood of maintenance and generalization, incorporates the target motor skill into a variety of other motor behaviors, promotes opportunities for social interactions, and increases the probability that children will acquire behaviors for recreational and leisure time activities. Marlowe (1979, 1980) describes a method called *game analysis* that can be used for adapting and designing games for children with different abilities including various handicapping conditions.

Sensory Integrative Therapy

Another approach to treatment is the sensory integrative therapy developed by Jean Ayres. When discussing sensory integration, the theory should be separated from the treatment procedures. The theory is built on the notion that motor interactions with the environment are the primary source of knowledge and perception and are the basis for adaptive and conceptual responses (Ayres, 1972a, 1979). Piaget, Kephart, Getman, and others have designed their theories on similar propositions. Ayres' theory is unique in that she places more emphasis on "lower" senses and on the integration of those systems. Ayres (1972a, 1979) uses a broad definition of the word *senses,* including the vestibular, tactile, proprioceptive, olfactory, auditory, and visual. The *vestibular* sense provides information about position or orientation in relation to the pull of gravity, maintenance of positions, and balance. The *tactile* sense is the sense of touch; the *proprioceptive* sense provides input from the muscles and joints about the body's position, balance, and changes in balance. *Olfactory* is the sense of smell, *auditory* the sense of hearing, and *visual* the sense of sight. "Sensory integration is the organization of sensations for use" (Ayres, 1979, p. 5). The relationship between the brain and the senses is complex in Ayres' theory. The brain orga-

nizes sensations from environment; integrated senses assist in "nourishing" or directing the brain in responding to the environment. When senses are integrated or organized as a whole, the brain is able to receive meaning from the sensations. Ayres believes performance of adaptive responses results in further sensory integration, which in turn leads to more complex adaptive responses.

When sensory input is not organized there is unorganized input to the brain, and as a result, learning difficulties occur. Lack of integration is assessed by "experienced observation" and by the *Southern California Postrotary Nystagmus Test* (Ayres, 1975) and the *Southern California Sensory Integration Tests* (Ayres, 1972b). From data gathered with these tools, Ayres (1972c, 1979) has postulated that a number of different sensory integration dysfunction "syndromes" exist.

Sensory integration therapy is designed to integrate the various systems by providing controlled or facilitated sensory inputs (preferably from multiple modalities) and allowing self-initiated stimulation. The lower sensory systems (vestibular, tactile, and proprioceptive systems) are the primary emphasis of therapy (Ayres, 1972a). Ayres (1979) believes children normally pass through a sequence of stages or levels particularly receptive to various types of sensory stimulation. Thus, stimulation of the lower systems is an attempt to duplicate those experiences. Treatment activities include allowing and encouraging the children to experience a variety of textures through touch. Techniques such as brushing the muscles, pushing and pulling the joints, and vibrating muscles are sometimes used. Children receive vestibular and tactile stimulation by playing on scooter boards, bolster swings, and "large collections of equipment for swinging, spinning, rolling, climbing, crawling, riding, and other full body movements" (Ayres, 1979, p. 148).

The primary emphasis of educational research has been on learning disabled children (Ayres, 1972c, 1972d; de Quiros, 1976); however, some has been conducted to determine whether children with learning disabilities also have sensory integration dysfunctions (e.g., Ayres, 1972c).

Attempts to use sensory integration with other populations have been made; for example, with retarded children (Bonadonna, 1981; Clark, Miller, Thomas, Kucherawy, & Azen, 1978; Kantner, Clark, Allen, & Chase, 1976; Montgomery & Richter, 1977) and cerebral palsied children (Chee, Kreutzberg, & Clark, 1978). Clark and Shuer (1978) describe and present a rationale and suggestions for using sensory integration therapy with retarded children. In spite of the interest, methodological problems plague research with sensory integration therapy and retarded children. Thus, generalizations about the effectiveness of the therapy are very limited and questionable.

Methodological problems make it very difficult to conclude that sensory integration therapy is an effective treatment for handicapped children. Thus, teachers should carefully evaluate sensory integration therapy. Methods for such evaluations have been described (Hacker, 1980a, 1980b; Martin & Epstein, 1976; O'Neill & Harris, 1982; Wolery & Harris, 1982).

FINE MOTOR SKILLS

Fine motor skills, particularly those required for accurate and efficient use of the hands and fingers, develop in a relatively predicable fashion. Hand and finger development includes the progression from pronation to supination, from proximal to distal, and from ulnar to radial.

Pronation is observed when the palm of the hand faces the floor while the child is in an upright position. *Supination* is observed when the palm is turned to face the ceiling (Cohen & Gross, 1979). Initially infants exclusively use pronation; however, as they develop, they also acquire the ability to supinate the arm, greatly increasing the number of functional behaviors.

Development also proceeds in a *proximal to distal* fashion. Initially infants are flexed and cannot accurately extend their arms or move their hands well. As they mature, control of extremities and the ability to reach and grasp become apparent.

The ulnar to radial principle involves the hand. The "little finger" side of the hand is the *ulnar* side and the thumb is the *radial* side (Livingston & Chandler, 1977). This principle influences the development of grasp patterns.

The developmental sequence of grasp patterns is displayed in Figure 15.7. At birth infants have a *reflexive palmar grasp*. This grasp is stimulated when an object comes in contact with the palm and involves closing the fingers around the object. The thumb may

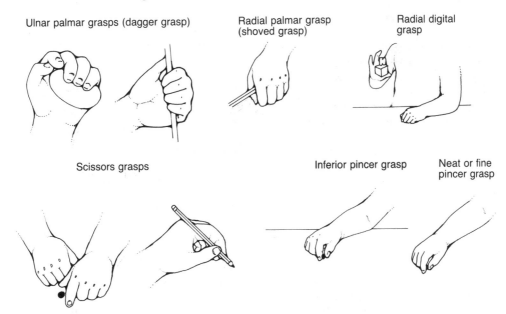

FIGURE 15.7
Developmental sequence of grasp patterns.   *Source:* Livingston & Chandler, 1977.

wrap around the object in the same or opposite direction as the fingers. However, the thumb is not important in this grasp and is not used in opposition (Livingston & Chandler, 1977).

The *ulnar palmar grasp* and all subsequent grasps are volitional rather than reflexive; that is, the child can use them in the absence of direct object stimulation. The little finger and ring finger and on occasion the middle finger are used to secure the object against the palm. The thumb is not used in opposition to the fingers (Livingston & Chandler, 1977). The ulnar palmar grasp is sometimes called the dagger grasp because the manipulandum (grasped and manipulated object) protrudes from the ulnar side of the hand like a dagger (Molloy, 1972).

The *radial palmar grasp* is the next to develop. The index and middle fingers hold the manipulandum against the palm of the hand (Livingston & Chandler, 1977) and the thumb may be used. This grasp is also called the shovel grasp because the manipulandum may protrude from the radial side of the hand similar to grasping a shovel (Molloy, 1972).

The *radial digital grasp* involves the thumb used in opposition to the middle and index fingers, frequently at the base of the fingers (Cohen & Gross, 1979). The movement of the manipulandum away from the palm of the hand as in the radial palmar grasp indicates the proximal-to-distal direction of development.

The *scissors grasp* involves the thumb in opposition to the *side* of the index finger. The point of contact on the index finger is usually farther out (more distal) toward the end of the finger than the radial digital grasp (Livingston & Chandler, 1977; Molloy, 1972).

The *pincer grasp* involves picking up small objects with the thumb in opposition to the *ends* of the index and/or the middle fingers. The first pincer grasp to develop is the *inferior pincer grasp* (Livingston & Chandler, 1977). The child must rest an arm on a surface. The *neat* or *fine pincer grasp* develops later and does not require resting the arm on a surface.

The development of grasp patterns from the reflexive palmar grasp to the fine pincer grasp is accomplished in normally developing children within the first year of life (Cohen & Gross, 1977). However, the child's ability to use these grasps is refined throughout the preschool years. The strength, speed, and coordination of these grasp patterns increases as children grow older.

Assessing Fine Motor Skills

Fine motor skills may be assessed through norm- or criterion-referenced assessments. Many criterion- and curriculum-referenced tests include a fine motor domain. Several norm-referenced measures have been developed to assess perceptual-motor skills (eye-hand coordination). These tools include the Developmental Test of Visual Perception (DTVP) (Frostig, Lefever, & Whittlesey, 1966), Purdue Perceptual-Motor Survey (PPMS) (Roach & Kephart, 1966), Developmental Test of Visual-Motor Integration (VMI) (Beery & Buktenica, 1967), and others (Salvia & Ysseldyke, 1981). Unfortunately, reliability is very low for many of these measures (Salvia & Ysseldyke, 1981). Also, the items on these tests were not selected because of their instructional usefulness. Thus teachers should be wary of using these instruments to design or evaluate interventions for children.

Most criterion- and curriculum-referenced measures, such as those described in Chapter 2, provide a finer motor section listing skills that are more useful instructional targets. Basic fine motor and writing skills drawn from two such instruments (D'Eugenio & Moersch, 1981; White, Edgar, Haring, Affleck, Hayden, & Bendersky, 1981) are listed in Table 15.6.

Perceptual Motor Training

A number of authors (such as Kephart, Barsch, Getman, and Frostig) have developed training regimens commonly called *perceptual-motor programs* (Hallahan & Cruickshank, 1973). These programs are based on the notion that certain perceptual and/or perceptual-motor abilities are prerequisites for academic achievement (Hammill & Wiederholt, 1973); thus, children who show deficient academic achievement may lack adequate perceptual and perceptual-motor abilities. Other assumptions are that some children have identifiable perceptual-motor problems, a prescriptive program of various exercises could alleviate these problems, and as a result of the remediation of these problems, children's academic performance would improve.

TABLE 15.6
Selected fine motor items from uniform performance assessment system (White et al., 1981) and developmental programming for infants and young children (D'Eugenio & Moersch, 1981)

General Age Range	Basic Fine Motor Skills	Writing Skills
0–6 months	Reaches for object held 6–8 inches away Grasps easily held object when presented Picks up one cube or toy in hand at same time	
6–12 months	Picks up small object using a rake, finger-thumb or pincer grasp Places cube or toy from one hand into the other Puts cube into container	
12–24 months	Puts ring on stick Puts peg in pegboard	Scribbles
24–36 months	Turns pages of book, singly Strings beads Pounds peg through a board Snips paper held by tester Places shape in cut out of shape Takes apart and puts together puzzle with 3 adjacent pieces Builds 2–6 cube tower	Draws vertical and horizontal strokes imitatively Makes continuous circle (loop) stroke after watching model Initiates zig-zag strokes
34–48 months	Cuts across 2-inch-wide paper while holding it Builds 8 cube tower Builds 3-block bridge in imitation Takes apart and puts together puzzle with 7–15 adjacent pieces	Exhibits hand preference Initiates drawing a circle Initiates drawing a "+"
48–60 months	Copies parquetry block design	Traces line within ¼ in. of original line Imitates drawing square Draws person with 3 parts

TABLE 15.6 (continued)

TABLE 15.6 (continued)
Selected fine motor items from uniform performance assessment system (White et al., 1981) and developmental programming for infants and young children (D'Eugenio & Moersch, 1981)

General Age Range	Basic Fine Motor Skills	Writing Skills
60–72 months		Exhibits mature pencil grip Draws person with 5 parts Can copy first name Prints name without model

The theoretical assumptions of perceptual-motor training, the methodological adequacy of the studies related to the effectiveness of training, and the actual effectiveness results of training have been seriously questioned (Hammill & Wiederholt, 1973; Ysseldyke, 1973). Hammill and Wiederholt (1973) reviewed research related to Frostig's training program and concluded that it "has no effect on reading and has a questionable effect on school readiness and perception itself" (p. 44). In relation to perceptual-motor training in general, Salvia and Ysseldyke (1981) state the following:

There is a tremendous lack of empirical evidence to support the claim that specific perceptual-motor training facilitates the acquisition of academic skills or improves the chances of academic success. Perceptual-motor training will improve *perceptual-motor* functioning. . . . There is no support for the use of perceptual-motor tests in planning programs designed to facilitate academic learning or remediate academic difficulties (p. 367).

Thus, in designing instructional programs for young handicapped children, little support can be given for the use of perceptual-motor assessment tools or the practice of training activities to facilitate later academic achievement.

Selecting Materials for Fine Motor Training

Nearly every preschool program has a variety of materials frequently referred to as "fine motor materials" or as "manipulative toys." Common examples are puzzles, blocks, shape sorting toys, clay, peg boards, form boards, crayons, threading and stacking toys, nesting cups, and construction sets. Often time is devoted to these materials without careful consideration of the objectives, child's needs, or the sequences through which children can meet the objectives. Teachers should clearly identify the purposes for which they use manipulative toys, including facilitating grasp acquisition and refinement (proficiency); eye-hand coordination; specific arm movements while maintaining grasps on objects; independent play; persistence at tasks (see Chapter 7); social skills such as turn-taking; and cognitive skills such as part-whole relationships, size, form, and color relationships, and problem solving.

Many manipulative materials can be used to assist children in developing and practicing proficient grasping. An assessment of the child's functional grasps should be done by comparing his or her grasps to the sequence of grasps in Figure 15.7. Materials should then be provided to stimulate the use of the given target grasp, with emphasis on grasping a variety of rather than one or two objects.

When children begin to use a pincer grasp proficiently, present functional activities such as fastening clothing and opening milk cartons. In addition, more time should be spent on activities to develop proficiency in using pencils, such as coloring and painting. Milone and Wasylyk (1981) describe the grasps and strokes necessary for painting.

When using manipulative toys to teach eye-hand coordination, the teacher should remember that eye-hand coordination means the eyes guide the hands and the hands in turn guide the eyes. Thus, to facilitate this mutual guiding and following, the teacher should be sure the child looks at the toys while manipulating them. Many children manipulate toys in a haphazard manner without looking at what their hands are doing and thus do not learn eye-hand coordination. Toys that require progressively more eye-hand coordination should be used as children acquire this skill. The eyes also guide other movements of the body such as reaching, tool use, foot movements, and locomotion. DeOreo and William (1980) describe the relationships between vision and motor skills.

If training is to stimulate arm movements, select toys that produce a result when moved. For example, a mobile produces an interesting sight when touched. A toy hammer produces a sound and the object pounded may move or change form. Several arm movements are needed to facilitate functional manipulation of objects in the environment. These are hand-to-mouth movement, slapping, pushing, shaking, poking, pulling, and wrist rotation. In addition, grasped objects frequently must be held while the movement occurs and some movements must be performed with both arms at the same time (Molloy, 1972). Select materials that stimulate the targeted arm movement.

Finally, materials and skills used in fine motor training should be functional. Skills should be taught when the child has acquired the necessary developmental precursors. However, at issue is whether the materials used in teaching should be real or artificial. For example, when teaching a basic self-help task such as buttoning a shirt, should the teacher use an artificial aid such as a buttoning board? Or should realistic materials such as buttons and an enlarged buttonhole be employed? The child may not generalize from the buttoning board to the real task; thus training using the artificial materials may be more lengthy than necessary. It is also difficult to approximate real task conditions of buttoning by using a board, particularly since relative positions of persons and materials will be different. Therefore, the more efficient instructional strategy would be to use the real materials, modifying them to the needs of each child. Artificial materials should be used sparingly.

Another example related to the training of functional motor skills is in the area of writing. Many teachers require children to draw certain shapes in preparation for writing letters. A common shape included on many assessment tools is a rectangle with diagonal lines connecting the corners. This skill alone is not very functional since children are never asked to draw that shape in the real world (except when taking a test!). This skill is taught because it is on the tests and because it is assumed to be good practice for teaching writing. But why not go ahead and begin simple letter writing? Many letters are much simpler and more functional to write than this rectangle. Given the limited amount of teaching time coupled with children's developmental delays, teachers should focus on *developmentally appropriate* yet *functional* skills.

Direct Instruction of Skills

Although children learn many motor skills through day-to-day experience, many handicapped children will need direct instruction to learn or refine those skills. The direct instruction process in teaching fine motor skills is similar to that used in teaching other motor skills. An appropriate skill is targeted, expected levels of performance are specified, and instruction begins. Teacher assists are often provided, either through physical prompts and manipulations or cues or models.

For example, Tawney et al. (1979) make several suggestions for helping teach a child to grasp. These suggestions include the following:

1 Place your hand over the child's wrist and squeeze, causing his fingers to curl. Gradually decrease your pressure.
2 To increase strength in hands, fingers, and wrist, guide the child to push his hand through water or sand. Gradually decrease your guidance.
3 Use objects with sticky surfaces (e.g., double-backed tape) at first.
4 Gradually increase the distance the object is placed from the child.
5 Use toy clickers and other attractive stimuli to increase the child's attention on the object (pp. 161–167).

Backward chaining (see Chapters 3 and 16) is a useful strategy for teaching some fine motor skills and involves helping the child perform the first steps in a sequence of behaviors, using the last task as the teaching target. Once the child learns the last step, the next to the last step is taught, and so forth, until the child masters the entire sequence. For example, the backward chaining procedure is used in the following sequence of steps to open a small carton of milk.

1 Locate correct side for opening.
2 Place thumbs underneath flap and other fingers on top and side of carton.
3 Pull opening apart.
4 Release.
5 Hold the bottom of the carton with one hand.
6 Grasp spout with other hand.
7 Pull spout out.

The teacher physically assists the child in performing all but the last step in the sequence. Once the child has learned to pull the carton open, he or she is asked to grasp the spout independently.

Guidelines and strategies for teaching children to manipulate toys are in Chapter 11, and those for teaching basic dressing skills that require fine motor movements are in Chapter 16.

LeBlanc, Etzel, and Domash (1978) describe an errorless learning procedure for teaching children to write. The child initially traces the word or letter. In subsequent training sessions, portions of the letters are gradually faded

FIGURE 15.8
Example of an errorless learning procedure to teach a child to write the word *cat. Source:* Le Blanc, Etzel, and Domash (1978).

until the child writes the word or letter from memory. An example of steps for writing the word *cat* is displayed in Figure 15.8.

SUMMARY

This chapter described procedures for assessing and teaching motor skills to young handicapped children. The basic areas of motor development—reflexes, reactions, and tone, gross motor skills, and fine motor skills—were identified.

Knowledge of reflexes, reactions, and tone is important because many preschool programs have children with these problems. Teachers should be aware of the techniques and equipment used by therapists in working with children with severe motor impairments.

Teaching locomotion and fine motor skills requires the basic steps of behavioral specification of objectives, task analysis, intervention, and evaluation. Teachers should attempt to insure that most motor skills taught will be functional.

Finally, the importance of consulting with therapists when developing instructional program plans for young handicapped children was emphasized. Various methods were described for implementing consultation between therapists and teachers (Connolly & Anderson, 1978; Mitchell & Lindsey, 1979) and between therapists, teachers, and parents (Harris, 1980; Sasano, Shepard, Bell, Davies, Hansen, & Sanford, 1977). Consultation is also important in determining the need for and appropriate form of therapy. In addition, teachers can obtain specific information concerning positioning, handling, lifting, and carrying children. Utley et al. (1977) and Finnie (1975) describe general procedures for positioning and handling, but teachers should seek confirmation from therapists about the applicability of given procedures to specific children, especially infants; non-ambulatory children; and children whose primitive reflexes are not integrated and with undeveloped automatic reactions, with abnormal tone (hypertonic or hypotonic), and with physical disabilities or deformities.

In addition to therapists, the adaptive physical educator can provide much helpful information on normal and abnormal motor development and can be particularly useful in designing recreational activities requiring specific motor skills.

REFERENCES

Andrews, M., & Down, J. Guidelines to positioning and adaptive equipment. In N. G. Haring (Ed.), *The experimental education training program*. Seattle: The Experimental Education Unit, 1977.

Ayres, A. J. *Sensory integration and learning disorders*. Los Angeles: Western Psychological Services, 1972. (a)

Ayres, A. J. *Southern California Sensory Integration Tests*. Los Angeles: Western Psychological Services, 1972. (b)

Ayres, A. J. Types of sensory integrative dysfunction among disabled learners. *The American Journal of Occupational Therapy*, 1972, *26*, 13–18. (c)

Ayres, A. J. Improving academic scores through sensory integration. *Journal of Learning Disabilities*, 1972, *5*, 23–28. (d)

Ayres, A. J. *Southern California Postrotary Nystagmus Test*. Los Angeles: Western Psychological Services, 1975.

Ayres, A. J. *Sensory integration and the child*. Los Angeles: Western Psychological Services, 1979.

Bayley, N. *Manual for the Bayley Scales of Infant Development*. New York: The Psychological Corporation, 1969.

Beery, K. E., & Buktenica, N. *Developmental Test of Visual-Motor Integration*. Chicago: Follett, 1967.

Bigge, J. L., & O'Donnell, P. A. *Teaching individuals with physical and multiple disabilities*. Columbus, Ohio: Charles E. Merrill, 1976.

Bijou, S. W. The prevention of retarded development in disadvantaged children. In M. J. Begab, H. C. Haywood, & H. L. Garber (Eds.), *Psychosocial influences in retarded performance* (Vol. 1). *Issues and theories in development*. Baltimore: University Park Press, 1981.

Bleck, E. E. Cerebral palsy, In E. E. Bleck and D. A. Nagel (Eds.), *Physically handicapped children: A medical atlas for teachers*. New York: Grune & Stratton, 1975.

Bleck, E. E., & Nagel, D. A. (Eds.). *Physically handicapped children: A medical atlas for teachers*. New York: Grune & Stratton, 1975.

Bobath, B. A neuro-developmental treatment of cerebral palsy. *Physiotherapy*, 1963, *49*, 242–244.

Bobath, B. The treatment of neuromuscular disorders by improving patterns of coordination. *Physiotherapy*, 1969, *55*, 18–22.

Bobath, B. Motor development, its effect on general development and application to the treatment of cerebral palsy. *Physiotherapy*, 1971, *57*, 526–532.

Bobath, K., & Bobath, B. The facilitation of normal postural reactions and movements in cerebral palsy. *Physiotherapy*, 1964, *50*, 246–252.

Bonadonna, P. Effects of a vestibular stimulation program on stereotypic rocking behavior. *The American Journal of Occupational Therapy*, 1981, *35*, 775–781.

Bragg, J. H., Houser, C., & Schumaker, J. Behavior modifications: Effects on reverse tailor sitting in children with cerebral palsy. *Physical Therapy*, 1975, *55*, 860–868.

Brazelton, T. B. *Neonatal Behavioral Assessment Scale*. Philadelphia: J. B. Lippincott and Spastic International Medical Publications, 1973.

Bunker, L. K. Motor skills. In M. E. Snell (Ed.), *Systematic instruction of the moderately and severely handicapped*. Columbus, Ohio: Charles E. Merrill, 1978.

Campbell, P., Green, K. M., & Carlson, L. M. Approximating the norm through environmental and child-centered prosthetics and adaptive equipment. In E. Sontag (Ed.), *Educational programming for the severely and profoundly handicapped*. Reston, Va.: Council for Exceptional Children, 1977.

Capute, A. J., Accardo, P. J., Vining, E. P. G., Rubenstein, J. E., Walcher, J. R., Harryman, S., & Ross, A. Primitive Reflex Profile: A pilot study. *Physical Therapy*, 1978, *58*, 1061–1065.

Chandler, L. S., Andrews, M. S., & Swanson, M. W. *Movement Assessment of Infants: A Manual*. Rolling Bay, Wash. 1980.

Chee, F. K. W., Kreutzberg, J. R., & Clark, D. L. Semicircular canal stimulation in cerebral palsied children. *Physical Therapy*, 1978, *58*, 1071–1075.

Clark, F. A., Miller, L. R., Thomas, J. A., Kucherawy, D. A., & Azen, S. P. A comparison of operant and sensory integrative methods on developmental parameters in profoundly retarded adults. *The American Journal of Occupational Therapy*, 1978, *32*, 86–92.

Clark, F. A., & Shuer, J. A clarification of sensory integrative therapy and its application to programming with retarded people. *Mental Retardation*, 1978, *16*, 227–232.

Cohen, M., & Gross, P. *The developmental resource: Behavioral sequences for assessment and program planning* (Vol. 1). New York: Grune & Stratton, 1979.

Connolly, B. H., & Anderson, R. M. Severely handicapped children in the public schools: A new frontier for the physical therapist. *Physical Therapy*, 1978, *58*, 433–438.

Cooper, R. G. *Principles of development*. Westwood, Miss.: The Paper Book Press, 1977.

DeOreo, K., & William, H. G. Characteristics of visual perception. In C. B. Corbin (Ed.), *A textbook of motor development* (2nd ed.). Dubuque, Iowa: Wm. C. Brown, 1980.

D'Eugenio, D., & Moersch, M. S. (Eds.). *Developmental programming for infants and young children*. Ann Arbor: University of Michigan Press, 1981.

de Quiros, D. Diagnosis of vestibular disorders in the learning disabled. *Journal of Learning Disabilities*, 1976, *9*, 50–58.

Dodds, P. Creativity in movement: Models for analysts. *Journal of Creative Behavior*, 1978, *12*, 265–273.

DuBose, R. F. Working with sensorily impaired children, Part I: Visual impairments. In S. G. Garwood (Ed.), *Educating young handicapped children: A developmental approach*. Germantown, Md.: Aspen Systems, 1979. (a)

DuBose, R. F. Working with sensorily impaired children, Part II: Hearing impaired. In S. G. Garwood (Ed.), *Educating young handicapped children: A developmental approach.* Germantown, Md.: Aspen Systems, 1979. (b)

Dubose, R. F., & Deni, K. Easily constructed adaptive and assistive equipment. *Teaching Exceptional Children,* 1980, *12,* 116–123.

Eipper, D. S., & Azen, S. P. A comparison of two developmental instruments in evaulating children with Down's syndrome. *Physical Therapy,* 1978, *58,* 1066–1069.

Evans, E. D., & McCandless, B. R. *Children and youth: Psychosocial development.* New York: Holt, Rinehart and Winston, 1978.

Eyman, R. K., Silverstein, A. B., & McLain, R. Effects of treatment programs on the acquisition of basic skills. *American Journal of Mental Deficiency,* 1975, *79,* 573–582.

Finnie, N. R. *Handling the young cerebral palsied child at home.* New York: Dutton, 1975.

Folio, R., & DuBose, R. F. *Peabody Developmental Motor Scales* (rev. experimental ed.). Nashville: Institute on Mental Retardation and Intellectual Development, 1974.

Ford, F. Normal motor development in infancy. In E. E. Bleck & D. A. Nagel (Eds.), *Physically handicapped children: A medical atlas for teachers.* New York: Grune & Strattion, 1975.

Fraiberg, S. *Insights from the blind.* New York: Basic Books, 1977.

Fredericks, H. D., Riggs, C., Furey, T., Grove, D., Moore, W., McDonnell, J., Jordan, E., Hanson, W., Baldwin, V., & Wadlow, M. *The teaching research curriculum for moderately and severely handicapped.* Springfield, Ill.: Charles C. Thomas, 1976.

Freides, D., Barbati, J., Van Kampen-Horowitz, L. J., Sprehn, G., Iversen, J., Silver, J. R., & Woodward, R. Blind evaluation of body reflexes and motor skills in learning disability. *Journal of Autism and Developmental Disorders,* 1980, *10,* 159–171.

Frostig, M., Lefever, W., & Whittlesey, J. *Administration and scoring manual; Marianne Frostig Developmental Test of Visual Perception.* Palo Alto, Calif.: Consulting Psychologists Press, 1966.

Garwood, S. G. Physical and physiological bases of handicaps. In S. G. Garwood (Ed.), *Educating young handicapped children: A developmental approach.* Germantown, Md.: Aspen Systems, 1979.

Gesell, A., & Amatruda, C. S. *Developmental diagnosis: Normal and abnormal child development: Clinical methods and pediatric applications.* New York: Hoeber, 1942.

Goldenson, R. M. *Disability and rehabilitation handbook.* New York: McGraw-Hill, 1978.

Haavik, S., & Altman, K. Establishing walking by severely retarded children. *Perceptual and Motor Skills,* 1977, *44,* 1107–1114.

Hacker, B. Single subject research strategies in occupational therapy: Part I. *The American Journal of Occupational Therapy,* 1980, *34,* 169–175. (a)

Hacker, B. Single subject research startegies in occupational therapy: Part II. *The American Journal of Occupational Therapy,* 1980, *34,* 169–175. (b)

Hallahan, D., & Cruickshank, W. *Psychoeducational foundations of learning disabilities.* Englewood Cliffs, N.J.: Prentice-Hall, 1973.

Hammill, D., & Wiederholt, J. L. Review of the Frostig Visual Perception Test and the related training program. In L. Mann & D. Sabatino (Eds.), *The first review of special education* (Vol. 1). Philadelphia: Journal of Special Education Press, Grune & Stratton, 1973.

Hardiman, S. A., Goetz, E. M., Reuter, K. E., & LeBlanc, J. M. Primes, contingent attention, and training: Effects on a child's motor behavior. *Journal of Applied Behavior Analysis,* 1975, *8,* 399–409.

Harris, S. R. Transdisciplinary therapy model for the infant with Down's syndrome. *Physical Therapy,* 1980, *60,* 420–423.

Harris, S. R. Effects of neurodevelopmental therapy on motor performance of infants with Down's syndrome. *Developmental Medicine and Child Neurology,* 1981, *23,* 477–483.

Harris, S. R., & Tada, W. L. Providing developmental therapy services. In S. G. Garwood & R. R. Fewell (Eds.), *Educating handicapped infants.* Rockville, Md.: Aspen Systems, 1983.

Homme, L. E., DeBaca, P. C., Devine, J. V., Steinhorst, R., & Rickert, E. J. Use of the Premack principle in controlling the behavior of nursery school children. *Journal of the Experimental Analysis of Behavior,* 1963, *6,* 544.

Janssen, C., & Guess, D. Use of function as a consequence in training receptive labeling to severely and profoundly retarded individuals. *AAESPH Review,* 1978, *3,* 246–258.

Johnson, J. L. Programming for early motor responses within the classroom. *AAESPH Review,* 1978, *3,* 4–14.

Kantner, R. M., Clark, D. L., Allen, L. C., & Chase, M. F. Effects of vestibular stimulation on Nystagmus response and motor performance in the developmentally delayed infant. *Physical Therapy,* 1976, *56,* 414–421.

Kasari, C., & Filler, J. W. Using inflatables with severely motorically involved infants and preschoolers. *Teaching Exceptional Children,* 1981, *14,* 22–26.

Langley, M. B. Working with young physically-impaired children, Part A: The nature of physical handicaps. In S. G. Garwood (Ed.), *Educating young handicapped children: A developmental approach.* Germantown, Md.: Aspen Systems, 1979.

LaVeck, B., & LaVeck, G. D. Sex differences in development among young children with Down syndrome. *The Journal of Pediatrics,* 1977, *91,* 767–769.

LeBlanc, J. M., Etzel, B. C., & Domash, M. A. A functional curriculum for early intervention. In K. E. Allen, V. A. Holm, & R. L. Schiefelbusch (Eds.), *Early intervention—a team approach.* Baltimore: University Park Press, 1978.

Lindsey, D., & O'Neal, J. Static and dynamic balance skills in eight year old deaf and hearing children. *American Annals of the Deaf,* 1976, *121,* 49–55.

Livingston, S. S., & Chandler, L. S. Fine motor development hand skill development. In N. G. Haring (Ed.), *The experimental education training program.* Seattle: Experimental Education Unit, 1977.

Marlowe, M. The games analysis intervention: Procedures to increase the peer acceptance and social adjustment of the mentally retarded child. *Education and Training of the Mentally Retarded,* 1979, *14,* 262–268.

Marlowe, M. Games analysis: Designing games for handicapped children. *Teaching Exceptional Children,* 1980, *12,* 48–51.

Martin, J., & Epstein, L. Evaluating treatment effectiveness in cerebral palsy: Single subject designs. *Physical Therapy,* 1976, *56,* 285–294.

McCandless, B. *Children and adolescents: Behavior and development.* New York: Holt, Rinehart and Winston, 1961.

McCarthy, D. *Manual for the McCarthy Scales of Children's Abilities.* New York: Psychological Corporation, 1972.

Milone, M. N., & Wasylyk, T. M. Handwriting in special education. *Teaching Exceptional Children,* 1981, *14,* 58–61.

Mitchell, M. M., & Lindsey, D. A model for establishing occupational therapy and physical therapy services in the public schools. *The American Journal of Occupational Therapy,* 1979, *33,* 361–364.

Molloy, J. S. *Trainable children: Curriculum and procedures.* New York: John Day, 1972.

Montgomery, P., & Richter, E. Effect of sensory integrative therapy on the neuromotor development of retarded children. *Physical Therapy,* 1977, *57,* 799–806.

Neisworth, J., Willoughby-Herb, S. J., Bagnato, S. J., Cartwright, C. A., & Laub, K. W. *Individualized education for preschool exceptional children.* Germantown, Md.: Aspen Systems, 1980.

O'Brien, F., Azrin, N. H., & Bugle, C. Training profoundly retarded children to stop crawling. *Journal of Applied Behavior Analysis,* 1972, *5,* 131–137.

O'Neil, D. L., & Harris, S. R. Developing goals and objectives for handicapped children. *Physical Therapy,* 1982, *62,* 295–298.

Piaget, J. *The origins of intelligence in children.* New York: Norton, 1952.

Roach, E. F., & Kephart, N. C. *The Purdue Perceptual-Motor Survey.* Columbus, Ohio: Charles E. Merrill, 1966.

Robinson, N. M., & Robinson, H. B. *The mentally retarded child* (2nd ed.). New York: McGraw-Hill, 1976.

Russo, L. M. Fun stuff: Having a ball. *The Exceptional Parent,* 1979, *9,* 55–58.

Salvia, J., & Ysseldyke, J. E. *Assessment in special and remedial education* (2nd ed.). Boston: Houghton Mifflin, 1981.

Sasano, E. M., Shepard, K. F., Bell, J. E., Davies, N. H., Hansen, E. M., & Sanford, T. L. The family in physical therapy. *Physical Therapy,* 1977, *57,* 153–159.

Swanson, M. W. Early motor development: Assessment and intervention. In B. L. Darby & M. J. May (Eds.), *Infant assessment: Issues and applications.* Seattle: Western States Technical Assistance Resource, 1979.

Tawney J. W., Knapp, D. S., O'Reilly, C. D., & Pratt, S. S. *Programmed environments curriculum.* Columbus, Ohio: Charles E. Merrill, 1979.

Tilton, J. R., Liska, D. C., & Bourland, J. C. *Guide to early developmental training.* Boston: Allyn and Bacon, 1977.

Utley, B. L., Holvoet, J. F., & Barnes, K. Handling, positioning, and feeding the physically handicapped. In E. Sontag (Ed.), *Educational programming for the severely and profoundly handicapped.* Reston, Va.: Division on Mental Retardation of the Council for Exceptional Children, 1977.

Vander Zanden, J. W. *Human Development* (2nd ed.). New York: Alfred A. Knopf, 1981.

Venn, J., Morganstern, L., & Dykes, M. K. Checklists for evaluating the fit and function of orthoses, prostheses, and wheelchairs in the classroom. *Teaching Exceptional Children,* 1978, *11,* 51–56.

Westervelt, V. D., & Luiselli, J. K. Establishing standing and walking behavior in a physically handicapped, retarded child. *Physical Therapy,* 1975, *55,* 761–765.

White, O., Edgar, G., Haring, N. G., Affleck, J., Hayden, A. H., & Bendersky, M. *Uniform Performance Assessment System.* Columbus, Ohio: Charles E. Merrill, 1981.

Wolery, M. R., & Harris, S. R. Interpreting the results of single subject research designs. *Physical Therapy,* 1982, *62,* 445–452.

Wolinsky, G., & Walker, S. A home safety inventory for parents of preschool handicapped children. *Teaching Exceptional Children.* 1973, *6,* 82–86.

Ysseldyke, J. E. Diagnostic-prescriptive teaching: The search for aptitude-treatment interactions. In L. Mann & D. Sabatino (Eds.), *The first review of special education.* Philadelphia: Journal of Special Education Press, Grune & Stratton, 1973.

S elf-help skills are behaviors that result in independent functioning in caring for one's basic survival needs and conforming to related social mores. Basic self-help skills are eating, self-feeding, toileting, and dressing/undressing; more advanced skills include, among others, grooming, bathing, clothing care, house cleaning/keeping, food preparation, and related social skills such as table manners (Bender & Valletutti, 1976). Although all of these skills are important, teachers of young handicapped children are primarily concerned with teaching self-feeding, eating, toileting, and dressing/undressing. This chapter describes these skills and procedures for facilitating their acquisition and use.

CHARACTERISTICS OF SELF-HELP SKILLS

Self-help skills have several characteristics pertinent to teaching preschool handicapped children. They are composed of behaviors that can be learned; thus, they can be taught (Osarchuk, 1973; Westling & Murden, 1978). Frequently, processes such as toileting or chewing are thought to be due to physiological or biological maturation. Admittedly, some maturation is required; for example, a child must be able to perform precise, independent movements of the jaw, lips, and tongue before he or she can successfully chew solid foods (Colangelo, Bergen, & Gottlieb, 1976), and certain sphincter muscle strength is necessary before toilet training. However, maturation alone may not be sufficient for the acquisition of many self-help skills by handicapped youngsters. For instance, a child may independently and precisely move his or her tongue, lips, and jaw, but still not chew, or a child may have considerable sphincter muscle control but not toilet at the appropriate times and places. Further, those behaviors thought to be due to maturational forces may be amenable to instruction. Kohlenberg (1973) found the sphincter muscle pressure of a 13-year-old encopretic (pants soiling) boy could be increased when he was reinforced with coins for exerting more pressure. Considerable evidence also suggests the effectiveness of behavioral procedures in teaching self-help skills to handicapped persons (Azrin & Armstrong, 1973; Azrin & Foxx, 1971; Bensberg, Colwell, & Cassell, 1965; Horner &

16

Acquisition and Use of Self-Help Skills

Keilitz, 1975; Matson, DiLorenzo, & Esveldt-Dawson, 1981). This effectiveness appears to be a direct result of the training rather than of increases in staff-to-child ratios or general enhancement of the environment (Murphy & Zahm, 1975). Thus, teachers of young handicapped children must assume responsibility for training self-help skills rather than waiting for maturational forces. Further, teachers must be competent in the use of behavioral procedures. The primary focus of this chapter is to describe the training procedures teachers can use in fulfilling this responsibility.

In addition, teaching self-help skills is a reasonable educational endeavor (Snell, 1980). In the past, teaching skills such as self-feeding, dressing, and toileting was considered a family function. However, with improved teaching procedures, increases in the number of severely handicapped children in educational settings, and the passage of P. L. 94–142 requiring an individualized and appropriate education, teachers have assumed more responsibility for teaching self-help skills. Teachers who do so not only increase children's ability to care for themselves, allowing them to function independently, but also decrease the number of behaviors that point out the differences between handicapped and typical children. For example, a child who is 6 years old and does not feed herself is more obviously different from typical children than the 6-year-old handicapped child who does.

Another characteristic is that normally developing children gradually acquire the basic self-help skills through the preschool years (Cohen & Gross, 1979). For example, when Tim was about 12 months old, he frequently pulled off his socks, but he did not tie his shoes until he was 6 years old. In the meantime, he learned to feed himself, put on and take off his clothing, and toilet himself. Similarly, when Tony was 2 years old he urinated in the toilet if he was taken, but he was 4 years old before he consistently slept through the night without wetting the bed. Steve fed himself with his fingers when he was 8 or 9 months old, but he was 5 before he could hold a piece of meat with a fork and cut it with a table knife. Because of the gradual acquisition of self-help skills, teachers of preschool handicapped children must be familiar with procedures for teaching a broad range of skills, and they will likely have self-help objectives regardless of the children's age or functioning level.

Also, simply being able to perform given self-help skills is usually not sufficient for those skills to be used in a functional manner. For example, Deborah can put on her shoes, but it takes her 5 minutes to do it. Rachael can feed herself with a spoon, but she spills about half of the food. Deborah and Rachael must become more proficient before the skills will result in independent functioning. Thus, when teaching self-help skills, teachers must ensure children can perform the behaviors proficiently. *Proficiency* is a combination of accuracy and speed (Gentry & Haring, 1976).

Still another characteristic is that most self-help skills are used on a regular but low frequency basis. For example, children put on their shoes almost daily, but during the course of the day they may put them on and take them off only one or two times. Similarly, if Lori is learning to feed herself with a fork, she will likely only eat three meals a day and perhaps one or two of those meals will not require the use of a fork. Since training in self-help skills should occur during natural times (learning to self-feed during meals or learning to undress when getting ready to go to bed) and since the behaviors occur at a low frequency, teachers of young handicapped children must frequently involve parents and other caregivers in training. Lance and Koch (1973) surveyed 107 parents of young handicapped children and asked them which self-help skills were the most important and the most difficult to teach. From most to least important, parents ranked the skills as toileting, eating, dressing, and washing and grooming; in order of most to least difficult to teach, parents ranked them as toileting, dressing, eating, and washing and grooming. Thus, early childhood special educators will likely have to train and support parents as they teach these skills. Parent training and involvement and support for parents during training have resulted in increased levels of self-help skills in handicapped children (Cullen, Cronk, Pueschel, Schnell, & Reed, 1981; Latham & Hofmeister, 1973; Mendelsohn, 1978; Tyler & Kahn, 1976).

Finally, most functional self-help skills are a series or chain of many individual behaviors

(Bensberg, 1965). For example, drinking from a cup involves the steps of locating the cup's position, reaching for the cup, grasping it, lifting it from the table, moving it toward one's mouth, placing it on the lower lip, tilting the cup to allow the liquid to enter the mouth, closing one's mouth, swallowing, removing the cup from the lip, placing the cup on the table, and releasing one's grasp. Thus, a simple behavior such as taking a drink from a cup involves at least 12 steps. Children must perform the small individual steps of each behavior proficiently and in the correct sequence. However, drinking from a cup is, of course, only one part of the more complex task of eating a meal independently. To eat a meal independently, children must combine several chains of behavior in an organized manner. For example, they must drink from a cup, eat with a spoon and/or fork, cut or spread with a knife, wipe their face with a napkin, and pass food to the next person. In addition, these behaviors are frequently performed in social situations that may require conversation. Thus, the teacher must be familiar with procedures for training behaviors into complex chains of behavior that can be performed in social settings.

A summary of the characteristics and implications for teaching is listed in Table 16.1.

EATING AND SELF-FEEDING

Since maintenance of life depends upon nutrient intake, eating and learning to feed oneself are critical behaviors. In spite of their

TABLE 16.1
Characteristics of self-help skills and implications for teaching

Characteristics	Implications for Teaching
Self-help skills are learned behaviors.	Teachers must teach self-help skills rather than wait for maturational forces to produce them.
	Teachers must be competent in using behavioral procedures.
Teaching self-help skills is a reasonable educational objective.	Learning self-help skills results in more independence.
	Learning self-help skills decreases the differences between handicapped and typical children.
Self-help skills are acquired throughout the preschool years.	Teachers must teach a broad range of self-help skills.
	Teachers will likely have self-help objectives for most of their children.
Acquisition of self-help skills is insufficient for using them in a functional manner.	Teachers must ensure child can perform self-help skills proficiently.
Self-help skills are used on a regular but low frequency basis.	Teachers need to involve parents in teaching self-help skills.
Most self-help skills are chains of many behaviors.	Teachers must be competent in teaching chains of behavior.

importance, they can be difficult to teach. This section describes procedures for assessing children's eating and self-feeding skills, general guidelines for feeding children and teaching self-feeding, and methods for teaching swallowing, chewing, and utensil use.

Assessing Eating and Self-Feeding Skills

The basic approaches specifically designed to assess eating and self-feeding skills are the developmental or maturational approach and the functional approach.

Developmental or maturational approach Normally developing children acquire eating and self-feeding skills over a number of years. These milestones are fairly consistent across children and have been well described (Cohen & Gross, 1979; Gesell & Ilg, 1937; Gesell, Ilg, Ames, & Rodell, 1974). When using the developmental approach, the teacher observes the child eating or self-feeding and compares the child's performance to the described milestones. Usually the teacher records those observations by writing a descriptive narrative (Campbell, 1977) or using checklists. Instructional targets are identified for emerging skills; that is, ones that are neither mastered nor extremely advanced for the child's current developmental level. A sample of eating and self-feeding milestones is shown in Table 16.2.

The milestones illustrated in Table 16.2 reflect a progressive acquisition of control over mouth, hand, and arm movements. When assessing a young handicapped child's eating and feeding skills, the teacher should focus on the child's movements rather than the child's age level or the age level of a given skill (Powell, 1981). The teacher should also assess the child's head and trunk control.

Teachers can readily observe movements of the arms and hands and control of the head and trunk. Movements of the oral musculature (mouth) are more obscure yet equally important. The type of food (liquid, strained, mashed, and so on) given to the child is determined in part by the development of the oral musculature (Campbell, 1977). In addition, failure to learn some skills (such as biting and chewing) in the proper sequence may result in later difficulties in learning (Illingworth & Lister, 1964). Finally, attempting to give children foods that are too advanced for their oral musculature may result in avoidance and disruptive or other maladaptive feeding behaviors.

The developmental milestones of the oral musculature are characterized by a decrease in the intensity of reflexes such as the rooting and sucking reflexes; by more independent movements of the tongue, lips, and jaw; and by more precise movements of these body parts (Cohen & Gross, 1979). Well developed movements of the oral musculature are not only important eating behaviors but also necessary for the development of clear speech (Colangelo et al., 1976; Nelson, 1979).

The primary weakness of the developmental approach is the *assumption* that proficient oral muscle movements are prerequisite behaviors to self-feeding. Some handicapped children are capable of self-feeding without demonstrating proficient oral muscle movements. With minimal training they can feed themselves and thereby become more independent, although their lip, tongue, and jaw movements may not be precise (Campbell, 1977). In addition, the use of the developmental approach to assess eating and self-feeding may suggest waiting for maturational forces to produce the desired behavior, when in fact many children will never acquire these skills naturally or will do so at a very slow rate.

Various early childhood special education curricula and accompanying assessment tools use the developmental approach, however. Examples include the *Developmental Pinpoints* (Cohen & Gross, 1979), *Portage Guide to Early Education* (Bluma, Shearer, Frohman, & Hilliard, 1976), *Washington Guide to Promoting Development in Young Children* (Powell, 1981), and the *Learning Accomplishment Profile* (LeMay, Griffin, & Sanford, 1977). Some of these manuals recommend the use of checklists for recording information rather than the narrative form. Checklists specify skills requiring instruction. Checklists, however, may obscure the quality of the child's movement.

Functional approach The functional approach involves specifying a series of behaviors that result in a desired self-feeding or eating skill. The series of behaviors or steps leading to each desired behavior is generated by adapting developmental milestones or by task analyzing the terminal behaviors. These steps are clearly specified in measurable

TABLE 16.2
Developmental milestones
for eating and self-feeding

Description of Feeding Behavior	Approximate Age of Accomplishment
Sucks and swallows	A few hours after birth
Opens mouth widely as spoon presented	4–6 months
Opens and closes mouth as food manipulated within mouth; makes smacking noises with tongue against palate	4–6 months
Learns to chew, establishes readiness for table foods	6–7 months
Holds and manipulates a spoon or cup in play	7 months
Picks up bits of food with thumb and first two fingers; self-feeding still messy	7–8 months
Opens mouth before spoon is actually presented; tongue held well within the mouth may be depressed	7–8 months
Removes food quickly from spoon by pressing lips against spoon and drawing head away	7–8 months
Feeds self cracker	9 months
Bites off correct amount; table foods are easily chewable	9–10 months
Self-management of the cup	16 months
Grasps spoon pronately near bowl; dips rather than scoops it into food; apt to turn spoon en route to mouth, spilling contents frequently. Uses fork	16 months
Demonstrates pronate grasp of spoon; holds spoon horizontally, raising elbow as he lifts spoon to mouth; spoon aligned to mouth half point, half side and may turn after it enters the mouth	18 months
Demonstrates supinate grasp of spoon handle. Inserts bowl of spoon in mouth sideways or by its point with good rotation at the wrist and little, if any, spilling	3 years
Holds cup by handle in adult fashion; no longer needs free hand to help	3 years
Spreads butter on bread with knife	3–4 years
Eats skillfully with fork. Cuts with knife	4–5 years

Source: Cohen and Gross (1979)

behaviors that allow efficient identification of instructional targets. The child's performance is compared to the list of steps (i.e., the task analysis) (Knapczyk, 1975). Usually, a checklist accompanies the task analysis. An example of a task analysis for wiping one's face with a napkin is as follows:

1 Child is positioned for eating so he or she can move one arm.
2 Child moves hand to the napkin (napkin may be placed on the lap or the table).
3 Child grasps the napkin.
4 Child maintains grasp on napkin and moves arm to the mouth.
5 Child wipes mouth with the napkin.
6 Child returns the napkin to the table or lap.

According to Campbell (1977, 1979), the primary weakness of the functional approach is that of merely noting the presence or absence of the behavior and not accounting for the quality. *Whether* the child performs the behavior is given more attention than *how* he or she performs it. Many children can perform given behaviors using abnormal patterns of movements. The functional approach usually does not identify those patterns. Thus, inappropriate remediation techniques may be used and important remedial goals not identified.

Several preschool curricula and accompanying assessment tools use the functional approach. Examples include the *Behavioral Characteristics Progression* (BCP) (Santa Cruz Schools, 1973), *The Teaching Research Curriculum for Moderately and Severely Handicapped* (Fredericks, Riggs, Furey, Grove, Moore, McDonnell, Jordan, Hanson, Baldwin, & Wadlow, 1976), the *Wabash Center Guide to Early Developmental Training* (Tilton, Liska, & Bourland, 1977), the *Programmed Environments Curriculum* (Tawney, Knapp, O'Reilly, & Pratt, 1979), and the *TARC Assessment System* (Sailor & Mix, 1975).

Because of the weaknesses in the developmental and functional approaches, Campbell (1977) proposed the *strong-inference approach* to be used in conjunction with the developmental and functional approaches. This approach identifies and generates possible reasons for children's eating or feeding prob-

lems. The underlying assumption is that if eating and feeding problems are identified and reasons proposed, then specific remedial or training procedures will be indicated. This assumption is invalid for domains such as language, social, and cognitive development. For example, it is probably impossible to identify why a given child rarely initiates social interactions, fails to search for objects he or she observed being hidden, or does not greet others when they enter the room. Further, even when possible reasons are identified, rarely do the reasons lead to specific training strategies. However, the assumption of the strong-inference model may be valid for eating and self-feeding problems. For example, Denise frequently gags and vomits when eating. Possible reasons for such behaviors are a hypersensitive tongue that elicits the gagging reflex, especially if lumpy food is used, certain environmental conditions such as noisy, confusing, interrupted feeding times, allergies to certain foods, general behavior problems, especially noncompliance with adult requests, and strong dislikes for certain foods (Morris, 1974). If Denise's gagging and vomiting behaviors are due to a hypersensitive tongue rather than noncompliance, then treatment procedures are quite different.

Other eating and self-feeding problems include refusal to eat solid foods, narrow range of food preferences, refusal to drink from a glass, poor jaw control, pushing food out of the mouth with the tongue, poor lip closure, lack of chewing, excessive drooling, and high muscle tone in trunk and neck while eating (Morris, 1974). Diagnostic and training procedures for these and other eating/self-feeding problems are described by Mueller (1975); Schmidt (1976); Stainback, Healy, Stainback, and Healy (1976); and Utley, Holvoet, and Barnes (1977). The strong-inference approach in combination with the developmental or functional approach for assessing feeding and eating skills can provide the direct link between specific problems and training strategies.

A complete assessment of eating and self-feeding should include the child's muscle tone; primitive reflexes; head and trunk control; sitting balance; grasp and release; hand to mouth behavior; oral skills such as tongue movements, swallowing, and lip movements and closure; and the type of food the child accepts

(Schmidt, 1976; Utley et al., 1977). Because of the complexity of these skills, the teacher should solicit the help of a physical or occupational therapist when conducting assessments of children who display particular eating and feeding problems.

Eating and self-feeding assessment tools
Besides the developmental and functional checklists, relatively few assessment tools exist for eating and self-feeding. Two tools are the *Balthazar Scales of Adaptive Behavior I* (Balthazar, 1976) and the *Eating Assessment Tool* (EAT) (Schmidt, 1976, 1977).

The *Balthazar Scales of Functional Independence* is a checklist for eating, dressing, and toileting. The eating scale is composed of five "classes" (subsections), including dependent feeding, finger foods, spoon usage, fork usage, and drinking. Through direct observation, the rater estimates the proportional occurrence of the child's eating behavior. For example, if the child eats appropriately with a fork on approximately 7 of 10 trials the estimated proportion would be 7. This assessment tool also includes an "eating checklist." The rater indicates information such as whether the child serves himself, the type of food eaten, the use of a knife, the child's positioning during feeding, whether adaptive devices are used, and how much supervision is required.

The Balthazar Scales are intended for determining treatment effectiveness and for instructional program planning. Because of the rating scale format and the use of observer estimates of time, reliability or interobserver agreement should be calculated frequently. Norms for each scale are provided, although the diversity within the norming sample results in the norms having only limited usefulness (Proger, 1973). The Balthazar Eating Scale does not assess motor skills such as head and trunk control, mouth movements, and reflexes. Thus, its usefulness is similar to other functional checklists such as those described by Tilton et al. (1977).

The *Eating Assessment Tool* (EAT) is composed of five parts, including gross motor skills and posture during feeding, oral skills, eye-hand coordination, feeding behavior, and other. Each section contains items measuring something different: *gross motor and posture* measures head and trunk control and

sitting balance; *oral skills*, swallowing, and lip, jaw, and tongue movements; *eye-hand coordination*, hand-to-mouth behavior and finger and spoon feeding; *feeding behavior*, the child's interest and attention to eating and social behavior; and *other*, environmental factors such as parent involvement, medications, feeding schedule, and records of the child's weight. Direct observation is used to rate the 67 items, each of which is rated on a 1–4 scale with a *1* indicating the behavior seldom occurs and a *4* indicating that it almost always occurs. The EAT assists in instructional program planning. It emphasizes oral and other motor skills; unfortunately, no data are presented on its reliability or usefulness.

Guidelines for Teaching Eating and Self-Feeding Skills

Since each child's eating and self-feeding programs should be based on individual assessments of abilities, specific training guidelines applicable to all children cannot be listed. However, some guidelines can be used and are included in this section.

Consult with physical and occupational therapists. Physical and occupational therapists are trained to assess and promote development of the appropriate motor behaviors. Their consultation is especially important with children with cerebral palsy and other physical disabilities (Harris, 1980; Tyler & Chandler, 1978). Therapists can provide information on positioning; assessment and treatment techniques for stimulation of tongue movements, chewing, lip closure, and swallowing; inhibition of primitive reflexes; and adaptive equipment (Barnes, Murphy, Waldo, & Sailor, 1979; Campbell, 1979; Finnie, 1975).

Position the child properly for eating and self-feeding. Proper positioning will facilitate normal muscle tone and symmetry (Tyler & Kahn, 1976); inhibit primitive reflexes; facilitate normal movement patterns (Utley et al., 1977); stabilize head and trunk control and compensate for the lack of sitting balance (Mueller, 1975); and facilitate sucking, swallowing, and chewing (Stainback et al., 1976). Although individualized positioning should be prescribed for each child with considerable motor involvement, certain general rules should be followed. Correct and incorrect positions

A. Half-sitting position for the child with some sitting balance. Remember to put the food in front of him. If the child still needs support, an infant seat can be used resting against the table edge.

B. When sitting balance improves, sit the baby up straight with his legs abducted and his hips well flexed. you may still have to control him from the shoulders.

A. **Wrong.** The cup is presented from above and the child is tilted back.

B. **Right.** The child is in a sitting position for drinking, with the trunk and head well forward, the beaker is presented from the front.

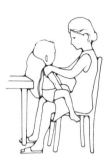

A. **Wrong.** The baby is placed in front of mother on a foam rubber wedge, which rests against the table edge. Without control and when the spoon is presented from above the baby will push his head back and cannot swallow properly.

B. **Right.** If you put your hand flat with pressure on the baby's lower chest and present the spoon from the front, you help him to control his head and to swallow.

FIGURE 16.1

Correct and incorrect feeding positions. *Note:* From "Feeding" by H. Mueller. In N. R. Finnie (Ed.), *Handling the Young Cerebral Palsied Child at Home* (2nd ed.). New York: Dutton, 1975, 117, 118, & 123. Copyright 1975 by Dutton. Reprinted by permission.

are shown in Figure 16.1. The child should be fed with his or her face at midline rather than looking to the left or right. Also, in most cases, feed the child in an upright position to keep the food from sliding down the throat without proper swallowing and reduce the chances of choking (Mueller, 1975). Children's heads should also usually be tilted slightly forward (Wehman, 1979); this position can be accomplished by rolling up and placing towels behind the back of the neck. However, do not push the head forward from behind as this will stimulate an extension of the neck and back (Utley et al., 1977).

Another rule of positioning is that *all* children's feet should be supported and hips flexed. Children's feet should be stable on the floor, on blocks on the floor, or on the foot rests of their wheelchairs. The flexing of the knees and hips helps inhibit extensions of the trunk, neck, and arms that make swallowing and self-feeding difficult. Finally, the hands of some physically involved children should be kept at midline. Cuff bands filled with sand can be used to secure the hands in place (Utley et al., 1977; Wehman, 1979).

The trainer's position should also be considered. Trainers should only hold those children they can comfortably lift and move during feeding. Attempting to hold children who are too heavy may result in dropping the child, straining muscles, and general discomfort. When training certain feeding skills such as lip closure, the trainer should be positioned to the side or in front of the child. When training the child to use utensils, the trainer should stand behind the child. Standing behind the child will allow the trainer to use natural movements when prompting the child's arm and hand movements (Snell, 1978). Regardless of the precise positions, Powell (1981) suggests they should be comfortable to both child and trainer, facilitating a relaxed and pleasant atmosphere.

Carefully select the foods to be presented to the child. The child's nutrient intake and the functioning level of the oral musculature should be considered when selecting foods. Handicapped children often exhibit a very narrow range of food preferences that may interfere with adequate nutrition (Pipes, 1981). When such circumstances exist, the usual procedure is to alternate bites of foods they readily eat with foods they do not eat. The preferred food acts as a reinforcer for the less preferred food. Leibowitz and Holcer (1974) describe a procedure they used with a young handicapped child who ate a very narrow range of foods and exhibited considerable disruptive behaviors when other foods were introduced. After a reinforcement preference test with a variety of foods, ice cream was identified as a reinforcer. During training a number of procedures were used simultaneously: the lights in the room were turned off when she had a

tantrum or screamed; praise and withdrawal of the spoon were used when the tantrums ceased; ice cream was placed on the tip of the spoon with small bits of other foods toward the back of the spoon; and alternate bites of ice cream and other foods were given. These procedures resulted in relatively rapid acceptance of a regular diet. Multiple trainers and settings were used to establish generalization of the eating behavior.

Increasing the variety of foods children eat is important for establishing adequate diets and for normalizing children's behavior. Pipes (1981) describes procedures for identifying children who may be at risk for nutritional problems, procedures for assessing nutrient intake, and adequate diets for various ages.

The types of food presented during feeding will be determined in part by the child's oral musculature. A sequence of children's oral motor movements and the type of food they should be given are shown in Table 16.3.

Use adaptive equipment and when possible fade its use. Physical and occupational therapists can assist teachers in determining the types of adaptive equipment necessary. For eating and self-feeding, common adaptive equipment includes spoons that have built-up handles or handles that extend around the back of the hand or have velcro tape allowing the child with a weak grasp to hold them,

TABLE 16.3
Oral motor movements and the type of food to give children

Oral Motor Movements	Type of Food
Child opens mouth, sucks, swallows.	Strained foods
Child opens mouth, sucks, swallows.	Mashed/chopped foods
Child munches food placed between side teeth with up and down tongue movements—tongue not involved.	Semisolid foods
Child uses rotary jaw movements to "chew" food placed between side teeth.	Solid "chewy" foods
Child uses lateral (side-to-side) tongue movements when chewing.	Solid "chewy" foods
Child bites and chews with lateral tongue movements.	Table foods

swivel and bent spoons, plates that secure themselves to the table with suction devices or have built-up lips to facilitate scooping, cups with cut out edges to keep the head from moving back during drinking, and many other devices (see Figure 16.2). These devices are available commercially, but many can be constructed by the teacher or therapist. These devices should be used to facilitate independent functioning. With some children they will be relatively permanent adaptations;

with others, the adaptive equipment can be faded as the child gains more control of arm and hand movements. Examples of additional adaptive equipment for eating and self-feeding can be found in Barnes et al. (1979); Hall and Hammock (1979); Largent and Waylett (1975); Magnusson and Justen (1981); Nelson and Ranka (1975); and Trefler, Westmoreland, and Burlingame (1977).

Use behavioral techniques to establish eating and self-feeding behaviors and control-

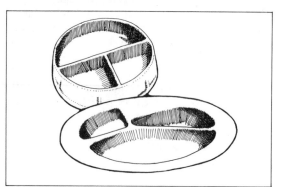

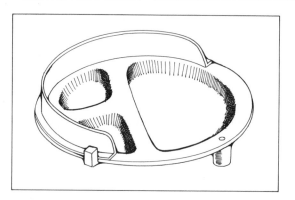
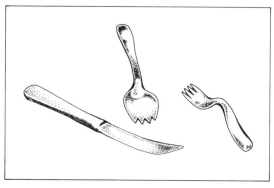
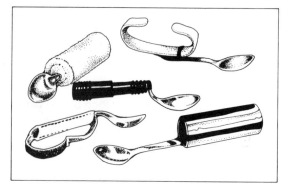

FIGURE 16.2
Adaptive devices for eating

related problems. Numerous studies document the use of operant techniques in teaching eating and self-feeding behaviors. Common techniques include reinforcement for desired behaviors, timeout from positive reinforcement for undesired behaviors (removal of food, physical restraint, and moving the person away from the table), graduated guidance (physical prompting and fading), and verbal cues (Westling & Murden, 1978). Trained behaviors included discriminating finger from non-finger foods (Miller, Patton, & Henton, 1971), spoon feeding (Berkowitz, Sherry, & Davis, 1972; Song & Gandhi, 1974), use of utensils other than spoons (Nelson, Cone, & Hanson, 1975; O'Brien & Azrin, 1972), napkin use and table manners (Azrin & Armstrong, 1973), general dining room behaviors such as getting food trays, taking appropriately sized bites, and eating at a normal rate (Mann & Sobsey, 1975), and behaviors needed to eat in public (van den Pol, Iwata, Ivancic, Page, Neef, & Whitley, 1981).

Various feeding and eating problems have been treated with behavioral procedures. Some examples of these behaviors, the treatment procedures and corresponding references are shown in Table 16.4. However, remember that behavioral procedures should be used in conjunction with techniques developed by physical and occupational therapists. Further, many of these studies were neither conducted with young children nor in home settings. Most used severely retarded institutionalized adolescents and adults as subjects.

Train eating and self-feeding at the appropriate times. Select the appropriate eating times by feeding the child when he or she is

TABLE 16.4
Problems related to eating and self-feeding treated with behavioral procedures

Behavior Problem	Treatment Procedure	Reference
Food stealing	Overcorrection Reinforcement, verbal reprimands, and physical restraint	Azrin & Wesolowski, 1974 Henrickson & Doughty, 1967
Refusal to eat foods other than baby foods	Normalizing oral muscle tone, eliminating baby foods, reinforcement, and scheduled presentation of foods	Holser-Buehler, 1973
Failure to eat a variety of foods	Reinforcement, timeout, and alternating bites of preferred and non-preferred foods	Leibowitz & Holcer, 1974
Sloppy eating	Timeout Timeout and reinforcement	Barton, Guess, Garcia, & Baer, 1970 Martin, McDonald, & Omichinski, 1971
Rumination and vomiting	Satiation (giving child more to eat) Overcorrection Contingent lemon juice	Jackson, Johnson, Ackron, & Crawley, 1975 Singh, Manning, & Angell, 1982 Sajwaj, Libet, & Agras, 1974
Refusal to eat	Reinforcement with liquids	Hatcher, 1979
Severe tongue thrust	Reinforcement and pushing tongue back in mouth	Thompson, Iwata, & Poynter, 1979

hungry and not fatigued (Powell, 1981). This will increase the likelihood that the child will receive the food without resistance (Stainback et al., 1976). Training feeding or drinking skills when a child is not hungry or thirsty *or* is quite tired may result in frustration for both the trainer and child.

Feeding training should be conducted only during real feedings. For example, if Wayne is learning to feed himself with a spoon, having him practice moving the spoon without food to his mouth is meaningless. Restricting eating and self-feeding training to natural times will result in relatively few training opportunities during the day. In addition, during long meals children begin to get full toward the end and training activities become less successful. To alleviate these difficulties, Azrin and Armstrong (1973) divided the three long meals per day into several shorter ones. By shortening the time and increasing the number of meals per day, Azrin and Armstrong were able to increase the number of training opportunities and eliminate the problem of children becoming full and therefore less receptive to training. If shorter meals are impossible, conduct training and introduce new procedures during the early portions of meals (Utley et al., 1977). Gradually the amount of time the new procedure (or food) is used can be increased to include the entire meal.

Also, select feeding times with minimal distractions (Stainback et al., 1976). While the goal of feeding training may be to have children eat with the family or other children when at school, sometimes such environments result in considerable distractions for the trainer and child. When such conditions exist, feed prior to or just after the family meal. Follow this recommendation with children who take a long time to feed, require considerable relaxation before feeding will be successful, and require considerable trainer attention.

Make mealtimes relaxing and enjoyable learning experiences. For many children, the mealtime task is not learning to eat or feed themselves, but rather to do so in an acceptable manner. With such children, mealtimes should be spent learning to try new foods, eating with the appropriate sized bites, wiping their mouths with napkins, chewing with their mouths closed, taking acceptable sized portions, passing bowls to the person sitting beside them, saying "Please" and "Thank you," and carrying on conversations while eating. These skills are best taught through modeling and reinforcement. To use these procedures the teacher should eat with the children, model the desired behaviors, and note and provide reinforcement when the children perform these behaviors. The teacher's role moves from one of providing direct instruction to being a model and facilitator of the desired behaviors. Teachers should also provide verbal prompts such as "Brian, you need to wipe your mouth with your napkin," but care should be taken not to nag children about desired behaviors. Conversation can be prompted by asking the children about the events of the day and by commenting upon the food they are eating.

During snacks and other mealtimes, teachers should use the incidental teaching procedures described in Chapter 13. Thus, the child would have an opportunity to practice concepts and skills learned at other times in the day. For example, if Allen is learning to identify objects as "big" or "little" and requests another piece of apple, then the teacher could show him a large and small piece and say, "Which piece is big?" After Allen answers, the teacher could give him an opportunity to choose the piece he wants.

Methods for Teaching Eating and Self-Feeding

Many children, especially mildly handicapped and at risk children, will learn to eat and self-feed by watching other people eat and with the usual instruction provided by most parents. With more severely handicapped children, however, direct teaching may be required.

When teachers are feeding severely handicapped children, they may need procedures for getting them to open their mouths, close their lips, swallow, and chew. For children who do not spontaneously open their mouths, or who do not open their mouths when the teacher does and presents the spoon, the teacher may choose to use jaw control procedures such as those shown in Figure 16.3. Utley et al. (1977) recommend applying a quick firm upward movement under the jaw. The upward motion stimulates the child to perform the countermotion; that is, lower the jaw or open the mouth. Once the child's

A. Jaw control as applied when the child is on your right side with your arm around his head: thumb on his jaw joint, index finger between chin and lower lip, middle finger behind chin applying constant firm pressure

B. Jaw control as applied from the front: thumb between chin and lower lip, index finger on jaw joint, middle finger applied firmly just behind the chin

FIGURE 16.3

Jaw-control grasps. *Note:* From "Feeding" by H. Mueller. In N. R. Finnie (Ed.), *Handling the Young Cerebral Palsied Child at Home* (2nd ed.). New York: Dutton, 1975. Copyright 1975 by Dutton. Reprinted by permission.

mouth is open, the half-filled spoon should be inserted directly at midline. Push the spoon down on the child's tongue about halfway back in the mouth. Food placed on the front of the tongue will increase tongue thrusting and food placed too far back on the tongue will stimulate the gag reflex (Morris, 1974). Remove the spoon without scraping the teeth or the roof of the mouth. Such scraping may stimulate a bite reflex. If the child does bite down on a spoon, do not pull it from the mouth but flex the neck forward and wait until the child's mouth opens.

Once the food is in the mouth and the utensil is removed, the child's lips should be closed. Lip closure can be accomplished by standing behind the child and placing your index finger on his or her upper lip, your middle finger below his or her lower lip, and the ring finger under his or her chin; the index and middle fingers are then firmly pushed together. To stimulate lip closure, Schmidt (1976) recommends tapping the outside of the lips during times other than feeding. Stainback et al. (1976) recommend placing a finger on the upper lip under the nose and pushing firmly several times per day, lightly stroking the lower lip, and gently pulling out on the lower lip and releasing it. Lip closure facilitates swallowing and keeps the child from pushing the food out with a tongue thrust.

Swallowing must be learned by some severely handicapped children. It can be stimulated by increasing saliva in the mouth through massaging the outer gums when the jaw is closed, upward stroking of the throat when food is in the mouth, establishing lip and symmetrical jaw closure, and using small bites of semisolid liquids (Stainback et al., 1976). Mueller (1975) stresses that a slight flexion of the neck forward during feeding develops good swallowing.

Chewing is developed by placing small pieces of chewable food between the child's side teeth, helping the child close his or her mouth using jaw control if necessary, and pushing up on the child's chin with the middle finger and applying constant pressure (Mueller, 1975). Stainback et al. (1976) recommend putting strips of bread crust between the child's side teeth, closing the mouth, and breaking off the bread to give the child the experience of biting with the teeth. For foods that will not break, tug slightly on such foods so the chewing action is stimulated (Stainback et al., 1976; Utley et al., 1977). Mueller (1975) and Stainback et al. (1976) strongly state that the teacher should not "work" the child's jaw up and down as in chewing, but rather apply consistent pressure with jaw control. Utley et al. (1977) recommend moving the jaw in, up, and down once or twice *before* the meal when the child does not have food in the mouth.

Mueller (1975), Stainback et al. (1976), and Utley et al. (1977) provide additional recommendations. They also discuss sucking and teaching children to drink from a cup. Morris (1974) discusses several procedures and management techniques for treating specific eating problems.

When teaching children to feed themselves with utensils, begin with the finger feeding, and then move to using spoons, and finally to using forks. Hand-to-mouth behavior is a prerequisite for self-feeding. During self-feeding, the child's position should facilitate head and trunk control and maximize appropriate arm movements (Banerdt & Bricker, 1978). The teacher should be positioned behind the child to physically prompt natural arm movements (Snell, 1978). Sticky foods such as mashed potatoes, yogurt, and spaghetti should be used rather than slippery foods that fall off the spoon. Foods the child readily eats should also be used. The teacher should place his or her hand over the child's hand that holds the spoon. The spoon should be scooped into the food, lifted straight up a few inches, moved to the mouth, in the mouth, and back to the table. The teacher could fade the full physical manipulation by using graduated guidance, fading the position of the prompt, or using backward chaining starting with the spoon going into the child's mouth. See Chapter 3 for discussions on prompting and fading prompts.

When children begin to independently feed themselves, they will be quite messy; but the messiness will decrease as they become more proficient. Sometimes children will drop the spoon and begin eating with their hands or will throw the spoon. The occurrence of such behaviors can be decreased by removing the plate and spoon for a few seconds (Westling & Murden, 1978).

TOILETING SKILLS

Toileting has received considerable attention in the child development literature. Freud, for example, considered toilet training as a source of parent-child conflicts that produced disorders lasting into adulthood. As a result, toileting acquired a certain mystique that sometimes made teachers hesitant to initiate toilet training activities. However, in recent years professionals have begun to view toileting as a social skill that can be learned like other social skills (Foxx & Azrin, 1973). Such a viewpoint makes the task of toilet training more straightforward. However, it can result in inappropriate behaviors and negative child-trainer interactions. Thus, toilet training should be implemented carefully and the trainer should note and respond appropriately to maladaptive behaviors.

Ellis (1963) asserted that toileting was a "conditionable behavior." Since that time several attempts have been made to develop efficient toilet training procedures for handicapped persons, particularly retarded persons in institutions (Azrin & Foxx, 1971; Baumeister & Klosowski, 1965; Giles & Wolf, 1966; Mahoney, Van Wagenen, & Meyerson, 1971; Marshall, 1966; Osarchuk, 1973). Additional procedures have been described for handicapped and nonhandicapped children outside of institutions (Azrin & Foxx, 1974; Fredericks, Baldwin, Grove, & Moore, 1975).

In this section, prerequisites for independent toileting, procedures for measuring the prerequisite behaviors, general guidelines, and methods for day and nighttime toilet training are described.

Prerequisites for Independent Toileting

In order for a child to independently take care of toileting needs, he or she must be able to retain urine and feces, which requires sphincter muscle control. The child must also be able to release urine and feces at will, and get to the bathroom. Before beginning training, the teacher must be sure that the child can hold waste material and release it at will. Getting to the toilet can be established in the later stages of training.

The child should also be free of medical problems that interfere with independent toileting. These include recurring urinary tract infections, other urological disorders, and paralysis that makes sphincter muscle control impossible. In addition, the teacher must check with the parents to insure they are willing and able to follow through with toilet training. Usually parents are eager for toilet training to begin, but in some instances family circumstances (possibly temporary) make attending to the training difficult. Examples include the impending birth of a sibling or disruptions to family life when some member is ill. Finally, for toilet training to be successful the child must be under instructional control. At issue is whether the child complies with adult requests. Unlike other self-help skills such as using the spoon or putting on a coat, urination and defecation cannot be prompted physically. Thus, if the child is noncompliant, toilet training efforts will probably be unsuccessful. Given that teachers of severely handicapped children have identified noncompliance as the most frequent behavior problem, it is likely that many children needing toilet training will be noncompliant (Wehman & McLaughlin, 1979).

Measurement of Prerequisites

With most nonhandicapped children, chronological age is an adequate predictor of toilet training readiness. Nonhandicapped children between 24 and 30 months can usually be trained without extreme difficulty. However, with handicapped children, chronological age is frequently a poor predictor of toilet training success, although P. S. Smith and L. J. Smith (1977) suggest that retarded persons over 25 years of age are toilet trained slower than those under age 20. Further, retarded children with social ages as measured by the Vineland Social Maturity Scale of 2–2.5 years are trained faster than those with social ages between 1.5 and 2 years. Azrin and Foxx (1974) state that even for nonhandicapped children the toileting prerequisites (bladder control, physical readiness, and instructional readiness) should be tested. For bladder control they suggest these questions "1) Does my child urinate a good deal at one time rather than dribbling throughout the day? 2) Does he often stay dry for several hours? 3) Does he appear to know he is about to urinate as indicated by his facial expressions or by special postures he adopts?" (p. 43). Physical readiness is determined by whether the child can pick up objects with the hands and move from room to room without assistance. Instructional readiness is measured by asking the child to follow a series of commands such as touching the eyes and mouth, sitting down, standing up, imitating simple movements, and placing familiar objects together on command. A nonhandicapped child is considered ready for toilet training if he or she completes 8 out of 10 of these tasks.

For handicapped children, Snell (1978) recommends that training can be initiated if the child regularly urinates or defecates "within certain daily time periods" (p. 234); if there are daily stable periods of 1–2 hours of dryness; and if the child is old enough (moderately retarded children should be 2½ years of age; severely retarded children should be 5 years of age). Fredericks et al. (1975) recommend beginning training if the child is 1½–4 years old and when a consistent pattern of urination is noted in at least two time periods per day.

The decisions teachers make to determine a child's readiness are shown in the flow chart in Figure 16.4. Essentially, the child demonstrates sufficient bladder control if he or she consistently is dry for 1–2 hours and consistently soaks as compared to dampening the

diaper. The parents are interviewed to determine the presence of medical problems and their willingness and ability to follow through with the training. The child's medical records may also indicate the presence or absence of medical problems. Finally, a determination is made concerning instructional control by observing the child's level of compliance with adult requests throughout the day and asking the child to follow simple directions and imitate simple motor movements.

General Guidelines for Toilet Training

Once it has been determined that the child is ready for toilet training, several general guidelines should be followed regardless of the training method used.

Train daytime rather than nighttime toileting. Children generally acquire daytime toileting before staying dry during the night. Children and trainers are more alert, and thus are more efficient, during the day. Nighttime training should begin after the child is toilet trained during the day.

Begin training with bladder rather than bowel control. Children urinate more frequently than defecate. Thus, if we are training bladder control we will have more opportunities within the space of a day to reinforce the child for urinating in the toilet, and if correction procedures are used, the child will have more opportunities to meet with those procedures. Children will learn more quickly if they meet with the reinforcers and correction procedures several times within a short time span than relatively few times over several days. In addition to this increase in training opportunities, children frequently urinate and have bowel movements at approximately the same time. If the child learns to use the toilet for urination, it is likely that he or she will incidentally learn to use the toilet for bowel movements. If not, training for bowel movements can be initiated after the child learns to urinate consistently in the toilet. Also, the number of times the child needs to urinate in a day can be artificially increased by having him drink more fluids. This is an important part of a rapid method of toilet training to be described later. It is much more difficult to increase the number of bowel movements per day, although it has been attempted (Giles & Wolf, 1966).

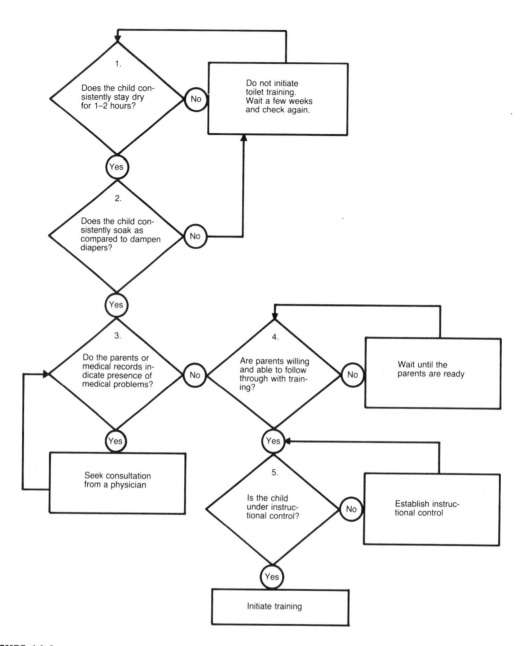

FIGURE 16.4
The decision points for determining whether a handicapped child is ready to be toilet trained

Train the child to sit on rather than stand by the toilet to urinate. Although boys eventually need to stand by the toilet to urinate, begin toilet training with boys sitting. Toilet training usually requires the child to remain near (on) the toilet for a few minutes "waiting for the urine to come." When a child is seated, he must get up and then wander away, but when the child is standing it is much easier to just walk away. Thus, sitting helps keep the child near the toilet. Further, boys have notoriously poor control of the direction of their urine flow and are apt to turn away from the toilet at the beginning of or during urination. This can result in urine falling on the floor, wall, trainer, and anything else within its range. Having children seated on the toilet helps avoid this. However, even when boys are seated their urine may not flow into the toilet so stand to the side while they are waiting to urinate. Some potty seats have shields to control this problem, but they are not completely successful, and because handicapped children are usually older than nonhandicapped children when they are toilet trained, their legs are bigger and are often scratched getting up or sitting down when the shield is on the seat. Finally, children should learn to have bowel movements when they urinate in the toilet. Boys who initially learn to urinate while standing by the toilet will require additional training to sit when they need to have a bowel movement. This training is usually initiated soon after they have their first bowel movement while standing by the toilet. Having them seated during initial training will eliminate some of these problems.

Train the child to indicate a need to go to the bathroom in the later stages of toilet training. The child should be trained to simply go to the bathroom when the need arises rather than having to tell someone he or she needs to go. However, in many classrooms and in other public situations, children must indicate they need to use the bathroom. The behavior of "requesting to use the bathroom" should be taught after the child has started to use the bathroom consistently. It is unrealistic to expect children to ask to do something they have never done before or do not do on a regular basis. However, throughout training use the family's words for going to the bathroom. As the child masters urination he or she can be trained through imitation and questioning to request going to the bathroom. The request may be vocal, some nonvocal sign, or a signal such as pointing to the bathroom.

Methods of Toilet Training

Independent toileting involves many skills including the following:

1 Indicates need to use toilet (if necessary).
2 Moves to bathroom.
3 Unfastens pants (if necessary).
4 Pushes pants and underwear down.
5 Gets on the toilet.

6 Maintains sitting balance on toilet.
7 Eliminates urine or feces.
8 Reaches and gets toilet tissue.
9 Wipes self until clean.
10 Disposes of toilet tissue.
11 Gets off toilet.
12 Flushes toilet.
13 Pulls up underwear and pants.
14 Washes and dries hands.

Methods used to establish toileting are described in this section, and include the traditional schedule method, the distributed practice or improved schedule method (Fredericks et al., 1975), and the massed practice or rapid method (Azrin & Foxx, 1974; Foxx & Azrin, 1973).

The traditional schedule method The traditional schedule method of toilet training can be accomplished by taking an extensive baseline (3–30 days) to determine when the child is wet and dry. This may involve checking the child's diaper every 15–30 minutes throughout the day. When a stable pattern of urination is identified, the teacher takes the child to the toilet a few minutes before each time the child has been consistently wet in baseline. If the child urinates while on the toilet, he or she is reinforced; if the child does not urinate within a few minutes, he or she is returned to regular activities.

Another use of the traditional schedule method is to take the child to the bathroom on a regular basis; for example, every hour or every half hour. The consequences for the child's toileting behavior are the same as those described in the first use of this method.

The traditional schedule method of toilet training handicapped children is quite slow and requires considerable effort by the trainer. Typically, the child has frequent trips to the toilet that do not result in urination and thus no reinforcement is given.

The distributed practice procedure—improved schedule method This method was developed by Fredericks et al. (1975) to minimize the effort expended by the trainer during training.[1] It is similar to the traditional

---

[1]The Fredericks et al. procedure was designed for use by parents, but can be used by parents and teachers working together. In this section the term *trainer* is used to signify anyone doing the training—parents, teachers, or both.

schedule method but with improvements. Fredericks et al. (1975) describe this procedure as involving the following steps:

1 establishing a baseline record of the child's urination and defecation behavior;
2 using that record to decide the most appropriate times of the day at which to conduct training;
3 selection of reinforcers to use during training;
4 conducting the training;
5 maintaining records during training;
6 expanding training to other periods of the day;

7 helping the child to learn to indicate toileting needs (p. 3).

The baseline data are collected each half hour throughout the day for 14 days. For each half hour the trainer records the child's urinations and bowel movements, their location (toilet or pants), meals and liquids given to the child, and whether the child was dry. A sample data collection sheet and legend are shown in Figure 16.5. After all data are collected, two times at which the child is most

Name: _____   Month: _____

Date	1	2	3	4	5	6	7	8	9	10	11	12	13	14	15	16	17	18	19	20	21	22	23	24	25	26	27	28	29	30	31
7:00–7:30																															
7:30–8:00																															
8:00–8:30																															
8:30–9:00																															
9:00–9:30																															
9:30–10:00																															
10:00–10:30																															
10:30–11:00																															
11:00–11:30																															
11:30–12:00																															
12:00–12:30																															
12:30–1:00																															
1:00–1:30																															
1:30–2:00																															
2:00–2:30																															
2:30–3:00																															
3:00–3:30																															
3:30–4:00																															
4:00–4:30																															
4:30–5:00																															
5:00–5:30																															
5:30–6:00																															
6:00–6:30																															
6:30–7:00																															
7:00–7:30																															
7:30–8:00																															
8:00–8:30																															
8:30–9:00																															

Coding Symbols:

✔ = Dry pants
○ = Urination off potty
⊗ = Urination in potty
△ = Bowel movement off potty
⊿ = Bowel movement in potty
⊿ = Urination and bowel movement in potty
X = On potty; nothing
M = Meal given to child
● = Liquids given to child

Daily comments:

FIGURE 16.5

Data sheet and legend for the distributed practice toilet training procedure.

Note: From *Toilet Training the Handicapped Child* by H. D. Fredericks, V. Baldwin, D. N. Grove, and W. G. Moore. Monmouth, Oreg.: Instructional Development, 1975. Copyright 1975 by H. D. Fredericks. Reprinted by permission.

likely to be wet are identified. If the data are too erratic, then 14 more days of data should be collected. Step 3 is to select reinforcers. Fredericks et al. (1975) recommend using powerful reinforcers and restricting their use to the toilet training project. After selection of the two training times and reinforcers, training is initiated. The child should be taken to the toilet at the two times he or she is most likely to be wet. During this period, data are collected only at these two times. The trainer should consistently use a cue such as "Let's go potty" throughout training. The child is seated on the toilet for 10 minutes or less if he or she urinates. As soon as the urination occurs, the child should be reinforced. If the child does not urinate within 10 minutes, he or she should be dressed and allowed to play for 5 minutes. The child is then placed back on the toilet for 5 more minutes. If urination occurs the child is allowed off the toilet and reinforced. If not, the child should be dressed and returned to the daily activities. When the child urinates in the toilet 50% of the times for either training time for two consecutive weeks, the trainer should begin to collect more baseline data to identify times for expanding training. Expanding training to one or two additional times should be done when the child urinates on 75% of the possible days at either of the two training times for two weeks. This expansion is continued until the child urinates at 75% of the opportunities throughout the day. At this point the child is trained to indicate the need to use the toilet. The trainer models the cue phrase such as "Go potty." The child is trained to imitate the modeled phrase, and once it is learned, the trainer adds the question, "Where are you going?" The child is trained to reply, "Go potty." The actual words should be the phrase used by the family, and signs or conventional gestures could also be used.

The Fredericks et al. (1975) procedure relies heavily on reinforcement. The emphasis on reinforcement is also seen when the toilet trained child begins to have accidents. If the child has daily accidents that occur at a consistent time, Fredericks et al. (1975) recommend adding prompts to cue the child to use the bathroom before the time when the accident usually occurs. Those prompts are gradually faded. If accidents occur throughout the day, the trainer may want to increase the reinforcement for eliminating in the toilet, have the child clean himself up, or add in reinforcement for staying dry for specific periods. These periods are gradually increased until the child is dry for the entire day.

The distributed practice or improved schedule method relies heavily on reinforcement, is designed to reduce the effort expended by the parent, and avoids the use of punishment. The procedure, while simple and relatively effective, is slow. However, when toilet training for a given child is desirable but not a pressing need, it is a viable option and certainly is more useful than the traditional schedule method.

The massed practice or rapid method Foxx and Azrin developed the massed practice method (Foxx and Azrin, 1973; Azrin & Foxx, 1971). It was originally developed for institutionalized retarded persons (Foxx & Azrin, 1973) and was expanded into the "less than a day method" for young nonhandicapped children (Azrin & Foxx, 1974). Although there are some differences between the two methods, their basic structure is similar.

The rapid method establishes self-initiated, independent toileting within a very short time period. This was accomplished with retarded persons in 4–6 days of intensive training and in nonhandicapped children in about 4–5 hours. *Independent toileting* means that, without aid, the child will move to the bathroom, take down his or her pants, urinate, flush the toilet, or empty the bowl if a potty chair is used, and pull up his or her pants. The training occurs during the day and lasts for several hours. It generally requires one teacher for one or two children. Other basic components are as follows:

1 The amount of liquid the child drinks during training is increased, thereby increasing the number of times the child will need to urinate and the number of potential opportunities to reinforce correct toileting.
2 The child is seated on the toilet for a set period of time (e.g., 10 minutes) and is then off the toilet for a set period of time.
3 The child is immediately reinforced for urinating in the toilet. Reinforcement frequently includes presenting praise, liquids, and edibles.

4 The child is reinforced on a regular basis (every 10 minutes) for staying dry when off the toilet.

5 Graduated guidance is used to prompt the child to move to the toilet, take down his or her pants, pull up pants and so on. Prompts are faded as quickly as possible.

6 When accidents occur, the trainer does four things: the child is verbally reprimanded for wetting; positive practice trials are provided that involve the child moving to the toilet, taking down his or her pants, sitting down on the toilet for about a second, standing up, pulling up pants, moving to another part of the room, and repeating this process several times; opportunities are provided for the child to feel his or her wet pants; and the child is required to take off wet pants, wash them, and put them in the appropriate receptacle. As described in Chapter 12, overcorrection is an aversive procedure and may result in tantrums, crying, and other emotional behaviors. Therefore, it should be implemented consistently, correctly, and with care. While punishment procedures should be avoided, overcorrection can sometimes be used since independent toileting is so critical.

7 Prompts to move to the toilet are decreased as training progresses.

8 During maintenance, the child is regularly reinforced for staying dry, and the consequences for accidents remain essentially the same except trials for feeling wet pants are eliminated.

The less than a day procedure includes more verbal rehearsal, reliance on more verbal reinforcement, and having the child toilet train a wetting doll. The rapid method for retarded persons includes a urine sensing device connected to the child's training pants and another urine sensing device on the toilet to detect the urine flow as it begins.

Choosing a method Based on the descriptions alone, one could not adequately implement the distributed or massed practice methods. This section will describe the research related to and differences among the various methods. Readers should also study the respective manuals.

Fredericks et al. (1975) report positive results in 9 years of using the distributed practice method with many handicapped children. No study compares the Fredericks et al. method to the traditional schedule method or to the massed practice (Foxx and Azrin) methods. However, several studies have been made on the Foxx and Azrin methods.

Williams and Sloop (1978) used the rapid method of toilet training retarded children (Foxx & Azrin, 1973) with similar subjects and found essentially the same results. Butler (1976a) assisted a mother in using the Foxx and Azrin (1973) procedures to toilet train a 4½-year-old boy with spina bifida meningomyelocele. The number of accidents was significantly reduced, although the training did not control the "dribbling" characteristic of spina bifida children.

Smith (1979) compared the Foxx and Azrin (1973) procedure with no pants alarm and positive practice replaced with timeout; a schedule method with increased fluid intake and no punishment for accidents; and a method similar to the timing procedure described by Mahoney et al. (1971) and Van Wagenen, Meyerson, Kerr, and Mahoney (1969). The subjects were 5–18-year-old profoundly retarded persons. The methods similar to Foxx and Azrin's and to Mahoney et al. were superior to the schedule method. Further, Foxx and Azrin's procedure was slightly superior and easier to use than the Mahoney et al. method. Sadler and Merkert (1977) compared the Foxx and Azrin (1973) method to a traditional schedule method in a day treatment center. The subjects were 14 severely and profoundly retarded 7–12-year-olds. The Foxx and Azrin method resulted in quicker toilet training that in some cases generalized to home settings. However, considerable time was required by the staff members who questioned whether the Foxx and Azrin method was worth the time and physical effort.

Kimmel (1974), in a review of *Toilet Training in Less Than a Day* (Azrin & Foxx, 1974), discussed concerns about the lack of research showing that parents using the book alone could toilet train their children; the fact that the skills needed by parents to accomplish the procedure might not be adequately described; and the possibility of parents not being prepared for behaviors such as tantrums and avoidance that might occur as a result of the procedure. Based on these concerns Butler (1976b) provided three weekly meetings to parents who planned to use the book. As a result, 39 of 49 parents were able to successfully toilet train their nonhandicapped children. Matson and Ollendick (1977) used two groups, one receiving only the book and the other receiving the book and supervision during training. There were five mothers in each group; four of the five in the book-plus-supervision group successfully trained their nonhandicapped children; in the book-only group, only one of the five was able to train her child. Thus, Kimmel's (1974) concerns seem well founded. From this research, several consistent findings are apparent. As reported by Azrin & Foxx (1974), children over 25 or 26 months of age are more quickly trained than younger children (Butler, 1976b; Matson & Ollendick, 1977). Also, some children, perhaps 20–30%, stop wetting the bed as a result of the training. Tantrum and avoidance behavior do occur during positive practice (Butler, 1976b; Matson, 1975; Matson & Ollendick, 1977). Finally, parents were more successful when assistance other than the manuals was available. The early childhood special educator should be aware that parents may need consultation if they use the book.

Published reports of the less than a day procedure with handicapped children could not be located. However, from the authors' own experience with preschool handicapped children, the results range from self-initiated toileting to little success. The most common result is that the children will urinate in the toilet if taken (Wolery & Conley, 1976).

When selecting a toilet training method, teachers should consider several factors. The traditional schedule method is apt to be very slow and may be totally ineffective. The Fredericks et al. distributed practice method should be used if the trainer has a limited amount of time to devote to toilet training and powerful reinforcers exist. The Foxx and Azrin procedure can be used given a skilled trainer and 2–5 uninterrupted days. However, the trainer should expect some tantrum behavior during positive practice. Remember that implementing the Fredericks et al. (1975), the Foxx and Azrin (1973) training the retarded procedure, or the Azrin and Foxx (1974) less than a day procedure requires careful study of the respective manuals. Also, when conducting toilet and other training activities, opt for procedures that do not require punishment. The effort, effectiveness, and efficiency of the methods are compared in Table 16.5.

Nighttime Toilet Training

Frequently, handicapped and nonhandicapped children wet their beds (nocturnal enuresis) even after they are toilet trained during the day. With some children, particularly boys, this condition persists into adolescence. Kolvin (1975) suggests 17% of the 5-year-old, 11% of the 11-year-old, and 2% of the 15-year-old children have nocturnal enuresis. Although incidence rates for handicapped children living at home are not readily available, incidence rates for adult retarded persons range between 41.5% (Smith, 1981) and 70% (Azrin, Sneed, & Foxx, 1973).

TABLE 16.5
Comparison of three methods of toilet training

| Method | Rank Order | | |
	Effectiveness	Efficiency[a]	Effort Required by Trainer
Traditional Schedule	3	3	2
Distributed Practice (Fredericks et al.)	1–2	2	1
Massed Practice (Foxx & Azrin)	1–2	1	3

[a]*Rank order* refers to a relative value of each of the three procedures, with 1 indicating the most value. *Efficiency* refers to the amount of calendar time for training.

With children free of medical problems, basic behavioral treatments for nocturnal enuresis include the urine alarm technique (O. H. Mower & W. M. Mower, 1938), dry-bed training (Azrin et al., 1973; Azrin, Sneed, & Foxx, 1974), the four phase system described by Fredericks et al. (1975), and the retention control procedure (Doleys, 1977). Although the early childhood special educator may not be directly involved in controlling nocturnal enuresis, parents frequently ask questions about it. Thus, a brief summary of these procedures is presented.

The *urine alarm system* is commercially available and is quite popular. This system has a disposable fiber sheet between two foil sheets that are placed under the child's bed sheets and connected to the alarm. When the child urinates, the moisture completes an electrical circuit between the two foil sheets and sounds the alarm, awakening the child. Estimates of initial success vary between 75% (Doleys, 1977) and approximately 84% (Sloop, 1970). However, many families stop using it before the enuresis is controlled (Azrin & Besalel, 1979), and relapses are common when the procedure is withdrawn (Taylor & Turner, 1975). It is somewhat successful with institutionalized retarded persons, and a recent adaptation involving increases in fluid intake, reprimands for wetting, changing the bed when wet, and reinforcement for staying dry throughout the night is slow but quite successful (Smith, 1981).

Fredericks et al. (1975) describe a *four phase procedure*, but present no evaluation data. Each phase, unless successful, is used for 10 days. Phase I involves going to the bathroom before bedtime and reinforcement for staying dry. Phase II involves reduced liquid intake two hours before going to bed and reinforcement for staying dry. Phase III involves the same procedures as Phase II with the addition of awakening the child at the parents' bedtime. Phase IV involves determining when the child usually wets and awakening him or her before that time. This awakening is gradually moved closer to the morning or bedtime. As with the Fredericks et al. (1975) daytime procedure, the nighttime procedure relies heavily on reinforcement.

Azrin et al. (1973, 1974) developed a *dry-bed training* procedure similar to their daytime rapid method of training. It involves the use of the urine alarm, increased fluid intake, practice getting up and going to the bathroom at bedtime, hourly awakenings to urinate, verbal rehearsal of procedures, reinforcement for staying dry, and overcorrection when accidents occur. The overcorrection involves the child changing the bed sheets and practicing getting up and going to the bathroom 20 times. This procedure has been successful with adult retarded persons (Azrin et al, 1973) and nonhandicapped children (Azrin et al., 1974). The procedure is less effective when used without the alarm (Azrin & Thienes, 1978) and in some cases ineffective (Bollard & Nettelbeck, 1981; Nettelbeck & Langeluddecke, 1979). When compared to the urine alarm alone it is superior (Bollard & Nettelbeck, 1981) and effective when administered by parents (Bollard & Nettelbeck, 1981; Bollard & Woodroffe, 1977). Azrin and Besalel (1979) described the procedures with some changes in a manual for parents. The changes are the addition of retention control during the day and hourly awakenings only until one o'clock in the morning. Evaluation of the parent manual resulted in considerable success (Azrin & Besalel, 1979).

The *retention control* procedure is based on the notion that the bladders of enuretic children are smaller (Muellner, 1960). The capacity of the bladder can be increased by waiting before urinating, attempting to hold more urine, and being reinforced for waiting and holding (Doleys, Ciminero, Tolison, Williams, & Wells, 1977). Unfortunately, increasing the capacity of the bladder does not necessarily change toileting behaviors (Doleys, 1977). Thus, the procedure alone is a weak treatment.

Of the nighttime methods, data seem to indicate that the dry-bed training is the most effective. This statement must be made with caution because of the lack of data with the Fredericks et al. procedure and lack of comparative studies with young handicapped children.

DRESSING AND UNDRESSING SKILLS

Dressing and undressing are skills that can result in independent functioning. In this section, several issues are discussed including the general developmental sequences, assessment of dressing and undressing, prerequisite skills for dressing, general guidelines for training dressing, and adaptive clothing.

General Developmental Sequences

Children learn to dress themselves over a number of years. The order in which they learn to take off, put on, and fasten various items of clothing varies depending upon the construction of the clothing, experience, and the child's motor abilities. However, children generally learn to take off before putting on specific garments. Cohen and Gross (1979) provided detailed sequences and age levels for each item of clothing. From about 7–12 months children begin to cooperate during dressing by holding out their arms or sticking out their feet. By the end of the second year, children begin to find and push their arms through armholes as well as lift their feet to go into pants legs. At approximately 1 year, children pull off a loose pullover shirt and sometimes push down wet or soiled pants. During the first part of the second year they take off socks and shoes, and during the second half of that year they take off their coats and other front-opening garments. During the third year, they learn to put on socks, shoes, pants, and coats and other front-opening garments. Items such as buttoning, zipping, and snapping are learned during the third year, while lacing and tying shoes are learned from the fourth to sixth years.

Prerequisite Behaviors and Assessment of Skills

Assessment of children's dressing abilities is primarily accomplished through use of the functional approach by direct observation using checklists frequently derived from task analyses of various dressing skills (Knapczyk, 1975). Frequently those checklists accompany curricula or are criterion-referenced tools. Examples are the *Brigance Inventory of Early Development* (Brigance, 1978); *Learning Accomplishment Profile* (LeMay et al., 1977); *TARC Assessment System* (Sailor & Mix, 1975); *Uniform Performance Assessment System* (White, Edgar, & Haring, 1978); *Wabash Curriculum* (Tilton et al., 1977); *Portage Guide to Early Education* (Bluma et al., 1976); and

the *Teaching Research Curriculum* (Fredericks et al., 1976). These and similar manuals assess children's dressing skills by having the assessor note how the child performs steps in putting on and taking off given garments and completes various fasteners such as buttons, and the level of assistance the child requires (if any) in completing various dressing tasks. The levels include independent functioning, verbal prompts, gestural prompts, models, partial physical prompts such as tapping or nudging, and full manipulation by the trainer (Gentry & Haring, 1976; Knapczyk, 1975).

Several additional motor and social skills should also be assessed. The teacher should consult with occupational and physical therapists (Marx, 1973) when assessing motor skills, including observation of children's arm movements. The accuracy of volitional arm movements, range of motion, and ability to move both arms are important. Information about the accuracy of arm movements will assist the teacher in determining whether to attempt instruction with various items of clothing. Evaluation of the range of motion and ability to use both arms will assist in selecting the sequences to be used in training. Children's grasp patterns should also be assessed to identify the type of grasp patterns, the strength of those grasps, and the child's ability to grasp while simultaneously moving the arms. To put on and take off many types of clothing the child will need a grasp to be used in pulling. This only needs to be a palmar grasp, but it must be strong and maintained when the arms are moved. Children also need a grasp for pushing off garments such as pants and socks. The child must place his or her thumb between the body and the clothing and push with the arms while maintaining a thumb inside the garment. To put on socks and some shoes, and secure and undo most fasteners, the child must have a fairly well developed pincer grasp, especially since many of the fasteners (buttons and zippers) on children's clothing are smaller than adults'. The ability to guide the arm and finger movements with the eyes is especially desirable when securing and undoing fasteners.

The child must also have well-developed static balance and automatic reactions including equilibrium, righting, and supportive responses. Finally, the motor assessment should include the child's primitive postural reflexes. These reflexes may necessitate special positioning during dressing to inhibit their occurrence.

In addition, dressing assessment should include social skills. Children should understand and comply with task requests and have imitative skills. Noncompliant children will present problems. Children who do not understand basic task requests will require more physical prompting than those who benefit from verbal, signed, or gestural cues. Similarly, children who do not imitate will require prompts other than models. Compliance, basic understanding of instructions, and imitative abilities are desirable and will influence the teacher's choice of instructional procedures.

Thus, when assessing children's ability to dress and undress, observe a number of skills. These include the child's ability to put on and take off items of clothing and fasten and unfasten buttons, snaps, zippers, buckles, laces, and ties. Further, assess the child's arm and hand skills, eye-hand coordination, balance, automatic reactions, and primitive postural reflexes. Desirable social skills include understanding task requests, compliance, and imitation.

General Guidelines for Training Skills

Several general guidelines for teaching dressing skills are described and related research is noted. Some of these guidelines are specific to training dressing and undressing, while others are also applicable for training more advanced self-help skills such as grooming, housekeeping, and others.

Train dressing and undressing at natural times. As with feeding, dressing skills should usually be taught when the child has a reason to dress and undress. For example, a young handicapped boy was able to put on and take off his clothing very slowly in the classroom. Training was initiated to increase his dressing and undressing rate, but one evening the boy went home with his teacher. When bathtime came the child was instructed to get undressed, which he did within seconds and then quickly climbed into the bathtub. His undressing rate in a natural setting was much faster than in a classroom setting.

However, children rarely dress and undress at school. This problem can be overcome by training parents to teach their children to dress and undress, conducting special dressing sessions at school, incorporating dressing into daily routines, and employing rapid methods for training dressing.

Parents of young handicapped children ranked toileting and eating skills as more important than dressing skills, but ranked dressing as the second most difficult self-help skill to teach (Lance & Koch, 1973). Thus, parents may need considerable assistance. Some parent training manuals include directions for teaching dressing (Baker, Brightman, Heifetz, & Murphy, 1976a, 1976b; Baldwin, Fredericks, & Brodsky, 1973; Hart, 1974). Besides reading such books, the method described by Shearer and Shearer (1977) can be used. This method involves setting goals for the child with the parent, demonstrating how to teach the skill, watching the parents try it, and providing feedback on their performance. In some cases, however, more specific training may be needed.

Fowler, Johnson, Whitman, and Zukotynski (1978) present a model for more intensive training. They trained a mother to teach her aggressive, noncompliant, profoundly retarded daughter to perform selected preacademic and self-help skills. Detailed steps of the tasks were written on index cards and different cards made for each task. Each card had verbal directions and prompts the mother was to use for each step, the child's possible responses, and the mother's responses to the child's correct and incorrect responses. A trainer also provided feedback and praise to the mother. Changes occurred in the child's preacademic, self-care, and social behaviors and coincided with changes in the mother's behavior.

If parents are unable to do the needed training or both parents and teachers decide to teach the skill, sessions can be conducted at school. This is not the preferred method, but during initial acquisition it is frequently necessary. From the limited data available, this training (at least for severely handicapped children) should be conducted in one-to-one sessions (Alberto, Jobes, Sizemore, & Doran, 1980). A place in the classroom that provides privacy should be selected. These sessions should conform with methods described later in this chapter.

Another strategy for teaching dressing is to incorporate dressing training into daily classroom routines. Times that children naturally dress include taking off and putting on coats and sweaters when arriving and departing or when going out and coming in from playing outside; pushing down and pulling up pants when toileting; taking off socks and shoes at naptime or before engaging in active indoor activities. Dressing skills can be incorporated into dramatic play activities and "dress-up" activities. Teachers can provide clothing to fit over the children's outer clothing or use costumes that require dressing and undressing. These situations can be contrived to increase the amount of dressing and undressing. Allow time for the children to dress and undress without being hurried.

Still another strategy that may be useful is an intensive method developed for training dressing skills to profoundly retarded adults (Azrin, Schaeffer, & Wesolowski, 1976). However, no published reports could be found with children as subjects, so follow these recommendations with care. Azrin et al. (1976) provide anecdotal information about an attempt to use it with children. The method involved a number of departures from usual behavioral approaches to teach dressing, but the most radical was to increase the training sessions to 2 or 3 hours and to offer two such daily sessions. The average training time required for the subjects to learn to dress and undress was 12 hours. The longest training time was 20 hours over four days.

Azrin et al. (1976) report that changes may be needed to make the procedure effective for children. "First, the snack treats may not be as useful as reinforcers for children as they are for adults because of the greater prevalence of 'food finikiness' of children" (p. 32). Second, children tended to engage in more tantrum behavior that was treated with required relaxation and resulted in a decrease in tantrums. Third, children tended to have a "greater desire for activity" (p. 32); thus, activities were used as a reinforcer and the bed rest used with adults was eliminated.

Train in accordance with the sequences of difficulty. Certain sequences of difficulty should be followed when training dressing and undressing. One sequence is that nonhandicapped children learn to take off before putting on most garments (Cohen & Gross, 1979) because it is easier. Thus, when training handicapped children to dress and undress, begin by training them to take off given garments. They do not have to be trained to take *all* their clothing off before learning to put it on; however, there is a greater likelihood of success if they are first trained to remove a specific garment.

Another sequence is that putting on and taking off clothing is easier than securing and undoing fasteners. The buttons, snaps, zippers, and ties on young children's clothing are frequently small and difficult to manage, sometimes even for adults. Train manipulation of these objects after children have learned to put on and remove their clothing. However, when training children to secure and undo fasteners, real or adapted clothing items such as vests (e.g., Edgar, Maser, & Haring, 1977) should be used rather than dressing dolls and boards. The clothing should be in the proper spatial relationship to the child. For example, when you tie your shoes, the toe faces away from you; thus, train children to tie shoes with the toe facing away from them. Real clothing items such as adult shoes should be used so the child can place his or her entire foot and shoe inside when learning to lace and tie. If, in the beginning, learning to fasten and unfasten is done in the correct spatial relationship to the child's body, then generalization to the child's clothing is more likely.

It is much easier to put on and remove loose-fitting clothing. When training young handicapped children to dress and undress, begin with clothing that is about two sizes too large. After the child masters putting on or removing this loose clothing, start training with clothing that fits more tightly. If the training is being conducted at school, the teacher should ask the parents to furnish a loose fitting set of clothing to keep in the classroom. The clothes can be used for dressing training and as a spare outfit when toileting and other accidents occur.

Assist parents in selecting and adapting clothing to promote independent functioning.

Many adaptations in clothing can allow the child to be more independent. For example, elastic bands can be used in place of zippers and snaps for all types of clothing. Tube socks alleviate the problem of getting the sock heel positioned correctly. Slip-on shoes are easier for children to put on than lace and tie shoes. Snaps and velcro fasteners are easier to manage than buttons (Michaelis, 1979). Other adaptations include such modifications as sewing reinforcements into garments to reduce wear caused by braces. Suggestions and directions for making adaptations, and drawings of various adaptations are described by Hoffman (1979); Bare, Boettke, and Waggoner (1962), and Kernaleguen (1978). When adapting clothing, make sure that the handicapped child does *not* appear different from others.

Train to maximize acquisition and generalization. Acquisition of dressing skills appears to be more efficiently taught during one-to-one sessions than group training sessions (Alberto, et al., 1980). Including parents and others in the training and using multiple settings may facilitate generalization (Stokes & Baer, 1977). Several additional procedures should also be implemented. The desired skill should be task analyzed (Westling & Murden, 1978) to identify the steps the child needs to perform to complete the dressing skill. Task analyses for various items of clothing can be found in Copeland, Ford, and Solon (1976); Baker et al. (1976a, 1976b); Fredericks et al. (1976); and many other curricula.

Once steps have been identified, use and fade physical prompts by backward or forward chaining (see Chapter 3). Backward chaining, sometimes referred to as reverse chaining, is the more common method (Snell, 1978; Westling & Murden, 1978). Full manipulation of the child is given on all steps until the last step, which the child performs independently. As training progresses, prompts are faded to the next to last step, and then the third step from completion, and so on until the child performs the task without assistance. In forward chaining, fading begins with the first step in the sequence and then assistance is provided on other steps. As training progresses, the child does the second step independently, and then the third, and so on until the child performs the task without assistance.

Backward chaining is used so the child is reinforced at the end of the task for independent skill completion. To reinforce independent functioning in the forward chaining procedure, the trainer must interrupt the chain. Azrin et al. (1976) used forward chaining in addition to intensive reinforcement in the rest of the sequence. An alternative to backward or forward chaining is graduated guidance (see Chapter 3). In graduated guidance, the skill is taught as a complete sequence on each trial; thus, the child participates with each step. Steps are chained together more efficiently. Failure to chain the steps together as one behavior will decrease the likelihood that the skill will be functional and generalize to similar garments and other settings (Cuvo, 1973). Sulzer-Azaroff and Mayer (1977) provide a more complete discussion of chaining. When using physical prompts to teach dressing, the trainer should be positioned behind the child, allowing the trainer to prompt the child to use more natural movements (Snell, 1978).

Because of physical limitations or other reasons, some children may benefit from alternative sequences. Brett (1960) describes specific alternative sequences for hemiplegic (paralysis affecting one side of the body) children. These sequences may also be useful with other children. Brett's (1960) sequence for taking off a pullover shirt with one hand is compared to another sequence for the same skill using two hands in Table 16.6. Brett (1960) presents sequences for each item of clothing. Other alternative sequences are also provided in a paper titled, "Dressing techniques for the cerebral palsied child" (no name, 1954). Finnie (1975) provides detailed guidelines for dressing the physically handicapped child.

SUMMARY

In this chapter the self-help skills of eating/self-feeding, toileting, and dressing/undressing were described as chains of learned behaviors that are reasonable educational goals and are learned throughout the preschool years. These skills must be acquired so they can be used functionally on a regular but low-frequency basis.

Eating and self-feeding can be assessed through the use of the developmental or functional approaches, but attention should be given to why children present eating problems. Guidelines for teaching eating and self-feeding include the following: consult with therapists when developing and implementing feeding programs, position the child properly for eating and self-feeding, carefully select the foods to be presented to the child, use and fade adaptive equipment, use behavioral techniques to establish eating and self-feeding behaviors and to control related problems, train eating and self-feeding at the appropriate times, and make mealtimes relaxing and enjoyable learning experiences. Procedures for teaching swallowing, lip closure, chewing, and spoon-feeding were also described.

Children's readiness for toilet training should include the ability to retain and release urine and feces. In addition, factors such as medical history, instructional control, and parents' willingness to follow through with training should be considered. When toilet training is initiated, follow several guidelines: train daytime rather than nighttime toileting, begin training with bladder rather than bowel control, train the child to sit cn rather than stand by the toilet to urinate, and, in the laters stages, train the child to indicate he needs to go to the bathroom. These guidelines should be followed with any of the traditional, distributed practice, or massed practice toilet training methods. The distributed and massed practice procedures are the preferred methods. Nighttime toileting procedures were also described.

Dressing and undressing skills are frequently assessed by using checklists that correspond to task analyses of taking off and putting on various items of clothing. Prerequisite skills for dressing and undressing include development of volitional arm movements, equilibrium reactions, and grasp patterns. Guidelines for teaching dressing and undressing include training at natural times, training in accordance with the sequences of difficulty, assisting parents in adapting clothing, and training to maximize acquisition and generalization.

TABLE 16.6

Comparisons of task analyses for removing a pullover shirt

Task analysis for removing a pullover shirt for hemiplegic children (Brett, 1960)	Task analysis for removing a pullover shirt requiring two hands
1. Starting at top back, gather shirt up [in hand], lean forward, duck head and pull forward over head. 2. Remove from good arm and then from affected arm.	1. Grasp the sleeve end of the left arm with the right hand. 2. Pull left sleeve out and away from the body while simultaneously bending the left arm. 3. Move the left arm down the front of the stomach and out the bottom of the shirt. 4. Pull the left side of the shirt up over the left shoulder. 5. Grasp the end of the right sleeve with the left arm. 6. Pull right sleeve out away from body, & pull right arm out of sleeve. 7. With both hands, pull shirt off the head.

Source: The task sequence on the left was adapted from G. Brett, Dressing techniques for the severely involved hemiplegic patient. *American Journal of Occupational Therapy*, 1960, *14*, 262–264.

REFERENCES

Alberto, P., Jobes, N., Sizemore, A., & Doran, D. A comparison of individual and group instruction across response tasks. *Journal of the Association for the Severely Handicapped,* 1980, *5,* 285–293.

Azrin, N. H., & Armstrong, P. M. The "mini-meal"—a method for teaching eating skills to the profoundly retarded. *Mental Retardation,* 1973, *11,* 9–13.

Azrin, N. H., & Besalel, V. A. *A parent's guide to bedwetting control: A step-by-step method.* New York: Simon & Schuster, 1979.

Azrin, N. H., & Foxx, R. M. A rapid method of toilet training the institutionalized retarded. *Journal of Applied Behavior Analysis,* 1971, *4,* 89–99.

Azrin, N. H., & Foxx, R. M. *Toilet training in less than a day.* New York: Simon & Schuster, 1974.

Azrin, N. H., Schaeffer, R. M., & Wesolowski, M. D. A rapid method of teaching profoundly retarded persons to dress. *Mental Retardation,* 1976, *14*(6), 29–33.

Azrin, N. H., Sneed, T. J., & Foxx, R. M. Dry bed: A rapid method of eliminating bedwetting (enuresis) of the retarded. *Behavior Research and Therapy,* 1973, *11,* 427–434.

Azrin, N. H., Sneed, T. J., & Foxx, R. M. Dry-bed training: Rapid elimination of childhood enuresis. *Behavior Research and Therapy,* 1974, *12,* 147–156.

Azrin, N. H., & Thienes, P. M. Rapid elimination of enuresis by intensive learning without a conditioning apparatus. *Behavior Therapy,* 1978, *9,* 324–354.

Azrin, N. H., & Wesolowski, M. D. Theft reversal: An overcorrection procedure for eliminating stealing by retarded persons. *Journal of Applied Behavior Analysis,* 1974, *7,* 577–581.

Baker, B. L., Brightman, A. J., Heifetz, L. J., & Murphy, D. M. *Early self-help skills.* Champaign, Ill.: Research Press, 1976. (a)

Baker, B. L., Brightman, A. J., Heifetz, L. J., & Murphy, D. M. *Intermediate self-help skills.* Champaign, Ill.: Research Press, 1976. (b)

Baldwin, V. L., Fredericks, H. D., & Brodsky, G. *Isn't it time he outgrew this? A training program for parents of retarded children.* Springfield, Ill.: Charles C. Thomas, 1973.

Balthazar, E. E. *Balthazar Scales of Adaptive Behavior I.* Palo Alto, Calif.: Consulting Psychologists Press, 1976. (b)

Banerdt, B., & Bricker, D. A training program for selected self-feeding skills for the motorically impaired. *AAESPH Review,* 1978, *3*(4), 222–229.

Bare, C., Boettke, E., & Waggoner, N. *Self-help clothing for handicapped children.* Chicago: National Society for Crippled Children and Adults, 1962.

Barnes, K. J., Murphy, M. Waldo, L., & Sailor, W. Adaptive equipment for the severely, multiply handicapped child. In R. L. York and E. Edgar (Eds.), *Teaching the severely handicapped* (Vol. 4). Seattle: American Association for the Education of the Severely/Profoundly Handicapped, 1979.

Barton, E. S., Guess, D., Garcia, E., & Baer, D. M. Improvements of retardates' mealtime behaviors by timeout procedures using the multiple baseline technique. *Journal of Applied Behavior Analysis,* 1970, *3,* 77–84.

Baumeister, A., & Klosowski, R. An attempt to group toilet train severely retarded patients. *Mental Retardation,* 1965, *3,* 24–26.

Bender, M., & Valletutti, P. J. *Teaching the moderately and severely handicapped: Curriculum objectives, strategies, and activities.* Baltimore: University Park Press, 1976.

Bensberg, G. J. (Ed.). *Teaching the mentally retarded: A handbook for ward personnel.* Atlanta: Southern Regional Education Board, 1965.

Bensberg, G. J., Colwell, N., & Cassell, R. H. Teaching profoundly retarded self-help activities by behavior shaping techniques. *American Journal of Mental Deficiency,* 1965, *69,* 674–679.

Berkowitz, S., Sherry, P. J., & Davis, B. A. Teaching self-feeding skills to profound retardates using reinforcement and fading procedures. *Behavior Therapy,* 1971, *2,* 62–67.

Bluma, S. M., Shearer, M. S., Frohman, A. H., & Hilliard, J. M. *Portage guide to early education: Manual.* Portage, Wis.: Cooperative Education Service Agency, 1976.

Bollard, J., & Nettelbeck, T. A comparison of dry-bed training and standard urine-alarm conditioning treatment of childhood bedwetting. *Behavior Research and Therapy,* 1981, *19,* 215–226.

Bollard, R. J., & Woodroffe, P. The effect of parent-administered dry-bed training on nocturnal enuresis in children. *Behavior Research and Therapy,* 1977, *15,* 159–165.

Brett, G. Dressing techniques for the severely involved hemiplegic patient. *American Journal of Occupational Therapy,* 1960, *5,* 262–264.

Brigance, A. *Inventory of early development.* Wobarn, Miss.: Curriculum Associates, 1978.

Butler, J. F. Toilet training a child with spina bifida. *Journal of Behavior Therapy and Experimental Psychiatry,* 1976, *7,* 63–65. (a)

Butler, J. F. The toilet training success of parents after reading *Toilet training in less than a day. Behavior Therapy,* 1976, *7,* 185–191. (b)

Campbell, P. H. Daily living skills. In N. G. Haring (Ed.), *Developing effective individualized educational programs for severely handicapped children and youth.* Washington, D.C.: Bureau of Education for the Handicapped, 1977.

Campbell, P. H. Assessing oral-motor skills in severely handicapped persons: An analysis of normal and abnormal patterns of movement. In R. L. York and E. B. Edgar (Eds.), *Teaching the severely handicapped* (Vol. 4). Seattle: American Association for the Education of the Severely/Profoundly Handicapped, 1979.

Cohen, M., & Gross, P. *The developmental resource: Behavioral sequences for assessment and program planning* (Vol. 1). New York: Grune & Stratton, 1979.

Colangelo, C. Bergen, A., & Gottlieb, L. *A normal baby: The sensory-motor processes of the first year.* Valhalla, N.Y.: Blythedale Children's Hospital, 1976.

Copeland, M., Ford, L., & Solon, N. *Occupational therapy for mentally retarded children.* Baltimore: University Park Press, 1976.

Cullen, S. M., Cronk, C. E., Pueschel, S. M., Schnell, R. R., & Reed, R. B. Social development and feeding milestones of young Down syndrome children. *American Journal of Mental Deficiency,* 1981, *85,* 410–415.

Cuvo, A. J. Child care workers as trainers of mentally retarded children. *Child Care Quarterly,* 1973, *2,* 25–37.

Doleys, D. M. Behavioral treatments for nocturnal enuresis in children: A review of the recent literature. *Psychological Bulletin,* 1977, *84,* 30–54.

Doleys, D. M., Ciminero, A. R., Tollison, J. W., Williams, C. L., & Wells, K. C. Dry-bed training and retention control training—a comparison. *Behavior Therapy,* 1977, *8,* 541–548.

Dressing techniques for the cerebral palsied child. *American Journal of Occupational Therapy,* 1954, *8,* 8–10; 37–38.

Edgar, E., Maser, J. T., & Haring, N. G. Button up: A systematic approach for teaching children to fasten. *Teaching Exceptional Children,* 1977, *9,* 104–105.

Ellis, N. R. Toilet training and the severely defective patient: An S–R reinforcement analysis. *American Journal of Mental Deficiency,* 1963, *68,* 93–103.

Finnie, N. R. *Handling the young cerebral palsied child at home.* New York: E. P. Dutton, 1975.

Fowler, S. A., Johnson, M. R., Whitman, T. L., & Zukotynski, G. Teaching a parent in the home to train self-help skills and increase compliance in her profoundly retarded adult daughter. *AAESPH Review,* 1978, *3*(3), 151–161.

Foxx, R. M., & Azrin, N. H. *Toilet training the retarded: A rapid program for day and nighttime independent toileting.* Champaign, Ill.: Research Press, 1973.

Fredericks, H. D., Baldwin, V. L., Grove, D. N., & Moore, W. G. *Toilet training the handicapped child.* Monmouth, Oreg.: Instructional Development Corporation, 1975.

Fredericks, H. D., Riggs, C., Furey, T., Grove, D., Moore, W., McDonnell, J., Jordan, E., Hanson, W., Baldwin, V., & Wadlow, M. *The teaching research curriculum for moderately and severely handicapped.* Springfield, Ill.: Charles C. Thomas, 1976.

Gentry, D., & Haring, N. G. Essentials of performance measurement. In N. G. Haring and L. J. Brown (Eds.), *Teaching the severely handicapped* (Vol. 1). New York: Grune & Stratton, 1976.

Gesell, A., & Ilg, F. L. *Feeding behavior of infants: A pediatric approach to the mental hygiene of early life.* Philadelphia: J. B. Lippincott, 1937.

Gesell, A., Ilg, F. L., Ames, L. B., & Rodell, J. L. *Infant and child in the culture of today: The guidance of development in home and nursery school.* New York: Harper & Row, 1974.

Giles, D. K., & Wolf, M. M. Toilet training institutionalized, severe retardates: An application of operant behavior modification techniques. *American Journal of Mental Deficiency,* 1966, *70,* 766–780.

Hall, K. W., & Hammock, M. Feeding and toileting devices for a child with arthrogryposis. *American Journal of Occupational Therapy,* 1979, *10,* 644–647.

Harris, S. R. Transdisciplinary therapy model for the infant with Down's syndrome. *Physical Therapy,* 1980, *60,* 420–423.

Hart, V. *Beginning with the handicapped.* Springfield, Ill.: Charles C. Thomas, 1974.

Hatcher, R. P. Treatment of food refusal in a two-year-old child. *Journal of Behavior Therapy and Experimental Psychiatry,* 1979, *10,* 363–367.

Henriksen, K., & Doughty, R. Decelerating undesired mealtime behavior in a group of profoundly retarded boys. *American Journal of Mental Deficiency,* 1967, *72,* 40–44.

Hoffman, A. M. *Clothing for the handicapped, the aged, and other people with special needs.* Springfield, Ill.: Charles C. Thomas, 1979.

Holser-Buehler, P. Correction of infantile feeding habits. *American Journal of Occupational Therapy,* 1973, *26,* 331–335.

Horner, D. R., & Keilitz, I. Training mentally retarded adolescents to brush their teeth. *Journal of Applied Behavior Analysis,* 1975, *8,* 301–309.

Illingworth, R. S., & Lister, J. The critical or sensitive period with special reference to certain feeding problems in infants and children. *Journal of Pediatrics,* 1964, *65,* 839.

Jackson, G., Johnson, C., Ackron, G., & Crawley, R. Food satiation as a procedure to decelerate vomiting. *American Journal of Mental Deficiency,* 1975, *80,* 223–227.

Kernaleguen, A. *Clothing designs for the handicapped.* Edmonton: University of Alberta Press, 1978.

Kimmel, H. D. Review of *Toilet training in less than a day. Journal of Behavior Therapy and Experimental Psychiatry,* 1974, *5,* 113–114.

Knapczyk, D. R. Task analytic assessment of severe learning problems. *Education and Training of the Mentally Retarded,* 1975, *10,* 74–77.

Kohlenberg, R. J. Operant conditioning of human anal sphincter pressure. *Journal of Applied Behavior Analysis,* 1973, *6,* 201–208.

Kolvin, I. Enuresis in childhood. *Practitioner,* 1975, *214,* 33–45.

Lance, W. D., & Koch, A. C. Parents as teachers: Self-help skills for young handicapped children. *Mental Retardation,* 1973, *11,* 3–4.

Largent, P., & Waylett, J. Follow-up study on upper extremity bracing of children with severe athetosis. *American Journal of Occupational Therapy,* 1975, *29,* 341–347.

Latham, G., & Hofmeister, A. A mediated training program for parents of the preschool mentally retarded. *Exceptional Children,* 1973, *39,* 472–473.

Leibowitz, M. J., & Holcer, P. Building and maintaining self-feeding skills in a retarded child. *American Journal of Occupational Therapy,* 1974, *28,* 545–548.

LeMay, D. W., Griffin, P. M., & Sanford, A. R. *Learning Accomplishment Profile Diagnostic Edition* (rev.). Chapel Hill, N.C.: Chapel Hill Training and Outreach Project, 1977.

Magnusson, C. J., & Justen, J. E. Teacher made adaptive and assistive aids for developing self-help skills in the severely handicapped. *Journal for Special Educators,* 1981, *17,* 389–400.

Mahoney, K., Van Wagenen, R. K., & Meyerson, L. Toilet training of normal and retarded children. *Journal of Applied Behavior Analysis,* 1971, *4,* 173–181.

Mann, W. C., & Sobsey, R. Feeding program for the institutionalized mentally retarded. *American Journal of Occupational Therapy*, 1975, *29*, 471–474.

Marshall, G. R. Toilet training of an autistic eight-year-old through conditioning therapy: A case report. *Behavior Research and Therapy*, 1966, *4*, 242–245.

Martin, L., McDonald, S., & Omichinski, M. An operant analysis of response interactions during meals with severely retarded girls. *American Journal of Mental Deficiency*, 1971, *76*, 68–75.

Marx, M. Integrating physical therapy into a cerebral palsy early education program. *Physical Therapy*, 1973, *53*, 512–514.

Matson, J. L. Some practical considerations for using the Foxx and Azrin method of toilet training. *Psychological Reports*, 1975, *37*, 350.

Matson, J. L., Dilorenzo, T. M., & Esveldt-Dawson, K. Independence training as a method of enhancing self-help skills acquisition of the mentally retarded. *Behavior Research and Therapy*, 1981, *19*, 399–405.

Matson, J. L., & Ollendick, T. H. Issues in toilet training normal children. *Behavior Therapy*, 1977, *8*, 549–553.

Mendelsohn, M. B. Behavioral training by paraprofessionals for families of developmentally disabled persons. *AAESPH Review*, 1978, *3*, 216–221.

Michaelis, C. T. Why can't Johnny look nice, too? Revisited. *The Exceptional Parent*, 1979, *9*, 9–14.

Miller, H. R., Patton, M. E., & Henton, K. R. Behavior modification of a profoundly retarded child: A case report. *Behavior Therapy*, 1971, *2*, 375–384.

Morris, S. E. Program guidelines for children with feeding problems. Milwaukee: Curative Workshop, Deemer-Kiwanis Children's Division, 1974.

Mowrer, O. H., & Mowrer, W. M. Enuresis: A method for its study and treatment. *American Journal of Orthopsychiatry*, 1938, *8*, 436–459.

Mueller, H. Feeding. In N. R. Finnie (Ed.), *Handling the young cerebral palsied child at home* (2nd ed.). New York: E. P. Dutton, 1975.

Muellner, S. R. Development of urinary control in children. *Journal of the American Medical Association*, 1960, *172*, 1256–1261.

Murphy, M. J., & Zahm, D. Effects of improved ward conditions and behavioral treatment of self-help skills. *Mental Retardation*, 1975, *13*, 24–27.

Nelson, C. E., & Ranka, J. L. CHRC eating aid. *American Journal of Occupational Therapy*, 1975, *29*, 362.

Nelson, G. L., Cone, J. D., & Hanson, C. R. Training correct utensil use in retarded children: Modeling vs. physical guidance. *American Journal of Mental Deficiency*, 1975, *80*, 114–122.

Nelson, N. W. *Planning individualized speech and language intervention programs.* Tucson: Communication Skill Builders, 1979.

Nettelbeck, T., & Langeluddecke, P. Dry-bed training without an enuresis machine. *Behavior Research and Therapy*, 1979, *17*, 403–404.

O'Brien, F., & Azrin, N. H. Developing proper mealtime behaviors of the institutionalized retarded. *Journal of Applied Behavior Analysis*, 1972, *5*, 389–399.

Osarchuk, M. Operant methods of toilet behavior training the severely and profoundly retarded: A review. *Journal of Special Education*, 1973, *7*, 423–437.

Pipes, P. L. Assessing food and nutrient intake. In M. L. Powell (Ed.), *Assessment and management of developmental changes and problems in children* (2nd ed.). St. Louis: C. V. Mosby, 1981.

Powell, M. L. *Assessment and management of developmental changes and problems in children* (2nd ed.). St. Louis: C. V. Mosby, 1981.

Proger, B. B. Test review no. 12 Balthazar Scales of Adaptive Behavior: Section 1. *Journal of Special Education*, 1973, *7*, 95–101.

Sadler, O. W., & Merkert, F. Evaluating the Foxx-Azrin toilet training procedure for the retarded children in a day training center. *Behavior Therapy*, 1977, *8*, 499–500.

Sailor, W., & Mix, B. J. *The TARC assessment system.* Lawrence, Kans.: H & H Enterprises, 1975.

Sajwaj, T., Libet, J., & Agras, S. Lemon-juice therapy: The control of life-threatening rumination in a six-month-old infant. *Journal of Applied Behavior Analysis*, 1974, *7*, 557–563.

Santa Cruz Schools. *Behavioral characteristics progression.* Palo Alto, Calif.: Vort, 1973.

Schmidt, P. Feeding assessment and therapy for neurologically impaired. *AAESPH Review*, 1976, *1*, 19–27.

Schmidt, P. Eating skills assessment and remediation. In N. G. Haring (Ed.), *The Experimental Education Training Program: An inservice program for personnel serving the severely handicapped.* Seattle: Experimental Education Unit, 1977.

Shearer, M. S., & Shearer, D. E. Parent involvement. In J. B. Jordan, A. H. Hayden, M. B. Karnes, & M. M. Wood (Eds.), *Early Childhood education for exceptional children.* Reston, Va.: Council for Exceptional Children, 1977.

Singh, N., Manning, P. J., & Angell, M. J. Effects of an oral hygiene punishment procedure on chronic rumination and collateral behaviors in monozygous twins. *Journal of Applied Behavior Analysis*, 1982, *15*, 309–314.

Sloop, E. W. *Conditioning treatment of nocturnal enuresis among the institutionalized.* Unpublished doctoral dissertation, Florida State University, 1974.

Smith, L. J. Training severely and profoundly mentally handicapped nocturnal enuretics. *Behavior Research and Therapy*, 1981, *19*, 67–74.

Smith, P. S. A comparison of different methods of toilet training the mentally handicapped. *Behavior Research and Therapy*, 1979, *17*, 33–43.

Smith, P. S., & Smith, L. J. Chronological age and social age as factors in intensive daytime toilet training of institutionalized mentally retarded individuals. *Journal of Behavior Therapy and Experimental Psychiatry*, 1977, *8*, 269–273.

Snell, M. E. (Ed.). *Systematic instruction of the moderately and severely handicapped.* Columbus, Ohio: Charles E. Merrill, 1978.

Snell, M. E. Does toilet training belong in the public schools? A review of toilet training research. *Education Unlimited*, 1980, *2*, 53–58.

Song, A. Y., & Gandhi, R. An analysis of behavior during the acquisition and maintenance phases of self-spoon feeding skills of profound retardates. *Mental Retardation*, 1974, *12*, 25–28.

Stainback, S., Healy, H., Stainback, W., & Healy, J. Teaching basic eating skills. *AAESPH Review*, 1976, *1*, 26–35.

Stokes, T. F., & Baer, D. M. An implicit technology of generalization. *Journal of Applied Behavior Analysis*, 1977, *10*, 349–367.

Sulzer-Azaroff, B., & Mayer, G. R. *Applying behavior-analysis procedures with children and youth.* New York: Holt, Rinehart and Winston, 1977.

Tawney, J. W., Knapp, D. S., O'Reilly, C. D., & Pratt, S. S. *Programmed environments curriculum.* Columbus, Ohio: Charles E. Merrill, 1979.

Taylor, P. D., & Turner, R. K. A clinical trial of continuous, intermittent and overlearning "bell and pad" treatments for nocturnal enuresis. *Behavior Research and Therapy*, 1975, *13*, 281–293.

Thompson, G. A., Iwata, B. A., & Poynter, H. Operant control of pathological tongue thrust in spastic cerebral palsy. *Journal of Applied Behavior Analysis*, 1979, *12*, 325–333.

Tilton, J. R., Liska, D. C., & Bourland, J. C. *Guide to early developmental training.* Boston: Allyn and Bacon, 1977.

Trefler, E., Westmoreland, D., & Burlingame, D. A feeding spatula for cerebral-palsied children. *American Journal of Occupational Therapy*, 1977, *31*, 260–261.

Trott, M. C. Application of Foxx and Azrin toilet training for the retarded in a school program. *Education and Training of the Mentally Retarded*, 1977, *12*, 336–338.

Tyler, N. B., & Chandler, L. S. The developmental therapists: The occupational therapists and physical therapist. In K. E. Allen, V.A. Holm, & R. L. Schiefelbusch (Eds.), *Early intervention: A team approach.* Baltimore: University Park Press, 1978.

Tyler, N. B., & Kahn, N. A home treatment program. *American Journal of Occupational Therapy*, 1976, *30*, 437–440.

Utley, B. L., Holvoet, J. F., & Barnes, K. Handling, positioning, and feeding the physically handicapped. In E. Sontag (Ed.), *Educational programming for the severely and profoundly handicapped.* Reston, Va.: Division on Mental Retardation of the Council for Exceptional Children, 1977.

van den Pol, R. A., Iwata, B. A., Ivancic, M. T., Page, T. J., Neef, N. A., & Whitley, F. Teaching the handicapped to eat in public places: Acquisition, generalization, and maintenance of restaurant skills. *Journal of Applied Behavior Analysis*, 1981, *14*, 61–69.

Van Wagenen, R. K., Meyerson, L., Kerr, N. J., & Mahoney, K. Field trials of a new procedure for toilet training. *Journal of Experimental Child Psychology*, 1969, *8*, 147–159.

Wehman, P. *Curriculum design for the severely and profoundly handicapped.* New York: Human Sciences Press, 1979.

Wehman, P., & McLaughlin, P. J. Teachers' perceptions of behavior problems with severely and profoundly handicapped students. *Mental Retardation*, 1979, *17*, 20–21.

Westling, D. L., & Murden, L. Self-help skills training: A review of operant studies. *Journal of Special Education*, 1978, *12*, 253–283.

White, O. R., Edgar, E. B., & Haring, N. G. *Uniform Performance Assessment System.* Seattle: University of Washington, 1978.

Williams, F. E., & Sloop, E. W. Success with a shortened Foxx-Azrin toilet training program. *Education and Training of the Mentally Retarded*, 1978, *13*, 399–402.

Wolery, M. R., & Conley, O. S. *Toilet training in less than a day: Myth or reality?* Paper presented at the State Council for Exceptional Children Annual Meeting. Reston, Va., March 1976.

Subject Index

Author Index